The Collapse of Antiquity:

Greece and Rome as Civilization's Oligarchic Turning Point

Michael Hudson

www.michael-hudson.com
www.islet-verlag.de

Cover design by Miguel Guerra

Index by Ashley Dayman

Typeset by Global University for Sustainability

Hudson, Michael, 1939-
The Collapse of Antiquity: Greece and Rome as Civilization's
Oligarchic Turning Point

ISBN 978-3-949546-12-9 paperback
ISBN 978-3-949546-11-2 hardback

Acknowledgements

In producing this book I have been enormously aided by my copy editor Ashley Dayman, who has doubled as proof-reader and fact checker. The publishing team at Global University for Sustainability under Kin Chi Lau's direction has been wonderfully patient and conscientious in typesetting the book, headed by Jin Peiyun and Kelven Cheung.

I have had help with Latin translations from John Siman, who also helped with fact checking and discussing the Roman context for the debt struggles that this book describes. I received helpful criticism from John Weisweiler and his colleagues at the 2016 meeting in Tübingen, Germany, on "Debt: The First 3500 Years," that brought ancient historians together to discuss David Graeber's book *Debt: The First 5000 Years*. I wish that David were still here to continue our many years of discussion about how societies through the ages have dealt with the evolution of debt and how they have coped with the crises that it has caused.

My publisher Cornelia Wunsch has designed the format for all my books published by ISLET and handled the technical details. She has also provided great scholarly help over the years in analyzing the Near Eastern context for the subsequent Western economic development.

Gunther Kopcke invited me to give my first paper on debt in antiquity at the 1990 conference he organized on *Greece: from the 10th to 8th centuries BC*. It was held at the Institute for Fine Arts in New York City, where we earlier had co-taught a course on those centuries. That paper, published in 1992, forms the take-off point for this book, describing the transmission of interest-bearing debt from the ancient Near East to the West.

For over 31 years I have been discussing this book with my wife Grace, who has been wonderfully supportive in protecting my time from distractions and helping in innumerable ways. I could not have finished it in a timely fashion without her constant help.

Contents

III. Epilogue

Preface

This history of debt and the social strains it caused in Greece and Rome is the second volume in my planned trilogy on how societies through the ages have dealt with relations between debtors and creditors. The way in which economies have handled credit and debt arrangements, especially those relating to land tenure and debt servitude, determines whether or not a creditor oligarchy will gain power to monopolize the land and concentrate wealth and political power in its own hands.

Bronze Age Near Eastern rulers proclaimed Clean Slates cancelling personal debts to save their subjects from falling into debt bondage and losing their self-support land to creditors on more than a temporary basis. No such tradition developed in classical Greece and Rome, despite half a millennium of social revolts trying to cancel debts and redistribute land to needy families.

What happened when economic life was disturbed and debts could not be paid

Early economies operated on credit – that is, debt. These debts were not the result of money loans. Rather, they arose by individuals buying food, beer and agricultural inputs on credit during the course of the crop year, much like running up a tab at an ale-house to be settled on payday. In early times, "payday" was the harvest, and was one of the few occasions when money actually was used – to pay for the expenses (debts) run up during the year. The payment was in grain, measured out on the public threshing floor. A bushel of grain was monetized by making it equal to a shekel of silver, at least for paying debts to the palace and other creditors. This was society's first use of formal money.

But sometimes the weather was bad, floods or droughts occurred, crops failed or warfare interrupted the harvest. When there was little crop to collect, rulers suspended tax collection and also annulled the debts that had accrued during the crop year. Their main concern was to restore economic balance so families could resume providing the palace economy with crops and corvée labor. Not to have cleared away the backlog of debts would have been to leave a residue of debt that would have turned smallholders into bondservants to their creditors. That would have led to economic collapse and revolt, or defection to other communities.

Creditors for their part (often within the palace bureaucracy) vied
with the palace to take for themselves the labor and crops of their
debtors. But it was not in the ruler's interest to see indebted citizens
forfeit their land or its crops, or to fall into bondage to work off their
debts to private creditors, leaving them unable to perform corvée labor
duties for the palace and serve in the military. Paying debts with one's
labor or crops did occur in normal times. But upon taking the throne,
rulers proclaimed Clean Slate amnesties, cancelling personal crop debts
so as to start their reign in balance. They also issued new Clean Slate
proclamations when wars were over, and suspended debt collection in
times of drought or flooding.[1] Restoring an idealized *status quo ante* of
fiscal and economic balance in this way kept indebted citizen-cultiva-
tors free of bondage, and prevented creditors from competing with the
palace for labor and crop surpluses, and from ultimately rivaling and
replacing strong rulers.

My first volume of the trilogy, *"... and forgive them their debts,"* reviewed
how it was politically easy for Near Eastern rulers to save their indebted
subjects from more than temporary loss of liberty, because the most
important agrarian debts being annulled were arrears owed to the
palace and its collectors. Rulers saw creditors using their own loans
and advances to appropriate the labor services and crop yields of their
debtors as threats having the potential to become an independent oligarchy rivaling the palace in power.

The rise of independent oligarchies is what happened in classical
Greece and Rome in the first millennium BC, and it has become the distinguishing feature of Western economies ever since. Greece and Rome
had no palace rulers at the time interest-bearing debt was brought to the
Aegean and Mediterranean lands around 800-750 BC. Many chieftains
became creditors and used debt leverage to become local despots. Many
were unseated by the 7th- and 6th-century "tyrant" reformers in Corinth
and other Greek city-states. But new elites emerged and monopolized
control of politics and law-making to block the ability of popular leaders
or other civic authority to cancel debts and redistribute the land, or even
to enforce the few laws that were passed to protect debtors.

The emergence of financial and landholding oligarchies made debt
peonage and bondage permanent, supported by a pro-creditor legal
and social philosophy that distinguishes Western civilization from what

---

[1] Commercial and other business debts were left intact to take care of themselves,
being contracted among wealthy individuals who could afford to lose wealth
without losing their rights as citizens.

went before. Today it would be called neoliberalism. Ever since Rome, creditor claims have been protected by governments, not annulled, while land can be permanently forfeited to creditors, who become strong enough to avoid the social and fiscal obligations originally attached to the land.

This volume describes how this state of affairs was brought into being in antiquity over the course of five centuries, often by violent suppression of popular revolts and by targeted assassination of leaders seeking to cancel debts and redistribute land to smallholders who had lost it to large landowners. What was in effect a long popular revolution failed to stop the debt dynamics and monopolization of land that eventually impoverished the Roman Empire's population at large, ultimately tying clients to the land of their patrons and, more lastingly, bequeathing a creditor-based body of legal principles to the modern world.

Debt dynamics and the resulting concentration of wealth in the hands of an economic oligarchy "free" from public oversight to restore economic balance has been the main force polarizing and impoverishing society through the ages. Today, a "free market" implies increasing dependency for debtors and families that do not own their own homes or means of self-support. The economic polarization is made more extreme when normal income, production and related economic activity is interrupted.

The sequel to the present volume, *The Tyranny of Debt*, will trace the course of debt in the modern era. My theme throughout this trilogy is that a distinguishing feature of Western civilization has been its rejection of any political authority with the power to restore economic balance when the accumulation of debt grows in excess of the ability to pay.

The economic fallout from today's Covid-19 pandemic has highlighted both the flaws in this Western approach, and the merits and logic of the pre-classical way of coping with the debt dynamic when economic activity is interrupted. Economic balance needs to be restored in order for the normal circulation of production and income to occur without being distorted by allowing creditor claims for debt payment, landlord claims for rent and government claims for taxes to create a debt burden that operates as a financial wedge that drastically alters society's distribution of wealth and income.

Maps

Classical Greece

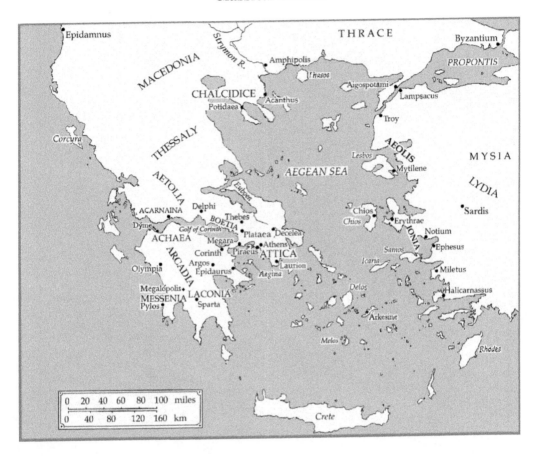

Ancient Italy

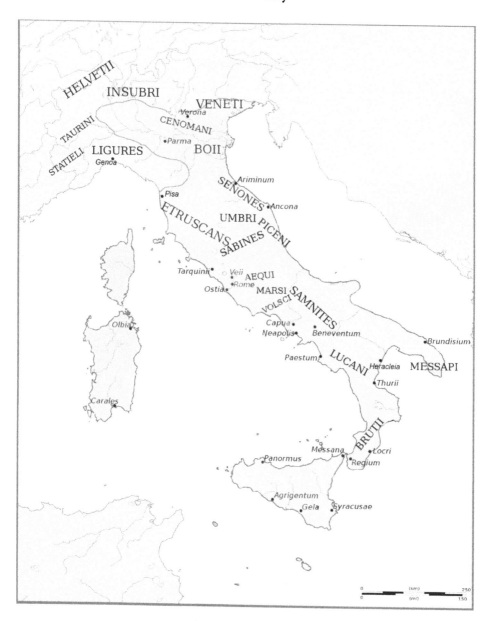

Asia Minor

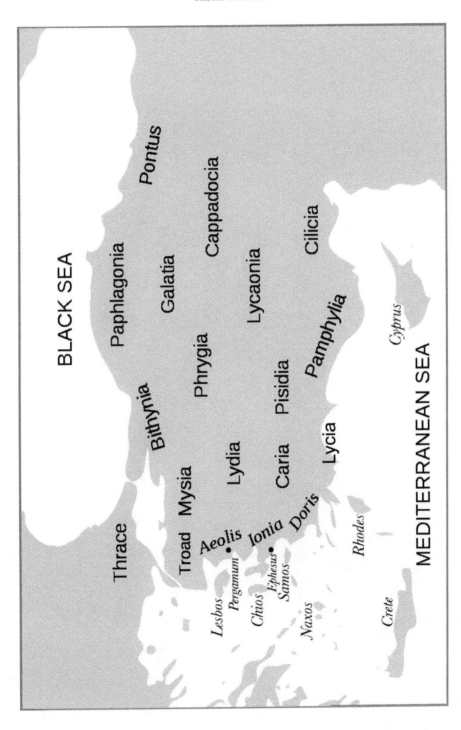

Roman Empire

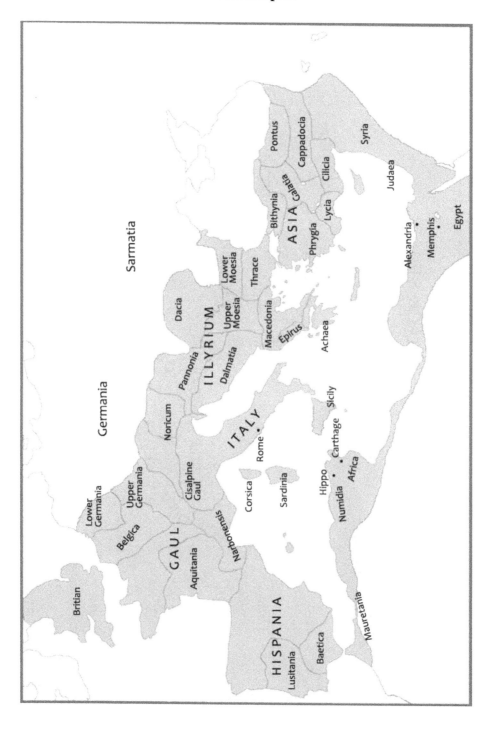

Introduction

The Social Darwinist philosophy of economic determinism has an optimistic circular reasoning: Any given society is assumed to be the product of natural selection favoring policies that best maximize productivity and prosperity. This logic assumes that today's Western civilization must be an outcome of past successes in an ascending line, with classical Greece and Rome being a progressive leap from the Near Eastern palatial economies to Western Europe and the modern West. It is from this self-congratulatory perspective that today's institutions of individualism and security of credit and property contracts (favoring creditor claims over debtors, and landlord rights over those of tenants) are traced back to classical antiquity as positive evolutionary developments, moving civilization away from "Oriental Despotism."

Modern ideology celebrates what made classical Greece and Rome different from what went before. They are treated as founding these Western traditions of individualism and secure creditor and property rights, not as ushering in a new form of oligarchic despotism that broke "free" of the royal and civic overrides that earlier societies had put in place to ensure economic balance and resilience. Laws providing security for credit and property rights, and opposition to kingship (the term applied to reformers threatening debt relief and land redistribution), are portrayed as going together with individualism and democracy to promote the survival of the fittest and most efficient.

The reality is that Rome's predatory oligarchies waged five centuries of civil war to deprive populations of liberty, blocking popular opposition to harsh pro-creditor laws and the monopolization of the land into latifundia estates. But the dynamics that drove labor into clientage and ultimately into serfdom have been downplayed by modern historiography that focuses more on Rome's military conquests and biographies of its leading consuls and emperors than on its struggles over debt and land tenure.

Rome as a "failed state" and what that implies for Western civilization

Antiquity's wealthy families, warlords and political elite appropriated most of the public land conquered from defeated regions, and acquired most of the domestic land by violence, seizure and foreclosure on indebted smallholders who encountered hard times. Rome's generals, governors, tax collectors, moneylenders and carpetbaggers squeezed out silver and gold in the form of military loot, tribute and usury from Asia Minor, Greece and Egypt. But Roman conquests are typically depicted as bringing order and progressive administrative organization akin to what the French have called their *mission civilisatrice*, an allegedly civilizing mission.

Yet the Greek and Roman economies ended in austerity and collapsed after having privatized credit and land in the hands of *rentier* oligarchies. Roman oligarchic ideology aimed at *preventing* kings or populist reformers from being strong enough to restore liberty and land to debtors. As in today's world, *rentier* elites sought to prevent any public regulation, debt cancellation and land redistribution that would threaten their power. Greece was destroyed by Rome's military oligarchy, which accused Catiline, Caesar and earlier advocates of ameliorating the debt crisis of "seeking kingship," as if the would-be reformers were merely seeking personal power, not trying to save Rome from its predatory elites. The oligarchs' idea of liberty was their right to appropriate land and other wealth by depriving debtors, other citizens and conquered populations of *their* liberty.

Rome's law of contracts established the fundamental principle of Western legal philosophy giving creditor claims priority over the property of debtors – euphemized today as "security of property rights." Public expenditure on social welfare was minimized – what today's political ideology calls leaving matters to "the market." It was a market that kept citizens of Rome and its Empire dependent for basic needs on wealthy patrons and moneylenders – and for bread and circuses, on the public dole and on games paid for by political candidates, who often themselves borrowed from wealthy oligarchs to finance their campaigns.

These pro-*rentier* ideas, policies and principles are those that today's Westernized world is following. That is what makes Roman history so relevant to today's economies suffering similar economic and political strains. The same dynamics are concentrating wealth in the hands of today's *rentier* oligarchies, which are imposing austerity by driving the population at large and even the public sector deeper into debt.

There is a tendency to view the oligarchic victory in Greece and Rome as inevitable and even natural, simply because that is how history turned out. But without seeing how antiquity's pro-creditor principles polarized and stifled its development, we will fail to recognize how our own epoch continues to be shaped by the legacy of antiquity's failure. The West remains largely a product of Rome's collapse, not its nonexistent democratic success. Antiquity's history provides an object lesson in the policies to avoid, not to emulate. But it is these very policies that survive at the core of the West's legal system and its individualistic philosophy of liberty to pursue economic gains at the expense of the broad public interest.

Debt as antiquity's major polarizing force

Throughout recorded history the most destabilizing dynamic has been the tendency of societies to polarize between a creditor oligarchy monopolizing land and other wealth, and an indebted clientage at the bottom. The major distinguishing feature of every civilization has been the way it has coped with debts that grow and tend to exceed the ability of many debtors to pay. If there is no intervention to restore balance by some authority acting from outside or "above" the market, economies will tend to polarize between creditors and debtors, patrons and clients.

Rome's own historians Livy, Sallust, Appian, Plutarch, Dionysius of Halicarnassus and Diodorus Siculus emphasized the subjugation of citizens to debt bondage as oligarchies used force and violence to monopolize the land and take control of governments. Most discussion focused on personal wealth ambition leading to socially destructive hubris. The Delphic oracle, poets and philosophers warned against the greed of creditors acting at the expense of society at large. Solon and Socrates, Stoics and Christians warned that wealth addiction and its money-love was the major threat to social harmony and hence to society.

The changing historiography of antiquity to reflect modern neoliberal ideology

The historiography of classical Greece and Rome reflects the modern world's own politics and ideology. Despite today's intensifying debt problems, recent historians have shown less concern with the role of debt in antiquity's decline and fall than did antiquity's own historians. A book published in 1984 became noteworthy for citing 210 causes of Rome's collapse.[1] Debt is conspicuously missing – and continues to be downplayed.

Historians writing in the late 19th and early 20th centuries focused on debt and land struggles, and were more critical of Rome's oligarchy than are more recent writers. Today's popular mainstream depicts antiquity as bequeathing democracy to the Western world. There has been a growing interest in the history of money and coinage, but debt relations, the resulting creditor power and land monopolization and the machinations of oligarchic political control have received less emphasis.

---

[1] Demandt 1984.

One reason is purely antiquarian. Coins and hoards have left an empirical record. In contrast to the abundance of Sumerian and Babylonian clay debt tablets describing royal Clean Slate proclamations and lawsuits to deal with creditor ploys to evade them, no such archives or even a clear legislative record survives for Greece and Rome. Our richest sources of information are dramatizations of debtor revolts in Rome, Greece and Asia Minor, but historians do not have clear debt laws for Greece prior to the 4th century BC, or for Rome even as late as the turbulent 1st century BC and early Empire. Apart from some notorious cases of usury, seizure of temple and civic property, and foreclosure on the arcades and other public property of indebted cities, there is little documentation of debts, especially on the personal level.

With few records of debt agreements, legal cases or even key Roman laws, it is understandable that most historians look where the light is brightest: to reports of Rome's military victories, its politicians and generals, and the melodrama of its celebrity emperors. To be sure, the past half century's scholarship has broadened our understanding of the early Greek reformer-tyrants, Roman kings and public finance. Yet the Greek debt crises discussed by Tarn (1923) and Fuks (1984), and the broad impact of debt, land tenure and tight patrician control of politics and the courts emphasized by Theodor Mommsen, Arnold Toynbee and Moses Finley, are disappearing in recent popular histories of classical antiquity. It is nearly a century since Tenney Frank began his five-volume *Economic Survey of Ancient Rome* (1933-1940), and no similar broad economic history of Greece has been attempted, above all where debt and its social conflicts are concerned.

Neoliberal economics downplays debt problems and hence those of ancient history

Recent classical histories tend to follow mainstream economics in focusing on productive lending that creates enough gains for borrowers to repay lenders without destabilizing basic social relationships. "According to the neoclassical model," notes Sitta von Reden, "credit has economic consequences only if it is used as capital for investment into productive enterprise. So-called consumption loans taken out to cover deficits and personal expenses are of little significance in this approach."[2] Instead of recognizing that economic polarization typically results from the

---

[2] Von Reden 2012:279. Most historians of coinage have related it mainly to prices, in accordance with the Quantity Theory of Money attributing price inflation to

accrual of debts as an inherent dynamic, today's mainstream economic theory treats debt as part of a system characterized by mutual gain, with borrowers making a voluntary choice to take on debt to improve their position – by buying land or other property, not losing it.

However, the major causes of debt for most people throughout antiquity were arrears for taxes, fines and cultivation costs that could not be paid in times of bad weather, disease and military disruption, or as a result of personal injury, sickness or accident. Debtors were obliged to work off their debts with their own labor, including most notoriously by sexual submission to their creditors. Roman law denied clients any rights to sue their patrons, and clients were obliged to support their patron's social spending. Debtors had little voice in drafting laws governing their obligations or through serving on juries, because Rome was never a democracy. Its legal and political systems established an oppressive power relationship that enabled moneylenders, tax collectors and related officials to push much of the population into clientage, which became irreversible when families lost their self-support land. Rome's indebted plebs found their only recourse to be walkouts ("secessions") in 494, 449 and 287 BC, winning modest gains, which the courts – manned by the oligarchy – typically refused to recognize.

Few recent classicists follow Rome's own historians in describing how its debt struggles and land grabs were mainly responsible for the Republic's decline and fall. Historians in the 19th and early 20th centuries followed classical economists in seeing progress as a movement to free society from *rentier* landlords and bankers extracting land rent and interest from the work of others. But historians following more modern views of market exchange and wealth downplay how debt dynamics led to the concentration of money, land and political power that destroyed the ancient economy's ability to sustain growth. Recent writers are reluctant to see debt as a major problem requiring writedowns to save economies from polarizing, and assume that "secure" credit contracts are a precondition for prosperity, regardless of the insecurity imposed on debtors.

The recent New Institutional Economics sidesteps the problem of widespread inability to pay arrears to creditors, tax collectors or landlords when the flow of the harvest and other economic activity is disrupted, or simply as a result of debts mounting up in the normal course of

---

currency debasement increasing the volume of coinage. More money is held to inflate prices proportionally. Bernard Laum's 1952 analytic synthesis of money and debt remains more comprehensive than most mainstream English-language discussion.

life.[3] Overlooking the political struggles that erupt when debts cannot be paid, Douglass North singles out the "security of contracts and property rights" as the key to economic progress. In practice this means the priority of creditor claims over the land and other property of debtors, and even their liberty. Sweden's central bank awarded North the neoliberal "Nobel" Economics Prize in 1993 for emphasizing this sanctity of financial claims on debtors and the ensuing rights to foreclose.[4]

Part of the appeal of this New Institutionalism is precisely its reluctance to acknowledge the society-wide effect of debts growing exponentially and leading to monopolization of the land by creditors. From the creditor's vantage point, the sanctity of debt claims and the legal right to foreclose are thought to be an intrinsic element of the natural order. In antiquity this meant that land tenure for smallholders was subordinate to the right of creditors to take their land, with creditors often using force, political assassination and control of politics and the courts to reduce indebted smallholders to clientage and loss of personal liberty. Today's academic economics isolates such phenomena as "exogenous," that is, extraneous to its models of exchange and wealth distribution. North's logic celebrating the rule of contract law that rationalized antiquity's polarization is reminiscent of Cicero's pleading that writing down debts would threaten property rights and the oligarchy's "confidence" that its appropriation of land would not be threatened by reformers.

To define a free market as including the freedom for creditors to insist on the "sanctity of debt" necessarily means a loss of liberty for debtors. But tolerance for an increasingly heavy debt overhead, enforced by pro-creditor "sanctity of debt" laws (and the consequent polarization of the ownership of land and other wealth as the magnitude of debt grows faster than the means to pay), is largely what has made Western civilization "Western." At least that is the spirit of most recent scholarship. Peter Temin notes that: "*The Cambridge Economic History of the Greco-Roman World* was based more on Douglass North than Moses Finley," and attributes Rome's success (and that of any economy) to its ability to provide the afore-mentioned security of contracts.[5]

---

[3] In contrast to the late 19th- and early 20th-century institutionalist school focusing on how *rentier* privileges emerged and consolidated their position (see Hudson 2011).

[4] For the prize's anti-regulatory, anti-government ideology see Offer and Söderberg 2016.

[5] Temin 2013:viii.

That is today's dominant ideology. Yet one might have expected today's debt crises from Greece to Argentina, and indeed from the United States to Europe, to have created more of an interest in how antiquity failed to alleviate its own debt problems. The financial dynamic that engulfed the Roman economy would seem to provide a clear warning against today's overriding directive that all debts must be paid, without regard for how this polarizes and hollows out economies.

The lesson to be drawn from antiquity is that creditor oligarchies seek to monopolize income and land in predatory ways that bring prosperity and growth to a halt. "The greed of creditors," wrote Plutarch, "brings neither enjoyment nor profit to them, and ruins those whom they wrong. They do not till the fields which they take from their debtors, nor do they live in their houses after evicting them."[6] Such concerns are what prompted Plutarch to write his biographies of Solon in Athens, Agis and Cleomenes in Sparta, and Roman reformers advocating the need to cancel debts in order to save society from creditors abusing their power to impoverish the indebted society at large. The volume of debt tends to expand exponentially, increasingly beyond the ability to pay, as debt service is plowed into new lending. Land pledged as collateral is forfeited when debtors fall into arrears and creditors are allowed to foreclose.

What are the ultimate causes of Rome's polarization and collapse?

Rome's toppling traditionally is dated to its sacking in 410 AD, followed in 476 by the deposition of its last emperor, derisively named Romulus Augustulus. But barbarians always were at the gates. Rome was weakened from within. If we look for the underlying causes of why it was weakened, we find century after century of oligarchic excesses.

Rome's civil war of 133-27 BC ended with the Senate Optimates fighting amongst themselves after having destroyed the plebeian opposition. Toynbee pushed the turning point back to the patrician land grab of Rome's *ager publicus* after the Punic Wars ended in 201. Hannibal's legacy was the spread of slave-stocked latifundia throughout Italy and Sicily.

To many Roman-era historians the die was cast already when the patricians overthrew Rome's kings in 509 and imposed a one-sided constitution and pro-creditor laws. The kings had offered immigrants a sufficiently attractive life to draw them from the surrounding region and motivate them to fight for the city. But elections under the Republic were limited to a choice of personalities, and reformers were blocked.

---

[6] Plutarch, *Moralia* 829 (Loeb Classical Library, 1936 X:327).

Attempts to establish more democratic rights were met by century after century of political assassination, with the killers being celebrated as heroes. By the 1st century BC the typical option for smallholders driven off their homesteads was to seek employment as mercenaries.

This book finds even deeper seeds for antiquity's collapse: specifically, in the way it adopted interest-bearing debt around the 8th century BC from the Near East without the tradition of Clean Slates. That tradition of debt cancellation and restoration of land that debtors had lost was designed to restore social balance and block the emergence of creditor oligarchies in the palace economies of the Near East. It was in those economies that interest-bearing debt first emerged, accompanied by the safety valve of royal Clean Slate proclamations that enabled them to avoid the irreversible debt bondage and concentration of land ownership that impoverished classical antiquity.

Today, these palatial economies whose rulers were empowered to issue proclamations of liberty would be called managed economies. Karl Wittfogel used the term "Oriental Despotism," implying governing structures antithetical to ideas of freedom and liberty. It is true that royal planning was not democratic. However, Near Eastern rulers recognized how polarizing the accrual of interest-bearing debt was, and protected most of the population's liberty from bondage by periodically reversing personal debt accruals and restoring land tenure rights.

What made Greece and Rome different from what went before was their rejection of this Near Eastern tradition of economic renewal. Instead of restoring balance by periodically reversing the accrual of personal and agrarian debts ("circular time"), classical oligarchies made debt foreclosure irreversible, so that land rights and personal liberty were lost irrevocably to creditors.

Whatever dates we choose to mark antiquity's fatal turning points, the key reason for its decline was the way in which it handled the problem of debtors falling into dependency, and the ensuing concentration of land ownership, monetary wealth and political power in creditor oligarchies. The pro-creditor ideology of Rome's oligarchy has survived to shape modern legal systems and economic ethics. The demand that all debts must be paid, without concern for the effects on debtors or on fiscal, economic and social stability, remains congenial to today's financial interests and has become ingrained in modern economic thought. It is not based on the evidence of economic history but reflects today's pro-creditor version of free-market ideology.

Given this prevailing ideology, this book no doubt will be characterized as a revisionist history of antiquity. What is ironic is that I have followed what antiquity's own historians and philosophers themselves emphasized: the conflict between creditors and debtors, won by increasingly powerful creditors at the cost of destroying the society that they managed. The kind of market that they designed and administered looked only at their short-term tactical gains, lacking the context of long-term viability that had guided earlier kingdoms which, ironic as it may seem, were more economically "democratic" than democratically elected oligarchies have proved to be.

Summary

Classical antiquity's historical records start around the 7th century BC. Greece was emerging from a Dark Age after the palatial economies using Linear B collapsed ca. 1200 BC as a result of what seems to have been severe climate disruption. Antiquity's subsequent trajectory cannot be understood without appreciating how its debt practices, money and the charging of interest, along with the associated monetary weights and measures, and even much myth and ritual, were brought to the Aegean and Mediterranean lands from the Near East by Syrian and other Levantine traders around the 8th century BC. These Near Eastern economic practices were adopted in a new social and economic context, without palatial overrides. With no tradition of debt cancellation and land redistribution to restrain personal wealth seeking, Greek and Italian chieftains, warlords and what some classicists have called mafiosi imposed absentee land ownership over dependent labor,[1] binding indebted clients to the land and obliging them to work off chronic dependency in the form of labor service (Chapter 1).

Economic polarization between creditors and debtors intensified by the 7th and 6th centuries BC as monopolization of the land forced populations into clientage. Some members of the ruling families (often from their minor branches) led revolts that redistributed land and cancelled debts, much as Near Eastern rulers had done, and sponsored laws to standardize the administration of justice, along with sumptuary legislation to discourage extravagance. These reformers were called tyrants; the word's negative connotation was applied above all by those who opposed debt cancellation and land redistribution in subsequent centuries.

Corinth produced a classic dynasty. The reformer-tyrant Cypselus (ruled ca. 657-627) and his son Periander (627-585) built temples and sponsored the Pan-Hellenic games and similar festivals, financed by the proceeds of state investment in commercial infrastructure. Like-minded reformers were Theagenes (ca. 600) in Megara, Orthagorus and his grandson Cleisthenes (ca. 600-560) in Sicyon, and Polycrates (538-522) on the island of Samos (Chapter 2).

---

[1] The term "mafiosi" is used by MacMullen 1974:12 and van Wees 2000 to describe how a few families established economic power over labor on the land that they gained control of.

Sparta remained relatively free of debt strains for many centuries. Local elites held most of the land in Sparta proper. When they conquered neighboring Messenia in the 7th and 6th centuries, they turned its population into serflike helots, who were forced to produce food and other needs for Sparta's infantry of *homoioi* "peers." This arrangement minimized the need for money, markets and hence debt as Sparta was economically self-contained (Chapter 3).

Solon cancelled debts in Athens in 594, but refrained from redistributing the land. Peisistratus and his sons (561-510) undertook public spending along the lines that tyrant-reformers had done in other Greek cities. At the end of the 6th century Cleisthenes shifted the basis of Athenian political representation and participation from clan membership to geographic locality, while preserving the citizenry's political status and military categories based on the landholding dividing lines that Solon is reported to have introduced (Chapter 4).

Athens' monetary reserves came mainly from its Laurion silver mines. Citizens voted to coin the mines' output to build the navy that defeated Persia's ships at Salamis. Ephialtes and Pericles strengthened the democracy, but the loss to Sparta in the Peloponnesian War (431-404 BC) led to a brief rapacious oligarchy that ran up heavy debts. The subsequent democracy agreed to pay these debts to demonstrate Athens' opposition to the debt cancellations being advocated throughout Greece (Chapter 5).

Chapter 6 traces the evolution of Greek public finance. As in the Near East, temples stored and displayed their communities' savings, headed by military booty cast into gold and silver statues, metallic garments and various votive offerings. Temples melted down this bullion and struck coins for civic authorities to hire mercenaries and build ships in war emergencies. This bullion was expected to be paid back upon the return to peace, making it the first formal public debt arrangement. Temple bullion also was used to finance the construction of public monuments. By the 4th century BC, however, many cities were so financially strapped that they had to rely on wealthy philanthropists or other elite to save their public property from decay. Cyme (in southern Italy) and Arkesine (on the island of Amorgos) pledged and forfeited their public arcades and infrastructure to creditors.

Describing wealth as addictive, Theognis of Megara and Solon, Plato and Aristotle framed the discussion of debt in the context of *pleonexia* (wealth addiction) or *philarguria* (love of silver) leading to predatory and socially injurious behavior. Athenian political and moral philosophy, poetry and drama denounced wealth addiction and money-lust as leading to hubris, which was defined as aggressive greed injuring the body politic. In Plato's *Republic*, Socrates proposed that only administrators without wealth or property should be appointed to govern society so that they presumably would not be prone to hubristic greed and defend pro-creditor rules (Chapter 7).

But by the 3rd century BC, aristocracies throughout Greece were monopolizing land and monetary wealth in the face of rising indebtedness for the rest of society. After Sparta defeated Athens in 404, the influx of silver destabilized its "in-kind" requisitioning system that had minimized the need for monetary exchange. Sparta's wealthiest families obtained most of the tribute. Most Spartan citizens fell into the ranks of "Inferiors."

To reverse this situation and revive Sparta's military power, Agis IV (245-241), Cleomenes III (235-222) and Nabis (207-192) promoted debt cancellation and land redistribution. Their policy was akin to that of the 7th-century "tyrants" in Corinth, Megara and other cities. Sparta's oligarchy responded by executing Agis, exiling Cleomenes, fighting Nabis, and joining neighboring oligarchies to invite Rome to intervene and prevent Spartan and other attempts to cancel debts and redistribute land (Chapter 8).

No written Roman narratives have survived from the archaic era. The standard histories of the Roman *rex* (a chieftain or "king") were written after the Republic had collapsed. Recent scholarship describes Rome's late kings as similar to Greece's 7th-century tyrants in sponsoring civic building programs and attracting immigrants from the surrounding territories. They were overthrown around 509 BC by a patrician coup whose leaders accused kings in principle of being prone to hubris.

More likely, the kings were opposed for keeping the wealthiest families in check. The oligarchy's real complaint was against any power strong enough to build up a public sector independent of Senate control and, in particular, to block the emerging oligarchy's subjugation of clients and debtors to bondage. Although written from the vantage point of the civil warfare and debt crises that marked the 1st century BC, the basic outline of what occurred under the kings is generally accepted (Chapter 9).[2]

What had been a century of expansion and conquest under Rome's kings gave way to half a century of oligarchic austerity, less public building and not very successful warfare. Led by Appius Claudius Sabinus (who

---

[2] Summarizing the "common body of tradition that outlined the main developments in the history of the city," Cornell 2005:52 has noted that "Cicero, Diodorus, Dionysius and Livy agree closely with one another on all fundamental points (and often in matters of fine detail)." See also Cornell's 1995 *Beginnings of Rome*.

had been granted patrician rank when he brought his wealth and a contingent of Sabine followers to Rome just before the oligarchic coup), the Senate sought to prevent any moves that might lead toward popular democracy. Its harsh overreach led to Secession of the Plebs in 494 over the debt and land crisis. The walkout was resolved by creating the office of popular tribunes to protect Roman citizens, but the tribunes were not empowered to initiate laws. The population at large never managed to achieve meaningful participation in lawmaking or the courts (Chapter 10).

A new crisis erupted ca. 450 BC when Appius Claudius Crassus picked ten men (decemvirs) to draft new Roman laws. Their harshly pro-creditor laws, the Twelve Tables, prompted the plebs to secede again in 449. But this did not deter the Senate from tightening its control and killing politicians accused of "seeking kingship," that is, supporting popular demands for debt relief and land grants from Rome's *ager publicus* won in wars with neighboring Italians (Chapter 11).

Chapter 12 describes the subsequent debt revolts that forced passage of the Licinian-Sextian law in 367 to limit the interest rate and the monopolization of public land. Half a century later the Poetelia-Papiria law banned *nexum* debt slavery. These laws protecting debtors had to be passed again and again, because the Senate refused to enforce them and Rome's patrician-run courts ignored them.

Rome's Second Punic War against Carthage (218-201) saw military contractors engage in large-scale fraud and violently block the Senate from prosecuting them. It also became an occasion for endowing the wealthiest families with public land when the Roman state treated their ostensibly patriotic donations of jewelry and money to aid the war effort as retroactive public debts subject to repayment. After Rome defeated Carthage, they demanded reimbursement for what they had given. The only asset the treasury had available was the rich land of *Campania* south of Rome. The wealthiest families arranged for the Senate to assign them most of this *ager publicus* instead of allocating it to war veterans as had been the tradition (Chapter 13).

Rome's conquest of Greece, Macedonia and Carthage in the mid-2nd century provided a vast supply of slaves, and Rome levied only minimum taxes after 167 BC. Most slaves were put to work on plantations in Sicily and elsewhere in Italy, setting the stage for Rome's three major slave wars (in 135, 104 and 73 BC) and for its century of civil war from 133 to 27 BC as the conflict between creditors and debtors came to a head. Tiberius Gracchus and hundreds of his fellow reformers were killed in 133, followed by his brother Gaius in 121. Such assassination of politicians seeking to limit creditor power became almost normal oligarchic policy in Rome down through the murder of Caesar, fearing that popular leaders would seek support by cancelling debts owed by the poor (Chapter 14).

Affluence from Rome's foreign tribute and rents led to a wave of lending among Rome's wealthy families to buy land. But a financial crisis occurred when tribute from Asia Minor was interrupted. Creditors called in their loans, forcing sales and crashing the land bubble. In 89 BC the praetor Asellio was killed for trying to enforce earlier Roman laws protecting debtors. The crisis finally was resolved by writing down loan balances by 75 percent to reflect the degree by which land prices had fallen. That stabilized the purchasing power of loans in terms of land, the major collateral and object of Roman lending to the well-to-do (Chapter 15).

Rome's conquest of Asia Minor and its rapacious demands for tribute led to the outbreak of the Mithridatic Wars (88-63 BC), which started when a reported 80,000 Romans were killed in the Vespers of Ephesus. Rome sent a series of generals who looted the province, imposed reparations, and allied themselves with publican tax collectors to strip its temples and civic assets. Senate attempts to stop the corruption and illegal seizure were stymied by the tax collectors' control of the courts (Chapter 16).

Sulla's looting of Asia Minor and Greece enabled him to bring his booty-laden troops back to Rome in 82 and impose an oligarchic constitution that rolled back the few gains plebeians had made in earlier centuries. His reign of terror let his supporters kill his opponents and confiscate their property, headed by that of families who had backed the popular general Marius. Widespread debt defaults occurred, including by wealthy individuals who had borrowed heavily to buy land or political office. By 63, many well-to-do as well as poor debtors supported Catiline's plan to assassinate Cicero and other opponents of debt cancellation, but their revolt was defeated by the Senate's army (Chapter 17).

Led by Cato, Cicero and Cato's son-in-law Bibulus, the Senate opposed any popular reform, even the distribution of land to war veterans. That led Pompey to break with the Senate oligarchy and join with Crassus, Rome's richest man, and Caesar to create the First Triumvirate (60-53), allying themselves with the popular assembly and tribunes. Seeing that the only way for a reform program to succeed was by armed force, Caesar arranged for a five-year military command in Spain and Gaul, which later was extended to ten years. He obtained enough wealth and loyal troops to march on Rome and gain power in 49 (Chapter 18).

Caesar's rise to power was the last opportunity to restore balance. During 49-44 (the chronology is not clear) he sponsored a bankruptcy law that alleviated the distress of indebted landowners by writing down their debts in proportion to the 25 percent fall in land prices. But he resisted the widespread debt cancellation that many Romans without property had anticipated. That moderation did not deter the Senate oligarchs from killing him, fearing that he might use his popularity to "seek kingship" by enacting more populist reforms. The ensuing infighting brought the Republic to an end when Caesar's adopted heir Octavian defeated his rivals Brutus, Cassius and finally Antony in 31 BC at the Battle of Actium and then had the Senate designate him princeps and augustus in 27 BC (Chapter 19).

The Senate lost power and became merely a ceremonial elite as army leaders gained control. Smallholders who lost their land found their major employment option to be joining armies as mercenaries under generals promising them booty and, as veterans, settlement on new plots of land. But Rome's Empire was basically a coda for the way in which the Republic had established its rules for credit and land tenure. The wealthiest families plowed most of their rents and interest into more land appropriation and usury, and passed the tax burden onto local officials and small landholders. By the time Emperor Hadrian felt obliged to burn the tax records to abolish arrears in 118 AD, as Marcus Aurelius would again do in 178, the major beneficiaries of such debt amnesties were the rich who had managed to delay paying their taxes (Chapter 20).

The Western Empire fell apart when there was no more land for the taking and no more monetary bullion to loot. Roman demands for tax revenues forced smallholders into debt to private creditors and landlords, leading them to lose their land to the creditor oligarchy, which opposed any state power capable of taxing it or restoring widespread land tenure. By the 5th century AD there was no more talk of land redistribution or debt cancellation. As the Late Roman Empire became a predatory free-for-all, its End Time produced so deep a revulsion against luxury amidst a world of poverty that martyrdom increased. By the 4th century the Christian Church was able to ban the charging of interest by members of the priesthood, and in due course by the lay population, without opposition from the wealthy (Chapter 21).

But Christianity's character changed as it became Rome's state religion under Constantine. Instead of its earlier critique of economic greed as sinful, the Church accepted the Empire's maldistribution of land and other wealth. The new official religion merely asked that the wealthy be charitable, and atone for personal sin by donating to the

Church. Instead of the earlier meaning of the Lord's Prayer as a call to forgive personal debts, the new sins calling for forgiveness were egotistical and, to Augustine, sexual drives especially. The financial dimension disappeared (Chapter 22).

Chapter 23 traces how Rome's oligarchic ideology and legal traditions have shaped those of the West. Today's protection of creditors and opposition to public regulation has its roots in Rome's oligarchy sanctifying the obligation of debtors to relinquish their land and personal liberty to creditors. To accept the views of Rome's own historians criticizing these oligarchic debt dynamics would call into question our own Western practice of following similar pro-creditor policies and free-market philosophy. This modern-day pro-creditor ideology has shaped recent economic interpretations of antiquity, which show increasing sympathy with Rome's oligarchic policies. Rome's decline and fall is blamed mainly on its predatory Empire, not on its debt dynamics and the failure of its internal struggles to promote domestic prosperity by reforming debt bondage and restoring the citizenry's means of self-support.

A Chronology of Debt Crises and Land Struggles in Greece and Rome

8th century BC: interest-bearing debt is transmitted from the Near East to Greece and Italy without the tradition of Clean Slate debt cancellations.

Mid-7th-mid-6th centuries BC: Popular reformers ("tyrants") come to power in Corinth, Megara, Sicyon and other Greek cities, overthrowing landed aristocracies (often including their own clan members), redistributing land and cancelling debts.

Early 6th century BC: Sparta defers a political crisis over debt and land distribution. Its "Lycurgan laws" abolish silver as money and redistribute the land conquered from Messenia, turning its population into helots to serve Spartan citizens.

594: When Athens succumbs to a similar debt and land crisis, Solon (ca. 638–558) is given powers to act as *archon* ("premier"). He cancels debts, bans personal debt bondage for Athenians, and also alien landowner-ship (thereby preventing foreign creditors from foreclosing), but avoids the land redistribution carried out in other cities.

509: Rome's last king, Tarquin Superbus, is overthrown. The Republic bases government on oligarchic rule. The resulting class conflict imposes austerity.

508: Cleisthenes restructures Athens' tribes and voting system on a geographic basis, diluting oligarchic control and paving the way for subsequent democracy.

494: First secession of the Roman plebs, mainly debtors who refused to fight until their subjugation was alleviated. Plebeian tribunes are intro-duced, but the Senate rigidly maintains intransigent power.

486: Spurius Cassius introduces an agrarian law in Rome, leading to his murder in 485.

482: Athenians vote to use the fiscal surplus from Laurion's silver mines to build their navy.

450-449: Rome's Twelve Tables retain the *nexum* institution of debt-servitude, but limit interest rates to 8 $\frac{1}{3}$ percent ($1/12^{th}$) per annum and impose a fourfold penalty for overcharging. But creditors repeatedly violate this tradition, and the law had to be reiterated in 357.

449: Second secession of the Roman plebs, resolved by the Valerio-Horatian laws.

439: Spurius Maelius is murdered for proposing land distribution to the plebs and Latin allies.

390: Gallic armies sack Rome, leaving famine in their wake as crops are destroyed.

384: M. Manlius Capitolinus, the first Roman patrician to act as a populist, is murdered for defending debtors by selling off public land to redeem their debts, accusing senators of embezzlement and urging them to redeem debtors.

380-378: To deal with the land grabbing by Roman elites, two censors are appointed to conduct a property census. But the Senate blocks it.

367: Rome's Licinian-Sextian law limits personal land holdings to only 500 iugera (125 hectares). The legislation permits debtors to deduct interest payments from the principal and to pay off the balance in three years instead of all at once.

357: Maximum interest rates in Rome are fixed at $1/12^{th}$, an ounce per pound (=$8\frac{1}{3}$ percent). A public commission is appointed in 352 to lend funds to save bankrupt Roman debtors from bondage and loss of their lands (revived during the 217 Punic War emergency).

ca. 356 to 350: The Greek military writer Aeneas Tacticus writes in his manual of military strategy that the way to defend a town is to promise to liberate debt servants and cancel the debts. Likewise for generals mounting an attack, the way to get a town to surrender or its army to defect is to make the same promise to cancel debts and free the bondservants.

347: Rome's legal interest rate is cut in half, to $4^1/6$ percent $(1/24^{th})$, and a moratorium is declared on existing debts, which are to be paid off in four equal installments. To ameliorate matters further, the *tributum* war tax is suspended.

342: The plebeian tribune Lucius Genucius moves to ban outright the charging of interest, but the ban, if it really happened, soon becomes a dead letter.

326 or 313: After popular riots, Rome's Poetelia-Papiria law bans *nexum* debt-servitude.

289: Mint and *tresviri monetales* (office of treasurer overseeing the minting of coins) are established in Rome.

287: When debt problems lead Rome's plebeians to secede once more, Quintus Hortensius is made Dictator to resolve matters. His *lex Hortensia* erased the political distinction between plebeians and patricians, giving the plebeian assembly some additional power relative to that of the Senate.

280-250: Uprisings aimed at debt and land reform on the islands of Naxos, Amorgos, Ceos and Syros are put down by Macedonia's oligarchic Corinthian League.

264-241: First Punic War with Carthage, followed by a second war in 218-201.

245-241: Sparta's king Agis IV attempts debt and land reform.

235-222 Cleomenes III reigns as king of Sparta, fights against the Achaean League starting in 229, and introduces his debt and land reform in 227, seeking to return to the legendary Lycurgan egalitarian ethic, and to restore a free land-tenured peasant army. He is defeated by Macedonia at Sellasia in 222.

225-224: Corinth revolts to support Cleomenes against the oligarchy, hoping for a debt cancellation, but Cleomenes fails to proclaim it, and Macedonia drives him out of northern Greece back to Sparta.

220-217: The "Social War" in Greece, by Sparta and its Aetolian League allies against Macedonia, with revolutionary sentiment in the Aetolian League headed by impoverished debtors.

207-192: Nabis rules Sparta and exiles many of its leading creditor families, and promotes debt cancellation in neighboring parts of Greece.

201: After Rome levies huge reparations on defeated Carthage after the Second Punic War, wealthy contributors to the war effort in 210 demand repayment, representing that their donations actually were loans. The money is to be paid in three installments.

200: With its treasury bare after paying two installments, Rome has only the public land to turn over, above all the rich *Campania*. Instead of being settled by war veterans as had been customary, this land is turned over to wealthy war-contributors in lieu of payment of the third installment. It is to be taxed at only a nominal rate. Beginning in 198, foreign slaves are imported *en masse* to cultivate the resulting latifundia.

193: The Sempronian law extends Rome's Twelve Tables' $8^{1}/_3$ percent interest-rate ceiling to cover non-Romans within the expanding imperial Republic's provinces.

192: Nabis is defeated when oligarchic cities call in Roman aid. Sparta is forced into the Achaean League. Greece passes into the Roman sphere of influence after the Peace of Apamea in 188.

179: Perseus, last Macedonian ruler of the post-Alexandrine Antigonid dynasty, starts his reign by an amnesty for exiles and cancels debts owed to the palace. This leads to Roman opposition, fearing the spread of demands for debt cancellation throughout Greece.

176: Rome delegates Appius Claudius Pulcher to write down debts in Aetolia and Thessaly to prevent their defection to Perseus.

168: Rome defeats Perseus at Pydna, ending Macedonian monarchy after Perseus tries to hold local support by advocating a debt cancellation.

167: The flow of booty from Greece enables Rome to stop taxing Italian land owned by its citizens (although Latin and Italian cities still had to pay the *tributum* tax). Rome incorporated Greece into its Macedonian province after the Battle of Corinth in 146.

144: Leaders of Dyme are put to death for burning the public archives and debt records.

133: Attalus III of Pergamum bequeaths his kingdom to Rome. Aristonicus, the local claimant, mobilizes the population against Rome, promising to cancel their debts and establish a "City of the Sun" (Heliopolis), a political ideal probably influenced by the Stoic philosopher Blossius. Aristonicus is defeated in 130 and in 129 Pergamum becomes a Roman province, named "Asia." Rome defeats local armies by poisoning the water supply. After looting local temples, it burdens Asia Minor with huge reparations debts, paving the way for over half a century of warfare. Regular tribute starts in 126.

133-27: Rome's domestic civil war is fought largely over the debt issue. In 133 the brothers Tiberius and Gaius Gracchus sponsor land reform on the public domain (in particular to limit the extent of large estates and distribute land to the poor). They also sponsor a financial reform, creating a class of *publicani* "knights" to act as creditors and financiers, so that senators will not perform this function. Tiberius Gracchus is murdered by oligarchic senators in 133, the first tribune to be killed.

123-121: Tiberius's brother Gaius Gracchus, continuing their reform program, becomes tribune, but he and his fellow tribune M. Fulvius Flaccus and their supporters are killed in 121 when they occupy the Aventine.

111: The oligarchic Agrarian Law declares all occupied public domain to be the property of existing holders, defeating plebeian hopes for land reform.

100: The tribune L. Appuleius Saturninus, supported by the consul Gaius Marius, sponsors a land-settlement reform, but the Optimates oppose it. After the leading Optimate candidate, Gaius Memmius, was beaten to death during the voting, Marius's allies Saturninus and G. Servilius Glaucia were killed, along with many of their supporters to prevent a popular revolt.

92: After serving as legate to Q. Mucius Scaevola (consul in 95) to help clean up the predatory behavior of *publicani* and moneylenders in Asia, P. Rutilius Rufus is put on trial for maladministration in a notorious travesty of justice by the *equites* fighting back against his attempts to block their extortionate practices. He chooses exile from Rome, settling in Smyrna whose inhabitants welcome him, and remaining there until his death after 78.

89: The praetor Asellio is murdered for sponsoring restoration of the Twelve Tables law punishing creditors fourfold for charging excessive interest (over $8^1/_3$ percent). Debtors were agitating for "new account books," that is, a Clean Slate debt cancellation.

88: The Vespers of Ephesus: As many as 80,000 Romans are killed in Asia Minor in retaliation against Roman tax farming and moneylending. During 88-85, Mithridates of Pontus turns what had begun as a local war in 92 into a region-wide war against Rome.

86: The consul L. Valerius Flaccus (filling out the term of Marius, who died in office) sponsors the *Lex Valeria de aere alieno* reducing debts by three-quarters. That reflected the degree to which land prices had fallen, establishing the correlation between land valuation and debts that would underlie Caesar's *cessio bonorum* in 49.

86-85: The Roman general Sulla, having marched on Rome to seize power in 88, sacks Asia Minor and imposes a huge tribute, forcing many cities and much of the population into debt to Italian bankers. This helps make Sulla the richest man in Rome by 83. His army takes over the city again and kills many of his opponents during his dictatorship of 82-79.

73-71: Slave revolt led by the Thracian war-captive Spartacus.

70: Rome declares a moratorium on Asia Minor's war tribute, which had multiplied six-fold from the 20,000 talents imposed by Sulla in 84 to 120,000 talents, despite the fact that 40,000 talents already had been paid out (not including the looted treasure of Asia Minor's temples). The local Roman general, Lucullus, sets a 12 percent interest rate and decrees that where interest payments have exceeded the original principal, the debt is to be considered paid. Debt service is limited to a quarter of the debtor's income.

63-62: Catiline's debt revolt. He and some three thousand supporters are killed in battle. A major plank of their program (which Cicero called a "conspiracy") is a cancellation of debts.

60: In the ensuing civil war, Pompey, Crassus and Caesar form the First Triumvirate. The next year, in 59 BC, Julius Caesar becomes consul. He writes down by a third the debts owed by the *equites* to the treasury on their Asia contracts.

56-50: Brutus makes a loan to the Cypriot city of Salamis at 48 percent annual interest, and sends his envoy Scaptius to serve on the staff of his father-in-law, Appius Claudius Pulcher, to command a cavalry and besiege the Salmatian officials in their senate house, starving five to death. When Cicero follows Appius as governor of Cilicia, Brutus asks him to empower Scaptius to resume collection. Having decreed the legal interest rate of 12 percent, Cicero refuses to agree, but dodges the issue by leaving matters for his successor to adjudicate.

49: Caesar marches on Rome and defeats Pompey and his supporters. He allows debtors to deduct interest payments from their principal, and introduces Rome's first bankruptcy law, but it alleviates debt pressures only for the wealthy. His *cessio bonorum* saves them from having to sell off their property under distress conditions by letting them turn over real estate at pre-civil war prices. To support collapsing land prices, Caesar also directs that two-thirds of all capital assets must be held in the form of Italian real estate. This is not much help to the landless and smallholding population at large. The demagogues Coelius Rufus and Milo are killed after leading a popular insurrection advocating debt cancellation.

47: P. Cornelius Dolabella likewise advocates cancellation of debts, but his supporters are killed when barricading the Forum. This is the final defeat for Rome's indebted poor. Henceforth, lending is concentrated mainly among the wealthy.

44: Caesar is appointed dictator for life, but is killed in the Senate by oligarchic leaders.

31: Octavian defeats Antony at Actium, and in 27 the Senate gives him the titles augustus and princeps.

27 BC-AD 235: The Roman Principate, the first phase of the Roman Empire: Twelve emperors in 262 years.

AD 1st century: Jesus attempts to revive the Mosaic tradition of the Jubilee Year. He devotes his first sermon (Luke 4) to announcing that he has come to proclaim a Jubilee Year bringing debt forgiveness and land redistribution in accordance with Leviticus 25.

AD 33: A financial crisis results from emperors hoarding coinage in the imperial treasury, aggravated by private hoarding and a drain of bullion to the East (largely to purchase luxuries). Tiberius re-imposes the traditional interest-rate ceiling, and Caesar's decree that two-thirds of all personal capital be invested in Italian real estate. This leads to widespread foreclosure on mortgages as lenders convert their financial claims into land. Tiberius decrees that debtors are obliged only to pay two-thirds of debts that are called due, but his measures nonetheless aggravate the general financial crisis.

AD 1st century: The colonate tenant-farming system emerges, with latifundists leasing parcels of land to *coloni*. Declining Roman warfare reduces the capture of slaves, raising their price after the 2nd century. That prompts large landowners to adopt patron-client arrangements, using debt leverage to lock labor into a state of peonage. Smallholders who run into debt are obliged to become *coloni* or seasonal migrant workers.

AD 1st-4th centuries: Persecutions of Christians. Roman authorities persecute Christianity not so much as a religion as a potentially revolutionary moral program opposed to Roman landlordship and creditor power. Persecution peaks in 303-304 under Diocletian. Galerius ends the persecution in 311.

AD 118: Hadrian burns the records of tax arrears – which by this time are owed mainly by the wealthier landholding families.

AD 178: Marcus Aurelius emulates Hadrian's burning of the tax and debt records.

AD 4th century: The colonate ossifies into feudalism, with *coloni* tied to the land. The first reference to serfs being bound to the soil in the Theodosian Code of 438 is a ruling from 322.

AD 321: Constantine makes Christianity Rome's state religion.

AD 311-417: Donatist movement against Roman creditors in North Africa, and then against Augustine and other Christian officials loyal to Rome and its client oligarchy.

AD 325: The Council of Nicaea bans the practice of usury by members of the Christian priesthood.

AD 354-430: Augustine serves as Bishop of Hippo and fights the Donatists to establish firm pro-Roman control of Christianity. Making it Rome's official state religion under pro-Roman control removes the early Christian advocacy of debt cancellation, refocusing the concept of sinfulness from the economic sphere to the personal sphere of individual egotism, above all with a sexual connotation reflecting Augustine's idiosyncratic focus on humanity's original sin.

AD 408: Alaric besieges Rome with an army that includes many debtors who had left the city to join him. He besieges it again in 409 and eventually sacks it in 410.

AD 430: Vandals take Hippo, and Augustine dies in the siege.

AD 476: Deposition of Romulus Augustus formally ends the Roman Empire.

The money-lender ... attacks your liberty and brings suit against your honor. If you will not pay him, he duns you; if you have funds, he won't accept payment; if you sell, he beats down the price; if you will not sell, he forces you to do so; if you sue him, he meets you in court; ... if you go to his door, he shuts it in your face; if you stay at home, he installs himself there and keeps knocking at your door.

— Plutarch, "That We Ought Not to Borrow," *Moralia*[1]

---

[1] Plutarch, *Moralia* 829E (Loeb Classical Library, 1936 X:322-323).

1

How Interest-Bearing Debt was Brought to Greece and Italy, 8th Century BC[1]

Economic historians used to assume that interest-bearing debt is so natural and widespread that it must have evolved spontaneously everywhere. But contrary to what was believed until quite recently, charging interest is not a spontaneous and universal phenomenon. There is no hint of it in the Linear B tablets of Mycenaean Greece or Crete ca. 1600-1200 BC. Its absence in these Bronze Age records strongly suggests that the practice was brought to the Aegean along with other commercial innovations from Phoenicia and Syria around 800 BC, when merchants from these regions appear to have begun organizing their trade with Greece and Italy, using temples as commercial embassies much like the Assyrians did a millennium earlier.[2]

The basic economic practices of modern civilization originated in the Bronze Age Near East – the fractional weights and measures that formed the basis for money and credit, interest-bearing debt and contractual enterprise arrangements, along with a cultural-religious awareness of the dangers posed to society by the arrogance of wealth, and the inevitability of Nemesis-like retribution for hubris.

When Levantine traders sailed westward early in the first millennium BC, they introduced the charging of interest and related financial innovations to the Greek and Italian chieftains with whom they dealt, and who adopted these practices without the palatial checks and balances that had made debt bondage only temporary in the Near East.

From 2500 to 1600 BC, Sumerian and Babylonian rulers had proclaimed royal tax and debt amnesties to clear the backlog of agrarian arrears and other personal debts that disrupted social balance when crops failed from floods or drought, or when military campaigns dis-

---

[1] This chapter is based on Hudson 1992.

[2] See "*... and forgive them their debts,*" Chapter 14 ("Diffusion of Trade via Assyrian Merchants: 1900-1825 BC") for Cappadocia in what is now central Turkey, and Chapter 20 ("Usury and Privatization in the Periphery: 1600-1200 BC") for the Hittites in Asia Minor.

rupted the normal flow of life. Even under normal conditions, debts tend to mount up beyond the ability of debtors to pay. Near Eastern rulers recognized that if left unchecked, this accumulation of debt would force indebted subjects to fall into bondage and owe their labor to creditors to work off their debts, making debtors unavailable to provide the palace with corvée labor for public projects or even to serve in the army. The rulers' interest therefore lay in reversing undue polarization between creditors and debtors. Clean Slates cancelled personal agrarian debts, reversed personal debt bondage and returned self-support land to debtors who had lost it. That tradition became the Mosaic Jubilee Year in Judaea, and Egypt's Rosetta Stone memorialized a debt amnesty. Herodotus cites examples from numerous kingdoms in the first millennium BC.

Liberating debtors in this way was not an aim of the aristocracies that emerged in the Aegean and Italy. Rather, the leading families used rural credit to obtain dependent labor, and ultimately to monopolize the land. Debt bondage became irreversible, creating popular resentment that led to civil warfare from the 7th century BC onward.

Absence of indigenous interest-bearing debt in archaic Greece

The phenomenon of monetized debt was so alien to the West in the early first millennium BC that Plutarch reports that borrowers in Knossos were obliged to go through the ritual of snatching the money being lent, "so that, if they default, they could be charged with violence and punished all the more."[3] The law of theft evidently was the only legal principle available to exact payment in line with established collection practices. The earliest Greek inscription relating to charging interest is from Eleusis ca. 435-430 BC,[4] although early literary records also referred to interest-bearing debt.

Even in Ugarit (active until ca. 1190 BC in what is now northern Syria), merchants differed from their Babylonian counterparts primarily in that "money-lending operations, so characteristic for the Babylonian *tamkaru* [merchants]," appear rarely, being "very poorly represented in the hitherto published business documents from Ugarit."[5] Enslavement for personal debts seems not to have occurred. When land was foreclosed for debt, foreign creditors were obliged to relinquish it to Ugarit's

---

[3] Plutarch, "Greek Questions," in *Moralia* 303B.

[4] Cavaignac 1908:42-44 and Bogaert 1968.

[5] Astour 1972:26.

ruler, who compensated them for their monetary losses. The effect was to keep land tenure local, transferring family property into royal hands, not to foreign creditors.[6]

It thus is doubtful that commercial or agrarian interest played a role in Bronze Age Greece. Its palaces had little need of credit balances with outsiders, or with domestic creditors. If shortfalls in scheduled deliveries of taxes or other payments occurred, there is no evidence that they were financed by third parties, with or without interest. In the Linear B archives, Moses Finley observes, "[n]o word on any existing tablet has been read which can confidently be taken to mean 'to buy,' 'to sell,' 'to lend,' or 'to pay a wage' (or the corresponding nouns). Furthermore, Ventris and Chadwick note that they 'have not been able to identify any payment in silver or gold for services rendered,' and that there is no evidence 'of anything approaching currency. Every commodity is listed separately, and there is never any sign of equivalence between one unit and another.'"[7]

Economic surpluses cited in the Homeric poems take the form of booty, not commercial enterprise. We find gift exchange as part of the reciprocity ethic, but not transactions involving formal commercial or agrarian debt. There is no mention of interest as a stipulated return. The anthropologist Sarah Humphreys points out that in the *Odyssey* the only male slave whose origin is explained – the shepherd Eumaeus – was captured and sold as a child. Male slaves are as rare in Hesiod as in Homer. Women might be bought, but they are foreigners (mainly captured war prisoners), not debt pledges.[8]

"It is difficult to imagine a formal system of interest payments within the close-knit community described in [Hesiod's] *Works and Days*," notes Paul Millett. "The whole system of generalized reciprocity detailed by Hesiod depended on the preservation of good relations between neighbors who were apparently on a more or less equal footing. Any person who tried to insist on interest payments would quickly find himself excluded from communal activities. Imposition of interest is possible only for people who are in some way outside the community – either in terms of physical distance, or because a higher level of prosperity (or breeding) puts them on a different social plane." Interest is an intrusion

---

[6] Heltzer 1984:183-185.

[7] Finley 1981:206 and 198, citing Ventris and Chadwick 1956:113.

[8] Humphreys 1978:161, citing the *Odyssey* 15.40384.

in "a closed, self-contained system, with simple mechanisms for main-taining short- and medium-term equilibrium."[9]

"What is strikingly absent from Archaic Greece is any kind of wide-spread professionalism or concentration in trade," Anthony Snodgrass summarizes; "other civilizations had their commercial class, often estab-lished in a commercial quarter of a city, or even comprising the main population of a trading settlement – what the Greeks called an *emporion*. But in Greece we have to look hard to find any of these elements." There was no mercantile class such as Mesopotamia's *damkars*. "Real trading-posts were few, remote from the Greek homeland and usually inhabited at least in part by non-Greeks."[10]

Near Easterners brought the classical weights and measures to Greece as part of the commercial system involving interest-bearing debt.[11] In Italy, the Phoenician and Greek presence is well documented on the island entrepôt of Ischia, near the Gulf of Naples in Etruria south of Rome.[12] In both Greece and Italy, interest at first seems to have been charged mainly by outsiders. That hardly is surprising, because banking was not a profession for aristocrats. The main early banking business was money changing, carried out by metics (foreign residents in Greece) or slaves.

How interest-bearing debt and money was brought to the Aegean

The first wave of Near Eastern mariners sailing westward into the Aegean occurred in the 10th century BC. Carians from Asia Minor settled on Samos, whose Heraion temple was rich in Levantine and even Mesopotamian objects. Near Eastern offerings to Aegean temples gained momentum from the 8th century to about 650. They included North Syrian bronze cauldrons, conical stands and related banquet utensils, gold and silver jewelry with granulation, filigree and punchwork, and Phoenician metal jugs.[13]

---

[9] Millett 1991:46-47.

[10] Snodgrass 1980:136

[11] Berriman 1953 points out that the carat originally was the weight of a carob grain, *ceratonia siliqua*, a tree native to the Mesopotamian meridian, weighing 1/60th of a shekel. The Greek term is *keration* ("small grain").

[12] Ridgeway 1993 reviews the establishment of trade with the Etruscans by Phoenicians and Euboean Greeks (from Eretria and Chalcis) in the 8th century BC on Ischia/Pithecusae.

[13] Francois de Polignac, Glen Markoe, Oscar Muscarella and Ingrid Strøm discuss these donations in Kopcke and Tokumaru 1992.

The major recipients of such *orientalia* were Pan-Hellenic temples dedicated to Apollo, whose oracle at Delphi helped coordinate Greek commercial diplomacy and colonization. Shrines dedicated to Hera, Artemis and Athena also received donations. Prestigious Near Eastern artwork also is found in cemeteries and settlements near temples, reflecting the sanctified role of temples as cosmopolitan intermediaries for contact between traders and local tribes or headmen. Their mediating "neutral ground" role in early trade and credit was much like that of Delphi or Delos in Hellenistic times.[14] In the tradition that began with Sumerian temples overseeing honest alloying of silver, temples were the central institutions to coin money (the word derives from Rome's Temple of Juno Moneta), and served as storehouses for public savings, lending their resources to palaces in times of war or kindred economic need.[15]

Bronze Age records illustrating the diffusion of interest-bearing debt are found in Assyria's trade colony of Kanesh in central Asia Minor after 2000 BC. Like the Dark Age Greeks, local Anatolians had little reason to develop monetary debt standards. Assyrian trade missions introduced commercial debt and interest charges, along with contractual legal forms and the use of weighed pieces of silver as "money of the world." This Assyrian trade provides a model for how temple embassies were established to provide contractual formalities for extending credit and settling obligations. Their quasi-public role was necessary to establish ongoing commercial trade and provide goods to Anatolians on credit.

Klaas Veenhof has described how Anatolians became "indebted for the value of the merchandise entrusted to them for sale in local markets." They normally had to pay a much higher rate of interest than did Assyrian traders amongst themselves. Anatolians also had "to provide securities, frequently joint liability by a plurality of debtors. The cooperation only rarely went beyond such elementary and fairly risk-free transactions; more developed forms like partnerships, agencies or investments are almost never attested."[16] Also, Veenhof adds: "Some of the better known Anatolians, represented in exclusively native documents and in some Assyrian texts, function primarily as local money-lenders,

---

[14] In Hudson 1999 I describe how temples functioned as "neutral zones" in peripheral regions, protecting and sanctifying commercial undertakings. For a description of commercial cults in Hellenistic Delos see Rostovtzeff 1941 II:790-791.

[15] I trace the transmission of monetary silver from the ancient Near East to the Aegean in Hudson 2019. See Chapter 6 below for the monetary functions of Greek temples.

[16] Veenhof 1982:148-149.

active in loan operations and in buying and selling (debt-)slaves, at times also as suppliers of cereals. They may have carried on their business on the fringe of the large-scale commercial activity of the Assyrians."

This is how interest-bearing debt most likely was transmitted to Greece and Italy. It seems that Phoenicians and other Near Easterners at Samos, Argos, Delphi, Olympia and Delos were important in introducing economic practices. Greek traders frequented Al Mina on the Syrian coast after around 800 BC, and "in eastern Spain and on the Sea of Azov, there were places actually named 'Emporion,'" but this trade was dominated by non-Greeks.[17]

The island and mainland communities that Near Eastern traders encountered in the Aegean and Italy in the 9th and 8th centuries BC were not yet monetized, and lacked a legal tradition to govern commercial relations. Most production was on a subsistence basis to meet basic needs, with some conspicuous-consumption goods used mainly for ritual burials and gift exchange. No doubt Dark Age Greece and Villanovan Italy had "anthropological" debts such as *wergild*-type fines for personal injury. But trade credit requires money as a means of payment, and a public institution such as a temple to sanctify a commercial mentality of equity and fairness, and to provide oversight and administration. Greece and Italy adopted Near Eastern commercial practices by organizing trade via commercial bodies centered in temples, which provided recourse to settle disputes between foreign traders and local parties, promoted the sanctity of contracts and protected the safety of merchants on their travels. It probably was under the tutelage of these temple-centered commercial bodies that the practice of charging interest was introduced.

The major local Aegean and Mediterranean customers of Near Eastern traders would have been clan heads and larger landholders. And just as they paid interest on debts owed to Near Eastern traders, they started to extend interest-bearing loans to their own local cultivators, who fell into various forms of clientage, as had occurred a thousand years earlier in Anatolia when Mesopotamian merchants established trade outposts.

Extending commercial credit practices to the agricultural sphere

Greeks and Italians adopted Near Eastern formalities to deal with collateral and security – for instance, to decide what would happen if a merchant was prevented from paying his creditors because his ship was

---

[17] Snodgrass 1980:136.

lost or his caravan robbed. "In the domain of maritime law," the financial historian Raymond Bogaert summarizes, "Greek law seems to have
stemmed from that of Phoenicia, especially in the concept of *contrat d'af-
frètement* (insurance), a conception traceable back to the Babylonians."[18]

Initially it would have been in commerce that the practice of charging
interest was adopted in Greece and Italy, but Humphreys sees the
logic of attaching land as collateral for agricultural debts as kindred to
backing commercial credit arrangements with collateral: "The *nautikon
daneion* [commercial shipping loan] and the mortgage of land [were]
different institutions, transacted through different relationships, and belonging to different systems of thought and behavior, even though they
could be described by the same general word, *hypotheke*,"[19] collateral
pledged for a loan or advance.

Commercial and agricultural debts had a common root: the main
creditors would have been the well-to-do landowners setting up workshops and producing export crops and handicrafts.[20] That would explain
how the practice of charging interest proliferated from the sphere of
commercial exchange to agriculture. Recipients of the initial infusion of
silver from foreign trade would have bolstered their power by acting as
creditors to cultivators on the land, establishing clientage relationships.

What became most important over the course of antiquity were the
conditions under which debt obligations were secured by the debtor's
personal freedom or land rights. Even without interest charges, indebtedness forced many cultivators into patron/client relationships that
enabled oligarchies to build up their power in Sparta, Corinth, Sicyon,
Megara, Etruria and other regions, triggering the backlash of popular
revolts in the 7th and 6th centuries' "Age of Tyrants" described in the
next chapter.

Setting interest rates in new contexts

No ancient language had separate words to contrast "interest" from
usury. In all languages the word used for interest was derived metaphori-
cally from the idea of birth or "newborn." (See Chapter 12 for Aristotle's
discussion of the implications.) Greek *tokos*, "offspring," was similar to
Latin *faenus* and Mesopotamian *mash*. And along with the transmission
of charging interest came the idea of setting its rate by the local unit-frac-

---

[18] Bogaert 1968:146. See also p. 156.

[19] Humphreys 1978:151-152.

[20] Bravo 1977:65. See also Bravo 1974.

tion for ease of calculation. What was "born" was not a new calf or goat, but the smallest unit in each society's number system, starting with $1/60^{th}$ per month (1 shekel per mina) in the Near Eastern sexagesimal system.

Greek and Egyptian mathematics was based on the decimal system. Greek temples, for instance, were accustomed to receiving a tithe (*dekate*) of war booty[21] – the unit-fraction, one-tenth, which became a typical annual rate of interest. Other Greek rates were 1 percent per month, or one drachma per mina. In Athenian agriculture the 1:6 ratio of obols to *drachmae* ("handfuls") was reflected in the obligation of *hektemoroi* ("sixth-parters") to pay 1/6th of the crop yield to landholders.[22] In Rome's duo-decimal system the rate of interest was an *uncia* per *as* – $1/12^{th}$ annually (8⅓ percent in decimalized terms), surviving today in the troy ounce.

No early documentation has survived to indicate just when interest began to be charged on Greek and Italian debts. Local economies were only partially monetized. "The earliest appearance of *tokos* as interest in a source with a secure date," Millett finds, is not in a financial document but one of Pindar's *Olympian Odes* (X.5-9), composed ca. 475 BC. Yet "the formalizing of interest was complete by the later fifth century," as shown for instance in the plays of Aristophanes.[23] By that time we find the estates of orphans being lent out at interest, and thriving commercial lending for trade ventures. Charging interest had become so widespread that it seems to have been there all along.

Yet Humphreys describes the still-alien character of interest-bearing debt to the Greek world. "Bankers, often ex-slaves, stood outside the social circle."[24] Extending credit at interest historically has been done more by outsiders than among peers. Within their own ranks, aristocrats provided mutual support by extending interest-free *eranos* loans, as it was considered ungentlemanly for the well-to-do to charge interest to each other, or even to engage directly in moneylending. In contrast to the officials and merchants who became the major creditors in Babylonia, wealthy Greeks and Romans assigned their slaves the task of investing

---

[21] See for instance Pritchett 1979.

[22] Millett 1991:104-105 gives examples for Greek debt. Hudson 2000 explains the unit-fraction norm for charging interest. Ancient economies typically had different interest rates for commercial and agrarian debts, with the agrarian interest rate often being based on the sharecropping rate, *e.g.*, one-third in Babylonia.

[23] Millett 1991:46.

[24] Humphreys 1978:152. See especially Andreau 1999. Loans to the state and commission arrangements were made mainly by the wealthiest families, however, as described in Chapter 6 below.

their masters' savings (and also the slave's own *peculium*) in usurious activities; these slaves often acting on behalf of their masters or silent partners who controlled the land but did not want to dirty their hands with business deemed anti-social throughout antiquity. By the time we hear of mercantile credit and usury on a large scale, in 4th-century Athens, the major creditors are foreigners, metics (foreign residents in Greece) and slaves or freedmen such as the banker Pasion and his son Apollodorus, Phormion, and the Delos *trapezites* Philostrates of Ascalon.[25]

The spread of usury destabilizes the Greek and Italian economies

The wars with Persia early in the 5th century catalyzed the spread of interest-bearing credit, while the need to pay cultivators who became mercenaries helped spur the development of coinage. Urbanization was also gaining momentum, expanding the market for monetized trade in grain and olive oil. Yet we must rely almost entirely on lawsuits, poetry and plays to see how credit and interest were transforming Greek economic life.

What we *do* hear about, of course, are the debt revolts and demands for land redistribution led by reformer-"tyrants" from the 7th century down through Solon's reforms in Athens in 594. By the 4th century the word "tyrant" had come to imply an autocratic policy, yet recent scholarship sees the tyrants as sponsoring the reforms that catalyzed the evolution toward democracy.

In the Near East, royal debt cancellations saved economies from the widespread bondage and loss of the debtor's land rights that became the main dynamic leading to oligarchic power in Greece and Rome. Accusing debt amnesties and land redistribution of being threats to liberty, not its preconditions, oligarchies overthrew Sparta's kings in the 3rd century BC, and killed Roman reformers urging debt and land relief. The ensuing buildup of debt and monopolization of the land led to antiquity's economic collapse.

What made Western oligarchies different from the palatial economies of the Near East

The conflict between creditors and debtors was mitigated in the Mesopotamian homeland by rulers proclaiming Clean Slate edicts cancelling agrarian debts, freeing bondservants and restoring lands to those who had forfeited them or sold them under economic duress. The practice

---

[25] Bogaert 1988. The word *trapezites* comes from Greek *trapeza*, table or bench (French *banc* > bank). The corresponding Latin word for bench and banker was *mensa*.

is documented throughout Mesopotamia for a thousand years, from ca. 2500 to 1600, and even in the first millennium BC, debts owed to the palace were traditionally given an amnesty when new rulers took the throne.[26] Hammurabi (who ruled from 1792 to 1750 BC) proclaimed numerous Clean Slates, and Babylonia's *andurarum* acts provided the model for the cognate Mosaic Jubilee Year (*deror*) in Leviticus 25.

Such royal authority was absent in the West. Greece and Italy had no tradition of proclaiming debt cancellations, and there was much less civic need for corvée labor to build infrastructure, which was paid for by public expenditure (most notably by the 7th- and 6th-century "tyrants"). Creditor claims on the labor of debtors therefore did not interfere with public work to anywhere near the degree that would have occurred in the Near East without debt amnesties.

The absence of a process to wipe out personal debts when they threatened to strip debtors of their land – and hence, their economic self-sufficiency, personal liberty and citizenship rights – explains why financial polarization occurred more irreversibly in Greece and Italy than in the Near East. The debt dynamic leading to widespread transfer of land and other wealth to creditors has been a constant throughout subsequent Western history. Adopting interest-bearing debt without the safeguard of occasional debt relief was like introducing a new plant or animal species into an environment lacking native resistance or predators. Usury proliferated in the same way that smallpox and African killer bees did when they were introduced to the Western Hemisphere.

The way in which credit relations were introduced in classical antiquity was repeated in the Middle Ages. Once again it was temples – the Knights Templars and Hospitallers, founded in the 12th century AD as banking orders to help finance the Crusades – that played a major role in legitimizing interest-bearing credit. Likewise, when European conquistadors introduced interest-bearing debt to Africa and South America, tribal chiefs ran into debt to European colonial merchants. Their debts were deemed to be owed by the entire tribal community, and were settled by transferring its land and mineral rights to creditor powers.

A similar corrosive effect occurred when Western economists re-introduced interest-bearing debt to the former Soviet economies in the 1990s. Their socialist revolutions had eradicated *rentier* interest and land rent. But when interest-bearing debt was re-introduced in 1991, no regulatory checks were in place to create a workable symbiosis between creditors

---

[26] I provide a long list of such acts in *"... and forgive them their debts"* (2018). See also Chapter 8 below.

and the rest of the economy. (Such checks had been unnecessary under Soviet socialism, so discussion of credit regulation had been minimal.) The upshot was an epidemic of grabitization and foreclosures of land, natural resources and hitherto public infrastructure, leading to depopulation and capital flight.

It took many centuries for modern Europe and North America to develop legal and political resistance to keep the proliferation of debt in check. But as in classical antiquity, creditor interests fought back, and today a financial oligarchy is once again stripping the economy's assets and revenue. Greece since 2015 is especially noteworthy in experiencing the same debt dynamic that two thousand years earlier plunged it and the Roman Empire into widespread debt foreclosures, austerity, forced sell-offs of public assets at distress prices and a flight of labor causing depopulation.

Ancient philosophy warned against monetary greed, above all by creditors

When today's economists discuss antiquity, they tend to retroject modern ideology celebrating individual self-interest and the sanctity of debt back in time, as being timeless and universal. There is scant recognition of how the leading ancient lawgivers recognized the need for debt cancellation and land redistribution. Moses, Hammurabi, Lycurgus and Solon are reported to have cancelled debts, although only Hammurabi and Solon are attested as actual individuals.

Although local headmen in the Aegean and Mediterranean found usury a means to obtain land and clients as trade revived in the 8th century BC, most "tyrants" are reported to have invited philosophers to their courts to criticize money-greed and explain why they needed to limit the dynamics of debt and concentration of land ownership. A war or crop failure was all that it took for creditors to find an opening to obtain land or labor pledged as collateral for loans, reducing the citizenry (which constituted only about a third of most classical populations) to dependency and ultimately to bondage. Early monarchs, reform-minded members of the elite in the 7th and 6th centuries BC, and Sparta's final kings in the 3rd century BC recognized that a viable economy with a citizen army required laws to prevent the rich from depriving citizens of their land. Such laws were a precondition for securing service in the military as well as for the citizenry's self-support.

The mythical Lycurgus is credited with having created archaic Sparta's laws redistributing land in the conquered Messenian territories in equal *kleroi* plots to its citizen-infantry (see Chapter 3 below).

Plutarch's biography of Lycurgus says that he cancelled debts, and even banned money so as to prevent debts from building up. Herodotus 6.59 reports that: "The Lacedaemonians resemble the Persians in this: when one king is dead and another takes office, this successor releases from debt any Spartan who owes a debt to the king or to the community. Among the Persians the king at the beginning of his reign forgives all cities their arrears of tribute."[27] Herodotus describes the Spartan tradition as being of ancient origin, but seemingly only applying to debts owed to the monarchy and the community.

Solon cancelled personal debts and banned debt slavery for Athenians in 594 (discussed in Chapter 4). These experiences show that such acts in the Greek city-states were always the result of political confrontation (*stasis*) between debtors and creditors, not a normal tradition as had been the case in the Near East.

Summary

Ever since the Bronze Age, the timeless principle has been that if governments do not control the financial system, creditors will gain control of the government and impose policies to enrich themselves by reducing their debtors to clientage. That has given rise to the eternal conflict between financial oligarchies and reformers. The richer the cities and states of classical antiquity grew, the more their economies polarized as the wealthy translated their financial power into political power to block protection for debtors and the poor. Oligarchs used violence and political assassination to prevent reformers from mobilizing support to cancel the debts that kept the lower orders in bondage and pried away their land.

Classical antiquity failed to solve the problem of how to provide credit without permanently stripping debtors of their personal liberty and land. Creditors monopolized as much land as they could, and obtained labor by using credit to oblige debtors to work off what they owed. Their success reflected the absence of a central authority to subordinate creditor claims when they threatened large sectors of the population with loss of their land rights and personal freedom.

The Bronze Age Near East likewise had experienced tension between palace rulers and an emerging landowning creditor oligarchy threaten-

---

[27] Cecchet 2017:132, citing Godley's translation, modified, of Herodotus 6.59. She adds that Asheri 1963 cites Persian monarchic *philanthropa*-decrees as providing debt relief to demonstrate the new ruler's spirit of generosity. This was a widespread practice of monarchies in the pre-Hellenic Near East and, later on, became a custom of Egypt's Hellenistic kings.

ing to gain at the expense of social stability. Near Eastern rulers could not afford rising agrarian debt diverting the erstwhile taxable crop surplus away from the palace or temples, and labor away from corvée service to the community and military service in the army. Private creditors therefore were viewed as a rising threat to palatial power and its fiscal needs. Near Eastern rulers addressed this problem by regularly proclaiming Clean Slate debt cancellations, albeit in circumstances where most of the debts being cancelled were owed to the palace.

The debt tensions of Greece and Rome occurred in a different political context to that of the Near East. Unlike the Bronze Age Near East, classical antiquity's agrarian and other personal debts were owed almost entirely to private creditors. They opposed any policies that would check their growing wealth, and that attitude led them to oppose any central authority having power to reign them in. The result was that the debt strains and polarization between these private creditors and their debtors intensified. It is at that point that most modern writing of classical history begins – with the overthrow of narrow elites whose monopolization of the land had reached an intolerable excess.

Part I: Greece

They say that hares at one and the same time give birth to one litter, suckle another, and conceive again; but the loans of these barbarous rascals give birth to interest before conception; for while they are giving they immediately demand payment, while they lay money down they take it up, and then lend what they receive for money lent. ... And then they make a laughing-stock forsooth of the scientists, who say that nothing arises out of nothing; for with these men interest arises out of that which has as yet no being or existence.

– Plutarch, "That We Ought Not to Borrow," *Moralia*[1]

The oracles of Delphi, the poetry of Theognis of Megara and Solon of Athens, the plays of Aristophanes and the philosophy of Socrates warned against money-lust and wealth addiction (*pleonexia*) threatening social balance and well-being by leading to hubristic behavior on the part of the rich and powerful. These warnings did not deter oligarchies from concentrating land ownership and credit in their own hands throughout all of Greece from the 6th through 1st centuries BC.

Greek city-states had different aetiologies and political dynamics – oligarchic Sparta with its helots and *homoioi* citizen-"equals" still subject to a landholding oligarchy, Corinth and other Isthmian cities whose archaic aristocracies were overthrown by reformer-tyrants, and Athens with Solon's debt cancellation in 594 followed by the democratic reforms of Cleisthenes, Pericles and Ephialtes. The Peloponnesian War (431-404) was part of a centuries-long fight between oligarchies backed by Sparta (followed by Macedonia and Rome) against democracies allied with Athens.

Oligarchies gained the upper hand by the 4th century BC. Many Greek cities from Macedonia in the north to the Peloponnese in southern Greece experienced civil warfare over demands for land redistribution and debt cancellation.

---

[1] Plutarch, *Moralia* 829B-C (Loeb Classical Library, 1936 X:325). In other words, they get something for nothing. Debtors often have interest taken out in advance.

2
Reformers Cancel Debts and Redistribute Land, 7th and 6th Centuries BC

Dark Ages and Intermediate Periods are free-for-alls in which central authority weakens, enabling well-placed opportunists to grab what they can. From Mesopotamia to Egypt such interregnums saw economic life "liberated" from palace authority. That occurred in Sumer at the hands of Sargon's Akkadians ca. 2300 BC, and Babylon fell ca. 1600. Egypt's First Intermediate Period (2181-2055) saw the Old Kingdom's temples pillaged, and records disappear in the Second Intermediate Period's chaos from 1650 to 1550.

A similar turmoil occurred in the Aegean and Levant after 1200 BC at the end of the Late Bronze Age. Palaces burned down and towns were abandoned in a region-wide devastation.[1] The Sea Peoples often are blamed, but many groups were in motion and local uprisings are attested. Administrative structures disappeared, along with syllabic writing. Much of the land was depopulated over the next five centuries, leaving survivors and invaders to appropriate palatial or communal land and workshops for themselves.

Many local headmen called themselves *basilae*. In Bronze Age Mycenaean kingdoms it had meant a local manager of an estate subject to a *wanax* "king." "In any Mycenaean state there would have been a great many *basileis*: not four or five, but forty or fifty," notes Robert Drews. "These minor officials were provincial, that is, they were in residence not in the palace itself but in various parts of the kingdom."[2] It seems that many kept their local managerial power after the palatial economy collapsed.

Walter Donlan has shown that what seemed to be closed family kinship clans controlling political life actually were "follower groups" that "originated in the early Dark Age as loosely organized political/

---

[1] Cline 2014:72 describes the devastation as "a rolling event, taking place between approximately 1225 and 1175 BC or, in some places, as late as 1130 BC."

[2] Drews 1983:112-113 and 116-117.

military associations."[3] They had to be open, as success lay in attracting new members and supporters, as Rome's early kings did so successfully.

The leading families concentrated religious authority in their own hands by controlling hereditary priesthoods, and secular power followed as they monopolized legal power as judges. As the land filled up again, debt dynamics and the resulting land transfers reduced much of Greece to nearly serf-like dependency on these elites. The rising disorder from this oppressive over-reaching by elites led members of some families to lead revolts to create a more acceptable political order under their own leadership.

Ambitious leaders gain supporters and power by reforming closed aristocracies

Not until the 5th century do we begin to get firm dates and events. In the absence of written records and reliable history dating from this early period we must rely on what was written many centuries later to describe the 7th- and 6th-century revolts that brought populist leaders to power in Corinth, Sicyon, Megara and other cities. Almost no records exist to explain how the early problematic debts came into being, but most of the surviving history of this early period is about the debt revolts and demands for land redistribution that extended down through Solon's reforms in Athens in 594. The leaders who brought reforms were called "tyrants." By the 4th century the word had come to imply an autocratic policy, yet, as recent scholarship has emphasized, the tyrants set in motion the reforms that led to democracy.

Various scenarios have been suggested to describe what ended local aristocratic dynasties such as the Bacchiads in Corinth. A popular 20th-century approach explained the emergence of democracy by emphasizing the use of iron weaponry raising the role of the hoplite infantry relative to that of the aristocratic cavalry. Synchronized fighting tactics were said to have paved the way for democratic representation as soldiers demanded a share of power to reflect the organization of hoplites into phalanx formations. But Hans van Wees criticizes this idea of a middle-class hoplite army as "a myth based on an isolated and ill-founded ancient generalization."[4] An organized hoplite militia had not yet devel-

---

[3] Donlan 1985:297-298, citing Roussel 1976 and Bourriot 1976.

[4] Van Wees 2004:60. He adds that only after the Persian Wars does evidence begin to suggest something close to an egalitarian militia employing standard weapons in a unified manner.

oped to the point where it was in a position to dictate new laws in Sparta, Corinth, Athens and other cities in the 7th and 6th centuries.

Support from hoplites and cultivators, craftsmen and merchants – or at least their non-opposition – certainly was necessary to break free of the closed elites, but their political influence was limited. Most writers follow Aristotle in describing the early moves toward democracy as being led by a fight among the elites themselves. Most reformers emerged from within the leading clans, for how else would they have had the resources and connections to organize a political takeover? Snodgrass finds that "the whole episode of the rise of tyranny appears to have been conducted on the level of aristocratic power-politics. The tyrants themselves were almost always dissident aristocrats, who exploited the unpopularity of their fellows in the ruling class, killed or exiled those currently in power, and often recalled to favor other recalcitrants."[5]

The problem with the pre-tyrant regimes was that their selfishness and exploitation blocked the growth of civic prosperity. Strabo described Corinth's Bacchiad clan "as tyrants themselves" acting "in general without rules."[6] Van Wees characterizes the elites in early cities such as Megara as timocracies – rule by the wealthy, typically mafia-type groups holding power secured by gangs of armed supporters.[7] Greg Anderson concurs: "State institutions were weak (like Western sheriffs not well empowered to block gangs). Private 'armies' of allies and retainers, attempts to seize power by force, assassinations, exiles, and property appropriation accordingly proliferated ..."[8] Backed by such force, the elites wielded their power above all as creditors holding their clients in debt.

The "Age of the Tyrants" was one of revolution against such predatory elites. Many populist leaders were low-ranking aristocrats, often from the minor branches of the leading families, who "took the demos into their camp," as Aristotle put it.[9] A typical example was Cypselus

---

[5] Snodgrass 1980:112. Sarah Morris 2003:11 (citing Thucydides 1.113) follows Thucydides in describing this rivalry as stemming from the rising commercial prosperity that enabled families to acquire money or a following of clients as a base for political power. In this view, tyrants emerged "as an event precipitated by an accumulation of power and wealth within the governing elite."

[6] Strabo, *Geographica* 378 (ca. 23 AD), cited by Salmon 1984:191.

[7] Van Wees 2000:52-53 and 63-65. Earlier, MacMullen 1974:12 called them mafiosi.

[8] Anderson 2005:183. He adds that bearing arms in public continued as normal practice until the 520s. They sound much like America's Wild West.

[9] Aristotle was referring above all to Cleisthenes, who reformed Athenian tribal and voting systems ca. 508 BC. Anderson 2005:186 and 175 characterizes such

mobilizing support from Corinth's disaffected well-to-do against his Bacchiad family. Leaders with a similar background included Pheidon of Argos and Solon, a less affluent member of the Athenian elite. He was named archon because Athenian elites feared that the revolts occurring all around them (including earlier in their own city) would redistribute their land if they did not at least end the threat of debt slavery.

Plutarch's comment about the strains that led to Solon's reforms in Athens in 594 applies equally well to the upheavals that took place throughout Greece during the 7th century: "The disparity between rich and poor reached such a high point, and the city was in an altogether perilous condition, that it seemed as if the only way to restore order and stop the turmoil was to establish a tyranny."[10] Economies were polarizing as cultivators were driven into debt, in many cases facing bondage or various kinds of serfdom such as Athenian *hektemoroi*. Socrates described tyrants as arising when people "with the least" gathered around a leader promising to redistribute land and cancel the peoples' debts.[11] Survival as a viable society required unseating the most recalcitrant elites and replacing them with a new political system of government.[12]

The creation of the Cypselid dynasty of Corinth is the best documented example. A member of the Bacchiad clan is said to have had a lame daughter, Labda, and the only husband that the family could find for her was Eetion, from the Petra district and outside the otherwise strictly endogamous clan. When they had no children, Eetion went to consult Delphi. "As soon as he entered, the Pythian priestess spoke these verses to him: 'Eetion, worthy of honor, no man honors you. [But] Labda is

---

individuals as a "community of dissent" who recognized "that their societies could not succeed in a militarily hostile world without extending government to include the population at large, including the hoplite infantry." He concludes that "a growing number of scholars would now see 'tyranny' as an important and perhaps a necessary transitional stage in the steady journey of the Greek polis from 'aristocratic' rule to full citizen government."

[10] Plutarch, *Life of Solon* 13.2.

[11] Plato, *Republic* 8 at 565d-566a. Aristotle, *Politics* 5 at 1310b14-16 and 29-31 describes them as demagogues with extraordinary power, initially emerging from within aristocratic factions, although Sagstetter 2013:18 notes, citing *Politics* 5 at 1306a6, 1308a19 and 1310b12: "According to Aristotle, tyrants almost always gained power by championing the people against the rich," and tended to gain power where oligarchies were most extreme.

[12] Mossé 1969:88.

with child, and her child will be a millstone [*olooitrochos*, a crushing rock] that will fall upon the rulers and will bring justice to Corinth.'"[13]

The Bacchiads heard of this oracle and tried to kill the child, Cypselus, but he survived. According to the narrative of his childhood, which reads like a standardized birth of a mythical hero, he overthrew the Bacchiad aristocracy and expelled its leaders (but not its less prosperous members who did not oppose his reforms). That was in line with normal Greek and Roman tradition exiling families considered to be a threat to social peace, this being what Thrasybulus did in Miletus when he exiled the old "royalist" families.

The early 7th-century poet Archilochus used the word *turannis* in a poem about Gyges of Lydia in Asia Minor, a bodyguard for its king, whom he killed to gain the throne.[14] The word soon was applied to outsiders who replaced entrenched dynasties. The term is best translated as "demagogy," which retains the populist *demos* root. But history is written by the victors – the landed oligarchies in Greece and Rome, which felt threatened by revolts led by lawgivers or reformers. They gave the word "tyrant" a negative connotation, and writers unsympathetic to democracy gave an autocratic meaning to the word.

What subsequent oligarchies found so "tyrannical" was the assertion of public power restraining the privileges of the wealthy by driving the dominant families into exile and, much as Near Eastern rulers had done, redistributing their land and cancelling the debts that had deprived many clients of their liberty. That led oligarchies to denounce reformers who advocated cancelling debts and limiting the land grabbing of creditor elites as being "immoderate" and power-hungry, as if *they* rather than creditor elites were hubristic. The Cypselids of Corinth, the Orthagorids of Sicyon and the Peisistratids of Athens in the 6th century were portrayed as power-seeking and overseeing anarchy, not as preparing the ground for their city-states' commercial takeoffs and progress toward democracy.

---

[13] Herodotus 5.92. See Gray 1996 for a discussion of the mythic character of this story.

[14] Ogden 1997:120 and 271, fns11-15, citing Aristotle, *Rhetoric* 2 at 1418b23, *Moralia* 470c, and *Etymologicum Magnum* and *Etymologicum Gudianum* s.v. *turranos*. He adds (p. 150) that some tyrants called themselves *basileus*, perhaps trying to recall an idealized past that had been usurped by the aristocrats who ran the major Greek towns. He suggests that perhaps *turranis* was Gyges's official title. Sealey 1976:38 points out that the word "tyranny" seems to have been the Lydian word for "king" or "pasha," connoting ostentatious wealth.

Corinth's tyrant-reformers were typical in seeking support and averting a counter-revolution by creating more equitable regimes. "It was through tyranny that most Greek states had their first taste of radical policies," Snodgrass has summarized, "and, conversely, there were few leading progressive states which had not passed through a phase of tyranny at some stage in the Archaic period, though usually it was of fairly brief duration."[15]

The Greek financial historian Andreas Andreades has pointed to the re-evaluation by "writers observ[ing] that the tyrants brought about praiseworthy social and economic reforms, developed agriculture, industry, commerce, and colonization, encouraged literature and the fine arts, contributed to the development of a Pan-Hellenic spirit through the reverence for the great shrines and oracles, and saved Hellenism in Sicily." Noting that the era of Peisistratus (ruler of Athens for most of 561-527) was considered to be Athens' "golden age," Andreades endorsed Gustave Glotz's judgment that "countries which did not know tyranny (such, *e.g.*, as Sparta and Boeotia) were retrogressive."[16]

Debt cancellation and land redistribution as the common denominators of reforms

The most common characteristic of tyrants was their ability to mobilize support against oppressive hereditary elites. The early tyrants are renowned most of all for confiscating the land of the leading families that had monopolized it. "Confiscations are recorded as having been made use of by nearly all tyrants," notes Andreades, citing Cypselus, Polycrates, Theagenes, Dionysius, Lygdamis, Pittacus, Aristodemus, Cleinias, and Pythagoras of Ephesus.[17]

Lists of the Seven Sages typically include four tyrants – Periander of Corinth (ruled 627-585), Pittacus of Mytilene (640-568), and Cleobulus of Lindos (6th century), followed by Solon (638-558) – for praising moderation and promising to bring justice, *dikē*, to their cities. Treating

---

[15] Snodgrass 1980:96.

[16] Andreades 1933:12, citing Glotz 1930. Kelcy Sagstetter's 2013 dissertation surveys how modern scholarship describes the reformer-tyrants in an increasingly favorable light, introducing written laws to reverse the maldistribution of land, money and power. She concludes (p. 14.): "Many scholars now see tyranny as an important transitional phase from traditional oligarchies to democracy, and there have been earnest attempts to rehabilitate the reputations of various individual tyrants, in particular the Peisistratids of Athens."

[17] Andreades 1933:119H.

the drive to accumulate wealth as a disease that led to hubris, they were known for criticizing the greed and money-lust (*pleonexia*) that was causing social confrontation (*stasis*).[18]

The most typical reform of "tyrants" was to cancel debts and redistribute land. In Argos, Pheidon overthrew the local aristocracy and is said to have redistributed land to equalize its distribution. A generation later, Corinth became the richest Greek city-state under Cypselus (ruled 657-627) and his son Periander, who cancelled debts, redistributed the land and exiled the families that had monopolized it. In Mytilene the denunciation of Pittacus by aristocratic writers suggests that he emulated the policy of other reformers and drove out the old aristocracy, redistributed their lands and cancelled debts. From Herodotus and other biographers, one can distill a "portrait of the tyrant as champion of egalitarian justice and opponent of aristocratic overreaching," notes Leslie Kurke.[19]

Aristotle reports that Peisistratus gained the support of many Athenian rural poor by paying off their debts with his own money, and Cicero describes Rome's legendary king Servius (said to have ruled from 575 to 535) as strengthening his position by also doing this. Diodorus says much the same thing of Servius's predecessor Tarquinius Priscus (616-579).[20]

Later writers accused tyrant-reformers of obtaining their rule by force, but Anderson notes that: "When violence was used, it was directed against rival leaders not against the 'state' as a whole."[21] Aristotle observed that tyrants rarely dispensed with guards to defend themselves and their supporters *against* the assassination and violence that wealthy elites have used throughout history to protect their privileges.[22]

---

[18] Popularizing (and romanticizing) the lives of the early tyrants, Diogenes Laertius wrote in the 3rd century AD that they often traveled and met each other. He depicted their philosophy as a proto-Stoic ethic of forbearance against the egotistic wealth of the ruling autocracies they overthrew. The poet-tyrant Cleobulus of Lindos on the island of Rhodes was known for his aphorisms "Avoid injustice" and "Moderation is the best thing." The other major sage was the mathematician Thales of Miletus, who helped free inductive science from mythology.

[19] Kurke 1999:67-68.

[20] Pseudo-Aristotle, *Athēnaiōn Politeia* ("Constitution of Athens") 16.2, Cicero, *De Re Publica* 2.21, and Diodorus 8, Fragment 13. See Ure 1922:216 and 221-222.

[21] Anderson 2005:198.

[22] Aristotle, *Politics* 5 at 1315b27-28. Aristotle, *Rhetoric* 2 at 1357b30-36 describes Dionysius of Syracuse being "appointed a bodyguard similar to Peisistratus's *korynephoroi*," and cites Theagenes of Megara (ca. 600) to illustrate his assertion that men who would become tyrant typically ask for bodyguards.

Ste. Croix points out that "Solon's great work might have been largely nullified had not Peisistratus, using violence to overcome aristocratic resistance, enforced Solon's constitution."[23] Cypselus ruled without bodyguards, but his son Periander revived the practice, although he was credited with a perhaps apocryphal saying that the best protection was the support of the people, not bodyguards.

Restructuring politics and voting systems

Matters would have regressed if reformers had not extended citizenship to a broader segment of the population than just elders of the leading family lineages and landholders. "In several cities," Snodgrass summarizes, "the tyrant's desire to increase the numbers of his adherents may have led him to extend citizenship more widely – to the landless, to the disenfranchised, to foreigners."[24] This drive led to constitutions that standardized voting rights and military status by dividing the expanded citizenry into three, four, eight or twelve civic "tribes" (literally a division into thirds) – uniform voting districts based on geographic locality instead of family pedigree.[25]

Lewis Henry Morgan's *Ancient Society* (1877) found this allocation of an expanded citizen body into standardized tribes to be the essence of civilization's urban revolution, forming the basis for civic duties, tax obligations and political rights. He credited Cleisthenes with creating Athenian democracy in 507 by shifting the basis of voting and military rank to local demes instead of blood relations in phratries. In Rome, the almost mythical king Servius likewise is said to have reorganized the voting system along geographic lines. However, Morgan's view of the urban revolution did not discuss debt relations and how the privatization of land tenure led to oligarchies.[26]

---

[23] Ste. Croix 2004:81-82.

[24] Snodgrass 1980:97.

[25] Salmon 1984:206-207 notes that Corinth's tribal organization was eightfold, giving rise to the proverb "eight of everything." Van Wees 2018b:251 points out that Sparta replaced its "kinship-based army by a force consisting of units recruited across kinship and local boundaries."

[26] Neither did Engels in his elaboration of Morgan's analysis in *Origin of the Family, Private Property and the State* (1884; English translation 1902).

Reformer-tyrants as "straighteners"

A common reform of "tyrants" after unseating despotic regimes was to "bring justice" in the form of written rules of law and courts. The poetry of Theognis of Megara (6th century BC) depicted the guiding idea as "straight" order, connoting moral, political and ultimately economic equity, "more straight ... than a carpenter's pin and rule and square ... *dikē*-'judgment' must not 'veer' from straightness."[27] Thus, classical antiquity's reformers who overthrew despotic aristocracies acted as "straighteners," with tyrants being characterized "as *euthunter*, 'straightener,' the bringer of justice and law."[28] This was the same metaphor used by Babylonian rulers who proclaimed *misharum* Clean Slates annulling rural debts, bringing "straight order" with connotations of distributive justice.

The historiography of the 7th and 6th centuries in this regard has changed radically over the past two centuries, both regarding the role of the tyrants as reformers bringing justice and as reformers introducing coinage and civic building. Kurke describes the pre-tyrant aristocracies as refraining from creating public coinage or standardizing prices because they preferred to conduct exchange on a personal basis, favoring their own powerful status according to circumstances. The introduction of coinage by tyrant-reformers was a political act that replaced the old elite's arbitrary demands and pricing with a more equitable and standardized system based on law.

Coinage helped bring justice by standardizing taxes, fees and remuneration rates for civic investment and employment. This idea of establishing standardized rules applying to all citizens was reflected in the ancient Greek word for money, *nomisma*, derived from *nomos*, Greek for law, and "[w]hether we etymologize it (with Will) as 'process or result of lawful distribution' or (with Laroche) as 'convention,' the term *nomisma* points to the political function of coinage, either as a means of effecting redistributive justice or as an institution of consensus."[29]

Kurke lists the Cypselids, the Phrygian king Midas's Kymaian wife, Hippias of Athens (the son of Peisistratus) and Polycrates of Samos as reformer-tyrants who organized exchange by striking coins.[30] Civic coinage thus was invented not by individuals bartering, but by reformers who took control of trade and finance away from the autocratic families.

---

[27] Nagy 1985:37, quoting Theognis 805-806.

[28] Kurke 1999:67-68, citing McGlew 1993:81-86.

[29] Kurke 1999:41, citing von Reden 1995:173-174.

[30] Kurke 1999:67-68.

Many 19th-century writers thought that debt crises and widespread rural distress resulted from the introduction of coinage, as if debt and commerce required silver to be coined. But coinage had not been necessary for the preceding two thousand years of the Near Eastern commercial takeoff, which used silver minted and overseen by the temples with quality assurances. The problem all along was elites who monopolized the land and held its cultivators in debt. Indeed many of the "tyrants" who introduced coinage were known for cancelling debts and redistributing land as part of their sponsorship of standardized economic relations.

The transition to more egalitarian politics required a democratization of law courts. Aristotle ascribed the long reign of Sicyon's tyrants to their willingness to place themselves at least partially under the rule of law as part of the demos. "Such radical measures as property-tax and the institution of circuit judges, as well as redistribution of land, are attributed to these rulers."[31] A major reform was to inscribe written laws that were the same for everyone, replacing the leeway for judges to indulge in arbitrary bias or favoritism. Peisistratus inaugurated the practice of judges traveling throughout rural Attica to ensure that citizens had access to proper legal protection,[32] and the key Athenian innovation was to choose juries by lot. By contrast, Roman courts drew judges from the senatorial oligarchy, flagrantly ruling in their own self-interest, as Appius Claudius is said to have done in 450 BC,[33] spurring a second Secession of the Plebs (see Chapter 11).

To check excessive wealth and luxury spending, above all for ostentatious funerals, the 7th- and 6th-century reformers passed sumptuary legislation. The classic example was Sparta's "Lycurgan" austerity. Herodotus (5.92) relates a legend about Periander ordering the most splendiferous clothes of Corinth's wealthy women to be burned. The city's anti-luxury laws remained in force until the 4th century. Periander even is reported to have restricted the ownership of slaves, but this may have referred to preventing creditors from enslaving fellow Corinthians for debt.[34]

---

[31] Snodgrass 1980:114, citing Aristotle, *Politics* 5 at 1315b14, singling out Cypselus and Peisistratus.

[32] Pseudo-Aristotle, *Athēnaiōn Politeia* 16.5.

[33] Note fn23 in Chapter 9 below discussing Mommsen's questioning of the portrayal of Appius Claudius and his descendants.

[34] Salmon 1984:200 comments that the source of this report is the often confused history by Nicolaus of Damascus written in the 1st century BC. What actually may have been meant, he suggests, is that "Periander outlawed debt slavery, like Solon

Tyrants were especially renowned for their public building programs. Aristotle attributed such projects to their proclivity for ostentatious display, but their investment in harbors and other infrastructure helped their cities become thriving commercial centers. Herodotus (3.60) credited Polycrates of Samos, who ruled the island from 538 to 522, for the three great feats of Greek engineering: the Heraion temple to Hera, the long Eupalinos aqueduct tunnel to provide the city with water, and a quarter-mile deep-water harbor mole to support its naval trade. In Corinth, Periander built the *diolkos*, an enormous causeway to transport ships across the Isthmian land bridge to the Peloponnese, after having tried unsuccessfully to dig a canal across the Isthmus. Revenues from the resulting harbor trade helped pay for his public spending. Because direct taxes on personal income and wealth were regarded as tribute imposed on unfree populations, tyrants relied mainly on indirect levies such as tariffs and excise taxes on commercial revenue-generating investment.

Pan-Hellenic ceremonies and civic religion

The major building expense in most cities was the construction of temples and other public cultural and sports venues. Pan-Hellenic and local games were accompanied by building programs for temples and sports arenas that provided urban employment. Public games brought tourist spending, a major source of revenue. Cypselus and Periander built Corinth's great Temple of Apollo and also the Poseidon temple on the neighboring Isthmus, which became the site for one of the four major Pan-Hellenic games. Strabo cited "the revenue brought by the crowds attending the Isthmian Games" as a major contributor to Corinthian prosperity.[35]

Aristocratic families controlled local cults to help sanctify their privileges, typically handing down wooden effigies of deities of their ancestor-and-property patron gods from father to eldest son, along with title to the family's land. Corinth's Bacchiad aristocracy sponsored an annual festival managed by the family priesthood to celebrate their putative heroic ancestors. Such hereditary priesthoods were a traditional mecha-

---

in Athens. That is not what our sources say; but they may represent distortions of just such a measure." That would be in keeping with the common characteristics cited by Plutarch, Aristotle *et al.* regarding the tyrants cancelling debts and liberating bondservants (along with redistributing land).

[35] Snodgrass 1980:117, citing Strabo, *Geographica* 8.6.20.

nism of aristocratic control throughout antiquity.[36] Reformers replaced these clan-based priesthoods with civic religion having its own rituals and traditions. Cypselus replaced Corinth's Bacchiad festivals with a recitation of the Homeric epics. In Athens, Thucydides describes Peisistratus as instituting the Panathenic Festival ca. 566, and later building the Temple of Olympian Zeus and the *Enneakrounos* in the Agora and the sanctuary of Demeter and Kore at Eleusis.[37]

Tyrants hired foreign artisans to decorate and work on their temples and other civic buildings, and also brought musicians, philosophers, poets and courtesans to create a prestigious civic life. The poet and *kitharode* (singer and lyre-player) Arion, credited with the invention of the dithyramb (an ecstatic hymn honoring Dionysus), lived at the court of Periander in Corinth. The lyric poet Anacreon composed numerous odes for Polycrates of Samos. Simonides (who invented a system of mnemonics and is said to have added the letters ω, η, ξ, ψ to the Greek alphabet) was a guest of Peisistratus's son Hipparchus as chorus leader and trainer, and his nephew Bacchylides, the lyric poet, joined the court of Hieron of Syracuse, which also attracted the poet Pindar and the dramatist Aeschylus.[38]

Many tyrants had ties to Delphi, a meeting place for Greek elites that Anderson describes as a classical "Davos" where elites established their ties to each other, as they also did through their participation in games at Pan-Hellenic centers.[39] After Delphi's oracle forecast that Cypselus

---

[36] See Morris 2003:13: "Priesthoods were often hereditary (in Athens, the Eumolpidae and Eteoboutidae) and linked to power (in Samos: Herodotus 3.142), as elite families retained privileges in civic ritual that offered avenues to power and popularity or used them to gain power (Gelon of Sicily, son of Telines the priest: Herodotus 7.154)." A notable example of such political control occurred in Rome, whose aristocracy appointed augurs given an omen-reading privilege to halt Senate voting when democratic moves seemed imminent.

[37] Thucydides 2.15.5 and Aristotle, *Politics* 5 at 1313b18-25. Andreades 1933:117 suggests that the reason why the Olympiaeum was left unfinished for many centuries (until Hadrian finally completed it) was that Zeus was "Peisistratized" as a result of Peisistratus representing himself as the god's favorite. For the reformers' building programs and festivals see Sagstetter 2013:150, citing Kolb 1977:99-138, Salmon 1997:32-38, Shapiro 1989, and Raaflaub 2003:9-94.

[38] Andreades 1933:118-119 notes that these large budgetary items prevented tyrants from building up treasure. One perhaps not incidental effect was to deter rivals from attempting to seize it, especially during the tyrant's absence.

[39] Anderson 2005:183-184, adding (p. 90) that tyrants from Corinth, Megara, Mytilene and Sicyon were "prominent members of the Panhellenic chariot-racing

would "bring justice (δικαιώσει) to Corinth," he reciprocated by building its treasury, and his dynasty made lavish dedications to Delphi as well as to Olympia.[40] An allied ruler, Cleisthenes of Sicyon (who ruled ca. 600-560), was a major backer of Delphi in the First Sacred War (590).

Moral philosophy warning against wealth addiction and hubris[41]

Reformers, poets, dramatists and philosophers warned that wealth addiction and *pleonexia*, "the desire to have more," were leading to hubris. The Delphic oracle warned Sparta that this was the only thing that would threaten its survival. No philosopher endorsed classical antiquity's increasingly pro-creditor laws and oligarchic opposition to reform, and none viewed personal greed as an "incentive" to enterprise and progress.

Thrasybulus of Miletus (in Asia Minor, opposite the island of Samos) expressed the idea of "straight order" laconically to a herald sent by his Corinthian ally Periander. Herodotus reports that he led the man to a field and cut off the highest ears of grain with a scythe.[42] Periander understood this as advice to cut the wealthiest and most aggressive members of Corinth's aristocracy down to size (now called the Tall Poppy Syndrome) by exiling or otherwise excluding them.

The metaphor of cutting down sheaves of grain so that the field would be equal in height has been echoed through the ages as a response to the hubristic drive for wealth. Tracing the root of the word *hubris* to an overgrowth of plant life, Nick Fisher cites Aristotle's description of "*hybristai* and arrogant (*hyperephanoi*), affected by the possession of wealth."[43] He finds that denunciations of hubris "form part of a sustained drive in a number of Greek archaic states to restrain the competitive tensions and abuses of aristocrats through laws and community action. ... in almost all

---

set to which most ambitious, accomplished Greek elites aspired to belong." After Cylon of Athens won the *diaulos* at Olympia in 640, Theagenes of Megara chose him "to be his son-in-law, and Cleisthenes of Sicyon was himself a noted competitor in the Panhellenic games." Tyrant-reformers cemented mutual support for each other by intermarriage, and often militarily as well.

[40] Anderson 2005:191, citing Herodotus 1.14.2. For Delphi's oracle regarding Cypselus see Herodotus 5.92.2.

[41] Chapter 7 discusses wealth addiction and hubris in detail.

[42] Sealey 1976:49, citing Herodotus 5.92. Aristotle (*Politics* 3 at 1284a26-33 and 5 at 1311a) reverses the roles, and depicts Periander as sending this advice to Thrasybulus.

[43] Aristotle, *Rhetoric* 2 at 1390b32-91a19 and 1383a1-3, discussed in Fisher 1992:20.

of our texts *hybris* is seen as above all the fault of the rich and powerful,"
specifically those who achieved their wealth by impoverishing the citizenry at large. In general, "the rich ('fools blessed with fortune') believe
that their wealth gives them a claim to being treated as superiors, and
the means to deal with any resistance ('everything can be bought'), and
hence treat others with *hybris* and contempt, leading them into injustices." The role assigned to Zeus and other gods was "to punish *hybris*,
and uphold *dikē* and *eunomia*."[44]

In Greek dramaturgy, poetry and philosophy from Hesiod to Plato,
"*hybris* is used repeatedly as a contrary of *dikē*, to indicate behavior that is
variously violent, criminal and anti-social."[45] The earliest Greek reforms
and moral philosophy are documented in the poetry of Solon and Theognis
of Megara. Theognis denounced bad men who "destroy the *demos* and give
justice to unjust men for the sake of private gain and power."[46]

> ... this city is pregnant, and I am afraid lest it give birth to a man who
> will be a straightener of our wicked ὕβρις. [hybris] For the townsmen are
> still prudent, but the leaders are inclined to fall into great wickedness.[47]

The critique of *hybris* developed into a Stoic philosophy that was especially critical of usury reducing the poor to debt dependency and

---

[44] Fisher 1992:129 and 493-495. *Eunomia* means literally "good law." Isocrates
accused Sparta's oppression of the helots as hubristic, in line with the Homeric
treatment of *hybris* as "a major crime, endangering the cohesion of the community
as well as the essential self-esteem and identity of the individual."

[45] Fisher 1992:69 and 127.

[46] Describing the leading tyrants as poets, Sagstetter 2013:105 notes: "The writings
of Pittacus, Periander, and Cleobulus (to name a few) are not preserved, but
Diogenes Laertius (1.78) credits these tyrant-poets with similar subject matter and
many of the same themes as the laws and poems of Solon. Pittacus, for example,
wrote poetry on prudence, hard work, the supremacy of law, and the need to
accept one's lot in life. ... Periander wrote a 2,000-line didactic poem, part of which
explicitly outlined proper behavior for tyrants. He said that tyrants should concentrate on making citizens loyal through benevolence rather than threats, noting
that it was just as dangerous to be dispossessed by force as to retire of one's own
accord ... Periander further cautioned against greed, rashness, and the transience
of wealth." (She also cites Diogenes Laertius 1.97.) West 1972 includes Pittacus and
Periander in his corpus of elegiac poets.

[47] Theognis 38-51. See Figueira 1985. Van Wees 2000:62 notes that Theognis
"ruefully acknowledges, in lines adapted from Solon, that 'to wealth there is no
apparent limit for mankind, because those of us who now have the greatest livelihood are eager to have twice as much' (227-9)."

clientage. Plutarch cites an echo of what seems to have been Megara's debt revolt, probably under Theagenes in the late 7th century: an annual festival celebrating Megara's freedom from debt ca. 540, the *palintokia*, "the return of interest (*tokos*) which they had chanced to have paid their creditors."[48] The term *tokos* for interest is not found before the last quarter of the 5th century, so what occurred is most likely to have been a debt cancellation. The logic may have been that creditors already had received the equivalent of their principal back in the form of the interest they had received.[49] Historians are still debating whether the agrarian debts that Solon cancelled bore interest. Even without interest charges, debts would have led to bondage for cultivators unable to pay their stipulated obligations. After all, the Merchant of Venice's pledge of a pound of flesh to Shylock was a zero-interest loan.

Cancelling debts and redistributing land echoed through the ensuing centuries. Around 365 BC in Heracleia, in Pontus on the Black Sea, the oligarchy recalled Klearchos from exile to deal with a popular debt revolt. Said to have been a pupil of Plato and also Isocrates, Klearchos decided to take power for himself by sponsoring a debt cancellation and redistributing the land. After he had ruled for thirteen years, surrounding himself with bodyguards to ward off constant attempts to kill him, Sparta finally deposed him by force in 353.[50]

---

[48] Plutarch, *Greek Questions* #18 in *Moralia* 295D, based on an Aristotelian study of Megara's constitution. See also Aristotle, *Politics* 5 at 1305a24 and Plato, *Republic* 8 at 562D. Theagenes is said to have confiscated estates from his enemies and used them to reward supporters or pay for public works projects such as the aqueduct (Sagstetter 2013:155). Plutarch says that Theagenes married his daughter to the Athenian tyrant Cylon and was exiled by a political reaction, but the new government retained many of his reforms.

Athenaeus, *Banquet of the Sophists* 14.629-630 (ca. 200 BC), also reports a dance to celebrate Syracuse's debt cancellation, perhaps under Dionysus I (late 5th century). But Millett 1991:253, fn41 thinks that the term to describe it (*chreon apokopē*) is a confusion with 'meat stealing' (*kreon apoklopē*).

[49] That logic was implicit in Hammurabi's laws ca. 1750 BC, freeing bondservants after three years of service. Babylonia's annual interest rate on grain debts was one-third, so the creditor would have received his full principal by the time three years had elapsed. By Plutarch's day another term for cancelling back interest existed: *prosagoresantes*.

[50] Sagstetter 2013:157, citing Diodorus, *Bibliotheca historica* 15.81.5 and Justin, *Epitome of Pompeius Trogus* 16.4-5.

Oligarchies fight to prevent new reformers from gaining "tyrannical" power

The aristocratic idea of "equality" was limited to equal rights among the wealthy. They made interest-free *eranos* loans to each other as mutual aid, but did not extend this practice to society at large. Their concept of liberty was freedom for creditors to turn citizens into clients and debt servants.

Today's euphemistic economic vocabulary would call such lending to smallholders – under contractual terms enabling creditors to appropriate land and reduce debtors to servitude – a "free market," and celebrate it as an expression of individualist gain-seeking. It was indeed that, but the Age of Tyrants viewed patronage and credit practices that reduced debt-ridden individuals to dependency as an attack on *dikē*. But as oligarchies re-appeared, the prevailing vocabulary became euphemistic. As Moses Finley wryly noted: "*Eunomia* became an ambiguous term: 'good order' slid into 'stable government' and *eunomia* became a catchword of propagandists against political change, in particular change to democracy."[51]

Each Greek and Italian city sought to resolve the problem of closed elites in its own way. In Athens, Solon enacted the first debt cancellation that is attested in detail (although its vocabulary is so archaic as to be ambiguous), but left landholdings in place (see Chapter 4). As the next chapter will discuss, Sparta reduced neighboring Messenia to helotage to support its *homoioi* citizen-army, while its oligarchy's leaders maintained their own landholdings in Sparta itself.

Roman kings opened their city to immigrants, whom they armed to conquer neighboring Italian towns run by more closed elites (see Chapter 9). But like the oligarchic regimes that increased their power in Greece from the 5th century onward, the increasingly prosperous Roman elites opposed the spirit of the 7th- and 6th-century royal reforms, and overthrew Rome's kings and transferred political control into the hands of a narrow senatorial class for the duration of the Republic.

Despite the moves by reformer-tyrants to reduce inequality, money-lending enabled oligarchies to re-emerge. Aristotle explained that what "used to be called democracies" turned into mild or moderate constitutional states (*politeias*) controlled by *rentier* oligarchies that depicted the 7th-century and subsequent tyrants as overthrowing liberty, not as catalysts for classical democracy. The victors "established a 'timocracy' based on wealth, in which, along with the nobles, those who had gained

---

[51] Finley 1982:27 and 254, fn6.

some affluence shared in the government."[52] Greece ended up being conquered by oligarchic Sparta and Macedonia, and ultimately by Rome.
Today's world is still living in the aftermath.

---

[52] Andreades 1933:114, and Aristotle, *Politics* 4 at 1297b; see also 3 at 1274b-1278b.

3
Sparta's Oligarchy Defers an Early Political Crisis, 6th Century BC

Having left almost no monuments, inscriptions or chronicles prior to the 2nd century BC, Sparta's early history was written entirely by foreigners, headed by Herodotus, Xenophon, Plato and Aristotle.[1] Much later, Plutarch's *Parallel Lives of the Greeks and Romans* became the most popular source. Like many narratives written in late antiquity, he cast Greek and Roman history as a moral fable of his own epoch's debt dynamics destroying a hypothetical archaic state of equality. His idealized "Lycurgan" constitution based on equal land ownership, subsequently undermined by money-lust, actually was the program of kings Agis IV and Cleomenes III cancelling debts and redistributing land in the 3rd century BC.

This "Spartan mirage" is a mythologizing of the "original" Lycurgan laws that had made Sparta so dominant in the 5th century BC, when it ruled Greece despite the small size of its free population.[2] But Sparta always had wide economic inequality, gaining a reputation by the early 7th century "as a *polis* in which only the wealthy counted." Indeed, "the acquisitive behavior of the rich and the impoverishment of poor citizens

---

[1] Regarding Sparta's dearth of historical records, Toynbee 1969:158 notes that the further back in time a narrative is set, the more free rein is given to political bias. The would-be archaist's political zeal "may tempt him to use his imagination to fill in the lacunae." The papers in Anton Powell's 2018 *Companion to Sparta* review the vast modern scholarship trying to untangle and reconstruct Sparta's history. The major critiques of the mythology are François Ollier, *Le mirage spartiate* (2 vols., 1933-1943), Eugène Napoleon Tigerstedt, *The Legend of Sparta in Classical Antiquity* (2 vols., 1965-1974), Elizabeth Rawson, *The Spartan Tradition in European Thought* (1975), and most recently Mogens Herman Hansen, *The Imaginary Polis: Symposium, January 7– 10, 2004* (2005), esp. Stephen Hodkinson, "The Imaginary Spartan Politeia," pp. 22–81. See also Powell and Hodkinson 2002, and Hodkinson and Morris 2012.

[2] Writing ca. 75 AD, Plutarch drew on the histories by Ephorus from the 4th century BC and the 3rd-century Stoic writer Phylarchus, who popularized the reforms of Cleomenes III. Hodkinson 2000 reviews Plutarch's anachronisms.

provoked a civil war focused on demands for a redistribution of land" in a long 6th-century revolution.[3]

What made Sparta's economy unique

To avoid being overthrown like other oligarchies in the 7th- and 6th-century revolts that erupted throughout Greece (and also apparently in Italy), Sparta's oligarchy enacted a unique set of reforms, now dated to the 6th century. While other Greek city-states founded colonies and Rome used its *ager publicus* to settle army veterans, Sparta assigned land conquered from neighboring Laconia and Messenia to its fighters as standardized allotments (*kleroi*). The defeated Messenians were reduced to serflike helot status, turning over a reported half of the crop on their assigned *kleros* land to Sparta's citizens, who thus were able to avoid manual labor and devote their time to military practice (mainly to keep the helots subdued), as well as sports and leisure.[4]

Called "Equals" (*homoioi*), each citizen had a similar public status, using crops from land farmed by the servile helot population to make standardized contributions to the common meals (*syssitia*) to reduce at least the appearance of inequality in everyday life. But Sparta did not restrict the acquisition of property by its oligarchy, whose wealthiest families protected their interests politically by controlling Sparta's "upper house," the *gerousia*. Composed of elders over the age of sixty, its members were drawn from the ranks of Sparta's elite and held veto power over its two kings.[5]

The result was that Sparta became an oppressive *rentier* state vis-à-vis the helots, but averted the resentment and upheavals that unseated aristocracies in other polities in the 7th and 6th centuries by avoiding extreme public displays of wealth. In addition to organizing group

---

[3] Hodkinson 2018:46, noting (p. 30) that the phrase "sixth-century revolution" comes from Moses Finley.

[4] The helots were not ethnically different, and spoke the same Dorian dialect as the Spartans (Thucydides 4.3.3). Spartan children by them were called *mothax* "step-brothers." See fn45 below.

[5] Sparta was the only Greek polity with kings – a dual kingship by the Agiad and Eurypontid dynasties. Oliva 1971:27 compares them to Rome's two consuls, each able to veto the other, thereby requiring broad agreement for any innovation. Sparta's five ephors were elected to "advise" its kings – or overrule them, as they did Cleomenes III in 227. Hodkinson 2018:48 notes: "According to Aristotle (*Politics* 5.1306a18-19), the choice of members was *dynasteutikē*, 'dynastic,' limited to a narrow range of families."

common meals, Sparta enacted anti-luxury laws that limited conspicuous spending at funerals and other rites of passage. Such laws were
a common reform throughout Greece "as part of a reaction across the
Greek world to increasing inequality and the development of 'luxurious'
lifestyles." Van Wees dates this "culture of austerity" as coming at the
end of the sixth century, ca. 515-500 BC.[6]

The myth of equal land distribution

The most serious distortion of Sparta's history is Plutarch's description
of Lycurgus convincing wealthy families to divide up the land equally
among its citizens:

> There was an extreme inequality among them, and their state was
> overloaded with a multitude of indigent and necessitous persons, while
> its whole wealth had centered upon a very few. To the end, therefore,
> that he might expel from the state arrogance and envy, luxury and
> crime, and those yet more inveterate diseases of want and superfluity, he
> obtained of them to renounce their properties, and to consent to a new
> division of the land, and that they should all live together on an equal
> footing; merit to be their only road to eminence.[7]

Nearly all our early information comes from Herodotus, Thucydides,
Xenophon, Plato and Aristotle, who "make no mention of equality in the
holding of land in Sparta, and Cicero, too, is equally silent; ... even in the
time of the Persian wars mention is often made of rich and poor, and from
that time on we have many witnesses to such inequality."[8] Plato's *Republic*,
written in the aftermath of the Peloponnesian War in the 380s or 370s,
"depicted Sparta as the archetypical oligarchy, driven by greed and competition for wealth (544c, 545a), a system inimical to equality of property."[9]

---

[6] Van Wees 2018a:203 and 2018b:253-254. He elaborates (p. 255): "The classical
system of communal dining was introduced ca. 515-500 in a program of reform
which assigned 9,000 citizens to mess-groups of fifteen members of different ages,
families and economic statuses."

[7] Plutarch, *Lycurgus* 8. Contra this passage and Polybius 6.45.3-4 and 6.48.3, Hodkinson 2000 demonstrates that large estates survived the reforms, and were greatly
extended in the 4th century after Sparta defeated Athens, causing a land and debt
crisis by the mid-3rd century (discussed below in Chapter 8).

[8] Andreades 1933:46, 38 and 40, citing Cicero, *De Officiis*, 2.23 and *De Re Publica* 3.9,
and Jannet 1873.

[9] Van Wees 2018a:207. He adds (p. 215): "Plato (*Republic* 548ab) pictured Sparta
and Crete as 'timocracies' where citizens 'wildly worship gold and silver, [but hide
it] in storerooms and domestic treasuries ... and behind the courtyard walls of their

Toynbee notes that Herodotus and Xenophon mention wealthy Spartans, and that Aristotle observed that "the inequality in the distribution of property is one of the reprehensible features of Spartan life. ... Consequently, the country has fallen into the hands of a small minority."[10] Sparta was always Greece's most oligarchic state, with some families always "more equal than others." The only land that was distributed was in Messenian territory. Sparta's elite retained "their ancestral freeholds in the original nucleus of Sparta's city-state territory,"[11] a retention that a fable by Aesop seems to have described:

> Having become a general over the other wolves, a wolf was establishing laws for everyone, so that he would place in the middle whatever each took in the hunt and give to each an equal share, so that they would not resort to eating each other out of need. But an ass approached and, shaking his mane, said, "It is a fine sentiment that comes from a wolf's mind, but how is it that you put yesterday's hunt in your [own] lair? Come put this in the middle and apportion it." But upon being challenged the [wolf] dissolved the laws.[12]

The wolf in this fable is Sparta's oligarchy, dividing up the Messenian prey equally while keeping for themselves "yesterday's hunt," the land in Sparta itself. "There was no fundamental redistribution of land or alteration to the system of private property ownership," Hodkinson concludes. "The uneven distribution of property remained and became increasingly severe from the fifth century onwards."[13]

---

dwellings – in a word, in private nests within which they may squander a fortune in spending on their wives and the rest.'"

[10] Toynbee 1969:310, citing Herodotus 6.61, Xenophon, *Hellenica* 6.4.11 and Aristotle, *Politics* 6 at 1270a. Van Wees 2018a:204 concludes: "The notion that Lykourgos had divided Spartan territory equally amongst all citizens seems to have been formulated first in 243 BC" by Agis IV, claiming that his reforms were a return to the "true" Lycurgan system. In sum, (p. 207), "apart from five revolutionary years during the reign of Kleomenes III, Sparta had no equality of landownership at any time."

[11] Toynbee 1969:232. Van Wees 2018:203 notes that since Hodkinson 2000, "It is now widely accepted that equalization of property was a myth, never attempted in archaic or classical Sparta."

[12] Cited in Sagstetter 2013:138, #228 in the numbering of Aesop's fables by Chambry 1926.

[13] Hodkinson 2018:46.

Public austerity and Sparta's oligarchic "equality" among its homoioi

Laws to keep funeral and wedding spending simple instead of expensive shows of status were typical reforms enacted throughout Greece in the 6ᵗʰ century. By imposing uniformity of dress and education, Sparta went further to deter resentment against the wealthy lording it over less affluent citizens.[14] Although its workshops had produced luxury ceramics and other art for the wealthy in the 8ᵗʰ and early 7ᵗʰ century, "after ca. 525, Lakonian figurative pottery was no longer produced, yet no Attic or other foreign pottery was imported to take its place; only locally-made black-glaze or plain pottery was used."[15]

Sparta's rules discouraging conspicuous consumption were capped prior to 500 by the "public messes with their culture of regulated eating and drinking."[16] Groups of fifteen men, "Equals" (*homoioi*), took their *syssitia* meals with one another, sharing a basic diet so that "the rich, being obliged to go to the same table with the poor, could not make use of or enjoy their abundance."[17] At these meals, "the exclusive use of pottery was a powerful sign of material moderation in Sparta," as "elsewhere in classical Greece, gold, silver and bronze tableware were an integral feature of elite symposia."[18]

Minimizing wealth distinctions in these ways made Sparta superficially appear "a democracy because the regime has a number of democratic-looking traits," noted Aristotle in the 4ᵗʰ century. "There is the educational system, to start with. The children of the rich are brought up like the children of the poor, and the kind of education that they are given is

---

[14] Plutarch, *Moralia*, amplified in *Lycurgus* 10.

[15] Van Wees 2018a:213-214. He adds (p. 244) that Sparta had limited public building, so prominent elsewhere in Greece. Handicrafts were simple and were obtained in large part from the *perioikoi*, "dwellers around."

[16] Van Wees 2018a:226.

[17] Plutarch, *Lycurgus* 10. Plato's *Republic* and More's *Utopia* were based on Sparta. Nearly all such utopias have been authoritarian and micro-managed to impose austerity. But van Wees (2018a:204) notes that "Despite the philosopher's best efforts to make the meals seem austere, Spartans consumed generous quantities of a variety of foods. Modern scholars often speak of 'rations,' but Dikaiarkhos reveals that diners were not restricted to fixed quantities of barley or wine." Van Wees points out that well-to-do members typically added more varied foods.

[18] Van Wees, 2018b:243. Flower 2002:197, citing Murray 1993:175 and Cartledge 2001:73-74, emphasizes that *homoioi* "means not 'the equal ones,' but 'the similar ones.' ... Individuals who are similar dress alike, act alike, eat alike, but are not necessarily equal in terms of possessions and status."

within the reach of the poor as well. ... It is not apparent who is rich and who is poor."[19] But display was prominent behind closed doors, and it was clear who was wealthy. They supplied figs, cheese, meat and other niceties to *syssitia* with members from the richest families,[20] provided horses for the cavalry, and often won the four horse-chariot races at Olympia in the 5th and 4th centuries.[21]

Rejecting commercial exchange and silver money

Prior to its reforms Sparta had a typically Greek culture and, as noted above, produced luxury ceramics for a cosmopolitan elite class. But Sparta was economically self-contained from ca. 500 until the 4th century BC. Its economy was based on non-market requisitioning, and thanks to its own iron mines, good ceramic clay and even some copper, Sparta did not need money for foreign trade. The *perioikoi* ("dwellers around") produced its handicrafts, including arms, while its wine was "locally-produced rather than imported, the tableware and furniture plain rather than ostentatious."[22] And it did not need bullion to pay for foreign military adventures as long as its infantry was used for domestic policing of the helots, who produced its food.[23]

This self-sufficiency helped Sparta avoid the debt problems that plagued other Greek cities. Sparta's self-sufficiency provided its *homoioi* hoplites with just enough to support themselves, although citizens lost their status and became "Inferiors" if they failed to make the prescribed contributions of food and wine.[24]

---

[19] Aristotle, *Politics* 4 at 1294b. Austerity was especially harsh for the young. The *agoge* system of military training allowed young men only one cloak a year, and if Plutarch's report is accurate, they had to make their own beds from rushes gathered from the riverbank.

[20] Van Wees 2018a:204 and 2018b:241. "Men's and boys' regulation meals," he adds (p. 203), "were supplemented by 'after-dinner dishes' donated either by the richer members or by successful hunters."

[21] Christien 2002:181, citing Herodotus 6.61 and Xenophon, *Hellenica* 6.4.11 and *Lakedaemonion Politeia* (*Spartan Constitution*, henceforth *Lak. Pol.*) 14.3.

[22] Van Wees 2018a:203:

[23] The neighboring *perioikoi* seem to have been independent and self-governing, supporting themselves on their own land. Although not citizens of Sparta, they fought with its army as hoplites.

[24] "Citizens who defaulted on their obligations could be relegated to the ranks of 'Tremblers' and 'Inferiors,' but they still seem to have kept their places in the phalanx," notes Snodgrass 1980:109. However, the term *hypomeiones*, "Inferiors" or

Viewing commerce and moneylending as society's main destabilizing force by leading to wealth addiction (money-love) – considered to
be a symptom of corrupt alien influence – Sparta's "Lycurgan" ethic
rejected the drive for pecuniary *chrēmatismos* (money making) and barred
the hoplite *homoioi* from "having anything to do with vulgar trades."[25]
"Why, then, should money-making be a preoccupation in a state where
the pains caused by its possession exceed the pleasures it gives?"
Xenophon asked (*Lak. Pol.* 7.6). That was in line with Greek moral philosophy viewing commercial gain-seeking as injuring the body politic
by fostering *hubris*. An oft-cited Delphic oracle warned: "Love of money
[φιλοχρηματία, *philochrēmatia*] will destroy Sparta, nothing else."[26]
    Credit did not become a serious form of exploitation until the 3ʳᵈ
century. "From Herodotus onwards," van Wees finds, "we have allusions
to Spartans, including the kings, lending and borrowing, and there was
apparently a distinctive Spartan way of recording such transactions.
Given the rate at which inequality of property developed, many poorer
Spartans will have borrowed from the rich in an effort to hang on to
their citizenship, and among non-citizens even more families will have
been in need of extra money."[27] Still, such debt long remained a relatively marginal phenomenon.
    Banning gold and silver deterred foreign contact with "behaviors asso-
ciated with archaic aristocrats (*hybris* [arrogance], *pleonexia* [greediness],
and *truphē* [luxury])."[28] But Sparta's avoidance of foreign commerce,
along with its rejection of silver and gold coinage after its Messenian wars,
made it seem so archaic that Aristotle dated the "Lycurgan" reforms to
the 8ᵗʰ century, others to the 9ᵗʰ century or even earlier.

"Lesser Spartiatae," is attested only once, by Xenophon, *Hellenica* 3.3.6. Aristotle,
Politics 2 at 1271a27-37 cites poor Spartans unable to meet their payments.

[25] Plutarch, *Lycurgus* 24 and Herodotus 2.167. This attitude was widely held (see
Figueira 2002). Plato (*Republic* 8 at 550E) believed that *khrēmastike* (acquisitiveness)
subverted respect for *aretē* (excellence). See Chapter 7 for a discussion of wealth addiction.

[26] Diodorus Siculus, *Bibliotheca historica* 7.12.5-6. The oracle has been ascribed to
Tyrtaeus; see his *Fragments* (Loeb Classical Library, 1999:43). The root is *chrema*, as
in Aristotle's discussion of *chrematistics*, monetary wealth (see below, Chapter 7 and
Chapter 12). In a similar vein, Solon's poetry (Solon 4) warned that greed might
destroy Athens. See Irwin 2005, and Plutarch, *Moralia* 239-240.

[27] Van Wees 2018a:212.

[28] Figueira 2002:141.

Sparta's iron money apparently was used mainly to pay fines to the
state, such as for failing to contribute one's crop quota for the *syssitia*
meals. Bulky and heavy, the flat round iron *pelanors* were deprived
of practical use by being plunged into vinegar when heated red-hot,
making them brittle and blistered. As Xenophon tried to explain the
Spartan rationale, *pelanors* were so cumbersome

> that even a sum of ten minae could not be brought into a house without
> the master and the servants being aware of it: the money would fill a
> large space and need a wagon to draw it. Moreover, there is a right of
> search for gold and silver, and, in the event of discovery, the possessor is
> fined.[29]

Pointing out that Sparta was by far the largest economy of its time not
to mint bullion, Figueira describes the *pelanors* as "'counter-money' and
'anti-money' ... not as a forerunner of coinage in gold or silver, but as
'invalidating all gold and silver money.'"[30] Yet "Spartans were certainly
not prevented from 'making money' from their landed estates," notes
van Wees. "Inequality of landownership meant that in reality some
citizens had huge agricultural surpluses while others could barely scrape
together their mess contributions, and many fell below the citizenship –
or indeed the subsistence threshold."[31]

As van Wees summarizes the scale of this private-sector economy,
"wealthy Spartan citizens disposed of large surpluses of grain, wine
and other produce as well as herds of livestock; they had a convenient
outlet in the large commercial center in the middle of the city, and they
regarded the right to buy and sell in this market as a high privilege."[32]
Writing in the early 4th century, Xenophon described Sparta's agora
"as a bustling market, so commercially active that stalls selling different

---

[29] Xenophon, *Lak. Pol.* 7.5-6. However, van Wees (2018a:208) points out, Herodotus
"does not even hint that it was illegal to own precious metal: his stories concern
only the immoral means by which it was acquired."

[30] Figueira 2002:138-140, citing Plutarch, *Lysander* 17.1-2 and *Lycurgus* 9.1; see also
Moralia 226C. He points out (p. 149) that "Sparta lacked ordinary channels of dis-
semination, like paying wages," and adds (p. 151) that silver coins did not spread
widely until the last few decades of the 500s, so Xenophon and Plutarch were
anachronistic in attributing the ban on coinage to the initial "Lycurgan" reforms.
No hoards in Peloponnesus were found before the 480s (p. 150). But neither has
any archaeological trace of iron *pelanors* been found (p. 143), and "contemporary
sources do not ever attest anyone utilizing iron money in any transactions."

[31] Van Wees 2018a 211.

[32] Van Wees 2018a:212-213.

kinds of products were grouped into zones," with public business conducted alongside market transactions, but having only about 40 citizens
there at a given moment, although "as many as 4,000 non-citizens." [33]
The "Lycurgan" reforms thus are unlikely to have banished commerce,
credit or the possession of bullion. "Only Plutarch, *Moralia* 226b attributed a cancellation of debts to the lawgiver; this was omitted from
his *Lykourgos*, and implicitly denied in his *Agis* 10."[34]

Spartan fiscal policy

Sparta's lack of monetization retarded the creation of an integrated
public budget. Its administered economy sustained itself on a break-
even basis as the land cultivated by helots supplied the food for its
common *syssitia* meals. State revenue took the form of various contribu-
tions-in-kind, including the skins from sacrificial animals as well as "a
boar from the litter of all the sows" so that "the king might never lack
victims for the sacrifice in case he needed to consult the gods."[35] Sparta
thus was a *rentier* state without being monetized or debt-financed.

This in-kind system left Sparta without the means to meet expenditures requiring foreign payments in silver. That lack led it to withdraw
early from the war against Persia (499-449), and made it reluctant to
enter into the Peloponnesian War against Athens, whose finances were
at their peak in the 5th century. The seeming irony, notes Andreades,
is that "this most warlike people was never ready for war," except do-
mestically against Messenia's helots. "Every unusual expenditure found
the Spartans totally unprepared," aggravated by Sparta's aristocracy
dodging the few fiscal obligations that existed.[36]

Sparta's oligarchy, like that of Rome, minimized the role of public
spending. Sparta had no public expenditures for theaters, statues or
public dramatic or even religious performances, although its leading
families contributed to the temples of Olympia and Delphi. It did not
build colonnades or other public buildings of the sort that characterized
most Greek cities, or even walls like the long defensive walls of Athens.

---

[33] Xenophon, *Lak. Pol.* 3.3.5-7, cited in Hodkinson 2018:44.

[34] Van Wees 2018a:205. See also 212-213 and 228, fn13.

[35] Andreades 1933:58-59, citing Xenophon, *Lak. Pol.* 15.5, Plato, *Alcibiades* A18, and
Athenaeus, *Banquet of the Sophists* 4.22. Citizens who could not meet their scheduled contributions from the land and helots assigned to them became second-class
or "inferior" citizens (see also fn24 above).

[36] Andreades 1933:61-62 and 65-70, citing Pseudo-Aristotle, *Oeconomica* 2.2.9.

Nor did Sparta have dockyards, for it was not a maritime city. And whereas Athens had about 20,000 citizens serving in a public capacity in the 5th century, Sparta had no such paid administrators. Even the ephors served without pay, typical of the oligarchic practice of guaranteeing that public offices would remain in the hands of a ruling class wealthy enough not to have to earn income.[37]

Sparta's recruitment of helots leads them to fight for their liberty

Sparta's army was deployed mainly for police action to keep the helots down and maintain its supremacy over southern Peloponnesia. Herodotus (9.28-30) reported that it provided 5,000 hoplites at the Battle of Plataea in 479, supported by 35,000 helots – seven (including one lightly-armed man) for every Spartan, accounting for half the Greek force of 69,500 troops that defeated Persia's army led by Xerxes. Helots were hired to carry their master's arms, were given half-rations, and were emancipated after their military service. Some served as suppliers, and others seem to have bought their freedom with what they earned by selling their crops.

Aristotle compared the helots to "an enemy constantly sitting in wait of the disaster of the Spartans." An uprising occurred in 470, led by thousands of the helots who had learned Spartan tactics fighting the Persians.[38] The crisis peaked when the ephors killed Sparta's general Pausanias, accusing him of conspiring to free the helots and make them citizens if they would support his takeover, and even of allying himself with Persia to make himself ruler of Sparta and hence Greece. The conflict ended with a truce that allowed the rebels supporting Pausanias to emigrate.[39] The Third Messenian War (468-458) soon followed, and intensified when a serious earthquake in 465 provided an opportunity for the helots to rise up in a decade-long fight.

Antagonism between Sparta and Athens meanwhile was leading up to what would become the Peloponnesian War (431-404). Sparta's king Archidamos II (469–427) tried to prevent it from entering war with

---

[37] Andreades 1933:71-72. There was no dole for the poor.

[38] Aristotle, *Politics* 2 at 1269a37-39 and Raaflaub 2007:126.

[39] Flower 2002:203 and 207, citing Thucydides 1.132.4, 1.138.3 and 1.103. Herodotus 5.32 called Pausanias "tyrant" of Greece. This apparently was not the first time that Spartan elites had sought to mobilize the helots. Cleomenes I (519-490 BC) had promised to make them citizens to overpower the ephors. See Oliva 1971:146, citing Dickens 1912.

Athens as pressure mounted in 428. He warned that war would involve a monetary drain, and that in contrast to Athens, Sparta had little silver. Noting the resistance of Sparta's landowners to taxes, he pointed out that: "We neither have public funds nor do we readily contribute from our private resources" (Thucydides 1.80).[40] But Archidamos's warning was in vain.

The ensuing war ended Sparta's control over the helots. Athens created a haven for them on the island of Pylos, threatening Sparta with loss of its supply of cultivators to feed its army. Sparta tricked some 2,000 helot leaders into an infamous massacre in 425:

> The helots were invited by a proclamation to pick out those of their number who claimed to have most distinguished themselves against the enemy, in order that they might receive their freedom; the object being to test them, as it was thought that the first to claim their freedom would be the most high spirited and the most apt to rebel. As many as two thousand were selected accordingly, who crowned themselves and went round the temples, rejoicing in their new freedom. The Spartans, however, soon afterwards did away with them, and no one ever knew how each of them perished. (Thucydides 4.80)

Sparta won the Peloponnesian War largely by recognizing Persia's sovereignty over the Greek cities in Asia Minor in exchange for Persia paying the wages of Sparta's naval crews, which were recruited for a drachma a day, twice the three-obol wage offered by Athens.[41] After a seven-year standoff with Athens during the Peace of Nicias, 421-414, Persia's prince Cyrus gave Sparta a subsidy to build up its naval fleet under the command of Lysander. Fighting resumed, much of it in Sicily where Sparta's general (*strategos*) Gylippus organized resistance to Athens' Delian League. His army defeated that of Athens in 414, and the war's last major battle occurred in 405 when Lysander's fleet destroyed that of Athens at Aigospotamoi, near the Hellespont (modern Istanbul).

Lysander installed regimes loyal to Sparta throughout Greece, typically in groups of ten administrators (*dekarchies*) with a Spartan *harmost*

---

[40] What was Sparta's advantage, Archidamos asked. "Is it in our money? There we have a far greater deficiency. We neither have it in our treasury, nor are we ready to contribute it from our private funds."

[41] Andreades 1933:65-70. He comments that for receiving 5,000 talents over time, Sparta became Persia's vassal-state, but turned against it after the Athenians had been defeated. Sparta was able to continue the Peloponnesian War by levying tribute on the defeated Athenian League members. See also Chapter 5 for further discussion of the Peloponnesian War, including Athens' financing of it.

ambassador commanding a military garrison.[42] This caused resentment against Sparta for ending Athenian domination only to make its former allies part of Sparta's own empire.

Matters were worst in Athens. It had lost control of the sea, and was obliged to pay heavy tribute to Sparta. It was stripped of most of its defenses, its fleet and its Long Walls between the city and its port, Piraeus. Many of its soldiers were sold off into slavery. Athens was not destroyed, but Lysander imposed a regime of thirty oligarchic supporters of Sparta – the notorious Thirty Tyrants (404/3) led by Plato's follower Critias. They killed democratic leaders, grabbed their land and fortunes, and left a legacy of Athenian debt in their wake (see Chapter 5).

Sparta's major allies, "especially Boeotia and Corinth, had bitterly opposed the terms of peace agreed with Athens at the end of the War, and in particular Sparta's decision not to destroy Athens," Thucydides reports.[43] At home, Sparta also suffered as its victory destabilized its domestic economy.

Sparta's postwar monetary inflow creates social instability

Sparta's foreign wars required money, first to fight Persia and then Athens. Being self-sufficient in essentials, its domestic economy could get along with only an iron currency, but empires needed silver and gold ("money of general currency" with exchange value, *koinon nomismatos*) to wage war abroad. As Polybius (6.49.7-10) pointed out:

> As long as their ambition was confined to governing their immediate neighbors, or even the Peloponnesians only, they were content with the resources and supplies provided by Lakonia itself, having all material of war ready to hand ... But directly as they took in hand to dispatch naval expeditions, or to go on campaigns by land outside the Peloponnese, it was evident that neither their iron currency, nor their use of crops for payment in kind, would be able to supply them with what they lacked if they abided by the legislation of Lycurgus; for such undertakings required money universally current, and goods from foreign countries. Thus they were compelled to wait humbly at Persian doors, impose tribute on the islanders, and exact contributions from all the Greeks.[44]

---

[42] Xenophon, *Hellenica* 3.4.2, 3.5.13 and 6.3.8, and Plutarch, *Lysander* 13.

[43] Thucydides 3.82.1 and Xenophon, *Hellenica* 2.2.19, cited and discussed in Roy 2018:365.

[44] See Christien 2002:172, and Figueira 2002:145-147, citing Diodorus 7.12.8 to the effect that: "The 'Lycurgan' system held the upper hand until it first proved ill-suit-

Sparta's military victory led to an immense inflow of tribute from
Athens after 404. This "influx of owls" – the image embossed on the
Athenian coins used to pay tribute – destabilized the distribution of
Spartan land and wealth, which was further aggravated by well-placed
Spartans bringing back to Sparta the silver booty that they had gained
by acting as *harmost* proconsuls or as mercenaries throughout Greece,
sometimes leading foreign armies. "The date at which Lacedaemon
[Sparta] was first attacked by social disease," wrote Plutarch (*Agis* 5), "co-
incides with the moment at which she overthrew the Athenian empire [in
404] and gorged herself with the precious metals."

Lysander in 405 consigned to Gylippus between 1000 and 1500 talents
of silver tribute and booty to bring back to Sparta. But 300 talents
turned out to be missing. The money had been wrapped in sacks, each
bag having a token recording how much it contained. When the shortfall
was discovered, Gylippus was accused of having taken some silver from
each, unaware of the security check.[45] He fled Sparta and the ephors
condemned him to death.

When Lysander brought home the rest of the war booty in summer
404, a debate (discussed below) arose over whether Sparta should use
it only for public purposes and limit its use in private transactions.
Personal possession of precious metals "was nothing new in 404," notes
Hodkinson. "What was new, however, was the vast scale of monetary
wealth becoming available to leading citizens from their overseas
commands" and by working as foreign mercenaries, commanders and
harmost proconsuls. Their positions "rested not on popular election, as
with the posts of the ephorate and Gerousia, but on appointment and
cooptation ... by patronage, personal influence and the cultivation of
connections – social networking in which the possession of wealth was
an essential ingredient."[46]

---

ed for war with Athens; it then accepted a weakening of monetary and sumptuary
restrictions; and finally it collapsed through the demoralization of greed."

[45] Diodorus 13.105.8-9 and Plutarch, *Lysander* 16.1f. Gylippus, Lysander and the
Spartan naval commander Callicratidas were said to have had helot mothers,
making them *mothax* "step-brothers" sponsored by wealthier Spartan families
and given full military training, usually in the less aristocratic navy. Hodkinson
2000:427 concludes that Gylippus already had become rich in Sicily, where Syra-
cusans had accused him of avarice in 414-413.

[46] Hodkinson 2000:429-430, citing Plutarch, *Lysander* 17 and Christien 2002:176-
179, emphasizing (p. 181) that although Sparta was still basically a non-monetized

Shortly before a new war with Persia ended in 394 a Spartan military leader, Cinadon, sought to break the oligarchy's power by mobilizing helots to overthrow it. He promised to give more rights to Sparta's *hypomeiones* ("Inferiors"), and perhaps to *perioikoi* and even the helots, although he was unable to mobilize these three groups in a common cause. The ephors accused him of organizing a revolt and forced him to name his accomplices, whom they killed after torturing them and dragging them through the city.[47]

The greed of the ensuing oligarchy led to widespread reports throughout Greece of Spartan avarice. Serving abroad, especially as *harmosts*, gave well-placed Spartans "considerable opportunities for private gain," Xenophon noted. "In the past they were afraid to appear to have gold, whereas nowadays there are some who even pride themselves in possessing it."[48]

The silver and gold that Lysander and other Spartan soldiers and commanders brought home must have amounted to immense sums over several generations.[49] Landowning families without "access to foreign posts (for example, members of the Gerousia and households without men of the right age)" feared that the fortunes being brought by military commanders, mercenaries and *harmosts* from Greek cities, Sicily and Asia Minor would threaten their status by shifting power to the wealthy.[50]

It seems that this was the context for the myth arising, "reported by Xenophon (*Lak. Pol.* 7.4-6), that Lycurgus ... had banned the use of

---

economy, there was much wealth at the top.

[47] The story is told by Aristotle, *Politics* 5 at 1306:b33-35, and Xenophon, *Hellenica* 3.3.5-11. Cinadon was said to be an "Inferior," a status usually reflecting failure to pay the stipulated *syssitia* dues, as noted above. Hodkinson 2000:436 finds that they outnumbered full Spartiates by this time.

[48] Hodkinson 2000:426, citing Xenophon, *Lak. Pol.* 14.2.3. Pointing to mercenary service abroad as a source of many Spartan fortunes (p. 434), he lists "Agesilaos in Asia and Egypt in the 360s; Gastron and Lamios in Egypt ca. 350; Archidamos III in Crete and Italy in the 340s and 330s; Thibron in Athens and Crete in the late 320s; Akrotatos in Sicily in 315; Kleonymos in Italy and Corcyra in the late 300s; Xanthippos in Carthage in 255."

[49] Boeckh 1842:29, citing Plutarch, *Nicias* 28 and *Lysander* 16-18, and Diodorus 13.106. Xenophon, *Hellenica* 3.2.6 states that 470 talents flowed into Sparta.

[50] Christien 2002:182. See also Flower 2002:193. As an example of how money tended to corrupt society, Plutarch told a story of king Anaxander (640-615 BC), explaining that the reason why Sparta did not accumulate money in the public treasury was "so that those made the guardians of it may not become corrupt," *Moralia* (Loeb Classical Library, 1931 III:299).

gold and silver in Sparta."[51] Idealizing a money-free economy, Plutarch described a lust for silver (*philarguria*) when "coinage first flowed into Sparta, and with it, greed and a desire for wealth ... Lysander, though incorruptible himself, filled his country with the love of riches and with luxury, thus subverting the laws of Lycurgus."[52]

Plutarch's biography of Lysander (17.2) states that when the new ephors elected in autumn 404 summoned the assembly to debate the use of the war booty, "it was Skiraphidas (according to Theopompus), or Phlogidas (according to Ephorus), who declared that they ought not to receive gold and silver coinage into the city but to use their ancestral [iron] currency." The assembly reached a compromise: It banned the personal use of precious metals within the domestic economy, imposing capital punishment on violators, but Sparta's treasury could accumulate silver to hire mercenaries and support oligarchic regimes in cities loyal to it. "Thorax, a friend of Lysander and a well-known soldier, was condemned for possession of money. By putting him to death, Lysander's enemies signaled their determination that the victors would not profit from their victories."[53]

But owners of monetary fortunes found a grab-bag of opportunities. The ensuing polarization of wealth led to dissatisfaction among poorer Spartans, who felt threatened with being reduced to "Inferiors" and losing their citizenship status. "Sparta was troubled by major change in society: large losses in citizen manpower; growing use of men from the non-Spartiate classes – above all, of helots who, once promoted to trusted roles, could never again be relegated to their former humble position; and the recourse to mercenary soldiers, something which was always very expensive."[54]

Democratic revolts against oligarchies supported by Sparta

Sparta's new war with Persia ended after the defeat of its navy in 394 at the Battle of Cnidus in Ionia, ending its brief period of naval supremacy but leaving it the dominant power in Greece. After the "King's Peace" of

---

[51] Ruzé 2018:324.

[52] Plutarch, *Lycurgus* 30.1.

[53] Christien 2002:181. The details are related in Plutarch, *Lysander* 19.4. Hodkinson 2000:427 states that "Thorax's acquisition of the silver probably took place either from the spoils of Aigospotamoi or during his time at Samos among the fanatical pro-Spartan oligarchs." According to Jones 1967:39, "part of the Spartiate's mess contribution was in Aeginetan Obols."

[54] Ruzé 2018:322.

386 ended its war with Corinth (395-387), Sparta installed loyal oligarchic regimes throughout the Peloponnese. In Arcadia, a center of democratic politics, "[t]he city of Mantineia was razed and its inhabitants
dispersed into villages by the Spartans after a war in 385. Initially, says
Xenophon, there was resentment; 'but since the landowners ... had an
aristocratic government and were rid of the troublesome demagogues
[*i.e.*, advocates of democratic economic reforms], they became pleased at
what they [the Spartans] had done.'"[55]

However, Argive rebels drove out the local oligarchies that Sparta had
put in place, confiscating their property and condemning over 1,200
men to death. Tegea asked the Arcadians to form a confederacy, which
appointed a popular council of 10,000 men. Many of the wealthiest
Arcadians (Diodorus says 1,400) fled to Sparta and neighboring Pallan-
tium, but were captured and killed. Sparta's king Agesilaus retaliated by
invading Tegean territory.

That drew Thebes into the fighting. Sparta had defeated it in 382
and put local oligarchs in power. Democratic Theban leaders took
refuge in Athens, but returned in 379 to drive out the Spartan garrison
and helped found the Second Athenian League in 378. Ultimately,
the Theban general and statesman Epaminondas decisively defeated
Sparta's army in 371 at the Battle of Leuctra in Boeotia. Of Sparta's
force of seven hundred hoplites, four hundred were killed (Xenophon,
Hellenica 6.4.15).[56]

That was the final blow to Spartan hegemony over Greece. Sparta
lost its dominance, polarizing and shrinking as rapidly as it earlier had
risen. In 370, Epaminondas led the Theban army against Sparta itself,
looting Laconia and attracting many helot and *perioikoi* defectors. Sparta
lost Messenia in 370/69, and most of its Peloponnesian League allies
defected by 366. It offered helots their liberty and attracted a reported
six thousand military volunteers, but the Thebans helped many of the
remaining helots to break away. No longer supported by an enserfed
class, most Spartan citizens had to farm their own land, cook and make
their own clothes.

Hodkinson estimates that Sparta's military losses deprived it of two-
thirds of its land, "some 90,000 ha ... leaving the Spartiates with less

---

[55] Snodgrass 1980:47, citing Xenophon, *Hellenica* 5.2.7.

[56] Oliva 1971:195 and Diodorus 15.57-58; see also 15.56.4: "More than four
thousand Lacedaemonians fell in the battle, but only about three hundred Boeotians. After the battle they made a truce to allow for taking up the bodies of the
dead and the departure of the Lacedaemonians to the Peloponnese."

than 50,000 ha in Lakonia. ... Any ordinary citizen household which had a sizeable portion of its holdings in Messenia would have suffered a loss of sufficient magnitude to threaten its capacity to meet its mess dues."[57] Citizens began to fall into the ranks of "Inferiors."

After the winter of 370, democrats in Tegea killed or exiled the pro-Spartan oligarchs and led Arcadian cities to meet with other Greeks at Delphi. "The Thebans were much less anxious than the Arcadians to promote democracy," summarizes one recent historian of this period. Oligarchs took control in the Achaean cities and allied with Sparta. But by the end of the 360s the Tegean and Mantinean democrats formed "an Arcadian confederacy that was broadly democratic and anti-Spartan in sentiment. ... The Tegean-Megalopolitan bloc had the support of Messenia, Sikyon, Argos, and above all Boeotia and its allies from central Greece."[58]

With a much diminished helot population to exploit, Sparta suffered widening inequality. This apparently (according to van Wees) was stemmed by a land reform around 370/69 creating indivisible "ancient shares" producing a fixed tribute, probably less than half the crop so as to ease the burden on the few remaining helot cultivators in the hope of deterring them from deserting the land.[59]

No records survive to quantify the magnitude of debt, but it is clear that the influx of tribute and booty led to a "relentless pursuit of additional landholdings" during the 4th century, which became so severe by the 3rd-century BC that Sparta experienced a new wave of revolutions recalling those of the 7th-century (as Chapter 8 will describe).[60]

Summary

By imposing helotage on the Messenians it conquered, Sparta managed to avoid the revolutions and reforms that led to democratic politics of one form or another in other parts of Greece in the 7th and 6th centuries. Yet despite having promoted a citizen-infantry of *homoioi* holding standardized *kleroi* plots on Messenian land and long avoided agrarian usury, Sparta became Greece's most unequal and oligarchic economy.

Looking over the course of Greece from the 7th century BC through Sparta's loss of independence to Rome in 195 BC and Athens' similar

---

[57] Hodkinson 2000:437.

[58] Roy 2018:367-369, citing Xenophon, *Hellenica* 6.5.6-10.

[59] Van Wees 2018a:207-208.

[60] Hodkinson 2000:432-433, citing Aristotle, *Politics* 5 at 1307a19-20 and 34-36.

loss in 146, no city-state was able to avoid a social explosion leading to cancellation of debts or redistribution of land. Athens managed a halfway solution when Solon cancelled debts and banned outright enslavement of debtors, but refrained from redistributing land. Attempts at integrated debt and land reform still lay ahead for Sparta under Agis IV, Cleomenes III and Nabis in the late 3rd century BC. Agis was killed, Cleomenes was exiled, and Nabis was defeated when the Achaean League's oligarchies called on Rome to put down the Spartan kings' program of debt cancellation and land redistribution.

4
Solon Bans Debt Slavery in Athens, 594 BC

A thens remained one of the most aristocratic cities in Greece down through the 7th century BC, resisting the reforms that were being enacted in Corinth, Sicyon, Megara and Sparta. A coup was attempted in 632/1 by Cylon, an Olympic victor in 640, but no historian has found records of any economic program or reforms that he may have proposed. He had married the daughter of neighboring Megara's tyrant Theagenes and, backed by troops supplied by Megara, his main concern seemed to be to secure its control over the island and port of Salamis located between Megara and Athens.

Enough of the Athenian *demos* came in from the countryside to force Cylon's troops to take refuge in the Temple of Athena on the Acropolis.[1] After Cylon escaped, his followers were promised safe conduct by Megacles, an archon from the wealthy Alcmaeonid family. But they were treacherously murdered, causing the family's leading members to be exiled for having committed a sacred "stain" or "pollution" (*miasma*, the Curse of Cylon).

A decade later, ca. 622/1, rising discontent led Athenian leaders to protect their interests by choosing Dracon as lawgiver. Only his "draconian" law for manslaughter has survived, but other laws were said to include harsh rules toward debtors and exile for offenders.[2] These laws were the opposite of those introduced by reformer-tyrants in other Greek cities to resolve the period's debt and land crisis.

Diodorus (1.79.5) pointed to the contradiction in early Athenian laws that allowed debtors to be seized and reduced to bondage, yet prohibited creditors from taking their military equipment, plows and other

---

[1] Thucydides 1.126 and Oliva 1981:133.

[2] *Athēnaiōn Politeia* ("Constitution of Athens") 7.1. Apparently written by a student of Aristotle and probably published between 350 and 325, this remains the major source for the works and laws of Dracon, Solon and other Athenian leaders. Henceforth it is abbreviated as *Ath. Pol.* The city's local histories (*Atthides*) and literary sources are in the character of pamphleteering, projecting the political struggles of later times – mainly from the oligarchic perspective – back onto early Greek history.

tools of trade pledged as security for loans.[3] How could debtors continue performing the basic agricultural and military functions expected of citizens if they owed their labor services to their creditors?

Little epigraphic or other documentation survives to explain how these early debts came into being, or what (if any) interest they bore. Neither Naphtali Lewis (1941), Kurt von Fritz (1943), J. V. A. Fine (1951) nor Finley (1952 and elsewhere) have ventured to guess whether the debts owed by *hektemoroi* ("sixth-parters") bore interest. Most payments were still being made in kind in Greece's pre-monetary economy well into the 6th century. The debt burden would have been oppressive even without interest charges, just as the pound of flesh in Shakespeare's *Merchant of Venice* was pledged on an interest-free loan.

Thomas Figueira emphasizes that client/patron obligations were the context for early Greek debt and rental arrangements: "Loans were usually in foodstuffs or in seed grain, provisions for life itself. Borrowing was seldom a one-time affair, as marginal farms were repeatedly in need. In this atmosphere, loans were not quantified (in this regard, the absence of coinage is significant) and tended to become open-ended. Thus, a form of bondage was created with the obligations of the debtors being political, religious, and/or fiscal."[4] As a result: "To be a debtor was not a contractual situation but entailed a castelike status. To lend or borrow was a hereditary role." In a similar vein, Moses Finley describes the typical marginal cultivator as "poor and essentially defenseless against bad harvests and famine, against war and its depredations, against the one-sidedness of the law. When his luck was bad his only defense was to put himself *in fidem*, in the power of the powerful."[5]

Historians have proposed a variety of scenarios to describe how early Athenian land tenure led to indebtedness. The main question is whether the rural *hektemoroi* ("sixth-parters") who were central to Solon's reform were renters, sharecroppers, or quasi-serfs whose status could be reduced to that of outright slaves. Did they have to pay one-sixth, or keep only one-sixth for themselves? Most agree on the former, given the stony character of Athenian soil, but Hans van Wees believes they were able to "keep only an economically barely viable sixth."[6]

---

[3] Fisher 1992:72.

[4] Figueira 1985:147-148.

[5] Finley 1981:161.

[6] Van Wees 2006:379.

What is clear is that this quasi-serflike loss of personal liberty was viewed as a debt relationship, or at least as having originated in some kind of archaic debt. That arrangement was what Solon did away with.

Solon's appointment as archon in 594

The Athenian economy was impoverishing most citizens while concentrating land ownership and political control at the top. "An elite of 10-20% of the population controlled sufficient land and labour not to have to work, while the remaining 80-90% of the population [did] not have enough land to survive without additional income."[7] The poor faced slavery if they did not flee, and the aristocracy feared that civil war might lead to their expropriation and exile, as had occurred in Corinth. It was normal practice in such situations for cities to appoint a single person over their affairs, a referee to act as archon to prevent a populist "tyrant" from mobilizing followers to gain power.[8] Solon was elected as a moderate, having neither "joined in the exactions of the rich" nor involved himself as a champion of the poor. In contrast to Cylon's backing of Megara's control of Salamis, Solon had gained renown for his poems advocating Athenian military action to secure the naval base for its trade in olive oil and pottery. Alleviating economic resentment was a precondition for recruiting the armed force needed to secure Salamis.

Solon came from an aristocratic family but was not particularly wealthy. His father is said by Plutarch to have risen by trade, but ruined his estate by extending kindness to others. His mother was a cousin of Peisistratus's mother, probably from the Hills, the poorer section of Athens and the one most favoring reform. Plato's mother also was said to be a relative, and Solon's brother was an ancestor of Critias, one of the oligarchy's Thirty Tyrants installed by Sparta after the Peloponnesian War.[9]

---

[7] Van Wees 2006:396 and 366. This 80/20 principle is known as the [Vilfredo] Pareto Distribution, formulated in 1909 stipulating a historically constant proportion of 20 percent of the population possessing 80 percent of the wealth. A mathematical corollary was that 10 percent would have 65 percent of the wealth, and 5 percent would have half the national wealth.

[8] Kelcy Sagstetter's dissertation *Solon of Athens* (2013) provides a bibliographic review. She cites (p. 19) Aristotle (*Politics* 5 at 1301b18-20, 25-28; 3 at 1285a31-34; cf. 3 at 1285b25-26) regarding "a class of tyrants called *aisymnetes* who were elected to powerful office, including Phalaris of Agrigentum and the Ionian tyrants." They "often arose because of social *stasis*. ... For the elective tyranny of Pittacus see Aristotle, *Politics* 1.1285b25-26)." See also Moore 1975:215.

[9] Plato, *Timaeus* 20e and Diogenes Laertius 3.1 (*Life of Plato*).

Solon's critique of oligarchic hubris

Like reformers in other Greek cities, Solon's poetry criticizing the hubris of the wealthy helped establish his reputation as a sage. In Fragment 4 of his major poem, he wrote that the wealthy "do not understand how to hold back their satiety," despite there being plenty to go around.[10] Hubristic individuals "appropriate, unjustly, the property of others." As Josiah Ober translates Fragment 4 in modern prose:

> It is the citizens themselves who, by their act of foolishness and subservience to money, are willing to destroy a great city, ... the people's leaders ... are certain to suffer much pain as a result of their great arrogance. For they do not know how to restrain excess or to conduct in an orderly and peaceful manner the festivities of the banquet that are at hand ... they grow wealthy, yielding to unjust deeds ... sparing neither sacred nor private property, they steal with rapaciousness ... and they have no regard for the august foundations of Justice, who bears silent witness to the present and the past and who in time assuredly comes to exact retribution.[11]

Sara Forsdyke points to the parallel between Theognis of Megara's statement that "personal wealth brings with it public harm" and Solon's rebuke of those who destroy the city "on account of their desire for wealth" (Fragment 4.5-6), and who "grow wealthy through unjust acts" (Fragment 4.11). The problem, Solon wrote (Fragment 13.71-73), is that wealth is addictive: "There is no apparent limit of wealth laid down for men. Those of us who possess the most seek to double it."[12] The result is that "excess breeds insolence, when great prosperity comes to men who are not sound of mind" (Fragment 6).

Such views were part of a centuries-long Greek critique of wealth addiction and hubris. Solon's reference to wealthy individuals "not sound of mind" became the takeoff point for Socrates' argument about whether it was just to repay socially destructive creditors (*Republic*, Book 1, discussed below in Chapter 7).

Whom did Solon liberate?

Solon wrote that he removed the *horoi*. The word meant "'limit,' 'boundary,' 'definition,'" typically translated as boundary stones. *Horoi*

---

[10] Sagstetter 2013:109. All that survives of Solon's poetry is what was quoted in the works of others.

[11] Ober 2006:458. For another translation see Fisher 1992:69.

[12] Cited in Forsdyke 2006:337.

were "slabs of marble, limestone, volcanic rock, or other available stone driven into the ground at the appropriate spots. They were used for private estates, city limits, state boundaries, temple and cult properties, and graves. The visible half might be entirely blank. But most often it was engraved either with the single word *horos* or with an additional word or phrase naming the god of a temple or giving some equally distinctive bit of information."[13]

On the basis of Solon's poetry accusing the wealthy of not sparing sacred or public land, van Wees suspects that these stones demarcated land grabbed by force, foreclosure and/or legal stealth from the public domain as well as from private holders.[14] By the 4th century BC they indeed came to signify the debts owed by cultivators, making them what Finley termed "hypothecation-stones." But recent scholarship shows that the *horoi* of Solon's time were not "mortgage stones," because *hektemoroi* debtors appear to have been statutory tenants who held sharecropping rights as long as they paid their (probably) one-sixth of the crop.[15] They were a kind of sharecropper, not landholders who had forfeited their property for debt. In contrast to the 4th-century *stelai*, it therefore is unlikely that Solon's *horoi* recorded mortgage debts.[16] Rather, well-to-do landowners established patronage relationships in which debts built up. Cultivation was extended by clients providing labor services on the patron's land, ultimately leading to a state of dependency or outright bondage, losing to their patrons whatever land tenure they may have had.

Most early debts were secured by the cultivator's labor, not the land. "Debt was a deliberate device on the part of the creditor, to obtain more dependent labor," concludes Finley. Labor was the resource in

---

[13] Finley 1951:4-5. No *horoi* have survived from Solon's period, only from later times.

[14] Van Wees 2006:380, suggesting that Solon's removal of the boundary stones may have ended the *illegal* seizure of public or communal lands. Blok and Krul 2017:615 agree.

[15] Finley 1983:268. Plutarch's discussion (*Solon* 3.2), written seven centuries later, distinguishes between the status of *hektemoroi* and that of Athenian debtors in general, relying on *Ath. Pol.* 2.2. Bintliff 2006:328 agrees that a class of sharecroppers, *kakoi*, worked their own holdings as well as those of the *agathoi*, the "good men," the top 3 classes in Athenian society, as discussed below. The *kakoi* were the fourth and lowest class, a tied labor force probably making up half or more of the Athenian population. Solon would have removed the *horoi* only for the holdings of these poor, but in that case, "the *kakoi* were perhaps still duty bound to work the fields of the *agathoi*."

[16] Ober 2006:454.

shortest supply.[17] Debtors had to keep working and pay the crop yield to their creditors until the debt was paid off. This is known as antichretic interest, which had a long pedigree in Sumer and Babylonia.[18]

After decades of studying the Athenian *hektemoroi*, Finley threw up his hands and acknowledged that they "constituted a distinct status whose roots are lost in the Dark Age of Greek history, men who worked land on terms of a fixed rent of one sixth of the crop, presumably not free to leave it, but not caught up in what we normally refer to when we speak of a debtor-creditor relationship."[19] They were not slaves but "dependent or involuntary labor," or simply "tenants in arrears."[20] The vicissitudes of weather and the harvest caused them to be chronically in arrears.

The main protests occurred when *hektemoroi* fell behind on their crop obligation, or borrowed food, seed or other supplies and were unable to pay their debts, and fell into bondage. Prior to Solon's reforms their creditor-patrons could sell them to foreign slave dealers as outright chattel slaves. What made matters urgent, according to Solon's poetry, was the fear of debtors being sold outside of their community, away from their families and acquaintances. That "was an affront to traditional sentiment and violated the principle of solidarity of the citizen group."[21] They felt their precarious clientage position was unfair and unnatural, no better than war slaves. They wanted their land free of debt, but Athens had no conquered territory to distribute to them, and its oligarchy fought against parting with any of its own land.

As long as debtors remained attached to their own familiar land, they may have hoped their position was merely temporary, or at least only

---

[17] Harris 2002:427 points out that land was not in short supply at that time: "The archaeological evidence does not support the view that overpopulation in Attica in particular or Greece in general led to extensification of land as Andrewes, French, Gallant and others have argued. ... there was no expansion into less productive areas of Attica during the seventh or sixth centuries; this process occurred in the fifth and fourth centuries."

[18] See for instance Steinkeller 2002:124.

[19] Finley 1983:156.

[20] Finley 1973:69-70.

[21] French 1964:16. Finley 1973:67 emphasizes that the struggle by the *hektemoroi* and indeed, cultivators in other cities, "was never looked upon, either by themselves or by our ancient authorities on the subject, as a slave revolt. They were citizens reclaiming their rightful place in their own community, having been reduced to a form of servitude that they felt had wrongly become chronic rather than merely temporary and escapable under normal conditions."

nominal in view of the limited ability of their creditors to further exploit them. But customary social constraints were weakening, and marginal cultivators were in danger of losing their rights as citizens. That is what led Solon to ban enslavement for debt arrears (or by illegal force) to work land that the wealthy had unjustly appropriated and enclosed:

> Many fixed landmarks I removed, and made those free that were once a slave. Many brought I back to their God-built birthplace, many that had been sold, some justly, some unjustly, and others that had been exiled through urgent penury, men that no longer spake the Attic speech because they had wandered so far and wide; and those that suffered shameful servitude at home, trembling before the whims of their owners, these made I free men.

It is not clear how in practice Solon might have redeemed debtors who had been sold abroad.[22] What is most important to recognize is that he enforced legal recognition of the fact that the status of bondservants was much better than that of outright slaves. Between outright slavery and liberty was the intermediate category of bondage for nominally free debtors who retained their legal rights as citizens, *e.g.*, not to be treated as slaves by being sold or mistreated by their creditors. Athenian debtors retained their rights as citizens and membership in their tribal units.

According to Blok and Krul, the problem was that "the Athenian elite raided the Attic countryside, fetching booty and individuals whom they then sold abroad." This enslavement of Athenians was illegal, and a major cause of the *dysnomia* cited by Solon in Fragment 4.[23] Masters

> could beat them [their slaves], chain them up, starve them (Xenophon *Memorabilia.* 2.1.16), employ them as prostitutes ([Demosthenes] 59.18-23), or even castrate them (Herodotus 8.105). All money earned by slaves belonged to the master ([Demosthenes] 53.20), and likewise all contracts made by the

---

[22] In the Bronze Age Near East, Hammurabi's laws required temples to redeem debtors sold abroad. Babylonian merchants were to purchase their freedom, presumably to be reimbursed. Sagstetter thinks that Solon's claim is a fourth-century interpolation from *Ath. Pol.* 2.2. Oliva 1971:44, citing Aristotle, *Politics* 2 at 1269a-36-37, points out that throughout much of Greece, debtors could be sold as slaves without hope of redemption. "It is said of the *penestai* that they allowed the Thessalians to enslave them under certain conditions," but "they were not 'to be taken away from their country, nor killed.' In return they bound themselves to work the land and hand over a certain amount of their produce. Some were even said to be richer than their masters." The word *penestai* derives from (*pénēs*), "poor," as in English "penury."

[23] Blok and Krul 2017:616-617

slave were the responsibility of his master (Hyp. *Ath. passim*). If the master fell into debt, he could offer to hand over his slave to the creditor as compensation ([Demosthenes] 53.20-1), or if the master had his property confiscated by the polis, the *poletai* would seize his slaves and sell them.[24]

Solon's *seisachtheia* ("shedding of burdens") is the best attested debt cancellation among early Greek cities. He banned outright debt slavery for Athenian citizens, although not the obligation of debtors to work off their debts as free men owing labor service. As Edward Harris has emphasized, "debt-bondage is not a permanent status: the debt-bondsman remains under the control of the creditor only until his debt is paid off. The creditor does not have all the rights exercised by an owner, just the right to his services for a certain period of time," a practice that continued "long after Solon's legislation. ... The law granted creditors the right to seize borrowers who failed to repay their loans and to hold them until they were able to work off their debts. Yet at the same time, the law protected the freedom of debtors by denying creditors the ability to sell them into slavery as a way of recovering their loans."[25]

The ensuing century's prosperity enabled Athenians typically to earn enough to stay out of debt. But debt bondage is found elsewhere (as in Bithynia, where it was imposed by Roman publican tax collectors and others; see Chapter 14 below).

Solon's political reforms

Solon fulfilled the aristocracy's hope to avoid the land redistribution that had occurred in Corinth, Sicyon and other cities. This left many of the poor disappointed according to the most detailed treatment of his reforms, the *Athēnaiōn Politeia* (11.2), written by one of Aristotle's students. Subsequent oligarchic writers celebrated Solon as a model precisely because of his moderation in *refraining* from redistributing the Athenian elite's landholdings. Solon was unsympathetic to those who resented him for not redistributing the land: "They that came for plunder had rich hopes, reckoning every man that he would find himself great prosperity ... Vain were their imaginings then, and now they are angered with me and all eye me askance as if I were an enemy."[26]

---

[24] Harris 2002:415-416. The *pōlētaí* (sellers) were officials responsible for selling public contracts (including for tax collection) and confiscated property.

[25] Harris 2002:417, 425-426 and 429-430. For an example, see p. 421 citing Menander's play *Heroes*.

[26] Fragment 36, quoted in *Ath. Pol.*

Yet popular disappointment over him leaving the wealthy with their land intact was so strong that he left Athens for ten years, visiting Egypt, the court of Croesus in Lydia and other realms. That left a political hiatus in Athens, where policy disagreements among the elite prevented any archon from being elected for two years after 593.[27]

Aristotle considered three measures to be Solon's most important steps toward democracy. First was his *seisachtheia* (banning of debt slavery and cancellation of debts). Second came popular access to the law courts. Establishing the right of all classes to appeal to jury courts for redress solved the problem of aristocratic judges acting arbitrarily.[28] The third reform was to expand membership in the Areopagus Council, which set the agenda for discussion by the popular assembly (*Ekklēsia*).[29] The old board of *exegetai* was drawn from the ranks of the *Eupatridai* "well-born."[30] Solon left the Council's authority in the hands of the largest landholders, but it seems to have played a diminishing role until finally being phased out by the 5th-century reforms of Ephialtes discussed in the next chapter.

Solon defined the qualification for public office in terms of four classes, ranked by their agricultural production and hence landholding. He grouped the top three classes together as the "good men" (*agathoi*): the "five hundred bushel men" (*pentakosiomedimnoi*), "horsemen" (*hippeis* equipped for the cavalry) with more than 300 bushels, and "yoke men" (*zeugitai*) with a team of oxen "yoked" to harvest their fields, producing more than 200 bushels. Van Wees estimates that these three classes comprised the richest 15 to 20 percent of citizens. Only they were eligible for public office and membership of the Areopagus.[31]

Solon's fourth class comprised the *thētes*, composed of laborers, sharecroppers and those dependent on loans. These poor (*kakoi*, literally "bad men") were not eligible for public office, and were admitted only

---

[27] *Ath. Pol.* 13, cited in Wallace 2007:72-74.

[28] *Ath. Pol.* 9-10, discussed by Sagstetter 2013:80.

[29] *Ath. Pol.* 8.4 and Plutarch, *Solon* 19.1. Plutarch claimed that the poor wanted Solon to make "all men equal and alike in their livelihoods," but this ideal only developed later.

[30] The Areopagus Council is said to have backed Peisistratus and his populist reforms: Wallace 2007:64, citing Diogenes Laertius 1.49-54.

[31] Van Wees 2006:367-368, citing *Ath. Pol.* 26.2 and 47.1. He estimates that Cleisthenes' Council of Five Hundred (*Boulē*) was also drawn from the richest 15 to 20 percent of the population, in keeping with Pareto's Distribution cited above (fn7) as characterizing most economies from ancient to modern history.

to the popular assembly and law courts. This meant that about 80 to 85 percent of adult men "were still formally excluded from all office."[32] It took until 457 for *zeugitai* hoplites to become eligible for the archonship, and *thētes* never qualified. So Solon was far from creating a modern political democracy or seriously checking oligarchic power. As Raaflaub notes, what modern jargon calls a "meritocracy" remained oligarchic: "The traditional aristocracies had such an enormous advantage in education, training, experience, organization, and social and political connections that, despite economic changes and political reforms, even in democratic Athens the members of wealthy but not old aristocratic families only reached positions of higher influence many generations after Solon had formally replaced birth by wealth as the criterion for holding high office."[33]

The English historian William Cunningham recognized a century ago that Solon's reforms were more "a prelude to a period of intense social discord" than a resolution. Solon "did not succeed in saving the peasantry, for the class he tried to protect were driven from their holdings, not as slaves, but as bankrupt freemen" to swell the crowd of Athenian wage-earners much like what England's 16th-century smallholders and villains experienced when they were driven off the land into a life of urban poverty. "The genuinely free peasant had no protection against a run of bad harvests, against compulsory army service, against the endless depredations in civil and foreign wars."[34]

Replacing aristocratic religion by public festivals and drama

Solon reflected the anti-luxury ethic typical of nearly all Greek cities in his period by passing laws "against excessive expense on funerals. These were the main occasions for aristocrats" to glorify their family status with "ostentatious and divisive demonstrations." As an alternative to such rites, Solon introduced "an annual state festival in honor of the dead, the Genesia. ... Religion, along with much else, was now being pressed into the service of the community as a whole, that is, of the state rather than of any one faction, class, family or individual."[35]

---

[32] Van Wees 2006:351-352 and 376. See also Wallace 2007:61.

[33] Raaflaub 2005:20.

[34] Cunningham 1911 I:102. See also French 1964:25, and Finley 1963b:251, 255 and 263.

[35] Snodgrass 1980:118-119 and 115-116. Sparta and other cities also passed anti-luxury laws.

Democratizing religion was a key to democratizing laws. Solon's festival calendar helped create "a religion of the State" not controlled by the nobility's leading clans, and not one that they could use to impede reforms "by raising religious difficulties," explains Felix Jacoby. Creating a civic religion required weakening "the position of the aristocracy in matters of cult. ... It was a religious change of the first order when *e.g.*, according to the new constitution, the first three archons, who all had religious duties, were chosen from the new class of the *pentakosio-medimnoi*, not from that class which until then had alone carried out the intercourse with the gods."[36]

Throughout Greece during the 7th and 6th centuries, tyrants had been taking control of the major Pan-Hellenic festivals out of the hands of local aristocracies. At Olympia, Pheidon created a public organization to replace control by the Argive elite. Cleisthenes of Sicyon did the same at Delphi. In Athens, Peisistratus would expand the Great Panathenaia, the four-yearly festival of Athena, and also would move the Dionysus festival to Athens, away from the Eleutherai under control of the Boeotian confederation. Snodgrass cites the common use by Greek tyrants "of propaganda through religion and myth," including "the institution and enlargement of state cults and festivals, to the detriment of the exclusive, family-based cults which widely prevailed."[37] Subsequent Athenian leaders would further secularize and democratize control of religion.

Religious festivals and drama dealt openly with the hubris of the rich and their wealth addiction, frequently treating the elite with derision. Public comedy evolved out of the Dionysus festival and "the ribald songs sung by tipsy revelers in the procession (*komos*)." According to classical tradition, it was under Peisistratus that Thespis "added a story told by a narrator to the framework of choruses, thus laying the foundations of the dialogue between the actor and the leader of the chorus."[38] The first tragedy is said to have been performed at the Great Dionysia ca. 536-532.

These festivals, an Athenian innovation that later flourished under Aristophanes and others (see Chapter 5), involved a large public expenditure, absorbing "probably a fifth of the total internal revenue" to provide food and drink for their sacrifices and feasts, and also funding

---

[36] Jacoby 1949:58, adding: "Among the people as distinct from the nobles, there existed [in archaic times] no association of clans; each individual family stood by itself with its many religious duties."

[37] Snodgrass 1980:115-116.

[38] Oliva 1981:177.

to build temples.[39] Thucydides (6.54.5) reports that Peisistratus imposed a 5 percent income tax to finance this expenditure. The tax would have been paid mainly in crops, inasmuch as the earliest Greek coinage dates to just before 560 and was not widely adopted until later in the century.

The Peisistratids (561-510)

Idealizing Solon for not threatening oligarchic control, Greek elites applied the label of "tyrant" broadly to populist and democratic reform-ers. Challenging oligarchic rule was deemed to be a tyrannical abuse of liberty, a euphemism for the freedom of creditors and aristocrats to do as they pleased.

Solon criticized the *demos* for wanting a strong ruler, but that was the only way to break the oligarchy's power, given their large landholdings and monetary wealth that enabled them to control the political system. The *demos*, especially cultivators furthest from Athens (and hence the poorest), supported Peisistratus in the hope that he would have the power that earlier Greek reformer-tyrants had in other parts of Greece.

The past few decades have reversed the stereotype of Peisistratus that biased classical history for over two thousand years. Under his rule, 561-527 (with two interruptions) and that of his son Hippias (527-510), Athens became more commercial and prosperous. "In Athens his tyranny came to be praised as a golden 'age of Kronos,'" states Wallace.[40] Hatzfeld describes him as "the real founder of Athenian greatness."[41]

A recent survey has noted that Peisistratus was like 7th-century tyrants in that "[a]lmost all activities listed by Herodotus in Peisistratus's rise to power can be regarded as those of a private aristocrat who is busy accumulating power, prestige and influence."[42] He hoped to found a

---

[39] Andreades 1933:231, cited by Snodgrass 1980:117. Although Peisistratus was said to have spurred building programs in Athens, little archaeological trace has survived. Subsequent oligarchies may have dismantled traces of his memory, much as Roman patricians destroyed the houses of reformers they assassinated. Boersma 2000 doubts that he had a consistent building policy.

[40] Wallace 2007:75-76, citing *Ath. Pol.* 16.2-3 and 16.7, and Aristotle, *Politics* 5 at 1305a.

[41] Hatzfeld 1966:75-76.

[42] Sancisi-Weerdenburg 2000:10. As noted in Chapter 2, Peisistratus was de-nounced as a tyrant for saving debtors by lending them his own money to protect them from insolvency, and defending himself with bodyguards instead of letting himself become a victim of political assassination.

hereditary dynasty, and directly appointed archons rather than leaving them to be chosen by lot. But details about the commercial flowering of Athens during his rule are sketchy beyond two of his institutions supporting the peasantry: "first, a kind of agricultural credit-bank to lend small landowners the funds necessary to improve their equipment or augment their holdings; secondly, the institution of circulating tribunals to save the peasant those journeys to town which, whatever his country, make the course of justice unpalatable to him."[43]

Cleisthenes transforms civic organization in 508 BC

The rule of Peisistratus, Hippias and their successor Cleisthenes shows the extent to which Athenian politics was still a struggle among the most powerful families. Ambitious leaders "brought the demos into their camp," as Aristotle put it, by promising the citizenry enough benefits to gain their support.

Foreign support played an important role. Solon's reforms in 594 had included an amnesty for exiles, allowing the Alcmaeonids to return after their murder of Cylon's followers in 631. But many members remained in exile, and others left when Peisistratus gained power. In exile the family retained its great wealth, while making allies across the Aegean in Asia Minor and Persia.

Alcmaeon, son of Megacles (the grandfather of Cleisthenes) who was himself personally exiled under the "Curse of Cylon," moved to the Lydian court, and found an opportunity to promote his family's return to Athens by winning the bid to rebuild Delphi's temple, which had burned down in 548. Herodotus (5.62) describes Alcmaeon as doing much more impressive construction than the contract required, and as using his family's money to induce the priestess to urge Spartans visiting the oracle that it was their duty to liberate Athens from the Peisistratids.

Incited by the Alcmaeonid family, led at the time by Cleisthenes (born ca. 570, and in his sixties when he took control, apparently after serving as archon in 525/4), Sparta's king Cleomenes I (ruled 519-490) sent an army to drive out Hippias in 510. But upon reaching Athens its leaders learned that the Alcmaeonids had bribed the oracle. They invited Hippias and his followers to return to the city, telling them (according to Herodotus): "We acknowledge to you, our comrades in arms, that we

---

[43] Hatzfeld 1966:75. Sancisi-Weerdenburg 2000 cites the main sources for the period of Peisistratid rule: Herodotus 1.59-64; 5.55-57, 62-65; 6.39, 103; Thucydides 1.20; 6.54-60; *Ath. Pol.* 13-18; and Plutarch, *Solon* 29-30.

made a mistake. On the strength of certain oracles, which have proved to be a swindle, we expelled from their country men who were our friends [*i.e.*, the Peisistratids], men who undertook to keep Athens dependent upon us; these gone, we put power into the hands of an ungrateful rabble ... which turned against us and flung us out, ourselves and our king, with every mark of insult."[44]

Cleomenes I forced Cleisthenes into exile, and then attempted to dissolve the Council (*Boulē*) and transfer its power to Isagoras and his three hundred followers, backed by installing a military force on the Acropolis. But the *Boulē*, supported by the Athenian people, revolted and besieged the Acropolis, driving the pro-Spartan faction from the city (Herodotus 5.72). Cleisthenes was invited to return from exile and take the leadership of Athens.

He then instituted his fundamental democratic reforms of the Athenian constitution. To weaken the political control of the four hereditary aristocratic tribes, Cleisthenes organized Athens into ten new, geographically scattered tribes (*phylai*) drawn from 139 local subdivisions called demes (*demos* singular, *demoi* plural — whence the word democracy). Each of the new tribes contained a similar mixture of wealthy urban demes, commercial coastal demes and the poorer inland demes.[45] Cleisthenes also reformed the Council (*Boulē*), expanding it to 500 male citizens (fifty from each of the ten new tribes) and gave it the power to set the agenda for the Athenian popular assembly (*Ekklēsia*).

Opposing Cleisthenes' reforms and hoping to restore Isagoras, Sparta's oligarchy sent a new army in 506, allied with Boeotia to the

---

[44] Herodotus 5.91. See also 5.66 and 6.124, and the commentary by Forrest 1966:191, 204, 146 and 158. Hippias did not take up the Spartan invitation to return to Athens, and was said to have taken refuge in the Achaemenid Empire, where he was welcomed and received land grants along with other Athenians.

[45] As Herodotus 5.69 noted: "Cleisthenes added the demos to his following, though he had totally spurned it before." Cleisthenes' mother Agarista was the daughter of his namesake, Kleisthenes of Sicyon, who had renamed the tribes into which Sicyon was divided. Herodotus 5.67 states that he called his own tribe *archelaoi* ("Leaders of the People"), giving the older tribes derogatory names. This kind of restructuring no doubt helped inspire Cleisthenes' redivision of the Athenian population into geographically based "tribal" divisions instead of hereditary clan membership. In that respect his reform was the capstone of the dynamic sponsored by earlier reformer-tyrants. *Ath. Pol.* says that men of the plain wanted an oligarchy, and men of the coast wanted the middle constitution. The plain surrounding Athens probably contained the largest number of wealthy families, and Peisistratus's hilly region east of Attica contained the smallest number.

north and Chalcis on the island of Euboea to the northeast. Athens' army defeated Sparta and its two allies. The Boeotians then backed Aegina in launching an unsuccessful naval war against Athens, and Sparta intervened again in 504, this time seeking to restore Hippias, "whom they themselves had expelled in 510 and who was now living under Persian protection."[46] The attempt failed.

Cleisthenes disappears from history after Athenians rejected his policy of seeking Persian support against Sparta. But his reforms paved the way for what became Athenian democracy in the generation of Ephialtes and Pericles in the 5th century.

---

[46] Snodgrass 1980:198. See Herodotus 5.75.

5
From Democracy to the Thirty Tyrants, 508-404 BC

The word *dēmokratia*, literally "people rule" (*demos* + *kratos*), seems to be first documented ca. 462 BC.[1] Herodotus associated the word with rule of the *demos*, *plethos* ("mass") or *homilos* ("crowd"), and with *isonomia* (equality under the law, *nomos*). Athenian babies began to be named Democrates around this time, but no children were given names with the root of oligarchy, *olig-* ("few").[2]

Following Cleisthenes' reforms in 508 BC, the 500 members of the Council (*Boulē*) were selected by lot from male citizens who were at least 30 years old and belonged to one of the three wealthiest property classes (the *pentakosiomedimnoi*, *hippeis* and *zeugitai*).[3] The *thētes* were not eligible, but the popular assembly (*Ekklēsia*) continued to be open to all Athenian citizens, regardless of class, as it had been since the reforms of Solon. It continued to have the power to declare war, to elect generals (*strategoi*), and to nominate and elect magistrates (*árchontes*).

The aim was to prevent a narrow wealthy class from controlling government. By contrast, Rome's constitution weighted voting power heavily by one's property class, while senators appointed generals and other officials and controlled the courts, excluding the general population from juries.

Athenian citizens were paid for serving in all public offices and as jurors – and by the 4th century even for attending the theater. Offi-

---

[1] Forrest 2000:280.

[2] Rhodes 2000:124-125.

[3] Archons also were chosen randomly by lot, as were jurors from 487/6 onward: Moore 1975:177 and 207. *Boulē* members could not serve consecutively, but they could be selected by lot more than once. The main exception to selection by lot was where military expertise was concerned, recognizing that this was specialized. Military commanders were elected. See Moore 1975:45 and 201, citing *Ath. Pol.* 41: "There are ten *strategoi*, who once were elected one from each tribe, but are now elected from the whole people. ... Also elected are ten regimental commanders, one for each tribe." The Areopagus also seems to have been an exception to selection by lot until Ephialtes' reforms in 462/1.

cials were answerable to state tribunals run by the citizenry at large to prevent corruption. Administrators found to have mishandled public funds were subject to imprisonment and "the so-called infamy, or exclusion from the rights and privileges of the commonwealth."[4] These reforms aimed to avert the kind of oligarchic self-dealing that occurred most notoriously in Rome, where public positions became profit-centers for corrupt self-dealing. Cicero's denunciation of Rome's governor in Sicily, Gaius Verres ca. 70 BC, provides a repertory of the opportunities available to rapacious officials (see Chapter 17).

These democratic reforms were strengthened in the 5th century as a result of the Persian War (499-449) and the Peloponnesian War (431-404) obliging Athens to employ the lower classes as rowers, construction workers and other urban labor. Athens moved the Delian League treasury to the Acropolis in 454, charging League members for the cost of much public construction in Athens and its naval protection against both Persia and oligarchies backed by Sparta. After Ephialtes was killed in 461, leadership of Athens passed to the pro-democracy general Pericles (461-429), who spent the allies' money on building programs employing labor at public cost.[5] He also introduced payment for Assemblymen and jurors – a policy that Plato later accused of making Athenians "lazy, cowardly, loquacious and avaricious."[6]

Personal debt relations in Athens

Expanding trade in grain, olive oil, pottery and other handicrafts required credit and money. Coinage spread rapidly, catalyzed by the Persian Wars obliging Greece to pay naval oarsmen and infantry fighters. But the 5th century is still dark as far as documentation of personal debt is concerned, especially among the lower classes. Even the 4th century's debt records are limited to lawsuits among the well-to-do who had enough money to hire Demosthenes and other rhetoricians to plead their case. The scant primary documentation that has survived indicates that general prosperity enabled Athens to avoid a new debt

---

[4] Boeckh 1857:450-451 and 505-506. Debtors owing money to civic authorities were excluded from office, being "deprived of many active political rights until they had cleared the debt."

[5] Andreades 1933:234.

[6] Andreades 1933:253-254, 258-259 and 263, citing Plato, *Georgias* 515e. Later, Athens established the Theoric Festival Fund (*theorikon*) to help poorer citizens pay for admission to the theater of Dionysus. Aristotle accused this of being simply a means of giving money to the poor with no equivalent return.

crisis, and that its bankers and the largest creditors were not a significant part of the debt problems that later developed. As Paul Millett summarizes lending and borrowing in Athens:

> whatever modern theory might seem to suggest, Greek bankers were not
> primarily money-lenders. The extension of credit was only one of a range
> of services which included safe keeping of deposits (including valuables
> and documents), acting as witnesses and guarantors, and changing money.
> Also, bankers – usually non-citizens themselves – would typically lend
> to those who were either outside the community of citizens by reason of
> birth, or had forfeited its protection by failing to respect social norms. As
> a result, bankers in Athens were not seen as a threat to the citizen solidar-
> ity that was considered essential for the well-being of the polis.[7]

Kirsty Shipton finds that the wealthiest Athenian families, those listed
among the ranks of trierarchs (responsible for outfitting trireme ships,
discussed below), accounted for 42 percent of the documented lenders,
and were half of the bank depositors as well as "half of the known borrowers of bank credit."[8] Greek bankers (*trapezitai*) and private moneylenders lent mainly to well-to do borrowers able to pay.

Foreigners made about a third of bank loans, mainly investments in
"bottomry" commercial shipping. The court pleadings of Demosthenes
and others indicate that half the non-bank loans were for trade, a fifth
for war, and a quarter for domestic use – to buy slaves, pay ransom,
perform state liturgies, or for conspicuous consumption for dowry or
funeral expenses. Few loans were for industry – mining and blacksmith-
ing. In the relatively small sample that Shipton found, the largest borrowers of loans from bankers and wealthy investors were the trierarch
families themselves.[9]

Banking activities were combined with ordinary business undertakings, as was the case in contemporary Babylonia with the Egibi and
Murashu firms, but much commercialized banking in Greece was left to
outsiders. The major Greek banker (*trapezites*) by the 4th century BC was
the alien metic Pasion who, "like many of his contemporary Greek and
oriental colleagues, had his own ships, his agricultural plots and houses
in Attica, in addition to his bank and his banking business. He directed
a shield factory in Athens and even hired out, against a fee, domestic
articles which he must have acquired as forfeits for unpaid debts; for

---

[7] Millett 1991:217.

[8] Shipton 2008:96-97, 108 and 112. See also Cohen 1992.

[9] Shipton 2008:103.

blankets, clothes, silver bowls, and similar articles were among his collection."[10]

Silver had been used as money for two thousand years in Babylonia, which had minimized debt bondage, so the introduction of coinage was not itself a novel cause of the debt crises that developed in Greece and Italy. The debts of the poor resulted not so much from debtors borrowing money as from arrears that accrued as a result of poor families being unable to pay crops for expenses and fees that arose during the year. A family disaster, sickness or death, or a member called away to fight and perhaps to be injured or killed, or sick or injured livestock, or simply an inability to pay for advances of agricultural inputs, led to indebtedness that became a threat to the cultivator's liberty and land tenure.

The absence of debt revolts in Athens in the 5th and 4th centuries was largely a result of its rising prosperity and progressive tax system, above all its policy of raising money for large expenditures by imposing *leiturgoi* on the wealthiest families, and also by the leasing revenue that Athens obtained from its silver mines at Laurion and the subsidies from its military allies against Persia (and later against Sparta). Less affluent Athenians received money for public employment and civic service, and also were relatively free of tax burdens. However, less prosperous cities were unable to avoid a debt crisis as the Peloponnesian War heated up. In Corcyra, Thucydides (3.81.4) reports that in 427:

> During seven days that Eurymedon [an Athenian general backing the "democratic" faction against the oligarchs] stayed with his sixty ships, the Corcyraeans were engaged in butchering those of their fellow citizens whom they regarded as their enemies: and although the crime imputed was that of attempting to put down the democracy, some were slain also for private hatred, others by their debtors because of the monies owed to them.[11]

Thucydides (3.82.1) adds that the threat of economic warfare, largely over the debt issue, soon came to dominate the conflict with Sparta: "Later on ... the whole Hellenic world was convulsed; struggles being everywhere made by the popular chiefs to bring in the Athenians, and by the oligarchs to introduce the Lacedaemonians [Spartans]." In a summary comment that frames his discussion of Corcyra, Thucydides concluded:

---

[10] Heichelheim 1964:82.

[11] Thucydides was related by marriage to Cimon and took a pro-oligarchic position. Fuks 1984:48-55 suspects that much of his subsequent Book 84 emphasizing debt problems in his discussion of Corcyra is a later interpolation.

The cause of all these evils was the lust for power arising from greed and ambition. ... The leaders in the cities ... on the one side with the cry of political equality of the people, on the other of a moderate aristocracy, sought prizes for themselves in those public interests which they pretended to cherish, and ... in their acts of vengeance they went to even greater lengths, not stopping at what justice or the good of the state demanded, but making the party caprice of the moment their only standard ...

Athenian money creation from its silver mines

Most early public revenue came from rents from public land, mines, ports, buildings and slaves, as well as from tariffs levied on trade, and fines. Direct taxes on land or labor were rejected throughout antiquity as tribute imposed on subject populations. Athens limited such taxes to foreign-born metics and other non-citizens.[12]

Public revenue needs were kept down by the fact that the largest expense, that of the military, was financed by the soldiers or cavalrymen themselves as part of their citizenship duties. Athens obliged the wealthiest families to bear the cost of leiturgoi, headed by the duties to outfit trireme ships (the trierarchy obligation) and civic gymnasia, and to stage dramatic choruses and similar activities.

Athens also had an extraordinary source of revenue that other Greek cities lacked: its silver mines at Laurion. The site had been mined for thousands of years, mainly for lead and copper, but a new vein of silver was discovered in 483. Unlike the earlier shallow veins that were close to the surface, the new silver lode was deep underground. Its supply of silver enabled Athens to avoid having to tax the economy at large or run a trade surplus. Athens literally mined its own money, coining the famous silver "owls" from 480 onward. Operation of Laurion mining was leased to private bidders in exchange for a share of the profits, yielding a reported 100 talents to the city.[13] The bidders who won the concession came from the wealthiest families (those from whom trierarchs and other major liturgy-bearers were appointed).

---

[12] Andreades 1933:126-127 provides an overall review.

[13] It is not clear how much income the private operators made. The state either collected a fixed share of the metal produced or was paid a fixed rent for leasing the mine. Xenophon's *Constitution of the Athenians* (Moore 1975:48) states that mine leases ran for 3 or 10 years, for a specified price plus 1/24th of the value of the metal mined. Andreades 1933:269-270 notes that by 345-323, great fortunes were amassed by those in charge of the mines.

A debate occurred in 482 over what to do with this public revenue from Laurion. The Alcmaeonid leader Aristeides advocated that it should be distributed to Athens' citizenry – a reported 10 drachmae per man – much like Alaska's oil royalties today are distributed among the state's residents. But Themistocles, having already led an effort to develop the Piraeus shipping port, wanted to use the revenue to build a navy – "two hundred ships for the war, that is, for the war with Aegina," the neighboring island that was growing into a seafaring rival of Athens (Herodotus 7.144).

The *Athēnaiōn Politeia* (*Constitution of Athens*) 12 shows the usual elitist bias of denigrating democracies for pandering to the passions of the poor, who allegedly live in the short run and vote in their own narrow interests. The text describes Themistocles as not saying what he would use the money for, but recommending:

> that a talent should be lent to each of the hundred wealthiest Athenians. If the people approved of what it was spent on, the expenditure should be borne by the state; if not, they should recover the money from those who had borrowed it. The proposal was approved on these terms, and he had a hundred triremes built, one by each man. This was the fleet with which they fought the barbarians [the Persian fleet] at Salamis.[14]

Athens built 330 warships at public expense by the time it defeated Persia's fleet at the Battle of Salamis in 480. To pay for their provisioning, crew and upkeep, Athens assigned the trierarchy, its highest *leiturgia* obligation, to the wealthiest landowners, while building the navy provided employment in the shipyards and many lower-class *thētes* were hired as rowers.

How funding public expenditures by leiturgoi *promoted economic democracy*

Cities from Greece to Asia Minor shared a political philosophy that wealth was to be used to benefit the citizenry at large. The richest

---

[14] Moore 1975:45 and 56. The implication is that the wealthy families did not choose to distribute the public revenue to the population at large. Democratic versions say that the population was enlightened enough to put Athenian military needs above their own self-interest. Most historians endorse Herodotus's figure of 200 triremes built, some ships perhaps from subsequent leasing revenue. Prior to this time Athens had no war fleet of its own, only private ships and those funded by the 50 *naukraroi* districts created by Cleisthenes. Creating a navy with the Laurion mine proceeds replaced this local financing system.

families – in practice, the largest landowners – were obliged to bear the cost of the major categories of civic spending. For Athens these costs were headed by outfitting and maintaining naval vessels, hiring and training choruses for the major public music-drama festivals, and providing oil and other operating expenses for gymnasia (one of the major gathering places for the elite).[15]

Treating wealth as being granted provisionally for its holders to use in the public interest was made compatible with aristocratic values through the prestige it bestowed on those who served as trierarchs, gymnasiarchs and *choregoi*, especially by allowing them to directly manage the ships, gymnasia and choruses they funded.[16] Down through Roman times a patriotic rivalry existed among the wealthiest citizens to demonstrate their public spirit by competing for excellence in what might be called conspicuous philanthropy, an extension of their own personal creativity. It was an opportunity to gain renown for the liturgy holder's own trireme, drama or chorus.

A *choregos*, for instance, provided training and costumes for choruses of men and boys to perform tragedies, comedies and "various dances and the dithyramb ... the most expensive of all the liturgies, involving a chorus of fifty and the most expensive aulos-players." The springtime Dionysia festival "was a particularly fine opportunity for a wealthy man to spend heavily and thus earn prestige with his fellow citizens. Further expenditure could be incurred by hiring extras, and a generous *choregos* could make all the difference to the success of a play; it is said that Nicias never failed to win the prize when he was *choregos*."[17] Other *leit-*

---

[15] See Jones 1966b:220-221. Describing Asia Minor, Magie 1950:62 summarizes characteristics common throughout most Greek cities: A gymnasium "was usually provided not only with places for exercise, both indoors and in the open, and with baths, hot and cold, but also with lecture-halls and sometimes even a library, and with rooms for general conversation. Thus, as supplying needs of various kinds, the gymnasium became the center of the social life of the community." The gymnasiarch "also had to provide, often at his own expense, for the care of the building and its equipment, for the heating of the baths, and, at times, for the lighting of the rooms after dark. A duty of especial importance ... was that of furnishing the oil used both as a cleanser and as a lubricant by those who exercised in the place; the cost, apparently a large item, was sometimes met by appropriations from the city-treasury, but usually it was supplied by some generous donor or, more often, by the gymnasiarch himself."

[16] Van Wees 2013, Gabrielsen 1994 and Pritchett 1974 provide a general overview.

[17] Moore 1975:194 and 196.

ergoi included the *sitesis* (for grain and flour to provision the polis), *lampadarchia* (for torch races), and *hiera periodos* (for religious processions).

Many liturgy payers bragged about how they spent more than the officially required minimum.[18] Kleinias, son of Alcibiades, provided his own ship and crew at Salamis, for instance, despite not being required to do so as a trierarch (Herodotus 8.17).[19] The aim was "to win the favor of the populace. ... [and] many fortunes were squandered. From this arose the terms to 'expend lavishly' on liturgies or choregies. One who did not undertake [such excessive expenditures] could not expect the support of his fellow citizens or even their lenience in political and other trials that were then so common. Isocrates in his *Areopagiticus* looks back with longing to the time when the liturgies did not take their rise in vainglory and were not a source of strife."[20]

Leiturgoi were not strictly proportional to wealth. "Under Periander in 357/6 the 1200 richest Athenians were obliged to become trierarchs, distributed into 20 symmories of 60 men each, to spread the costs. The result was ... almost a per capita arrangement."[21] The outcome was a standard minimum levy for each liturgy category.

A striking innovation was to permit challenges by landowners assigned to perform a liturgy. One could "allege that another citizen was wealthier and more able to bear the expense than he. He therefore chal-

---

[18] Gabrielsen 1994 describes the competitive generosity of Athenian elites in performing these functions. Moore 1975:49 cites Xenophon's *Constitution of the Athenians* as pointing out that liturgies "had the advantage that they [the rich families] were personally involved: the trierarchs who maintained the triremes also sailed on them, and their own safety therefore depended, at least to some extent, on not 'economising.' ... To provide a tragic chorus could well cost half a talent, a dithyramb distinctly more, and to maintain a trireme could cost nearly a talent; by comparison, a poor family could live on 1/20th of a talent a year."

[19] Cited in Butera 2010:57, who points out (p. 55) that because of the heavy burden of such maintenance, "trierarchs, unlike those who performed other liturgies, were granted a two-year respite from liturgical obligation after their year of service, instead of the more common one-year exemption." A man could not be required to perform more than one liturgy at the same time, nor be named to bear the same liturgy in successive years. His performance gave exemption for a fixed period.

[20] Andreades 1933:130-132 and 293, citing Isocrates, *Areopagiticus* 20. See also Thomson 1964:11.

[21] Andreades 1933:324-325. Demosthenes made these *leiturgoi* more proportional to landed wealth.

lenged him to exchange property or accept the liturgy."[22] An attempt to emulate this policy was made in England in the early 20th century. The "Peoples' Budget" of Liberal Party leader H. H. Asquith (1908-1916) proposed a 20 percent tax on the land's annual increase in value. Each titleholder was to estimate a fair price for his land. If it seemed high, the treasury would use it as the tax base; if too low, the government would buy the land. The House of Lords blocked that move as part of its opposition to land taxation in the constitutional crisis of 1909-1910.

The Delian League vs. oligarchic Sparta's control of Delphi

Defeating Persia's much larger infantry and naval forces in 490, 480 and 479 gave Athens the momentum to create the Delian League in 478, with a common fund for mutual defense to drive the Persians out of the Aegean, finally doing so in 449. Two decades of peace and prosperity ensued, but rivalry was looming between Athens and Sparta as sponsors of democracy or oligarchy respectively.

In the background, Persian agents sought to influence Delphi, whose oracle was described by Thucydides and Herodotus as being prone to bribery. Its prophecies had discouraged the Greeks from fighting Persia in earlier times, urged Sparta and its allies to overthrow Athens' Peisistratids, and promised Sparta victory in the Peloponnesian War.[23] By the war's outbreak in 431, Delphi, Olympia and other temples had fallen under the sway of Sparta's Peloponnesian League. For Athens, the temple island of Delos became strategically important as Athens "began to aim at supremacy, for the acquisition of which religion is a powerful instrument."[24]

---

[22] Moore 1975:194. If the man elected to the exchange, "complete lists of property, except for holdings in the mines at Laurion which were exempt from assessment for the purposes of liturgies, had to be filed within three days of the challenge by both sides."

[23] The reason why Athens as well as Sparta "put up trophies and sent offerings of the soils to Delphi" at the war's outset in 432 was that two of its citizens, Pleistoanax and his brother Aristocles, had bribed the priestess to give biased oracles to the Spartan delegations that had come on official visits. (Thucydides 1.15 and 126; 4.134 and 5.16). Olmstead 1948:41-43, 153-156 and 249, especially p. 42, observes that after 547 "both Apollo of Miletus and Apollo of Delphi for the next half-century remained consistent friends of the Persians."

[24] Boeckh 1857:531-532, citing Thucydides 5.16, and Herodotus 1.50-52, 85-90; 5.61-62 and 6.124.

Thucydides (1.96-99) describes how Athens, in establishing the Delian League in 478,

> assessed the various contributions to be made for the war against Persia, and decided which states should furnish money and which states should send ships – the object being to compensate themselves for their losses by ravaging the territory of the King of Persia. At this time the officials who became known as 'Hellenic Treasurers' were first appointed by the Athenians.

The Delian League, however, soon transformed its member states from contributors of ships to payers of tribute to Athens (although the islands of Chios, Lesbos and Samos only provided ships, not money). When Naxos sought to withdraw in 470, Athens invaded it and subsequently moved the Delian League treasury to Athens in 454.

Democratic reforms under Ephialtes and Pericles

An earthquake in 464 provided Sparta's helots with an opportunity to rebel (as noted in Chapter 3). Sparta asked for help, and the leading conservative Athenian politician, Cimon, supported the aid request. But the democratic leader Ephialtes argued that oligarchic Sparta was a looming rival. Cimon prevailed, and led an Athenian contingent to help Sparta in 463/2. But the Athenian troops were so appalled by Sparta's treatment of its helots that Spartan leaders soon asked Cimon to leave, fearing that his troops might encourage the helots' struggle for liberty. The soldiers returned to Athens, and the fight between Ephialtes' democratic supporters and Cimon's pro-oligarchic faction was renewed. It ended with Cimon being ostracized for his pro-Spartan advocacy.

Cimon's exile enabled Ephialtes to introduce more radical democratic reforms to break the oligarchy's monopoly on policymaking. His first target was the Areopagus, whose membership was restricted to the wealthiest classes, with members holding office for life. Immune to the democratic principle of choice by lot, the Areopagus was a bastion of Cimon's power. In 461, Ephialtes opened membership in the Areopagus, *Boulē* and even the archonship to the broad Athenian population, and shifted nearly all policy decisions to the *Boulē* and popular assembly (*Ekklēsia*), limiting the power of the Areopagus to judgments regarding the sacrilege of blood-guilt for murder.[25]

---

[25] Rhodes 1972:210 describes the shift of political power away from the Areopagus to the *Boulē*.

Members of the oligarchy retaliated by killing Ephialtes, and leadership passed to his prominent associate Pericles, who led the ensuing democratic flowering in Athens.[26] The generation 461-429 has become known as the Age of Pericles. A group of aristocrats mounted a coup in 458/7, hoping to prevent the archonship from being opened to the third property class, the *zeugitai* to which most hoplites belonged. But they were defeated.

Under Pericles the conflict between democratic Athens and oligarchic Sparta intensified as Athens spent three years, 460-457, building long defensive walls. Thebes allied itself with Sparta, while Argos shifted its allegiance to Athens. In 451, Pericles introduced a citizenship law limiting citizenship to men whose parents were both native-born Athenians. The aim was to exclude the aristocrats, who were busy arranging foreign marriage alliances. Cimon's own mother, for instance, was the daughter of Olorus, king of Thrace.[27]

Athenian "democratic imperialism"

Athenian expenditures mounted rapidly during the 5th century, above all for the wars with Persia and Sparta, and because citizens began to be paid for public services, in addition to being hired to work on public construction. Pericles spent between 6,000 and 8,000 talents on the Temple of Nike Apteros among others, parts of the long walls, docks, the Parthenon, Chryselephantine Athena and two gold Victories. Prior to the tribute from Athens' Delian League allies, its annual public revenue amounted to only about 1,000 talents.

The 448 Callias Peace Treaty committed Persia not to interfere with Greek cities in Asia Minor and Cyprus. Sparta pried Euboea and Megara away from the Delian League alliance in 447, and attacked Athens the next year. The fight was settled in 445 by the so-called Thirty Years Peace, which lasted 15 years, until 431. During this period Athens consolidated its control over the Delian League, whose treasurers were all Athenian. They collected annual tribute of about 400 talents, contributing

---

[26] *Ath. Pol.* 26.2. See Rhodes 2000:119, 121 and 124, citing *Ath. Pol.* 23 to 25, and Plutarch, *Pericles* 10.7-8. Finley 1963:77 notes that the silence about Ephialtes' life and murder "is sufficient commentary on the tendentiousness of Greek writers, a one-sidedness with which the modern historian must grapple all the time, and never more than in the study of the history and functioning of the Athenian democracy." For more details of the reforms of Ephialtes and Pericles, see Rhodes 1972:210.

[27] *Ath. Pol.* 26.1, Plutarch, *Cimon* 4.1 and Moore 1975:53.

as much as two-thirds of the Athenian budget.[28] The money was paid in Athenian four-drachma "owls," the period's most prevalent silver coins.

Moore's commentary on the *Athēnaiōn Politeia* implies that "more than 20,000 people made their living from the empire," prompting Athenians to move into the city and live off this influx of silver.[29] The Parthenon was built largely with Delian League tribute during 447-432. The tribute received from its allies enabled Athens to avoid imposing new taxes on its own citizens.

By 425, Athens had tripled the Delian League's annual tribute to over 1,200 talents, which continued until it finally was defeated by Sparta in 404.[30]

Introduction of the eisphora *tax to pay for the Peloponnesian War (431-404)*

The tribute arrangement did not pacify either Athens' allies or wealthy Athenians, who bore the brunt of domestic taxation and whose reluctance to pay the levies led them to advocate an early resolution of the Peloponnesian War. Echoing Plato's criticism of oligarchies as being "too grasping to want to pay the expenses of a war" (*Republic* 8 at 551e), Thomsen blamed Athens' loss to Sparta largely on this attitude of tax avoidance by the rich contributing to their pacifism.[31]

Until the Peloponnesian War, Athens had received "so much booty from the Persians and contributions (*thoroi*) from its [Delian League] allies that it was scarcely ever forced to levy any *eisphora*."[32] The city-state had established a reserve fund of 6,000 talents, but by 428 this had shrunk to just around 945 talents. Hence, the steeply progressive *eisphora* tax was imposed,

---

[28] Andreades 1933:268. He calculates that over 90 percent of Rome's budget in the 1st century BC came from tribute levied on its provinces. By the time Egypt paid tribute under Augustus, Italian taxes represented less than 5 percent of the Roman budget.

[29] Moore 1975:48-49. Each of the ten Cleisthenic tribes provided 600 jurors, each paid by the city, creating a pool of six thousand receiving enough income to support their families.

[30] Pausanias, *Description of Greece* 8.52, quoted in Boeckh 1857:513, Thucydides 1.96-99 and 2.9, and Hatzfeld 1966:64. See also Forrest 1955:39.

[31] Thomsen 1977:144. He also (p. 140) blames the oligarchic revolution of 411 largely on "the political scheming among the wealthy citizens." Andreades takes the same position. See also Hodkinson 2000:433.

[32] Thomsen 1977:136-137 discusses the origins of the *eisphora* tax in the 6th-century *naukraric* system of Cleisthenes' day.

being levied on personal wealth (of all forms) for the first time in 428 to raise 200 talents to fund the war. It was followed by a *proeisphora*, obliging the wealthy to advance the scheduled tax payment to the government.[33]

Thētes were exempted, as were artisans. (Metics were said to have paid a sixth.) The *zeugitai* class only had to pay 16 2/3 talents in 428/7, compared to 50 talents for the *hippeis* and 100 talents for the *pentakosiomedimnoi*. A few years later, in 425/4, rising Delian League payments enabled Athens to discontinue the *eisphora*, but the tax had to be renewed when the Dekeleian War broke out in 413.[34]

Athens' defeat by Sparta

The key to understanding the Peloponnesian War and subsequent Greek conflicts of the 4th and 3rd centuries is to recognize that the opposing alliances were between oligarchic cities on the one hand and democracies on the other. Sparta supported oligarchies such as the Achaean League and Macedonia, and Delphi was part of the Sparta-Persia alliance against democratic Athens and the Delian League.

The "Thucydides trap" theory recently in vogue trivializes this conflict as one simply of geopolitical rivalry, depicting the War as resulting from Spartan jealousy of Athens as a rising rival.[35] But the conflict was domestic as much as foreign, because it was fundamentally about democratic attempts to limit oligarchic wealth. There was no commercial rivalry between Sparta and Athens, because Sparta was not a commercial economy. The conflict was between oligarchic and democratic power and the alliances resulting from domestic class antagonisms. This conflict existed within both Athenian and Spartan society, not merely between the two.

Athens and other democratic cities had their own creditor elites, who shared Sparta's fear of democracy. In 411, after its Delian League allies withdrew support in the wake of Athens' loss in Sicily, wealthy Athe-

---

[33] The only exception was for the wealthiest families' investment in the Laurion mine leasing. Andreades 1933:80 points out: "The word *phoros*, corresponding exactly to Latin *tributum*, was a sum paid by a subject for the exclusive advantage of the conqueror." The basis of public finance thus "was a permanent and systematized form of 'gathering in the spoils,' stretched out over time."

[34] Thomsen 1964:251-253.

[35] The Thucydides Trap is a theory proposed by Graham Allison's 2017 book *Destined for War: Can America and China Escape Thucydides's Trap?* Allison and much recent popular discussion postulates that war between a rising power and an established power is inevitable.

nians staged a coup, egged on by Alcibiades, a former Athenian general working for Sparta after being exiled by his home city. Their aim was for Sparta to end the war and ally itself with the Athenian oligarchy, freeing them from the *eisphora* and other wartime taxes that fell mainly on themselves, and ending civic spending on the lower classes. Toward that end they installed a council of the Four Hundred, and restricted the popular assembly (*Ekklēsia*) to 5000 landowners (*Ath. Pol.* 19).

The coup was thwarted, as was a parallel attempt at Athens' naval base on Samos, but Sparta conquered Athens seven years later, in 404. Sparta's *strategos* Lysander worked with Athenian oligarchs to appoint a military junta subsequently known as the Thirty Tyrants, notorious for confiscating the property of democratic leaders and wealthy targets alike during the regime's tumultuous eight months of power. "When the Thirty had tightened their grip on the city, there was no type of citizen they did not attack. They killed those remarkable for wealth, family or reputation, aiming to remove any potential threat and to lay their hands on their property. After a short time they had killed no less than fifteen hundred men."[36]

Claiming to restore the "ancestral constitution," the Thirty downgraded the *Boulē*'s five hundred citizens into a merely "advisory" group whose views had no official weight.[37] To provide a patina of legitimacy they appointed 3,000 loyalists as official voters and 300 "lash-bearers" to break up any resistance, while depicting themselves "as champions of freedom and lawful government," meaning their authority to nullify policies not in their own interest.

The *Athēnaiōn Politeia* 37-38 describes this reign of terror as driving democrats to take refuge in Thebes. Among the exiles was the Athenian trierarch Thrasybulus, who organized a resistance in 403 and attacked a northern Attica fortress, Phyle, and seized the Piraeus port area.

---

[36] *Ath. Pol.* 35, quoted by Moore 1975:178, who likens the Thirty to "a modern Latin-American military junta" (p. 267). He notes that "Diodorus is the first surviving writer to use the term 'the Thirty Tyrants.'" Their two leading members were Critias, a student of Socrates, and Theramenes. For a specialized study see Krentz 1982. Cecchet 2017:141, fn14 cites "Lysias 12.6–8 (the Thirty decide to arrest ten metics in order to have their property confiscated); Isocrates 18.5–6 (confiscation of the money of a citizen by the Ten, the successors to the Thirty); pseudo-Aristotle *Ath. Pol.* 35.4 (seizure of the estates of wealthy citizens condemned to death by the Thirty); Xenophon *Memorabilia.* 2.7.2 and Diodorus Siculus 14.4.4 (confiscation of the lands of some citizens by the Thirty)."

[37] *Ath. Pol.* 35.2, in Moore 1975:78, citing Xenophon, *Hellenica* 2.3.2 and 11.

Sparta had disarmed the local citizenry so that it could not support the insurgents, but the Athenian exiles from Thebes seized the Munichia hill area around the Piraeus and defeated the Thirty. "The men from the city returned after the battle, met in the Agora the next day, and deposed the Thirty and elected ten citizens with full powers to bring the war to an end."

The oligarchy's 3,000 designated voters were given amnesty except for the Thirty (including Critias), the Eleven (the executioners), and the governors of the Piraeus. However, instead of redistributing the land of the Thirty and their main supporters, the new civilian government left it in the hands of the oligarchy and even committed to repay "the money the Thirty had borrowed from the Spartans for the war, although the [peace] agreement had specified that the men of the city and those of the Piraeus should repay their debts separately."[38] During their rule "the tyrants had obtained a loan of a hundred talents from Sparta. At the end of the struggle this money had to be paid back. Even though the agreement between the two former opponents laid down that each party should fulfill its economic commitments, the *ekklesia*, to express the new conciliatory spirit, voted that all Athenians should unite in paying this debt."[39]

That bailed out the oligarchy's leaders by paying the debts that The Thirty had run up during their brutal eight months in power. This was done ostensibly to promote concord, but the debt bailout probably aimed at preventing a new wave of violence against the democracy. Ober favorably contrasts Athens' payment of the debt to "the bad tendency of other democratic governments to confiscate private property," suggesting that it was aimed at maintaining a good reputation for repayment of loans by showing fiscal responsibility.[40] But the democracy had just met the oligarchs' demand to be freed from their own responsibility!

That double standard would remain a constant throughout the balance of antiquity. A pleading by Demosthenes *Against Timocrates* (ca. 353 BC) cites an oath that Athenian jurors were obliged to take since 401, which concluded with the pledge: "I will not allow private debts (*chreon idiom*) to be cancelled, nor lands nor houses of Athenian citizens to be redistributed."[41] Moritz Hinsch points out that debt crises "were

---

[38] Moore 1975:82 and 72, citing *Ath. Pol.* 40.

[39] Thomsen 1964:178, citing Demosthenes 20.12.

[40] Ober 2015:515. For other Athenian discussion about the repayment see the sources cited in Migeotte 1984:19-23.

[41] Demosthenes, *Against Timocrates* 24.149. He also cites restoring exiles as a crime against democracy, although Solon was also much lauded for such an amnesty.

most absent from the very region where money, credit and enforceabili-
ty were most entrenched."[42] The *Athēnaiōn Politeia* 60.2-3 points out that
when democracy was restored, the new regime "did not even make a
redistribution of the land," a typical policy of democracies overthrowing
oligarchies.

The explanation for such moderation is that Athens used its public
revenue to subsidize its poorer citizens. Public employment provided
a source of income for the needy, while temples advanced emergency
loans. It was in the most rural and least commercialized parts of Greece
that debt revolts broke out, from Sparta to Argos and the Corinthian
Isthmus in the 3rd and 2nd centuries.

An oligarchic attempt to rewrite Athenian history to reject debt cancellation

After Thrasybulus ousted the Thirty Tyrants and restored democracy
in 403, the *demos* seems to have retained opposition to debt cancellation,
accepting the oligarchic claim that its advocates were liable to be tyrants
or aspirers to kingship. The pro-oligarchy speech writer Andocides (died
ca. 390 BC after being exiled from Athens) claimed that the democracy
was best upheld by affirming the validity of decisions in private suits, "to
avoid canceling debts and reopening of such lawsuits, and to ensure the
enforcement of private contracts."[43]

That set the stage for an oligarchic re-writing of Athenian history in
the 4th century seeking to persuade the *demos* to oppose debt cancellation
as being the policy of tyrants, and to expunge from history any acknowledgement that cancelling personal debts had helped Athens develop a
thriving economy. Most classical descriptions of the supposed "ancestral constitution," not only of Solon but also of Draco (whose harshness
was admired by the oligarchy), derive from the "moderate" 4th-century
version of early laws rejecting debt cancellations as radical. Felix Jacoby
has shown that local Athenian histories (*Atthides*) are in the character of

---

Millett 1991:257, fn19, and 21 attributes such pledges not to the pro-Spartan
tyranny imposed in 404, but to the restored democracy's desire to avoid a renewal
of civil warfare over the debt issue.

[42] Hinsch 2016:16.

[43] Andocides, *On the Mysteries* 1.88 (ca. 400 BC). See Cecchet 2017:129. Timocrates
proposed to let debtors to the state go free from prison if they provided a surety
for their obligation, thus saving them from being held until they had paid their
debts. Democrates claimed that this would benefit wealthy citizens more than poor
debtors who had no such guarantors.

party pamphleteering by oligarchic or democratic partisans.

In accord with the oligarchy party, Androtion (ca. 344/3), a follower of the oligarchic Isocrates, even denied that Solon actually cancelled debts in 594, claiming that he merely revalued the coinage, weights and measures to make them more easily payable.[44] But there was no coinage in Solon's time. This attempt at rewriting history, Jacoby concluded, reflected "the terror of the propertied classes" at the demands for debt cancellation that were being "raised again in the fourth century."[45] The ensuing narratives about the 7th- and 6th-century tyrant-reformers, written three centuries after the events and with little more documentation than we have today, reconstructed history in a pro-oligarchic light, sidestepping their positive achievements and denouncing their land redistribution, debt cancellation and economic defense of the poor as "tyranny."

Aeschylus had written in *Eumenides* (performed in 458): "Not a life of anarchy nor the rule of tyranny: take the middle way endowed by gods." In practice the "middle way" meant leaving the wealthy with their privileged role and not giving democracy "too much," defined as any reform of the existing property regime. As Aristotle remarked: "A further consequence of the fact that all aristocratic constitutions are oligarchic in character is that the notables are more grasping, for example at Sparta, where properties keep coming into the hands of a few."[46] Interest-bearing debt was the main cause of such concentration of wealth, and like Plato and the Stoics, Aristotle condemned usury. (There was no ancient word in Greek, Latin or any other ancient language to distinguish interest from usury.)

The next two centuries saw all Greece, from Athens to Sparta, experience deepening economic strains over rising indebtedness in the face of weak taxing power by cities. The next chapter describes the fiscal transition of cities from creditor to debtor status throughout the Greek world.

---

[44] Plutarch, *Solon* 15.2 = FGrHist 324 F 34.

[45] Jacoby 1949:74, adding that Androtion also was probably responsible for depicting Solon as the founder of the Areopagus. Moore 1975:56-57 and 73 also finds a pro-oligarchic bias in the 4th century against democratic reforms by Aristotle and the author of the *Athēnaiōn Politeia*. Jones 1986:75-96 also discusses how 4th-century Athenians rejected debt cancellation and land reallocation.

[46] Aeschylus, *Eumenides*, lines 696-699 and Aristotle, *Politics* 5 at 1307a34-36, cited in Hodkinson 2000:433.

6
Public Finance, from Temples to Oligarchs

Mycenaean palatial economies (1600-1200 BC) were mainly agricultural and pastoral, with little occasion for using precious metals. Public revenue derived from the royal estate (*temenos*) and its economic privileges. Palatial treasure hoards, like those of Judah, Asia Minor and Persia, stemmed from booty seized from foreign lands, and from commerce conducted or taxed by the king, to whom foreign merchants were expected to give gifts (*dotine*) for the privilege of trading.

Andreades's *History of Greek Public Finance* describes the Homeric-era palaces as resembling European feudalism in their "relatively small number of public expenditures in the ordinary meaning of the term. ... the requirements of the prince are also the requirements of the state, which has few needs apart from those of its ruler."[1] Public officials in Homeric times were general assistants such as heralds. Economic life was not yet monetized, so instead of being paid, they lived as members of the king's household (*oikos*), sharing in whatever war spoils the king might obtain. All who played a role in administering palace affairs, as well as minstrels and other court adherents, ate at the palace *oikos* table, along with the community's elders who chose to attend.[2]

To the extent that there were obligations for payment, gift exchange was the most important, especially with visitors from afar. The cost of military campaigns was limited as armies lived off the land of the areas they invaded in search of slaves and booty. Losers were expected to ransom as many of their kinsmen or countrymen from slavery as they could.

The absence of monetary debt or even a monetary common denominator, is a key characteristic of the basically self-sufficient Mycenaean and subsequent Greek Dark Age economies (1200-800 BC). The palace and temples had no regular expenditures and hence required little regular taxation, being self-sufficient with their own land and work-

---

[1] Andreades 1933:6-8. Austin and Vidal-Naquet 1977:41-42 cite Homer, *Odyssey* 2.337-347 to show that the role that temples and palaces played for their communities evolved out of the private storerooms on archaic manorial estates, and chieftains' households in yet earlier times.

[2] Andreades 1933:9, 12-14 and 20.

shops.[3] There was no fiscal apparatus, so clan leaders – the largest land-holders – performed the major administrative and judicial tasks.

War was the major source of temple treasure, typically a tithe of the booty. For thousands of years Mesopotamian palaces met extraordinary military expenses by borrowing temple silver to pay mercenaries and defray other war expenditures. Greek city-states followed this practice, making temples the earliest creditors to civic authorities, minting coinage in Athens during the Peloponnesian War and in many other cities.[4]

Evolution of civic budgets from surplus to deficit

Normal fiscal revenue after the Greek Dark Age took the form of taxes, rents and other payments for advances of land, mining rights or other assets during the year. But by the Hellenistic period following the death of Alexander the Great in 323 BC, Greek cities were becoming increasingly dependent on private loans and contributions. Partly this reflected the resistance of the emerging oligarchies to taxation. By the 2nd and 1st centuries BC entire realms were obliged to pledge their land and infrastructure as collateral to creditors and Roman tribute takers.

From the Bronze Age Near East to classical Greece and Rome, land tenure seems to have been apportioned according to the obligation of its holders to serve in the military.[5] In the classical period, when the cavalry and infantry bore the costs of arming and training themselves, military and political status was based on one's tax-paying ability. Hence land ownership was the determinant of military class (the original meaning of class). The landed nobility thus played the major military role as well as dominating civic regimes and religious administration.[6]

Early fiscal obligations to the palace or temples initially were owed in kind, mainly food (grain in Mesopotamia, livestock and their meat in the Aegean lands). Silver was the basic medium to pay temples and palaces for commercial advances. As economies grew more complex and trade became more important, a monetary standard had to be created as

---

[3] See Andreades 1933:6-10 and 172-174.

[4] I review the historiography of the origins of money in payments to temples and palaces in Hudson 2019.

[5] The papers in Steinkeller and Hudson 2015 provide a discussion of the allocation of Neolithic and Bronze Age land tenure. Obligations to perform corvée labor duties to work on public infrastructure were especially important in the Near East. See also Hudson 2021.

[6] Weber 1976:69.

a fiscal management measure to denominate and standardize the fiscal obligations owed to the palace and temples. The prestige of silver for donations to temples or to one's ancestors in funeral rites helped make it acceptable to public collectors, leading it to become general-purpose money, especially for paying debts.

Greek cities defrayed much of the cost of waging the Persian War (499-449) without borrowing. As Chapter 5 has described, Athens paid for building the ships that defeated Persia at Salamis in 480 with silver from its mines, while trierarchs covered their operating expenses. Persia financed its navy partly from its domestic gold mines, and increasingly from its empire's annual tribute. Herodotus (3.89) reports that for Persia in the reign of Cyrus (559-530) and his son Cambyses II (530-522), "there was nothing fixed about the tribute, but they used to collect gifts."

Cyrus's son-in-law Darius (521-486) was the great innovator regularizing the annual payment of tribute, imposing it as an annual tax of 14,560 talents. Nearly a third came from India in the form of gold dust (Herodotus 3.94), enabling Persia's royal mint to strike its gold darics (named either from the Old Persian word for gold, *dari*, or for Darius).[7] Persia's next gold coins were issued during the final decade of the Peloponnesian War (431-404). This coinage helped standardize the tribute owed by the satrapies that Darius had established.

Alexander's military conquests flooded the entire regional economy with money coined from looting the temples along the routes of his conquests. It was becoming normal practice for generals to carry coin-making equipment with them to melt down booty to pay their troops their share. Most of this wealth was concentrated in the hands of an oligarchy whose leaders sought to minimize its tax liability by curtailing public social spending and privatizing the social and financial role hitherto played by temples as creditors. The 3rd and 2nd centuries BC would see cities rely increasingly on money provided by the wealthy, partly as civic-minded contributions but increasingly as interest-bearing loans.

Debt character of early gold coinage, owed to the temples for war financing

Temples built up their treasure by receiving a tithe (or sometimes more) of war booty, and by philanthropic donations. As in the Near East, the

---

[7] Herodotus 4.166 wrote that Croesus of Lydia may have issued gold coins before Cyrus conquered his kingdom in 546. See Gardner 1918:86-87 and Andreades 1933:91 and 97-98. The daric was very pure, with only about 3 percent alloy. The main mint is said to have been at Sardis in Lycia.

major Greek and Roman temples were storehouses for their community's savings, sometimes of food and weapons but especially of treasure in the form of bullion. As the overseers of weights and measures, temples became the official refiners of precious metals and regulators of their purity. That made them the official issuers of coinage, often minted to meet the demands of war emergencies by melting down the bullion contained in their statues and votive offerings.[8]

J. P. Morgan is reported to have said: "Gold is money. All else is credit." But the gold coins issued by Greece and then Rome down through the 2nd century BC were struck from offerings and ornaments that civic authorities borrowed from temples, such as when Athens borrowed from the Temple of Athena on its Acropolis. This bullion-money was indeed a form of credit inasmuch as it was supposed to be repaid when peacetime conditions permitted, ideally out of booty and reparations paid by defeated lands.

Recognizing that warfare was a constant fact of life, cities built up temple hoards during periods of prosperity, to be lent to civic authorities in times of need and restored when the emergency was over. "In framing a constitution," Aristotle wrote (*Politics* 2.7 at 1267a), "it is essential to have regard to acquiring strength for war ... A nation's wealth is part of its strength; for it is essential that there should be resources sufficient not merely for its internal needs but also to meet external dangers."[9] A Greek city-state's temples were the main repository of civic wealth for meeting such dangers. But city-states had an obligation to return what they borrowed, with temple treasurers keeping track of the metal melted down from statues, garments of the gods and other contributions.

In the Samian War (440-439), for example, "the 3,000 talents paid to Athena and the smaller sum paid to the Other Gods represent the repayment, with interest, of the sums borrowed."[10] After the war, Athens

---

[8] Laum 1952 emphasizes the symbiosis of fiscal and monetary policy and its linkages with religion from archaic times through Rome. Most subsequent studies segregate these topics from their relation to debt.

[9] As Chapter 3 has noted (Thucydides 1.80), Sparta's king Archidamos II pointed out at the outset of the Peloponnesian War that his own realm lacked monetary savings, leaving Athens better prepared.

[10] Rhodes 1972:92, noting (p. 93) "the 5th-century formality of treating withdrawals as borrowings, on which interest had to be computed." Oppenheim 1949:172, 175 and 186 notes that gold thread and small gold rosette squares or decorations were sewn onto the fabric of the ceremonial garments of the gods, a practice followed in Athens and elsewhere. The Bible, Book II Kings 12:17 and 18:14-16, describes

demanded reparations of 1,200 to 1,400 talents from Samos "in install-ments at regular intervals," probably borrowed from the goddess Hera.[11] A century later, the bullion used to mint the coins issued by Philip of Macedon to pay mercenaries in his Sacred War (356-346) was restored to Delphi upon the return to peace, to be cast into new images for the sanctuary whose temple and treasures had been looted by the Phocians.

Andreades describes the separation of temple and state budgets as "more apparent than real, for the temples had become essentially an ap-pendage of the state, being early subjected (in Athens in the 6th century) to the scrutiny of the state, while at the same time their administrators were chosen by the *demos* and were accountable to it like all public servants."[12] Civic and temple finances certainly were symbiotic. The Parthenon's ten Treasurers of Athena were selected by lot from each of the city's ten tribes (*phylai*), and were responsible directly to the *demos* (*Ath. Pol.* 47). Also on the Acropolis with the Temple of Athena was the Treasury of Other Gods. The latter's bullion was drawn on by Athens' public treasury before that of Athena, whose treasure was the city-state's last resort.[13]

---

temple gold being sent to Syria to pay it not to attack Jerusalem. "Hezekiah cut off the gold from the doors of the temple of the Lord, and from the pillars which Hezekiah king of Judah had overlaid, and gave it to the king of Assyria."

[11] Thucydides 1.117, Meritt 1937:35-38 and Gomme 1956 I:31-33 and 356.

[12] Andreades 1933:192. On p. 169 he calls advances from the Temple of Athena in the Parthenon "pretended" loans (which German classicists called *Scheinanleihen*), because in reality: "This treasure belonged rather to the state than to the goddess, and the measures which were taken to return this looked rather toward a re-estab-lishment of the treasure than to the repayment of a debt. The fact that these loans were made by the decree of the people, that is to say by the simple decision of the borrower, as well as that the interest was purely nominal and was rarely actually paid, is enough to prove that we are dealing here with a transaction that has only the semblance of a loan." In his compilation of Greek documentation of public debts, Migeotte 1984:4 likewise views borrowings from local temples as internal fiscal operations, because the city-temples were basically public in character, ad-ministered by elected or appointed civic treasurers, accountants and related fiscal officials. For earlier elaboration see Boeckh 1857:222 and Curtius 1870:108-109.

[13] Morris 2003:16 notes: "The Acropolis became a fusion of Archaic Panhellenic shrine with imperial city. The citizens themselves acknowledged this, when they agreed to pay the costs rather than have Pericles do so and take full credit, like an archaic tyrant (Plutarch, *Pericles* 14)." Allied tribute was stored in the Parthenon, formerly contributed to a religious league centered on Delos.

The earliest documented public borrowing from temples dates from 432-422, following a decree by Kallias in 434 for 3,000 talents from Athena. This loan was repaid with interest after the Peace of Nicias in 421. Borrowing by city-states from their temples was thus the first form of public borrowing in Greece. The accounting formalities for such temple advances to city-states provided the basic contractual model for subsequent civic borrowing from private Hellenistic creditors.

Borrowing other than from city-temples

The first borrowing beyond one's own city-temples was from foreign temples, and in due course from allied city-states. Athens controlled the island of Delos and its shrines, while Sparta and Corinth dominated Delphi and its Temple of Apollo. When Corinth's representatives took stock of the Peloponnesian League's resources in 432 at the Allied Congress in Sparta, shortly before its war with Athens' Delian League, they pointed out that they could finance their sea power by supplementing existing resources "from the funds at Olympia and at Delphi. If we borrow money from there we shall be able to attract the foreign sailors in the Athenian navy by offering higher rates of pay. For the power of Athens rests on mercenaries rather than on her own citizens" (Thucydides 1.121).

On the eve of the Peloponnesian War in 431, Pericles urged the Athenians to keep a tight hold on payments from their Delian League allies, calculating that:

> the strength of Athens derived from the money brought in by their payments, and success in war depended principally upon conduct and capital. ... Apart from other sources of income, an average revenue of 600 talents of silver was drawn from the tribute of the allies; and there were still 6,000 talents of coined silver in the Acropolis, out of 9,700 that had once been there, from which the money had been taken for the porch of the Acropolis, the other public buildings, and for Potidaea. This did not include the uncoined gold and silver in public and private offerings, the sacred vessels for the processions and games, the Median spoils, and similar resources to the amount of 500 talents.
>
> To this he added the treasures of the other temples. These were by no means inconsiderable, and might fairly be used. Nay, if they were ever absolutely driven to it, they might take even the gold ornaments of

Athene herself; for the statue contained 40 talents of pure gold and it was all removable. (Thucydides 2.13)[14]

This latter sum "might be used for self-preservation, but every penny of it must be restored," in the same or even a better quality.

During the Peloponnesian War, Greek cities issued coins struck from gold borrowed from their temples – Syracuse in 413, with its Sicilian allies Gela, Camariac and Arigentum following suit during 406/5, "struck from golden images and dedications melted down during great stress."[15] In 413 the Athenian general Nicias offered to reimburse Syracuse for all the expenses that it had incurred in the war, and to pledge Athenians as hostages, one for each talent owed, if Sparta's general Gylippus would let the Athenian army go (Thucydides 7.83.2). But Gylippus rejected the truce offer, and Athens lost the war in 404, after having indeed melted down its own Winged Victory statues on the Acropolis to strike gold coins in 407 after its navy was defeated at Notium. (Again under stress in 339-330, Athens issued more gold coins from new golden Victory figures.)

The final years of the Peloponnesian War saw cities lend to allies. In 412/1, Lydia's satrap Tissaphernes negotiated a naval subsidy from the Lacedaemonians, to be repaid at the end of the war (Thucydides 8.58.5-6). In Athens, the democracy repaid Sparta for its support of the Thirty Tyrants during their rule in 404/3, as Chapter 5 has noted.[16]

---

[14] Modern scholarship sets the gold's weight at 44 talents, that is, about 1,100 kilograms (2,400 pounds), following Philochorus, who seems to have quoted directly from the inscriptions and archives on the Acropolis and who therefore is to be preferred (see Dinsmoor 1934). Eddy 1977 describes the statue, sculpted by Pheidias, as having removable gold plates on top of bronze plates around a wooden base, with the face and arms made of ivory. In addition, there was ceremonial equipment consisting of chariots, jewelry and other items used in major festival processions to the gods. Removability of golden garments had become common already in Bronze Age Mesopotamia, as noted by Oppenheim 1949. Moore 1975:284 comments on *Ath. Pol.* 47: "Although it was removable, there is no evidence that the Athenians ever used any of this gold even in the darkest days of the Peloponnesian War, and it was therefore presumably still there in Aristotle's day. Gold statues of Victory were an accepted way of 'storing' surplus revenue. Ten are known in the late fifth century, of which eight were melted down to make gold coins in 407/6; others are mentioned in the fourth century, notably those in Plutarch, *Moralia* 841D: '(Lycurgus) constructed gold and silver ceremonial vessels for the city and gold Victories'; the date was 334."

[15] Gardiner 1913:185-186. See also Head 1887, and Warren 1863.

[16] Migeotte 1984, Nos. 23 and 1 provides the extant documentation for these two examples.

Athenian tax policy reflects the emerging strains between democracy and oligarchy

The Athenian democracy imposed a wartime *eisphora* tax on property holders, and extended it to include metics in 378/7. But it soon was replaced by a non-progressive flat tax that favored the well-to-do citizens by abolishing the tax system based on the Solonian income classes.[17] A progressive tax was restored when warfare with Sparta broke out again in the 370s. In 373/2 the wealthy classes once again were obliged to bear the heaviest burden, above all via the *proeisphora*. "By this arrangement, the three hundred richest Athenians, who already had to perform liturgies, especially the trierarchy, were obliged to advance to the treasury the total *eisphora* amount levied, and had then afterwards to collect it themselves from the individual taxpayers."[18]

Athens thus avoided the problem of tax arrears by obliging 300 designated wealthy families as a group to pay the *proeisphora* tax collectively. Its advantage was that if wealthy Athenians tried to conceal their fortunes, the state didn't lose, because the *eisphora* was an overall quota for the group and any shortfall had to be met by the other taxpaying families.

War remained the major force pushing public finances into deficit. Triremes were antiquity's most expensive weapons, until Athens introduced quadriremes (ships with four layers of rowers) around 330, and quinqueremes five years later. No longer able to be financed by the temples and Pan-Hellenic shrines that had served as the major public creditors in the 5th century, cities found themselves obliged to start borrowing from wealthy individuals.

Fiscal stratagems from the pseudo-Aristotelian Oeconomica

As Bernard Laum has noted, liturgies develop where the wealthy are socialized.[19] But the rise of oligarchies saw the wealthy become increasingly predatory as creditors, land monopolists and public administrators, acting and ruling in their own narrow interest instead of promoting overall prosperity and economic balance. However, strong rulers were

---

[17] Thomsen 1964:254, citing Thucydides 3.19.

[18] Thomsen 1964:255-257. He makes the same point in Thomsen 1977:135 and 142. Rhodes 1972:150 writes that men obliged to pay the *eisphora* and presumably the *proeisphora* who were unable to meet their quota lost their civic rights until they had paid. The *Boulē* had the right to imprison them or confiscate the property of their guarantors.

[19] Laum 1952:217.

able to use various stratagems to finance their public spending. The second book of Aristotle's *Oeconomica*, compiled by one of his followers in the late 3rd century BC, describes fiscal devices to raise money. "Nearly all the 'expedients' mentioned," Andreades summarizes, "refer to difficulties which tyrants, generals or cities of the second rank found in paying their soldiers."[20]

A typical ploy was to requisition jewelry and precious metal. When a Persian satrap Mausolus (377-353) in Caria (Asia Minor) received a demand for tribute from Artaxerxes II, he called together a number of well-to-do men, who contributed liberally. "With this example before them, they who were wealthier than these, partly in shame and partly in alarm, promised and paid much larger sums than the others" (*Oeconomica* 2.2.13-14).

The mutual-aid ethic still survived, but such contributions had to be enforced. Ephesus, "being in need of funds, passed a law forbidding their women to wear gold, and ordered them to lend the state what gold they had in their possession." It also sold rights to citizens to donate new pillars for the Temple of Artemis (*Oeconomica* 2.2.19).

Dionysius of Syracuse (405-367), famous as an occasional sponsor of Plato, devised various ploys to induce citizens to contribute to the local temple, from which he then borrowed. On one occasion he declared "that Demeter had appeared to him, and bade him convey all the women's ornaments into her temple." He collected those of his own household and announced that all other citizens "must now follow his example, and thereby avoid any visitation of the goddess's anger. Anyone who failed to comply would be guilty of sacrilege. ... all the citizens brought in whatever they had. Then Dionysius, after sacrificing to the goddess, removed the ornaments to his own treasury as a loan which he had borrowed from her." He decreed that "any women who desired to wear gold should make an offering of a fixed amount in the temple" (*Oeconomica* 2.2.20).

Dionysius developed the habit of going to the temple and removing its votive offerings simply by saying, "I accept it." When such stratagems led his subjects to protest that they were broke, he brought out the furnishings of his palace and offered them for sale, pretending to be in need of money. "At the sale, he had a list made of the articles and their purchasers; and when they had all paid, he commanded everyone to bring back the article he had brought" (*Oeconomica* 2.2.41).

The Athenian general Chabrias used a similar ploy in Egypt in 359 when he served as advisor to the pharaoh Teos (360-359, sometimes

---

[20] Andreades 1933:83-85.

transliterated as Tachos). He recruited ten thousand Greek mercenaries to defend Egypt against Persia. They demanded their pay in cash, but Egypt's economy was only partially monetized. On the advice of Chabrias, Teos

> informed the priests that most of them must be discharged, since the expense of the war enforced the closing of certain temples. Naturally, each temple gave a bribe to remain open. After collecting large sums of money from each, [Teos] issued fresh orders: Each temple was permitted to retain as an act of grace one-tenth of its revenues, while the remaining nine-tenths was to be a forced loan which, it was promised on the faith of the government, would be repaid at the end of the war.

Teos imposed new taxes, including collecting the tithe on maritime imports and manufactures that his father Nectanebo I had granted to the temple at Neith. "All gold and silver in private possession was called in. From the precious metals were struck coins to pay the mercenaries; a gold daric bearing the name Tau [for Teos] in Greek letters and the helmeted Athena and her owl has survived. Those who thoughtlessly surrendered their hoards were 'commended' to the monarchs who were supposed to repay them from the local taxes." However, when Teos invaded Phoenicia and Palestine on his way toward Mesopotamia, his brother (serving as regent of Egypt) "took advantage of the universal hatred for the tax 'reforms' by declaring his own son Nectanebo II king," who reigned for nearly twenty years (359-340) and rebuilt the temples.[21]

Condalus, Persian satrap at Lycia, thought up one of the more memorable stratagems:

> Noticing that the Lycians were fond of wearing their hair long, Condalus proclaimed that a dispatch had arrived from the King ordering him to send hair to make forelocks for his horses; and that Mausolus had therefore instructed him to shave their heads. However, if they would pay him a fixed sum per head, he would send to Greece for hair. They were glad to comply with his demand, and a large sum was collected, the number of those taxed being great.[22]

---

[21] Olmstead 1948:417-420, citing pseudo-Aristotle, *Oeconomica* 2.2.25 and 37, and Schur 1926:281-283. Chabrias returned to Athens, where he was made general for the year 357.

[22] *Oeconomica* 2.2.14. See Andreades 1933:108. On p. 175 he explains why this ploy worked: In medieval times, "Baldwin II, the king of Jerusalem, gave his beard as

Clazomenae, a Greek city near Smyrna on the coast of Asia Minor, moved toward modern public finance techniques by monetizing its debt. It paid 20 percent interest to its mercenaries each year (4 talents on a total of 20) but lacked the resources to pay the principal. So it struck an iron coinage assigned a value of 20 talents, bearing the same face value as silver, and made it legal tender, *e.g.*, for paying taxes and other public fees (the basic modern definition of general-purpose money). The city exchanged this iron coinage with its citizens for silver of equal nominal value (*Oeconomica* 2.2.12). That was not the same thing as the debasement of coinage, because the Clazomenians paid "interest out of the revenue to those who had advanced the silver; and little by little distributed repayment among them, recalling at the same time the currency of iron" (*Oeconomica* 2.2.6).

The Euboeans developed a policy akin to today's tax-anticipation notes by pledging their public revenues to Demosthenes of Athens, subject to payment of interest on advances. In Rhodes, Memnon (380-333) likewise assigned its scheduled tax revenue to creditors, and Orchomenos (in Boeotia) mortgaged the revenue from its cattle pastures to a neighboring Elatean creditor ca. 230-210 BC.[23]

The shift to borrowing from the wealthy instead of taxing them

Xenophon's *Ways and Means* (354 BC) proposed attracting private loans by offering the same 20 percent return that investors received for commercial ventures:

> Anyone whose contribution amounts to ten minae may look forward to a return as high as he would get on bottomry, of nearly one-fifth ... That is to say, a subscription of one mina will put the subscriber in possession of nearly double that sum, and that, moreover, without setting foot outside Athens, which, as far as human affairs go, is as sound and durable a security as possible.
>
> Moreover, I am of opinion that if the names of contributors were to be inscribed as benefactors for all time, many foreigners would be induced

---

a pledge, the beard being an adornment to which the people of the East give great significance." Apparently the same was true of hair on top of the head.

[23] *Oeconomica* 2.2.29, 25 and 12. For the text and commentary of the Orchomenos borrowing see Migeotte 1984:48-53 (No. 12) and http://www.attalus.org/docs/other/inscr_126.html. Andreades 1933:171 notes that when Memnon contracted "short-term loans which were to be liquidated ... through taxes that were to be collected in the near future ... when the taxes had been got in he refused to keep his promise, arbitrarily changing the short-term loans into long-term ones."

to contribute, and possibly not a few states, in their desire to obtain the right of inscription; indeed I anticipate that some kings, tyrants, and satraps will display a keen desire to share in such a favor.[24]

Some creditors were willing to reduce or even forego their claims in exchange for a public inscription of gratitude for their generosity as public benefactors (*euergetes*). In Samos, the wealthy Boulagoras used his fortune to bail out the city from a food shortage ca. 240. He made interest-free loans to some of the needy, and paid for other public functions. An inscription (SEG I 366) shows the extent to which Samos (like other cities) had become fiscally dependent on such creditors:

> ... elected director of the gymnasium by the people according to the law, on account of the deficiency of the gymnasiarch, he supervised the good-conduct of the ephebes and the youths fairly and nobly; and ... promised to advance the money required for these things from his own resources, (a sum) not much less than 6000 drachmas; and when a shortage of grain beset the city and the citizens, due to the urgency of the need, appointed three commissions to buy grain, he showed no lack of zeal and love of honor, but in the case of the first commission he advanced all the money to be put out at interest, according to what the *demos* decreed, in the case of the second he promised the same amount as those who contributed the most, and in the case of the third he not only provided all the money to be lent out from his own resources, but also, when the grain was brought into the city and the grain-buyer had contracted a loan on it, he came before the assembly and promised, since there was no source whence the money would be repaid, to pay off the loan for the city as well as the interest and all the other expenses, and he did this quickly and reimbursed the lender without making any contract with the city for this money or requiring guarantors to be appointed for him, but considering more important the common good and that the *demos* might live in prosperity; and in all other matters he continues to show himself zealous and kind both to the *demos* in general and individually to each of the citizens, [giving] the best [counsel] and reconciling those with differences and lending without interest from his own

---

[24] Xenophon, *Ways and Means: A pamphlet on Revenues*. Bottomry was a form of maritime trade financing where a loan at interest (and sometimes a share of profits) was made for the purposes of a voyage, with the ship pledged as security for repayment of the loan on successful completion of the venture. Such loans were not repayable if the ship was lost. (See the discussion of similar Roman financing practice in Chapter 13 below.) Xenophon's proposal would have paid the same interest rate as bottomry loans, but risk-free.

resources to many of those who are in difficulties; in order, then, that we may be clear in honoring good men and in urging many of the citizens to the same attitude, be it resolved by the *demos*: to praise Boulagoras son of Alexis for his virtue and his good-will toward the citizens, and to crown him with a gold crown at the tragedies during the Dionysia, and for the *agonothetes* to look after the announcement; and for the *exetastai* to have this decree inscribed on a stone stele and set up in the sanctuary of Hera; and for the treasurer of the sacred funds to provide the expense from the money he has on hand from fines.[25]

The translators note that Boulagoras did not permanently part with his money, but simply allowed Samos "to use his capital for a time." He was to be repaid at some point.

The best that cities could do was to heap ceremonial praise on wealthy creditors, appealing to their public spirit in the hope that they would advance funds on terms less onerous than those typical for commercial loans. Cancellation of interest or interest-free loans are widely attested, but debt relief *in toto* was infrequent. Wealthy individuals preferred to lend at interest, secured by public property as collateral. It became more difficult to rely on philanthropy as civic finances deteriorated in the 3rd century BC.[26]

Another civic option in the Hellenistic period was to create a public bank to attract deposits by offering various investment opportunities. In Miletus (in Asia Minor, and home of the tyrant Thrasybulus and the philosopher Thales) an inscription from 283/2 reports that the city needed money to cover its budget deficit. Unable to persuade the citizens to agree to pay an *eisphora* tax, the city offered to sell annuities. For each 3,600 drachma subscription, a citizen (called a "giver") was "to receive 30 drachmas every month for as long as he/she lives – that is to say, the giver actually receives a monthly-paid annuity. ... At the death of the giver, payment of their annuity ceases and the city treasurers are to pay 150 dr. for the burial of the deceased."[27]

Some 39 subscribers were given the choice of naming a recipient. They named 25 minors and only 12 adults. Miletus raised 140,400 drachmas in this way, from "precisely the people most likely to be liable to payment

---

[25] Bagnall and Derow 2008. The text also is translated in Austin 1981:194-196, and Austin and Vidal-Naquet 1977:64 provide a summary version.

[26] Cecchet 2017:127.

[27] Gabrielsen 2008:126. He lists (p. 119) seven Hellenistic cities with public banks: Athens, Cos, Delos, Ilion, Lampsacus, Miletus and Tenos. But he only accounts for 37 subscribers, not 39.

of the *eisphora* tax." By making loans, investors "harvested a profit of 10 per cent per year in the form of a monthly paid, life-long annuity." No wonder they preferred to make such loans instead of being taxed!

Growing fiscal dependence on wealthy creditors (often foreign)

As noted above, Alexander's conquests flooded the Greek world with money coined from the loot taken from the temples along the path of his conquests. Despite the resulting commercial prosperity, ongoing warfare exhausted civic treasuries and caused "the steadily progressing impoverishment of the middle classes" and smallholders. The growth of private fortunes in the 4th and 3rd centuries saw Greek democracies overthrown, first by Spartan and Persian-backed oligarchies and then by Macedonia. After Macedonia's rise, difficulties in obtaining money "became almost a regular thing"[28] for cities as they were less able to tax their citizens. The rising wealth in private hands was directed more to personal gain-seeking than to public social programs.

Oligarchies reduced the taxes and contributions that had characterized the archaic mutual-aid ethic, while squeezing lower-income taxpayers. Much as Xenophon had proposed in his *Ways and Means*, the wealthy favored financing public budgets by lending on commercial terms. Gabrielsen describes the Hellenistic period's fiscal shift: "the overall share of public borrowing becomes larger at the expense of the share of tax revenue. ... increasingly, the tax-payer (*ho eispheron*) was transforming himself into a public lender (*ho daneistes*) – and correspondingly, the payer of tax in advance (*ho proeispheron*) into a lender of money in advance (*ho prodaneistes*)."[29] Such lending "was often coated with a layer of euergetism," as if creditors were doing their cities a favor.

Their terms became more onerous by the 3rd century. Foreclosure procedures that initially had been developed for land pledged by private debtors were imposed on civic property. Customs duties and other tax revenues were pledged as collateral for loans, and cities pledged their public land, gymnasia, market colonnades, and even in some cases the wealth of citizens and residents to creditors. Andreades describes, the terms of the newer loan contracts as being harsher than

> even the greediest of usurers would ... dare to demand today [1933]. So, according to Strabo (13.4.6), the people of Cyme [Cumae, in southern Italy] gave their colonnades as security, accepting the condition that in

---

[28] Andreades 1933:170 and 88, citing Aristotle, *Politics* 1.4.4 and Cavaignac 1923.

[29] Gabrielsen 2008:125.

case of non-payment of their debt, lingering in these colonnades should be forbidden. ... one rainy day the creditors, taking pity on the inhabitants, proclaimed through the herald that they permitted the use of the colonnades.[30]

Citizens lost the right to use this public space. Equally oppressive were the terms imposed on Arkesine, on the Cycladic island of Amorgos, in exchange for a loan by a Naxos creditor. An inscription records that around 300, the city sent two officials on a mission to Naxos and borrowed three talents of Attic silver from Praxikles at 10 percent interest. This rate was not unusual, but what made this inscription so noteworthy are the penalties guaranteeing Praxikles against all risks for the mortgages he obtained on

> all the public property of the city and the private property belonging to the Arkesineans and those dwelling in Arkesine, within the land and overseas.
>
> The treasurers who collect the revenues of the Arkesineans will pay the interest each year. If they do not pay, let those who do not pay be liable to Praxikles for 150 per cent of the money owed from their own private resources, (this money to be recoverable) by all manner of execution.

Arrears were to mount up at compound interest, including the late-payment 50-percent penalty from the personal property of Arkesine's treasurers. The Arkesineans had to pay back the principal within six months from the time Praxikles (or whomever he designated) demanded it, "in Attic or Alexandrian coin, which the city uses, [guaranteed against all risk], whole, genuine, uncut (?), undamaged, free of all imposts wherever Praxikles orders," without requiring him to go to court to enforce his terms.

> If they [the treasurers] do not pay back the money according to the written terms, the Arkesineans agree and covenant to owe to Praxikles six talents [that is, double the original principal]; and it shall be permit-

---

[30] Andreades 1933:173, citing Polyaenus, *Stratagems in War* 3.11.5 and Appian, *Mithridatic Wars 63,* as well as *Oeconomica* regarding Cnidus, Cyme and other indebted cities. Schepens, *et al. FrGrH* 1999:421 note: "Eurypylus and Dicaeocles of Cnidus in the 21st book of his *Diatribes,* and also the orator Demochares [nephew of Democrates] in his speech *For Sophocles Against Philon,* say that Euaeon of Lampsacus lent money to his native city, taking the Acropolis as security." Ure 1922:281 cites Athenaeus 11.508-509 to the effect that when Lampsacus defaulted, Euaeon wanted to become tyrant. The Lampsacenes rose up and cast him out, after paying him the money they owed.

ted to Praxikles, free from all penalty, to exact this money by all manner
of execution from the public property of the Arkesineans, and from the
private property of the Arkesineans and those dwelling in Arkesine, both
the whole amount from one individual and from all alike, in whatever
way he can, just as from the losers of a final court decision in (before)
the umpire city in accordance with the *symbolon* of the Naxians and Arkesineans [*i.e.*, without Praxikles having to bring a lawsuit]. And whatever
Praxikles seizes or exacts is not to be to the credit of the Arkesineans
toward the repayment of the money they owe.

And the Arkesineans also release from penalty and from liability to
court action any who exact the money at Praxikles' behest. If any of the
Arkesineans or of those dwelling in Arkesine obstructs the exactors or
interferes with the exaction in any way or under any pretext whatever, let
him pay as penalty to Praxikles a talent of silver, and [let him be liable
for exaction] of this money, just as if he had lost a final court decision
to Praxikles in (before) the umpire city in accordance with the *symbolon*,
and let this money not be to the credit of the city toward the repayment
of the loan. And if any injury or expense arises in the exaction of the
money, let this be (the responsibility) of the city of the Arkesineans, and
let the city pay back this money along with the rest of the loan.

The Arkesineans agree that nothing shall have precedence over this
contract, neither law nor decree nor resolution nor *strategos* nor any
other magistrate who renders a decision at odds with what is written in
this contract nor anything else at all by any device or under any pretext
whatsoever, but that this contract is to be valid wherever the lender or
those acting on his behalf produce (it).

The Arkesineans agree to have this contract inscribed at Arkesine in
the public archive [and in the] sanctuary of Hera on a stone stele within
sixty days from the time when the *daneistai* announce ...[31]

The translators comment that "not only is everything owned by all
the citizens of Arkesine pledged as security to Praxikles but also everything owned by the metics (resident aliens) as well," giving him the
right to seize the foreign assets of Arkesine metics as well as its citizens,
even property on ships at sea.[32] It is as if the mayor of New York City

---

[31] Bagnall and Derow 2008:121-122 #72, Praxikles' Loan to Arkesine, late 4th/early
3rd century, from *Syll.*3 955. The stone inscribed with this contract is in the Epi-
graphical Museum in Athens, and is illustrated in Migeotte 1984, Plates II and III
(see fn33). The inscription "is discussed by Tarn [1923:108-110] and provides a fair
indication of the uncertainty of the times."

[32] They add: "This may be related to the provision about overseas property, as
Tarn suggests (1923:110): 'For metics were often traders and ship-owners; and the

and all its residents (local and foreign alike) were obliged to pledge their personal wealth against the city's borrowing.

Creditors had broken free from social constraints obliging them to use their wealth in the interest of their communities. And from their point of view, notes Migeotte, "the severity of creditor conditions regarding collateral reflects precautions resulting from the local revolutions cited by Tarn and numerous civic insolvencies." He also notes: "The contract between Orchomene and Nikareta gives the creditor the right of seizing not only the goods but also the persons of four magistrates and ten guarantors. ... We have no other example of personal execution for public credit, except perhaps for the testimony of Cicero regarding Salimine on Cyprus, thanks to a few cavalry squadrons."[33]

Domestic corruption was another major factor sapping public finances. Already by the end of the 4th century an Athenian demagogue, Lachares, hired mercenaries to loot the city's treasury, whose

> great series of official inventories of the various chambers of the Parthenon comes to a sudden termination. The reason for this, obviously, was the disappearance of the precious offerings recorded in the inventories, because of the depredations of Lachares. By means of a *coup d'état* in 300 BC he established himself as 'tyrant' at Athens ... for nearly five years. For the payment of his mercenaries a precedent had been set during the Sacred War (356-346), when the Phocians paid their mercenaries by melting gold offerings at Delphi, to the value of 4000 talents, and silver offerings of more than 6000 talents. (Diodorus 16.56) So Lachares, according to four passages which have come down to us, melted down the golden shields dedicated on the Acropolis, the golden Nikes, and even the removable gold from the image of Athena herself; as it was laconically expressed, 'Lachares left Athena nude.' (Pausanias 1.25.7)[34]

The fiscal squeeze occurred throughout Greece and Asia Minor. Ephesus and other cities mortgaged their theaters and gymnasia, other

---

right given to Praxicles to seize metics' property as well as citizens' property really means the right to seize any ship belonging to any inhabitant of Arkesine without enquiring as to the owner's status. If he insisted on this right, he must have thought that his security over property in Arkesine itself might become valueless; and only one thing could make it valueless, a revolution and cancellation of debts.' At issue, however, may be Arkesinean holdings on the small islands nearby."

[33] Migeotte 1984:194 and 396. He translates and discusses the contract (No. 13) on pp. 166-194. Chapter 8 below describes the 3rd-century revolts.

[34] Dinsmoor 1934:96-97, citing IG I$_2$, 232309 and II$_2$, 1370-1492.

buildings and even their walls to pay the indemnities imposed by Sulla in the Mithridatic Wars (88-63 BC, discussed below in Chapter 16). Interest charges on public borrowing, which were 10 to 12 percent in the 4th century, reached 48 percent in the 1st century BC at the hands of Brutus and other wealthy Roman officials, creditors and tribute collectors who stripped away the reserves held in city treasuries and temples. Loans typically were made for five years or less, with the debt being doubled if not repaid within the stipulated time frame.[35]

What began as the *noblesse oblige* of leading families to defray the expenses of their communities thus gave way to creditors gaining control of the state to concentrate land and other means of production in their own hands. Today's neo-oligarchic New Institutional Economics celebrates this as creating a "market economy" based on "security of contracts," meaning the security of creditor claims on the property of debtors, public and private. Percy Ure cites a relevant quip from Boswell: "Sir, the way to make sure of power and influence is by lending money confidentially to your neighbours at a small interest or perhaps at no interest at all, and having their bonds in your possession."[36] The New Institutional Economics endorses the expansionary path of debt financing as the bulwark of sound economic progress. But that is the dynamic that plagued entire cities and provinces by the 1st century BC, depleting public wealth in the same way that creditors foreclosed on the land of smallholders who fell into debt.

As Chapter 7 will describe, leading philosophers and the political correctness of the day saw the concentration of wealth as harming society, not helping it. The socially destructive behavior of creditors was the problem that framed Plato's *Republic* (ca. 380 BC). At the outset, Socrates asks whether it is morally right to pay creditors. The answer, he suggests, depends on what they do with the money. Noting their tendency to succumb to abusive hubris as they fall prey to wealth addiction, he asks whether it might be possible to create a government not ruled by the wealthy but by enlightened rulers acting only in society's overall interest. To do this, he concluded, they must not be allowed to possess fortunes of their own – but also should not be from "the poor."

Such speculation proved fanciful in practice in his oligarchic epoch. The Hellenistic Era submerged the Greek economies in debt. Debt-

---

[35] Andreades 1933:172 and 174. Part II below reviews Rome's predatory oligarchic fiscal policy.

[36] Ure 1922:281-282, citing Aristotle, *Politics* 7 at 1307 alluding to Orosius 4.6, and Dr. Johnson, *Boswell*, ed., Fitzgerald, I:422.

strapped cities came to rely on wealthy individuals to act as public benefactors (*euergetai*) to enable them to maintain their public services. But that was not a dependable solution to the debt problem, notes Paul Veyne: "The *euergetai* wished, first and foremost, to please themselves," often by commissioning self-promoting statues to be erected around their city. Many *euergetai* were demagogues such as Molpagoras, at Cius (on the Propontis), whom Polybius described as "flattering the populace, by inciting the rabble against men of means, by finally killing some of the latter and banishing others whose property he confiscated and distributed among the people, soon attain[ing] by these means to supreme power." The main issue at stake in the Hellenistic epoch remained the social struggle over "cancellation of debts and redistribution of landed property," especially during "famines (when corn was in short supply, or rather was too dear, there were riots in the cities)."[37]

---

[37] Veyne 1990:95, citing Polybius 15.2.1, 6.17, 7.10 and 13.1.

7

Plato, Aristophanes and Aristotle on Money-Lust, 4th Century BC

Delphi's warning that lust for monetary silver (*philarguria*) was the only thing that could destroy Sparta was echoed by Plato, Socrates and other philosophers who accused wealth addiction of leading to greedy behavior by the wealthy that impoverished society at large. Creditors were singled out for reducing debtors to bondage and taking their land.

Near the outset of Plato's *Republic* (1 at 331c-d, written ca. 380 BC), Socrates (who had been put to death nearly twenty years earlier, in 399) discusses the morality of repaying debts in circumstances where this would lead to anti-social consequences. Cephalus, a businessman living in the commercial Piraeus district, states the typical ethic that it is fair to pay back what one has borrowed. Socrates asks if it would be just to return weapons even to a man who has become a lunatic. If such a madman is intent on murder, Socrates asks, will not returning his weapon to him enable him to commit unjust acts?

In view of the likely adverse social consequences, paying back such a creditor would be wrong. The morality of repaying debts depends on what creditors will do with their returns, and how their actions affect society. Book 8 of the *Republic* elaborates upon this discussion, describing how wealth leads its owners to act in ways detrimental to society.

Wealth addiction

In contrast to 20th-century price theory assuming diminishing "marginal utility" for each additional unit of a specific consumer good, Greek philosophy saw monetary wealth as being insatiable, becoming ever more addictive. In Aristophanes' last play, *Ploutos* ("Wealth," written in 388), the character Karion observes that one may become over-satiated with food – bread, sweets, cakes, figs and barley – but no one ever has enough wealth. His friend Chremelos (the root of whose name is *chrema*, exchange value and hence money-wealth) observes:

> Give a man a sum of thirteen talents,
>   and all the more he hungers for sixteen.

Give him sixteen, and he must needs have forty,
or life's not worth living, so he says. (lines 189-193)

Money-lust and greed are insatiable and hence infinite. Chremelos
says that he loves wealth more than he loves his wife and only son (lines
250-251), but recognizes that: "Our life nowadays can only be described
as madness or lunacy. Many wicked men are rich having amassed
wealth unjustly, while many others, though scrupulously honest, are
poor and hungry" (lines 500-504).[1]

Quoting from a poem of Solon – "No bound is set on riches for men"
– Aristotle (*Politics* 1 at 1256b) described the drive to acquire commercial gains as addictive. As a Roman proverb expressed it: "Money is like
sea water: The more you drink, the thirstier you get." The more money
a rich man has, the more driven he is to accumulate yet more, without
limit. Ecclesiastes 5:10 says: "Whoever loves money never has money
enough; whoever loves wealth is never satisfied with his income."

Jean-Pierre Vernant has summarized how Greek dramatists portrayed
the greed for money as a disease of the psyche: "Ultimately, wealth has
no object but itself. Created to satisfy the needs of life, as a mere means
of subsistence, it becomes its own end, a universal, insatiable, boundless
craving that nothing will ever be able to assuage. At the root of wealth
one therefore discovers a corrupted disposition, a perverse will, a *pleonexia* – the desire to have more than others, more than one's share, to have
everything. In Greek eyes, *ploutos* (wealth) was bound up with a kind of
disaster."[2]

To illustrate how wealth addiction warps personal character, Aristotle
cited the legend of King Midas of Phrygia. Praying to Dionysus that everything he touched would turn to gold, Midas found that he could not
eat without turning his food to gold. "What a ridiculous kind of wealth
is that which, even in abundance, will not save you from dying with
hunger," observed Aristotle (*Politics* 1 at 1257b).

Wealth addiction leads to destructive hubris

Idealizing the golden mean, the famous inscription near the entrance of
the Delphi temple urged: "Nothing to excess." The most characteristic
excess was addictive money-wealth. A Greek proverb warned that excess
(*koros*) was so addictive that it led to *pleonexia*, the compulsion to obtain
more and more wealth. This compulsion led to *hubris*, an obsessive and

---

[1] See David 1984:41.

[2] Vernant 1982:82.

arrogant trampling on the rights of others, taking what rightfully belongs to them. Socrates suggests that the unjust person "will strive to get the most he can for himself and from everyone" (Plato, *Republic* 1 at 349c).

Nick Fisher traces the development of this idea: "In Hesiod, *hybris* is used repeatedly as a contrary of *dikē* ["justice"], to indicate behavior that is variously violent, criminal and anti-social," most notoriously among rich "fools blessed with fortune."[3] For Homer, *hybris* "is a major crime, endangering the cohesion of the community," as well as the individual's personal psyche. The tendency of money-wealth to become socially corrosive is what led Zeus and the other gods "to punish *hybris*, and uphold *dikē* and *eunomia*," good order and laws.[4]

Aristotle contrasted the social instinct for reciprocity with the pleasure of hubristic acts "making others feel one's superiority by hurting or insulting them, and it is more likely to occur among those blessed by the gods of fortune (while lacking moral virtue) ...; the rich and the young were specifically mentioned in the definition as typically *hybristai*." Such hubris was a problem that mainly plagued the rich: "the connection with the idea of *koros* or too much good fortune is not far away."[5]

Men commit the most serious crimes because "their aims are extravagant," observed Aristotle (*Politics* 2.7 at 1267a), "not just to provide themselves with necessities. Who ever heard of a man making himself a dictator in order to keep warm?" And recognizing that "poverty produces faction and crime" (*Politics* 2.6 at 1265b), he concluded that democracy would be corrupted if creditors and others amassed wealth by impoverishing their fellow citizens: "the duty of a true democrat is to see that the population is not destitute" (*Politics* 6 at 1320a).

Socrates (*Republic* 4 at 421d) suggests that wealth is as destructive as the poverty it causes. "Will a potter who's gotten rich still be willing to attend to his art? And will he become idler and more careless? Doesn't he become a worse potter then? And further, if from poverty he's not even able to provide himself with tools or anything else for his art, he'll produce shoddier works ... Then from both poverty and wealth, the products of the arts are worse and men themselves are worse."

---

[3] Fisher 1992:20-21 and 69.

[4] Fisher 1992:493.

[5] Fisher 1992:19, citing Aristotle, *Rhetoric* 2 at 1383a1-3: Individuals "who feel they have nothing left to be afraid of ... are *hybristai*, contemptuous (*oligoroi*) and bold – and it is wealth, strength, having many friends, or power which makes them like that." For a discussion of how the pseudo-Aristotelian *Athēnaiōn Politeia* (*Constitution of Athens*) 5.2-3 criticized the hubris of the wealthy, see Nagy 1985:43.

Aristotle and subsequent Stoics advocated that rulers should prevent poverty by ensuring that citizens had enough land to be self-sustaining. That could not be achieved when citizens fell deeply into debt and land holdings were widely unequal – and this was the reality of classical Greek society, despite the principles of balance and moderation underlying its ostensibly democratic moral philosophy.

The hubris of wealth addiction vs. the morality of moderation

The concept of balance permeated Greek philosophy. That of medicine, for instance, sought to prevent disease by keeping the body's four humors in balance so as not to let any one part gain at the expense of the others. The social analogy was to limit appetites, avoid ostentatious luxury and refrain from abusing power. The fundamental Greek democratic principle was that public officials should protect the polis from too great a concentration of wealth as well as against poverty. Guiding mottos were "Neither too much nor too little," and "Avoid and hate all mean advantage, and seek for equality." The Stoic ethic held that citizens should conduct themselves like well-behaved guests at a group meal, with self-restraint and a concern for the welfare of their companions.

In Athenian drama the basic tragic flaw was over-reaching, leading to punishment by Zeus, Nemesis or other deities. Aeschylus's chorus in *Agamemnon* (458 BC) warns that "the swarthy Furies stalk the man gone rich beyond all rights."[6] Most tribal cultures studied by anthropologists similarly constrain the egotism of chiefs and other powerful individuals. The typical ethic is to "pound down the nail that stands up too high," sometimes called the "tall poppy syndrome."

But rising Greek prosperity undermined the traditional symbolic equality of portions. In *On Drunkenness*, Chamaeleon of Heracleia (ca. 350-275 BC) wrote: "If those who enjoy power and wealth esteem this devotion to drunkenness above everything else, it is not to be wondered at" that they demand ever larger wine cups. "This is why the larger forms of drinking-cups grew to be the fashion among the persons in power. But this ... is a recent invention, imported from the barbarians."[7]

---

[6] The chorus continues: "with a twist of fortune grind him down, dissolve him into the blurring dead; there is no help. The reach for power can recoil, the bolt of god can strike you at a glance." Plato and Aristotle describe this downfall as being the fate of entire political systems, from oligarchy to democracy.

[7] Chamaeleon of Heracleia, *On Drunkenness*, cited in Athenaeus 11.461.

In a similar vein Plutarch's *Table Talk* (2.10 at 644) later observed: "The custom of distributing portions of the meat was abandoned when dinners became extravagant; for it was not possible, I suppose, to divide fancy cakes and Lydian puddings and rich sauces and all sorts of other dishes made of ground and grated delicacies; these luxurious dainties got the better of men and the custom of an equal share for all was abandoned."[8]

The logic of sumptuary legislation against luxury was based on the belief that drinking and feasting without constraint tended to corrupt. A typical image of wealth addiction was to be drunk with wealth, seeking to amass as much land and money as possible, without regard for the social consequences.

Interest rates, birth metaphors and the unnatural character of charging interest[9]

When Scholastic Canon law banned interest charges in the 13ᵗʰ century, the most important text was Aristotle's *Politics* (1.10 at 1256, written ca. 350): "The taking of interest is contrary to nature because money by nature cannot produce anything and is intended only to serve the purpose of exchange." Cattle give birth to calves, but inasmuch as money is "barren metal," it is unfair for creditors to charge interest as if money were animate and productive by itself.

From Bronze Age Mesopotamia through classical Greece and Rome, the words for interest signified an offspring, such as a newborn goat (*mash* in Sumerian) or calf (*tokos* in Greek). The prefix *fe* in the Latin word for interest *fenus* connotes the birth-related ideas of female (originally "to suckle"), fecundity and fertility. All these words depicted the generation of interest as the birth of an offspring. Yet usury typically was personified as the opposite of procreation – as sodomy, or at best a sterile old man, as in the story of how Rome's Poetelia-Papiria law against usury came to be passed after a creditor abused a young boy pledged to his household for debt (see Chapter 12). This sexual metaphor of homo-

---

[8] Murray 1990:139 notes that "Solon connects the *hubris* of the wealthy with their feasting: 'they know not how to restrain their *koros* or to order their present *euphrosunai* [the delights of the *symposion*] in the quiet of the feast' (Fragment 4.9-10 West)." He adds (p. 142): the whole of Demosthenes 21 is built around the typical relationship between wealth and hubristic behavior.

[9] See also Chapter 12 below, under the heading "Usury as 'sterile,' extractive and predatory" (fn18), for a reiteration and elaboration of this discussion in the context of Rome.

sexuality and the inability to procreate survived into medieval Europe. In 1306, Philip the Fair accused the Knights Templar of buggary as an excuse to seize the wealth of their Paris Temple.

The widespread dislike of interest, Aristotle explained (*Politics* 1.8-9 at 12156b-1258b), "is fully justified, for the gain arises out of the currency itself, not as a product of that for which currency was provided. Coinage was intended to be a means of exchange, whereas interest represents an increase in the currency itself." That seemed to be unnatural, Aristotle continues: "Hence its name, *tokos* ('offspring'), for each animal produces its like, and interest is currency born of currency. And so of all types of business this is the most contrary to nature."

What really was "born" in the case of interest-bearing credit in antiquity was the local society's unit-fraction after a specified period of time, typically a lunar month ending with the new moon, the date on which Greek debt service was owed. The idea goes back to Mesopotamia, where a shekel ($1/60^{th}$ of a mina) accrued or was "born" of each mina every month.[10] A "baby" unit (1 shekel per mina) of silver-interest accrued (was "born") when the crescent moon, patron deity of silver, was born, so a shekel loaned out doubled in 60 months (five years).

Aristophanes' *Clouds* (first staged in 423) opens with Strepsiades unable to pay the debts that his son has run up. He laments "that day which more than all the rest I loathe and shrink from and abominate ... that hateful Old-and-New day" on which his debt payments will fall due, but without him having earned the means to pay.[11] To extricate himself, he urges his son to attend Socrates' school, the Thinkery, to be taught rhetorical tactics and "unjust speech" to beat his creditors by making the weaker argument appear stronger and more just.[12]

Strepsiades (attending the Thinkery himself) asks one of his creditors from what source debts are to be paid. "How is it just that you recover your money, if you know nothing of meteorological matters? Money can no more increase from day to day than the sea can increase its size from the influx of rivers" (lines 1283-1295), assuming the sea's volume of water to be constant. So where were interest payments to come from?

The exponential growth of money lent out at interest was seen to be especially extractive, compounding without limit. It was along this line that Socrates criticized the wealthy. They "insert their sting – that is,

---

[10] I survey the semantics in Hudson 2000a.

[11] *Clouds*, line 113. See Meritt 1961:40.

[12] Lines 116-118. For a discussion see Nichols 1987:9, 20 and 23.

their money – into someone else who is not on his guard against them, and recover the parent sum many times over multiplied into a family of children."[13] But while extracting interest for the creditor, the loan itself was not procreative for the debtor. It typically did not generate an income with which to pay the debt.

The contrast between market price and use value

Money lent out at interest was different from tangible means of production. The root meaning of "capital" is "head" (from Latin *caput*), as in a head of cattle yielding calves. Tools and other forms of capital were means to make things, while money's proper function was to serve as a means of payment, facilitating market exchange for families that did not produce their own food and other necessities. Aristotle extended his contrast between productive capital and money by juxtaposing household management (*oikonomos*), based on use values, to the commercial acquisition of money-wealth (*chrematistike*).[14] To obtain wealth simply through mercantile exchange value (*chrema*), amassing monetary gain as an objective in and for itself, was "unnatural," because it "is not productive of goods ... the end is sheer increase" for its own sake. And further, while unnaturally increasing their own wealth, creditors drive their debtors into poverty, reducing large numbers of citizens to debt bondage and stripping away their means of self-support and hence ability to procreate.

The destructively selfish wealth-and-power ethic

Along with admonishing the aim of purely monetary gain (the taking of interest) as unnatural, Aristotle saw wealth addiction (*pleonexia*) and hubris as characterized by creditors living on interest paid out of other people's effort and product, and being averse to getting their own hands dirty.

Aristophanes' *Ecclesiazusae* ("Women in Parliament," written in 391 BC) depicts women taking control of the government to ban private wealth and promote equal pay and similar equality, claiming that after

---

[13] Plato, *Republic* 8 at 555d-556b (Jowett translation).

[14] Lowry 1987:230-232 notes: "The whole profit-motivated market process which we now call the 'economy' was regarded by Aristotle as *chrematistics* and *external* to his *oikonomia*. His political economy was directed to an analysis of the management and satisfaction of the needs of the household and state and not to the study of a market oriented toward profit maximization." Modern economics shields its eyes from the predatory behavior of wealth. It views the profit motive as leading to economic equilibrium, not destabilizing society as a result of wealth addiction.

all, they do most of the work. The character Blepyros expresses the hope that theft will disappear once citizens are provided with life's necessities and the means of self-support.

But a Wealthy Man appears and urges that the new laws be ignored. Attending a feast at which the invitees are expected to contribute food, he brings nothing, and tries to persuade others to adopt his anti-social attitude. The play proceeds to describe how the oligarchic character flaw of wealth addiction prevents poverty from being eradicated. "Prosperity did not actually stop the wealthy from stealing more and more; on the contrary, they proved to be the biggest thieves,"[15] paraphrases one commentator. As long as the tendency for money-wealth to be addictive and socially destructive remains, "preventing highway robbery by removing the problems of hunger and cold, cannot ... be a panacea for social ills."[16]

Characterizing protectors of debtors as "tyrants"

In practice, the seemingly moderate advice of Aeschylus: "Not a life of anarchy nor the rule of tyranny: take the middle way endowed by gods" (*Eumenides,* lines 696-699, 458 BC) meant leaving the wealthy with their privileges and power. The "middle way" always meant "don't give democracy too much." Although criticizing the destructive behavior of creditors, Plato and Aristotle considered debt cancellation and land redistribution to be the program of tyrants seeking power by pandering to the intemperate mobocracy (*ochlocracy*) of the poor, ending up falling subject to the same hubris as the wealth-addicted rich. Deeming the poor the "worst classes" (*kakoi*), Plato had Socrates say: "Wherever you see beggars in a city, there are somewhere concealed thieves and cut-purses and temple robbers and similar experts in crime" (*Republic* 8 at 552d).

Aristotle followed suit, writing that citizenship should be limited to the well-to-do leisure class, excluding craftsmen, most of whom were metics or freedmen.[17] He endorsed Solon's Athenian constitution pre-

---

[15] *Ecclesiazusae,* lines 608 and 667-668, cited in David 1984:12. Elsewhere in the play Praxagora asks, "Where did the lender get the money from in the first place ... Obviously, he's a thief!"

[16] David 1984:11-12, citing Aristotle, *Politics* 6.5 at 1320a, with a further discussion.

[17] Sagstetter 2013:64 points out that Plato "claimed that 'work' crushed souls and deformed bodies" (*Republic* 6 at 495d-e). Aristotle (*Politics* 6 at 1328b-1329a) wrote: "The citizen must not lead the life of mechanics or tradesman, for such a life is ignoble and an enemy of virtue. Neither must they be farmers, since leisure is necessary both for the development of virtue and the performance of political duties."

scribing that the leading lawmakers be chosen from among the wealthiest landowners, assuming that their interest would lie in preserving a prosperous and well-balanced body politic. Productivity was not yet sufficiently advanced to support all citizens in the comfort and leisure necessary to enable them to participate in time-consuming management of public affairs (and military practice).[18] It thus was necessary to have some citizens specializing and experienced in civic management. But the assumption that the wealthiest landowners would act to preserve a prosperous and socially balanced polis was inconsistent with Plato's and Aristotle's own critique of *pleonexia*.

What stood in the way of creating a less selfish, more fair and resilient economy was the oligarchic *rentier* class, to which these landowners belonged and whose worldview Plato and Aristotle themselves characterized as one of wealth addiction and hubris. Plato's and Aristotle's students came from this class and hardly could be expected to want its wealth and privileges curtailed or taken from their own families. Oligarchies from Athens and Sparta to Rome blocked public policies aiming to save society at large from being injured by debt and land monopolization.

Socrates debates how wealth corrupts politics

Book 1 of Plato's *Republic* centers on a debate between Socrates and Thrasymachus about how the strong rule over the weak. Their discussion posed Western civilization's most important political question. If rulers are drawn from the class of large landholders and creditors, aspiring to monopolize economic gains for themselves and their class at the expense of the citizens they govern, how can they be prevented from abusing their control of government to impoverish society?

Socrates' ideal is for legislators to be like good craftsmen: Just as doctors or sea captains seek the well-being of their patients or crew, public officials are supposed to promote the welfare of society as a whole.[19] But Thrasymachus points out that:

---

[18] Moore 1975:147 and 150, citing *Ath. Pol.* 2.5 and Fustel de Coulanges, and noting: "That is why Spartans left the mean or mechanical trades to the *perioikoi*."

[19] Duplouy and Brock 2018 point out that Aristotle (*Politics* 3 at 1279a-b) said that although well-run states were those that had the welfare of their citizens at heart, rulers tended to act in their own interest. "The correct (*orthai*) forms of government are those which have the welfare of the governed at heart, whereas those who aim only at the rulers' good are 'deviations' (*parekbaseis*)." But *rentier* oligarchies were inherently self-centered and exploitative. That was the norm, not a "deviation," given the dominance of such oligarchies in classical antiquity.

injustice, on a grand enough scale, is superior to justice in strength and freedom and autocratic power; and 'right' ... means simply what serves the interest of the stronger party. ... in every case the laws are made by the ruling party in its own interest; a democracy makes democratic laws, a despot autocratic ones, and so on. By making these laws they define as 'right' for their subjects whatever is for their own interest, and they call anyone who breaks them a 'wrongdoer' and punish him accordingly.[20]

Socrates defends his ideal:

The physician, as such, studies only the patient's interest, not his own. ... the business of the physician, in the strict sense, is not to make money for himself, but to exercise his power [to heal] the patient's body. The ship's captain, again considered strictly as no mere sailor but in command of the crew, will study and enjoin the interest of his subordinates, not his own. ... And so with government of any kind: no ruler, in so far as he is acting as ruler, will study or enjoin what is for his own interest. All that he says and does will be said and done with a view to what is good and proper for the subject for whom he practices his art.

But this ideal is turned upside down in practice, Thrasymachus replies:

You imagine that a herdsman studies the interests of his flocks or cattle, tending and fattening them up with some other end in view than his master's profit or his own. So you don't see that in politics, the genuine ruler regards his subjects exactly like sheep, and thinks of nothing else, night and day, but the good he can get out of them for himself.

The reality, he says (*Republic* 1 at 343a-d), is that "to be 'just' means serving the interest of the stronger who rules ... A just man always has the worst of it. Take a private business: when a partnership is wound up, you will never find that the more honest of two partners comes off with the larger share." It is the same with public officials: Dishonest administrators enrich themselves at society's expense. So the unjust become happier than the just. A political system run by the strongest and richest

rewards wrongdoing with supreme welfare and happiness and reduces its victims, if they won't retaliate in kind, to misery. That form is despotism, which uses force or fraud to plunder the goods of others, public or private, sacred or profane, and to do it in a wholesale way. If you are caught committing any one of these crimes on a small scale, you are punished and disgraced. They call it sacrilege, kidnapping, burglary,

---

[20] Plato, *Republic* 1 at 342d-e. I use Cornford's translation, 1941.

theft and brigandage. But if, besides taking their property, you turn all your countrymen into slaves ... your countrymen will call you the happiest of men and bless your name, and so will everyone who hears of such a complete triumph of injustice. (*Republic* 1 at 344a-c)

A double standard is at work. "When people denounce injustice, it is because they are afraid of suffering wrong [as victims], not of doing it."[21]

Socrates accuses democracy of leading to tyranny, as if there were no alternative

Book 8 of the *Republic* is basically a lecture by Socrates about how oligarchy gives way temporarily to democracy, which must end in tyranny and a new oligarchy. He outlines a cyclical view of political stages, with each stage decaying as the class in power acts selfishly and succumbs to hubris (*Republic* 8 at 555a-556a) and the debt issue primarily responsible for the shift from oligarchy (rule by the wealthy few) to tyranny (*Republic* 8 at 566a and 573e).

Socrates starts by explaining how oligarchy arises out of the aristocracy consolidating its political control by establishing a property qualification for office, and using force to prevent laws being enacted to limit its members' power and money-lust. Society bifurcates into two classes, rich and poor, "always conspiring against each other."

The rich fear incorporating poorer citizens in the army, because:

> the poor man, lean and sunburnt, may find himself posted in battle beside one who, thanks to his wealth and indoor life, is panting under his burden of fat and showing every mark of distress. 'Such men,' he will think, 'are rich because we are cowards'; and when he and his friends meet in private, the word will go round: 'These men are no good: they are at our mercy.' (*Republic* 8 at 556e)

In addition, Socrates elaborates, "their fondness for money makes the wealthy unwilling to pay taxes." They take land from the less affluent, whom they reduce to a pauperized class, "neither trader, nor artisan, nor horseman, nor hoplite, but only poor, helpless creatures. ... the drone and pauper element in the state." The ruling class even devours its own members, foreclosing on their land and disenfranchising them, this occurring as spendthrift youths who have inherited property lose their

---

[21] Henry Fielding drew the same moral in the first full-length English-language novel, *The History of the Adventures of Joseph Andrews and of his Friend Mr. Abraham Adams* (1742): "Nobody scarce doth any good, yet they all agree in praising those who do. ... All rail at wickedness, and all are as eager to be what they abuse."

estates to creditors, who walk around "pretending not even to see those whom they have already ruined."

To avert this "negligence and encouragement of licentiousness in oligarchies" by creditors inserting the parasitic "sting of their money into any of the remainder who do not resist" (*Republic* 8 at 555d-556b), Socrates suggests a law "commanding that most voluntary contracts should be at the contractor's risk." Debtors who could not pay would have their debts forgiven, as creditors would bear the risk of the debtor's inability to pay. That was as close as Socrates got to picking up the point he had made in Book 1: that it would be wrong to pay debts to creditors who would use the money in destructive ways, reducing the citizenry to debt dependency and stripping away their land.

Obliging creditors to bear the risk had long been the norm in trade financing. From Mesopotamia to Greece and Rome, mercantile lending to shippers accepted the basic principle of creditors sharing in the risk of the debtor's inability to pay. Creditors and investors lost when a ship sank. That made trade financing basically a form of maritime insurance. (Chapter 13 describes the frauds that Roman shippers developed to abuse this principle.) But there was no similar law obliging creditors to share in the risk of non-payment of agrarian credit. Creditors were permitted to foreclose on the property of their debtors. Socrates warned that this financial threat left the people (*demos*) to "conspire against the acquirers of their estates and the rest of the citizens, and be eager for revolution."

Not expecting Greek ruling elites to enact his proposals, Socrates outlined the political dynamic that Aristotle described in Book 5 of *Politics*: Some aristocrats would seek power over rivals by "taking the multitude into their camp." Younger members of the ruling oligarchy, especially those from less affluent branches who had run into debt, were most likely to lead such a revolution.

However, Socrates warned, a democratic city was one in which "a thirst for liberty gets bad cupbearers for its leaders and is intoxicated by drinking too deep of that unmixed wine," a frequent metaphor for the "immoderate" policies of cancelling debts and redistributing land.[22] Expressing his contempt for democracy's "anarchic temper," he concluded: "The climax of popular liberty is when the slave bought with money, male or female, is just as free as his or her purchaser; nor must I forget

---

[22] Pseudo-Demosthenes 17.15 (ca. 336 BC) mentions debt cancellation, confiscations of property, land distribution and liberation of slaves as the typical revolutionary program threatening Greek oligarchies. Cited in Cecchet 2017:131.

to tell of the liberty and equality of the two sexes in relation to each other" (*Republic* 8 at 562a-568a).

Socrates thus shared the prejudice of his Athenian students and friends in characterizing advocates of cancelling debts or limiting land-holdings as incipient tyrants. Leaders claiming to "protect the people" would pander to the intemperate tastes of democratic mobs and become hubristic, succumbing to luxurious feasting, drinking and "insatiate lust for wealth and the neglect of everything else for the sake of money-making." The poor are too impatient to elect moderate public servants, and back a tyrant whose own ambition would lead him to consolidate his power by persecuting his opponents. "Some he kills and others he banishes, at the same time hinting at the abolition of debts and partition of lands ... At first, in the early days of his power, he is full of smiles ... liberating debtors, and distributing land to the people and his followers. ... But when he has disposed of foreign enemies by conquest or treaty and there is nothing to fear from them, then he is always stirring up some war or other in order that the people may require a leader."

Socrates proposes a new ruling class in his own image, without money or land

Socrates found wealth addiction to be the underlying explanation for bad economic relations. The *Republic*'s discussion is thus primarily about how ideal rulership is prevented by the reality that leaders are chosen from the most powerful families, and hence are most prone to be corrupted by money-lust, especially in the case of creditors seeking wealth at the expense of society at large.

The excesses that Socrates saw among the richest Athenians seem to have led him to renounce wealth-seeking himself. Plato's *Apology* reports that at his trial Socrates stated that he considered money-making and property a waste his time, diverting him from being useful. He did not accept payment from his students, expressing disdain for the heavy fees that Sophists charged. As he explained (Xenophon, *Memorabilia of Socrates* 1.13): "It is common opinion among us in regard to beauty and wisdom that there is an honorable and a shameful way of bestowing them. For to offer one's beauty for money to all comers is called prostitution. ... So is it with wisdom. Those who offer it to all comers for money are known as sophists, prostitutors of wisdom."

Aristophanes (*Clouds*, lines 103-104) characterizes Socrates as a "barefoot vagabond" and Plato's *Phaedrus* (229) likewise describes him as always going about barefoot. Xenophon (*Memorabilia* 1.2-5 and 1.10) records the prosperous Antiphon as bewildered by the fact that Socrates's "meat and drink are of the poorest: the cloak you wear is not only a poor thing, but is never changed summer or winter; and you never wear shoes or tunic. Besides you refuse to take money, the mere getting of which is a joy, while its possession makes one more independent and happier."

Socrates replies that, "because I refuse to take it, I am not obliged to talk with anyone against my will." He concludes: "You seem, Antiphon, to imagine that happiness consists in luxury and extravagance. But my belief is that to have no wants is divine; to have as few as possible comes next to the divine." Socrates explains that he is rich (*ploutein*) in real wealth, which he defines as satisfaction with what he has.

Conversely, Socrates explains, wealthy people are "poor" because their money-addiction makes them feel hungry for more as money becomes an end in itself instead of serving its "natural" function to facilitate exchange. He describes his extravagant friend Critobulus as actually being poorer, if one defines wealth as satisfaction with what one has.

> Socrates: I certainly think I have no need of more money and am rich enough. But you seem to me to be quite poor, Critobulus, and at times, I assure you, I feel quite sorry for you.
>
> Critobulus (laughing): And how much, pray, would your property fetch at a sale, do you suppose, Socrates, and how much would mine?
>
> Socrates: Well, if I found a good buyer, I think the whole of my goods and chattels, including the house, might readily sell for five minae [about $100]. Yours, I feel sure, would fetch more than a hundred times that sum.
>
> Critobulus: And in spite of that estimate, you really think you have no need of money and pity me for my poverty?
>
> Socrates: Yes, because my property is sufficient to satisfy my wants, but I don't think you would have enough to keep up the style you are living in and to support your reputation, even if your fortune were three times what it is.[23]

Considering money-love to be the lowest part of the soul (*Republic* 9 at 581c-d), Socrates contrasts the pleasure of lovers of economic gain to that of lovers of wisdom (philosophers) or of military victory: "The financier will affirm that in comparison with profit, the pleasures of honor or of learning are of no value except in so far as they produce money." But philosophers and public-spirited men "regard the pleasure that comes from money as vulgar and low ... [for] the lover of gain is under no neces-

---

[23] Xenophon, *Oeconomica* 2.2-4, translated by R. C. Marchant (1929).

sity of tasting or experiencing the sweetness of the pleasure of learning the true natures of things."

Socrates's logic was that oligarchy corrupts the personal moral values of the wealthy by unleashing the addictive and anti-social dynamic of greed, a lust that becomes compulsive and impoverishes the rest of society. By embracing greed and promoting a false view of how economies and societies actually function, the oligarchic worldview leads to behavior that tends to polarize society instead of promoting prosperity. The drive for monetary gain is inherently short-term on the broad social scale. It is not sustainable but ends eventually in a crisis.

Socrates elaborated his own self-imposed poverty into the political ideal of a ruling class of Guardians who would live like him and reject wealth. To keep them immune from being sucked into the vortex of wealth addiction, he proposed that they be banned from having gold or silver coinage or ornaments. "In the first place, none must possess any private property save for the indispensable ... Secondly, none must have any habitation or treasure house that is not open for all to enter at will" (*Republic* 3 at 416d).

To compensate for their not being allowed to own substantial property or money, Socrates recommended that the Guardians would "receive an agreed stipend from the other citizens as the wages of their guardianship, so measured that there shall be neither superfluity at the end of the year nor any lack." Their diet would be organized like Sparta's *syssitia* meals, "a common mess like soldiers on campaign ... in such quantities as are needful for athletes of war, sober and brave."

Plato's *Laws* (5 at 736c-737a) adopts this emphasis on personal abstinence. The main foundation of the security of a state "consists in renouncing avarice by the aid of justice." Specifically, a "rule of moderation" was to be based on the principle "that poverty consists not in decreasing one's substance but in increasing one's greed."[24]

> Just as we said that the colony of the Heraclidae was fortunate in avoiding fierce and dangerous strife concerning the distribution of land and money and the cancelling of debts (so we are similarly lucky); for when a State is obliged to settle such strife by law, ... no way is left save what one might term that of "pious aspiration" and cautious change,

---

[24] Plato disdained charging interest and usury (*Laws* 5 at 742c) and urged minimizing the role of money, as Sparta did. He only endorsed interest charges as penalty fees on broken civic contracts with craftsmen, "one obol on each drachma for every month of arrears; and actions for these cases shall take place before the tribal courts" (*Laws* 11 at 921b-d).

little by little, extended over a long period. ... there must already exist a supply of men to effect the change, who themselves, on each occasion, possess abundance of land and have many persons in their debt, and who are kind enough to wish to give a share of these things to those of them who are in want, partly by remissions and partly by distributions.

This was accepted as the "political correctness" of the time. Realizing the political prejudices of the Academy's students, Socrates and Plato limited their discussion to explaining why wealth addiction led to bad public policy. Describing himself as a gadfly, giving his own kind of "sting" once and a while to spur philosophical discussion, Socrates's perspective was that of a critical outsider. After warning that usury and money-love injured society, Socrates stopped short of concrete reforms to limit their current abuses. To have advocated outright debt cancellation, as Sparta's Agis IV and Cleomenes III would do in the late 3rd century BC, would have seemed abhorrent to most well-to-do Athenians. Yet the ideal of a ruling class without property and money of its own was so unrealistic as to be a harmless threat to the status quo.

By blaming populist leaders for bad policies, Socrates sidestepped the point that Peter Brunt has made with regard to Rome's civil war (133 to 27 BC): "Perhaps no *populares*, at least after the Gracchi, were sincere; perhaps all sought only to satisfy their ambition or that of their leader. But again, their personal motives, which it may be hard to determine, are less significant than the real grievances and genuine discontents on which they could play."[25] Like most of their aristocratic contemporaries, Socrates and Plato show disdain for populist reformers seeking to cancel debts. To the *rentier* oligarchy, the "demos" did not mean all citizens ("all native males, irrespective of class"), but just the lower classes. That was a snobbish distinction, however, only "drawn by critics or opponents of democracy, not by democrats themselves."[26]

Socrates let himself be condemned to death by Athenians who resented the fact that his students and adherents at Plato's academy were wealthy aristocrats, including members of the pro-Spartan oligarchy of the Thirty, most notably Critias (first cousin of Plato) and Charmides (Plato's uncle) who led the dominant aristocratic faction.[27] Socrates did not protest that these aristocrats were the opposite of the kind of

---

[25] Brunt 1971a:95.

[26] Ober 2007:94.

[27] I. F. Stone's 1988 book *The Trial of Socrates* surveys the conservative aristocratic leanings of Socrates to explain the democratic motivations in bringing him to trial.

Guardians he advocated. They were precisely like his critic Thrasyma-chus accused them of being at the outset of the *Republic*, using power to support their own narrow self-interest.

The economically destructive rule of oligarchies became increasingly evident as Greece and Rome succumbed to debt crises and oligarchic military attacks against democracies from the 4th century BC onward. When Sparta's kings finally sought to cancel debts, Greek oligarchies called on Rome to defeat the effort – and Rome went on to destroy Greece and Macedonia and turn them into subject tribute-paying provinces.

8
Agis, Cleomenes and Nabis Cancel Sparta's Debts, 3rd Century BC

W. W. Tarn described the Hellenistic Age – the three centuries spanning the death of Alexander the Great in 323 to the future Augustus's Battle of Actium in 31 BC – as "a prosperous time for the upper classes in most places" but with the lower classes "definitely worse off." Art and drama, trade and fine cuisine flourished, but wages were down and prices were rising, especially for food and housing. The gulf between rich and poor widened as indebtedness rose and land passed into the hands of the wealthy. "Underneath the brilliant civilization of the third century lies the fear of social revolution ... a rising of the 'have-nots' against the 'haves' to the cry of division of the land and cancellation of debts. Debt in fact was often at the bottom of the whole business."[1]

Macedonia's oligarchic Corinthian League put down repeated uprisings aiming at debt and land reform on the islands of Naxos, Amorgos, Ceos and Syros during 280-250. And on the Greek mainland,

> at Athens the jurymen had for centuries taken an oath not to vote for division of land or cancellation of debts; the threat colors many passages in Aristotle; Isocrates had said bluntly that men feared their fellow-citizens more than a foreign enemy. But with the advent of Macedonia, precautions had been substituted for fears. In the treaties made in 335 between Alexander and the States of the League of Corinth it was provided that the Council of the League and Alexander's representative were to see to it that in no city of the League should there be either confiscation of personal property, or division of land, or cancellation of debt, or liberation of slaves for the purpose of revolution. We have here both the complete programme of the social revolution under four heads, and an interstate guarantee against it; if revolution breaks out in any city it is to be repressed by the full force of Macedonia and the Panhellenic League.[2]

---

[1] Tarn 1923:112, 115, 117, 108 and 127.

[2] Tarn 1923:127-128. The Corinthian League (sometimes called the [Pan-]Hellenic League) was created by Philip II of Macedon in 338 to coordinate his war against

In contrast to the Near East's abundance of family archives preserved on clay tablets, we lack records of Greek land transfers, marriage contracts and wills that would enable us to quantify the buildup of debt that led to popular calls for reform. Public records from this period are also sparse, but a decree survives "from 306, in honor of Antigonus I, cancelling all non-sacred debts on the island of Ios. ... In the early third century, all the citizens of Itanos on Crete swore an oath not to cancel debts."[3]

Aeneas Tacticus's *On the Defense of Fortified Positions* (ca. 356 to 350 BC) reflects the debt problem that was worsening. He advised generals to secure a city's loyalty by winning over "debtors by a reduction or complete cancellation of interest, and, especially in cases of danger, of some part of the principal, or even all of it when necessary." His modern translator notes: "More than half his military admonitions are directed towards preventing treachery and forestalling revolution. The men for whom he wrote his manual were clearly in constant danger of the enemy within their own gates, a peril which became more rather than less acute when armed foes without were threatening the very existence of the state."[4]

Mikhail Rostovtzeff has summarized the debt strains that were gaining momentum from Athens and Sparta to Rome:

> The war-cry was the immemorial one of redistribution of land and abolition of debts. ... In the fourth century the fear of a social revolution was constantly present to the minds of Aristotle and Isocrates, and in 335 the league of Corinth formed a sort of association for protection against it. It is significant of conditions in Greece during the third century and later that a clause forbidding the redistribution of land and the cancellation of debts was introduced into the oath of the citizens of Itana in Crete.[5]

Persia. Macedonia's Antigonus III Doson (229-221) revived the League to fight against Sparta in 224.

[3] Millett 1991:252, citing IG xii 5.168 for Ios and SIG4 526.21-24 for Itanos. He adds: "An undated anecdote preserved by Aelian (*Varia Historia* xiv.24) describes murderous attacks on their creditors in Corinth and Mytilene (the consensus is for a fourth-century date)."

[4] Aeneas Tacticus, *On the Defense of Fortified Positions*, Chapter 14.

[5] Rostovtzeff 1926:2.

Sparta's debt crisis

The crisis was most acute in Sparta, which had become the most polar-ized oligarchy in Greece by ca. 250. The influx of booty and monetary tribute following its victory over Athens in 404 had catalyzed the concentration of wealth as land became subject to market forces. As helots defected, labor had to be hired and food paid for. *Syssitia* arrears mounted up, reducing poorer citizens to the status of impoverished "Inferiors," forcing them to sell their land to the wealthy (see Chapter 3).

With these poorer citizens unable to maintain their status as *homoioi* as their land was burdened with mortgage debts (*klaria*), only about seven hundred full citizens were left with *kleros* land and able to pay their *syssitia* food contributions, shrinking the citizen-army accordingly. Plutarch describes the wealthiest hundred families as owning most of the land.[6] His biographies of Agis IV, Cleomenes III, Nabis and the Achaean commander Aratus describe the widespread calls for debt cancellation and redistribution of land over the last half of the 3rd century BC.[7]

Plutarch's faith in a golden age of Spartan equality obliged him to explain how its land had become concentrated in so few hands. He blamed a single individual in the early 4th century, the ephor Epitadeus, "headstrong and of a violent temper." To avoid having to bequeath his *kleros* lot to his son, Epitadeus supposedly introduced a rhetra law per-mitting Spartans to give their land to anyone they might choose. This

> satisfied a private grudge of his own ... but his fellow citizens welcomed it out of greed, made it valid, and so destroyed the most excellent of institutions. For the men of power and influence at once began to acquire estates without scruple, ejecting the rightful heirs from their inheritances; and speedily wealth streamed into the hands of a few and poverty ruled the polis.[8]

Citing Herodotus, Hodkinson shows that "the right of gift supposedly introduced by Epitadeus was already in operation at the time of the accession of King Agesilaos II" in 398, catalyzed by the inflow of money after Sparta's victory over Athens, and then by the loss of Spartan land when Messenia became independent after 369.[9] Plutarch (or his source,

---

[6] See David 1981:152-153.

[7] These sources have received scholarly analysis by Miltiadis Michalopoulos (2016), following the books by Pavel Oliva (1971) and Benjamin Shimron (1972).

[8] Plutarch, *Agis* 5.2-3.

[9] Hodkinson 2000:90-91 and 424-425 summarizes the recent scholarship. See also Schütrumpf 1987. Hodkinson noted later (2018:43) that: "Landowners could

Phylarchus) seems to have made up the story of Epitadeus, whose "very name means literally someone 'who acts in his own interests,' and the character Epitadeus is credited correspondingly with having proposed a bill to satisfy his personal interests. Mythical or fictive characters often have a name in line with their acts."[10]

Aristotle (*Politics* 1270a18-21) pointed out that the presumed loosening of Sparta's "ancestral constitution" to permit owners to cloak the sale of land as a gift or to bequeath it freely (with the purchase price deemed to be a gift, and land reciprocated as a counter-gift) "inevitably leads to the same result as if it had been allowed to come into the market," namely, forced sales and forfeitures of land. He also blamed the large dowries given to Spartan girls for the concentration of female land ownership. Plutarch wrote that by the mid-3rd century, propertied women owned 40 percent of Spartan land as a result of remaining unmarried or becoming widows.[11]

"The only possible salvation for Sparta" once it lost its foreign tribute, concluded Toynbee, was "a social revolution,"[12] and specifically a debt cancellation. In Sparta, as in the Near East, this was advocated by palace rulers, not by populists. But as was the case elsewhere in Greece, the oligarchy stood firm and used violence to prevent this.

Agis IV seeks to redistribute land and cancel debts

Matters came to a head with the struggle between Leonidas II (254-235) and his young co-king Agis IV (245-241), whose mother and grandmother were said to be members of Sparta's wealthiest family. Agis's ambition was to restore Sparta to its former power and replenish its hoplite army. To do this, he recognized, it was necessary to cancel the *klaria* mortgage debts and endow new citizens with new plots of their own.

Younger Spartans supported Agis, as did the "Inferiors" who had lost their right to qualify to vote. Less affluent Spartan *homoioi* were falling into arrears while wealthy Spartans were investing their growing supply of silver in loans to well-to-do Spartans borrowing to buy the land being

---

also disinherit their natural heirs, wholly or partially, by passing on their landed property to a third party through lifetime gifts or testamentary bequests." Selling one's land, however, was viewed as dishonorable.

[10] Nafissi 2018:110.

[11] Hodkinson 2000:439. Hodkinson 2000:98 disputes the validity of Plutarch's claim "that Lycurgus had prohibited the giving of dowries, since large dowries had also contributed to the unequal redistribution of land."

[12] Toynbee 1913:259.

sold under distress conditions. Many wealthy citizens also saw the need for reform. One of them, Lysandros, was elected chief ephor in 243/2, and sponsored Agis's plan to divide Laconia's land into 4,500 inalienable lots for citizens, and another 15,000 carved out from neighboring territory to incorporate *perioikoi* and other appropriate foreigners into Sparta's army. To clear the slate for vesting this self-support land and restoring Sparta's archaic *syssitia* messes so Spartans could live like they supposedly had done in an idealized Lycurgan epoch, Lysandros proposed to cancel all debts.[13]

This seems to be the first time that debt appears in the documented discussion of Sparta's economy and its polarization. Leonidas backed the families and the women who had inherited large estates in opposing this land redistribution. The 28-member *gerousia*, composed of the wealthiest citizens, rejected the proposal in a narrow vote. But Agis and his supporters gained support from an oracle in a temple located on *perioikoi* land, and convened the popular assembly, where he backed his reforms by promising to donate his own land to the city, along with 600 talents of silver. His wealthy friends and their relatives followed suit with their own land.

Leonidas accused Agis of aiming to establish a personal tyranny, with the aid of mercenaries and *perioikoi* to be given land (Plutarch, *Agis* 7.5). He also claimed that the proposal was contrary to the laws of Lycurgus, whom he said had not cancelled debts or included foreigners in Sparta's political body. Agis replied that a debt cancellation was implicit in the Lycurgan abolition of foreign money – assuming that borrowing or arrears would have had to be monetized, not simply owed in crops or cast iron.[14]

Other opponents of Leonidas accused him of having lived at the Seleucid court in Asia Minor for many years and falling under foreign influence by marrying a Lydian wife who bore him two sons. (She claimed to be the daughter of the region's ruler, Alexander's Macedonian general Seleucis I Nicator.) Leonidas tried to turn the tables by accusing Agis of following foreign philosophers whose ideology was alien to Sparta. But he was attacked and was obliged to take refuge in a temple.

---

[13] Plutarch, *Agis* 8. Flower 2002:196 adds that this plan "was eventually carried out by Cleomenes (Plutarch, *Cleomenes* 11), who created a citizen body of 4,000 men. It is hardly coincidental that in Plutarch's life of Lycurgus (8.16) we find the statement that Lycurgus himself had made a similar distribution, even if the original number of lots was a matter of dispute." See Stewart 2018:391 for a discussion.

[14] Plutarch, *Agis* 10 describes this debate.

When new ephors were elected for the administrative year 242/1, they ruled that the proposal by Lysandros and Mandrokleidas (another supporter of Agis) to cancel debts and redistribute the land was illegal. The reformers protested that ephors never had been given authority to oppose kings. But of course, that was precisely their role – at least, to block kings from acting against the oligarchy. Ephors often had blocked any alliance between Sparta's kings and the elected *gerousia* to reform the Spartan laws in ways not deemed to be in the oligarchy's interest.[15] They freed Leonidas from the temple, but the ephor Lysander claimed to have seen an astronomical omen against him. Leonidas went into exile, yielding the throne to his son-in-law Cleombrotus II (whose reign turned out to be very brief, 242-241).

Seeing that the only way to enact his program was by force, Agis gathered his supporters and marched into the market place with the new king Cleombrotus, "removed the ephors from their seats, and appointed others in their stead," including his uncle Agesilaus, a large landowner. "Then they armed a large body of young men and set free all who were in prison, thus striking fear into their opponents, who thought they would put many of them to death. Agis then burned the records of debts and mortgages (*klaria*) in Sparta's agora."[16]

At this juncture Agis was persuaded by Agesilaus to accept a fatal compromise. The uncle had bought much property on credit, and was glad to sponsor a debt cancellation. He convinced Agis that this alone would be the easiest way to introduce his program, leaving land redistribution for later. But delaying the land reform weakened support from Sparta's population who wanted land, especially the "Inferiors" and *perioikoi*. Burning the *klaria* mortgage records helped indebted absentee owners such as Agesilaus, but most owners did not want to see their holdings given away.

---

[15] Oliva 1971:125-132 notes that the list of ephors began around 753 with five members, elected annually. The ephor Chilon (556/5) played a major role in establishing their power to overshadow that of the kings, ostensibly to make sure that Sparta's kings would keep their oath to preserve the existing laws, not introduce reforms. Chilon maneuvered against tyrant-reformers in Sicyon, and helped found the Peloponnesian League to oppose democratic reforms and Athenian leadership.

[16] Plutarch, *Agis* 12. It is not clear whether Agis's debt cancellation only annulled mortgages on land or applied to other personal debts as well. Most prisoners were guilty of political protest, or simply of poverty. That would explain why Cleomenes III later freed prisoners in Alexandria at the end of his life.

The resulting discontent saw Agis accused of abandoning his promises, much like what had occurred in Athens after Solon refrained from redistributing land when he cancelled debts. Agis sought to build up his image by leading a military campaign up to the Corinthian Isthmus to support his Achaean League allies in 241. Agesilaus was left in charge of policy at home, where he proclaimed an intercalary month to extend the fiscal year so that he could impose a special tax. That prompted a revolt, and Leonidas was invited back to Sparta to reclaim his throne. He appointed new ephors who opposed reforms threatening the oligarchy.

When Agis reached Corinth, the Achaean *strategos*, Aratus of Sicyon, told him that the fighting was over, and asked him to take his troops home.[17] When Agis returned to Sparta and refused to recant his reforms, the new ephors appointed by Leonidas sentenced him to death. Agis and Cleombrotus sought refuge in a temple, but were lured out and arrested by the ephor Amphares and condemned to prison. Agis's relatives demanded that he be tried before his fellow citizens, but the ephors refused, and Leonidas mobilized troops to keep crowds away from the prison.

Plutarch (*Agis* 19-20) wrote a melodramatic scene of Agis – still only twenty years old – being led away to be strangled. Amphares then let Agis's mother Agesistrate and grandmother Archidamia into the prison, where they were killed. It seems likely that they had used their wealth to support Agis's reform program and had mobilized other families to do so.

Cleombrotus was exiled (joined by his wife Chilonis, Leonidas's daughter). Agesilaus went to Egypt, and Lysandros (who had encouraged Agis's debt cancellation) also went into exile. Agis's brother Archidamos fled to Messenia, leaving Leonidas to rule for six more years, until 235. He sought to solidify his control by marrying off his 18-year old son, Cleomenes III, to Agis's widow Agiatis.

That turned out to be a classic case of unintended consequences after Cleomenes became king in 235.

Cleomenes III (235-222) seeks to complete Agis IV's reforms

Perhaps convinced by his wife, Cleomenes adopted her former husband's reform program. At some point he invited the Stoic teacher Sphairos of Borysthenes to Sparta. Sphairos is said to have studied under Zeno of

---

[17] Plutarch, *Agis* 14-15. Stewart 2018:392 says that Aratus "appears to have been alarmed at the overtly communal features of Agis's regime, and perhaps feared the spread of his ideas to the poleis of his Achaean League."

Citeum, whose ideal republic was an egalitarian utopia, with men and women dressing alike and living in Spartan austerity.[18]

Militarily, Sparta was challenged by Megalopolis on its northern border. Founded in 371 by a group of Arcadian villages after Sparta had lost to the Thebans at Leuctra, it became Arcadia's first large urban town. In the year Cleomenes became king it joined the Achaean League against Sparta. The League's army was commanded by Aratus, who was seeking hegemony over the southern Peloponnese.

The ephors asked Cleomenes to secure the border area against Megalopolis in 229, six years into his reign, and he mobilized troops to prepare for what became known as the Cleomenean War against the Achaean League, 229-222. That gave him the opportunity to gain acclaim as general, on top of his social reform program to rebuild Sparta's army. His troops defeated those of Aratus at Leuctra, wiped out Achaean garrisons throughout Arcadia, and defeated Achaean resistance at Dyme, forcing the Achaeans to surrender the Acrocorinth citadel on the northern Isthmus, commanding the entry to southern Greece.[19] These victories led Ptolemy III of Egypt to shift his alliance from Macedonia to Sparta as a counterweight to the Achaean League.

Fresh from these victories, Cleomenes led his troops back to Sparta in 227. Seeing that the ephors sought to block his reform plan, he killed four of them along with some of their supporters at their *syssitia* meal. He also consolidated Sparta's dual kingship in his own hands when Agis IV's son, the 13-year-old Eudamidas III (241-228), died. He invited Agis's brother Archidamos to return to Sparta as its second king in 228/7, but Archidamos soon was killed, either by supporters of Cleomenes or by the oligarchy fearing that he was supporting Cleomenes' program.[20]

Earlier kings had challenged the ephors' authority, only to have the leading landholders reassert their dominance. Agis's challenge had

---

[18] Diogenes Laertius, *Lives of the Eminent Philosophers* 2.7. For Sphairos's *Polity of the Lakedaimonians* and related influences, see Michalopoulos 2016.

[19] Michalopoulos 2016:41-58 gives a detailed summary of the Cleomenean War. Aratus was the uncle of Polybius, whose account of Agis and Cleomenes is as negatively biased as that of Plutarch is positive.

[20] Plutarch says that he was killed upon his return to Sparta, but Oliva 1971:274-275 notes that Polybius 5.37 wrote that Archidamos quickly left Sparta upon his first return, but then tried to come back and was killed by Cleomenes. Michalopoulos 2016:27 suggests that he was killed by oligarchic opponents of Agis's reforms who feared that he would form an alliance with Cleomenes.

cost him his life, but Cleomenes proved more successful. He repeated the reformers' claim that early kings had created the ephors merely to serve as deputies, and that he was restoring the ancestral constitution by removing all their seats except one, which he kept for himself. He listed the names of eighty citizens to be exiled, including many prominent *gerousia* members.

Cleomenes then proclaimed his debt cancellation. The earlier act of Agis may have been reversed after Leonidas returned (although the mortgage documents had been burned), and in any case new debts would have accrued. To gain popular support, Cleomenes emulated Agis's populist strategy by donating his own family wealth to a public fund, and "all the rest of the citizens did the same, and the land was parceled out" along Lycurgan lines, establishing 4,000 *kleroi* lots (500 fewer than Agis had proposed), with 15,000 for *perioikoi*.[21] Cleomenes even assigned lots to the families he had exiled, promising that they could return once the new constitution was firmly established.

The program was radical, and as Flower has noted: "If Agis and Cleomenes wanted their reforms to be acceptable and effective, they had to be attributed to Lycurgus. Their system of land tenure was so unprecedented that even historical continuity had to be invented."[22] Although Cleomenes wanted to equally apportion movable property as well as land, "so as to do away completely with all inequality and disparity,"[23] he found too much resistance to redistribute ownership of such property, so he demurred.

Cleomenes sought to give citizenship to *perioikoi* supporters, as Agis had sought to do, and recruited impoverished *hypomeiones* and even mercenaries into Sparta's army to mobilize enough soldiers to embark on a new war against the north, quickly defeating Argos and much of the Argolid. The Achaean commander Aratus asked Macedonia's king Antigonus III Doson (229-221) for support, warning that Cleomenes was urging cities to "abolish wealth" by seizing land from the oligarchies.[24] The next year, in 226, Mantinea's citizens indeed asked Cleomenes to free their city from Achaean control. He drove the Achaeans out, but

---

[21] See Plutarch, *Cleomenes*, 10.6 and 18.2 for his debt cancellation, and 11.1 for his land redistribution.

[22] Flower 2002:200-202.

[23] Plutarch, *Lycurgus* 9.1 and *Apophthegmata Laconica* (Lycurgus).

[24] Plutarch, *Cleomenes* 16.5-6 blames the nobility's pro-creditor prejudice for Aratus's stance.

"restored to them their [former] laws and constitution," appointing local oligarchic leaders instead of reformers to act as his proxies.[25]

Pressing north in 225, he attacked Aratus's base in Sicyon without success, but then conquered Argos and moved on to Corinth, supported by rebels advocating a Spartan-style debt cancellation. The city surrendered to Cleomenes, and a crowd gathered to turn Aratus over to him, however the commander managed to escape on horseback.

After confiscating Aratus's property in Corinth, Cleomenes invaded Sicyon, trapping Aratus there in the spring of 224. With the Achaean League on the verge of collapse as cities seemed about to defect, Aratus saw that his only hope was to make a deal with the League's traditional rival Macedonia, led by Antigonus. Aratus turned the fort at Acrocorinth over to Antigonus and paid Macedonia a military subsidy.

Like Agis, Cleomenes wanted to restore Sparta's legendary strength. But its former power had been achieved by conquering foreign territory and oppressing helots, and that state of affairs could not be reinstated. He was able to provide democratic rights and egalitarian "Lycurgan" practices only to a small portion of the population, not even to the *perioikoi*. Most seriously, he did not turn the war against the Achaean League and Macedonia into a social war to free their populations from debt and redistribute the land. Instead of winning cities over to his side by inciting a region-wide social and economic revolution, Cleomenes aimed only at reviving Sparta's own military dominance.[26] Outside of Sparta, the Argive population became disgruntled with Cleomenes, because he "had not brought about the abolition of debts which they expected."[27]

Antigonus III Doson defeats Cleomenes and re-installs Sparta's exiled oligarchy

Later in 224, Antigonus mounted a force of 20,000 infantry and 1,300 cavalry to relieve Sicyon, driving Cleomenes back to Sparta, regain-

---

[25] Plutarch, *Cleomenes* 14.1. See Shimron 1972:45-46 and Michalopoulos 2016:203.

[26] Oliva 1971:258 comments that in neighboring Peloponnesian cities, the poor "seem to have thought, at first, that Cleomenes would free them from their wearisome dependence on landlords and usurers, that he would cancel their debts and give them land. ... but they soon realized that the Spartan king was pursuing only his own goals, political and military."

[27] Plutarch, *Cleomenes* 20.3. Michalopoulos 2016:50 and 203, fn171, and Walbank 1982:468: "there is not the slightest reference regarding the implementation of any social reforms in any city under Kleomenes' control, while there is strong evidence of the opposite: when in 226, with the help of the Mantineians, he won the city from the Achaean League he simply assigned to it its old regime."

ing control of Argos and taking away much of Sparta's territory in the southern Peloponnese. Cleomenes dug in by building defensive walls around Sparta for the first time in its history, and restored the *agoge* military training along with the common *syssitia* meals. He also raised funds to hire mercenaries by selling helots their freedom for five Athenian minas each. Monetizing economic life evidently had enabled helots to sell their crops for the money with which to buy their liberty. Plutarch reports that 6,000 helots did so, paying *in toto* some 500 talents of silver – to the government, not to their Spartan masters. A reported 2,000 joined Sparta's army, enabling Cleomenes to muster about 20,000 fighting men, including *perioikoi*, mercenaries and allies.

In May 223, Cleomenes sought to seize Megalopolis, but failed. Antigonus besieged Tegea and then looted Mantinea, selling its population as slaves or killing them, and then renamed the city Antigoneia. This barbarity was unprecedented and disturbed other Greeks, and Aratus's opponents blamed him for inviting in the Macedonians.[28] And indeed, after Macedonia's overwhelming force of 29,000 men destroyed Sparta's army at the fateful Battle of Sellasia in 222, the Achaean region became a dependency of Macedonia. The Achaean cavalry was commanded by Philopoemen, a rising leader from Megalopolis. In 209 he would be named *strategos* of the Achaean League, and later led the fight against Nabis.

Egypt withdrew its support for Cleomenes after Sparta's defeat, but he nonetheless went to the port of Gytheion and sailed to Alexandria.[29] Antigonus re-installed the oligarchic families that Cleomenes had exiled, and restored the ephorate by 220. The *gerousia* reasserted its power, acting in the oligarchy's interest. It seems unlikely that the debts that Cleomenes had cancelled were reinstated, but there may have been an attempt to do so, because a new revolt erupted in 219 (discussed further below), killing the new ephors along with members of Sparta's leading families.

Social revolution and counter-revolution continue throughout Greece

What is known as the Social War in Greece pit Sparta and its Aetolian League allies against Macedonia (220-217). The Aetolian League embarked on "a wave of revolutionary enthusiasm such as Greece had never seen," headed by impoverished debtors.[30] The Megalopolitan

---

[28] Plutarch, *Aratus* 45.4-6. See Michalopoulos 2016:55.

[29] Plutarch, *Cleomenes* 29.3, confirmed by Polybius 2.69.11, discussed by Michalopoulos 2016:73.

[30] Tarn 1961:136-137.

emissary to Macedonia, Cercidas, wrote a poem looking forward to the day when "the greedy rich will sink into poverty, and the poor ... be blessed with a stream of silver."[31] Attacking usurers, the poem complained that Justice (*Dikē*) and Order (*Themis*) seemed not to hear or see the injustices being perpetrated. Where, it asked, are the gods and Nemesis to sweep away the selfish gains that the wealthy have accumulated? A modern translation reads:

> If a man is a turd of a loan-shark, a real old die-for-a-penny
> who squanders it all out again, one who's the death of his fortune,
> why can't God just empty this man of his swine-wealth,
> and give to a thin-feeding, common-bowl cup-dipper
> all the man's damned expenditure? Has the eye of Justice been
> mole-blinded?[32]

The fact that Cercidas had commanded Megalopolis's infantry at Sellasia in 222 shows how deeply the cry for debt cancellation and land redistribution was felt outside of Sparta. Such sentiments prompted the Achaean League to mount a region-wide counter-revolutionary war after Macedonia's king Antigonus Doson died in 222, to be succeeded by the 17-year old Philip V.

The end of Cleomenes in Alexandria

In Egypt, Cleomenes claimed to have attracted a following among the 3,000 Peloponnesians and 1,000 Cretan mercenaries living in Alexandria, and hoped that Ptolemy III would back his return to fight against Macedonia. But Ptolemy died in 222, like his Macedonian adversary Antigonus. His successor, Ptolemy IV Philopator, left Cleomenes to languish under what seems to have been house arrest.

By 220, after pressing for two years for an army and fleet while warfare between Greek oligarchies and democracies gained momentum, Cleomenes saw his only option to be escape. A dozen supporters provided food and wine for his guards, and freed him and his allies to go into the streets and urge people to join them in a march on the jail to free prisoners. But it was locked and guarded, and Cleomenes failed to gain new followers.

Seeing that their cause was hopeless, Cleomenes and twelve of his supporters decided that suicide was the only way out. They died "one

---

[31] Cercidas, Fragment 2, in Knox 1929.

[32] Shipley 2000:184.

after another with their own daggers." When all the others were dead, Cleomenes' closest friend Panteus "pricked him in the ankle and, seeing his face twitch, he kissed him and sat down by his side." He then killed himself over the dead king's body. "Ptolemy ordered that the corpse be hanged on a cross and left exposed to the sight of the Alexandrian mob."[33] That story prompted Arnold Toynbee to depict this end for Cleomenes as a premonition of the Crucifixion, with his defiance of the ephors and accusations that they had usurped power and violated the sacred laws being akin to Jesus defying the Pharisees. Yet curiously, Toynbee draws no parallel between Cleomenes' debt cancellation and Jesus's announcement (Luke 4) that he had come to proclaim the Jubilee Year, nor between Cleomenes exiling Sparta's wealthiest oligarchic families and Jesus throwing the bankers out of the temple.

Back in Sparta, supporters of Cleomenes overthrew the pro-Macedonian regime that had exiled him. Aiming to revive his land distribution program, they killed the ephors at their meal along with some of their allies, and exiled their supporters in 219. Headed by the wealthy Lykourgos, they attempted to revive the dual kingship, but failed to gather widespread support and ended up fleeing the city.

A new leader from one of the royal houses seized power, Chilon (the same name as the leading 6th-century ephor). But he also was unable to mobilize support and left Sparta.[34] Lykourgos returned and led an invasion of Messenia in 218, prompting Philip V of Macedonia to invade Laconia. Fighting continued back and forth for the next decade between pro-debtor reformers and oligarchic elites.

Meanwhile, the First Macedonian War (214-205) broke out as Rome allied itself with Attalus of Pergamum and the Aetolians to block Macedonia from supporting Carthage. Rome invaded central Greece and soon gained control. In a sidelight to this conflict, the Achaean League *strategos* Philopoemen (having commanded the cavalry that helped beat Cleomenes at Sellasia in 222) defeated Sparta once again, this time at the Battle of Mantinea in 207, capturing Tegea north of Sparta, and besting Sparta's ruler Machanidas in one-on-one combat.

It was at this point that Nabis became regent for Sparta's three-year-old king Pelops. He soon disposed of the little boy and took the throne for himself. It was under his rule that Greece's civil war over debt and land reached a peak.

---

[33] Plutarch, *Cleomenes* 37.7. Toynbee's analysis in *A Study of History* (1939), Vols. 5 and 6 is reviewed in Michalopoulos 2016, Appendix D: "From Crucified Kleomenes to Crucified Jesus," pp. 165-171.

[34] Polybius 4.22-24 and 4.81.

Nabis (207-192) promotes debt cancellation and land redistribution beyond Sparta

Ruling alone instead of as part of Sparta's traditional dual kingship, Nabis distributed land to *perioikoi* and mercenaries who agreed to join his army. He financed a military buildup by selling off the treasure of Spartan temples and taxing the oligarchs heavily. He exiled many oligarchic families, rendering debts and rents owed to them uncollectible. And capping his program to "legitimize the rights of his supporters over the property of the previous owners," he "forced the wives and daughters of the exiled men to marry the new landowners."[35]

Polybius provides a visceral image of Nabis squeezing and bleeding Sparta's wealthiest families, most strikingly by an "Iron Maiden" to impale landowners who refused to pay the taxes he demanded.[36] The coffin-like cabinet was said to be painted to resemble Nabis's wife Apia, with her arms, hands and bosom covered with sharp iron spikes to impale recalcitrant oligarchs.

Nabis frightened neighboring oligarchies by creating an alliance against the Achaean League to spread his revolutionary program. Livy (32.38.9) characterized his proposal to Argos in 197 to cancel debts and distribute the land of oligarchs as "lighting two torches with which revolutionists could inflame the commons against the nobility." Nabis went to war against the Achaean League as soon as the First Macedonian War with Rome (214-205) ended, and tried to reconquer Messenia. But Philopoemen drove him back to Sparta, where Nabis set about rebuilding his army and resumed his raids against the Achaean League in 200.

When the League ended its neutrality and backed Rome against Macedonia in 198 in the Second Macedonian War (200-196), Argos withdrew from the League and expelled the Achaean garrison. To free Macedonian troops for fighting elsewhere, Philip asked Nabis to take control of Argos, and sought to seal the bargain by marrying his daughters to Nabis's sons.

Nabis asked Philocles, the leader of Argos and Corinth, to ally the two cities with Sparta, but Argos's leading families led its assembly to

---

[35] Michalopoulos 2016:226, citing Pausanias 4.39.10, and p. 96, citing Polybius 13.6.2-4 and 16.13.1, and Livy 34.35.7, 34.36.4 and 38.34.6. Livy's narrative is based on lost books by Polybius.

[36] Oliva 1971:282, citing Polybius 13.6.7, and Plutarch, *Aratus* 49 for Philip V's opposition to popular leaders and tyrants. Polybius, son of the Achaean League general Lycortas, was highly prejudiced, admiring Aratus and Philopoemen, favoring oligarchy and opposing the reforms of Cleomenes and Nabis.

aresist his offer. According to Livy, Nabis took over the city at night with his troops, imposing heavy fines on its wealthiest citizens and demanding their gold and silver. "Those who paid promptly were let go without insult or bodily injury; those who were suspected of concealing or holding back assets were punished and tortured like slaves."[37] Polybius wrote that Nabis's wife went to Argos "to strip the women of their jewelry and finery and take it back to Sparta," not to promote social revolution.[38]

Hoping to gain control of the Peloponnese, Nabis raised an army of ten thousand men (probably including emancipated helots) and rebuilt Sparta's fleet at Gytheion.[39] After capturing Megalopolis he allied himself with Rome, which he saw as a stronger power than Macedonia. The Roman proconsul T. Quinctius Flamininus – to whom the Senate had assigned control of Greek affairs in 197, the year in which Rome finally defeated Macedonia – welcomed Nabis's military support.

Achaean League oligarchies invite Rome to defeat Sparta's revolution

The next year Flamininus issued the Isthmian declaration announcing that Rome's conquest had provided "freedom for the Greeks." The Aetolians complained that they "were getting not freedom, but a change of masters" from Philip to Rome.[40] And to prove their point, despite Nabis's pro-Roman shift, Flamininus was so opposed to his policy of debt cancellation and land redistribution that he accused Nabis of tyranny at the meeting he convened at the Corinthian Games in 195.

Nabis replied that the people of Argos had invited him in, and said that he was called a tyrant merely "because I summon slaves to the enjoyment of freedom and establish the needy commons upon the soil." He pointed out that this was the same policy he had backed when Flamininus made alliance with him and saluted him as king, not tyrant. He explained that he was simply acting as his ancestors had done by

---

[37] Livy 32.38, reflecting Polybius's political bias against Sparta. For a discussion of Argos's role in the conflict between Sparta, Macedonia and Rome, see Eckstein 1987.

[38] Eckstein 1987:230, citing Polybius 18.17. Livy 32.40.10-11 describes Nabis's wife as inviting women "and partly by flattery, partly by threats, took from them not only their money but finally even their raiment and their whole feminine adornment as well."

[39] Michalopoulos 2016:55 cites helots as being incorporated into Sparta's army under Cleomenes in 223, and on six earlier occasions, in 425, 413, 412, 400, 396 and 394.

[40] Polybius 18.12 and 18.45.

increasing the population by freeing slaves and distributing land to the poor. He concluded:

> Do not weigh what is done in Lacedaemon on the scales of your own laws and institutions. You choose your cavalry and your infantry according to their census-ratings, and you desire that a few should excel in wealth and that the commons should be under their control; our lawgiver ordained that the state should not be in the hands of the few, whom you call the senate, and that no one order should predominate in the state, but he believed that by equalizing wealth and rank it would come to pass that there would be many to bear arms for the country.[41]

Flamininus replied that Nabis had occupied Argos by force after the popular assembly opposed him. Promising to liberate Argos from tyranny, Flamininus assigned it to Macedonia as part of Rome's peace agreement. But the city and the Aetolians supported Sparta, defining liberty as cancelling debts and redistributing land. That prompted Flamininus to march on Sparta, seize the port of Gytheion and destroy crops while recruiting Spartan exiles and dissidents for his army.

Instead of attacking well-fortified Sparta, Flamininus proposed a truce, which Nabis accepted. "Within ten days Nabis was to surrender Argos and the surrounding villages in its possession to the Romans. All emancipated slaves of Argos would return to their former owners. Nabis was forced to return the fugitives and his prisoners to the Roman allies, and the spoils he had confiscated from Messene to the city's inhabitants. He also had to return the property of the mercenaries who had defected to the Romans or their allies." Sparta was deprived of its fleet except for two ships, and of control over its coastal *perioikoi* cities, whose soldiers had provided a major military contingent. "Finally, he had to pay 500 silver talents in compensation, of which 100 talents was due immediately and the rest in eight installments of fifty talents," and supply five hostages, including his son Armenas. But at least Sparta was not obliged to let the wealthy families it had exiled return.[42]

After Flamininus withdrew his Roman troops from Greece in 194, Nabis fortified Sparta's walls with trenches and ramparts to prepare for new fighting with the Achaeans. He arrested and executed 80 people suspected of treason, along with helots deemed untrustworthy (Livy 34.27). The Aetolians encouraged Sparta to retake the port of Gytheion,

---

[41] Livy 34.31.17-19.

[42] Michalopoulos 2016:114, citing Livy 34.35.3-11.

which it did in 193. That prompted the Achaeans to invite Rome back
to Greece to support the oligarchies against Sparta and the Aetolians.

Once more Nabis was confronted by Philopoemen, who in the preceding year had again become *strategos* for the Achaean League, after
serving as a mercenary leader in Crete for five years. He asked for
Roman troops and was told to wait for their arrival, but he took the
initiative to attack Sparta by sea, and lost a two-day land battle. Flamininus then arrived and again invaded Laconia.

A standoff ensued after Nabis recaptured Sparta's neighboring territories in 192, destroying the Achaean fleet. He convened a Spartan
assembly to decide how to respond to Rome's advancing army. The
helots were afraid of being returned to their former owners if he was
defeated, and Spartans who had obtained the land of the exiles feared
losing it, so they urged Nabis to fight. He ended up losing to Rome's
much larger army.[43]

The Aetolians decided to assassinate Nabis to gain control of Sparta
for themselves. They sent a thousand cavalry members and arranged
for Nabis to inspect the assembled army. A group of Aetolian cavalry
members used their lances to kill his horse, throwing Nabis to the
ground, and then stabbed him with their lances. He died slowly in front
of his own men, as it took many such stabs to pierce his armor.

The Aetolians started to plunder Sparta, but its citizens fought back,
cornering the leaders and their cohorts in the palace and massacring them,
along with others who took refuge in a temple. A few escaped to Achaean
League cities, but they were treated as enemies and sold into slavery.[44]

Attempts at social reform continue in Sparta after Nabis's death

Henceforth the history of Sparta and the rest of Greece would be written
by historians of Rome, headed by Polybius, Livy (who based his history
of this period largely on Polybius), Pausanias and Diodorus Siculus.
Most historians of Sparta stop their narrative with Nabis's assassination
in 192. Philopoemen invaded and brought it into the Achaean League.
His allies seized Nabis's palace and estate, and offered to pay Philopoemen 120 talents, but he urged that the money be paid to Spartans to
gain their support for the new arrangement.

Civil warfare continued, and followers of Nabis overthrew and exiled
the pro-Achaean faction in 191. The Achaeans tried to force Sparta to

---

[43] Michalopoulos 2016:115, citing Livy 34.37.4-6.
[44] Michalopoulos 2016:121-122, citing Livy 35.36.

rejoin their League, but were met by a rebellion in 189 that executed thirty pro-Achaean supporters. Sparta's army attacked Las, southwest of Gytheion where many formerly wealthy anti-Nabis exiles had settled. They protested to Philopoemen, and he invaded Laconia in 188, joined by many exiles, to whom he hoped to give control of Sparta.

Insisting that the instigators of the attack be handed over, he promised that they would be safe pending a fair trial. Some 80 leading citizens went to the Achaean camp, including supporters to defend their safety. But the returned exiles incited the Achaean crowd to stone and chain the detainees, killing seventeen. Livy (38.31) reports that Philopoemen intervened to save the remaining 63, "not because he was concerned for their safety but because he did not wish them to be killed by an angry mob without a proper trial."[45] They were all killed the next day for resisting Achaean rule.

Philopoemen tore down Sparta's walls and killed or exiled opponents of the Achaean League, along with helots who had been liberated to serve in the army. Many who tried to stay were arrested, and 3,000 were sold into slavery. Philopoemen then ordered the return of the exiles banished by Cleomenes in 227, Lykourgos in 219 and Nabis in 207, expecting them to become Sparta's leaders supporting the Achaean League and the new oligarchic laws that replaced Sparta's "Lycurgan" tradition.[46] But the oligarchs whom the Achaeans put in place were so oppressive that even pro-Achaean Spartans and Messenians fought back, capturing and killing Philopoemen.

A citizen named Chairon emerged to revive Nabis's program of land redistribution, starting with what Nabis had set aside for the families he exiled in case of their return under the laws he had decreed. Later in the 180s, Chairon asked Rome's Senate to permit Nabis's exiled supporters to return. His request was granted, causing a turmoil leading to the old conservative exiles, who wanted their former land back, being driven out of the city once again.[47]

Seeing the Achaeans busy suppressing a Messenian revolt, Chairon sought to break Sparta away from the Achaean League. He failed to do so in 182, but the next year he tried once again to restore Nabis's program of land redistribution. That was the last known attempt at social reform in Sparta. The Achaeans intervened and condemned

---

[45] Michalopoulos 2016:126-129, citing Livy 38.31-34 and Pausanias 8.51.3-4

[46] Michalopoulos 2016:128.

[47] Michalopoulos 2016:130, and Oliva 1971:309, citing Polybius, Book 24.

Chairon to death. In 180 a final compromise allowed all exiles to return. The next year Sparta was permitted to rebuild its walls and restore some of its traditions.[48]

After the Seleucid military ruler Antiochus III (ruled 222-187) lost to Rome in 192-190, social conflict lasted another 25 years on Boeotia. Polybius describes its magistrates as "always contriving to abolish legal proceedings. Certain strategi even provided pay out of the public funds for the indigent, the populace thus learning to court and invest with power those men who would help them to escape the legal consequences of their crimes and debts." But

> after the peace between the Romans and Antiochus had been signed, the hopes of all those who had revolutionary aims were cut short, and there was a radical change of character in the various states. ... now it was common matter of talk in the different cities that a final end must be put to all the disputes between the citizens.[49]

Rome's intervention resolved this social conflict in favor of oligarchies. After defeating Sparta's kings and subsequent leaders who advocated debt cancellation, its army unseated Perseus who tried to preserve Macedonian power by sponsoring similar pro-debtor reforms. Rome turned the region into a tributary province, leaving austerity in the wake of its looting and destruction.

Ongoing Greek debt cancellations

The turmoil leading to debt cancellations in other Greek cities continued in the 170s. In Macedonia, Philip V's son Perseus (179-167), the last king of the Antigonid dynasty created after the death of Alexander the Great, started his rule by calling "back to Macedonia fugitive debtors and those who had been banished from the country either by sentence of the courts or for offences against the king. ... In Macedonia itself he relieved all who were in debt to the crown, and released those who had been imprisoned for offences against the crown. By this action he aroused the expectation of many, as it seemed to show that for the whole of Greece much was to be hoped from him" (Polybius 25.3).

This act catalyzed popular calls for debt cancellation throughout Greece. Diodorus describes how: "The cancelling of debts in Aetolia was emulated in Thessaly, and factional strife and disorder broke out in

---

[48] Oliva 1971:311-312, citing Pausanias 7.9.5.

[49] Polybius 20.6.1-2 and 22.4.1-2. See Veyne 1990:96.

every city. The [Roman] Senate assumed that Perseus was at the bottom of this turmoil." [50] By 176, Livy describes, he sought support from the Aetolians and others. Rome viewed this as inciting "the worse cause," and worried that Perseus would use the promise of debt cancellation in the same way that Nabis had done, to gain allies against Rome. It sent an embassy to the Aetolians and Thessalians headed by former consul Appius Claudius Pulcher to quell the debt protests and gain their support against Perseus:

> It was not only in Aetolia that disturbances had arisen through the heavy pressure of debt. The Thessalians were in the same condition, and the mischief had spread like an epidemic to Perrhaebia also. When news came that the Thessalians were in arms, the Senate at once sent Ap. Claudius to examine the situation and allay the excitement. He severely censured the leaders on both sides. The debt was swollen by illegal interest, and he reduced the amount with the consent of those who had made it so heavy, and then arranged that the amount legally owing should be paid off by equal instalments in ten years. Affairs in Perrhaebia were settled in the same way. (Livy 42.5.7-9)

Pergamon's ruler Eumenes II (197-159) went to Rome to assure the Senate that he was not planning an alliance with Perseus, and warned of the troubles to come if Rome did not back him against Perseus, whom he claimed had

> brought about universal confusion in Thessaly and Perrhaebia by holding out the prospect of a cancellation of all debts, so that he might crush the aristocracy by a body of debtors bound by their obligations to him. As you have remained quiet and allowed him to do all this, and as he sees that, as far as you are concerned, Greece has been handed over to him, he takes it for granted that he will meet with no armed opposition before he has landed in Italy. (Livy 42.13.9-10)

Local oligarchies preferred dependency on Rome as military enforcer to the risk of citizens rising up to demand freedom from debt and access to the land that the leading families were monopolizing. Still, Livy (42.14.5-10) describes Rhodian and other Greek leaders as worried that the effect of Eumenes' policy was to draw Rome into the region and support him against Rhodes and other cities. Their fears proved justified

---

[50] Diodorus Siculus 29.33. Cecchet 2017:35 notes that Diodorus used the term *chreokopia* for debt cancellation and that Thomas Middleton's *The Old Law* (1656) cites Solon as using this term, but Cecchet finds that: "The expression *chreon apokope* is more common in sources."

when the Third Macedonian War (171-168) saw Rome defeat Perseus at
Pydna in 168 and annex his kingdom a few years later as the Roman
province of Macedonia, later extended to absorb the rest of Greece (see
Chapter 14).

Contemporary debt and tax cancellation in Egypt

It is during this period that Egypt's Rosetta Stone – discussed in this
book's preceding volume, "... *and forgive them their debts*" – commemorated the cancellation of back taxes and other debts by the 13-year old
Ptolemy V Epiphanes in 196. After more than a century of rule, the Ptol-
emies were getting into the flow of ancient tradition. Encouraged by the
priesthood to act as "the living image of Zeus/Amon, son of the Sun,"
the young ruler crowned at Memphis proclaimed an amnesty on the
occasion of his coming of age and taking the throne.

The political context, notes Ogden Goelet, was that "the synod of
Egyptian priests who helped compose the text had been convened in the
aftermath of the final suppression of a lengthy native revolt."[51] Reminiscent of kindred proclamations that were traditional for pharaohs before
Alexander's conquest of Egypt, the inscription reports that "he has
remitted the debts to the crown which were owed by the people in Egypt
and those in the rest of his kingdom, which were considerable, and he
has freed those who were in the prisons and who were under accusation
for a long time from the charges against them," as well as remitting
various taxes and duties, including "the debts of the temples to the royal
treasury up to the 8th year" of his rule, 198/7 BC.[52]

Rostovtzeff describes this act as a *philanthropa* edict (royal good work)
belonging to a time-honored tradition. They "were first and foremost
proclamations of peace or grants of amnesty. They all began with the
same formula: the kings give general pardon to all their subjects for
'errors, crimes, accusations, condemnations, and charges of all kinds' up
to a certain date. ... There followed a general concession to all the population: a remission of taxes until a certain date."[53]

In a few centuries this would become the policy of Roman emperors.
But by that time the beneficiaries were mainly the wealthy.

---

[51] Goelet 2002:283, citing the review of the political situation leading up to the
decree in Quirke and Andrews 1988:7-8.

[52] The text is translated in Austin 1981:374-376.

[53] Rostovtzeff 1941:879-880.

Greece loses its independence to Rome

Rome's opposition to Greek reformers was much like Sparta's earlier support for oligarchies against democracies. During yet a new war with Rome in 147, the Achaean general Critolaus suspended debt collection, but his ruling expired when the war ended. Critolaus again sought to relieve debtors and quell popular dissent after Rome let Sparta withdraw from the Achaean League, but he was replaced by his predecessor Diaios when war broke out again with Sparta. Rome ended the Achaean League in 146 by destroying Corinth. The Senate directed the League to pay Sparta 200 talents in reparations, but never forced payment as Sparta fell back under a pro-Roman oligarchy.[54]

Greece lost its independence, and its subsequent history was determined by Rome's Senate and the proconsuls it appointed. By the time Augustus visited Sparta in 21 BC and participated in a ceremonial *syssitia* meal, the city had become a theme park serving tourists black broth and performing traditional dances. As a final coda, Emperor Hadrian visited Sparta twice, in 124/5 and 128/9 AD.

Summary

The leading reformers in both the 7th and 3rd centuries came from the top of the social pyramid – the Greek tyrants, the founders of Athenian democracy Solon and Cleisthenes, and Sparta's kings Agis, Cleomenes and Nabis. Their support for debt cancellation was countered by the violence and military force of oligarchic city-states, first that of Sparta, then Macedonia and then Rome. But after first fighting against reforms, Sparta and Macedonia eventually themselves tried to cancel their debts to hold the support of their citizenry, who wanted access to self-support land and relief from the debts that threatened to reduce them to inferior economic status and bondage. Rome ended up the ultimate power blocking debt cancellations, using force throughout the later Republic and Empire to impose pro-creditor laws and protect the monopolization of land and wealth.

---

[54] Toynbee 1969:226, and Oliva 1971:316-317, citing Polybius 38.11.10.

Part II

Rome

Have you money? Do not borrow, for you are not in need.
Have you no money? Do not borrow, for you will not be able to pay.
As the proverb says, "I am unable to carry the goat, put the ox then upon me," so, being unable to carry the burden of poverty,
you put the money-lender upon your back,
a burden difficult even for the rich to bear.
                                    – Plutarch, "That we Ought not to Borrow," *Moralia*[1]

Rome's legendary kings (753-509 BC) were akin to Greece's tyrant-reformers in protecting liberty and expanding prosperity for the population at large. That is the essence of democracy – yet it is rarely achieved in practice. In Greece it required overthrowing the autocratic families that monopolized land and wealth. Greek reformers cancelled debts, freed citizens from debt-slavery, redistributed land and in Athens set the stage for establishing a more democratic voting and judicial court system.

Rome never was a political democracy. But its kings provided land to attract runaways and immigrants from neighboring communities, building up an army. For many centuries Rome's kings prevented a creditor oligarchy from gaining power to turn debtors into clients and servile labor. But oligarchic families grew strong enough to overthrow Rome's last king in 509. For the next five centuries of the Republic (509-27 BC) the oligarchy fought to prevent reformers from establishing better rights for the commoners.

Roman records before ca. 200 BC were limited to archives held by Rome's leading aristocratic families and pontifices – terse and often obscure lists of consuls, temple building, military victories, grain shortages, and the titles of early laws. Many centuries later, the narratives by Livy (59 BC to AD 17), Sallust (86-35 BC), Dionysius of Halicarnassus (60

---

[1] Plutarch, *Moralia* 830 (Loeb Classical Library, 1936 X:329).

to 7 BC), Diodorus Siculus (90 to 30 BC), Plutarch (AD 46 to 120) and Appian (AD 95 to 165) provided melodramatic scenarios to describe the patrician coup in 509 BC, the cries for debt relief that led to Secession of the Plebs in 494 and again in 449, and the ensuing centuries of political struggles as land appropriation and monetary wealth at the top impoverished the commoners at the bottom.[2]

In line with the Stoic philosophy of their times, these historians followed the theme of classical tragic drama, in which Rome's hubris brought on its own decline and fall. Specifically, the oligarchy's intransigent self-seeking was described as polarizing the economy, mainly by getting borrowers into debt and expropriating their land, thereby undermining the economy from within. Theodor Mommsen, Arnold Toynbee and other classicists of the reform era reflect this common theme of the Roman historians.

Sallust and Appian described how moneylenders and military commanders devastated Rome's provinces and impoverished Rome's domestic population. The leading senatorial families monopolized the grabbing of foreign booty and tribute, and assigned conquered land (*ager publicus*) mainly to themselves while also absorbing the land of Roman smallholders. Centuries before the Empire formally dissolved, Tacitus described how this dynamic would end, in words attributed to the Celtic leader Calgacus ca. AD 84: Rome made the land a desert, and called it peace.

---

[2] All but Livy (from Cisalpine Gaul in northern Italy) wrote in Greek. Dionysius was from Asia Minor, Diodorus was a Greek from Sicily, Plutarch was from Boeotia in Greece, and Appian was from Alexandria. Raaflaub 2005:5 describes Livy's and Dionysius's "description of the monarchy and early Republic as prose epics or historical novels," based on oral myths while retrojecting Rome's debt and land crisis of the 1st century BC back to the founding of the Republic. The following chapters treat their narratives as plausible verbalizations and dramatizations to bring alive the brief summaries and reminiscences from which they seem to have worked.

9

From Rome's Takeoff to the Patrician Coup, 753-509 BC

Rome's foundation myth describes it as originating as a place of refuge in 753, but signs of habitation date already from ca. 1000 BC. What seems accurate is that a gathering area between some hills above the Tiber river was indeed populated by runaways, fugitives and exiles from neighboring Italian towns.[1] Recent studies describe the countryside as being run by *condottieri* and chieftains with their own armies, controlling the land and exploiting their subjects to such a point that they fled in order to obtain a better life.

The Roman gathering place was bad for mosquito-borne diseases and flooding, although good later for the boat trade that became a source of *portorium* tolls as the town grew by welcoming immigrants as a source of labor and military service. But its essence was not peaceful, and violence was woven into its foundation myth. Rome's eponymous founder Romulus is said to have been suckled with his young twin brother Remus by a she-wolf after their uncle ordered them to be thrown into the Tiber during a local family power grab. After gaining dominance by killing his brother, Romulus is said to have been killed, decades later, in a public assembly.

Peace was made by offering the Roman kingship to Numa, a Sabine, while the Sabines took a Roman leader. Numa is credited with introducing civil law to Rome, and his appointment started the policy of appointing foreigners as kings (*rex*, for which the term "headman" seems most appropriate in view of Rome's modest early size) instead of making them a hereditary dynasty or choosing them from the wealthiest families.[2]

---

[1] In his commentary on Livy, Ogilvie 1965 points out: "In the Greek world the right of asylum is commonly associated with the right of settlement." Such flight was common in Mesopotamia ca. 1400-1200 BC, where fugitives created their own communities, sometimes as bandits or hiring themselves out as mercenaries. They often were characterized by democratic mutual aid as among the *hapiru*. See Renger 1972 and Hudson 2018:172-173 for Mesopotamian examples.

[2] "No king of Rome inherited the throne from his father," notes Cornell 1995:141. "The last king, Tarquin the Proud, was the son of the elder Tarquin," but he took

The most likely motive to invite foreigners to rule Rome was that as outsiders, they would be freer to promote the broad civic welfare without prejudicial favoritism or taking sides in local family in-fighting. It seems that when a king died, the patricians administered the *interregnum* during which they selected the next king.[3] Anthropologists are familiar with tribes inviting foreigners to play such a role. Herodotus reports how Persia's Medes chose Deioces to become their ruler in the early 7th century BC as a result of his reputation for fair judgment.[4] That practice may help explain the most positive features reported for Rome's kings and the town's remarkable growth and power under their rule.

If Rome was indeed settled by immigrants seeking a better economic opportunity than was available elsewhere, the kings are likely to have sought to prevent an oppressive domestic aristocracy from emerging and developing into the kind of society from which the migrants had fled. Rome's reported third king, Tullius Hostilius (like Romulus, a Latin) "distributed to the poor citizens the vast and fertile royal lands that Romulus had reserved for himself and which were also enjoyed by Numa." These grants freed many of the poor from having "to work as menials on the property of others." Rome's fourth listed king, Ancus Marcius (like Numa, a Sabine) is said to have distributed conquered territories to veterans as public land (*ager publicus*).[5] That land-settlement policy would explain why Rome became central Italy's most dynamic town, and why land tenure became a long-term demand by the plebs.

Tarquinius Priscus, Rome's legendary fifth king (616 to 579), is usually said to have come from Etruria, but Fabius Pictor made him the son of a Corinthian Bacchiad, Demaratus, fleeing Cypselus's tyranny ca. 625.[6] In either case Tarquin probably became king by bringing wealth

---

the throne as a usurper rather than as an heir.

[3] For a recent discussion see Cornell 1995:251-252 and 143.

[4] Herodotus 1.97.3: "Since we cannot go on living in the present way in the land, come, let us set up a king over us; in this way the land will be well governed, and we ourselves shall attend to our business and not be routed by lawlessness." Deioces governed for a reported 53 years (727-675).

[5] Gabba 1991:177-178, citing Dionysius 3.1.4-5 and Cicero *De Re Publica* 2.33. Gabba describes Dionysius as a patrician who travelled from Halicarnassus to Rome after Octavian's victory in 30 BC, and finds his *Roman Antiquities* (he prefers the title *History of Archaic Rome*) more faithful to its sources than Livy's contemporary *History of Rome* 1.34.

[6] Pliny the Elder, *Natural History* 35.16.152, and Strabo, *Geographica* 5.219.

and followers with him. Rome's offer of kingship would have been a prime inducement to attract wealthy candidates.

Like the contemporary Greek tyrants in Corinth and elsewhere, Tarquin is said to have overseen the expansion of Rome's population and to have built the large Circus Maximus stadium, drained the swamps around Rome by constructing the great sewer system (the *cloaca maxima*), and used booty seized from the Sabines to build temples as Rome's population conquered the surrounding lands from which their forbears had fled.

In promoting public works and trying to limit rival power centers within the aristocracy, Tarquin and Rome's other kings followed a strategy similar to that of the Greek tyrants. In Cornell's reconstruction, they

> were essentially anti-aristocratic figures, who ruled in the interests of the lower classes, particularly the class of independent small farmers. They expropriated the wealth of their aristocratic opponents and redistributed it among their friends and supporters; at the same time they attacked their political privileges and extended civil rights to wider groups. This is precisely what is said to have happened under the later kings of Rome. Ancus Marcius was a patron of the plebs and was too easily swayed by the voice of the people, according to Virgil's famous characterization (*Aeneid* 6.815-6). Tarquinius Priscus canvassed for popular support and carried out reforms that angered the aristocracy. But the last two kings went much further. ... Servius's thorough reform of the state is best understood as an attempt to undermine the traditional bases of aristocratic power; and Tarquinius Superbus openly persecuted the aristocracy.

The reforms attributed to Servius

Servius Tullius, Rome's sixth king (assigned a reign of 578 to 534 BC), is credited with reorganizing Rome's voting classes and political system. His name implies that his father was a slave or war captive. Dionysius put into his mouth a long speech whose logic encapsulates the reform program that emerged over the next five centuries, much like an overture introducing an opera's major themes. Like Rome's other major classical historians, Dionysius was simply following the narrative spirit of Greek tragedy as described by Aristotle. The plots of such compositions were about the protagonist's tragic flaw – in this case that of Rome itself.

The great Roman narratives (today they might be called historical novels) aimed to awaken the audience to see how the flaw – usually a form of hubris – might affect their own fate. That was the context leading Dionysius to put an anachronistic warning about Rome's tragic flaw into the mouth of Servius, the king who was assigned the role of structuring Rome's economy. Dionysius implies that Servius's policy of debt forgiveness, if implemented, might have avoided the Republic's fate of economic polarization that resulted from its oligarchic character, above all the arrogant selfishness of its creditors injuring Rome's indebted citizenry at large. The epoch of kingship thus was juxtaposed to that of the Republic to show a falling away from a conciliatory policy of mutuality.

Dionysius describes Servius as summoning an assembly to increase his power at the expense of the patricians, and emulating Solon's ban on debt bondage in 594 as well as Peisistratus's reported practice of using his own money to bail out needy debtors:

> Hear from me now the benefits I myself have arranged to confer upon you and the reasons that induced me to summon this assembly. Those among you who already have debts which, through poverty, they are unable to discharge, I am eager to help, since they are citizens and have undergone many hardships in the service of their country; hence, in order that these men who have securely established the common liberty may not be deprived of their own, I am giving them from my own means enough to pay their debts.
>
> And those who shall hereafter borrow, I will not permit to be hauled to prison on account of their debts, but will make a law that no one shall lend money on the security of the persons of free men; for I hold that it is enough for the lenders to possess the property of those who contracted the debts.[7]

Rome, however, banned debt bondage (*nexum*) only in 326 or 313, almost three centuries after Solon's *seisachtheia* in 594. Dionysius even portrays Servius as advocating progressive taxation, promising to lower taxes for smallholders, the major factor pushing them into debt:

---

[7] Dionysius 4:8-10. Cornell 2005:48 notes that "Roman historians felt entitled to add rhetorical color and incidental detail to the traditional story in order to enliven the narrative. ... In the same way historians were expected to compose imaginary speeches to put into the mouths of leading historical figures." However, he emphasizes that regarding Livy and Dionysius, "no one has seriously suggested that they were downright dishonest." Cornell adds (p. 50) that for the major Roman and Greek historians, "the general structure of the narrative is remarkably uniform in all the sources, and only minor discrepancies are registered." The existence of early summaries meant that "the annalists had only limited scope for tampering with the received facts."

> In order to lighten the burden of the war taxes you pay to the public treasury, by which the poor are oppressed and obliged to borrow, I will order all the citizens to give a valuation of their property and everyone to pay his share of the taxes according to that valuation, as I learn is done in the greatest and best governed cities. I regard it as both just and advantageous to the public that those who possess much should pay much in taxes and those who have little should pay little.[8]

In the spirit of Plutarch crediting Lycurgus with establishing full equality among Sparta's *homoioi*, Dionysius's idealized version of Servius portrays him as an early endorser of the Stoic egalitarianism that developed centuries later, promising "to never cease to take thought for the equality of all the citizens."

Emulating Tullius Hostilius and Ancus Marcius, Servius is said to have proposed preventing patricians from appropriating land won in war, foreshadowing Tiberius Gracchus's program of 133 to distribute the *ager publicus* among those who had no allotments:

> I believe that the public lands, which you have obtained by your arms and now enjoy, should not, as at present, be held by those who are the most shameless, whether they got them by favor or acquired them by purchase, but by those among you who have no allotment of land, to the end that you, being free men, may not be serfs to others or cultivate others' lands instead of your own; for a noble spirit cannot dwell in the breasts of men who are in want of the necessaries of daily life.

It certainly is logical to assume that most early Romans simply wanted to avoid bondage and keep their land (or obtain some). Dionysius describes Servius as spending the next few days ordering that

> lists be made of all the debtors who were unable to keep their pledges, with the amount each owed and the names of the creditors; and when this list had been delivered to him, he commanded tables to be placed in the Forum and in the presence of all the citizens counted out to the lenders the amount of the debts.
>
> Having finished with this, he published a royal edict commanding that all those who were enjoying the use of the public lands and holding them for their own should quit possession within a certain specified

---

[8] Dionysius 4.9. Rome at the time of Servius did not yet have monetary means to value such land, which could be measured only in terms of its area and crop yield. The *tributum* war tax was not actually imposed until the war with Veii in 406 (Livy 4.59).

time, and that those citizens who had no allotments of land should give in their names to him....

While he was pursuing these measures, the patricians were growing indignant as they saw the power of the Senate being overthrown.

In Dionysius's narrative, Servius called an assembly and explained the political crisis to the crowd:

> The patricians are plotting against me and I have received information that some of them are conspiring to kill me, not because they can charge me with any crime, great or trivial, but because they resent the benefits I have conferred and am prepared to confer upon the people and feel that they are being treated unjustly.
>
> The money-lenders, for their part, feel aggrieved because I did not permit the poor among you to be hauled to prison by them because of their debts and to be deprived of their liberty. And those who misappropriate and hold what belongs to the state, finding themselves obliged to give up the land which you acquired with your blood, are as angry as if they were being deprived of their inheritances instead of merely restoring what belongs to others.[9]

This dramatization lays out a rationale for the Poetelia-Papiria law banning debt bondage a quarter-millennium later (see Chapter 12). Servius went on to accuse creditors "of abusing the poor, as they now do, as if they were so many purchased slaves." If the citizenry failed to support him, Servius warned, Rome's patricians would get control of affairs and "would treat wives, mothers and daughters and all the female sex like slaves."

Dionysius's narrative of Servius should be read as encapsulating the program that took many centuries to refine. Yet it basically is grounded in the kind of populist reforms that contemporary Greek tyrants and reformers had introduced. No doubt conflict was intensifying in Servius's Rome over debt and access to self-support land, leading the wealthy to oppose royal moves to block creditors from turning debtors and other poor into chattel slaves. That is the conflict which would simmer and often boil over throughout Roman history, framing its destiny as economic polarization intensified.

What seems most historically grounded is Servius's reorganization of Rome's voting structure, classifying citizens in terms of locality instead of "aristocratic clans, which had an exclusive membership based on birth." Replacing Rome's former threefold tribal division and organizing

---

[9] Dionysius 11.1-4.

the first census to define its citizenship made "membership in a tribe, and consequently entitlement to Roman citizenship, [depend] on residence and on registration at the census, which was organized locally."[10]

This reform anticipated those of Athens a generation later. But unlike the voting and office-holding reforms of Athenian tribes by Cleisthenes and Ephialtes that created a homogeneous participation in politics and the courts, Rome's tribal division into five classes was timocratic, that is, based on wealth. Voting rights, military service (the basic meaning of "class") and tax liability (headed by the *tributum* war tax introduced later) were weighted according to one's wealth in land, leaving the commoners (who in time became "plebeians," cognate to Greek *plethos*, "the many") with only marginal influence. "The citizens were distributed among the classes in such a way that the first class of wealthy citizens ... contained almost as many centuries [voting units] as the rest of the classes put together," despite their small numerical size.[11]

Rome's patricians overthrow the kings

Servius's restructuring of Roman society raises the question of how he gained the power to enforce his rulings, or even to propose them. Cornell finds the view of the emperor Claudius to be plausible. That view, supposedly based on Etruscan sources, described Servius as a military commander from Volci, a chronic rival of Rome in the hilly and swampy land to the southeast, and depicted Servius as bidding for support from Roman citizens, whose town he was trying to conquer.[12]

Alternatively, Servius may have made an alliance with Tarquinius Priscus, bringing his own troops to join those of Rome. Tarquinius may have given his daughter Tanaquil in marriage to Servius to seal such

---

[10] For details see Cornell 1995:179, whose Chapter 7 deals with "The Reforms of Servius Tullius."

[11] Cornell 1995:186. He adds (pp. 379-380): "The centuries, which functioned as voting units in the *comitia centuriata*, were so distributed as to ensure that the old could outvote the young, and the rich could outvote the poor." Within the centuries, seniors (older than 46) had over twice the weight of juniors, and "Proletarians who fell below the minimum property qualification for membership of the fifth class were enrolled in a single century, and were often not called upon to vote at all." Walsh 1974 cites Momigliano 1963:95-97 pointing out that Servius was 20 years behind Solon. Findings of Attic vases in Rome suggest that Servius would have heard of Solon's reforms as a means of holding a city together to avoid class war. See also Raaflaub 2005:23.

[12] Cornell 1995:130-141, citing Dionysius 4.9.8.

an alliance, rather than simply rewarding him as a court favorite, as appears in the histories of Livy and Dionysius. In any event, Servius's reforms led Rome's patricians to oppose royal power in principle for being inherently "tyrannical," their epithet for any policies checking their own greed.

The narratives of Servius's successor, Rome's last king, Tarquinius Superbus (the "Proud" or "Arrogant"), depict him as sponsoring major public works, headed by Rome's great *cloaca maxima* sewer, the Temple of Jupiter on the Capitoline Hill, and large seating for the public circus. They also accuse him of angering the population by working laborers to death, driving some to suicide. But what is not explained is how this labor was paid. Was it from the public treasury, spending treasure on which the wealthy class had set its eyes? The answer is important, because all indications are that Tarquinius was removed by the aristocratic elite, not by the lower classes.

The coup ca. 509 BC seems to have been violent. Later mythology framed it in terms of the traditional Greek association of hubris with wealth and power, accusing kings (and subsequent political leaders) in principle of being a danger to society. The "Rape of Lucretia" story describes Sextus, Tarquinius's son, as raping the wife of the consul Collatinus, and being avenged by the patrician aristocracy defending family values by overthrowing the monarchy.

The story became a rationalization for Rome's patricians replacing kingship with a republic. In contrast to the poetry of Theognis and Solon, and Greek philosophy warning of hubris, Rome's upper class depicted itself as being free of the pro-creditor violence and rapine that later would be exhibited from Appius Claudius in his Rape of Verginia (450 BC) to Verres, Roman governor of Sicily.

The standard historical narrative depicts Tarquinius as seeking Etruscan help from Lars Porsenna to return him to power. Lars may have occupied Rome after the Battle of Aricia in 504, and Rome fought off an Etruscan alliance at Lake Regillus sometime between 499 and 496 (Livy 2.19-20 and Dionysius 6.2-4). Many Etruscan sites show signs of warfare at this time, and Rome's Sant'Omobono temple and sanctuary, closely associated with Rome's kings, was burned down around 500, along with the Regia and Comitium.

If there was fighting with the Etruscans, why didn't Rome return to kingship after the conflict was over? The answer must be that the patricians decided to end the institution of kingship. Cornell attributes the local destruction not to fighting against Lars, but to "an oligarchic coup against a populist and tyrannical monarchy" that "restricted the growth of patrician power."[13] The coup was a reaction against the political power of kings to favor the poor by restraining the behavior of wealthy families.

Describing Tarquinius's hostility to the aristocracy, Livy (1.54) interjects a version of the story related by Herodotus (above, Chapter 2, fn41) about Thrasybulus of Miletus advising Periander to cut off the highest stalks of grain with a scythe. In Livy's version, Tarquinius takes a messenger from his son Sextus to his garden to reply to a message asking what to do about the town of Gabii that was resisting Rome. Tarquinius is reported to have cut down the tallest poppies – a symbolic gesture for cutting down the leading potential rivals in local aristocracies.

Reacting against public spending by the kings, Rome's oligarchy embraced an anti-government ideology as passionately as do today's anti-socialists. Much like the Greek oligarchs who accused reformers seeking popular support by cancelling debts and redistributing land of being "tyrants," Roman patricians accused reformers of "seeking kingship" by proposing debt reform and assignment of public land to settle the poor instead of letting patricians grab it for themselves. Such advocacy led to the most progressive reformers from the leading families being assassinated in political killings over the ensuing five centuries.

> In the republican period the very idea of a king was viewed with an almost pathological dislike. ... The tradition is very likely correct when it says that the first acts of the founders of the Republic were to make the people swear never to allow any man to be king in Rome and to legislate against anyone aspiring to monarchy in the future. What was truly repugnant to the nobles was the thought of one of their number elevating himself above his peers by attending to the needs of the lower classes and winning their political support.
>
> This explains why all the serious charges of monarchism (*regnum*) in the Republic were leveled against mavericks from the ruling elite whose only offence, it seems, was to direct their personal efforts and resources to the relief of the poor.[14]

This Roman fear of kingship is what Judea's upper class played upon when they sought to have Jesus condemned after he incited the hatred of the Pharisees and the creditor class with his first sermon (Luke 4), when he unrolled the scroll of Isaiah and announced that he had come to proclaim the Jubilee Year of the Lord, cancelling debts as called

---

[13] Cornell 1995:237-240.

[14] Cornell 1995:148-150.

for under Mosaic Law. They accused him of aspiring to be "king of the Jews," that is, "seeking kingship," the familiar epithet the Romans applied to leaders whom they feared might cancel debts, including Catiline and Caesar around Jesus's time.

Replacing Rome's kings with a patrician Senate

By preventing royal authority from protecting the indebted Roman poor and assigning them land, the patrician coup ended Rome's long expansion under the kings. The economy fell into recession as the patricians sought economic gains in ways that impoverished the population at large. The 5th century under their rule "is something of a blank," Cornell summarizes. "There is almost no known artifact or monument that can be safely ascribed to it."[15] Imports of Athenian pottery disappear from the archaeological record, and temple building comes to an end in 484 with the Temple of Castor. A half-century gap ensued until the Temple of Apollo was built in 431. "There is virtually nothing from Rome that can be dated to the period from ca. 474 to ca. 400 BC. ... The literary sources connect plebeian agitations with economic distress, and refer specifically to indebtedness, food shortages and land hunger."[16]

Even Rome's military prowess was impaired by the patrician class warfare against the men who were to serve as its soldiers. Rome suffered numerous defeats in its almost constant 5th-century warfare with its neighbors. That dried up public spending, because temples "were normally financed by war booty, and were therefore constructed as a consequence of successful campaigns."

The patricians imposed harsh debt-ridden austerity with pro-creditor laws and land grabbing. Unable to extract more revenue at home, their preference for brute financial and *rentier* exploitation through seizing foreign lands and extracting tribute characterized all subsequent Roman history. And the narrow Senate aristocracy locked in its hereditary monopoly of administrative power over religious, political and economic management throughout the Republic, 509-27, as Raaflaub has summarized:

> Around 500 BC, Rome's territory was comparable to that of Corinth. As in most Greek *poleis*, in Rome the earlier monarchy was replaced by an aristocracy consisting of a limited number of families that dominated the life of their community in every possible respect: economically, socially, militarily, in religion and jurisdiction, and, through the council,

---

[15] Cornell 2005:55.

[16] Cornell 1995:266.

public offices, and priesthoods, also politically. This group aimed at exclusiveness and tried to set up social and institutional barriers against potential competitors.[17]

Recognition of the self-defeating character of this class war led to a split within the patrician elite from 133 through the assassination of Caesar in 44 BC as the gap between the wealthy elite and the rest of the population widened. Attempts at moderation and reform ultimately failed.

Patron/client relationships, debt and economic polarization

The royal period was in many ways Rome's golden age, but it was ended by the patrician coup that divided the city into opposing camps. The ensuing polarization seems to have occurred as Rome's land filled up with its growing population. As long as land had remained available, the main scarce resource was labor. Families with land faced the problem of how to get workers to help cultivate it.[18] The path of least resistance was to create patron-client relationships, which tended to become hereditary.

By the time such arrangements took full shape, clients had no right to sue or contest the open-ended debts placed upon their shoulders. They had to bear the costs of their patron's feasts to celebrate his rites of passage, provide dowries for marriages, and even pay for his maneuvering for social status and expenditures to obtain public office, the major way to increase one's wealth and power. As Roman proverbs warned: "To accept a favor [*beneficium*] is to sell one's freedom," and "To ask a favor [an *officium*] is a form of servitude."[19] The most complete reconstruction of the patron-client relationship is that of Dionysius (*Roman Antiquities* 2.10), anachronistically attributing it to the outset of Roman settlement:

> The regulations which he [Romulus] instituted concerning patronage and which long continued in use among the Romans were as follows: It was the duty of the patricians to ... bring suit on behalf of their clients when they were wronged in connection with contracts, and to defend them against any who brought charges against them ... It was the duty of the clients to assist their patrons in providing dowries for their daughters upon their marriage if the fathers had not sufficient means; to pay their ransom to the enemy if any of them or of their children were taken prisoner; to discharge out of their own purses their patrons' losses in

---

[17] Raaflaub 2005:15.

[18] Livy 1.43 describes the categories of labor. See also Dionysius 4.16.

[19] Ste. Croix 1989:342, quoting from a collection by Publilius Syrus. See also Hopkins 1978:22-23.

private suits and the pecuniary fines which they were condemned to pay to the State, making these contributions to them not as loans but as thank-offerings; and to share with their patrons the costs incurred in their magistracies and dignities and other public expenditures, in the same manner as if they were their relations.

For both patrons and clients alike it was impious and unlawful to accuse each other in law-suits or to bear witness or to give their votes against each other or to be found in the number of each other's enemies; and whoever was convicted of doing any of these things was guilty of treason by virtue of the law sanctioned by Romulus, and might lawfully be put to death by any man who so wished as a victim devoted to the Jupiter of the infernal regions.

... the connections between the clients and patrons continued for many generations, differing in no wise from the ties of blood-relationship and being handed down to their children's children. And it was a matter of great praise to men of illustrious families to have as many clients as possible and not only to preserve the succession of hereditary patronages but also by their own merit to acquire others.

Although some reciprocity must have been necessary to attract early immigration, clientage became systematized as poorer citizens "entered class conflicts not as serfs but as debtors,"[20] summarized Max Weber a century ago. What may have seemed ostensibly a reciprocal relationship at first became increasingly exploitative after oligarchs replaced the kings in a way that made the poor increasingly dependent and denied them political and legal rights. Even when the commoners managed to obtain legal protection of their rights, the courts – manned exclusively by patricians – simply ignored laws limiting interest rates and creditor power. The only way to avoid clientage and debt slavery was to leave the city in a walkout, as occurred in 494, and to create institutions with the commoners' own officials and policy program.

From a mixed public/private economy to oligarchy

Following the patrician coup, many heroic reformers lost their lives or were driven into exile by the recalcitrant oligarchy for advocating more lenient debt laws and protection of smallholders. Such advocacy led to Spurius Cassius being killed in 485, Spurius Maelius in 439 and

---

[20] Weber 2013 [1909]:97. He adds (p. 25): "In Varro's time, another group was available for day labour – the peasants who had to work off debts (*nexi, obaerati*). In ancient times still another group was available as extra help in harvest time – the peasants who held land by favour (*precarium*)."

M. Manlius Capitolinus in 384. Unlike the Greek reformer-tyrants, the creators of Athenian democracy and rebels in other cities, such Roman reformers faced a more brutal and inexorable aristocracy, one descended from Rome's founding fathers, the families that gained power during the late 6th century to overpower the kings and privatize their control over lawmaking, credit and land tenure.

Most notable among the patricians was the Sabine leader Attus Clausus (Appius Claudius Sabinus, "the Sabine"). As a Sabine patrician he had advocated peace with the Romans, but upon failing to get his town to follow his leadership, he brought his wealth and a reported retinue of 5,000 armed clients to Rome ca. 504. He was accepted as a patrician (founding the Claudia gens) and granted senatorial status.[21]

Over the next five centuries Appius Claudius and his descendants sharing that name were intransigent in opposing democratic reforms and concessions to debtors and the poor.[22] Wherever their names appear in the histories of Livy and Dionysius, it is as a motif framing the history of Rome in terms of the Claudii leading the oligarchy in monopolizing land, money and political power, and in the Senate's most conservative and unyielding confrontations with the Roman populace.[23] Most historians also depict the Claudii as tyrants, in opposition to the moderation of the popular leaders, who ended up being murdered simply for advocating humanitarian improvements in the political rights and economic condition of debtors and other poor.

---

[21] Cornell 1995:144.

[22] Suetonius, *Life of Tiberius* 1-3 summarizes the clan's history.

[23] Mommsen 1911 I:475-476. (Appendix: "The Patrician Claudii"): "At the very beginning of his [Livy's] work (2.56) the Claudii are introduced as the *familia superbissima ac crudelissima in plebem Romanam.*" Mommsen believes that this picture is a late reconstruction originating with Licinius Macer, praetor in 68 BC, whose annals Livy and Dionysius took as the basis for their dramatization of Roman history as containing in its very seeds the conflict between the oligarchic Optimates and the Populares of the first century BC. But most historians find the Claudian family accurately reflected by Livy and Dionysius. Mommsen adds (p. 476): "Tacitus again speaks, just like Livy and Dionysius, of the *vetus atque insita Claudiae familiae superbia* (*Annals* 1.4); and Suetonius, in his *Lives of the Caesars* (*Tiberius* 2) says still more expressly, that all the patrician Claudii, with the exception of the tribune of the people P. Clodius, had been conservative (*Optimates*) and the most zealous champions of the standing and power of the patriciate as opposed to the plebs."

Overthrowing Rome's kings foreclosed democracy instead of cata-
lyzing Rome's development and self-feeding prosperity as occurred in
Greece with its public spending and civic checks and balances. Rome's
reliance on its citizen infantry did not lead to democracy. Instead, it led
to landlordship. The public domain created from the lands conquered
by Rome's citizen army was increasingly appropriated by the wealthiest
insider families. Rome's army was fighting for its own disenfranchise-
ment. Instead of being used to settle veterans, the best land was turned
into large estates stocked with war prisoners from the 3rd century on.

Rome's history of its legendary kings implies that they created an
attractive city whose immigrants came to expect that in exchange for
fighting to increase its territory and power, they would be protected by
the kings and assured self-support land of their own, and liberty from
debt slavery. And indeed, it was that expectation and its associated class
consciousness (if I may use that term) that led to the protests that broke
out, starting when the plebs staged their walk-out of Rome after the oligarchy overthrew the kings and tried to abolish the economic liberty
that the citizenry had come to expect as its natural right.

10
Secession of the Plebs and Broken Patrician Promises, 495-471 BC

Rome's mode of expansion was military, not commercial. It made war an economic enterprise, which started by conquering land from the neighboring Sabines, Latins and Volscians. These conquests led to two major domestic conflicts that raged for half a millennium: whether the conquered land should be distributed to veterans and the poor or appropriated by the patricians; and how to resolve the debts that mounted up when soldiers left their own plots of land to fight and when harvests were bad.

From the outset of the Republic (509 BC), indebtedness threatened smallholders with loss of their livestock, land and ultimately their personal liberty. Wealthy landowners expanded their holdings by extending credit to smallholders, who could pay only by working on the homes or estates of their creditors. The process often ended with creditors taking the debtor's land as well as his labor and that of his family members.

Debt collection was suspended in times of war. The problem was what happened upon the return to peace. After defeating its Latin neighbors in 495, Rome's wartime suspension of creditor lawsuits ended, and debtors began to be called into court. Their complaints gained momentum and a crowd gathered in the Forum. Dionysius (6.22) found it plausible to assume that they explained how they were unable to pay, "since their land had been laid waste during the long war, their cattle destroyed, the number of their slaves reduced by desertion and raids, and their fortunes in the city exhausted by their expenditures for the campaign." Creditors replied that they too had lost, and "refused to abate even the interest."

Election of Appius Claudius as consul in 495 led to a crisis. Republican Rome had two consuls to act as its major administrative officers. Election was for one year, and was not supposed to be served by the same man twice in succession. As the Senate's most uncompromising leader when it came to dealing with Rome's commoners, Appius urged the Senate to present a show of force to dash the hopes of debtors to avoid enslavement for non-payment. Meeting their demands, he warned, would enable them to "establish a pernicious power" over the aristocracy. "Why entrust the government to the people," he asked, "when we have it in our power to live under an aristocracy?"[1]

Hoping to move the complainers out of the city under military command – and claiming that news of Roman political dissension was emboldening its enemies – the Senate voted to attack the Volscians, and sought to enroll volunteers. Appius's more moderate co-consul, Publius Servilius, sought to avoid a confrontation, warning that "men in want of the daily necessities of life, if compelled to serve at their own expense, might get together and adopt some desperate course." He advised the Senate to avert conflict "by decreeing an abolition or diminution of the debts, or, failing that, by forbidding for the time being the hauling to prison of the debtors whose obligations were overdue." There were no public prisons, so he would have been referring to bondage in the homes of private creditors. Livy and Dionysius described what happened next.

How much of Livy's and Dionysius's narrative is valid?

Livy and Dionysius (echoed by Plutarch's life of Coriolanus) wrote plausible reconstructions based on scantily documented history to explain how the conflict between patricians and plebeians was shaped from the 5th century onward. Not being in the fortunate position of Thucydides writing about the Peloponnesian War in which he himself participated as a general, the clearly reasoned speeches they put into the mouths of Rome's kings, leaders and protesters of the 6th and 5th centuries BC reflect the arguments being put forth in their own time over the issues being contested.

Thucydides described his method as being "to keep as close as possible to the general sense of the words that actually were used, to make the speakers say what, in my opinion, was called for by each situation." But Roman historians writing during the end of the Republic and inception of its Empire had only the bare bones of stories, and a few chronological lists available to explain how their own polarized epoch came into being. They focused on debt and land tenure to create what seemed to be a plausible set of scenarios for how Rome ended up with its always simmer-

---

[1] Dionysius, *Roman Antiquities* 6.23. Book 2 of Livy's *History of Rome* also describes the patrician hostility toward pleas for debt forgiveness, but Dionysius provides more elaborate detail.

ing debt crises and civil war. Many details are anachronistic, but what undoubtedly occurred was the fight by creditors against debtors.

The economic interests of both groups are timeless. Much as modern monopolists and financiers call advocates of public regulation enemies of the "free market" – by which they mean a status quo benefiting the vested interests – creditors and large landowners historically have accused anyone seeking to check their power to be aiming at monarchic tyranny. Rome's patricians denounced the "tyranny of the mob" (ochlocracy) in rhetoric similar to that which they used in their opposition to kingship. They demonized reformers seeking public regulations as reducing their "liberty" to indebt the population and privatize public land for themselves.

The reconstructions of this Roman history by Dionysius, Livy and their contemporaries describe the class strategy implicit in the early patrician victories. They made the logic of Rome's debtors and other poor more explicit than would have been perceived and documented at the outset. It took many centuries for debtors to develop the ideals of public administration and the common weal, these taking form mainly after the 2nd century BC in Rome. The indebted smallholders – often prematurely called plebeians – translated their economic demands into a political program only gradually, summarizes Kurt Raaflaub. At first, "the plebeians almost exclusively fought for defensive goals: for protection, security, and fairness against the overwhelming economic, social, jurisdictional, and political power of the patricians and their magistrates. Economic grievances over the debt problem and the shortage of land and food on the one hand and dissatisfaction with magisterial arbitrariness and the demand for codification of law on the other were the dominant issues."[2]

But the logic seems clear enough to see that Dionysius and Livy simply added flesh to the skeletal bare bones that survived to provide a summary of what had happened.

Popular demands for debt writedowns and liberation from bondage

Debtors complained that the creditor lawsuits were treating them like a conquered population, and many refused to fight against the Volscians until their grievances were met. To summarize the reasons why Romans

---

[2] Raaflaub 2005:189. Commoners were not formally known as plebeians until the passing of the *lex Publilia* in 471.

fell into debt and how they were treated, Livy drew a melodramatic picture of an emaciated old centurion stumbling into the Forum:

> He bared his breast and showed the scars that bore witness to many campaigns in which he had borne an honorable part. ... He stated that whilst serving in the Sabine war he had not only lost the produce of his land through the depredations of the enemy, but his farm had been burnt, all his property plundered, his cattle driven away, the war-tax [*tributum*] demanded when he was least able to pay it, and he had got into debt. This debt had been vastly increased through usury and had stripped him first of his father's and grandfather's farm, then of his other property, and at last like a pestilence had reached his person. He had been carried off by his creditor, not into slavery only, but to an underground workshop, a living death.[3]

After the soldier showed his back with recent lash marks, an angry crowd gathered around the Senate house. The intransigent Appius urged "a display of authority on the part of the consuls," and recommended choosing one protestor for punishment to make an example, suggesting that "if one or two were brought up for trial, the rest would calm down" – the age-old tactic known as "killing the chickens to scare the monkeys."

The senators warned that a Volscian army was approaching the city, but this only made the debtors exultant. "They said that the gods were preparing to avenge the tyranny of the patricians; they encouraged each other to evade enrolment, for it was better for all to die together than to perish one by one" while the patricians kept the booty and land for themselves (Livy 2.24).

The Senate sent the more moderate consul Servilius to win popular support. He promised that debtors who signed up to fight would be freed from bondage, and that no creditor could "distrain or sell the goods of a soldier as long as he was in camp, or detain his children or grandchildren." Many joined, and drove back the Volscians, plundering slaves, cattle, arms, gold and silver. Servilius permitted the soldiers to divide it among themselves so that "every man might share in the booty, and he ordered them to bring no part of it into the treasury" (Dionysius 6.29). Presumably, creditors ended up with most.

The men returned to Rome "expecting the fulfillment of the promises the consul had made." But the Senate refused to honor them, while

---

[3] Livy 2.23, repeated in Dionysius 6.22. No *tributum* is reported to have been levied until the late 5th century BC.

Appius, as judge (senators alone were the judges and juries) imposed harsh sentences on debtors brought before him and handed them over to their creditors. He accused Servilius of stirring up sedition by supporting the multitude, "and charged him particularly with having brought no part of the spoils of war back to the public treasury, having instead made a present of it all to whom he thought fit." This complaint recalled that made against Tarquinius Superbus and other kings whose public construction programs prevented wealthy insider families from spending the treasury's money on themselves.

The crowd in the Forum demanded "that Servilius should either get an ordinance passed by the Senate" or protect them in his dual role as consul and commander of the soldiers. But he had no means to force compliance. "The patricians regarded him as a weak popularity-hunting consul, the plebeians considered him false, and it soon became apparent that he was as much detested as Appius." Seeing that "any prospect of help from the consuls or the Senate was hopeless," the commoners took matters into their own hands:

> Whenever they saw a debtor brought before the court, they rushed there from all sides, and by their shouts and uproar prevented the consul's sentence from being heard, and when it was pronounced no one obeyed it. They resorted to violence, and all the fear and danger to personal liberty was transferred from the debtors to the creditors, who were roughly handled. (Livy 2.27)

Dionysius's version (6.34) adds that, "assembling together a few at a time, they bound one another by oaths that they would no longer assist the patricians in any war, and that they would render aid jointly to every one of the poor who was oppressed." Nighttime meetings were organized to discuss secession.

Citizens refuse to fight without liberty from debt

Preparing for a Sabine war, the Senate decreed a military draft, but no one enrolled. The new consuls installed in 494 adopted Appius's hardline tactic. Ascending the tribunal, they called out the names of those ordered to serve.

> Not a single man answered to his name. The people ... declared that the plebs could no longer be imposed upon, the consuls should not get a single soldier until the promise made in the name of the State was fulfilled. Before arms were put into their hands, every man's liberty must be restored to him, that they might fight for their country and their fel-

low-citizens and not for tyrannical masters. A desperate conflict with the
plebs seemed inevitable. (Livy 2.28)

The Senate directed the consuls to put down any disturbance by
force, but civil disobedience was gaining strength. Whenever the consuls
"ordered anyone to be seized, the poor assembled in a body and endeav-
ored to rescue the one who was being carried away, and when the
consuls' lictors refused to release them, they beat them and drove them
off. If any of the knights or patricians who were present attempted to put
a stop to these proceedings, they did not refrain from beating them too."[4]

The senators saw the need to soften their hard line. Titus Larcius
(former consul and dictator as commander of the infantry, *magister
populi*, in 501/500) "considered that the time had passed for rewarding
only men who had fought [as Servilius had promised]. The plebs were
overwhelmed with debt, which could not be arrested unless there was
a measure for universal relief. Any attempt to differentiate between
the various classes would only kindle fresh discord instead of allaying
it." Dionysius (6.36) describes Larcius as anticipating Charles Dickens
by pointing out that the Romans "inhabit two cities, one of which is
ruled by poverty and necessity, and the other by satiety and insolence"
making "superior strength the measure of justice."

Order could only be restored by alleviating creditor demands. But
Appius, the previous year's consul, insisted on "never yielding to the
people," adding that "as long as I live, I will never propose an abolition
of debts as a favor to wicked men ... every evil and corruption and, in
a word, the overthrow of the state, begins with the abolition of debts"
(Dionysius 6.38). The Senate claimed that freeing soldiers or others from
debt liability "would destroy all credit." Urging that the debtors' right of
appeal be revoked, Appius asked the Senate to appoint a dictator "from
whom there is no appeal," hoping that he himself would be named.

When the senators were told that the Volscians, Aequi and Sabines
were arming themselves, they chose the more moderate Manius Valerius
as dictator. He issued an edict similar to the one Servilius had issued
prior to the Volscian war, freeing soldiers from debt (but not those who
would not enroll). He also appointed Quintus Servilius, the 70-year-
old brother of the former weak but sympathetic consul, as his second in
command (Master of the Horse). Summoning the people to an assembly,
Valerius acknowledged that when the consuls wanted to engage them

---

[4] Dionysius 6.34. (Livy paints the same picture.) Lictors were bodyguards armed
with clubs to protect public magistrates from attack.

to march against the enemy, one or the other would promise that the Senate would give them what they want, but "never carries out his promises." Vowing that he would not be a party to such deception, Valerius said that the Senate would resolve the debt issue and "grant everything else you can reasonably ask of them ... In the meantime let every possession, every person, and every right of a Roman citizen be left secure from seizure for either debt or any other obligation" (Dionysius 6.40-41).

Ten legions, composed of 4,000 men each, enrolled for the next round of fighting and won an easy victory with much booty. But when they returned to Rome, the senators once again double-crossed them, refusing to ratify the promise that Valerius had made to cancel their debts. "The moneylenders possessed such influence and had taken such skillful precautions that they rendered the commons and even the dictator himself powerless."

The younger, most radical senators demanded repeal of the plebeian assembly's role as a court of justice," blaming it for "destroying the power of the patricians." Valerius accused the senators of advocating "not what is most advantageous to the commonwealth, but what is pleasing to themselves at the present moment" (Dionysius 6.46):

> "I am accused of having turned over to the poor among you, without the consent of the Senate, the spoils taken from the enemy, in the desire to gain a private advantage for myself ... and of having disbanded the armies in spite of the opposition of the senators, when I ought to have kept you in the enemy's country occupied in sleeping in the open and in endless marching. I am also reproached in the matter of sending the colonists into the territory of the Volscians, on the ground that I did not bestow a large and fertile country upon the patricians or even upon the knights, but allotted it to the poor among you."

Saying that the Senate had misled him as well as the people at large, he resigned.

Secession of the Plebs in 494

The Senate sought to break up the ensuing protests by ordering "the legions to be marched out of the City, on the pretext that war had been recommenced by the Aequi." This ploy led the indebted poor, "at the instigation of a certain Sicinius Bellutus, to ignore the consuls and withdraw to the Sacred Mount, which lay on the other side of the Anio, three miles from the City. ... There, without any commander, in a regularly entrenched camp, taking nothing with them but the necessaries of life, they quietly maintained themselves for some days, neither receiving nor giving any provocation."[5]

Fearing that outright civil war would erupt, the senators sought to convince them to return. The implicit threat was that the seceders might join the Sabines or Latins and return to Rome to occupy it on behalf of another city, taking its land for themselves in a less polarized economy. Dionysius (6.45) put into the mouth of the seceders' spokesman Sicinius a reply that spelled out the inherent issue at stake:

> "With what purpose, patricians, do you now recall those whom you have driven from their country and transformed from free men into slaves? What assurances will you give us for the performance of those promises that you are convicted of having often broken already? Since you desire to have sole possession of the city, return thither undisturbed by the poor and humble. As for us, we shall be content to regard as our country any land, whatever it be, in which we may enjoy our liberty."

More Romans joined the Secession, including "those who were desirous of escaping their debts and the sentences and punishments they expected," Dionysius (6.46-47) continues. While the secessionists fed themselves from the fields surrounding the Sacred Mount, the Senate sent emissaries to ask "what they desired and upon what terms they would consent to return to the city."

An agreement was reached that the commoners would have two tribunes of their own, whose persons were to be sanctified as inviolable. They were not empowered to propose laws or affect policy, but only to protect commoners against the consuls, and debtors from being hauled into court and deprived of their land and liberty (Livy 2.33).

The patrician elite denounced even this modest authority. And unlike Solon's act in Athens a century earlier, the debts of Rome's rebellious poor were not forgiven.

The plebeian "state within a state"

This experience served as a proving ground for the Roman poor to consolidate their aims by creating what became a full-fledged organization as a parallel "state within a state," having its own administrative functions, officials and, in due course, plebiscites:

---

[5] Livy 2.32, basing his narrative on the *Annales* of Lucius Calpurnius Piso, plebeian tribune in 149 and consul in 133 at the time of the Gracchi, although opposing their reforms.

In the space of a few decades the plebeians created their own popular
assembly in opposition to the *comita centuriata*; they instituted their own
magistrates, ten tribunes and two aediles, who were both more numerous
and more effective than the patrician magistrates; and they founded
their own religious center, the temple of Ceres, Liber and Libera, which
in its triadic form emulated the Capitoline triad of Jupiter, Juno and
Minerva. In the temple of Ceres the plebs established an archive, something the patricians seem not to have had.[6]

Arnaldo Momigliano points out that the patricians spent the remainder of the Republic fighting against attempts to create anything like
Athenian democracy. Minimizing public administration as a means
of maintaining their own control, "[t]he patrician state had no officials
comparable to the plebeian aediles to look after its temples, markets and
archives."[7]

Coriolanus is exiled for trying to reverse the seceders' gains

In 493, the year following the Secession, Rome made a treaty with the
Latin towns and went to war against the Volscians, southeast of Rome.
A distinguished young soldier, Gnaeus Marcius, won the epithet "Coriolanus" for his siege of the town of Corioli. But at home Rome suffered
a famine, largely a result of the fields not being cultivated during the
Secession. The new consuls tried to buy grain from neighboring peoples,
but the Volscians blocked their merchants from selling to Rome, forcing
it to buy grain from Sicily, with some coming from Etruria up the Tiber
(Livy 2.34).[8] This posed a problem of what price to charge for the grain.

Many were of the opinion that the moment had come for putting
pressure on the plebeians, and recovering the rights that had been

---

[6] Momigliano 2005:178. Magistrates were elected, laws passed and trials held in
the Centuriate Assembly consisting of Rome's soldiers, but plebeians were not
allowed to hold magisterial office in the early years of the Republic. Neither their
tribunes nor aediles were technically magistrates, since they were elected solely by
the plebeians. Plebeian tribunes often attempted to block legislation unfavorable to
their order, but the patricians frequently thwarted them by gaining the support of
one or another of the tribunes, especially as wealthy plebeians emerged with interests akin to those of the patricians.

[7] Momigliano 2005:179. This oversight role of the plebeian aediles (the word
derives from *aedes*, temple) led to their being recognized as public functionaries.

[8] Livy and Dionysius report ten grain shortages during 496-411, probably drawing
on pontifical records. See Forsythe 2005:241, citing Ogilvie 1965:256-257.

wrested from the Senate through the secession and the violence which accompanied it. Foremost among these was Marcius Coriolanus.

"If," he argued, "they want their corn at the old price, let them restore to the Senate its old powers. ... why do I see a Sicinius in power? ... Am I, who could not put up with a Tarquin as king, to put up with a Sicinius? Let him secede now! Let him call out his plebeians, the way lies open to the Sacred Hill and to other hills. Let them enjoy the scarcity which in their madness they have produced!"

Coriolanus urged the senators not to lower the price of grain unless the commoners relinquished their newly won right to have their own tribunes. The commoners "flew to arms. Famine, they said, was being used as a weapon against them, as though they were enemies; they were being cheated out of food and sustenance. The foreign grain – their sole means of support – was to be snatched from their mouths unless their tribunes were given up in chains to Gn. Marcius," leaving the poor to "either die or live as slaves" (Livy 2.35).

The tribunes set a date to impeach Coriolanus, and when he did not appear on the day of trial, popular resentment led to his exile. He joined the Volscians, and led their army in an attack on Rome, showing that his patrician loyalty was not to his own community but to his class and its dominance through wealth and privilege.

The seceders never defected to another town, but always returned to Rome. Opportunity for real reform, however, had passed. Rome's wealthy were constantly at war with the poor, writing laws in their own favor and using political violence as their trump card.

Rome's oligarchy blocks democratic reforms

No middle ground was reached between the plebeians and patricians, because the "middle ground" and "moderation" are euphemisms for not seriously disturbing a status quo dominated by the vested interests. Moderate politicians such as the consul Servilius and the dictator Valerius made promises to the poor, which were only to be revoked by the patrician elite. Strong advocates of reforms benefiting debtors and other poor often were put to death for seeking "royalist" power.

In 486, for instance, Rome defeated the Hernici, a neighboring Latin tribe. After taking two-thirds of their land, the new consul Spurius Cassius proposed an agrarian law intended to give half the conquered territory to the Latins and half to needy Romans, who also were to receive public land that patricians had occupied (Dionysius 8.77). The patricians accused Cassius of "building up a power dangerous to liberty" by seeking popular support and "endangering the security" of aristocratic land ownership. When his annual term was over he was charged with treason and killed. His house was burned to the ground to eradicate memory of his land policy (Livy 2.41).

The fight over whether patricians or the needy poor would be the main recipients of public land dragged on for twelve years. By 474 the consuls were still refusing to enact Cassius's law and distribute land to the people. The commoners' tribune, Gnaeus Genucius, sought to bring the previous year's consuls to trial for delaying the redistribution. That year's two consuls, Lucius Furius and Gaius Manlius, argued "that decrees of the Senate were not laws continuing in force forever, but measures designed to meet temporary needs and having validity for one year only" (Livy 2.54 and Dionysius 9.37-38). This meant that the Senate could renege on any decree that had been passed, so that there was no standing permanent law – at least, none that did not benefit the patricians.

The tribune Genucius persisted by bringing a suit against the consuls in 473 for "not appointing the decemvirs [ten designated officials] directed by the Senate to distribute the allotments of land." Noting that twelve successive pairs of annual consuls had failed to proceed, he explained that the only way to compel the new year's consuls "to allot the land would be for them to see some others punished by the populace and thus be reminded that it would be their fate to meet with the same treatment."

The former year's two consuls responded by coming to the Forum dressed in mourning clothes, claiming that Genucius was seeking to make them scapegoats. On the date set for their trial, the commoners gathered and waited for Genucius to appear. "When at length his delay began to look suspicious, they supposed he had been frightened away by the nobles ... finally, those who had presented themselves at the tribune's vestibule brought back word that he had been found dead in his house." When the patricians bragged about putting an end to the commoners' policy threats, the popular leaders feared for their lives, seeing "how utterly ineffectual to protect them were the laws that proclaimed their sanctity" (Livy 2.54).

The new consuls resorted to the usual tactic to disperse the angry populace, calling for a levy of troops as an excuse to move the protestors out of the city. Resistance was led by a centurion, Volero Publilius, whom the crowd defended when the lictors sought to force him to enroll as a common soldier. The consuls themselves took flight, and Volero was elected tribune the next year. He "called an assembly of the populace and proposed a law concerning the tribunician elections, transferring them from the Assembly of the clans, called by the Romans the *curiate* assembly, to the tribal assembly" (Dionysius 9.40-41). That meant "depriving the patricians of the power of using their clients' votes to select what tribunes they liked," by enabling the plebeian assembly to elect tribunes without being subject to Senate or patrician veto (Livy 2.57-58).

The senators were split between those favoring confrontation (led by Appius Claudius, son of the earlier hardliner) and those seeking accommodation to keep the commoners loyal. "It was the opinion of Appius that the idle and needy populace should be kept employed in military expeditions abroad, in order that ... they might be least likely to be hostile and troublesome to the senators who were administering public affairs." He accused Volero's proposed law of "transferring the legitimate courts ... from the most incorruptible Senate to the vilest mob ... introducing tyrannical and unfair laws against the men of noble birth, without leaving to the Senate the power even of passing the preliminary decree concerning those laws."[9] His aim was to retain Rome's version of the Athenian *probouloi*, enabling the patricians to decide what could and what could not be discussed and legislated by the popular assembly and its tribunes.

Appius's attitude was so polarizing that in 471 the Senate supported Volero's *lex Publilia* without opposition. It is from the passing of this law that one can describe the commoners formally as plebeians with specified political rights, giving Rome's Struggle of the Orders its classical shape.[10]

Almost immediately the patricians counter-moved to negate as many plebeian gains as they could, continuing this effort over the last three-quarters of the 5th century. The codification of laws in the Twelve Tables in 450 locked in pro-creditor rules and did not help the plebeians more than marginally, with only nominal promises that the patri-

---

[9] Dionysius 9.43. He added that Appius, "domineering over them as if they were outcasts or foreigners or men whose liberty was precarious, uttered bitter and intolerable reproaches, upbraiding them with the abolition of their debts ... they showed no moderation and could not behave themselves like good citizens, but were always aiming at some selfish encroachment and violation of the laws."

[10] Some historians suspect that Livy conflated this episode with the *lex Publilia* enacted over a century later, in 339, to make plebeian policies – plebiscites – binding on all Romans including the patricians, and also to open the office of censor to plebeians. The aim was to reduce the political power of the *comitia centuriata* that had survived since the time of Roman kings.

cians failed to honor in practice. Ten commissioners were charged with reforming the Roman constitution. They prompted a Second Secession of the Plebs in 449 by trying to abolish the power of the plebeian tribunes.

11
The Twelve Tables and Struggle for Debt Reform, 462-390 BC

Rome's commoners made few economic gains during the 5th century. Excluded from holding office, they created their own assembly and elected their own tribunes to provide defense against the use of force by the patricians. The tribunes "had only one duty: to protect their fellow plebeians against abuse of power by the patricians and their magistrates," summarizes Raaflaub. "Originally everything must have been informal, based on despair, determination, solidarity, and the sacred oath."[1]

Two basic democratic reforms were needed: political rights for the commoners, including access to political office and juries; and a standardized body of law. In 462 the tribune Gaius Terentilius Harsa proposed a five-man commission to define and limit the power of consuls. The Senate kept postponing discussion of reform, and after eight years had passed, the tribunes asked the Senate in 454 to appoint "a body of legislators, chosen in equal numbers from plebeians and patricians to enact what would be useful to both orders and secure equal liberty for each" (Livy 3.32). The Senate insisted that only patricians be appointed, and named its own team to draw up the laws.

Two years later, in 452, the appointees said they were ready to make their recommendations. Livy and Dionysius thought that they went to Athens to review its laws, but no similarity exists at all. Rome had no democratic restructuring akin to the reforms of Cleisthenes providing equality among voters and equal access to public office and juries, to say nothing of Solon's *seisachtheia* ending debt bondage a century and a half earlier. Rome's one-sided oligarchic power was locked in place, above all via the debt laws that were at the heart of politics and land tenure.

The plebeians made a fateful concession in 451 to trust Appius Claudius Crassus (either the son or great-nephew of the original Sabine patrician Appius Claudius) to appoint a ten-member commission (decemvirs) with power to write the laws that became the Twelve Tables. Despite his reputation as an opponent of the plebeians, he posed as their

---

[1] Raaflaub 2005:195.

friend long enough to gain their support. Once appointed, he no longer needed to court popular favor. He named himself as the first decimvir and sponsored nine supporters (five of them said to be plebeians) to write the laws with him.[2]

The plebeians had demanded such a commission to escape from patrician rule, but the decemvirs aimed to terminate the popular assembly, tribunes and aediles by making a deal to open all remaining offices to plebeians.[3] The only plebeian demand that was met was to fix the laws and Senate decisions in writing, so as to lock in whatever promises were made, and thus limit the arbitrary power of magistrates. But the Twelve Tables that the decimvirs produced were Draconian and pro-creditor, reinforcing the oligarchy's economic power (Livy 3.37). The effect of codifying written statutory law was to make debt foreclosure and other practices uniform, but harsh.

Table III locks in creditor power

The Twelve Tables were formally promulgated in 449 and inscribed in bronze and displayed in the Forum. Cicero wrote that students were obliged to memorize the text, which seems to have been so well known that Livy doesn't bother to cite it.[4] However, the laws were not a comprehensive code in the modern sense. Reflecting the agricultural character of Rome's economy at the time, they did not deal "with commercial transactions, credit, industrial production or investment; all the clauses that deal with purchase are concerned with *res mancipi* – that is, real estate, draught animals and what are called 'rustic *praedial* servitudes' (rights to walk, to drive animals or carts, or to take water, through someone else's property)."[5]

Table III set out the rules for defaulting debtors. If a debtor failed to make a stipulated payment on time, he was taken into court and a judgment obtained against him. He had thirty days to come up with the money due. After that period had elapsed, his creditor could bind him in up to fifteen pounds of chains or wooden stocks, and either keep him

---

[2] Von Ungern-Sternberg 2005:76-77.

[3] See Cornell 1995:73, citing Livy 3.33, and the rest of his Chapter 11: "The Twelve Tables" (pp. 272-292).

[4] Cornell 1995:278, citing Dionysius 10.57.7, Diodorus 12.26.1 and Livy 3.57.10. The full text is available at https://archive.org/stream/thetwelvetables14783gut/14783.txt. Like Hammurabi's laws they took the form of "If this, then that."

[5] Cornell 1995:287.

at his own premise (being obliged to feed him at least one pound of grits daily) or let him live on his own, for sixty more days.

If the debtor could not raise the money by the end of that time, he was taken before the praetor's court in the public marketplace for three successive marketing days, and the amount of his debts publicly announced. On the third day his creditors were permitted to divide up his personal estate, literally "take their several portions" ("cut him into pieces"). This must have meant dividing up his property, because taking the proverbial pound of flesh would have spurred a popular outcry – not to mention losing the debtor's value as a bondservant or slave.[6]

Codifying the *nexal* law, Table III stated that any enslavement of defaulting debtors had to take place outside of Roman territory and that of Rome's Latin allies, by selling the debtors "across the Tiber" (*trans Tiberim*) in Etruscan territory. The alternative to "execution" or being sold abroad was to agree to work for the creditor or to "enter a *nexum* contract with a third party, to whom he (the debtor) surrendered himself as a bondsman in exchange for money with which he paid off his existing debts."[7] The sources imply that *nexum* was "the result of an agreement voluntarily entered into by the debtor."

The Twelve Tables set a maximum limit on the legal rate of usury – $1/12^{th}$ (one ounce per pound, *unciarium foenus*, the equivalent of $8^{1}/3$ percent).[8] This was Rome's first documented reference to an interest rate. Reflecting the contempt in which usurers were widely held, Table VIII punished them twice as severely as thieves: Creditors who charged higher interest than the legal rate were liable to pay fourfold damages, while thieves only had to make twofold restitution.[9]

These rules did not save debtors from losing their liberty, but at least "*nexum* was clearly distinct from sale into slavery," Cornell emphasizes, "first because the *nexi* ("bondsmen") retained their status as Roman citizens, and second because they continued to live at Rome." The best that plebeians could obtain was protection against being sold into

---

[6] Gellius 20.1.48-50 thought that *partis secanto* meant literally cutting the debtor into pieces, and "was surprised that there was no record of this cruel provision ever having been put into effect."

[7] Cornell 1995:281.

[8] The rate of $1/12^{th}$ reflected the year's division into 12 months. That became the basis for Rome's fractional system, making $1/12^{th}$ the easiest rate to calculate. See also Chapter 12 below and Hudson 2000a for how this calendrical basis of fractions reflected an annualized Near Eastern practice of $1/60^{th}$ (based on 30-day months).

[9] See Tenney Frank 1933:17.

slavery to Etruscans, as they were in no position to expect full debt cancellation.[10]

Smallholders with only a few acres could hardly avoid running into debt, especially when war drew them away from their farms. The effect of these laws was to create a framework for Roman loan-for-labor (*nexum*) contracts, similar to the typical character of the debt relationship in archaic agrarian societies. As Cornell summarizes:

> It may strike the observer as puzzling that moneylenders should have been prepared to advance loans to impoverished peasants who had no serious prospect of repaying them, and no security other than their own persons. The knowledge that one would be entitled to cut a defaulter into pieces is unlikely to have given much satisfaction. The explanation is that we are not dealing with moneylending, 'credit' and interest payments; rather, it is a matter of 'loans' made by wealthy landowners, often no doubt paid in kind, in the form of seed-corn or the bare means of subsistence. The purpose of the "loan," which was secured on the person of the debtor, was precisely to create a state of bondage. In reality it was a payment for the labour services of a bondsman, who effectively sold himself (or one of his children) to the "creditor." The very nature of the contract, *per aes et libram* [with copper and scales], was similar to a sale. From the lender's point of view the object of the exercise was to obtain the labor services of the debtor rather than profit through interest.[11]

The usurer (*faenerator*) "had the right to seize the person of the *nexus*" at any time, even before harvest.[12] Also, without a mandatory waiting period for the debtor to raise the money to pay, the creditor might collect his loan by "buying" the debtor's property at an arbitrary price that he himself set on the spot.[13]

Patrician character of the Twelve Tables

The Twelve Tables did not address the political crisis that led to the appointment of the decemvirs: the patrician blockage of plebeian par-

---

[10] Cornell 1995:281-282.

[11] Cornell 1995:282-283. This certainly was the case in Bronze Age Mesopotamia: see Steinkeller and Hudson 2015. On *nexum* (debt bondage), Cornell cites F. De Zuleuta, *Law Quarterly Review* 29 (1913):137-153, Watson, *Twelve Tables*:111-124, and J. Ennew, *Debt Bondage: a survey* (London 1981).

[12] Richard 2005:119.

[13] That was one of the abuses that Urukagina of Lagash (ca. 2350 BC) cited in his "reform" or "liberty" (amargi) text. I discuss this Near Eastern background in Hudson 2018, Chapter 9.

ticipation in lawmaking and the courts. Plebeians would continue to be excluded from the magistracies and priesthoods that administered Rome's political and legal system.[14] Table XI tried to permanently exclude plebeians from gaining access to these offices even by marriage, separating the orders by banning intermarriage between patricians and plebeians. (The law was soon repealed.)

Instead of a conciliatory move toward compromise with the plebeians by Appius Claudius and his appointees, the Twelve Tables focused narrowly on what debtors owed their creditors and how they would be punished for insulting those in authority or stealing their property. The laws were "a reaction of the few aiming at preserving their political influence as completely as possible," locking in a framework of pro-creditor rules to provide "a legal basis for existing property arrangements," and above all "to render ineffective any demand for cancellation of debts or distribution of land."[15]

Unlike Athenian juries selected by lot, patricians continued to run the courts exclusively, with no check on their arbitrary judgments or process to force the courts to make patrician usurers or land grabbers pay the penalties laid down for breaking the laws – or for that matter, to stop the Senate from simply refusing to enforce laws favorable to the plebeians. Creditors were deterred only temporarily from violating the maximum limit on interest rates, so the same laws had to be re-enacted again and again.[16]

The laws were Draconian toward the poor. "If a person has maimed another's limb, let there be retaliation in kind unless he makes agreement for settlement with him" (VIII.2). Likewise, Table III prescribes: "For pasturing on, or cutting secretly by night, another's crops acquired by tillage, there shall be capital punishment in the case of an adult male-

---

[14] Raaflaub 2005:195 and 203, citing Livy 6.11.9; 31.2; 32.1 and 34.2. Rome's legal formulae had long been kept secret, known only to elite patrician families. They "were decisive for any proper legal procedure, [and] were not published but remained under the well-guarded control of the *pontifices* for another 150 years." See also Eder 2005:263, fn36.

[15] Eder 2005:239-240.

[16] Some classicists believe that the legal cap on interest rates and other laws were passed only once, and infer that repeated similar laws must be confusion by the annalists. This view misses the reason why similar laws had to be passed again and again: namely, to try and force creditors to obey the law that they repeatedly and systematically violated. The modern equivalent of Rome's failure to prosecute would be the Obama Administration's principle of U.S. banks and other campaign contributors being "too big to jail."

factor ... he shall be hanged and put to death as a sacrifice to Ceres."
Younger persons were to be scourged or pay double damages.[17]

To prevent populist mockery of the elites, such as was found in
Athenian comedy performed on public occasions, the patricians used
the Twelve Tables to punish humor or personal political opposition
as if it were an attack on a person's body. "If any person has sung or
composed against another person a song such as was causing slander or
insult to another, he shall be clubbed to death."[18]

Rejection of the decemvirs leads to the Valero-Horatian laws

The attempt by the decemvirs to abolish the tribunate left the plebeians
with only one resort: to establish their own legal principles by threatening to leave the city once again, which they did in 449. This Second
Secession of the Plebs was said to have been triggered by a patrician
"Rape of Lucretia" attack on a defenseless woman by Appius Claudius.
Lusting after a plebeian girl, Verginia, he schemed to obtain her as his
sex servant by arranging for one of his clients, "M. Claudius, to claim
the girl as his slave," stating that the man claiming to be her father was
actually her kidnapper and barring "any claim on the part of her friends
to retain possession of her till the case was tried." Appius himself was
the judge at the trial to decide her fate, and naturally judged for his
client. To protect the girl's honor, her father stabbed her to death.[19]

This incident is said to have catalyzed plebeian resentment against the
patriciate. The plebeians called for the decemvirs to resign when their
one-year term was up, but the decemvirs refused to step down. Riots
ensued, and the plebeians and much of the army withdrew once again
to the Sacred Mount. That led many more conciliatory senators to react
against the extremism of the decemvirs. Livy (3.52.5-8) describes the
logic that led to a resolution: Many besides the two Senate negotiators
with the plebeians, L. Valerius Potitus and M. Horatius Barbatus,

> were now angrily asking, "What are you waiting for, senators? If the
> decemvirs do not lay aside their obstinacy, will you allow everything to
> go to wrack and ruin? ... Are you going to administer justice to walls

---

[17] Lewis and Reinhold 1951:112. Treating people according to their status was
common in Germanic and other wergild-type laws.

[18] Table VIII, in Lewis and Reinhold 1951:106.

[19] Livy 3.44.1. See also 3.47.5; 3.50.13 and 3.52.1. Von Ungern-Sternberg 2005:7-78
describes the various versions of this story.

and roofs? Are you not ashamed to see a greater number of lictors in the Forum than of all other citizens put together?

"What will you do if the enemy approach the City? What if the plebs seeing that their secession has no effect, come shortly against us in arms? Do you want to end your power by the fall of the City? Either you will have to do without the plebeians or you will have to accept their tribunes; sooner than they will go without their magistrates, we shall have to go without ours."

However, the negotiations for their return achieved nothing like the democratic power achieved in Athens. There was no debt cancellation, nor even limitations on being sold as slaves across the Tiber, as distinct from simply having to work off their debts as free men. There was not "it seems, a significant improvement in the plight of the debtors," summarizes Raaflaub. "Nor was the aristocratic monopoly of power institutionally restricted ... There was no mediator, no real compromise."[20] Rome's constitution remained aristocratic throughout Roman history as the aristocracy remained united in its opposition to raising the political and economic status of the commoners.

But at least in 449 the Senate responded to this Second Secession by restoring the former political arrangements, and Valerius and Horatius were elected as the year's new consuls. They formally promulgated the Twelve Tables at this time, and passed the Valerio-Horatian laws restoring the right of citizens to appeal (which the decemvir dictatorship had suspended), and confirmed the sacrosanct protective status of the tribunes. In an attempt to deter the breaking of senatorial agreements, the Valerio-Horatian laws called for all senatorial decrees and acts to be publicly recorded in the Temple of Ceres, the main plebeian temple, so that they could not be altered or falsified.

The plebeian assembly was officially recognized and its plebiscites could make laws binding on all Roman citizens – but subject to a Senate veto. This confirmation of plebiscites had to be re-asserted in 339 by the consul and dictator Q. Publilius Philo (the *lex Publilia*), and again in 287 (the *lex Hortensia*), evidently because the Senate went back on its promise.[21] Meanwhile, plebeian leaders were becoming wealthy enough to be co-opted by the patricians. Almost immediately, in 448 the patri-

---

[20] Raaflaub 2005:194.

[21] Cornell 1995:276, citing Livy 3.53.3, notes that "Roman reformers frequently re-enacted earlier statutes, even when these were still in force," *e.g.*, Tiberius Gracchus's revival of the law limiting to 500 iugera the public land that one citizen could occupy (see Chapter 14).

cians maneuvered to retain political control by co-opting five plebeians into their camp. As a result, only five tribunes were elected to fill the ten designated tribal positions, and a new plebeian protest led to passage of the *Lex Trebonia* forbidding the patricians from distorting future elections in this manner.

The attempt by Table XI to ban intermarriage led the plebeians to demand explicit and irrevocable political equality with the patricians. In 445 they demanded the right to have one of their class be elected as consul. The Senate balked, but permitted the Centuriate Assembly of fighting men to elect military tribunes with consular command authority (*imperium*), subject to the usual Senate veto of any outcome it did not like.

When the dust of the Second Secession had settled, P. A. Brunt asks:

> What had been achieved? In form, a greater measure of democratic control: that was to prove an illusion. Plebeians had been admitted to office. But by giving up their monopoly, the patricians perpetuated for themselves a share in power. A new nobility arose in which only a few plebeians were admitted, and which was as dominant as the patricians had been. Its economic interests and oligarchic sentiments were no different. The order of society was basically unchanged.[22]

Although ordinary Roman citizens were not able to "participate in politics to the same extent as the Athenian demos of the fifth and fourth centuries," notes Eder, and despite the fact that "the lower classes achieved only relatively small gains, the dangerous tensions seem to have been alleviated for a long time. ... Not until about eighty years later did the struggle break out again in Rome."[23]

It took until the late 4th and early 3rd centuries for the respective laws of Q. Publilius Philo and Quintus Hortensius to finally confirm that any law passed by the plebeian assembly would have full force of law over patricians as well as plebeians. Their laws confirmed the Valerio-Horatian laws of 449, and the *lex Hortensia* removed the last patrician and Senate check to plebeian rulings.

The assassination of Spurius Maelius in 439

A chronic problem preventing Rome's commoners from obtaining meaningful democratic rights was the ultimate veto: the murder of strong leaders who threatened the oligarchy. Throughout Roman history

---

[22] Brunt 1971a:58. This evaluation is also an underlying theme of Cornell and Raaflaub.

[23] Eder 2005:250, 292 and 248.

most political violence was against reformers advocating debt allevia-
tion and/or land distribution. It was by violence that the senators killed
Tiberius Gracchus and his supporters in 133 for opposing and trying to
reverse the illegal grabbing of public land. This violence inaugurated the
ensuing century of civil warfare that culminated in the murder of politicians from Catiline to Julius Caesar.[24]

Spurius Cassius had been put to death in 485 for advocating land
distribution (described in Chapter 10). The next two major martyrs
were Spurius Maelius in 439, and the patrician Manlius Capitolinus
in 384. The century spanning these three political killings saw Roman
politics increasingly polarized as a result of the deteriorating condition
of debtors and smallholders.

In 440-439, a decade after the Twelve Tables, a severe grain shortage
occurred. To relieve the resulting unrest and alleviate the debts of
commoners facing bondage, Spurius Maelius, a wealthy equestrian
merchant, used his own money to distribute grain to the hungry population, "measuring out a peck for two *denarii* instead of for twelve *denarii*,
and bestowing it without payment upon all those whom he perceived to
be utterly helpless and unable to defray the cost of even their daily subsistence" (Dionysius 12.1). The patricians "regarded him with suspicion,
thinking that no good would come to them from the man's prodigality;
and gathering together in the Forum, they considered how they ought,
in most seemly fashion and without danger, to force him to desist from
these political designs." Livy (4.13) reflects the patricians' fear that
this was "a very bad precedent," to which they attributed "still worse
motives" of political ambition to tyranny.

Maelius accused Rome's prefect of the grain market, L. Minucius
Lanatus, of doing nothing to help resolve the food shortage. Minucius
tried to blame Maelius for sending his friends and clients from Etruria to
Sicily to buy grain, bidding up prices in these regions. Maelius defended
himself by denouncing the selfish behavior of patricians "for taking no
thought ... for the needy" and refusing to use their own fortunes for the
good of Rome. Indeed, he pointed out, they "had even appropriated the
public land and had for a long time now enjoyed its use."

The patricians no doubt were upset that Maelius's act prevented high
food prices from forcing more families into debt and thus making the
plebeians more willing to surrender to patrician demands to roll back
the political rights they recently had won (recalling the tactic advocated

---

[24] It also was by violence that the mercantile suppliers of the Roman state blocked
attempts to prosecute them for fraud during the Punic Wars (see Chapter 13).

by Coriolanus noted above in Chapter 10). Accusing Maelius of using his popularity to establish a tyranny, Minucius warned the Senate that Maelius was mobilizing his followers and storing arms at his house to prepare for a fight. That persuaded the Senate to recall a former dictator, the octogenarian L. Quinctius Cincinnatus, known to be a patrician hard-liner. He issued an order for Maelius to stand trial for treason.

Minucius, the consuls and guards set out for the Forum after midnight, and when the crowd gathered in the morning, told them that a dictator had been chosen. Livy (4.14) describes Maelius as asking why this was done, as Rome was not at war and there was no domestic disturbance. The reply was given by C. Servilius Ahala, whom Cincinnatus had chosen as his second-in-command (Master of the Horse). The young man announced in front of the crowd: "An act of impeachment was brought against you yesterday before the Senate, Maelius, for attempting a revolution."

Maelius saw where this was leading, and turned to the crowd: "Plebeians, help me; for I am being snatched away by the men in power because of my goodwill toward you. It is not to a trial that I am summoned by them, but to death." The crowd rescued Maelius when Ahala ordered an officer to arrest him. In Livy's version, Ahala then chased Maelius and killed him. Returning to Cincinnatus, he said that he had done this because Maelius was inciting the crowd to riot. He was duly commended for saving the Republic from an ambitious man seeking to establish a kingly tyranny.[25]

Maelius's property was confiscated and his house razed to the ground, presumably to abolish all memory of his seeking the support of the poor by relieving them from famine at his own expense, as if this were an obligation of the wealthy or the state. In an attempt to recover its own popularity, the Senate enabled Minucius to "distribute the corn that had belonged to Maelius at the price of one 'as' per bushel; the plebs raised no objection to his being thus honored" (Livy 6.16).

Cornell notes that the two versions of the story by Livy and Dionysius "contain a sufficient number of unique details to make it unlikely that the whole story was a politically motivated fiction." To be sure, "in the pre-Gracchan period the tradition probably said no more than

---

[25] Livy, Dionysius and Cicero describe Ahala as acting in an official capacity. An alternative version (which Dionysius 12.2 says comes from Cincius Alimentus and Calpurnius Piso) has the assassin acting as a private citizen. In that version Maelius ran into a butcher shop, but was followed and "hacked to pieces, he died like a wild beast."

that Maelius had been killed by Servilius Ahala while trying to make himself king. But the calamitous events of 133 BC would have given the episode a new and startling relevance ... since it might have appeared to be a precedent for the action of P. Scipio Nasica, who had instigated the lynching of Gracchus and his followers."[26] Nevertheless, Cornell concludes: "A place called Aequimaeliuim was thought to mark the site of Maelius's house, which was razed to the ground on the orders of the Senate." Nearby was the column of L. Minucius who first warned the Senate of Maelius's supposed intentions to gain power.

Forsythe finds the details unbelievable because they are so standardized. But subsidizing grain prices or paying off the debts of supporters to gain popular support was in fact a standard political tactic from Greece to Rome. Later historians probably had a summary report "that the Roman state suffered from some crisis at that time, and that it was probably associated with a food shortage."[27]

The politics of debt, war and land appropriation were becoming standardized. When domestic protests threatened, patricians typically found a reason to send the populace out to fight. Waging war directed hopes for land and economic improvement at the expense of foreigners. Warfare suspended lawsuits over debt, freeing enlisted men from being sued by creditors as long as they continued fighting. Veterans usually were given land from conquered territories, so they were fighting to obtain their own means of self-support, and to acquire war prisoners to become their family servants.

In any event, the problem of famine was soon to end for a century as Rome conquered land from neighboring peoples. But plebeian debt and patrician land grabbing remained a constant source of complaint for all plebeian critics.[28]

The conquest of Veii, 406-396

The end of the 5th century saw Rome fight against Veii, ten miles north of the Tiber and the wealthiest Etruscan city. Rome began paying its

---

[26] Cornell 2005:50-52. See Livy 4.12-16 and 21.3-4, Dionysius 12.1, Cicero, *De Senectute* 16, and Ogilvie 1965:550-557.

[27] Forsythe 2005:239-240. Raaflaub 2005:29 likewise finds this story "heavily tainted by reinterpretations prompted by debates connected with Tiberius Gracchus's murder," retrojected back to the 5th century.

[28] Bernard 2016:318 notes that food shortages were reported in 508, 492, 477, 456, 453, 440, 428, 411, 392 and 383, but not for the remainder of the 4th century (until 299 BC). Debt crises took their place.

troops a salary for the first time, but obliged them to spend the winter building new quarters near Veii to prepare a siege. The plebeians denounced this as a ruse to prevent them from pressing for reforms at home while their debts mounted up as they were unable to till their land (Livy 5.2). Rome increased its military tax when Etruscan armies joined to support Veii, leading plebeian leaders to protest that "the reason why military pay had been established was that one half of the plebs might be crushed by the war-tax, and the other by military service" (Livy 5.10.6-7). The conflict was settled by the plebeians agreeing to pay the war tax in exchange for the right to appoint a plebeian consular tribune (Livy 5.12).

Rome seemed on the verge of defeat by 397 when it named M. Furius Camillus dictator (the first of what would be five times). He expanded Rome's army to include Latin and Hernican troops. They dug under Veii's city walls to enter through its underground drainage system, massacring the adult male population and selling its women and children into slavery. The sales proceeds were paid into the treasury (Livy 5.22).

The victory nearly doubled the size of Rome's territory. That revived the tension between Rome's oligarchy and commoners over how to dispose of the conquered land. The plebeians advocated using the 50,000 hectares across the Tiber to settle veterans and other poor families. As an alternative, the Senate voted to plant a colony on the more distant Volscian frontier, "and the names of 3000 Roman citizens were entered for it. Triumvirs appointed for the purpose had divided the land into lots of 3 7/12 iugera per man" (Livy 5.24). The plebeians wanted closer and more fertile Veientine land, and proposed incorporating Veii into Rome as a single state. Camillus led the opposition to the plebeians' plan, using the usual patrician tactic of delay (Plutarch, *Camillus* 7.4).

He had promised to donate a tenth of the captured booty to the Temple of Apollo at Delphi. But he broke this pledge and asked the Senate how to distribute the booty. Romans were invited to go to Veii and take whatever they could. The Senate later decided that inasmuch as many citizens had simply helped themselves, each should simply devote a tenth of whatever they had taken, as there were no records of the total seized. This became a lasting sore spot among the plebeians for the next few decades, suspecting that the patricians had kept the lion's share of the booty for themselves.

The Senate settled matters by sending a golden bowl to Delphi, but the argument over booty dragged on for another year. The plebeians vented their anger at Camillus by demanding that he pay a large sum

(15,000 *asses*). His friends offered to provide the money, but Camillus
chose to go into exile in 391. The Senate ruled that each plebeian should
receive 7 iugera of the Veientine territory (twice the original proposal),
not only family heads but also "all the children in the house, that men
might be willing to bring up children in the hope that they would receive
their share" (Livy 5.30.8).[29]

The Gauls sack and burn Rome

Gaulish bands had crossed the Alps into Italy soon after 400 BC. By 391
they were attacking Tuscan and Etruscan territories. The next year they
reached Rome, heavily defeating its army where the Tiber joined with the
Allia river. Many soldiers took refuge in Veii, causing the people remaining in Rome to panic when they thought that the few survivors who
returned to the city were all the troops that were left. The Gauls poured
in and killed the largely non-combatant citizens, and set the city on fire.

Those who were able mounted a last stand to defend the citadel (Arx)
on the steep Capitoline Hill.[30] The Gauls tried to sneak up to it, and
avoided waking the Roman sentries and even the dogs. But the sacred
geese of Juno began to honk, warning the Romans – hence, the name of
the temple subsequently built on the site - Juno Moneta, "the Warner."
Among the Romans defending the citadel was a patrician who had been
consul in 392, M. Manlius (later given the honorific name Capitolinus).
Other Romans joined him and they drove the Gauls back with stones
and javelins (Livy 5.47).

It was mid-summer, and the Gauls began to catch malaria from the
mosquitos breeding along the Tiber. Both armies were suffering from
famine, as Rome's grain had been burned or otherwise destroyed.
Seeing that the situation was a standoff, "a conference took place
between Q. Sulpicius, the consular tribune, and Brennus, the Gauls'
chieftain. An agreement was arrived at by which the sum of 1000
pounds of gold was fixed as the ransom" to pay the Gauls to leave (Livy
5.48). An argument arose over just how much a pound was supposed to
weigh, with the Romans accusing the Gauls of using unfair weights.

It was at this point that Camillus appeared with the troops he had

---

[29] Roselaar 2010:19-20 and 30-31 notes that Roman conquest of foreign land was
minimal in the 5th century, and really begins with Veii, although earlier public land
was used to settle the plebs while much was, as usual, occupied by the well-to-do.
Colonization ceased after the foundation of Sutrium and Nepet in 383.

[30] Livy 5.30 and 5.39 to 5.43. Some modern historians date the sack of Rome to 387.

gathered while in exile in Ardea, where he had given an inspirational speech to its citizens to support Rome. They had surprised and massacred the Gaulish army nearby. Camillus then mobilized the Roman troops that had retreated to Veii and led them to Rome. Upon hearing the truce that had been negotiated, he rejected it, claiming to be the only proper authority as dictator. "He then warned the Gauls to prepare for battle," and told the Romans to "win their country back by steel, not by gold." The Gauls were furious, and without pausing to plan a strategy of attack, they rushed at the Romans. Camillus outmaneuvered them and devastated their troops.

The withdrawal of the Gauls, coupled with Rome's military conquest of Veii, marks the point at which surviving Roman historical sources really begin. Livy started Book 6 of his *History of Rome* by pointing out that "the pontifical commentaries and public and private archives nearly all perished" when the city burned, leaving few written records for subsequent historians to consult.[31]

The aftermath of Rome's foreign conquest and the city's rebuilding led to new debt strains and demands for land redistribution throughout the 4th century. The next four centuries of Roman history were shaped by war making, land grabbing and rules governing debt dependency. These three dynamics determined which class would end up with most of the conquered territory, and how deeply the commoners would be indebted to the wealthy.

A series of six debt reforms started in 367 with the Licinian-Sextian Rogation providing debt relief and limiting the ownership of public land. This was followed in 357 by reiterating 1/12th as the legal interest ceiling. New laws adjudicated fair prices for transferring land to foreclosing creditors in 352, and in 347 the legal interest rate was cut in half and repayment schedules stretched out over three years. The Genucian law of 342 banned interest charges outright, and in 326 or 313 the Poetelia-Papiria law banned *nexum* debt slavery. These reforms were accompanied by the acquisition of at least nominal legal equality between the plebeians and patricians regarding access to the highest public offices.[32]

---

[31] Livy adds (6.10) that the Twelve Tables and some other records "were made accessible to the public, but those which dealt with divine worship were kept secret by the pontiff mainly in order that the people might remain dependent on them for religious guidance."

[32] Savunen 1993 provides a thorough enumeration of references to the literature and commentaries on the 4th-century's debt reforms discussed in the next chapter.

12

New Revolts Lead to the Banning of Debt Slavery, 390-287 BC

S eeing how thoroughly Rome had been burned by the Gauls in 390, the plebeian tribunes reiterated their proposal that Romans should migrate to Veii or simply incorporate its territory into that of Rome.[1] The war against Veii had attracted debtors into the army, and they sought to colonize the conquered land. But Camillus continued to oppose the move, pressing for rebuilding Rome within a single year, taking no time for urban planning. Streets were not laid out in straight lines, and buildings were constructed haphazardly over existing sewage and drainage routes.

By 387, three years after the great fire that had burned much of Rome, enough young Roman settlers had been granted farming plots in Veii to create four new rural tribes (bringing the total number to 25). The new tribes included the inhabitants of Capenae and Fidenae who had supported Rome in its war against Veii and then against the Gauls. This expansion averted pressure on the patricians to redistribute their own domestic land in Rome itself. However, the difficulty of eking out a living on the new settlers' modest 7 iugera lots, along with the levies imposed to rebuild Rome (which Livy 6.32 cited as the main cause), resulted in new debt strains that pushed indebtedness to a new extreme. That led to a wave of bondage, culminating in riots in 385 as popular antagonism deepened toward Camillus and his patrician allies.

Livy (6.27) explained the patrician policy throughout the 4th century as being to wage ongoing military campaigns to keep the plebeians "under arms and not allow them any breathing time in the city or any leisure for thoughts of liberty, or any possibility for taking their place in the Assembly, where they might listen to the voice of a tribune urging the reduction of interest and the redress of other grievances."

The Senate's fight against Manlius Capitolinus (386-384)

Livy attributed the riots in 385 to the "vast amount of debt [that] had been contracted owing to the expense of building, an expense most ru-

---

[1] Livy 5.49-50. See 5.24.7-9 for the similar earlier demand.

inous even to the rich." Patricians feared a new uprising by distressed debtors. "[I]t became, therefore, a question of arming the government with stronger powers" to write new debt laws and also to grant land to the plebeians.

As matters turned out, the advocacy for reform was soon led by a member of the patricians' own class, the defender of the Capitoline Hill Marcus Manlius Capitolinus.[2] Livy (6.11.6-9) described him as the first patrician to act as a populist (*popularis*), recognizing "that the laws of debt caused more irritation than the others; they not only threatened poverty and disgrace, but they terrified the freeman with the prospect of fetters and imprisonment."

Manlius escalated the showdown when he saw creditors seizing a renowned centurion, "carried off to chains and slavery just as though he had been captured by the victorious Gauls" (Livy 6.14). Paying the man's debt with his own money and sending him home, Manlius denounced "the tyranny of patricians and the brutality of usurers and the wretched condition of the plebs."

In Livy's narrative the released debtor showed the crowd his war wounds, complaining much like the veteran whose plight had triggered the First Secession of the Plebs a century earlier, and spelled out the point that Livy wanted to make about the burden of usury: "Whilst I was serving in the field and trying to restore my desolated home, I paid in interest an amount equal to many times the principal, but as the fresh interest always exceeded my capital, I was buried beneath the load of debt."

Manlius's popularity increased when he put his estate in the Veientine territory up for auction and used the proceeds to relieve Roman debtors. He then threw down the political gauntlet by accusing the patricians of taking for themselves the gold collected as ransom for the Gauls, of appropriating public land for themselves and of embezzling so much public revenue that if the money hidden away "were brought to light, the debts of the plebs could be wiped off."

His house became a gathering place for his supporters to outline their program of debt forgiveness and public land distribution. To counter these demands, the Senate appointed A. Cornelius Cossus dictator in 385. When he summoned Manlius to answer the charge that he was aspiring to kingship, "Manlius gave his party a signal that a conflict was

---

[2] Mommsen suspected that the story of Manlius having saved the Capitoline Hill from attack by the Gauls was a folk etymology, and thought that his cognomen Capitolinus more likely reflected where his prestigious home was located. See Hooper 1979:53-55.

imminent, and appeared before the tribunal with an immense crowd around him. On the one side the Senate, on the other side the plebs ... stood facing one another as though drawn up for battle" (Livy 6.15).

Calling for Manlius to back up his accusation, Cossus said: "I see that you have led your fellow citizens to expect that all debts can be paid without any loss to the creditors out of the treasure recovered from the Gauls, which you say the leading patricians are secreting. I am so far from wishing to hinder this project that, on the contrary, I challenge M. Manlius to take off from their hidden hordes those who, like sitting hens, are brooding over treasures that belong to the State." Failure to do so, he added, would result in Manlius being thrown into prison.

Manlius accused Cossus of "openly declaring himself the protector of the usurers against the plebeians." He suggested that if the patricians sought to draw support away from him, why not simply "release your fellow-citizens from the stocks, by preventing them from being adjudged to their creditors, by supporting others in their necessity out of the superabundance of your own wealth?" At the very least, he urged creditors to "deduct from the principal what has already been paid in interest." If that were done, he said, "then the crowd round me will be no more noticeable than that round anyone else."

He was imprisoned for inciting the crowd, which Livy describes as being so submissive to authority that "neither the tribunes of the plebs nor the plebeians themselves ventured to cast an angry look or breathe a syllable against the action of the dictator." Editorializing on the theme of why Rome had never developed a more fair and viable economy, Livy (6.17) blamed the failure of its plebeians for their timidity to fight to obtain the rights that the Greeks had won: "Men were heard openly reproaching the populace for always encouraging their defenders till they led them to the brink of the precipice, but deserting them when the moment of danger actually came. It was in this way, they said, that Sp. Cassius, while seeking to get the plebs on to the land, and Sp. Maelius, whilst staving off famine at his own cost from the mouths of his fellow-citizens, had both been crushed."

To alleviate the unrest, the Senate "ordered that 2000 Roman citizens should be settled as colonists at Satricum, and each receive two and a half iugera of land. This was regarded as too small a grant, distributed amongst too small a number. It was looked upon as a bribe for the betrayal of Manlius." Crowds gathered afresh and put on the garb of mourners, usually done only in times of great public calamity. The Senate feared that they were about to storm the prison to free Manlius.

Cowed by the tumult, it released Manlius in order to avoid a showdown (Plutarch, *Camillus* 36.4).

Rallying his followers, Manlius gave a speech into which Livy (6.18) writes a summary of what he himself thought should have been the logic guiding the plebeian demands – at least, as they had sharpened by the 1st century's civil war toward which Rome's 4th-century debt crisis was heading.[3]

> "How long, pray," he asked, "are you going to remain in ignorance of your strength, an ignorance which nature forbids even to beasts? Do at least reckon up your numbers and those of your opponents. ... You are much more numerous ... You have only to make a show of war and you will have peace. Let them see you are prepared to use force, they will abate their claims. You must dare something as a body or you will have to suffer everything as individuals. ...
>
> "Why is it that you display such spirit towards foreign nations as to think it fair and just that you should rule over them? ... Dictatorships and consulships must be leveled to the ground in order that the Roman plebs may lift up its head. Take your places, then, in the Forum; prevent any judgment for debt from being pronounced."

Seeing this show of force as an incitement to yet another Secession of the Plebs, "A great many [patricians] exclaimed that what was wanted was a Servilius Ahala, who would ... put an end to the internecine war by the sacrifice of a single citizen" (Livy 6.19). The Senate accused him of aiming at monarchy and condemned him to death for treason in 385.

Manlius described how he had led the fight to save Rome from the Gauls, and claimed to be saving it once again from its domestic enemy, the creditors. Livy (6.20.6) describes Manlius's real offense as being his

---

[3] Forsythe 2005:259-260 grants that: "As in the cases of Spurius Cassius and Spurius Maelius, the sedition of M. Manlius is overlaid with late annalistic inventions, which make it difficult to ascertain what actually happened." He finds that Manlius's speech to his supporters "contains obvious fictitious elements derived from the political violence and rhetoric of the late Republic, especially from the Catilinarian conspiracy of 63." Citing Livy 6.11-20 and Diodorus 15.35.3, he notes (p. 314) that the speech recalls the story by Livy 2.23 about the plight of an indebted centurion inciting the First Secession of the Plebs (above, Chapter 10). The story about Manlius's house being leveled "was probably used to explain the open area in front of the temple of Juno Moneta on the Arx (Livy 7.28.5). The site was kept unobstructed by any kind of building not because of Manlius's fate, however, but because the site was the augurs' Auguraculum, from which they were accustomed to take the auspices."

ability "to have produced nearly four hundred people to whom he had advanced money without interest, whom he had prevented from being sold up and having their persons adjudged to their creditors."

As Manlius grew more defiantly seditious, Camillus was again made military tribune. In 384 he adjourned the proceedings against Manlius and transferred the court outside the city to the Peteline Grove, from which there was no view of the Capitol where Manlius had rescued Rome by stopping the Gauls. "Manlius was convicted, carried to the Capitol, [where] the tribunes hurled him from the Tarpeian Rock, so the place which was the monument of his exceptional glory became also the scene of his final punishment" (Livy 6.20 and Plutarch, *Camillus* 36.6). His house on the Capitoline was razed and the Senate sought to erase popular memory of his fight against the oligarchy by decreeing that no patrician ever should live there. Forty years later, in 345, the temple and mint of Juno Moneta were built on the site. The Manlii clan promised that no subsequent member would be called Marcus.

Debt and land problems create pressure for new laws

Appropriation by patricians of most of the *ager publicus* that was carved out of the conquered territories left Roman land so crowded and unequally distributed that most landholdings were only 2 to 7 iugera (0.5 to 1.75 ha.), hardly enough to feed a family. Warfare, taxes, crop failures, personal emergencies and the obligations that clients owed their patron "to pay ransom, dowry, fines or the expenses of public office" forced families into debt dependency and clientage.[4] A new class of citizen smallholders emerged, composed of young couples no longer living on their extended-family homestead but being more dependent on market exchange for the necessities that their small plots did not produce. These smallholders ran into debt and lost their land through foreclosures or distress sales to owners of large and more productive estates.[5]

New revolts in 380 and 378 protested such land transfers and led to the appointment of two censors to conduct a census of the land owned by Roman citizens. But after one censor died and the other resigned, the Senate cited religious auspices to delay further work on the matter.

> The tribunes declared that such mockery was intolerable. "The Senate," according to them, "dreaded the publication of the assessment lists, which supplied information as to every man's property, because ... it

---

[4] Hopkins 1978:20-22.

[5] Bernard 2016:326 and 329-330.

would show how one half of the community was being ruined by the other half, while the debt-burdened plebs were all the time being exposed to
one enemy after another."[6]

The patricians resorted to their usual tactic of trying to send the plebeians out of the city to war, but the plebeian tribunes would not "permit
an army to be raised until an account was taken of the existing debt and
some method of reducing it discovered, so that each man might know
what he actually owed, and what was left for himself – whether his person was free" or headed to the stocks and bondage. The Senate sought
to divert citizens from pressing the debt issue by enrolling fresh legions
to fight with Praeneste, but the tribunes blocked the military recruitment. "Men whose names were called for enrolment refused to answer,"
and warnings that enemy troops were advancing only made them more
determined to force economic and political concessions.

The fact that war was not being waged meant that debtors who could
not pay their creditors were being hauled into court. Many "had no
means left on which to draw, and after judgment had been given against
them, they satisfied their creditors by surrendering their good name and
their personal liberty" to become bondservants (Livy 6.34), often in the
prison rooms that were a feature of many private estates.

In 376, G. Licinius Stolo and L. Sextius Laturanus were elected as plebeian tribunes and put three bills before the assembly. The first provided debt relief by scaling down debts. Interest already paid was to be deducted from the principal, and the balance was to be paid in three equal
annual installments. Addressing the patricians, Sextius and Licinius
asked (Livy 6.36.12):

> Is it your pleasure that the plebeians, crushed by debt, should sur-
> render their persons to fetters and punishments sooner than that they
> should discharge their debts by repaying the principal? That, they
> should be led off in crowds from the Forum as the property of their cred-
> itors? That the houses of the nobility should be filled with prisoners, and
> wherever a patrician lives there should be a private dungeon?

Their second proposal, agrarian reform, banned ownership of more
than 500 iugera (300 acres, just under half a square mile) of public land,

---

[6] Livy 6.27. The same situation occurred later in the wake of the Licinian-Sextian
law, when new censors were appointed to record ownership changes caused by the
debt crisis (Livy 7.22.6).

and forbade grazing more than 100 cattle.[7] "'Have you,' they asked, 'the audacity to demand that whilst two iugera are allotted to each plebeian, you yourselves should each occupy more than five hundred iugera, so that while a single patrician can occupy the land of nearly three hundred citizens, a plebeian's holding is hardly extensive enough for the roof he needs to shelter him or the place where he is to be buried?'" (Livy 6.36.11).

To gain the authority needed to enforce their debt reform and use conquered land to endow veterans and needy Roman poor, Licinius and Sextius demanded a third plank of their platform: at least one of Rome's two consuls should be a plebeian. They warned that "there would be no limit to the seizure of land by the patricians or the murder of the plebs by the deadly usury until the plebs elected one of the consuls from their own ranks as a guardian of their liberties."[8]

Livy wrote that the Senate deemed only aristocrats fit to serve as consuls, and "refused to allow either the reading of the bills or any other procedure which the plebs usually adopted when they came to vote. For many weeks the Assembly was regularly summoned without any business being done, and the bills were looked upon as dead." That drove Sextius to reply:

> Very good. Since it is your pleasure that the veto shall possess so much power, we will use this same weapon for the protection of the plebs. Come then, patricians, give notice of an Assembly for the election of consular tribunes, I will take care that the word which our colleagues are now uttering in concert to your great delight, the word "I FORBID," shall not give you much pleasure.[9]

Livy's history becomes questionable in describing this fight as lasting for an entire decade. He has been criticized on the ground that there is no Roman record of tribunes at that time being elected successively for even two years, to say nothing of ten. Forsythe suspects that Livy stretched a single year's turmoil into a decade-long fight, and points out

---

[7] Forsythe 2005:265 suspects that this land limit may be a retrojection, noting that the 500-iugera limit is the same as that cited in Tiberius Gracchus's agrarian law of 133 (Appian, *Civil War* 1.8-9 and Plutarch, *Tiberius Gracchus* 8-9). Similarly, this second proposal anticipated (or was retrojected by Livy to provide a precedent for) Tiberius Gracchus's complaint that although animals had their lairs, impoverished Roman citizens had no place to sleep.

[8] Livy 6.37.3. He explained (6.37.4): "There could be no fair or just administration as long as the executive power was in the hands of the other party, while they had only the right of protesting by their veto."

[9] Livy 6.35. Another translation can be found in Lewis and Reinhold 1951:118.

that blocking the election of military officials probably would have led Rome's enemies to attack.[10] What is affirmed, however, is that Licinius and Sextius made an all-or-nothing demand for their three-part program. Military levies could not be enacted without the assent of plebeian tribunes, and even military tribunes were blocked from being elected.

Opposition to the plebeian demands was led by Appius Claudius Crassus, a grandson of the old decemvir. Accusing Licinius and Sextius of seeking kingship for themselves as "Tarquinian tribunes," he claimed that their demand that one of Rome's two consuls should be a plebeian would "bring death" by denying the freedom of Romans to elect two patricians to the consulship.[11]

By 367 the plebeians threatened yet a new secession, and escalated the standoff that year by electing Sextius as Rome's first plebeian consul. "The patricians refused to confirm his appointment, and matters were approaching a secession of the plebs" (Livy 6.42.11). Affairs were settled when Camillus, whom the Senate had appointed dictator for the fifth time, "quieted the disturbances by arranging a compromise. The nobility made a concession in the matter of a plebeian consul, the plebs gave way to the nobility on the appointment of a praetor to administer justice in the city who was to be a patrician."

The Licinian-Sextian law of 367 provided the debt relief that the two plebeian tribunes had demanded. "What had been paid as interest should be deducted from the principal, and the balance discharged in three annual installments of equal size" instead of falling due all at once. As often occurred, however, this law seems not to have been widely enforced. The courts were under the control of senators, who ruled as they pleased.

---

[10] Forsythe 2005:263 says that re-election of the plebeian tribune for consecutive years was only introduced by the Gracchi after 133 or even as late as 110 BC. No earlier example of a plebeian tribune holding office for even two consecutive years is known. It also seems improbable that they could have blocked the election of leading magistrates for ten years.

[11] Livy 6.40.12. Appius, who would later be consul in 349, spelled out his complaint (6.40.18): "Is this what you call an equal distribution of honors, when it is lawful for two plebeians to be made consuls, but not for two patricians; when one must necessarily be taken from the plebs, while it is open to reject every patrician?" Appius earlier had denounced commoners protesting the winter siege of Veii (Livy 5.2). Mommsen noted that nearly every "Appius Claudius" figure in Roman history appears to have been moved by feelings of hatred toward the commoners. Members of the Claudian clan (*gens*) do not appear as generals leading military victories, but only as protectors of oligarchic privileges by blocking (or at least trying to block) democratic reforms.

Also ignored by the courts and treasury was the Licinian-Sextian law's limit on the amount of land that one person could possess. By 367, "it had become clear that the occupation of *ager publicus* was a problem, [and] a law was passed" limiting to 500 iugera the amount of land that an individual could own. However, "no attempts were made to deprive anyone of land in excess of the upper limit,"[12] so landless Romans did not get any such land.

Appian summarized how the law was widely ignored for many centuries: "No notice was taken either of the laws or the oaths; some who appeared to observe them made bogus transfers of land to their relations, while the majority completely ignored them." Plutarch wrote that for a short time this edict did help protect the poor to stay on the land they had rented. But later, "their rich neighbors began to transfer the leases to themselves under fictitious names, and then ended up by blatantly owning most of the land in their own names."[13]

Roselaar cites the report by Livy (10.13-14) on the edict's early enforcement that already in 298, "a large number of people were prosecuted by the aediles for possessing more than the legal quantity of land. Hardly anyone could clear himself of the charge, and a very strong curb was placed upon inordinate covetousness."[14] But the Punic War led to vast new land being conquered and made public, with the prize locations turned over to the wealthy (as the next chapter describes). The political fight over violations of the 500-iugera limit became a key plank of Tiberius and Gaius Gracchus in their attempt to distribute public land to needy Romans after 133.

Further concessions to debtor interests – but keeping the debts on the books

In 357, a decade after the Licinian-Sextian law was passed, the *lex Duilia Memenia de unciario fenore* reiterated the legal interest-rate ceiling of $1/12^{th}$, indicating that its regulation as stipulated in the Twelve Tables had been allowed to lapse during the preceding century, and that interest payments were not being credited against the debt principal that was

---

[12] Roselaar 2010:144. She concludes that this limit applied to privately owned as well as public land.

[13] Roselaar 2010:113, citing Appian, *Civil War* 1.8 and Plutarch, *Tiberius Gracchus* 8.2.

[14] Roselaar 2010:96-97, 100 and 104, pointing out that dating the 500-iugera limit from the Licinian-Sextian law is first attested in a speech by Cato, *Pro Rhodiensilbus* in 167, but that Livy seems to have relied on an annalistic source for making this connection.

owed. Also, there was no legal procedure to stop aggressive landowners from carving large estates out of Rome's *ager publicus* on which to settle their clients, ignoring the 500-iugera private ownership limit for the *ager publicus*. This land grabbing was becoming a source of great family fortunes for Roman elites.

Five years later, in 352, a debt crisis led to the appointment of a commission of five public bankers (*quinqueviri mensarii*; the Latin word for bank was *mensa*, a table or bench) to hold bankruptcy sales to value and transfer family land instead of enslaving the debtors. Imprisonment remained the fate of debtors unable to pay, but at least the less impoverished debtors did not have to sell their land or livestock for money in a distressed market or at low prices set by foreclosing creditors. Debtors were given an appraised valuation for their property to be credited against what they owed. Public bankers also were empowered to make loans against such assets in order to enable debtors to work their way out of debt by keeping their property, while owing the Roman treasury instead of private creditors.

Under this *lex de quinqueviris mensariis creandis*, creditors still gained land and livestock at the expense of debtors, but the latter avoided personal bondage – if (and only if) they had sufficient assets available to forfeit.

> The State assumed the responsibility for the liquidation of the debts, and five commissioners were appointed, who were charged with the management of the money and were hence called *mensarii* (='bankers'). ... Seated at tables in the Forum, they dealt with long-standing debts due to the slackness of the debtor more than to his want of means, either by advancing public money on proper security, or by making a fair valuation of his property. In this way an immense amount of debt was cleared off without any injustice or even complaints on either side. (Livy 7.21.5-8)

Another five years later, in 347, the legal rate of interest was cut in half, to $1/24^{th}$ (the equivalent of 4 1/6 percent; see Livy 7.27.3-4, describing the *plebiscitum de fenore semunciario*). A moratorium was declared on existing debts, which "were made payable, one-fourth down and the remainder in three installments; even so, some of the plebeians were distressed."[15] To further lighten the burden, the *tributum* war tax was suspended.

Livy (7.28.9) reports that the aediles prosecuted moneylenders in 344. The next year, in 343, Rome's campaign in Campania "marked the first

---

[15] Livy 7.21 and 7.27. Lewis and Reinhold 1951:117-121 conveniently collect the documentation.

time the republic carried war well beyond the confines of Latium," a foreboding of strains to come.[16] The plebeian tribune Lucius Genucius moved to ban the charging of interest outright in 342 (Livy 7.42). Tacitus and Appian affirm that interest charges actually were forbidden at this time. But if the ban really happened, it soon became a dead letter, as reflected in how self-righteously "creditors attacked and killed the praetor [Asellio] when he tried to enforce this old law in 89 in order to ease a financial crisis."[17]

The first plebeian censor, C. Marcius Rutilius, had been appointed in 351 (Livy 7.22), and in 339 the *lex Publilia* stipulated that one of the two censors must be a plebeian (Livy 8.12). Two years later, plebeians could qualify for all higher positions, and in 300 they became eligible for the priestly colleges. In 287 the *lex Hortensia* (described below) made plebiscites binding on all classes, and in 172 both consuls were plebeians for the first time. This became common, and was often backed by patricians as long as the plebeian candidates showed themselves to be suitably co-opted into the oligarchic elite.

Usury as "sterile," extractive and predatory[18]

As discussed in Chapter 7, around the time that these events were erupting in Rome, Aristotle (384-322 BC) provided an analytic schema by juxtaposing household management (*oikonomos*, what today is called the "real economy") to the commercial acquisition of wealth (*chrematistike*, the financialized market economy). "Natural" economies were based on use values. Tools and other tangible forms of capital were means to make things, not to amass money for its own sake. But to the extent that families had to buy necessities, they needed money. However, monetary commerce (*chrematistike*), "by which men gain from one another, is not productive of goods" (*Politics* 1 at 1258a-b). As money-wealth (*chrema*, exchange value) became an objective in itself, commercial exchange aiming at the acquisition of money undercut the "natural" system of production based on use values.

---

[16] Rosenstein 2004:29.

[17] Forsythe 2005:262. See Chapter 15 below and Appian, *Civil War* 1.54 for a discussion of Asellio's murder.

[18] This section reiterates and elaborates in the context of Rome the discussion of these matters in Chapter 7 under the headings "Interest rates, birth metaphors and the unnatural character of charging interest" (fn9) and "The contrast between market price and use value."

Quoting Solon's poem, "No bound is set on riches for men," Aristotle wrote that amassing financial wealth was not only "unnatural" but also addictive, the desire for it insatiable, in contrast to the appetite for food and other simple basic needs that quickly becomes satiated. "All those engaged in acquiring goods go on increasing their coin without limit ... the end is sheer increase." Wealth-seekers always want more (as Chapter 7 has discussed).

To illustrate how hubris warped personal character, Aristotle cited the legend of King Midas of Phrygia, who prayed to Dionysus that everything he touched would turn to gold. His prayer was granted, but Midas then found that he could not eat, because whatever he handled was turned into bullion. "And what a ridiculous kind of wealth is that," observed Aristotle, "which even in abundance will not save you from dying with hunger!" Midas ultimately turned his own daughter into gold – a metaphor for how commercial wealth-seeking gave priority to the inanimate over the living.

As markets and coinage developed, Aristotle explained, money emerged as a social convention (*nomos*, "law," the root of *numismatics*, the study of coinage). However: "Taking interest is contrary to nature because money by nature cannot produce anything, and is intended only to serve the purpose of exchange" simply as a means of payment (*Politics* 1 at 1256), not as a means to exploit citizens, much less reduce them to bondage. The general dislike of interest, he concluded, "is fully justified, for the gain arises out of the currency itself, not as a product of that for which currency was provided. Coinage was intended to be a means of exchange, whereas interest represents an increase in the currency itself. Hence its name, *tokos* ('offspring'), for each animal produces its like, and interest is currency born of currency. And so of all types of business this is the most contrary to nature."

Given that money is sterile and hence was commonly regarded as inappropriate to bear interest, it may seem puzzling that the ancient words for interest connoted birth and fertility – a calf (or birth in general, *tokos*) in classical Greek, and similarly a newborn kid-goat (*mash*) in Sumerian. Likewise, the prefix *fe-* in Latin *fenus* connotes the related ideas of *fe*male (originally "to suckle"), *fe*cundity and *fe*rtility. A *fae*nerator was a usurer. These words depict interest as an offspring of capital (from Latin caput, "head," as in a head of cattle).[19]

---

[19] Benveniste 1973 discusses the term "capital." The word *usufruct* ("use of the fruits," the basis of *usury*) has a similar connotation.

It is one thing for heads of cattle to yield offspring, but how can silver calves accrue to metallic money? As Shakespeare expressed the idea in *The Merchant of Venice*, how can one "take a breed from barren metal"? The explanation relates both to the monetary unit by which debts are denominated, and to the timing of the occasion for interest to accrue. Originally the word for calf or "birth" was used in connection with interest in a metaphoric sense: a fractional monetary unit was "born" (that is, accrued) with the monthly birth of a new moon.

Charging interest is first attested in the third millennium BC, in Bronze Age Mesopotamia. The Sumerians likened the accrual of interest to a baby being born. What actually was "born" was the basic "unit fraction" into which full units were divided. The Sumerian unit ("1") and its unit-fraction $(1/60^{th})$ originally were expressed by different sized D-shaped symbols. The word *gesh* and the symbol D signified either 1 (or $60/60^{ths}$) or 60. This system was applied to weights and measures. The shekel weighed $1/60^{th}$ of a mina, and Sumer's earliest attested commercial interest rate was one shekel per silver mina per month. This worked out annually to $12/60^{ths}$ per year – a fifth (20 percent) annually.[20]

Thinking of a "yield" of interest as a "baby" unit emerging from the older full-sized parent capital ("head") explains how silver could be lent out to yield offspring despite the fact that metal itself was barren. Minas lent out at interest gave birth to shekel-60^{ths} each month, generating a veritable herd of silver offspring, just as a Roman pound (*as*) yielded an *uncia* of interest each year.

Rome's 12-based (duodecimal) system still survives in today's troy ounce. The Twelve Tables set the interest rate at $1/12^{th}$ per year, reflecting the fact that the Romans divided their pound into 12 troy ounces, there being 12 *unciae* of metal in every *as*. Each year an *uncia* of interest had to be paid on each *as* of debt.[21] For many centuries the English likewise divided their shillings and feet into twelfths. The principle at work in setting early interest rates was pragmatic: ease of calculation.

Simplicity of computation explains the remarkable stability of ancient interest rates over time. From the third millennium, Mesopotamia's $1/60^{th}$ monthly rate (the "birth" of the new moon) remained in force for over a thousand years. Also stable for many centuries was Rome's

---

[20] I describe this metonymy in more detail in Hudson 2000a. Modern society retains the Sumerian division of hours and minutes into 60^{ths}.

[21] The Latin word for "pound" (*as*) is a cognate to Greek *heis*, "one." Each of the 12 *unciae* (ounces) was also a "one" (from *unus*, "unity"), making a big unit and a little unit.

official rate of $1/12^{th}$. These standardized rates were unresponsive to shifting supply and demand or to profit or productivity rates.

A debt revolt leads to the lex Poetelia-Papiria

Opposition to *nexum* debt bondage erupted in a new uprising in 326, which led to the *lex Poetelia-Papiria* (Poetilian Law). The legend of what brought matters to a head has survived as a dramatic personification of Aristotle's description of money as being sterile and charging interest as an "unnatural" act. The catalyst for this new debt revolt was in many ways like the old soldier whose abuse by his creditors was said to have incited the Secession of the Plebs in 494. This time the dimension of sexual abuse was added to the economic dimension of creditors reducing debtors to bondage. Livy (8.28-29) describes the treatment of a young boy given over as a debt pledge to a pederast seeking sexual gratification:

> This year (326 BC) was marked by the dawn, as it were, of a new era of liberty for the plebs; creditors were no longer allowed to attach the persons of their debtors. This change in the law was brought about by a signal instance of lust and cruelty upon the part of a moneylender. L. Papirius was the man in question. C. Publilius had pledged his person to him for a debt that his father had contracted. The youth and beauty of the debtor, which ought to have called forth feelings of compassion, only acted as incentives to lust and insult. Finding that his infamous proposals only filled the youth with horror and loathing, the man reminded him that he was absolutely in his power and sought to terrify him by threats. As these failed to crush the boy's noble instincts, he ordered him to be stripped and beaten. Mangled and bleeding the boy rushed into the street and loudly complained of the usurer's lust and brutality.
>
> A vast crowd gathered, and on learning what had happened became furious at the outrage offered to one of such tender years, reminding them as it did of the conditions under which they and their children were living. They ran into the Forum and from there in a compact body to the Senate-House. In face of this sudden outbreak the consuls felt it necessary to convene a meeting of the Senate at once, and as the members entered the House the crowd exhibited the lacerated back of the youth and flung themselves at the feet of the senators as they passed in one by one.
>
> The strongest bond and support of credit was there and then overthrown through the mad excesses of one individual. The consuls were instructed by the Senate to lay before the people a proposal "that no man be kept in irons or in the stocks, except such as have been guilty of some crime, and then only till they have worked out their sentence; and,

further, that the goods and not the person of the debtor shall be the security for the debt." So the *nexi* were released, and it was forbidden for any to become *nexi* in the future.[22]

Livy's story of the assault by Papirius on Publilius that inspired the Poetilian Law was, like the Rape of Verginia by Appius Claudius in 450, a counter-myth to the Rape of Lucretia in 509 depicting patricians as protectors of traditional morality. From 450 to 326 it was patrician creditors who exploited and raped debtors. Livy added a further dimension by personifying the sterility of usury (in contrast to procreative activity) described by Aristotle, portraying the pederast's extraction of interest as including "the boy's youthful bloom as added interest on his loan." Non-procreative sodomy continued to be used as a common metaphor for usurers into the 14th century AD, often with Biblical reference to usurers as Sodomites.

Livy called the abolition of *nexum* bondage "a new beginning of freedom." But although debt slavery no longer was legally enforceable under normal circumstances, working off debts in slave-like conditions persisted. The new law only meant that "it was necessary to take the debtor to court. If he could not or would not pay, the court would at all times authorize the creditor to hale him off in bonds to a private prison; in 216 many hundreds were released from this captivity to serve in the army." Smallholders who were taken into bondage forfeited their land rights and farm animals that were their means of self-support. "Some of the annalists' vivid descriptions of the debt-bondsmens' plight in the early Republic," notes Brunt, date from ca. 63 BC, by which time *nexum* had evolved into a new compulsion to work off one's debt.[23]

Meanwhile, oligarchic economic power had grown strong enough that the Senate felt able to permit increasing nominal political democracy. When debt problems provoked the plebeians to secede once more in 287, the plebeian Quintus Hortensius was made dictator to resolve matters. His *lex Hortensia* made plebiscites binding on all classes of Roman citizens by removing the requirement of Senate ratification for laws to be enacted. That raised the plebeian assembly's power relative to that of the Senate, theoretically erasing the formal political distinction between

---

[22] Regarding the *lex Poetelia Papiria de nexis*, Bernard (2016:320) notes that Livy (8.28) dates it to 326 while Varro (*Lingua Latina* 7.105) dates it in 313. "In both accounts, however, the law's force is identical." The discrepancy seems to derive from "competing attempts to reconcile authentic but independent documentary sources, probably separate lists of magistrates and of legal measures."

[23] Brunt 1971b:57 and 129.

plebeians and patricians. But by this time plebeian politicians had become as wealthy as many patricians, so the effect was to consolidate the
power of Rome's creditor oligarchy.

Summary: Rome's agrarian debt and land problem prior to the Punic Wars

"Roman warfare had become incompatible with the requirements of
small-scale husbandry long before Hannibal set foot in Italy," points out
Nathan Rosenstein. Debt problems increased as Rome extended its warfare beyond its nearby neighbors and for longer periods. "Evidence from
the annalistic tradition indicates that from at least the late fourth century onward Roman armies regularly campaigned well into the autumn
and winter months – long past the planting time for the fall-sown cereal
crops that formed the mainstays of the Roman and Italian diet."[24]

Slavery was becoming a significant source of agricultural labor. Indeed,
Rosenstein suggests: "The best explanation for the abolition of debt bondage at the close of the fourth century that ended the Struggle of the Orders is the hypothesis that chattel slavery came to substitute for a dependent labor force made up of Roman citizens on the estates of the rich."

Appian (*Civil War* 1.7) summarized how the wealthy turned conquered
lands into a windfall for themselves instead of being used to support
Rome's growing population, which indeed was being expropriated by
the wealthy and replaced by slaves:

> The rich, getting possession of the greater part of the undistributed
> lands, and being emboldened by the lapse of time to believe that they
> would never be dispossessed, absorbing any adjacent strips and their
> poor neighbors' allotments partly by purchase under persuasion and
> partly by force, came to cultivate vast tracts instead of single estates, us-
> ing slaves as laborers and herdsmen, lest free laborers should be drawn
> from agriculture into the army. At the same time the ownership of slaves
> brought them great gain from the multitude of their progeny, who in-
> creased because they were exempt from military service.

The displacement of smallholders and buildup of large estates was
occurring well before the wars with Carthage in the late 3rd century. But
the wars' aftermath accelerated the monopolization of land, especially in
southern Italy and Sicily. "The countryside around Rome had lost nearly the whole of its population of smallholders by the early second centu-

---

[24] Rosenstein 2004:19.

ry, a process that began well before Hannibal's invasion. The result was not their replacement by estates staffed by gangs of slaves, however, but rather desolation."[25].

---

[25] Rosenstein 2004:7-8. The war's military and provisioning needs created a market for crops, and this favored large plantations.

13

The Punic Wars End with a Financial Land Grab, 218-198 BC

In addition to being Rome's most profitable activity, war was its almost exclusive source of fiscal revenue. That was a radical change from other ancient states, which had long received booty, loot and tribute, but basically relied on a strong domestic revenue from crop yields and trade. "There is not a single Mesopotamian state, not even the Neo-Assyrian Empire," writes Michael Jursa, "for which tribute and war booty were the mainstay of public finance, nor can this be claimed for any phase in Egyptian history."[1]

Rome's most important prize was land confiscated from foreigners. This became *ager publicus*. Some was used to settle war veterans and some of the poor, but most ended up being transferred to Rome's wealthiest families. Wars also yielded booty in the form of slaves, bullion and trophies, and these captured assets likewise were not shared equally. Generals took most of the booty, and some of the bullion was consecrated in Rome's temples, ultimately to be monetized. The balance was distributed to soldiers, but often failed to compensate them for the cost of their being away from their land.

Hopkins calculates that Rome's ongoing wars kept an average 130,000 soldiers off the land, straining their ability to make ends meet and thus leading to arrears in their obligations. When wars ended, the courts were allowed to resume bankruptcy proceedings, enabling creditors to foreclose on land that debtors had pledged as collateral. Most debtors sold out or simply were driven off, especially after Hannibal's invasion of Italy in 219 sent many families running for safety to Rome.[2]

Rome paid its armies by levying a *tributum* tax, which was made proportional to one's wealth class.[3] The money was hoped to be repaid out

---

[1] Jursa and Moreno Garcia 2015:159.

[2] Hopkins 1978:56.

[3] Tan 2015:211-212 describes the *tributum* as "a levy on property that was defined by three important features: it was formulated as a kind of loan and could be repaid to the payer in part or as a whole; it applied specifically to the funding of

of the booty seized in battle. But when the Punic Wars were followed by new fighting in Macedonia, the treasury's cash-strapped condition led to a privatization sale of Rome's rich *Campania* land to settle the wealthy's Punic War contributions, which had been made as voluntary donations but were subsequently treated as having been loans. That transformed what initially was celebrated as a patriotic sacrifice into a land grab that remained a source of political conflict over the ensuing century, peaking in the attempt by Tiberius Gracchus in 133 to enforce laws limiting the amount of land that could fairly be appropriated.

The role of publican equites in Roman fiscal policy

Rome hired joint-stock companies (*societates publicanorum*) to undertake specific public projects. They were the only forms of limited-liability corporation permitted.[4] A public undertaking such as shipping food, military supplies or other cargoes or undertaking large-scale construction was called a *publicum*, and the businessmen who undertook it were *publicani*, wealthy investors operating through these joint-stock companies to spread the heavy costs and risks amongst themselves. Although they were called *equites* or knights, they were "the most unmilitary part of the population, and they inherited the title only because of the property qualification for the *equites equo privato*, *i.e.*, the cavalry who served with their own horses." Any Roman able to meet the property qualification of 400,000 sesterces "could call himself an *eques*, provided he were not a senator."[5]

Establishing themselves during the 3rd-century Pyrrhic and Punic wars as public contractors and tax farmers, the *publicani* "companies and not the bankers are the respectable investors of funds. ... [and] there

---

wars and was not demanded in years of peace. ... It was in essence a financial contribution by those who, though wealthy enough for military service, had not been called up (whether by chance or because of age, infirmity, etc.) and was hence the fiscal equivalent of conscription." No firm records show exactly when this fiscal arrangement began.

[4] Frank 1940:217. In contrast to the rules that governed these public corporations, Roman law held every partner of private undertakings – called *negotiatores* – "liable for the full amount of any debt ... [and] the partnership came to an end at the death of any partner." See also Frank 1933:102 and 148-157.

[5] Frank 1940:84, 208 and 148-150, and Fowler 1927:60-61 and 69-70. See also Badian 1983. At least by Cicero's time each member of a *publicum* was required to possess at least 100,000 *denarii*.

is no indication that they dealt with *argentarii*," that is, moneylenders.[6] Publican corporations did not engage in mercantile activities, as their officers were drawn from the wealthiest classes whose ethic eschewed commercial trade.[7] Senators were forbidden to engage in business directly, although they often participated in publican ventures as silent partners through freedmen or other clients.

Bidding fixed sums on government contracts for five-year periods for the right to collect public rents and taxes or undertake public construction projects, the companies were permitted to keep whatever they could make over and above the terms of their contracts. They normally received 10 percent of the gross revenue they collected, which typically worked out to a 50 percent return on their equity investment.[8] The ruling magistrate of each company changed each year, but a large staff of assistants provided better administration than the government could achieve, as Rome had no permanent bureaucracy and its relatively few public administrators held office only on an annual basis. This absence of oversight enabled the *publicani* in due course to charge "the taxpayers various fees when they could get away with it," including "fees for such spurious items as 'inspection' (*spectatio*), currency exchange (*collybus*), 'wax money' (*cerarium*), presumably for sealing official receipts, and a clerk's fee (*scribae nomen*) of 4 per cent; again we should assume that these charges were levied on the total tax collected."[9]

---

[6] Frank 1933:208

[7] Frank 1933:208: The only commercial or industrial companies were "such organizations as fish-packers and makers of pitch that took contracts from the state for utilizing public property." Weber 1909:317 observes that: "Exclusion of aristocrats from direct involvement in industry was common throughout Antiquity, but Rome was unusual in that this exclusion was extended to include tax farming and shipping; a senator might possess ships only of a capacity just sufficient to transport the products of his own estates. As a result senators could gain wealth only from political office, from the rents paid by their tenants, from mortgages assumed through the agency of freedmen (though this was forbidden, it was commonly done as early as Cato the Elder), and from indirect investment in commerce and shipping."

[8] Broughton 1938:542. Their income was not taxed. David Jones 2006:210-211 notes that: "Cicero suggests that the normal rate of commission was 10 per cent of the tithe collected, *i.e.*, 1 per cent of the total crop. The commission was, in any event, charged to the taxpayers, not to the government," citing Cicero, *2 Verrines* 3.116 regarding 6 percent of the total crop in Sicily, and *pro Rabino Postumo* 30 regarding 10 percent of tax collected.

[9] Jones 2006:211, citing Cicero, *2 Verrines* 3.181.

Monetary consequences of the Punic Wars

Just as the wars with Persia catalyzed the monetization of Greece's economy, the Punic Wars catalyzed the spread of Roman coinage, which was primarily military both in its sources of bullion (booty and reparations levies) and its uses (to pay soldiers, hire mercenaries and build ships). In the absence of early coinage, soldiers were paid a *stipendum* (< stipend), meaning a share of the booty.[10]

Rome minted its first silver coins in 280 to meet the needs of its war in southern Italy against Pyrrhus, king of Epirus. Silver booty from southern Italy was sent to the Temple of Juno Moneta to be melted down. "Since the theater of war, South Italy, had for several centuries been accustomed to silver money, the Romans were forced to break with their bronze tradition and – probably with Carthaginian help – issue the first two silver Romano-Campanian *didrachmas*," depicting the she-wolf suckling Romulus and Remus.[11] By 150, Rome was able to shift completely from bronze coinage to silver, the money in which its tribute was denominated.

Starting in 264, Rome waged three wars against Carthage, the former Phoenician colony that it finally destroyed in 146. The cost of mounting a sea fleet created much local Roman opposition. Polybius said that the taxes levied after Rome lost 700 quinqueremes early in the First Punic War (264-241) were so burdensome that Romans voted "to ban publicly funded fleets in 253 and again in 249; the navy that won the war in 241 had to be funded by voluntary loans from the elite."[12] By that year "there were no funds in the public treasury for this purpose," but wealthy individuals "undertook to provide a quinquereme fully equipped on the understanding that they would be repaid if all went well. In this way a fleet of two hundred quinqueremes was rapidly got ready" (Polybius 1.59.6-8).

When the war ended, Rome's naval commander Gaius Lutatius demanded that the Carthaginians pay 2,200 talents over twenty years (230 talents of silver annually, about 10,000 pounds), and later raised the

---

[10] Cornell 1995:288 notes that coins were only issued after ca. 300 BC. Servius is credited with designating the *as* (a pound of bronze) as the Roman monetary unit (Pliny the Elder, *Natural History* 33-43), and by the time of the Twelve Tables, "Payments in bronze are specified as penalties for certain types of injury in Table VIII.3-4." See Crawford 1974 I:35-37, and 1985:19, and Thomsen 1980:202-204.

[11] Thomsen 1957:261.

[12] Tan 2015:212, citing Polybius 1.39.7 regarding the 253 protest.

penalty to 3,200 talents over just ten years.[13] Carthage was obliged to withdraw from Sicily, and sought to avoid more war by paying a further 50,000 pounds of silver. But when Rome grabbed Sardinia, Carthage felt driven to open the Second Punic War (218-201). Hannibal crossed the Alps with his troops, horses and pack elephants in 216. Despite losing half his forces and supplies, he killed fifty thousand Roman soldiers at Cannae, its worst loss in history. The Roman camp surrendered and was obliged to pay a ransom, prompting a large issue of silver coins struck from Rome's remaining monetary reserves.[14]

Capua (near Naples) and other southern Italian cities defected, and although their senators, "and especially the leading members stood loyally by the alliance with Rome, the common people as usual were all for a change of government and for Hannibal" (Livy 23.14). Five years later, when Rome recaptured Capua in 211, it retaliated by imprisoning or killing the city's aristocrats, selling many of its citizens into slavery and confiscating their land.

The shortage of bullion became so severe by 216 that a financial commission was appointed (emulating an earlier such move in 351) to hold the loyalty of soldiers by lending them public funds to pay their debts. To replenish the treasury and pay for fresh oarsmen, the consuls proposed a new land tax in 210, but "there was such protest among the people, such indignation, that what was lacking for an uprising was a leader rather than fuel" (Livy 26.35). Romans complained that they had "nothing left. Their houses had been burned by the enemy, the slaves who tilled the soil had been taken away by the state, now by purchase at a low price for military service, now by impressing them as oarsmen."

After devaluing the bronze pound (*as*) repeatedly, in 211 Rome took 5,000 pounds of its gold reserves from the public treasury in the Temple of Saturn on the Capitoline Hill, near that of Juno Moneta, to coin a Mars/Eagle gold *denarius* denominated in *asses*.[15] Called the Aerarium,

---

[13] Tan 2015:210, citing Polybius 1.62.8, who explains (1.63.3) that the Romans "reduced the terms of payment by one half, added a thousand talents to the indemnity, and demanded the evacuation by the Carthaginians of all islands lying between Sicily and Italy."

[14] Rome's first gold coinage was issued to defray the war's costs in 217/6, some 51 years after the first silver coins were struck at the Temple of Juno Moneta. About four thousand pounds of gold were coined, starting with a Janus/Oath scene symbolizing the concord between Rome and its Italic allies.

[15] Thomsen 1957-1961 I:41 and 48, and III:264-265, citing Livy 48; 22.52-54 and 27.10-11. For details on the Aerarium see Livy 7.16 and 27.10. The special reserve

its name was derived from Latin *aes*, meaning at first a pound (*e.g.*, of bronze), then money, and subsequently a poll tax and tax in general.

Most silver and gold was in the hands of the wealthiest families. They were the only source of further war funding, but the Senate had no thought of taxing them with a new war levy or emulating Hellenistic forced loans and confiscatory levies such as are described in Book II of pseudo-Aristotle's *Oeconomica* (see Chapter 6 above). Instead, the consul for 210, M. Valerius Laevinus, proposed a show of patriotism to save the day (Livy 26.36): Each senator would bring in all his gold, silver and coined bronze, except for

> a ring for himself and for his wife and his children, and a bulla for a son, and those who have a wife or daughters may leave for each an ounce of gold. ... Let us leave 5,000 *asses* of coined bronze to each paterfamilias. All the rest of the gold, silver, coined bronze let us deposit with the bank commissioners, without first making any decree of the Senate, so that a voluntary contribution and competition in helping the republic may stir up to rivalry, first the spirit of the knightly order, and then of the plebeians as well.
>
> Agreement was so spirited that they actually thanked the consuls. The Senate then adjourned, and each man brought his own gold and silver and bronze into the treasury, while such rivalry was aroused to have their names the first or among the first men on the public records, that neither were the commissioners equal to the task of receiving nor the clerks to that of making the entries. The knightly order followed this unanimity of the Senate, the populace that of the knights. Thus without an edict, without constraint on the part of any magistrate, the state lacked neither oarsmen ... nor their pay.

The gold and silver was turned over to the Temple of Juno Moneta to strike the coinage that was spent to defeat Carthage. But this episode ended with a land grab by wealthy families when these ostensibly altruistic wartime donations made in 210 were re-classified in 201 as loans, and the consul Laevinus convinced the Senate to surrender Rome's most desirable public land in payment (described below).

---

fund (*aerarium sanctum*), based originally on war spoils and supplemented chiefly by a 5 percent tax on the value of all manumitted slaves (established by the *lex Manilia* in 357), was only to be touched in emergencies.

The publicani *fight to block prosecution for fraud*

Rome borrowed from publicans in 215 to supply Scipio's Spanish campaign. Three publican companies, comprising nineteen members, contracted with the state to supply the campaign, subject to the condition that they be exempted from military service throughout its duration, and that the state would take responsibility for any losses they incurred in shipping supplies. Rome promised to repay the borrowing out of the first money to come into the treasury.

Shipping loans were the main commercial vehicle throughout antiquity for "respectable" money invested at interest. Financing trade partnerships served as a kind of insurance, spreading the losses so as to make high average gains on balance. Already in Hammurabi's Babylonia, entrepreneurial merchants did not have to pay their debts to creditors when ships were lost at sea. Creditors shared in their borrowers' risk and misfortune – a principle not applied to personal usury collateralized by land.

Two publican contractors – Titus Pomponius Veientanus and Marcus Postumius of Pyrgi – devised a scheme to arrange shipwrecks and falsify the accounts of their cargoes so as to collect unwarranted funds from the state. "They would put small cargoes of little value into old, battered vessels, sink them at sea, after taking up the crews in small boats that were in readiness for the purpose, and then falsely declare that the shipments were far more valuable."[16]

When the praetor Marcus Atilius brought the fraud to light, the Senate was so protective of its fellow elite that it simply ignored the scheme. But matters came to a head in 212 when the two plebeian tribunes proposed a heavy fine on Postumius. "When the day came for his appeal, the people attended the assembly in such numbers that the open space on the Capitol was packed to capacity." Even Postumius's relative, the plebeian tribune Casca, did not rise to support him. But the publicans, seeing little support from Casca,

> determined to wreck proceedings themselves. Shoulder to shoulder, like troops breaking through the enemy's line, they thrust their way into the space left by the crowd when it was ordered to stand back, hurling insults as they went at people and tribunes alike. It had nearly come to blows, when the consul Fulvius called out to the tribunes ... 'that unless you dismiss the assembly at once there will be an insurrection.'
>
> The assembly was dismissed and a meeting of the Senate called. The consuls brought forward the matter of the lawless violence of the publi-

---

[16] Livy 23.48-49 and 25.3. See also Frank 1940:86, and Badian 1983:17-18.

cans which had led to the break-up of the assembly. Postumius of Pyrgi
... had robbed the people of their right to vote, wrecked the assembly,
degraded the tribunes, threatened his countrymen with battle, forced
himself and his friends in between the tribunes and the crowd deliber-
ately to prevent the tribes being called on to vote.

   ... Postumius's behavior ... was formally declared to be an act of
violence against the State and a most dangerous precedent. The two
Carvilii, as tribunes, promptly dropped proceedings for the fine and
brought a capital charge instead, adding an order that if Postumius
failed to furnish sureties he was to be arrested and taken to prison. Postumius did provide sureties but did not appear in person. The question
was put to the people, who returned a decision to the following effect:
'If Postumius fails to appear before the first of May ... then it shall be
understood that he is in exile; his property shall be sold and he shall be
refused water and fire.' The tribunes then began to bring capital charges
against all the men who had helped to stir up riot and sedition, ordering
them to produce sureties. Those who failed to do so were imprisoned at
once; then others who were in a position to do so were imprisoned too;
the majority avoided the risk by going into exile. So ends the story of the
tax farmers – a story first of dishonesty, then of the audacious means by
which they hoped to get away with it. (Livy 25.3-5)

   Such confluence of war, corruption and wealth-grabbing has persisted
through the ages, along with bold attempts to intimidate civic prosecutors.

The postwar land grab

The peace treaty ending the Second Punic War in 201 called for
Carthage to pay 10,000 talents (570,000 pounds of silver) as reparations
over fifty years, at the rate of 200 talents (11,400 pounds) each year.
After taking care of his troops, Scipio brought 123,000 pounds of silver
into the treasury, and another 43,000 pounds from Spain and 320,000
asses (pounds of copper) from Gaul.[17]

   The monetary influx inspired the wealthy former contributors to
Rome's war effort to depict their earlier patriotic acts as having been
loans. Laevinus, who had asked for the show of patriotism in 210 when
he and Marcus Claudius were consuls, insisted "that equity required
that the monies which had been contributed by private individuals
... should now at length be repaid." A military hawk, he hoped to use
Rome's revenue to wage new wars against Carthage and Macedonia

---

[17] Frank 1940:91, 94, 97, 128-130 and 146-50, citing Livy 30.45. War absorbed over
three-quarters of Rome's public revenue.

instead of using the money to pay creditors. He urged the Senate to return these earlier contributions by paying out Rome's future receipts of war tribute. A decree was passed "authorizing the repayment of the money in three installments, the first installment to be paid in cash by the consuls of the present year, the other two at two-yearly intervals" (Livy 29.16).

After the second installment was paid as scheduled in 202, the contributors came up with a bold ploy for the third and final payment falling due in 200:

> Many private citizens ... appealed to the senate because the consuls had declared that, since the treasury hardly sufficed for the new war [against Macedonia], which was to be waged with a great fleet and large armies, there was no money at their command with which to make the payment. The senate could not resist their complaints: If the state wished to use the money loaned for the Punic war for the Macedonian war, the petitioners argued ... what else could be the result than the confiscation of their property in return for an act of generosity, as if it had been a crime? (Livy 31.13)

The former contributors pointed out that Rome needed to keep its money to continue fighting, but had much public land available – the *ager publicus populi*, "public land of the people." So in lieu of cash payment, they asked their Senate friends to offer them land located within fifty miles of Rome. A precedent had been set in 205 when Rome sold valuable public land in the *Campania* to provide Scipio with money to invade Africa. The effect was to reverse the practice of settling war veterans on public land.

To cap the wealthy contributors' privatization scheme, this land was to be taxed at only a nominal rate "in attestation of its being public land, in order that, when the people should become able to pay, if anyone chose to have his money rather than the land, he might restore the land to the state." Nobody did, of course. "The private creditors accepted the terms with joy; and that land was called *Trientabulum* because it was given in lieu of the third part of their money" (Livy 28.46). Most land privatized in this way ended up as vast latifundia.[18]

---

[18] Roselaar 2010:128 notes that this *ager in trientabulus* "was expressly stated to have remained *ager publicus*," and as such could be taken away by the state if the buyer asked it to do so in exchange for the original monetary payment that was promised, so "its occupiers acquired virtually complete security of tenure on this land." *Campania* land was *ager censorius*, but the state didn't keep records, so "we do not know how much land belonged to this category." Roselaar 2010:293 points

Most fortunes in history have been obtained by obtaining public land and natural resources – by great thefts that in time came to be accepted as legitimate, as Balzac noted. Modern analogies would be the U.S. land grants to the railroads that vested the great American fortunes of the second half of the 19th century, and the vast natural resources given to post-Soviet oligarchs after the 1994 loans-for-shares swindle. In *Hannibal's Legacy*, Arnold Toynbee describes Rome's giveaway of its *ager publicus* after the Second Punic War as a fatal turning point deciding, "at one stroke, the economic and social future of the Central Italian lowlands."

The oligarchy's land grab endowed Rome's wealthiest families with the great latifundia estates that, as Pliny accused, ruined Italy.[19] It thus is remarkable that the Penguin translation of Livy's Books 31 through 45 (under the title *Rome and the Mediterranean*) omits the three key debt-related passages regarding the *Campania* land swap negotiated in 200 (Livy 31.13), Livy's reporting on the third and final debt payment in 195 to wealthy Roman families for their wartime contribution, met in part by taxing the priesthood and temple property (Livy 33.42), and his description of how foreign moneylenders were driven from Rome's provinces (Livy 32.27.4). A. H. McDonald's introduction to this Penguin edition (1976) claims that skipping these episodes enhances the continuity of Livy's text so as to "carr[y] the main narrative."[20]

But in doing so, this translation strips away Livy's emphasis throughout his *Roman History* on explaining how Rome fell under the sway of a self-dealing creditor oligarchy monopolizing the land and cultivating it mainly by slaves, not freemen. Only in the dual-language Loeb Classical Library can one find how Rome's monetary squeeze resulting from the Second Punic War led to the polarized land ownership that set the stage for the reform proposals of the Gracchi brothers later in the century.[21]

The land privatized into latifundia was cultivated largely by slaves

---

out that the *trientabulum* land was only a relatively small part of Rome's overall *ager publicus*, most of which would become privatized by the Gracchi after 133 BC (as discussed in the next chapter). She points out that most "land in the environs of Rome had already been privatized before 200," so the amount cannot have been large.

[19] Pliny the Elder, *Natural History*, criticizing the agricultural management treatises by Columella and others.

[20] Livy, *Rome and the Mediterranean* (1976), Introduction by A. H. McDonald, p. 1, fn1.

[21] Most of the key passages also can be found in the volumes of readings selected by Lewis and Reinhold 1955 I (see *e.g.*, pp. 163-165).

captured in the wars against Carthage and Macedonia. Captives who could not redeem themselves became subject to labor-contracts. *Redemptores* would pay their ransom and gain a right to their labor for five years.[22] Vast numbers of the prisoners captured in Macedonia, Greece and North Africa were sold to private buyers to work on the plantation estates being assembled, or in public mines or on public land. Displacing the formerly free population condemned the Central Italian lowlands "to become predominantly a country of underpopulated slave-plantations and overpopulated industrial towns."[23]

After defeating Philip V of Macedonia in 199 (and soon decisively in 197 and 196), Rome still had to find a means to pay its wealthy families for their 210 "gift," because not all claimants had been paid in 200. Contributors who had not availed themselves of the earlier opportunity to acquire public land were still awaiting the third payment in 195. Rome met part of the problem by taxing the priesthood, demanding payment of back taxes on their property. "The priests appealed in vain to the tribunes of the people, and the money was collected for the whole period in which it had not been paid" (Livy 33.42). The economic role of temples faded as a result.

Rome becomes a fiscal rentier state

Rome recovered about half the cost of its military conquests after 200 in the form of booty, along with war indemnities spread over many years as ongoing tribute. Publican companies collected the funds, partly by obliging conquered territories to borrow the money to pay Rome. The operations of these companies provided such lucrative investment opportunities for wealthy Romans (as described in the next chapter) that Polybius wrote in the mid-2nd century that "almost everyone in Italy seemed to be involved in some way with public contracts."[24]

Much of the money to pay these ongoing obligations to the *publicani* was advanced by moneylenders, initially Greeks who dominated Roman banking at the outset of the 2nd century largely because they were not subject to its anti-usury laws. To clear the way for Italian moneylenders to take over this business, Carthaginians, Greeks and other foreign

---

[22] Mitchell 1993 and Hudson 2010. Most of the slaves were Greek-speaking.

[23] Toynbee 1965 II:250-251; cf. 341-373.

[24] Frank 1940:206-208, 148-150 and 84, citing Livy 35.7 and 32.27, and Hopkins 1978:45, citing Polybius 6.17. For a general review of the *publicani* see Badian 1983, Nicolet 1966, and Fowler 1927:60-61 and 69-70.

lenders were driven from Sardinia in 198, and from other provinces soon thereafter. By 167, Rome had become a "fiscal state," levying ongoing tribute and taxing foreigners in amounts sufficient to enable it to end its own domestic *tributum* tax on land. Its military conquests thus were followed by a fiscal and creditor conquest of territories in the Republic's expanding empire.

Latifundia after the Punic Wars

"Roman allies who sided with Hannibal during his invasion of Italy were punished by having their land confiscated."[25] The appropriation of Capua's land was exemplary. Rome deprived the town of political liberty for having supported Hannibal, and "the mass of citizens were scattered with no hope of return." Roman rage, however, spared the "innocent buildings and city walls from burning and demolition," preserving them for Roman settlement (Livy 26.16). The Campania territory in the south, "well known to be the foremost in Italy in general fertility," was annexed to become the property of the Roman people (in practice, its oligarchy).[26]

Rome auctioned off this and other land that it annexed from conquered territories. Some land was allocated to colonists, but much was leased to whomever would pay rent to the state. Taxation and rent collection on such land was, however, negligent, as the wealthiest land appropriators were in charge, and occupation-tenure by the early leasers gradually became permanent by the time Tiberius Gracchus sought to reverse unlawfully large appropriations.

This was the point at which great latifundia began to be assembled. The rich outbid the poor at land auctions, typically ignoring the law that forbade holdings of over 500 iugera (125 hectares), while smallholders tended to fall into debt whose charges worked "either to deprive the possessor directly of his farm and to make him the bondsman if not the slave of his creditor-lord, or to reduce him through encumbrances practically to the condition of a temporary lessee of his creditor."[27] The result

---

[25] Hopkins 1978:59, citing Plutarch, *Tiberius Gracchus* 8.

[26] Hopkins 1978:55 and 59-60. Responding to the loss of land by smallholders, the Senate organized a program to resettle about 100,000 peasants (including women and children) from central Italy to more than twenty colonies established in Italy's extreme south and north in 194 and 177.

[27] Mommsen 1911:267, section 2.2. Plutarch attributed the dispossessions and debt problems faced by free Roman cultivators by the time of Tiberius to the practice of auctioning off annexed land.

was that both public and private land passed into the hands of Rome's wealthiest families.

Modern historians from Mommsen through Toynbee focused on Rome's land alienations to the wealthy, reflecting both the emphasis that their era's classical political economy placed on land rent and the focus of ancient historians who described how land appropriation and usury concentrated wealth at the top of Rome's steepening economic pyramid. Sallust (who lived from 86 to 35 BC) highlighted how most of the Roman oligarchy's takings derived from war, looting and corrupt insider dealing:

> When freed from the fear of Carthage ... there sprang up on all sides troubles, seditions, and at last civil wars. A small number of powerful men, whose favor most of the citizens sought by base means, exercised a veritable despotism under the imposing name, sometimes of the Senate, at other times of the 'People.' The title of good or bad citizen was no longer the reward of what he did for or against his country, for all were equally corrupt. But the more anyone was rich, and in condition to do evil with impunity, provided he supported the present order of things, the more he passed for a man of worth.[28]

The antagonism between the oligarchy and the population at large over the land and debt issues became more pronounced by the end of the 2nd century. Rome became more predatory and obtained wealth for its elites by stripping other regions – what David Harvey calls "accumulation by dispossession," not by increasing productivity and prosperity.[29] Looking back at how the Republic had ended up with an oligarchy that polarized and destabilized Roman society, Sallust quoted a letter from Mithridates to Arsaces, king of the Parthians:

> In fact, the Romans have one inveterate motive for making war upon all nations, peoples and kings: namely, a deep-seated desire for dominion and for riches. ... Do you not know that the Romans ... have possessed nothing since the beginning of their existence except what they have stolen – their home, their wives, their lands, their empire? ... no laws, human or divine, prevent them from seizing and destroying allies and friends, those near them and those afar off, weak or powerful, and from considering every government which does not serve them, especially monarchies, as their enemies. ... it is by audacity, by deceit, and by

---

[28] Sallust, Fragment I.10, translated in Austin 1981:227-228.

[29] Harvey 2003:158.

joining war to war that they have grown great. Following their usual custom, they will destroy everything or perish in the attempt.[30]

---

[30] Sallust, *Historiae* 4.69, translated by J. C. Rolfe 1960:435-441, quoted in Schavione 2000:84.

14

Rome's Empire Enriches its Financial Oligarchy, 2nd Century BC

Roman wealth was achieved at the expense of the territories it conquered. From the Second Punic War onward, summarizes Philip Kay, "Rome is best seen as a warrior state ... at war in every year from 218 to 157 and at peace for only four years in the whole of the second century." Going beyond simple one-time grabs of booty, land and slaves, Rome became a tribute-taking empire, imposing war indemnities mounting up to an estimated 27,280 talents – the equivalent to 630 metric tonnes of silver – between 201 and 152 from Greece, Macedonia, Spain and North Africa.[1] J. K. Davies comments that: Roman generals took their predatory behavior "to remorseless extremes, denuding region after region of all movable items of value." Livy describes a highlight, the three-day triumphal procession of T. Quinctius Flamininus in 194 to celebrate his victory over Philip V of Macedon:

> On the first day the procession displayed the arms, weapons, and statues of bronze and marble, more of which had been captured from Philip than received from the cities of Greece; and on the second day the gold and silver, wrought, unwrought, and minted. Of unwrought silver he had 43,270 pounds; of wrought silver there were many vases of all varieties, most of them embossed and some of remarkable workmanship; there were besides many fashioned from bronze, and in addition ten shields of silver. Of minted silver there were 84,000 Attic coins called "tetrachma," and the weight of silver in them is about equivalent to 3 *denarii* each. There were 3,714 pounds of gold, one shield made completely of gold, and 14,514 gold coins with the image of Philip upon them. On the third day 114 golden crowns, gifts from the cities, were carried past.[2]

---

[1] Kay 2014:21, 25, 30 and 42. (A tonne is a thousand kilograms.) Tan 2015 and 2017 classifies Rome as a tribute state whose economic surplus was monopolized by the oligarchy.

[2] Davies 2009:441, referring to Livy 34.52. Livy adds that the entire army was brought back to parade, each infantryman receiving 250 *asses*, each centurion 500, and each cavalryman 750, and that "in front of [Flamininus's] chariot there were

Foreign tribute accounted for nearly all of Rome's public revenue by the time it destroyed Carthage and Corinth in 146, spending an estimated three-quarters of its budget on the army at the start of the 2nd century, and nearly all by the mid-1st century.[3] Most of what remained was used to build civic monuments and temples. Almost none was used to expand social services or the public bureaucracy, despite the rising administrative complexity of Rome's empire, or to alleviate the social dislocations caused by the large estates taken from the public domain and stocked with war slaves.

Independently of what Rome's treasury received, its generals looted the temples and cities of conquered regions, and consuls vied for appointment to governorships, where a one-year tenure provided an opportunity to make a fortune to last a lifetime.

As noted in Chapter 13, investors in publican tax-collecting companies typically received a 50 percent return. Italian moneylenders also became part of the collection process by advancing the money to pay the tribute that Rome imposed. "The first attested instance of converting state payments into private loans was in 199," notes James Tan, "when the Carthaginians, trying to make the first payment of their indemnity with coins of just 75 percent purity, were forced to borrow the missing 25 percent."[4]

Italians were not initially subject to the limitations on interest rates that the Twelve Tables imposed on Romans. That exemption enabled Roman creditors to evade prohibitions against higher interest rates by transferring loans to Latin usurers or working via *socii* groups not subject to such restrictions. But such evasion was publicly denounced, with steps taken against it. Livy (32.27.3-4) reports that Cato the Elder, as praetor in Sardinia in 198, was "considered overharsh in his restraint of usury. The usurers were expelled from the island, and the expenses which the allies were accustomed to incur for the comfort of the praetors were cut down or abolished."[5]

Rome extended its civil code to non-Romans "after the great size of the debt contracted by this evasion was revealed by these public declara-

---

many noble prisoners and hostages, among whom were Demetrius, the son of King Philip, and the Spartan Armenes, son of the tyrant Nabis."

[3] Frank 1933:141 and 146. See the discussion by Kay 2014:25 and Hopkins 1978:37 and 41.

[4] Tan 2017:35, citing Livy 32.2.1

[5] Kay 2014:115, quoting Livy 35.7.2-5. The basic fraud was for a creditor to sell his loan to another, transferring accounts to allies not subject to Roman law.

tions." The plebeian tribune M. Sempronius Tuditanus ordered in 193 that "the laws relative to money lent between Roman citizens and the subjects of any of the allied states, or of the Latin confederacy, should be the same as those between Roman citizens." The Senate moved in 193/2 to avert foreign resentment by proposing "that the allies of the Latin confederacy should have the same law regarding the lending of money that applied to Roman citizens," that is, 12 percent per annum. The plebeian assembly supported the law, and the incoming aediles prosecuted some moneylenders.[6]

Roman fear of debt cancellation by kings or populist rebels

Rome's peace treaty with Macedonia in 197 required Philip V to surrender his naval fleet and pay an indemnity of 1,000 talents. The Roman army then turned its attention to Antiochus III, the Seleucid ruler of Alexander's conquests in Syria and Western Asia, defeating him near Magnesia in 190. Hannibal's two great Roman adversaries, Cornelius Scipio and his brother Scipio Africanus, pushed Antiochus back to Asia Minor and obliged him to relinquish all claims to the region north of the Taurus Mountains. The Peace of Apamea in 188 obliged him to surrender his fleet and pay 15,000 talents in twelve annual installments.[7]

In Macedonia, Philip's son Perseus (ruled 179-166) tried to recapture Greece in 171 after having begun his reign by calling back exiles and cancelling debts owed to the palace, as Chapter 8 has described. A Roman inscription accused him of "revealing his hatred toward the best men" by cancelling debts and sponsoring revolts.[8] That is what Mithridates VI would achieve a century later on a much broader scale throughout the entire region for a quarter-century, 88 to 63. A letter that Mithridates may or may not have written to mobilize eastern resistance

---

[6] Livy 35.7.5. The details of this law (and indeed, what it was called) have been lost, but Livy 35.41.9 describes how the treasury spent the fines imposed under the Sempronian law on the condemned usurers: "gilded four-horse chariots were set up on the Capitoline and in the inner room of the Temple of Jupiter, above the roof of the shrine, twelve gilded shields were also placed, and the same men built a portico outside the Porta Trigemina in the wood-dealers' quarter."

[7] The magnitude of the associated looting led the Senate to accuse Scipio Africanus of treason for embezzling 3,000 talents. His brother, Cornelius Scipio (awarded the title of Asiaticus for his victory over Antiochus), was also accused of the same offence and driven into exile, where he died in 183.

[8] Sherk 1984:18-19 #19. Letter to the Delphian Amphictyonies about King Perseus, 171/70 BC, SIG[3]643.

described Rome as "viciously hostile to every government not subject to Rome – especially monarchies."[9] Rejecting kingship at home, Rome's oligarchy also opposed it abroad, fearing that a strong local king or ruler might promote populist policies and mobilize debtors against Rome, as Mithridates indeed would do.

Rome defeated Perseus at Pydna in 168, after Perseus tried to hold local support by advocating a debt cancellation. Rome abolished the monarchy and declared the Macedonians free, although obliged to "pay Rome annually half of what they had paid to their king in direct tax." The Senate divided Macedonia "into four Republics without political or economic intercourse with each other. ... Greece could remain free as long as she was weak and disunited."[10] Stripped of their monetary reserves and driven into debt to pay the stipulated reparations and taxes, conquered regions were kept too weak to mount serious resistance to Rome, having no funds left to hire mercenaries or field a rebel army to defy Roman demands for tribute.

Keeping the profits of empire private instead of public

The inflow of tribute was so immense that by 167, the year after conquering Macedonia, Rome was able to stop taxing its citizens (although Italian cities had to continue paying the *tributum* tax). Given this revenue from the provinces it conquered, "Policy makers could have radically increased the resources of the treasury, but on the whole they decided not to," Tan points out. The Senate "consciously eschewed the opportunity to raise more money for the treasury," leaving citizens dependent on patrons instead of on public support. That opposition to "big government" left commoners with nowhere to turn except to the aristocracy. "By channeling Rome's new wealth away from the treasury and into their own estates, elite Romans retained control over society's economic surplus and reserved the right to decide how it would be spent."[11]

---

[9] Sallust, *Historiae* 4.69, attributing this accusation to Mithridates writing to the Parthian king Arsaces (70-57 BC). See Lewis and Reinhold 1990:235-236. The letter is cited in more detail in Chapter 13 above and Chapter 16 below.

[10] Scullard 1951:212-214, adding that imperial policy consisted of "rewarding the loyal, punishing the rebellious, establishing local pro-Roman leaders in control, and removing all suspect politicians so that no leaders would be left to organize political opposition." Collaborators "supplied their Roman master with lists of political suspects, so that leaders from Aetolia, Acarnania, Epirus, and Boeotia were deported to Rome for trial."

[11] Tan 2017:150 and 93, and Tan 2015:221-223.

Keeping the public treasury minimalist left nothing for populist politicians to take in case they might somehow mount a coup.[12]

The oligarchy's main social expenditure was that of candidates
seeking office by paying for public games to demonstrate their civic
spirit. That usually entailed going into debt to their creditors and donors
(such as Crassus in the next century).

The debt protests in Dyme

Almost immediately after Rome installed loyal local administrators in
Greece, resistance developed, above all by strapped debtors among the
well-to-do, along with the poor. After the Battle of Corinth in 146, the
year that Rome leveled Carthage, it merged Greece into the Macedonian province as part of its empire, selling a reported 300,000 Greeks
into slavery and allocating their land for Roman soldiers and allies to
colonize.[13]

In Dyme (southwest of the Corinthian gulf), after Rome had defeated
the region in 146, the proconsul Q. Fabius Maximus inscribed a marble
memorial, sentencing an anti-Roman leader Sosos to death for burning
the public archives and the debt records, seeking allies by supporting "a
cancellation of debts, and ... [writing] laws for the destruction of the [oli-
garchic] constitution given" to Dyme and other Achaeans.[14] The inscription depicts Dyme's protection of debtors as a "disruption ... alien to the
freedom restored to the Greeks in common and our policy."

These are Fabius's words (lines 15-16), but Roman records are so
sketchy that historians can only guess at just what actually was happen-
ing. For most of the 20th century, historians viewed the "Dyme affair"
as reflecting "a social-revolutionary or democratic struggle against
Roman-sponsored oligarchs ... For Rostovtzeff, 'The populace rose
against the propertied classes with elemental force. ... The cry was certainly for cancellation of debts ... and of contracts. ... New laws were
drafted and no doubt adopted by the new 'democratic' government....'
Fuks writes of a revolt of the 'masses,' the abolition of the 'existing
regime' ... by a revolutionary government' which instituted 'revolution-

---

[12] Tan 2017:165 and 185. See also Tan 2015:209.

[13] War slaves were put to work on plantations or consigned to work in mines and
private business undertakings.

[14] Sherk 1984:54-55 #50: Letter of Q. Fabius Maximus to the City of Dyme, 115
BC, SIG[3]684, dated 144.

ary rule.'" Larsen labeled it a "leftist revolution."[15] In these readings, populist leaders mobilized support from the indebted majority when creditors called in their debts to pay the tribute that Rome demanded.

But burning public records of land holdings and debts does not necessarily imply a change of regime or constitution, and the masses are nowhere in view. Kallet-Marx suggests that "the alleged perpetrators [were] members of the political elite," and that the arsonists aimed "to destroy census records and assessments of tribute" that would have fallen mainly on themselves.[16] In his reading, opposition likely occurred at the top of the social pyramid, inasmuch as Rome's exaction of tribute fell mainly on those who could pay the most. But the ruling class certainly sided with Rome by the time debt cancellation became a broad populist demand led by Mithridates VI. Rome "made sure that Greece was kept 'quiet' and friendly to her," notes Ste. Croix, "by ensuring that the cities were controlled by the wealthy class, which now had mainly given up the idea of resistance to Roman rule and in fact seems to have welcomed it for the most part, as an insurance against popular movements from below."[17]

Land grabbing leads to latifundia stocked with war slaves

At the end of each war, Roman soldiers traditionally received a share of the booty in money, and whatever they could plunder on their own. Starting in the early 2nd century they also received grants to feed their families for three months, extended to a few years by the mid-1st century.[18] But during this period Roman imperialism polarized its own economy by fighting wars that led to the wholesale capture of slaves, who then were put to work on the land being taken from captured territories and, increasingly, Rome's own smallholders. "In the old days, at the end of a campaign, or between fighting seasons," describes Hopkins, "peasant soldiers returned to their farms." From the 2nd century onward,

---

[15] Kallet-Marx 1995:148, citing Fuks 1984:282-288, Rostovtzeff 1941:757 and 1508-1509, and Larsen 1938:503.

[16] Kallet-Marx 1995:149-151.

[17] Ste. Croix 1989:344.

[18] Hopkins 1978:38. "Ideally, Roman soldiers shared all the booty," with half being detailed to collect it, the rest to stand guard. But such checks sometimes broke down.

Rome's peasant-soldiers "were fighting for their own displacement" by
the slave labor.[19]

The supply of inexpensive war slaves meant that large landholders no
longer had to obtain labor by turning indebted Romans into bondservants. They could buy war prisoners from pirate-traders or slave dealers
on the Delos market to work the plantations they were assembling in
Sicily and elsewhere. Appian (*Civil War* 1.7) described this situation
as setting the stage for the century to come: "[C]ertain powerful men
became extremely rich and the race of slaves multiplied throughout the
country, while the Italian people dwindled in numbers and strength,
being oppressed by penury, taxes, and military service. ... the land was
held by the rich, who employed slaves instead of freemen as cultivators."
Mommsen described small farms as disappearing "like raindrops in the
sea" as the supply of inexpensive war slaves provided an incentive for
large landowners "to buy out the small landholders, or, if they remained
obstinate, to seize their fields outright – in which case, as might be
supposed, matters were not always amicably settled. A particularly
favored method was to evict the farmer's wife and children while he
was absent on military service, and thus to make him comply with a *fait
accompli*."[20]

"The poor peasantry was extruded from the land," summarizes
Hopkins, especially the land around Rome that the wealthy wanted for
themselves. Colonization was one way to pay families to leave. "Either
they sold out or emigrated to colonies, or were violently thrown off, or lost
to creditors."[21] The Senate organized over twenty colonization programs
in 194 and 177 to resettle about 100,000 men, women and children from
central Italy, mainly in the far south and north. But average plot size in
the colonies was small, so the new settlers remained poor.

Little documentation survives of Rome's debt and land crisis that
mounted up in the years spanning the destruction of Carthage and
Greece in 146, and the in-fighting that led to the election of Tiberius
Gracchus in 133 and his brother Gaius a decade later. Livy's history
after 167 BC, from Book 46 onward, is lost, including his history of the

---

[19] Hopkins 1978:30. The concentration of land ownership gained momentum as
smallholders were squeezed out. Roselaar 2010:155-156 prefers the term villas for
the 2nd-century transition, on the ground that latifundia did not become dominant
until the 1st century BC.

[20] Mommsen 1958:33 and 91. See also the summary at the end of Chapter 12
above.

[21] Hopkins 1978:56, citing Livy 31.13 and 25.36.

Gracchi, Rome's inheritance of Asia Minor and Aristonicus's revolt there. The major surviving sources are Appian's *Civil War* and Plutarch's life of Tiberius Gracchus. These narratives depict the oligarchy as fighting to maintain its monopoly on politics, the courts and foreign affairs by blocking reforms (and their sponsors) which might disturb its control. Any proposal to create more resilience for the citizenry at large was viewed as a threat to the status quo of oligarchic power. Pliny noted the ideological intensity with which the modest ballot reforms calling for secret votes to elect magistrates (the Gabinian law of 139) and for jury decisions (the Cassian law of 137) were denounced by what Cicero condemned as populist threats to the elite's political liberty.[22] As Mommsen summarized, the Senate was happy to have "a government of aristocratic nobodies."[23]

The agrarian reform proposals of Tiberius Gracchus in 133

Tiberius Gracchus was born sometime between 169 and 164 into one of Rome's most prominent families. His father (also called Tiberius) was twice elected consul, and his mother was the daughter of Scipio Africanus, who had defeated Hannibal at Zama in 202. The younger Tiberius fought in Africa with Scipio's son (his mother's brother). In 133 he was elected plebeian tribune and became the most popular opponent of the Senate oligarchy. Along with his brother Gaius (nine years younger), he used the tribunate to promote reforms that modern democracies would find fair and normal, but which the Senate deemed to be an audacious attack on its prerogatives.

Tiberius's program contained three parts. His basic initiative was agrarian reform distributing land to the poor, to be paid for by his second proposal: using the treasure from Asia Minor that Attalus III bequeathed to Rome in 133. His third proposal sought to address the corruption of Senators appointed as governors who looted the provinces for themselves instead of passing their takings on to the treasury. He hoped to block this practice by diluting senatorial power over the courts – whose judgeships were filled by the Senate's 300 members – by adding

---

[22] Cited in Cicero, *De Legibus (On Laws)* 33-39.

[23] Mommsen 1958:20. His description of this period was grounded in the 19th century's own concern with the relationship between land tenure and its taxation, political reform, and the banking and credit system.

publicans and other *equites* to the judges' ranks.[24] The assumption was that as financial managers they would block official abuses. Neither Tiberius nor his brother Gaius (who ultimately assigned the *equites* to provincial jury courts) anticipated that the *equites* would be as corrupt as the Senate politicians who became governors.

Plutarch described Tiberius's agrarian reform as having been inspired on a trip through Tuscany when observing "the dearth of inhabitants in the country and that those who tilled its soil or tended its flocks there were barbarian slaves." To reverse the decline in Rome's free rural population and thereby revive its ability to serve in the citizen-army, Tiberius advocated distributing Rome's *ager publicus* to the poor. "The wild beasts that roam over Italy have every one of them a cave or lair to lurk in," he declaimed,

> but the men who fight and die for Italy enjoy the common air and light, indeed, but nothing else; houseless and homeless, they wander about with their wives and children ... they fight and die to support others in wealth and luxury, and though they are styled masters of the world, they have not a single clod of earth that is their own.[25]

Pointing to archaeological evidence of population growth in the 2nd century, Roselaar attributes the problems of many small farmers in central Italy to "increasing fragmentation of their private holdings, making it harder to support a family on them." Warfare was becoming less remunerative, no new colonization projects were implemented, and food prices may have risen after about 140. Many smallholders sold their land to work in Rome.[26]

Tiberius saw distribution of *ager publicus*, along with enforcement of the Licinian-Sextian law of 367 limiting personal land holdings to only 500 iugera (125 hectares), as the *solution* to the agrarian problem and the related problem of land grabbing by the powerful. The situation had been festering for quite some time as wealthy landowners occupied *ager publicus* in addition to their own landholdings. As Tan has summarized: "In 173 a consul, L. Postumius Albinus, was sent to establish the

---

[24] Plutarch, *Tiberius Gracchus* 16. See also Badian 1972:50, 54, 57 and 110. Publicans were members of the *equites*, the landowning equestrian class (see Chapter 13 above). It was left to Gaius Gracchus to implement this reform (see below).

[25] Plutarch, *Tiberius Gracchus* 8.7-9. This remains the richest description of Tiberius and his program. Plutarch depicted Rome's earlier history as a prelude leading up to the debt and land problems that Tiberius's program was designed to solve.

[26] Roselaar 2010:293-295.

borders between public and private land in Campania, since it was well understood that over some four decades neighboring landowners had been steadily encroaching on the public domain. In fact, it emerged that the state had never bothered issuing leases for this land and so farmers understandably began to employ it themselves. Postumius recovered 'a great part' of the ager Campanus, and the censors finally issued leases to farm the land."[27]

Plutarch describes subsequent censors as neglecting to renew these leases, enabling the interlopers to "continue using the land without contributing to the treasury's revenues." Wealthy buyers outbid the poor and evaded the Licinian-Sextian law when Rome put conquered lands up for auction, at first "by means of fictitious personages ... and finally held most of the land openly in their own names ... so that soon all Italy was conscious of a dearth of freemen, and was filled with gangs of foreign slaves, by whose aid the rich cultivated their estates." They offered "various arguments to defend their occupation of public land: holders had invested money in those fields, or had bought them thinking they were private; they had buried ancestors on them or used the land for dowries or as security on loans."[28]

Tiberius offered to buy them out at public expense, despite their breach of the Licinian-Sextian law, hoping that this would persuade them to accept his plan to redistribute plots of 30 iugera each to the needy. Each occupier could keep 500 iugera for himself and 250 for each son (up to 1,000 per family). Tiberius took his proposed law to the plebeian assembly for approval, bypassing the Senate as he anticipated that it would see his plan as a threat to its control of Roman affairs, and specifically to the land claims of many Senatorial families.

Senate leaders accused him of "introducing a re-distribution of land for the confusion of the body politic, and stirring up a general revolution," and persuaded the other plebeian tribune, Marcus Octavius, to veto the proposed land law. Tiberius countered by suspending state business, and held the vote a second time. Again, Octavius vetoed it. Tiberius then withdrew his offer to pay landholders anything at all for what they had taken in violation of the 500-iugera limit.

Popular support for public land distribution was so strong that the Senate felt obliged to create a commission in 133 to begin distributing it. Three men were designated to administer it: Tiberius himself, his

---

[27] Tan 2017:150, citing Livy 42.1.6 and 46.19.1-2.

[28] Tan 2017:150 and 154-155, citing Plutarch, *Tiberius Gracchus* 8.3 and Appian, *Civil War* 1.10.

brother Gaius and his father-in-law Appius Claudius Pulcher, who had
been elected consul in 143 and censor in 136.[29] By 128 a few thousand
citizens had received allotments in colonies throughout Italy.

The effect of Tiberius's reform was to complete the privatization of
nearly all that remained of Rome's *ager publicus*. Much of what was given
to small farmers was later swallowed up by creditors or lost in related
economic duress as wealthy landowners quickly increased their holdings
in excess of 500 iugera.

Attalus III of Pergamum bequeaths Asia Minor to Rome in 133

Tiberius planned to finance his agrarian reform program by using
Rome's windfall from a fateful event that occurred in the same year he
was elected tribune: when Pergamum's king Attalus III died in 133 he
willed his Asia Minor kingdom – or at least his royal treasury and estate
– to the Roman people.

Pergamum's rulers had been allies of Rome ever since Eumenes II
(197-159) had helped its army conquer Antiochus III at the Battle of
Magnesia in 190. Rome's imperial focus was on Greece and North
Africa, with little concern for lands to the east. To reward Eumenes
for his support, the Senate assigned Antiochus's Seleucid kingdom in
Asia Minor to him, including the rich Ionian coastal cities of Ephesus
and Smyrna. Pergamum became famous for its library and monumental sculpture, overtaking Athens as a cultural center, and Eumenes
expanded his realm inland, with Roman acquiescence.[30]

When Eumenes died in 159, his brother, Attalus II, became regent
for a boy said to be Eumenes's illegitimate son, who took the throne 21
years later as Attalus III (138-133). The new king never married after
his betrothed died, and indulged in a five-year "carnival of bloodshed
and murder," poisoning many whom he suspected of killing her. Not
finding supporters at home, he left a will bequeathing his royal land
to the Roman people, and an inscription making Pergamum a free
state. Temple lands and their villages, as well as cities such as Ephesus,
probably were also left free and "very much to their own devices in

---

[29] Plutarch, *Tiberius Gracchus* 13.

[30] Sherwin-White 1977:63-64 and Magie 1950:19. Rome's conquest of central
Anatolia extended east to the river Halys and north to Cappadocia.

internal affairs ... exempt from proconsular jurisdiction and interference, and in some cases from Roman taxation."[31]

Seeing Attalus's legacy as an opportunity to finance the settlement of war veterans and other needy poor, Tiberius advocated that the Pergamum treasure "should be given to the citizens who received a parcel of the public land, to aid them in stocking and tilling their farms."[32] This challenged the Senate's control over foreign affairs and the spending of provincial revenues and other public funds, initiating what became a century-long war over whether Rome's imperial revenue should be taken by the oligarchy or spent on social programs to benefit Rome's commoners.

Tiberius's reform proposals lead to his assassination in 133

Claiming that any redistribution of public land would be an attack on the "freedom" of Rome's oligarchy, senators and others who wanted this land for themselves, a Senate mob decided to kill Tiberius. Ste. Croix summarizes the oligarchy's use of violence as its ultimate political tactic:

> The Roman ruling class was prepared to kill without mercy anyone who seemed likely to prove himself a genuine popular leader and perhaps fulfill the role of a Greek tyrant of the progressive type. Such a man could be conveniently accused of aspiring to make himself king, *rex* – in the precise sense of the Greek *tyrannos*. ... In this tradition, Cicero accused Ti. Gracchus for trying to seize *regnum* for himself and succeeding "for a few months." The Tribune C. Memmius, a *popularis*, accused the patricians of dismissing anyone standing for popular rights as planning to make himself king.[33]

Tiberius warned his supporters that his life was in danger, and a few thousand men organized a protection detail. But they were not able to prevent a large group of senators and their allies from attacking and beating him to death in public with clubs and wooden planks. A

---

[31] Sherwin-White 1977:67, citing the bibliography in Edouard Will 1967. Magie 1950:23 and 27-29 provides details and references, and points out (p. 33): "The bequest did not include the lands belonging to those temples of the gods which lay within the bounds of the kingdom, or, obviously, the territories of the independent Greek cities of the coast. Nor did it include the city of Pergamum itself; for Attalus in his will 'left the city free, attaching to it also the civic territory which he adjudged to it.'" All this was nullified when Rome annexed the province in 129.

[32] Plutarch, *Tiberius Gracchus* 14. See also Magie 1950:147.

[33] Ste. Croix 1989:337, citing Sallust, *Bellum Jugurthinum* 31.8.

reported three hundred of his followers were killed and their bodies thrown into the Tiber.

This showdown in 133 inaugurated a generation of mass killings of popular leaders and their followers that would continue through the murder of Gaius in 121, the proscriptions of Sulla after 91 and his march on Rome in 83, the murder of Asellio in 89 and Catiline and his supporters in 62, capped by the Senate's assassination of Caesar in 44.

Gaius Gracchus creates a more elaborate populist program

With Tiberius dead, popular leadership passed to Gaius, whose father-in-law, Publius Crassus Mucianus, took Tiberius's place as tribune. The land law survived to the point where even Tiberius's opponent, the consul Publius Popillius, parceled out grazing lands for new settlers to farm. "The old land registers became the commission's Bible, and not only were occupations revoked without distinction between new and old, but in various cases private property to which the holder was unable to prove his title was also confiscated."[34]

The main administrative problem involved land in allied Italian communities. This was technically Rome's public domain, but wealthy Romans had been using it, as well as prominent local Italians. Tiberius's brother-in-law, the general and statesman Scipio Aemilianus, backed Latin insistence on blocking further distribution of such public land. He planned to take allocation authority away from Tiberius's commission and give it to the censors and consuls. But on the day he was to address relations with the Latins, he was found dead in his bed, presumably assassinated.

Fearing that Gaius would mobilize the constituency that had supported his brother, the Senate backed its own candidate for plebeian tribune, Livius Drusus. He sought to outbid Gaius for popular support by proposing that recipients of *ager publicus* need not pay any rent at all, and to settle 36,000 colonists in twelve new Italian colonies. Gaius did not become tribune until 123, when he was indeed elected by Romans who had supported Tiberius.

Gaius Gracchus assigns control of provincial courts to the publican equites

Upon being elected a decade after his brother, Gaius succeeded in implementing Tiberius's plan to assign control of the provincial criminal

---

[34] Mommsen 1958:54.

courts to the *equites*. He seems to have expected the publican *equites* to act as a progressive check on the governors whom the Senate appointed. In 123 he permitted publicans to bid for contracts to collect "tithes on produce, taxes on pasture and customs-duties" from the Asia province. That year also saw the plebeian assembly authorize Gaius to select the new judges, and the Senate agreed.[35] In accordance with Tiberius's plan, Gaius selected publican *equites*, thereby giving the tax farmers control of the courts. But as matters turned out, this enabled them to become just as rapacious as the governors that the Senate appointed.[36] Now the court that heard extortion cases (*res repetundae*) was in a position to condemn governors who acted to restrain the publicans' own financial misbehavior.

Publican companies collecting taxes in Asia and other provinces were allowed to keep whatever they could extract over and above what they guaranteed to pay the Roman treasury. Their agents "made sub-contracts with the several communities, which thus became responsible for the payment of their respective quotas,"[37] and had to pay interest on late payments. Asia's temples and basic infrastructure were stripped as rapacious publicans ignored these institutions' long-standing tax exemption and legal protection. The province's financial situation deteriorated as Roman violations disrupted public infrastructure spending and basic maintenance. Most protests against publican corruption were futile in the face of juries manned by the *equites*.

Complaints were made to Rome about *publicani* and their agents "asserting claims to all possible sources of revenue," including the land of free cities and temple estates, and reducing many subjects to slavery. When Rome's consul Marius asked Nicomedes III of Bithynia to contribute troops for his war against the Cimbri and Teutons in 104-102, the king told him "that he had not enough manpower left: most of his subjects had been sold off into slavery by the *publicani*. This reply came

---

[35] Plutarch, *Gaius Gracchus* 5.

[36] Hopkins 1978:46, citing Cicero, *De Legibus* 3.20 and Varro, Fragment 114R. Mommsen 1958:66-68, 73 and 238 describes the publican courts as creating "a despotism even more unscrupulous than that of the aristocracy."

[37] Magie 1950:162-164 and 33. Most companies based their headquarters in Ephesus, under a *magister* who remained in Rome. Italian moneylenders often were part of this system, organizing themselves in companies typically called "the resident Romans" or "the Romans engaged in business." Officials and treasuries in major cities bought land and other property outside of the former royal domains [of Attalus], which belonged nominally to the Roman People and were managed by the publican companies.

as such a shock to the Senate that it at once decreed that no citizen of an allied (*i.e.*, client) state should be held in slavery in a Roman province."[38]

The problem of publican corruption in the provinces had been festering for half a century. "The first permanent judicial tribunal established in Rome was set up (in 149) to deal with complaints by provincials of illegal extortion." But it only covered extortion involving an administrator's failure to pay the Roman treasury its due, not local extortion or illegal seizure. Subsequent tribunals were "plagued by domestic Roman political intrigues and collusions," and recouped only a small part of the grabbing.[39]

The worst abuses occurred in regions outside Rome's formal empire and hence beyond direct Senate oversight. "The *publicani* based in Asia had been adding to their gains by doing business outside the area under the control of a Roman governor. We can see, half a century later, that it might still be easier to get away with dubious means of making a profit in an allied kingdom than in a well-run province."[40]

One of the few positive outcomes occurred in the wake of *publicani* seizing the lakes near Ephesus and confiscating revenues from fishing rights belonging to the Temple of Artemis. "The famous geographer Artemidorus was sent to Rome by the temple-officials to present the case to the Senate," which upheld the temple's rights. Another favorable Roman response upheld the rights of the sanctuary of Athenia Polias at Priene to have the revenue from its salt works exempt from Roman taxation.[41]

In 95 the Senate sent the consul Q. Mucius Scaevola to Asia to deal with complaints about reprehensible publican practices, which included crucifying slaves who had contracted with their owners for emancipation. This was the first time a consul was sent to govern a peaceful province. Scaevola brought along his fellow consular jurist P. Rutilius

---

[38] Badian 1983:87, citing Diodorus 36.3. Magie 1950:197 and 1093, fn57 says that "there could not have been any *publicani* in the independent kingdom of Bithynia," so Nicomedes's resentment must have been against Roman moneylenders. Badian finds the easiest explanation to be "that the *publicani* had lent the King money and he had offered some of his subjects for security: he was presumably the owner of all men not living in cities. Client kings were always desperately short of money and eager to borrow." Nicomedes apparently felt that the Romans "were legally entitled to abduct his subjects," as he himself viewed them as his personal property. See also Finley 1977:161.

[39] Hopkins 1978:41.

[40] Badian 1983:147.

[41] Magie 1950:166.

Rufus. Together, they sought to clean up the corrupt activities of the tax farmers, protect temple and civic assets from unlawful seizure, and ban contracts made under the use or threat of force.[42]

The *publicani* in control of the courts were hesitant to attack Scaevola directly, and focused on Rutilius, who remained three months longer in Asia to enforce Scaevola's rules. The publican juries accused him of maladministration in office, *i.e.*, not permitting rapacity to continue at its normal rate. In 92 "he was convicted and sentenced to pay a sum greater than he could realize even by the sale of all his property."[43] He went into exile on Lesbos. Many free cities received him with gifts, and he was welcomed in Smyrna, where he spent the rest of his life, composing his memoirs and a history of Rome (subsequently lost).

This attack on officials who challenged publican behavior showed the tax collectors' power over that of "an innocent, indeed reputedly incorruptible acting-governor," notes Hopkins. It was "a warning to other governors to trim their sails" when it came to restraining publican asset stripping. "The knights' domination of the jury courts for more than a generation confirmed the power and wealth of the tax-farming companies. The increased competition between aristocrats for office (after 81 BC) ensured the continuance of what had become a tradition; senatorial administrators and tax-farmers colluded in getting rich at the expense of the weakest party, the conquered provincials."[44]

In retrospect we can see how naïve the Gracchi were to imagine that the tax collectors would prove less corrupt as judges than the governors and other magistrates sent by the Senate. Instead of publicans and senators acting as checks on one another, they joined forces to protect

---

[42] Badian 1983:89. Tan 2017:83 summarizes earlier attempts at reform, drawing on Livy 43.12 and 17.2-3: "The Senate was already attempting to clamp down on the reckless demands of its members as early as 171: it forbade officials in Spain from setting arbitrary prices for grain and insisted that no city in Greece should provide anything to Roman magistrates unless specified by the Senate." In 149 the tribune Lucius Calpurnius Piso sponsored the *lex Calpurnia*, establishing a court overseen by a praetor to prosecute corrupt governors extorting tribute from the provinces they ruled. The *lex Acilia repetundarum* in 123 of Gaius Gracchus was supposed to use the publican courts to check similar wrongful behavior, but the problem was illicit actions by the publicans themselves. "A *Lex Porcia* of 121 or 118 regulated the scope of a governor's requisitions, and by the time of the *Lex Julia* in 59, most forms of profiteering were the subjects of (imperfect) regulation."

[43] Magie 1950:174-175. Mayor 2010:171 notes that Rutilius was recognized as an exception to Roman rapacity, and was spared in the Ephesian Vespers of 88.

[44] Hopkins 1978:47.

their takings. Gaius's attempt at reform gave the publican *equites* "power without responsibility ... it could use that power irresponsibly, if not to govern the state (for that was not its purpose, nor in its power), at least to prevent it from being governed."[45]

The murder of Gaius and his followers in 121

Gaius's domestic policy promoted public welfare spending along the lines later emulated by Julius Caesar. Roman soldiers were to be clothed at public expense, and state granaries built and stocked to lower the price of grain for the poor. He also sought to construct roads and send out colonies.[46]

When Gaius was re-elected as tribune in 122, the Senate resorted to the same lethal violence its members had mobilized against his brother. When one of his bodyguards killed a bystander during a particularly tense confrontation, Gaius's enemies recruited a mob to attack his supporters, whom Gaius's fellow tribune M. Fulvius Flaccus led to safety at the old plebeian stronghold on the Aventine Hill. But the Senate mob attacked them and killed Fulvius. It then pursued Gaius to the Temple of Minerva, where he avoided being killed by the mob by having his servant help him commit suicide. The houses of both tribunes were plundered, and their severed heads delivered to the consul Opimius, "who gave their weight in gold to those who brought them."[47] About 250 of Gaius's supporters were killed and thrown into the river, followed by mass arrests. Some 3,000 were said to have been strangled in prison.[48]

The murder of Gaius Gracchus and his supporters inaugurated an oligarchic offensive that abolished the land commission in 119. In 111 a law was passed privatizing much of the remaining *ager publicus* and permitting its holders to sell it (previously forbidden by Tiberius Gracchus). The result was that "immediately the rich started to buy from the poor

---

[45] Badian 1983:91 and 96. As civil war raged after 88, Sulla restored control of the courts to the Senate, appointing 300 new senators to serve as jurors to replace the 300 *equites* that Gaius had added. The praetor L. Aurelius Cotta restored the *equites'* judicial role in 70.

[46] Plutarch, *Gaius Gracchus* 3-9, and Appian, *Civil War* 1.1-2, in Lewis and Reinhold 1951:256-260. See also Frank 1933:234-237.

[47] Appian, *Civil War* 1.3, in Lewis and Reinhold 1951:261. This fight led to public assemblies being armed.

[48] The details are reported in Plutarch, *Gaius Gracchus*, and Appian, *Civil War* 1.19-20.

or find pretexts to evict them by force."[49] The law was "the death knell of the Gracchan attempt to revive a class of peasant smallholders and a major victory for the latifundists in Italy and the provinces, since it removed all obstacles to the expansion of large private holdings."[50]

In 104 the tribune L. Marcius Philippus complained that only two thousand Romans were left who owned any property. He proposed an agrarian law "to distribute land to the poor in order to cut back the number of large estates, which still existed in great numbers. The only land which could be distributed was *ager occupatorius*, which apparently still existed. As it was, this law came to nothing, and the possessors retained their holdings."[51]

The next chapter will review the creditor alliance that murdered the praetor Asellio for proposing to restore pro-debtor laws in 89. That was the year in which Mithridates VI invaded Cappadocia, initiating the First Mithridatic War (89-85) to drive Roman tax collectors, creditors and other businessmen and administrators from Asia Minor and Greece (which Chapter 16 will describe). Greek and Asian resentment toward the Romans led to the Vespers of Ephesus in which a reported 80,000 Romans and their Italian allies were massacred in 88, seven years after the failed mission of Scaevola and Rutilius.

---

[49] Roselaar 2010:256-257 and 275, citing Appian, *Civil War* 1.27.

[50] Lewis and Reinhold 1951:256 (1990 ed., p. 275).

[51] Roselaar 2010:281, citing Cicero, *De Officiis* 2.21.73. *Ager occupatorius* was land occupied by a victor driving out the conquered people who had held it.

15
Revolts Against and Within Rome Lead to Financial Crisis, 91–86 BC

From the beginning of the Republic in 509 BC, running into debt had led smallholders to forfeit their land to foreclosing creditors. But as booty and tribute poured into Rome from Asia and other conquered territories, wealthy recipients lent out their takings to well-to-do borrowers to buy land as an investment. Land could be bought on credit if one had sufficient collateral to pledge and was deemed a suitable borrower by wealthy lenders. This novel practice of buying land on credit used debt as a means to acquire land, not lose it! Absentee landownership – and mortgage lending – became investment vehicles. And inevitably, land speculation bid up prices – leading to the first recorded land bubble.

However, this land bubble could only be maintained by Rome's military enforcing the collection of foreign tribute, taxes, debt service and land rents. Foreign resistance disrupted this affluence as revolts by Italian cities gained momentum from 91 to 89, and the liquidity crisis became more intense in 88 when a revolt by Mithridates VI interrupted tribute from Asia Minor. Creditors demanded payment from debtors unable to collect revenue from that province. Calling in their loans caused land prices to crash. Well-to-do investors joined the poor in demanding debt relief, which the Optimate oligarchy blocked by violence.

The "New Men" and their new army

The changing character of Rome's army shaped the political conflict that arose at this time between the Populares – the largely plebeian citizenry under Gaius Marius (157-86) – and the oligarchic Optimates led by L. Cornelius Sulla (138-78). At issue between these two men was who would lead their troops to Asia and loot enough money to gain control of Rome.

Marius was a "new man" (*novus homo*), born into a Latin equestrian family with Roman citizenship. Attracting support from the Metelli and other prominent families who recognized his leadership talents, he rose from military tribune to plebeian tribune, and married into the patri-

cian Julii family. His wife Julia (140-69) would become the aunt of Julius
Caesar.

Marius's victories in 109 under the consul C. Caecilius Metellus in
North Africa against the Numidian king Jugurtha gained him enough
popularity to break into the aristocracy's monopoly of high office, being
elected consul in 107 and re-elected annually from 104 to 100, and
again in 86. During these years he reorganized Rome's military system
by admitting landless men into the legions, starting with the army
he recruited to fight against Jugurtha in his first year as consul. The
army "did away with the property qualification formerly required, and
accepted the poorest citizens, if physically fit, for military service."[1]

This changed the army's composition to one based on landless volunteers, men who had been driven off their land and now sought employment and a share of the booty, and hoped to receive land grants for
themselves. Their interest lay in backing generals who were their paymasters and rewarded them well, and sometimes killing those who did
not. For the rest of Roman history down through the end of the Empire,
generals used their command to an unprecedented extent to enrich
themselves from conquered territories and lead soldiers personally loyal
to themselves to gain political power at home.

Marius's future nemesis, Sulla, was a minor aristocrat from the least
distinguished of the seven Cornelian patrician families. He was elected
quaestor for the year 107 (the year of Marius's first consulship). That
position traditionally was the first step toward higher office. When lots
were drawn to assign duties, he was chosen to serve under Marius in
North Africa, and was assigned command of the victorious cavalry.
Marius ultimately captured Jugurtha for Rome, and celebrated a
military triumph in 104, parading Jugurtha along with large stores of
wealth captured from North Africa.

In 103, at the start of his four consecutive consulships, Marius consolidated his popularity by allying with the tribune L. Appuleius Saturninus to assign land to his veterans. Saturninus was re-elected tribune in
100 (for the third time), along with G. Servilius Glaucia. But when the
leading Optimate candidate, Gaius Memmius, was beaten to death in
the political infighting, the oligarchic faction incited an attack in which
Saturninus and Servilius were killed, along with many of their supporters. Marius thought it best to leave Rome in 99 to travel to Asia, where
he met Mithridates VI. That encounter led him to seek command of the
Roman army, envisioning a war for eastern land and its wealth.

---

[1] Mommsen 1958:114. See also Keaveney 2005:50-52.

That same year, in 99, Sulla ran for a praetorship, largely on his military record with Marius. He lost, but was elected the next year to serve in 97, and was appointed proconsul to Cilicia to deal with pirates and restore Rome's ally Ariobarzanes to Cappadocia's throne.

The Social War between Romans and other Italians

In 95, Rome's conflict with its Italian neighbors over the distribution of *ager publicus* occupied by other Italians heated up. A generation earlier, in 125 when Gaius Gracchus had sought to distribute to Roman colonists this public land that Rome had allowed its allies to use, he tried to minimize conflict with the rest of Italy. As a tradeoff for Rome finally taking possession of this land for its own colonists and private owners, Gaius offered citizenship rights to the Italians.[2]

The problem was that most of the land that Rome proposed to re-appropriate had been farmed by wealthy local families. For these Italians, Roman citizenship, freedom from the *tributum* tax and the right to vote (for those who could afford to travel to Rome) was little compensation for what they lost, so no agreement was reached.

In Rome itself there was strong opposition to giving Italians equal citizenship status. In 95 the *lex Licinia Mucia* expelled all non-Roman Italians from the city. That spurred a revolt, and by 91 the conflict over whether to accept Latins and other Italians as citizens was dominating Roman politics.

The Populares advocated extending citizenship to the Italians, absorbing them into Rome's existing tribes when assigning their voting rights. The Optimates offered lesser second-class rights in newly created tribes. The Optimate tribune Livius Drusus went further and opposed any admission to citizenship for Italians. That stance – along with his attempt to take control of the extortion court away from the *equites* and restore it to the Senate in the wake of the Rutilius scandal in Asia – led to him being killed.

The conflict over *ager publicus* saw the Italians field twelve armies against Rome from 91 to 88, seizing many estates owned by Roman landlords. That left Romans who had bought this land on credit unable to pay their debts out of the rents they had anticipated. They had

---

[2] Roselaar 2010:6, 275 and 282, pointing out (p. 297) that: "It is likely that many Italian elites held a relatively high percentage of their land as *ager publicus*, since in many areas so much land had been turned into public land, not much else was available. This also meant that some of them had lost more land in the Gracchan reform than most Roman citizens had." See also Appian, *Civil War* 1.21 and 23.1.

pledged most of their property as collateral, but were unable to borrow more against it or sell what remained after seizure by the Italians at a high enough price to cover their debts. The ensuing Roman financial and real estate crisis has been well described in a classic article by Charles Barlow:

> Land held by the enemy was worthless as collateral, which led many creditors to call in their loans. At the same time the turmoil and social tensions led to the hoarding of coins, which in turn probably caused all land prices to drop. The declining land prices further undermined the credit structure, while the hoarding of coins caused money to disappear from circulation. The debtors could neither pay off their loans nor renegotiate them. By 89, with credit laboring under coin hoarding, falling land prices, and a shaken *fides*, the government faced a deepening debt crisis.[3]

The magnitude of the debts far exceeded the falling market prices for the land pledged as collateral. Bankruptcy confronted a large segment of Rome's political elite, with foreclosure threatening to reduce the reputation of families who had bought land on credit.

Meanwhile, the Italian states sought support in their fight against Rome from Mithridates, but he declined, evidently expecting Rome to leave him alone once he had driven its troops out of Asia in the anti-Roman revolt that he would commence in 88. "Had this Asiatic war broken out a year earlier," in 89 instead of in 88, commented Mommsen, "the simultaneous revolt of half of Italy would have constituted an immense peril to the Roman state."[4]

The murder of Asellio in a creditor riot

Trying to negotiate an agreement between Roman creditors and debtors, the urban praetor for the year 88, A. Sempronius Asellio, set about reviewing the history of Roman law in his function of ruling on civil actions involving debt collection. His solution was to impose a moratorium on debt collection.[5] To enable debtors to dispose of their land to pay their creditors in an orderly way, he proclaimed a moratorium (*exceptio*) on payments. In addition to basing his ruling on the Twelve Tables (VIII.18) requiring creditors to pay damages of four times the amount of the interest they had charged above the legal rate of $1/12^{th}$, he

---

[3] Barlow 1980:213-214. See Appian, *Civil War* 1.54, Livy 7.39-42, Scullard 1951:257 and Sampson 2013:51-52.

[4] Mommsen 1958:137.

[5] Frank 1933:268-269.

noted that the Genucian law of 342 banned usury outright. By blocking creditors from bringing legal action to demand payment, Asellio's moratorium would have let debtors save their property.

"It was said in debtor circles that the suffering multitude could only be relieved by 'new account-books,'" commented Mommsen; "that is, by cancelling the claims of all creditors against all debtors."[6] Even indebted aristocrats found themselves in favor of the kind of pro-debtor relief that they had long opposed when smallholders and the poor were the major victims of losing land (and liberty) through debt. But most creditors argued that enforcing the laws cited by Asellio would disrupt practices that had been customary for three centuries, during which time the Senate had refused to enforce laws that the oligarchy did not like.

The crisis was resolved extra-judicially, by force. Moneylenders, *equites* and other creditors gathered in the Forum, where the tribune Lucius Cassius led the crowd in stoning Asellio while he was offering a sacrifice to Castor and Pollux. Asellio tried to escape by running toward the Temple of Vesta, but his pursuers caught him and cut his throat. No investigation followed, and none of his killers were named or punished. "The money-lenders covered up everything" and blocked enforcement of his rulings, concluded Appian (54.1).[7]

The murder pushed the preceding half-century's oligarchic wave of political assassination to a level of normalcy. The violence had started with opposition to the Gracchi and their followers advocating land reform. Then came the killing of Saturninus and Servilius in 100 for seeking to give land to Marius's veterans. In 88 the creditor elite opposed debt relief even for wealthy members of their own class. Killing Asellio for trying to find some way to bring debts into line with the ability to pay established the oligarchic tradition of using killing as a normal political tactic free of punishment or even inquiry.

The scale of political assassination escalated through the 80s, with matters getting much worse as a result of the fighting against the Romans in Asia.

---

[6] Mommsen 1958:140. Also in 88, in order to deter the practice of going into debt to buy political support and favors, "the tribune Publius Sulpicius Rufus proposed that every senator who owed more than 2,000 *denarii* should forfeit his seat in the Senate."

[7] Sampson 2013:51 notes that: "Appian and the *Periochae* of Livy place his death in the Forum whilst Valerius Maximus states that he fled the Forum but was dragged from a shop he was hiding in and butchered." See also Badian 1969:475-481.

Rome strips Asia and drives its realms into debt, spurring a revolt

When Attalus III died in 133, the leading claimant for Pergamum's throne was Aristonicus, said to be yet another illegitimate son of Eumenes II. Refusing to accept Attalus's will disinheriting him, the prince took the name Eumenes III and started what became a four-year war against the armies that Rome sent to Asia to appropriate Attalas's treasure. The Roman consul P. Licinius Crassus Mucianus arrived in Asia in 131 to seize the bequest, but after his first attack failed at Leucae he retreated northward and was killed by the Thracians.

The region's landholders and urban property owners opposed Aristonicus, and the Ephesian navy defeated his fleet off Cyme on the Aeolian coast. Mithridates V of Pontus (ruled ca. 150-120) executed many supporters of Aristonicus, who retreated into the interior, pillaging towns and capturing booty. He was joined by the philosopher Blossius, who provided him with a Stoic rhetoric to attract debtors and other dispossessed, along with "slaves who were dissatisfied with their lot and ready to turn against their owners." Aristonicus called his followers Heliopolitans, "citizens of the City of the Sun," after a utopian novel by Iambulus describing an egalitarian island community in the ocean off Ethiopia.[8]

The Roman consul in 130, Marcus Perperna, quickly defeated Aristonicus and grabbed Attalus's treasure and shipped it to Rome, where it was sold at public auction. Aristonicus was sent in chains to Rome to be strangled in prison. Blossius killed himself when he saw that the cause he had idealized was lost. Rome annexed Pergamum the next year, calling it "Asia."

Manius Aquillius, Roman consul for 129, soon arrived in Asia and conquered much of it, imposing such heavy tribute that citizens of Pergamum and other cities had to borrow from Italian moneylenders. Crops failed as a result of the military requisitions, war damage and cultivators having abandoned their land to join Aristonicus. Matters were

---

[8] Magie 1950:148-153 and 1034-1036, citing Florus I 35.4, Strabo 14, Diodorus 2.55-60, Rostovtzeff 1941:807-808 and Broughton 1938:505. Dudley 1941:98-99 points out that Eunus, leader of Sicily's first slave uprising, which also occurred at this time (135-132), "called his followers 'Syrians' or 'Helipolitae.' ... Heliopolis – now better known as Baalbek – by the source of the Orontes, between the Lebanon and Anti-Lebanon ranges, was the seat of the great cult of the Syrian Sun-God. Sometimes as Baal, sometimes as Hadad with a consort Atargatis, his cult had been widespread throughout the Seleucid Empire, including Asia Minor."

saved in Pergamum when a citizen, Diodorus Pasparos, used his own resources to pay the promissory notes and interest levied on the city.[9]

Asia fell prey to Rome's publican tax collectors and the moneylenders in their train. It was Rome's richest province for many centuries, and obliged to pay more annual tribute than any other. Rome rewarded Mithridates V for his support against Aristonicus by giving Pontus control of Greater Phrygia. Neighboring Paphlagonia went to Bithynia's Nicomedes II (149-127), who also asked for Phrygia, but the Roman Senate denied his request, citing bribery.[10] Phrygia was declared nominally independent (although part of Asia) in 116, but Pontus's new king, Mithridates VI (ruled 120-63), soon conquered it and invaded Cappadocia, sealing his takeover by marrying off his daughter to its young king. He then absorbed Paphlagonia and established Galatia as a protectorate. This expansion set the stage for his long revolt from 88 onward against Roman misrule.

Sulla restores Optimate dictatorship and then leaves Rome to fight Mithridates

Rome's two consuls in 88, Sulla and Q. Pompeius Rufus, recognized the need for some action to resolve the debt crisis. Their *lex Cornelia Pompeia unciaria* restored the maximum limit on interest to $1/12^{th}$ (the legal maximum in the Twelve Tables), and wrote down debt by what seems to have been a tenth.[11] This evidently brought some relief to landlords who were in debt, but was not nearly enough to resolve the overall problem, which soon engulfed the creditor classes, including those who had invested in the publican tax-collecting companies before tribute from Asia was interrupted in 88 by Mithridates' revolt.

The Mithridatic War had started as a local affair in 92, and erupted into a regionwide revolt against Rome in 88. The wealthy as well as the poor in many cities throughout Asia Minor and Greece rose up in the Vespers of Ephesus, killing a reported 80,000 Romans and their retinue (described in the next chapter). In the absence of money from

---

[9] Magie 1950:160 and 1046-1048.

[10] Appian, *Mithridatic Wars* 12.56-57 and Justin, *Oriental History* 37.1.

[11] Frank 1933:269. Surviving Roman records are so brief and the language so obscure that there is confusion over just what the new law meant. "Probably two clauses were in the law: (1) the words *debitores decimam partam* seem to imply an immediate reduction of a tenth of debts, and (2) the same *unciaria lex* (a later appellation) refers to a maximum rate of interest of an ounce to the pound per month, *i.e.*, 12 per cent." See also Sampson 2013:52.

Asia, Rome's treasury met its fiscal needs by selling off public property, including the possessions of the pontifices, augurs and others, and raised 9,000 pounds of gold by selling "building sites on and near the citadel in Rome, which had remained unoccupied since ancient times."[12]

Some of the revenue flowing in from Rome's military conquests and rents had, in addition to being lent for land investment, been invested in shares in the publican tax-collecting companies, which found themselves in a deficit position as revenue from Asia fell short of what they had promised to pay the Roman treasury. A stock exchange in *partes* (participating non-management shares in the publican companies) had developed in the Forum in the 2nd century BC, and Polybius wrote that "there is hardly anyone who is not involved in the sale of these contracts or in the kinds of business to which they give rise."[13] So, when the war interrupted Asian tribute, financial and property markets across the board were threatened with disruption as a result of the interconnections between the Asian tribute, the tax-collecting companies and the credit that had helped fuel the rise in land prices.

Within Rome, the leaders of the two parties vied for control of Asian and other tribute by their own armies and political supporters. By the time Sulla was elected consul for the year 88, his main aim was for the Senate to grant him instead of Marius command of the army being mounted to oppose Mithridates. The Senate awarded him command over the army in Asia, but Marius asked the plebeian tribune, P. Sulpicius Rufus, to convene the popular assembly, which appointed Marius commander, after Sulpicius had first achieved the passage of an electoral franchise law to secure sufficient votes for Marius. Sulla accused Marius of buying his commission by promising to erase the debts of Sulpicius, who was reported to have become financially overstretched.

Sulla gathered the army that the Senate had authorized him to lead and marched on Rome to seize power. When Marius sent M. Junius Brutus (the father of Caesar's assassin) to ask why he was attacking, Sulla replied that he had come to deliver Rome from tyrants – the epithet used against the Gracchi and other populist leaders. His troops broke the symbolic rods of office carried by Brutus, beat him and sent him back to Rome. Sulla also rejected the next two embassies sent by the Senate, but offered to meet with Marius and the tribune Sulpicius Rufus in the Campus Martius, promising to halt his advance. Instead,

---

[12] Mommsen 1958:137.

[13] Polybius 6.17, cited in Badian 1983:45. See Hopkins 1978:5, and Fowler 1927:2-74, citing Deloume, *Manieurs d'Argent*.

he sent his commanders to seize the city gate and walls on the side of
the Esquiline Hill, and invaded the city. This was the first time that a
Roman military leader (if we exclude Coriolanus in the 5th century BC)
had marched on the city to take control by force of arms.

To avoid being stoned from neighboring houses, Sulla ordered his
troops to use blazing arrows to burn them down. In a battle that lasted
only one day he captured the Forum and drove out the forces that
Marius had placed there. Trying to rally his troops, Marius proclaimed
freedom for slaves who would support his cause, but none stepped
forward. He fled to Africa, where he remained popular for giving land
to his troops.[14]

Sulla's idea of "defending Roman liberty" was for the Optimates
to rule by violent autocracy. He decreed Marius, Sulpicius and ten of
their supporters to be public enemies. Sulpicius was caught and killed,
betrayed by a slave who was given his freedom as a reward, but then
hurled from the Tarpeian Rock for betraying his master.

Declaring Sulpicius's legislation null and void on the ground that it
had been passed by force, Sulla used his own force to amend the constitution to prevent any law from being brought to vote in the popular
assembly without the Senate's prior consent. Henceforth, a law would
have to be ratified by the *comitia centuriata*, whose voting classes were
weighted in proportion to landowning wealth. The *comitia populi tributa*
with its democratic equality of votes "would be idle and the *concilium
plebis* would concern itself solely with the business of electing tribunes,"
who were left with little authority.[15]

The conflict between supporters of Sulla and those of Marius was
resolved by re-electing L. Cornelius Cinna annually as consul for the
next four years, 87-84. Although a compromise candidate, he repealed
the laws that Sulla and Pompeius Rufus had introduced in 88.[16] When
he brought charges against Sulla, the latter avoided a trial by leading his
army out of Rome in 87 to loot Asia Minor and Greece in his war with
Mithridates.

After Sulla left Rome, Marius and many of the exiles who supported him returned in 86, bringing with them soldiers whom they had

---

[14] Plutarch, *Sulla* 9 and Appian, *Civil War* 7.

[15] Keaveney 2005:53-56.

[16] Julius Caesar married Cinna's daughter Cornelia probably in 83. They had one
daughter, Julia. Caesar's aunt Julia was, as noted above, the wife of Marius. Sulla
ordered him to divorce Cornelia, but he refused and was proscribed, escaping
Rome until Sulla relented. Cornelia died in 69 or 68.

recruited to fight against those that Sulla had left.[17] Having recruited four thousand slaves and convicts, as well as a reported six thousand Etrurians, Marius declared Sulla to be a public enemy, razed his house to the ground and forcibly removed his followers from office. Five former consuls were killed, and the corpses of many prominent conservatives were dragged through the streets.

The Valerian Law of 86

By 86, Rome's Social War with Italians raged alongside the war against Mithridates in Asia, and the conflict between debtor and creditor interests at home. Land prices fell by three-quarters as a result of the foreclosures and distress sales of property and hoarding of coinage, affecting wealthy as well as poor debtors.

Marius died suddenly (at the age of seventy) only half a month into his victorious return as consul in 86. His supporter L. Valerius Flaccus completed his term alongside Cinna. His Valerian Law (*Lex Valeria de aere alieno*) stopped the wave of foreclosures and distress sales by enabling debts that had been incurred in silver *sestertii* to be repaid in bronze or copper *asses*, coins worth only one-quarter of the silver *sestertius*.[18]

The effect was to remit three-quarters of Roman debts. This 75 percent debt writedown reflected the decline in land prices. Although creditors received only one quarter of their original loan, they still had the equivalent in purchasing power over land. They lost in nominal monetary terms, but not in land value. If they foreclosed, they still received the same property as before, so "in real values they may have lost almost nothing."[19] Creditors thus received the same amount of land that their original loan represented, while well-do-do debtors avoided bankruptcy and loss of reputation.

Government claims also were scaled back by three-fourths, reflecting the 1:4 ratio of bronze *asses* to silver sesterces. This benefited the *publicani*, who were squeezed by being required to pay the Roman treasury specific sums under their contracts to collect tribute in Asia and other provinces after payment was interrupted following the Vespers massacre of publicans and moneylenders.

---

[17] Sampson 2013:83-95 describes the fighting, citing Appian 1.67 and Plutarch, *Marius* 41.2.

[18] Frank 1933:269-271, citing Sallust, *Catiline Conspiracy* 33.2.

[19] Barlow 1980:216. See Sallust, *Catiline Conspiracy* 33.2 and Cicero, *Pro Fonteio* 1–5.

The Valerian Law seems to have been passed largely on the wave of public anger at the moneylenders' murder of Asellio three years earlier. Sallust reported that the writedown, the largest in Roman history, was enacted "with the consent of all good men," benefiting the *equites* and other well-to-do as well as less affluent debtors.[20] But the main beneficiaries were at the top of the economic pyramid. The Valerian Law benefited some poor debtors on their small farms, but the primary beneficiaries were absentee landowners; otherwise, the Senate hardly would have agreed to pass it.[21] But statistics are lacking on the magnitude of the debts of Rome's wealthy and poor alike, and even the area of public land and its rent is undocumented.

The merging of financial fortunes and real estate bought on credit had led to more concentrated land ownership, and would continue to do so for the next hundred years.

The aftermath

Flaccus was appointed governor of Asia in 85 to command the army that was intended to replace Sulla's troops, but he was murdered by his own troops who sought to avoid the fight. In 84, Cinna led an army against Sulla, but also was killed by his own soldiers, who saw that fighting would not yield any booty for them. Sulla made his own peace with Mithridates, obtaining heavy reparations and, after looting Greece, brought his booty-laden troops back to Rome and made himself dictator in 82. He settled a reported 23 legions comprising between 80,000 and 100,000 soldiers (an estimated 10 percent of Rome's citizenry according to the 70 BC census) on conquered land throughout Italy.[22] This further exacerbated Italian protests in the Social War and lay the groundwork for the debt crisis that erupted in 64-62 when Catiline waged a rebellion to cancel the debts into which many veterans had fallen.

The next chapter will describe how the long war against Mithridates in Asia affected the Roman as well as Asian economy. Chapter 17 then will describe Sulla's return to Rome with the loot and army that he accumulated in Asia, taking over Rome a second time and imposing an Optimate dictatorship.

---

[20] Sallust, *Catiline Conspiracy* 33.2. See Lewis and Reinhold 1951:305. By the Augustinian era Velleius Paterculus (ca. 19 BC – ca. AD 31) in his *Historiæ* 2.23.2 called this "a most dishonorable law."

[21] Frank 1933:232 and 270.

[22] Andreau 2012.

16
The Mithridatic Wars Against Roman Creditors, 88-63 BC

Rome's predatory behavior made Asia Minor and its surrounding regions fertile ground for Mithridates VI of Pontus to organize the largest war against Rome since that of Hannibal. Asia and Greece became a battleground for revolts against Roman officials and the moneylenders who accompanied them. The war paralleled Rome's own domestic civil war between its own debtors and creditors – with the debtors in the East being entire cities and provinces.

In 120, aged somewhere between 13 and 15, Mithridates Eupator VI inherited the throne of Pontus after his father, the powerful Mithridates V, was poisoned in a court intrigue. The teenager was protected and taken to the mountains and forests on the south shore of the Black Sea. Around 116-113 he returned and imprisoned his mother Laodice VI (a Seleucid princess acting as regent) and his younger brother whom she favored. To keep the throne in his immediate family, he married his 16-year old sister, Laodice "the Younger."

Appian describes Mithridates as a large man, judging from the size of his armor, "bloodthirsty and cruel to all – the slayer of his mother, his brother, three sons and three daughters." Yet he also "cultivated Greek learning ... and [was] fond of music" and reportedly able to speak all twenty-two languages of the regions he governed. He defeated all the leading Roman generals at one time or another – Aquillius, Sulla and Lucullus, as well as Fimbria, Flaccus, Cotta and Murena. Even when conquered after a reign of half a century "he left no avenue of attack against the Romans untried." Fighting at times with over 400 ships of his own, as many as 50,000 cavalry and 250,000 infantry, he "held communications with the leaders of the Roman civil wars, which were then fiercely raging, and with those who were inciting insurrection in Spain [against Sulla]. He established friendly relations with the Gauls for the purpose of invading Italy by that route also." Plutarch called Mithridates "the new Hannibal."[1]

His first campaign marched through Lesser Armenia and circled up along the east shore of the Black Sea around Colchis to the northern coast and Crimea, driving the Scythians out of Greek colonies in the region. Around 105 he made an alliance with Nicomedes III of Bithynia to divide Paphlagonia (west of Pontus). Rome was too busy struggling with its Germanic invaders in the Cimbric Wars (103-101) to protest much, and the region was still marginal to its concerns in Greece and Africa.

Around 102, Mithridates tried to annex neighboring Cappadocia in central Anatolia. His nephew, Ariarathes VI, had been granted the throne after Ariarathes's mother (Mithridates' older sister, Laodice the Elder) had poisoned Ariarathes's five brothers. Mithridates backed a local noble, Gordius, to kill the king. That made Laodice the regent. But Nicomedes took the initiative and invaded Cappadocia, which Laodice linked to Bithynia by marrying him instead of backing her brother. Mithridates responded by invading Cappadocia and installing the son of Ariarathes VI as Ariarathes VII, with Gordius as regent ca. 116. When the new king later protested Gordius's role, Mithridates led a large army into the kingdom and arranged a public conference, where "he stabbed the young man in full view of both their armies."[2] He then (ca. 101 or 100) proclaimed his own 8-year old son king of Cappadocia (later called Ariarathes IX), again under the control of Gordius.

Around 96, Nicomedes and Laodice (apparently backed by Cappadocia's nobility) asked the Roman Senate to replace Pontic control of Cappadocia by installing the second son of Ariarathes VI (and also nephew of Mithridates) as Ariarathes VIII. The Senate rejected this request and also that of Mithridates, ruling "that Cappadocia should be given freedom; that is, that the aristocracy or feudal lords should rule the country without a king."[3] Paphlagonia likewise was declared free, and Nicomedes was told to withdraw. Cappadocian barons asked to appoint one of their own, Ariobarzanes, as their king. The Senate agreed, and

---

[1] Appian, *Mithridatic Wars* 112 and 119. See also Pliny the Elder, *Natural History* 7.24, and Plutarch, *Lucullus* 5. Adrienne Mayor's biography of Mithridates (2010) provides a thorough biography and overview.

[2] Magie 1950:203.

[3] Sherwin-White 1977:71, citing Justin, *Oriental History* 38, the main source of this convoluted story. The chronology of the many changes in Cappadocia's kings during the 90s is somewhat sketchy.

remained his key backer against future attempts by Mithridates and Nicomedes to appropriate the kingdom.

Rome sent Sulla, just elected as a praetor, to restore Ariobarzanes. He was the first Roman administrator to appear east of the Halys river. But after he left, Mithridates again invaded in 95 and placed his son, the spurious Ariarathes IX, on the throne again. Ariobarzanes fled to Rome and urged the Senate to reinstate him, but by then Rome was busy fighting with its Italian neighbors.

When Nicomedes III died in 94, Mithridates invaded Bithynia and put the former king's illegitimate son Socrates on the throne. But the Senate recognized Nicomedes III's legitimate son, Nicomedes IV (94-74). Mithridates then allied himself with Tigranes of Greater Armenia and invaded Cappadocia again in 93/2. Driving out Ariobarzanes, who had regained the kingship, he again placed his own son on the throne for the third time.

In 90, Rome sent Manius Aquillius (who had been co-consul with Marius in 101) to restore the region's two pro-Roman client kings, Ariobarzanes in Cappadocia and Nicomedes IV in Bithynia. Mithridates acquiesced, but when Aquillius and his commissioners "rendered Mithridates a bill for damages ... he refused to pay [and presented] them in turn with a statement of the expenditures he had incurred."[4]

Aquillius's father (also called Manius Aquillius and himself a consul in 129) had incurred hatred in Asia a generation earlier by leading Rome's fight against Aristonicus and imposing high reparations debts and taxes on Pergamum. The son proved equally offensive. Seeing that Mithridates was not going to be an obedient client, he urged Ariobarzanes and also Nicomedes to invade Pontus. Neither was eager for such a war, but Nicomedes owed the Romans money. He promised them a large reward (bribe) if they restored him to power in Cappadocia, and would pay "other large sums which he had borrowed on interest from the Romans in their suites, and for which they were dunning him." He attacked Pontus and plundered it, seizing booty and retaining Roman support by using part of his spoils to repay their loans.[5]

Mithridates saw that a fight against Rome was inevitable. Negotiating an alliance with Thrace, the Scythians and other neighbors, he accumulated 300 warships and recruited steersmen and lookouts in Phoenicia

---

[4] Magie 1950:208. Mayor 2010:139-140 notes that Aquillius's father had fought Aristonicus's Citizens of the Sun and "had been tried in Rome for gross avarice, profiteering and bribery, but escaped punishment."

[5] Appian, *Mithridatic Wars* 11-13.

and Egypt.[6] He also hired a prominent Greek general, Archelaus, who brought with him the support of much of Greece. This consolidated a broad alliance from the Danube down to Armenia, Asia Minor, Syria, Greece and Africa, all of which regions were so oppressed by Roman greed that they were ready to join Mithridates in the event of a war.

By 89, Mithridates felt strong enough to again seize Cappadocia. After doing so, he sent an embassy to Rome to complain about the Senate's support for Nicomedes, and an envoy, Pelopidas, to warn Aquillius "not to start a major war without an official senatorial decree." Around this time, Diodorus wrote, Mithridates "promised Rome's enemies in Italy that when he had established his power in Asia he would come to their aid" to break the Romans.[7] But fatefully, they never combined their revolt with that of the East.

Despite the fact that war against Mithridates threatened to strain Rome's hold on its eastern and North African provinces, Aquillius affirmed his backing for Nicomedes and, without waiting for the Senate to authorize war, announced his intent to restore Ariobarzanes to Cappadocia's throne and even to invade Pontus. Aquillius, Cilicia's governor Quintus Oppius and Asia's governor Lucius Cassius rounded up three armies of 40,000 men each, alongside 50,000 soldiers of Nicomedes, to confront a force of almost equal size under Mithridates.[8]

Mithridates defeated the army of Nicomedes by driving scythe-bearing chariots "at great speed against the Bithynians, cutting some of them in two instantaneously, and tearing others to pieces. The Bithynians were terrified at seeing men cut in halves and still breathing, or mangled in fragments, or hanging on the scythes." Nicomedes's "camp was captured, together with his money, of which there was a considerable amount, and many prisoners. All these Mithridates treated kindly and sent to their homes with supplies for the journey, thus gaining a reputation for clemency among his enemies."[9]

The Roman generals had undertaken the war without a Senate decree, and evidently without good judgment. Mithridates won battle after battle, each time sending the defeated armies home with provisions. This, along with replacing the Romans by appointing his own local gov-

---

[6] Starting earlier, in 93, Mithridates minted coinage to pay for troops and arms.

[7] Diodorus 37.2.11, citied in Magie 1950:207 and 1100, fn21.

[8] Mayor 2010:143-146, citing Appian, *Mithridatic Wars* 15-16, points out: "Powerful, rogue commanders could now make war for their own gain, as the Senate's power waned."

[9] Appian, *Mithridatic Wars* 17-19.

ernors, increased his popularity as the East's protector against Rome. He gained further local support by freeing the port of Adramyttium from oligarchic opposition by killing the members of its city council.[10]

Rebels in Laodicea captured Cilicia's governor Oppius and turned him over to Mithridates, who paraded him seated on a donkey for ridicule (and later turned him over to Sulla). Aquillius tried to escape back to Italy, but rebels in Mytilene (on Lesbos) delivered him to Mithridates, who poured molten gold down his throat, deeming him the Roman ambassador most to blame for the war. That became a popular form of treating captured Roman generals. A generation later, in 53, the Parthian king poured molten gold into the severed head of the defeated Roman general Crassus at Carrhae, saying "Sate thyself now with the metal for which, when alive, thou wert so greedy."[11] These symbolic acts reflected the widespread hatred of Roman avarice.

Despite the fact that "almost all parts of Italy had seceded one after another" during its Social War with other Italians, Rome declared war on Mithridates. The civil war had depleted its treasury, and war with Asia promised to provide enough loot to replenish Roman finances. As Chapter 15 has described, the two consuls, Sulla and Marius, cast lots in 88 to see who would lead the campaign. Sulla won, but Marius maneuvered to obtain the command for himself, thinking "that this would be an easy and lucrative war." Then, six legions backed Sulla in capturing Rome, eager for war "because it promised much plunder, and they feared that Marius would enlist other soldiers instead of themselves." After his military coup Sulla set out against Mithridates.

With Rome's treasury depleted, he was obliged to tap the temples for funds, including "the treasures that King Numa Pompilius had set up for sacrifices to the gods,"[12] starting what would become a vast looting of temples from Greece to Asia Minor, leading the entire region to rise up against the Romans and other Italians. Sulla's looting succeeded in enriching himself and his troops, but the war crashed Rome's domestic financial markets – and in the process, intensified the war between creditors and debtors.

---

[10] Magie 1950:215.

[11] Appian, *Mithridatic Wars* 20-21 regarding Oppius and Aquillius, and Pliny the Elder, *Natural History* 33.14 and Cassius Dio, *Roman History* 40.27 regarding Crassus. Magie 1950 provides a general military review.

[12] Appian, *Mithridatic Wars* 22.

The "Vespers of Ephesus" (88 BC)[13]

Mithridates built up a naval fleet to attack Rhodes as part of a coordi-
nated attack on Romans in Ephesus, Pergamum, Adramyttium, Chios
and other cities in Asia Minor. He "wrote secretly to all his satraps and
the magistrates of the cities that on the 30th day thereafter they should
set upon all Romans and Italians in their towns, and upon their wives
and children and their freedmen of Italian birth, kill them and throw
their bodies out unburied, and share their goods with King Mithridates.
He threatened to punish any who should bury the dead or conceal the
living, and proclaimed rewards to informers and to those who should
kill persons in hiding. To slaves who killed or betrayed their [Roman]
masters he offered freedom; to debtors who did the same to their
[Roman] creditors, the remission of half their debt."[14]

Mithridates won the support of wealthy Ephesus, and also backing
from Magnesia and Mytilene. "The Ephesians even overthrew the
Roman statues which had been erected in their cities,"[15] and seized
Romans who had taken refuge in the sanctuary of Artemis and killed
them publicly. "The Pergamenes shot with arrows those who had fled
the sanctuary of Aesculapius, without removing them from the statues
to which they were clinging. The people of Adramyttium pursued into
the sea those who sought to escape by swimming, and killed them and
drowned their children." Estimates of the number of men, women and
children killed range from 80,000 to nearly twice that number.[16] Slaves
who had helped kill their Roman masters were spared, along with those
speaking languages other than Latin.

A recent biographer of Mithridates, Addrienne Mayor, points out that
although "historians had long assumed that the lowest 'rabble' must
have carried out the slaughter," scholars now "conclude that ordinary

---

[13] The most detailed report of the warfare in Asia is Appian's *Mithridatic Wars*. The
following pages are based mainly on Book 12 of his *Roman History* (*The Mithridatic
Wars*). Only a précis of Livy's history of these wars has survived.

[14] Appian, *Mithridatic Wars* 22-33, describing many examples of the widespread
hatred of Roman tax collectors and usurers.

[15] Appian, *Mithridatic Wars* 21.

[16] Magie 1950:1103, fn37 notes that Plutarch (*Sulla* 24.4) estimated 150,000 killed,
based on Sulla's memoirs, which most historians think exaggerated the number in
order to mobilize Roman fury at Mithridates. Most of the Romans who managed
to escape gathered on the island of Rhodes. Evidently sensing revolution in the
air, Romans had begun to move into cities with major amnesty temples before the
massacre.

people of all classes, ethnic groups, and walks of life participated in
the popular coalition to wipe out Romans. The killers were indige-
nous Anatolians, Greeks and Jews reacting to Rome's harsh rule and
corrupt system of taxation, which threw individuals and entire cities
into deep debt." Many of the Roman merchants, moneylenders, tax collectors, slave traders, entrepreneurs, shopkeepers and other settlers "had
acquired their land from native people bankrupted by Roman taxation."
Even Cicero wrote that "the Roman name is held in loathing, and
Roman tributes, tithes, and taxes are instruments of death."[17]

The massacre inspired mercenaries in Roman armies to defect to
Mithridates' side, along with Greek sailors on Roman ships and neigh-
boring Galatians and Phrygians who had been drafted or hired into the
Roman-Bithynian armies that invaded Pontus.

Mithridates' exploitation of Asia and Greece to raise funds

Mithridates resorted to extractive measures of his own to raise funds
for his wars. In 87 his general Menophanes looted Delos and burned it
to the ground after killing as many as 20,000 Italian merchants residing
there and selling their wives and children into slavery. That ended the
island's financial role. But instead of taking the treasures in its Temple
of Apollo for his own use, Mithridates sent them to Athens, whose
leaders had supported him, and denounced the Romans for closing their
public assembly, schools, theaters and courts.[18]

The rebellious citizens of Asia and Greece had not intended to
throw off their Roman tax collectors and creditors merely to clear the
path for a new warlord, but found themselves having to contend with
Mithridates as well as the Romans. In cities that opposed Mithridates
or gave him only lukewarm support, he "took for himself a share in the
confiscated Roman properties, [and] some ancestral treasures of the
Bithynian kings." He "seized 800 talents deposited by Jewish bankers in
the Temple of Asclepius (on Cos) and other island sanctuaries, and also
seized artworks left by Cleopatra III of Egypt." When Galatia revolted
and opposition arose in other cities, Mithridates sacked them, using the
booty to raise a new army against Sulla. He fined Chios 2,000 talents
and obliged its officials to collect, "with loud lamentations, the temple
ornaments and all the women's jewelry to complete the amount."[19]

---

[17] Mayor 2010:19.

[18] Mayor 2010:190. See also Jebb 1880:20.

[19] Broughton 1938:513-514 and Magie 1950:217-218, citing Justin, *Oriental History* 38.3.9.

Worst of all, many of the satraps he imposed on captured cities were as oppressive as the Romans had been. General Zenobius, whom Mithridates had placed in charge of Chios, was thrown into prison and killed when he tried to raise more funds from Ephesus.

Mithridates' populist strategy

Mithridates found his early allies against Rome to be the propertied classes that had borne the brunt of Rome's tribute demands, but Appian describes how he turned against affluent Greeks when they opposed his own confiscations. Mithridates "sent an army against the rebels and inflicted terrible punishments on those whom he captured. But as he feared other defections, he gave freedom to the Greek cities, proclaimed the cancelling of debts, gave the right of citizenship to all sojourners [foreign residents] therein, and freed the slaves. He did this hoping (as indeed it turned out) that the debtors, sojourners and slaves would consider their new privileges secure only under his rule." He enrolled 15,000 former slaves into his army, freeing those who had killed their masters as he had done against the Romans, and remitted half of what was owed by debtors who killed their local creditors. He set native troops free, "remitting tribute for five years, sharing his claims to the properties of Romans ... and aiding cities, for he gave 100 talents to restore Apameia after an earthquake."[20]

Wealthy elites in many cities responded by matching Mithridates' populist economic program. "In an effort to hold its lower classes, [Ephesus] cancelled debts to the city and to [the wealthy temple of the Persian nature-goddess] Artemis, except sums publicly lent on mortgages (on these she remitted the interest), voided all suits except those dealing with boundaries and inheritances, gave citizenship to such tax-equals, residents, sacred attendants, freedmen, and strangers as took up arms, and enrolled public slaves, freedmen and residents upon the same terms; holders of private obligations voluntarily released their debtors."[21]

Sulla with an outlaw army devastates Greece and Asia (87-84 BC)

Rome's Senate gave Sulla a relatively small force of five 5,000-man legions in 87 to fight Mithridates. But as Chapter 15 has noted, as soon as he left Rome, his opponent Cinna issued a decree nullifying his command and proclaiming him to be a public enemy. That left Sulla

---

[20] Appian, *Mithridatic Wars* 47 and Broughton 1938:513-514.
[21] Broughton 1938:514-515.

with a rogue army that engaged mainly in looting. The Senate soon sent its own army against him, while Cinna and Marius killed his supporters at home, seized his property and burned his house to the ground.[22]

Sulla and his troops spent the 87/6 winter in Greece building engines of war to destroy Athens. He blockaded the city, subjecting it to famine and let his soldiers plunder it and massacre its inhabitants, including women and children. Even its olive groves were cut down. The destruction was comparable to the Crusaders' sacking of Constantinople a millennium later, and left Athens little more than a backwater for the next few centuries.

At Chaeronea, Sulla used tactics that countered Mithridates' scythed chariots and killed over 100,000 of the 120,000-man army commanded by Mithridates' general Archelaus. He then devastated much of what was left of Greece, seizing booty and sacking the temples at Delphi, Olympia and Epidaurus of a reported 9,000 pounds of gold. This enabled Sulla to pay his army as he went along, while keeping most for himself.

At Delphi, Sulla melted down the gold lion donated by Croesus of Lydia weighing over 500 pounds, along with silver urns, golden bowls, jewels and weaponry. Respecting the classical principle that borrowings from temples in time of war had to be repaid, he promised Delphi's guardians that Apollo's treasures were simply "transferred to him for 'safekeeping.' If he found it necessary to melt down the god's property, Sulla assured them the 'loan' would be repaid." He later took half of Thebes' land and dedicated its rental income to pay back Delphi – in the process, punishing Thebes "on account of its frequent defections."[23]

Sulla bestowed "freedom" (that is, Roman suzerainty) on Ilium, Chios, Lycia, Rhodes, Magnesia and other cities that had remained loyal to Rome. But he stripped Ephesus of some of its territory, and condemned to death members of its upper classes who had joined Mithridates. During the winter of 85/4 he took away the independence of most Greek

---

[22] See Plutarch, *Sulla* 1, Appian, *Mithridatic Wars* 28-37, Keaveney 2005, and Mayor 2010:196 and 210.

[23] Mayor 2010:197-205, noting that Sulla plundered "the temples of Zeus at Olympia and Asclepius in Epidaurus. Selecting the most beautiful, precious art for himself, he melted down massive amounts of silver to pay his men and buy supplies." See Appian, *Mithridatic Wars* 24, 28-30, 34-38 and 42, and Larsen 1938:426-429. Pausanias's *Description of Greece* 9.7.4-6 reports that the Theban land was given back to Thebes, although some of its income may have been earmarked for the temples as an endowment. See Appian, *Mithridatic Wars* 54, Larsen 1938:365 and Magie 1950:221-223.

and Asian cities by making them Roman subjects, and hence owing taxes to it, and imposed reparations on them to pay the cost of the war.

The Vespers of Ephesus had killed or driven out "the *publicani*, whose exactions had done so much to madden the Greeks." Since "there now existed no machinery for collecting these moneys," Sulla's soldiers went around doing the job. "The guilty cities had to provide them with billets whose luxury bordered on the regal. Every host had to furnish his unwelcome guest with daily pocket money, four tetradrachmas for a soldier and fifty drachmas for an officer. The latter also had to be provided with two suits of clothes, one to wear in the house and one suitable for when he went abroad to parade himself before the citizenry in the town square. The host, too, had to provide an evening meal to which his guest might bring as many friends as he wished." The entire war indemnity that Sulla levied on the Greek cities that had supported Mithridates was collected in a single winter.[24]

At Ephesus, Sulla "issued a proclamation that slaves who had been freed by Mithridates should at once return to their masters. As many disobeyed and some of the cities revolted, numerous massacres ensued of both free men and slaves, on various pretexts. The walls of many towns were demolished. Many others were plundered and their inhabitants sold into slavery." In this way, "Sulla punished the partisans of Mithridates by annulling his radical measures, and re-established the group that had tended to favor Rome." Mithridates for his part "realized that he must eventually withdraw, and began methodically to strip the [Asia] province, its cities, and temples, of public and private funds so far as he could and thus to leave it bare for the Roman victor."[25]

While Sulla waged his destructive swath through the East, his adversary Marius died in 85. L. Valerius Flaccus (author of the Valerian Law) was appointed to lead Rome's "legal" army to conduct the war in Asia.[26] Sulla began to wind up his own looting of the region. When Mithridates sent his general Archelaus to negotiate peace in 85, Sulla already had bled the Asia province dry but had no ships, support or money from Rome. He agreed to peace if Mithridates would be content with his own ancestral land, return his prisoners of war, pay 2,000 talents to cover the cost of the war incurred on his account, remove his garrisons from the

---

[24] Keaveney 2005:93.

[25] Appian, *Mithridatic Wars* 61-63, Broughton 1938:517 and Magie 1950:327.

[26] Appian, *Mithridatic Wars* 73 and Sampson 2013:94.

occupied cities, and turn over his navy to Sulla for him to transport his soldiers back to Rome and re-assert his power there.

Mithridates agreed to these conditions, being reconfirmed as king of Pontus and even as a Roman ally, and not obliged to restore the loot that he had taken from Asia Minor and Greece. But the settlement was no put into writing, and only the Senate could formalize the so-called Peace of Dardanus. Mithridates returned to Pontus, leaving Sulla able to move against the Senate army led by Flaccus, who by that time had reached Bithynia.

Flaccus soon fell victim to a mutiny. His troops decided to back the deposed legate Fimbria and killed Flaccus. After casting his head into the harbor and leaving his body unburied, they went on a looting spree, plundering cities and rural districts as they advanced through Bithynia westward toward the Mediterranean coast.[27] Fimbria persuaded Ilium to admit him, and then ordered a general slaughter and burned the town, including "the ancient temple of Athena Ilias, the inviolability of which Rome had long acknowledged. With this act of sacrilege Fimbria's name was ever afterward connected."[28]

Sulla pursued him, and when Fimbria asked his troops for a pledge of loyalty, they refused and chose to join Sulla's army. Fimbria fled and ended up committing suicide in the Temple of Aesculapius in Pergamum in 84. Sulla restored Nicomedes to Bithynia's throne, and Ariobarzanes to that of Cappadocia.

But matters in Asia did not simply revert to the *status quo ante*. In Pergamum, Sulla condemned members of the upper class to death for having joined Mithridates. Summoning the province's leaders to Ephesus, he lectured them on how Rome earlier had driven out the Syrian king Antiochus, yet they had ungratefully supported Mithridates, "who broke faith with you and gave you your fill of rapine and slaughter, redistributed your lands, canceled debts, freed your slaves, appointed tyrants over some of you, and committed robberies everywhere by land and sea."[29]

As a result of these troubles, Sulla concluded, "for the sake of that fair repute that is ever dear to the Romans, I shall only impose upon

---

[27] Appian, *Mithridatic Wars* 52. Fimbria had been one of Marius's commanders who stormed Rome in 87, and commanded the force that killed the father and brother of the future triumvir M. Licinius Crassus.

[28] Magie 1950:221 and 226.

[29] Appian, *Mithridatic Wars* 51, 54-58 and 59-60. See also Diodorus 38-39 and the discussion by Mayor 2010:222-224.

you the taxes of five years [those which Mithridates had suspended], to be paid at once, together with what the war has cost me, and whatever else may be spent in settling the affairs of the province. I will apportion these charges to each of you according to cities and will fix the time of payment. Upon the disobedient I shall visit punishment as upon enemies." He demanded 20,000 talents, by far the largest charge imposed on any region up to that time. "To facilitate the levy Sulla reorganized the province [of Asia] into 44 districts, making each responsible for a fixed proportion of the whole sum," and designated Rome's publicans to collect the tithe.

Having laid waste to the entire region and "killed 160,000 men, recovered Greece, Macedonia, Ionia, Asia and many other countries" for Rome, Sulla ended his fighting in Asia in 85, took his loot and marched his army back to Rome as its richest man. Magie summarizes his career in Greece and Asia: "Contrary to the clause of the Treaty of Dardanus which guaranteed amnesty to the cities, he had deprived many of them of the freedom they had enjoyed since the coming of Alexander; he had imposed on the communities a fine which exhausted them financially for years to come; he had done nothing to protect the coast cities from the ravages of the pirates; and he left a vain and reckless legate [Murena] as governor of the bleeding and bankrupt province."[30]

Sulla's soldiers carried so much booty with them when Sulla brought them back to march on Rome that they refrained from robbing the Italian cities from Brundisium to Rome.[31] That wealth empowered Sulla to conquer Rome, wiping out his rivals who had supported Marius and introducing the first dictatorship in three centuries. As Sampson summed up matters, the war indemnity of 2,000 talents that Mithridates agreed to pay Sulla served, in effect, as the price of "funding an attack on Italy by a Roman general, which was itself a bonus for Mithridates, as Rome collapsing into civil war once more would give him a freer hand in Asia Minor."[32]

The Roman legions left in Asia to "keep order" were an on-going plague. Sulla's general Murena conducted raids throughout the province

---

[30] Magie 1950:340 and 1116. Pliny the Elder, *Natural History* 33.5.7 wrote that Sulla displayed 115,000 pounds of silver and 15,000 pounds of gold at his triumphal procession back in Rome. Magie estimates that Rome overall took some 15 million *denarii* from Asia Minor.

[31] Frank 1933:269, citing Appian, *Mithridatic Wars* 62-63, Plutarch, *Sulla* 25 and *Lucullus* 7 and 20.

[32] Sampson 2013:112.

from 83 onward, plundering cities and robbing their temples at will, including Cappadocia's Comana Temple. Matters reached their depth in Cilicia in 80, when the notorious Gaius Verres indulged "his art-collector's passion" to loot famous statues and paintings from the Temple of Hera on the adjacent island of Samos, as well as temples in Chios, Erythrae, Halicarnassus and Tenedos.[33] Governors and generals looted the temples, destroying their artistic creations, above all those made of silver and gold. Many cities in Asia did not recover until the rule of Constantine broke free of the West four hundred years later.[34]

Murena was joined by Mithridates' best general, Archelaus, who defected out of fear that his employer would turn against him for having negotiated the original peace settlement with Sulla. Murena launched a pre-emptive attack against Cappadocia in 83 and defeated some of Mithridates' cavalry. "When Mithridates made appeal to the treaty of Dardanus, Murena simply asked, 'What treaty?'" The Senate had not ratified the agreement.[35] Mithridates finally defeated Murena in 81, and Sulla endorsed his victory, ending what has been called the Second Mithridatic War.[36]

Mithridates reopens the war against Rome but is defeated by Lucullus

By 75, Mithridates was preparing for a third war, in alliance with Spain's governor Sertorius, who had fled Rome to organize opposition to Sulla. Hoping to attack Rome from both east and west, Sertorius and Mithridates raised a large fighting force in 74, including various enemies of Sulla. The widespread unrest by cities that had been bled by Roman tax collectors and their allies enabled Mithridates to reopen the war in 73 by invading Bithynia when Nicomedes died childless and bequeathed his kingdom to Rome. "Not only did these parts willingly receive him again," describes Plutarch, "but almost all Asia regarded him as their

---

[33] Magie 1950:340. He adds: "It is perhaps significant of the point of view in the Capital that ten years later Cicero, in his attempt to convince the jury of the heinousness of Verres's action, advanced the argument that, whereas many other Romans had robbed the provinces of works of art, they had always presented these to the Roman state, while Verres kept his plunder for his own enjoyment." See also Mayor 2010:228-230.

[34] Broughton 1938:518.

[35] Keaveney 2005:162. See also Magie 1950:340.

[36] Broughton 1938:525, and Appian, *Mithridatic Wars* 64-66.

salvation from the intolerable miseries which they were suffering from the Roman moneylenders and revenue farmers."[37]

The Roman consul for 74, Cotta, fled after losing 5,300 men in one fight compared to only 700 casualties for Mithridates' forces, along with the loss of 30 Bastarnian cavalry from Germany. Cities once again began to seize Roman *publicani* and put them to death, starting with the free city of Heracleia, the first stop of Mithridates. At Chalcedon he destroyed Cotta's entire fleet of 64 ships. That caused panic in Rome, as Asian and northern tribes were allying against it in a two-front conflict.[38]

It was at this point that L. Licinius Lucullus (Cotta's co-consul in 74) took command as Sulla's legate. He was a protégé of Sulla, and the only officer who had not deserted him when he marched on Rome in 88.[39] Helped by the fact that much of Mithridates' army had died of hunger and many of his ships were wrecked during the winter of 74/3, Lucullus waged guerilla warfare and conquered Mithridates decisively in 71/70. "More scrupulous than other commanders such as Cotta, [Lucullus] tried to spare the cities, but was partially frustrated by the depredations of the royal garrisons and by the desire of his own soldiers for booty."[40] The Roman soldiers fighting in Lesser Armenia were so intent on plundering what Mithridates had taken from Asia that they let him escape.

When the fighting ended in 70, the 20,000 talents levied on Asia by Sulla in 84 had accumulated so much interest that the balance due had risen sixfold, to 120,000 talents, despite the fact that 40,000 already had been paid, double the original indemnity. This growth in just fourteen years implies an interest rate of nearly 30 percent. The moneylenders recovered the gain, not the Roman treasury. The interest charges, penalties and property seized by creditors and publicans were privatized, creating personal fortunes that played an increasing role in Roman politics. As Tan emphasizes, "the provincials were tapped for more and more, paying extra fees, extra taxes, and immense rates of interest,

---

[37] Appian, *Mithridatic Wars* 68 and 71, and Plutarch, *Lucullus*. What is called the Third Mithridatic War lasted from 73 until Pompey's victory over Mithridates in 63, described below.

[38] Magie 1950:324-325. Upon returning to Rome, Cotta was expelled from the Senate for stealing war booty with which he had been entrusted (Broughton 1952:116 and 122). He had been sent to govern Bithynia after having served as co-consul with Lucullus in 74.

[39] Sampson 2013:199. Both Sulla and Lucullus had married into the prominent Metelli family.

[40] Broughton 1938:527.

while the treasury was allotted no more than the same old revenues. An empire built through public sacrifice yielded profits privatized for the elite."[41]

Publicans strip Asia's wealth

Sulla's violent demands and their aftermath destabilized Asia's economies irreparably. Having already been looted of all monetary means to pay, its cities were forced into the arms of Roman and Italian moneylenders. The typical arrangement called for tax farmers to "advance a predetermined sum to Rome in exchange for the right to maximize tax collection within the defined tax farm, and if taxpayers could not afford their obligation, then a banker would lend them the money for even greater profits over time, thanks to the interest charged."[42]

In other words, with the province unable to pay the reparations being demanded, Rome's publican *equites* paid the sum to the treasury in exchange for the privilege of taking whatever they could strip. They descended like locusts on the province. Asia's temples already had been looted and its cities sacked by Sulla. Members of its once-wealthy creditor class hardly could provide the money, because their loans had been cancelled either by Mithridates or by cities seeking to hold public support. "The cities, being in financial straits, borrowed at high rates of interest and mortgaged their theaters, their gymnasia, their walls, their harbors, and every other scrap of public property, being urged on by the soldiers with contumely."[43] A backlog of debts, personal as well as public, mounted up at usurious rates of interest as cities defaulted.

A byproduct of this devastation was the spread of pirates throughout the Aegean. Their ranks were swelled by men joining them rather than succumb to slavery as a result of the exactions by Sulla and Roman moneylenders. Even relatively wealthy men joined the pirates, who grew strong enough to attack entire islands and cities. Plutarch describes how they "built fortified roadsteads and signal stations, carried off wealthy citizens for ransom, treating Romans with special insolence, pillaged

---

[41] Tan 2015:217. He explains: "Tax-farming companies, moneylenders, and corrupt officials squeezed increasing profits from the provinces, but, because the treasury received fixed tributes from some provinces and predetermined contract prices from publicans, its share of imperial profits could not increase along with the increasing level of extraction."

[42] Tan 2017:75, citing Magie 1950:165-166 and 251-252.

[43] Appian, *Mithridatic Wars* 62-63. See Frank 1933:342-344 and 1940:518.

famous and wealthy shrines ... made their own accumulations of ship-building materials, timber, brass and iron, kept skilled artisans chained to their tasks, and gathered huge fleets of good vessels, skillful pilots and sturdy crews. Their wealth led to extravagant display, their power eventually made the Mediterranean unnavigable and closed to commerce."[44] Publicans campaigned to give the general and ex-consul Pompey adequate supplies and the right to requisition local provisions to fight the pirates when the *lex Gabinia* gave him command to pacify the region in 68/7. The resulting Mediterranean war lasted until 64.[45]

Despite the devastation wrought by the war against Mithridates and the interruption of commerce through piracy, Roman tax farmers and usurers imposed such extreme plunder and enslavement "that private people were compelled to sell their sons in the flower of their youth, and their daughters in their virginity, and the states publicly to sell their consecrated gifts, pictures, and statues," Plutarch describes.[46] Pompey imposed a settlement under which "the collectors of the tithe were no longer permitted to deal directly with the individual owners or cultivators of the land. They made their bargains under the supervision of the governor for definite sums with the separate communities, each community being then responsible for the collection and apportionment of the sum agreed upon." Levies were imposed on all economic activities, including pasture taxes and the customs revenue.[47]

Expanding well beyond the capacity of Asia to pay, the resulting debts posed a dilemma for Rome: Would it stand by the moneylenders

---

[44] Broughton 1938:519-521 and Plutarch, *Pompey* 24-25.

[45] Broughton 1938:523 adds that Pompey seized the pirate fleet, "capturing in all 846 ships ... and took 120 towns, forts and other bases, making captive about 20,000 pirates; about 10,000 had fallen in battle." In an attempt to ameliorate the economic conditions that spurred this piracy in the first place, Pompey settled some of the pirates into small and half-deserted cities of Cilicia to start a more peaceful life.

[46] Broughton 1938:561 and 545, and Plutarch, *Lucullus* 7 and 20, using his usual melodramatic imagery to add that: "At last men had to surrender to their creditors and serve them as slaves." Diodorus 5.38 made the point more elegantly, remarking that the Phoenicians had a talent for discovering sources of wealth, the Italians "a genius for leaving nothing for anybody else" (Cited in Ste. Croix 1989:356).

[47] Broughton 1938:537 and Frank 1933:343. Magie 1950:350 notes that "while it is not improbable that the tax-farming corporations sometimes engaged in money-lending ventures, this business, in general, was carried on by the banker, sometimes a native, but more often an immigrant from Italy" as opportunities for gain brought a new throng of Roman fortune-hunters to the Aegean.

at the cost of crippling the province? As Cicero wrote to his brother Quintus: "To all your good will and devotion to duty there is the serious obstacle of the publicans; if we oppose them, we shall alienate from ourselves and from the commonwealth an order that has deserved extremely well of us ... and yet if we yield to them in everything, we shall be acquiescing in the utter ruin of those whose security, and indeed whose interests we are bound to protect."[48]

Realizing how untenable a situation this was, Lucullus moved to free the cities from their arrears to Rome and the private debts that engulfed almost everyone who had been obliged to borrow from moneylenders to pay the taxes falling due. Lucullus enforced the legal 12 percent ceiling on interest rates, and decreed that where the accumulated interest already had come to exceed the principal, the debt was deemed to be paid off. "The third and most considerable order," Plutarch describes, was to limit debt payments to a maximum 25 percent of the debtor's income, until the debts were paid off, and that "if any lender had added the interest to the principal, it was utterly disallowed."[49]

These rulings helped ameliorate Asia's debt problem. In just four years, "all debts were paid and lands returned to their rightful owners," presumably by creditors who had taken them as collateral. Praising the policy of not pressing debtors beyond their capacity to pay, Plutarch described Lucullus as acting in the spirit of the goddess Artemis at Ephesus, who granted refuge in her sanctuary to debtors.[50]

But Lucullus's moderation "incurred the enmity of the knights and money lenders by reducing by fiat the debts of the Asiatic communities that had grown from the Sullan exaction of 20,000 talents 17 years before and the sudden explosion of provincial debts to them. And it was also known that he was not as willing to establish new provinces as were the knights; he had in fact given Syria and a part of Cilicia back to the Seleucides."[51] In fact, the break in the expected revenue for the *equite* companies led them to demand their own debt forgiveness from the Roman treasury of one quarter of what they had promised to pay. Seeking their support (and to show his own moderation), Caesar granted their wish when he became consul in 59 (see Chapter 18).

---

[48] Broughton 1938:539, citing Cicero, *ad Quintum Fratrem* I.1.32.

[49] Plutarch, *Lucullus* 20. Lucullus imposed a 25 percent tax on crops, and levied taxes on slaves and house property so that the economic burden fell on the cities as well as on the peasantry.

[50] Plutarch, *Lucullus* and *Moralia* 828 (Loeb Classical Library, 1936 X:321).

[51] Frank 1933:305.

Mithridates describes the predatory logic of imperial drives for control

A few anticlimaxes brought the Mithridatic wars to a close. Despite his defeat by Lucullus in 71/70, Mithridates sought aid from the Parthian leader Arsaces in 69 (in the letter cited in part in Chapters 13 and 14) to renew the fight against Rome. His letter has become famous as a description of the dynamic of Rome's imperial looting and money-lust. Reminding Arsaces of Rome's opposition to monarchies in its drive to subjugate all governments, Mithridates described the Romans as

> turn[ing] to the East only because the Atlantic Ocean ended their westward expansion. ... You [Arsaces] have great resources of men, weapons and gold. It is inevitable that Rome will make war on you to obtain these resources. Ask yourself, if Tigranes and I are defeated, should you really be better able to resist the Romans? There is no end to war with the Romans. They must be crushed.
>
> The Romans hate us as the avengers of all those they subjugate. ... Romans want power over all, but they always aim their deadliest weapons against those with the richest spoils. ... they will blot out everything or perish in the attempt.[52]

In 68, Roman moneylenders and publican tax collectors accused Lucullus of needlessly prolonging the war against Mithridates, and the Senate forced him to disband his troops.[53] Viewing Pompey as more likely to give them and Rome's moneylenders free rein, the *equites* threw their support behind the *lex Manilia* transferring the Asia command to Pompey in 66. In defending this transfer of command, Cicero praised Pompey's relative kindness as if this might change what had become Rome's *modus operandi*:

> Even if there be some men moderate and addicted to the practice of modesty and self-government, still, such is the multitude of covetous and licentious men, that no one thinks that these are such men. It is difficult to tell you, O Romans, how great our unpopularity is among foreign

---

[52] Quoted in Mayor 2010:305-306, based on Sallust, *Histories* 4.69. See Lewis and Reinhold 1990:235-236, and Cassius Dio, *Roman History* 36.1-3. Most historians find its eloquence genuine. Mithridates was well known for his oratory. In 88 he had made a public decree at Ephesus inverting Rome's euphemistic name for itself as the "common benefactor" with its inverse, "Romans, the common enemy of mankind" (quoted by Mayor 2010:154).

[53] See Mayor 2010:312: "In Rome, the Populares [joined with the *equites* and] denounced Lucullus for prolonging the war and stripping the palaces of Mithridates and Tigranes for his own profit."

nations, on account of the injurious and licentious behavior of those whom we have of late years sent among them with military command. For, in all those countries which are now under our dominion, what temple do you think has had a sufficiently holy reputation, what city has been sufficiently sacred, what private house has been sufficiently closed and fortified, to be safe from them? They seek out wealthy and splendid cities to find pretense for making war on them for the sake of plundering them.[54]

Cicero's speech closely echoes Mithridates' own letter. The reality, as Frank recognized, was that Pompey "seemed more likely to favor expansion that would profit the knights. Pompey did his work speedily, added Pontus and Syria to the list of provinces, and enlarged Cilicia and Bithynia, thereby extending Rome's income some 70 per cent and the field of operation of Roman capital very appreciably. He also enriched his officers and men and brought 50 million *denarii* into the treasury by way of booty."[55]

Seeing Italy aflame with the slave wars led by Spartacus while Pompey was busy fighting the pirates, Mithridates was joined by Armenia's king Tigranes in 68 to collect a new army, which easily reconquered Greece by defeating Rome's new provincial generals Fabius and Triarius in 67.[56] But when Pompey arrived, his army cornered Mithridates in a devastated region without provisions, forcing him to retreat east, to Armenia, and then north to the Scythians. In 65 he tried to circumvent Roman forces by a northern route to attack Italy via Europe. But one of his wives turned his treasure over to Pompey, and his son Machares also sided with Rome.

Mithridates' shrunken army was on its last legs, "killing plough-oxen for the sake of their sinews. He levied tribute on all, even those of the slenderest means." He still planned to invade Italy in league with the Gauls, hoping "that many of the Italians themselves would join him on account of their hatred of the Romans; for he had heard that such had been Hannibal's policy when the Romans were waging war against him in Spain, and that he had become in this way an object of the greatest terror to them."[57] But for the time being he survived by hit-and-run guerilla warfare along the Black Sea shore around Colchis ca. 65.

---

[54] Cicero, *pro lege Manilia* (*On Pompey's Command*) 22 and 64-65.

[55] Frank 1933:305-306, citing Plutarch, *Pompey* 45.

[56] Appian, *Mithridatic Wars* 87-90, 91-96 and 97-104.

[57] Appian, *Mithridatic Wars* 107-111.

He sought to negotiate peace with Pompey as he had done earlier with Sulla, but Pompey refused.

By the end of winter 63/2 the Mithridatic Wars were over. Mithridates, over 75 years old and deserted by his son Pharnaces and most of his troops, asked his loyal Gallic officer Bituitus to kill him by the sword so as to die nobly.[58] Victorious Pompey distributed 16,000 talents among his soldiers (1,500 Attic drachmae to each, with more to the officers), returning to Rome as a hero.

Rome's victory over Mithridates had far-reaching consequences for its own civil war. Sulla became as rapacious and murderous as dictator of Rome as he had been in Asia. And just as creditor demands drove the populations of Greece and Asia to fight back, rich as well as poor, Rome was engulfed in civil war as the plunder from the Mithridatic Wars, and from proscribed enemies of Sulla, helped finance Rome's policy war of oligarchy against democracy, creditors against debtors.

---

[58] Appian, *Mithridatic Wars* 116.

17

Rome's Land and Debt Crisis from Sulla to Catiline, 83-62 BC

Debt crises erupted more frequently after Mithridates stopped the flow of tribute in 88. From the Valerian Law in 86 to Caesar's bankruptcy laws in 49-44, well-to-do landowners who had invested in publican tax-collecting companies and bought property on credit became the most vociferous advocates for debt writedowns. Publican tax farmers fought to reduce their contractual obligations to the Roman treasury, and absentee landowners joined hands with smallholders as Rome's military and political conflict interrupted their ability to pay their mortgages. Many debtors from both sides backed Catiline after 63 as the Senate blocked debt relief.

Sulla's dictatorship and proscription of his enemies

Rome had feared invasion mainly from Mithridates, but (as Chapter 16 has discussed) the latter's peace with Sulla in 85 enabled the Roman general to be the one who invaded the city. Having distributed booty from Asia and Greece to his troops, Sulla landed at Brundisium and Tarantum on Italy's Adriatic coast in 83. Marching along the Appian Way toward Rome, his troops were not able to carry any more loot than that which they already had brought with them from Asia. "Not a soul was harmed. The crops were left untouched in the fields and not one farmhouse was fired or looted."[1]

Sulla was joined by the proconsul Metellus (a relative of his wife), Crassus and the young Pompey, who brought his own army. Moving toward Rome during 83 and 82, they defeated the armies that the consuls Scipio Asiaticus (a great-grandson of the 2nd century general with the same name) and Gaius Norbanus raised. After Marius's son (also called Marius) and Norbanus lost a reported 7,000 men, many of their soldiers defected to Sulla, who doubled his ranks by offering a full pardon to soldiers of Scipio's consular army who joined him. For endors-

---

[1] Keaveney 2005:108-109. See also Sampson 2013:118 for a narrative of these events.

ing this offer, Scipio was freed from the retaliation that Sulla directed against his other adversaries.

Sulla took control of Rome's key strategic sites in late 82, and his adversaries fled. While meeting with the Senate, he ordered a thousand Samnite captives from Antemnae (which had fought against him) to be massacred, showing how he would treat those who might hold out against him. The Senate not only reversed its decree of 87 declaring him a public enemy, but awarded him the power to treat his opponents as public enemies. The *lex Valeria* of 82, named for L. Valerius Flaccus (cousin of the Flaccus who authored the Valerian Law and fought Mithridates and had died in 84, he was *interrex* presiding over the Centuriate Assembly), appointed Sulla dictator, a position that had not been awarded since the end of the Second Punic War in 201. The appointment was permanent, not limited to the six-month term of former dictators, and Sulla was not obliged to resign when the consular year expired.[2]

Empowered to decree laws without needing approval from the Senate or plebeian assembly, Sulla nullified all legislation that had been enacted while he was in Asia during the consulships of Marius and Cinna. He thus became the tyrant seeking kingship that the oligarchy always claimed that it feared, but it made an exception seeing that unlike the Gracchi and other populist reformers, Sulla opposed popular rights. His laws stripped the tribunes of the power they had held for four centuries to initiate laws in the plebeian assembly, to summon the Senate, and to have *intercessio* power to block Senate acts.[3]

Sulla drew up lists of enemies who could be killed with impunity and have their estates seized. Their names were posted throughout Italy in June 81, headed by the consuls for the years 83 and 82, the younger Marius and about 1,600 *equites* who had profited from Cinna's rule. Thousands of other names followed, and anyone on the lists could be killed at will in order for the killer to receive a portion of their estates, which were sold at public auction with the net proceeds paid into Rome's depleted treasury. That gave opportunists a motive to kill and seize the estates of their personal enemies or even others not named by

---

[2] Vervaet 2004 summarizes Sulla's authority as dictator.

[3] Keaveney 2005:135-143. Also, Sulla's *lex Cornelia annalis* slowed the potential pace of reform to a crawl by forcing candidates "to proceed from office to office in a certain fixed and determined order. Thus nobody could be a praetor until he had first held the quaestorship, and one had to have been praetor [and at least 39 years old] before becoming consul" at a minimum age of 42. See also Mommsen 1958:176-177.

Sulla.[4] "A bounty was offered for every head brought in; and heads were actually brought to Sulla for inspection before the prize-money was collected from the quaestor. The atrium of his house was decorated with these grisly trophies and he displayed the head of the younger Marius in the Forum."[5]

Cassius Dio wrote that "Sulla's cruel tortures and killings of his fellow Romans surpassed even Mithridates' massacre of 88 BC."[6] And Mommsen noted that: "It sometimes happened that the assassination preceded rather than followed the placing of the name on the execution list. ... the culpable indulgence which Sulla displayed here as always toward those close to him, prevented punishment of even ordinary crimes perpetrated amid the disorder." The killers were exempt from punishment and counterclaims by their victims, whose "children and grandchildren were excluded from a political career."[7]

Sulla and his wife Metella are reported to have been the most blatant beneficiaries. "Sulla's daughter bought one of Marius's seaside villas for 300,000 sesterces and sold it on to Lucullus at a profit of over 3300 percent."[8] The family was "allowed to purchase without competition and sometimes had the purchase money wholly or partially remitted. One of his freedmen, for instance, is said to have purchased a property worth 6,000,000 sesterces for 2,000 ... an advocate asked whether the nobility had waged civil war solely to enrich their freedmen and slaves."[9] Sulla's wealth at its peak was estimated to be 170 million sesterces, making him the richest Roman.

---

[4] Keaveney 2005:126, Sampson 2013:146, and Mommsen 1958:198 and 178. The proceeds from the sale of confiscated estates were reported to total 350 million sesterces. Tan 2017:11 points out that the real value was higher, because the estates were bought at steep discounts. The standard work on Sulla's proscriptions is Hinard 1985.

[5] Keaveney 2005:124-126 and 134-135 gives a summary of the horrors, citing Plutarch, *Sulla* 30-31 and Appian, *Civil War* 1.95. Young Marius committed suicide when he was unable to escape. The tomb of his father was broken open and its ashes scattered.

[6] Mayor 2010:229, citing Cassius Dio, Fragment 30-35 and Plutarch, *Sulla* 27-34.

[7] Mommsen 1958:179-180. Catiline was accused of having profited by denouncing people, killing several *equites* and adding the name of his brother-in-law Q. Caecilius to the proscription lists retroactively. See Sallust, *Histories* 1.37 and Keaveney 2005:129.

[8] Tan 2017:11, citing Plutarch, *Marius* 34.2 and D'Arms 1970:27-28.

[9] Mommsen 1958:180 and 209-210.

Next to Sulla was Crassus, who accumulated his fortune largely through Sulla's proscriptions. He became a major buyer of confiscated real estate, forged a name to include on Sulla's list on at least one occasion, and had bailiffs drive smallholders off lands that adjoined his own. Plutarch reported that, seeing how prone Rome was to fire, Crassus organized 500 slaves into a fire brigade. They would hurry to the site of a building on fire, and Crassus or his representative would bargain with the owner over how much to charge to put the flames out. If the offer was not satisfactory, Crassus would let the property burn down and then buy it for a low price, rebuilding it as his own rental property.[10]

Focusing on the estates of the rebels from the Italian upper classes in Campania, Etruria and Umbria where resistance had been fiercest, Sulla declared land confiscated from his political enemies and Italians who had opposed him and Rome to be *ager publicus*, which he distributed to reward his strongest supporters.[11] Much land was bought at prices below actual value, paving the way for a vast increase in landed fortunes based on putting together large estates over the next decade.[12]

Sulla tore down the walls of towns that had opposed him, and resettled 23 legions (80,000 to 100,000 men) on land confiscated next to the towns to keep them in check. Appian (*Civil War*, 1.104) wrote that he gave 120,000 veterans homesteads throughout Italy, wherever he could grab land from existing owners and tenants. Adding to this gift funds from the proscriptions won the veterans' support as a virtual army in reserve to defend his new constitution.

However, many of these soldiers "proved to be unsuited to farming," and many were given marginal lands to begin with. They turned to banditry, and many joined Catiline's revolt two decades later. In the interim, the turmoil from banditry and land grabs led to the further enlargement of Roman villa estates at the expense of the dispossessed.[13]

In Rome itself, Sulla withdrew the right of freedmen to vote, but enrolled in his army 10,000 slaves of the victims of his proscriptions. He

---

[10] Plutarch, *Crassus* 2.3-4. Privatization of basic civic functions often involves corruption of this sort. I am told that in Hong Kong under the British, after seeing a brigade put out a fire with water hoses, the building's owner would ask the men to stop the hoses. The brigade leader then would bargain over how much to charge for turning off the water so as not to cause further damage to the building and its contents.

[11] Keaveney 2005:152, Mommsen 1958:183, and Hopkins 1978:36-37.

[12] Roselaar 2010:285-286.

[13] Sampson 2013:146-148.

ended the grain distribution that Gaius Gracchus had promoted, and doubled the number of senators to 600, packed with his supporters.[14] Then, after resolving the Social War by extending Roman citizenship to allied Italians, he stepped down as dictator in 81. He was elected to a second consulship for the year 80, and retired peacefully to write his memoirs. Sulla died in 78 and was given an extravagant state funeral celebrating him as the savior of Rome for having cleared away the followers of Marius who had challenged the oligarchy's power.

Cleaning up the abuses of Sulla's dictatorship

The incoming consul for 78, M. Aemilius Lepidus, began the process of reversing Sulla's legacy by removing 64 senators appointed by Sulla, starting with his most corrupt protégés. The power of plebeian tribunes to initiate legislation was restored, the grain dole was revived, and surviving families that were proscribed or exiled under Sulla were recalled. Their property was not returned to them, but Lepidus promised to return the land that Sulla had confiscated from the Italians.[15]

The next year, in 77, Caesar brought Sulla's partisan G. Cornelius Dolabella (consul under Sulla's dictatorship in 81) to trial for extortion as proconsul of Macedonia in 80-78. The most notorious governor, Gaius Verres, was prosecuted in 70 for looting and extortion in Sicily and elsewhere. The evidence presented in his prosecution, led by Cicero, illustrates the period's leeway for brutal grabitization.

> During a feast in 80 while serving as *legatus* under Dolabella in Cilicia, Verres (120-43) is said to have asked whether there were any attractive virgins that might induce him to prolong his stay. He was told that one man, Philodamus, had a beautiful daughter. Verres asked to stay at the man's house, and after dinner he asked the host to bring him his daughter. "There ensued a battle between the house slaves and those of Verres, in which one of Verres's official guards was killed." Verres brought the girl's father to trial for killing his guard, and packed the jury with Roman citizens to whom provincials owed money and who therefore needed the support of Verres to enforce their claims for payment. "The prosecutor was a moneylender too; the father could find no one who was willing to defend him and risk offending the governor. He was

---

[14] Badian 1983:99.

[15] Sampson 2013:212-213 and Roselaar 2010:285.

found guilty and executed."[16] Dolabella promoted Verres to pro-questor.

This event recalls the similar notorious misbehavior of Appius Claudius ca. 450 BC toward Verginia, and the Rape of Lucretia story that ended Roman kingship half a century earlier. It shows that the aristocracy's self-depiction as defending virtue against personal hubris and rapine was the reverse of reality. "Taking private profit from public office was built into the Roman system of provincial administration," concludes Hopkins. It was wrong only to take too much, or not to share it adequately with one's subordinates and the Roman treasury (or for generals, with one's troops).

Debt-financed land acquisition after Sulla

To most modern historians the debt issue seems to have been less pressing than recovery from Sulla's proscriptions and the slave revolt led by Spartacus in 73 (put down by Crassus in 71). Much of the problem stems from a lack of Roman financial and monetary data, even regarding the debt laws that seem to have been passed. "I know of no definition of the concept 'debt' to be found in the sources pertinent to the Republican period," writes Yavetz. The absence of documentation has left confusion as to just what sort of debts were sought to be cancelled by the widespread demands for *tabulae novae*, new account-books. "Not a single law pertaining to the abolition of debts has survived."[17]

By the time Pompey and Crassus were elected as Rome's two consuls in 70/69, complaints about debt strains are found primarily at the top of the economic pyramid. Ambitious Romans went deeply into debt to finance their campaigns for the consulship and lesser positions with an eye to obtaining a military command, governorship or other opportunity for exploitation. Paying for electoral support had long been normal, obliging most contenders to run into debt to their backers, of whom Crassus was especially prominent. Elections were notoriously rife with insider dealings and payoffs to obtain the reward of an army command and the wealth that a generalship or governorship brought. As Finley has described:

> the demands of politics ... and of conspicuous consumption ... involved the nobility as well as others, in moneylending on a stupendous scale.

---

[16] Hopkins 1978:41-42, based on Cicero, *Against Verres* 1.64-75. The father was executed in Laudicea's marketplace.

[17] Yavetz 1963:491, fn21. Taylor 1968 has hardly a word to say about the topic of debt.

Electoral bribery, an expensive life-style, extravagant public games and other forms of public largesse had become necessary ingredients of political careers. ... To borrow created a political obligation – until one was assigned a provincial governorship and recouped. Hence extortion in the provinces often became a personal necessity ... Only a few, such as Pompey and Crassus, were so rich as to be fairly immune from anxiety.[18]

Meanwhile, political violence in Rome was

becoming endemic in the city as in the countryside. Both the tribunes Gabinius and Manilius had already resorted to it. We begin in 66 to hear of hired gangs of thugs, partly composed of gladiators and runaway slaves. Sallust and Cicero both speak of a class of professional 'dagger-men' (*sicarii*). The law forbade men to carry arms with criminal intent on pain of death, but it hardly could be enforced. ... At the end of 66 the trial of Manilius had been broken up by force.[19]

This was the backdrop for the debtor-creditor relations that Mommsen described as reverting "almost to the point where they had stood during the worst of the social crises of the third century BC. The nominal owners held their lands virtually at the sufferance of their creditors." Debtors were forced either to vote for what their creditors demanded or

to declare war on property itself, to intimidate their creditors or get rid of them by conspiracy and civil war. On such relations was based the power of Crassus. Out of them arose the insurrections of Cinna, and still more definitely those of Catiline, of Coelius, and of Dolabella, closely resembling the Hellenic world's battles of a century before between those who had and those who had not.[20]

More recent historians have placed less emphasis on the debt issue. In 1973, Finley expressed his surprise at being "unable to find a systematic modern study of moneylending and moneylenders in this most critical period in ancient history."[21] Yet as Brunt noted around the same time, Cicero wrote that "the burden of debt had never been greater" by

---

[18] Finley 1973:53. Crassus defined wealth as the ability to support a legion on one's income (Cassius Dio, *Roman History* 40.60.1, and Pliny the Elder, *Natural History* 33.134). Crawford 2008:636 calls wealthy magnates such as Pompey and Crassus "alternative states."

[19] Brunt 1971a:127.

[20] Mommsen 1958:546-547.

[21] Finley 1973:187.

63. "Sallust describes 'wretched violence and cruelty of usurers of their fatherland.' Apparently, debt-for-labor contracts were spreading, in violation of abolition of *nexum* contracts."[22] Debt tensions were becoming untenable across Rome's economic spectrum, from the poor to the ruling elite who had borrowed to acquire more land and for their political careers and conspicuous consumption.

Catiline promises a debt cancellation (tabulae novae)[23]

The context in which L. Sergius Catiline (108-62) and his supporters emerged was one of indebtedness from the top to the bottom of Rome's economy, with a corresponding rise in desperation and violence. Catiline came from a lesser patrician family. Rising under Sulla and said to have enriched himself in the proscriptions in 82, he was elected praetor (probably in 68) and gained some wealth as a governing official in Africa (67-66).[24] He planned to run for consul in 65 after the winners, P. Cornelius Sulla (nephew of the former dictator) and P. Autronius Paetus, were disbarred for bribery. But an African delegation accused Catiline of the usual Roman corruption in office, and by the time he was acquitted (as almost always was the case) it was too late for him to run for election that year.

Catiline again avoided prosecution in 64 when Caesar, a judge in that year's homicide court, revoked Sulla's preemptive immunity for all crimes committed by men who had participated in his executions, especially those who brought the severed heads of their victims to Rome to claim a reward. Clearing his name enabled Catiline to run for the consulship for 63. Also running were Cicero and Antonius Hybrida (106-42, uncle of Mark Antony), who had served under Sulla in the Mithridatic

---

[22] Brunt 1971b:129, citing Sallust, *Catiline* 33. He adds: "Cicero tended to associate the '*egentes*' (needy) with the '*perditi*' (almost 'criminals'); he came near regarding poverty as a crime," and points out that "Cicero and other ancient writers ascribed the distress of the veterans solely to luxury and extravagance, implausible as a general explanation."

[23] The major sources are by opponents hostile to his program: Cicero's four *Catiline Orations* and Sallust's *Catiline* written two decades later. (Sallust married Cicero's first wife Terentia, but broke with him politically and personally.) Yavetz 1963 remains an excellent survey of the historiography of Catiline's political program.

[24] Plutarch, *Cicero* 17 and Cassius Dio, *Roman History* 37.30.4. See March 1989 and Hutchinson 1967:90 for details. Prominent among the ranks of his supporters were the senators P. Cornelius Lentulus Sura and C. Cornelius Cethegus, as well as Catiline's fellow candidate for consul in 62, G. Antonius Hybrida.

Wars and was supported in the election by Crassus and also by Caesar, who gained the praetorship.

Cassius Dio reports that Catiline and some tribunes already were advocating cancellation of debts, and a number of historians suspect that Caesar was sympathetic.[25] But with Catiline's criticism of Rome's vested interests becoming sharper, he lost by a small margin to Antonius and much more heavily to Cicero, who was supported by Pompey (away fighting in the Caucasus) and the oligarchic Senate core.

Catiline ran once again for the consulship in 63 (for office in 62), but by that time his views had made him an outcast among the wealthy classes who dominated Rome's weighted voting system. His rivals were D. Junius Silanus (stepfather of Brutus), S. Sulpicius Rufus (a litigious contrarian), and L. Licinius Murena (the son of the same-named father who had fought as legate under Sulla in the Second Mithridatic War).

July was the usual time for consular elections, but Cicero postponed it for a few months. Catiline appealed to voters by pointing to his own indebtedness, and promised to abolish their debts, redistribute land (much of it to be taken by proscriptions of wealthy landowners), democratize public offices and priesthoods, and spend war tribute on the population at large.[26] Cicero appeared in public wearing a breastplate, as if Catiline were threatening his life.

Such posturing by Cicero helped Silanus and Murena win. Sulpicius sued to overturn Murena's victory, claiming that he had bribed the voters. But "the jurors, chosen exclusively according to the *Lex Aurelia* from the Senate, the knights and the treasury officials," acquitted Murena, primarily so that Catiline would not become consul.[27]

Having tried the constitutional approach twice, Catiline saw that elections were won by creditor alliances and bribery, and concluded that the only way to advance his program was by armed revolt. The Optimates showed their own willingness to use force when Cicero warned that debt cancellation would indeed plunge Rome into bloodshed.

When Catiline later left Rome to take command of the army he raised for his revolt, Cicero described his major supporters as spendthrifts who refused to sell their property to pay their debts: "But what men has he

---

[25] Cassius Dio, *Roman History* 37.25.4. Mommsen 1958:270 accepts the claim that if Catiline became consul, Crassus was to be made dictator, and Caesar the Master of the Horse to raise a military force while Pompey was away from Italy.

[26] Sallust, *Catiline* 20-23. See Brunt 1971a:130 for a discussion.

[27] Hutchinson 1967:80-85 describes the election and how it showed Catiline that the political system was stacked against him and his program.

left behind! And what debts they have! And what influence! And what names!" He cited others hoping to have their mortgages wiped out in order to maintain their lifestyles, and veterans who had lost their farms in the settlements that Sulla had established.[28] From this time forward, notes Jean Andreau, the debtors facing default included "the senatorial elite, or at least a part of it ... The urban working classes and a certain number of poor or modest peasants were most likely chronically in debt, but this indebtedness did not become politically dramatic until the elite also fell into debt. The indebted senators had assets consisting of land, livestock, slaves, houses and valuable objects and, unless they sold a fraction of these assets, they would not be able to repay their creditors." Yet they refused to break up their landholdings, "because their dignity and their rank were founded on their estates."[29]

Cicero as consul for 63 had sought to deter his fellow consul Antonius from supporting Catiline's attempt to attract Populares to his camp. Seeing that Antonius needed money, Cicero offered the lucrative governorship of Macedonia and its opportunity for profiteering (which had been assigned to Cicero by lot) to Antonius when his consular term ended if he would stand aside and let Cicero act as sole consul. Antonius accepted the offer.

Sallust describes Catiline's support as coming largely from indebted veterans, the rural poor and urban plebs hoping to be allotted land that might be confiscated from the Optimates. To organize a revolt, Catiline "deposited arms, in convenient places, throughout Italy; he sent sums of money borrowed on his own credit, or that of his friends ... he is said to have attached to his cause great numbers of men of all classes, and some women who had contracted heavy debts" or perhaps wanted to get rid of their husbands.[30] He also gave money to Gaius Manlius, a centurion from Sulla's army, to recruit a small army of about ten to twenty thousand volunteers, and appealed to the poor throughout Italy to support a coup d'état.

Andreau traces the support for Catiline from these troops to Sulla's foundation of colonies a generation earlier on land seized from his enemies and from the neighboring Italians, especially in Arezzo and Fiesole in Etruria, where many of Sulla's veterans had been settled. These colonies were a failure for most veterans, whom Cicero dispar-

---

[28] Cicero, *Pro Murena* 50-51, cited by Ste. Croix 1989:352.

[29] Andreau 2012, citing Cicero, *Second Catiline* 4 and Sallust, *Catiline* 35.3-4.

[30] Sallust, *Catiline* 24.

aged as deplorables playing "at being large scale farmers by carrying out major construction and buying significant numbers of slaves. These unfamiliar rural exploitations drove them into debt, and the only conceivable way out was to join the conspiracy."[31] A letter from Manlius explained their plight in less scornful terms:

> We fight only to protect ourselves from wrong. We are poor and destitute; we have been driven from our lands by the violence and cruelty of moneylenders, who have robbed us of our reputation and fortunes. ... we have been deprived of the protection of the law of our ancestors which permitted a man to remain free even after he had forfeited his possessions. ... We seek only freedom, which no true man is willing to give up as long as he lives.[32]

Unlike the case of senators and other well-to-do who simply feared losing their reputations and prestige by being forced to sell their estates, Manlius explained, the land of smallholders already had been lost and the debtors were desperately trying to save their personal liberty. "The text shows that although (definitive and statutory) servitude for debt had been abolished in Italy, at least for Roman citizens, forced work for repaying debt still existed, on a temporary basis, until such time as the work carried out had compensated the sum of money owed. ... the possibility of such forced work, conceived as a violation of freedom, existed legally, even if it was not to be confused entirely with slavery."[33]

Cicero orders the killing of Catiline's leading organizers

Catiline left Rome in November 63, leaving P. Cornelius Lentulus Sura in charge.[34] Lentulus made what turned out to be a disastrous attempt to

---

[31] Cicero, *Second Catiline* 20, cited in Andreau 2012.

[32] Sallust, *Catiline* 33, in Frank 1933:307-309. Also available in Lewis and Reinhold 1951:272, and Forsythe 2018 II:212. Sulla had placed Manlius at the head of a colony of veterans settled about Fæsulæ, but he lost his property through debt. Countering Cicero's characterization of debtors as selfish spendthrifts, Manlius said that it was not debtors who were extravagant, but men "of dissolute principles and extravagant expectations ... [who] consulted the interest of the state no further than it was subservient to their own."

[33] Andreau 2012, citing Sallust, *Catiline* 37.4-9. Frank 1933:307-308 described Manlius's accusations as showing that "conservative praetors at times disregarded the old Papirian law to such an extent that peonage and imprisonment for debt were being permitted."

[34] Lentulus had been quaestor under Sulla in 81 despite his earlier support for Marius. He was praetor in 75, governor of Sicily in 74 and consul in 71, but the oli-

bargain with a group of Gallic Allobroges ambassadors who had come to Rome to ask for relief from the extortions of provincial governors. Along with other allies of Catiline, Lentulus promised to support their requests if their troops would join Catiline's coup.

But the debt issue was not paramount for the Allobroges at this time. Fearing that accepting the invitation to revolt would turn the Senate against them, they asked for advice from the Roman official they had been dealing with, Q. Fabius Sanga. He introduced them to Cicero, who asked them to get the proposed agreement in writing, signed by Lentulus and other leading conspirators.

The Gallic leaders obtained this and set out to leave Rome, ostensibly to join Catiline's camp. But as had been arranged with Cicero, they were stopped at the Mulvian bridge early on December 3. The signed papers were handed over to Cicero, who convened the Senate and produced the incriminating documents describing how Lentulus, the senator Cethegus and seven others had planned to assassinate him, some senators and even to set fire to much of Rome. When Cicero's allies searched Cethegus's house they found a cache of swords and daggers, evidently to provide to the fighters. Cicero ordered the arrest of Lentulus and Cethegus, the *equites* P. Gabinius Capito and L. Statilius, and a businessman, M. Caeparius. He had the incriminating documents copied and widely distributed.[35]

Cicero demanded that the five prisoners be executed for treason, and asked for dictatorial power to impose the "ultimate decree," the death penalty. He warned that delay might enable Catiline's supporters to rescue his lieutenants, and claimed that citizens arrested on charges of treason lost all their civil rights to a trial, because they had tried to mobilize an army to fight against the Roman state. But Caesar pointed out that Senate denial of the right to trial would violate the law of Gaius Gracchus dating from 123. He warned that any magistrate who put Roman citizens to death without trial should be brought before the popular court and outlawed. As an alternative, he recommended that the conspirators be exiled for life in Italian towns outside of Rome.

The public trial by jury that Caesar wanted would have given Catiline's colleagues an opportunity to explain before the people why the debt and land problems were forcing all classes, from patricians to small landholders, to resort to extra-legal means to overcome the Senate

---

garchic majority had removed him from the Senate in one of its purges.

[35] Appian gives the details. Cethegus had sided first with Marius and then with Sulla in the 80s before joining Catiline in 64. See Sallust, *Catiline* 17-18

blockage of relief. "Not only the conspirators, but the entire people approved Catiline's designs," reported Sallust.[36]

Cicero acknowledged that Catiline's agitation threatened Rome precisely because so many Romans, Italians and even trans-Alpine groups supported his program. "If you think you have before you only a few guilty men, you are mistaken," he claimed. "The evil is more widespread than you think. It has spread not only throughout Italy, but it has crossed the Alps and has crept into the provinces. It cannot be crushed by temporizing with it. Whatever remedy you decide on must be applied without delay."[37]

Other senators seemed to be leaning toward Caesar's proposal of exile, which the incoming consul, D. Junius Silanus, initially backed. But Cato supported Cicero's claim that any delay would put the Republic in danger of imminent attack by Catiline's army, and endorsed Cicero's demand to kill the accused without trial.[38] The Senate voted that they be killed immediately.

The knights who had congregated outside of the Senate to provide a bodyguard for Cicero drew their swords to threaten Caesar, who left the Senate under guard, and is said by Sallust to have stayed away for some time. Cicero then ordered the prisoners to be strangled in the Tullianum prison's dungeon on December 5, 63, just two days after being accused of treason.[39] The Senate celebrated by bestowing honors on Cicero. "On the motion of Quintus Catulus, seconded by Cato, he was given the great title of *pater patriae*, father of the country, the first to whom this honor had been given, although it was later appropriated by the Caesars."[40]

Meanwhile, Catiline had mobilized support in Etruria, which had been especially victimized by Sulla's land confiscations as a result of its attempt to revolt against Rome. He had an army of nearly ten thousand men recruited from throughout Italy, mainly from indebted landholders, families hoping to recover properties expropriated by Sulla, and

---

[36] Sallust, *Catiline* 39, quoted in Hutchinson 1967:79.

[37] Cicero, *Fourth Catiline* 3, quoted in Hutchinson 1967:145, who also (p. 16) cites Cicero's *De Officiis* 2.12 and 24. "'Never,' said Cicero himself, 'was debt greater.'"

[38] Cited by Sallust, this is Cato's only speech that survives. It marked his emergence as the Senate's main reactionary spokesman. Taylor 1968:125 notes that Cato, the great-grandson of Cato the Censor, was grandson on his mother's side of M. Livius Drusus, the tribune who fought against Gaius Gracchus by proposing rival demagogic laws.

[39] Sallust, *Catiline* 55.

[40] Hutchinson 1967:158-159.

from veterans who had not received the pensions and land they had been promised. But most of this army deserted when they learned that Catiline's Roman leaders had been caught and killed, and feared that the planned rebellion had missed its opportunity for success.[41]

Antonius demonstrated his loyalty to the Senate Optimates by leading an army accompanying that of the praetor Q. Metellus Celer to fight Catiline. Catiline retreated north to Cisalpine Gaul in modern Tuscany, but defections left his army with only three thousand men. When confronted by Celer's forces and those of Antonius in January 62, Catiline chose to fight his former sympathizer, perhaps hoping that Antonius might switch sides or at least let his troops escape.

Antonius indeed chose not to lead the battle, but assigned command to his Master of the Horse, Marcus Petreius, a former military tribune and soldier with thirty years' experience. He was an Optimate extremist, which is why the Senate had designated him to serve under Antonius to make sure that he would not defect to Catiline. Cassius Dio wrote that Petreius killed Catiline's entire army, including Manlius, at Pistoria.[42] Catiline is said to have rushed to the forefront of the attack, realizing that he would be killed but seeking at least to die bravely. His severed head was sent back to Rome.

The aftermath

Following the defeat of Catiline's rebellion, the plebs' tribune P. Clodius Pulcher passed a law prohibiting extrajudicial killings of Roman citizens, and Cicero was tried and exiled in 58 for killing Catiline's five supporters without a judicial trial – the crime that Caesar had warned him not to commit. Romans decorated Catiline's tomb with flowers.[43]

Petreius allied himself with Cato when Caesar became consul in 59, and went on to fight losing battles against Caesar in Spain in 49, and then in Africa supporting Pompey against Caesar. He finally killed himself, along with Pompey's ally King Juba of Numidia, to avoid being captured by Caesar's army at Thapsus (in modern Tunisia) in 46.

Cato sought to hold Utica (between Carthage and Hippo), and Plutarch describes him as reading Socrates' death scene as Caesar approached

---

[41] Sallust, *Catiline* 57.

[42] Mommsen 1958:287-288, Frank 1933:309 and Sampson 2013:230-232. Estimates vary as to the number of Catiline's army who were killed. Yavetz 1963:495 cites a range of estimates from 3,000 to 10,000.

[43] Cicero, *Pro Flaccus* 95.

from Thapsus and committing suicide by stabbing himself and painfully bleeding to death, finally having to tear out his own entrails.

Antonius was rewarded by receiving the governorship of Macedonia that Cicero had promised. His rule was so abusive that the local population rebelled after he tried to invade neighboring Moesia and was driven back without being able to seize any loot. He was removed in 60 and prosecuted by Caesar and Crassus in 59, fined and banished to the Ionian Greek island of Cephalonia. Yet Caesar evidently thought that Antonius might be reclaimed as a supporter and recalled him in 47, even backing his candidacy for censor (an election that Antonius lost).

As for the Allobroges, their role in acting as spies tricking Catiline's deputies did not win more lenient treatment from the Senate. They revolted two years later, but by that time Catiline's rebellion had failed and they had lost their chance to join the fight against Rome's oligarchy.

Two decades after Catiline's rebellion, the memory of how Cicero had treated Lentulus led the latter's stepson, Mark Antony, to demand Cicero's execution as a condition for joining Octavian and Lepidus in the Second Triumvirate, 43-33. Cicero was captured at his villa and decapitated. His hands, with which he had written the *Philippics* attacking Antony, were cut off and nailed along with his head in the Forum, recalling the practice of Marius and Sulla.

As a result of debt dynamics, the Roman Republic was polarizing much like the archaic Greek autocracies that ended up being toppled by "tyrants" in Sparta, Corinth, Megara, Athens and other Greek cities in the 7th and 6th centuries BC. In the face of the Senate Optimates blocking anything more than palliative measures (such as the grain dole), Catiline's revolt was headed by disaffected patricians who lacked a constitutional path to enact debt cancellation and land redistribution. Henceforth the beneficiaries of debt relief were limited to the wealthiest debtors. Caesar was followed by emperors who passed acts to alleviate the debts of estate owners who owed money to the treasury or to private creditors to buy land, but there was little relief for less affluent smallholders.

18

From Cato and Cicero to Pompey and Caesar, 65-49 BC

Catiline's following of indebted aristocrats and the poor was no match for the Senate Optimates. Cato's strategy was to filibuster and ultimately veto any proposal for reform, and to block any potentially popular politician-general from emerging.[1] His policy was so extreme that it led ultimately to just what he feared most: It became clear that the only way to achieve reform was to bypass the Senate by appealing to the popular assembly and its tribunes, and above all to gain command of an official army. The strident opposition of Cato and Cicero to popular reforms left no hope for achieving debt and land reform by legislative means. Only a domestic military revolt overpowering Senate troops could resolve the debt and land crisis.[2]

Caesar and Pompey seemed the most likely candidates to follow this path, given their popularity as consuls and generals, and their own personal wealth and financial backing. Oligarchic concern was directed against any politician who gained popular acclaim, fearing that political opportunism could lead them to acquire the power to bypass the Senate and support populist policies. Some senators hoped that Pompey might defend their interests against Caesar, who had faced mistrust from the oligarchic Senate since the beginning of his career, being descended from a family close to Marius, and rumored to have been close to most populist upstarts, including Catiline.

---

[1] Taylor 1968:130-131 and 119 summarizes the problem: "Cato stood out firmly and succeeded in using up so much time talking that for months not only the matter of the publicans but all senatorial business, including the affairs of Pompey, were at a standstill." Bibulus (married to Cato's daughter Porcia) helped Cato's "leadership of the Optimates, the coalition dominated by old Sullans, all of them members of the plebeian nobility."

[2] Yavetz 1963:498, citing the reform attempts by the tribune L. Appuleius Saturninus (stoned to death in 100 BC), M. Livius Drusus (assassinated in 91), the tribune P. Sulpicius Rufus (hunted down in 88 and his severed head sent to Sulla), and Quintus Sertorius (outlawed by Sulla and stabbed to death in 73).

But Pompey also was feared, precisely because of his popularity. Plutarch reports that in 48 BC, when leading the army sent to unseat Caesar, Pompey heard that the cavalry was discussing how, "as soon as they had routed Caesar, they must put down himself also. And some say this was also the reason why Pompey called upon Cato for no service of any importance, but even when marching against Caesar left him at the coast in charge of the baggage, fearing that if Caesar should be taken off, he himself also might be forced by Cato to lay down his command at once."[3]

What the Optimate leadership longed for, summarizes Lily Ross Taylor, was "the pre-Gracchan (or the Sullan) constitution, when the authority of the Senate had been predominant in the conduct of public affairs."[4] But given the unpopularity of Optimates among debtors and smallholders, all the Senate could do was to block anyone who looked popular enough to become consul and "seek kingship" (*regnum*) by being assigned command of an army after his year in office. That was the trajectory of Caesar after Cato, Brutus and other Optimates were unable to block the Senate from giving him a military command in Gaul. His rise led to the epoch of the emperors overpowering the Senate and leaving membership of it little more than a ceremonial status for the wealthy.

Mommsen set the stage for the historiography of Caesarism with his *History of Rome*, written in 1854 in the wake of Europe's 1848 revolutions. He likened the ability of Cato and his Optimate allies in the Senate to block debt and land reform to his own epoch's landed aristocracy using its control of the upper house of parliament (such as Britain's House of Lords) to block the more democratic Commons, the lower house. Rome's popular assembly had too marginal a role to rival Senate dominance, and in any case, advocates of debt cancellation and land redistribution were almost routinely assassinated or executed under the Senate's emergency death penalty (*senatus consultum ultimum*) by which Cicero killed Catiline's leaders.

Cicero denounced Caesar's rising popularity with the usual oligarchic epithet used against reformers: seeking kingship, meaning power over the oligarchy.[5] He reflected the Optimate spirit when, looking back

---

[3] Plutarch, *Pompey* 67, referring to the Battle of Pharsales in August 48, in which Caesar defeated Pompey's troops that were preparing to invade Italy from Macedonia across the Adriatic, unseat Caesar and restore Senate power.

[4] Taylor 1968:153.

[5] Cicero, *Philippics* 5.49. Mommsen 1958:292 thought that Caesar and Crassus must have had some knowledge of Catiline's conspiracy, having supported his candidacy for the consulship in 65 and allowed Catiline to be acquitted in 64. The

shortly after Caesar was killed in 44 BC, he wrote to a friend that: "I could wish that you had invited me to the banquet of the Ides of March: there would have been nothing left over!"[6]

Cicero bragged that as consul in 63 he had rescued the *faeneratores*, the usurers, by warning that cancelling debts would destroy the Republic's essence, the oligarchy's creditor power. Noting that "indebtedness was never greater" than at the outset of his consulship, he wrote that "debts were never liquidated more easily or more fully" than under his philosophy that "should a serious debt be incurred, we are not to allow the rich to lose their property," meaning their financial claims on the land (and labor) of their debtors.[7] Debts would be "extinguished" not by cancelling them but by legally enforcing payment by foreclosures and forced sales to cut off the debtor's "hope of defrauding the creditor" by leaving "no indebtedness of a nature to endanger the public safety." Cicero's ideal was for the economy to be debt-free, but at the cost of widespread forfeiture of land ownership at the expense of the indebted. That is indeed how the Roman Empire ended up.

Focusing on debts that were taken on to buy land, mainly by buyers sufficiently well-to-do to obtain credit based on their own assets and the newly-bought land as collateral, Cicero continued, asking rhetorically: "What is the meaning of an abolition of debts, except that you buy a farm with my money; that you have the farm, and I have not my money." These debts were not those of smallholders running into debt simply to survive. Blaming speculative borrowers, Cicero's *De Officiis* insisted simply that all debts should be paid:

> There is nothing that upholds a government more powerfully than its credit [*fides*, "good faith"]; and it can have no credit, unless the payment of debts is enforced by law. Never were measures for the repudiation of debts more strenuously agitated than in my consulship. Men of every sort and rank attempted with arms and armies to force the project

---

Senate rejected the accusations against them of complicity spread by Cicero and his friend Atticus. Cicero's informer Quintus Curius told the Senate that Catiline had said that Caesar knew of the plans for revolt (Hutchinson 1967:140). After Caesar demanded that Cicero provide further evidence and Cicero failed to do so, the Senate deprived Curius of all the rewards he had hoped to gain (one-quarter of the property of anyone convicted on their information).

[6] Cicero, *Letters to his friends* 12.4, to C. Cassius Longinus. See Brunt 1971a:145. The Ides of March was the date of Caesar's assassination in 44 BC.

[7] Cicero, *De Officiis* (On Duties) 2.84, dated 44 BC but published after Cicero was hunted down and killed the next year.

through. But I opposed them with such energy that this plague was wholly eradicated from the body politic.

Caesar's formative early rise

Aristotle explained how democracy emerged out of aristocratic society: A family head would take the people into his camp, as Cleisthenes did in Athens in 508 and as Caesar would attempt to do in Rome. The political antagonisms that ultimately brought down the Roman Republic were mainly among the wealthiest families, even within the Senate. But Caesar recognized that in addition to wealth and popular support, military force was required to enact basic reforms, and it had to be an official state army, not an informal force such as Catiline had recruited.

The way to gain command of such an army was to be elected consul, and that required extravagant amounts money, as Chapter 17 has discussed. "The demands of politics, as they were then being played," summarizes Finley, "and of conspicuous consumption, an element in politics, involved the nobility, as well as others, in moneylending on a stupendous scale [to engage in] electoral bribery, an expensive life-style, extravagant public games and other forms of political careers." Many Romans borrowed heavily to gain public office, hoping to repay out of the looting rights awarded upon retiring to lucrative commands or governorships in Asia or Macedonia – and for Caesar, Spain and then Gaul. "Hence extortion in the provinces often became a personal necessity, and all the time there was much tension, at this high level of Roman society, about money matters. Only a few, such as Pompey and Crassus, were so rich as to be fairly immune from anxiety."[8]

As Mommsen noted: "The princely wealth of that period was surpassed only by its still more princely liabilities. Around 62 BC Caesar owed 25,000,000 sesterces [according to Appian], after deducting his assets. Marcus Antonius owed 6,000,000 sesterces at the age of twenty-four, and 40,000,000 fourteen years afterwards." G. Scribonius Curio, elected tribune of the plebs in 51, "owed 60,000,000, Milo 70,000,000." Caesar paid off Curio's debts when the latter (formerly his adversary) joined his ranks.[9]

Caesar's rise began in 65 when he was elected aedile, an office whose task included oversight of the public games. Borrowing to

---

[8] Finley 1973:53.

[9] Mommsen 1958:546. See Cicero, *Letters to his friends* 8.7. The monthly interest rate doubled from 4 to 8 percent during these tumultuous years.

stage lavish entertainment, Caesar in 63 won sufficient popularity to be elected *pontifex maximus*, high priest and guardian of Rome's state religion, a lifetime post that he held until 44. In the election he defeated two prominent senators by a firm margin. Accusations of bribery against him led nowhere.[10]

Also in 63, Cicero was elected consul, but by December he was declared to have committed the extrajudicial murders of Catiline's followers. The tide was turning against the Optimates, enabling Caesar to be elected praetor in 62. Upon completing his term in office, he was appointed to govern Lusitania in southern Spain.

He was still in considerable debt and needed to satisfy his creditors, who were demanding payment before he could leave Rome to reap enough monetary reward to pay them. By this time, Plutarch noted, "the thoughtful and conservative part of the city attached itself to Pompey, the violent and volatile part supported the hopes of Caesar, while Crassus took a middle ground and drew from both." Caesar made a deal with Crassus to support him against Pompey in return for Crassus standing surety for 830 talents.[11] This placated his creditors, enabling him to leave Rome.

In Spain, Caesar marched west to the Atlantic Ocean, defeating the Callaici and Lusitanian tribes. He won local support by settling the conflict between debtors and creditors, ruling that a creditor should take only two thirds of the debtor's income each year until the debt was paid off. That left the remaining third for the debtor (usually a small landholder) to get by.[12] This protected land tenure from polarizing as a result of debt foreclosures.

Having appropriated enough wealth in Spain to settle his debts, Caesar secured the loyalty of his soldiers by enriching them as well. They gratefully acclaimed him *imperator*, an honorary title enabling him to ask the Senate to award him a public triumph. Nearing the end of his service, in 60, he planned to return to Rome to start his campaign for consul with his triumphal procession. But Cato had written a Senate law a few years earlier obliging candidates for office to register in person, and a long-standing Roman rule forbade generals from entering the city so as to avoid the prospect of a military coup.[13] If Caesar were to cele-

---

[10] Plutarch, *Caesar* 5.4 and 7.

[11] Plutarch, *Crassus* 7.6-8 and *Caesar* 11.1.

[12] Plutarch, *Caesar* 12.

[13] Taylor 1968:225.

brate a triumph, he would have to remain a soldier and stay outside of Rome until after the ceremony; to stand for election, he would need to lay down his command and enter Rome as a private citizen. He could not do both in the time available.

Caesar tried to solve the problem by asking the Senate for permission to register for the consular election *in absentia* before celebrating his triumph. Cato blocked his request, mounting one of his all-day filibusters on the last day that a candidate's announcement could be made. That obliged Caesar to relinquish his triumph in order to run for the consulship.[14]

Caesar ran alongside Lucius Lucceius, who agreed to put up the money to buy votes for their joint run against the third candidate, Cato's son-in-law M. Calpurnius Bibulus, who had been elected praetor alongside Caesar two years earlier. When Caesar's arrangement with Lucceius became known, "the aristocracy authorized Bibulus to promise the same amount, being seized with fear that Caesar would stick at nothing when he became chief magistrate, if he had a colleague who was heart and soul with him. Many of them contributed to the fund, and even Cato did not deny that bribery under such circumstances was for the good of the commonwealth."[15] Caesar was elected, but so was the obstructive Bibulus as his co-consul.

Cato then devised another legislative trick. Instead of assigning the new consuls command of the richest available provinces when they left office, the Senate selected the least important domain, Italy's woods and pasture lands. No army was assigned to them, and they offered none of the usual opportunities for personal remuneration.

Caesar renews his compact with Pompey and Crassus

Caesar countered by arranging peace between Crassus and Pompey, and the three agreed "that no step should be taken in public affairs which did not suit any one of the three."[16] This agreement basically continued the earlier First Triumvirate between the three men. Crassus had become the richest man in Rome, and held the votes of its monied classes. But he had fought with Pompey since their co-consulship in 70/69. Pompey held the soldiers' vote, and his military successes made him the most popular Roman after his victory ending the Third Mithri-

---

[14] Plutarch, *Caesar* 13 and *Cato* 31, and Suetonius, *Julius Caesar* 18.2.

[15] Suetonius, *Julius Caesar* 19. See also Plutarch, *Cato* 31.3. Cato himself was said to have spent money buying votes for Bibulus.

[16] Suetonius, *Julius Caesar* 19.2. See also Plutarch, *Caesar* 13-14.

datic War in 63. Like Caesar, he was confronted by Cato and the Optimates fearing his (or anyone's) popularity.

Together, the three realized that "with their enemies in control of the
Senate, they could achieve their ends only through the people. Thus, in
method if not in program they were ready to be *populares*, and Cicero
calls them that in his letters of 59."[17] Cato and his Optimates had
created precisely the alliance that they had sought to prevent.

Pompey had followed his victory over Mithridates by paying his
soldiers a reported 1500 Attic drachmas each, totaling 16,000 talents
(384,000,000 sesterces). He also had marched across Asia Minor in 63,
negotiating settlements and tribute to Rome by local cities, kings and
princes. Bringing 75,100,000 drachmas of silver coin and 700 ships to
Brundisium, he was cheered on his way to Rome by the inhabitants
of the cities he passed, joined by so many well-wishers that Plutarch
remarked that he arrived with such a large crowd that he would not
have needed an army for a Roman revolution.[18] Pompey was 45 years
old when he celebrated his triumph in Rome (his third).[19]

The *lex Gabinia* had given Pompey money and resources in 68/7
to fight the pirates, and the *lex Manilia* the following year gave him
command of the forces against Mithridates, but his popularity now led
the Senate's Optimates to fear that he might use it to establish a dictatorship like that of Sulla or "seek kingship." Crassus took his family and
gold safely out of the city and prepared to live in the East.[20] Yet Pompey's
aim was simply for the Senate to award land to his veterans and ratify
the settlements he had made in the East. Having every expectation that
the Senate would agree, he disbanded his army upon arriving in Italy.

---

[17] Taylor 1968:132.

[18] Plutarch, *Pompey* 42-43.

[19] The long two-day procession started with "two-horse carriages and litters laden
with gold or with other ornaments of various kinds, also the couch of Darius, the
son of Hystaspes, the throne and scepter Mithridates Eupator himself, and his
image, four meters high, made of solid gold, and 75,100,000 drachmas of silver
coin. The number of wagons carrying arms was infinite, and the number of the
beaks of ships. After these came the multitude of captives and pirates, none of
them bound, but all arrayed in their native costumes" (Appian, *Mithridatic Wars*
116). Plutarch, *Pompey* 45 notes that the captives led in the triumph included the
leaders of the pirates, the son of Tigranes the Great with his wife and daughter, a
sister and five children of Mithridates, Aristobulus II, the king of the Jews, and a
long parade of lesser hostages.

[20] Mommsen 1958:296.

Seeing Pompey as a potential threat to Senate supremacy, the consul Metellus Celer opposed a bill to allot farmland to Pompey's veterans and to some of Rome's urban poor reliant on the public grain dole. The other consul in 60, Lucius Afranius, yielded to Cato's obstructionism. This was despite Pompey having sponsored the campaigns of both consuls. Pompey made a final attempt to defuse Senate opposition by proposing to marry one of Cato's nieces and marry off his son to another niece, but Cato rejected it.

That led Pompey to seal an alliance against the Senate in 59 by marrying Caesar's only daughter, the 23-year old Julia.[21] As incoming consul, Caesar sponsored an agrarian law to settle some of Pompey's veterans as well as urban plebs on public land in Italy, largely around Capua. Additional land was to be bought from private owners, using funds from Pompey's campaign in Asia. To administer the distribution of this land, Caesar created a 20-member commission, including Crassus and Pompey but excluding himself so as to avoid any hint of corruption.

Such laws traditionally were put forward by a tribune, not a consul, but Caesar claimed that he was trying to ensure Senate support in advance. "Cato led the opposition, insisting in true Optimate style that there must be no change in the *status quo*."[22] He started one of his famous all-day speeches, but Caesar ordered him led away. Many senators followed Cato out, preventing a vote from being taken.

Caesar then adopted the tactic of Tiberius Gracchus and bypassed the Senate to put the measure before the Centuriate Assembly, composed largely of army veterans.[23] When his opponents threatened violence to block the popular vote, Pompey threatened to use his own force. When the time came for the Senate to ratify the law, Caesar and Pompey filled the Forum with their soldiers, and a large crowd gathered. Bibulus tried to suspend the voting, claiming to see bad omens that were supposed to suspend public business, making the law illegal – a delaying tactic that Mommsen called "political astrology."[24]

Caesar overruled Bibulus in his higher authority as *pontifex maximus*, leading the obstructionist to declare the rest of the year a sacred period

---

[21] Watts 2018:194-195. Metellus was the brother of Pompey's former wife Mucia, whom Pompey had married in 79 but just divorced in order to contract a new political marriage.

[22] Watts 2018:202, citing Cassius Dio, *Roman History* 38.2.2.

[23] Watts 2018:203, citing Cassius Dio, *Roman History* 38.2.2.

[24] Mommsen 1958:315-316.

in which no assemblies could be held or votes taken. But the crowd
drove Bibulus away and broke his insignia of consulship, the ceremonial
fasces carried by his lictors, and beat the tribunes allied with him. Cato
likewise was pushed away when he tried to force his way to the platform
to block the vote. He and Bibulus fled, and Caesar's bill was passed,
including "a clause that all senators were to take oath to adhere to it."[25]

Most senators took the oath, but the next day Bibulus asked the
Senate to annul the law, claiming that it was passed under the threat
of violence. Finding no support, he refused to swear an oath to uphold
the new law, as did Cato and Metellus Celer. But after holding out for
a while, they finally signed. Bibulus went home and "from that time
until the end of his term he did not leave his house, but merely issued
proclamations announcing adverse omens." Before every Senate vote he
sent a note to Caesar claiming that the day was sacred and that Caesar
was committing a sacrilege by taking action on it, making the entire
year's legal proceedings invalid. Cato and his closest supporters stopped
attending the Senate, and their allied Optimate tribunes likewise refused
to take part in public business for the rest of the year.[26] They were
simply ignored, leaving Caesar in full consular control.

The Triumvirate had overcome Senate opposition by governing via
the popular assembly and people as a whole. Among the next bills that
Caesar submitted were a dole for the poor and a second land law to distribute 6-iugera grants of fertile Campanian land to war veterans and
poor families with three or more children. However, the allotments were
"so small that there was no margin even with tax exemption, indeed a
near certainty of eventual failure."[27] Revenue to make up for the lost
budgetary rents on this Campania land came from the Asian tribute that
Pompey had negotiated.

---

[25] Taylor 1968:133, noting that: "Such a clause had been inserted in the land bill of
Saturninus in 100 BC, and Metellus Numidicus had been exiled because he would
not take the oath."

[26] Suetonius, *Julius Caesar* 20 and Watts 2018:204-205. See also Taylor 1968:134. To
show the people at large how obstructive the Senate was acting, Suetonius adds,
Caesar initiated the practice of compiling and publishing its daily acts and proceedings.

[27] Finley 1973:80-81 and Cassius Dio, *Roman History* 38.7. Plutarch, *Cato* 33 describes Caesar as proposing to divide "almost the whole of Campania among the
poor and needy. No one spoke against the law except Cato, and Caesar ordered
him to be dragged from the rostra to prison." Cato walked away, but Caesar was
able to see how unpopular his proposal was with the other senators.

Bailing out the publicans from their Asia contracts

Despite denouncing Catiline's program of cancelling debts for Romans of all classes, Cicero overcame his personal feelings and insisted that the debts of the wealthy *equites* be written down. They had lost their hoped-for gains on their Asia tax-farming contracts since Mithridates had disrupted the region's tribute payments by defeating Lucullus's army in 67. Each year since 61, the *equites* had petitioned the Senate to remit a third of what they owed the treasury, citing hardship for many debtors who had speculated on shares in their companies.[28] The Senate regularly shelved the question, with Cato heading the opposition to their request, on the principle that "a contract is a contract," leading Cicero to complain that Cato's principles were too ideological to be pragmatic.[29] As Ste. Croix elaborates the financial dynamics at work by 60 BC:

> the crash had two stages: first, those who had invested money in Asia could not repay their debts and were ruined; second, their creditors, unable to collect, could not repay their own debts, and so the effects of the crisis rapidly spread. Land prices probably began to fall again. When the creditors foreclosed, they put more land on the market just when the supply of money was short. This glut on the market, together with the shortage of money, caused land prices to drop swiftly. As the value of most collateral fell, more creditors probably foreclosed, and the collapse quickened. *Fides* had to give way, undermined by the Social War and the narrow supply of money.[30]

Cicero warned that a widespread financial crisis would occur if the *equites* and their companies lost their appeal:

> Coinciding with the loss by many people of large fortunes in Asia, we know that there was a collapse of credit at Rome owing to suspension of payment. It is indeed impossible for many individuals in a single state to lose their property and fortunes without involving still greater numbers in their own ruin. ... this system of credit and finance which operates at Rome, in the Forum, is bound up in and depends on capital invested in Asia. The loss of the one inevitably undermines the other and causes its collapse.[31]

---

[28] Frank 1933:310 and 345.

[29] Watts 2018:198

[30] Ste. Croix 1989:215.

[31] Cicero, *Lex Manilian* 19, cited by Frank 1933:305. See also Lewis and Reinhold 1951:344 [1990:373].

In other words, the *equites* were what today would be called Too Big to Fail. As matters turned out, Cato's early opposition to the *equites* had helped Caesar attract their support for his consulship for 59, by promising to support what the Senate was rejecting. His ally Crassus also backed a refunding of the money the *equite* companies had paid to the treasury, having "likely loaned some of the money these businessmen had paid up front" to secure the contract or invest in the companies. Caesar delivered on the Triumvirate's promise to endorse the *equites'* request to revise the Asia contracts. His law wrote down by one-third what they were obliged to pay the treasury. It was passed in April 59, a few weeks after his land law.[32] The *equites'* request was the most successful demand for debt relief, but it was not extended to the lower ranks of Rome's economic pyramid. "For this unexpected favor, which was far beyond their deserts, the knights extolled Caesar to the skies. Thus a more powerful body of defenders than that of the plebeians was added to Caesar's support through one political act."[33]

Caesar's popularity from these acts enabled his supporter, the tribune Vatianus, to sponsor a law giving him a five-year command of the provinces of Cisalpine Gaul (northern Italy) and the Illyrian peninsula extending from Romania and Bulgaria down through Macedonia to Greece, instead of the forests and pastures that Cato's followers had selected for him. The five-year command was longer than any previous command that had been assigned. To cap matters, when the governorship of Transalpine Gaul (southern France) became vacant, the Senate accepted Pompey's motion to add it to Caesar's command, providing him with four legions.[34]

These postings were renewed for another five years in 54, as the Senate apparently was glad to keep Caesar out of Rome. This period of his commands, 59-50, was the decade in which he gained the wealth and the loyal army that enabled him to seize power in 49. He enriched himself in the same way that Rome's political elite were doing whenever they were granted military or governing power. Indeed, Tenney Frank wrote: "Julius Caesar provided the ugliest example in Roman history of provincial looting for personal gain. He went to Spain heavily in debt in 61 (Appian, *Civil War* 2.8 says he owed 25,000,000 sesterces) and created

---

[32] Watts 2018:197, citing Cicero, *Letters to Atticus* 1.17.8-9.

[33] Magie 1950:253, citing Appian, *Civil War*.

[34] Watts 2018:206. See also Taylor 1968:135-137, based on Plutarch, *Caesar* 14, *Crassus* 14, *Cato the Younger* 32-33, *Pompey* 48; Cassius Dio, *Roman History* 38 and Suetonius, *Julius Caesar* 23.

wars that cleared him of debt. More wealth, immense, was taken from Gaul in 59-50, and he is said to have slain 400,000 and captured more. This is a minimum figure. He turned nothing over to the treasury, yet captured so much gold that its price fell 1/6."[35]

Such Roman rapaciousness is illustrated in greatest detail by Cicero's experience in 50 BC in Cilicia.

Rome's provinces become "debt farms" for usury

Cicero's backing of *faeneratores* continued after his consulship ended and he became governor of Cilicia, on the southern coast of Asia Minor and including the island of Cyprus. In he found himself asked to act on behalf of Brutus to enforce a loan made at 48 percent annual interest, four times the legal 12 percent rate.[36]

The transaction had its roots in 58, when Brutus had accompanied Cato to Cyprus and met its officials.[37] Five years later, in 53, his father-in-law, Appius Claudius Pulcher, was named proconsul for Cilicia after his year as consul in 54. Brutus was elected quaestor for 53, and chose to accompany Appius to Cilicia instead of joining Caesar in Gaul. He had a financial motive for this choice. Apparently in Rome he had followed up his earlier contacts and made a loan to officials of the Cypriot town of Salamis in 56. When Cicero became proconsul of Cilicia in 51, he came under the usual pressure on Roman officials to help collect debts incurred by provincials, and even to send in troops to enforce payment.

Brutus's demand for 48 percent annual interest was by no means unheard of, but it was illegal to make such loans to provincial envoys in Rome. Brutus obtained Senate dispensation to circumvent this restriction, and sent to Cyprus two envoys, Marcus Scaptius and P. Martinius, to serve on his father-in-law's staff to collect the money falling due. Appius appointed Scaptius prefect in charge of the Roman cavalry, to march on Salamis and collect the debt. When the Salmatian leaders took

---

[35] Frank 1933:325.

[36] Migeotte 1984:254-258 and 397 sees Brutus's loan as typifying the ability of creditors to bring pressure on Roman governors and other officials to intervene on their behalf. His collection of all then-known Greek documentation of civic debts includes those owed by Sardis (No. 99), Herakleon on Crete and Bargylia on the southwest coast of Anatolia (No. 105) as well as Bithynia on a debt of Nicea (No. 111). Brutus also solicited aid to collect a debt from Dyrrhachium on the Adriatic coast near modern Albania (No. 36).

[37] Brutus's mother Servilla was half-sister of Cato, and also was said to have been the mistress of Julius Caesar.

refuge in their senate house, Scaptius mounted a siege. After five officials had starved to death, the others were released, according to Cicero.

He wrote to his wealthy equestrian friend Atticus that when Brutus's
envoys asked him as the new proconsul to help collect the money still
owed by Salamis, he summoned the city's magistrates to Tarsus and discovered the exorbitant interest rate being demanded.[38] Brutus's agents
refused to lighten their demands for full payment at the 48 percent
rate, and insisted on 200 talents being paid. The Salmatian officials
replied that by their calculations only 106 talents was owed. When
Cicero sought to resolve matters in accordance with Rome's legal rate of
interest, Scaptius produced the Senate decree authorizing Brutus's loan,
showing Brutus himself to be the creditor.

Scaptius then asked Cicero to re-appoint him to the military position
that he had held under Appius Claudius to act as Brutus's local enforcer.
Cicero ordered the cavalry off the island and rolled back the interest
charge to 12 percent (he had issued an edict setting this rate), but then
dodged the issue by leaving the debt to his successor to handle.[39] His
final letter to Atticus concludes by worrying that public credit might not
recover from so scandalous a loan and the collection behavior demanded
of Roman officials on behalf of the usurers. "Lucius Lucceius, son
of Marcus, writes me a grumbling letter asserting that thanks to the
Senate, there is the utmost danger of these decrees leading to a general
repudiation." But such behavior by and for creditors had become built
into the imperial system. James Tan describes how this episode illustrates the

> standard practice for governors to use their administrative resources
> to further the private business interests of their friends. Assisted by the
> governor or his troops, debt collection could effect not just regular repay-
> ments but often also the seizure of mortgaged land ... As a private lender,
> the creditor had every right and every reason to demand land or some

---

[38] Cicero relates the story in his *Letters to Atticus* 5.21 and 6.1-6.3, written in 50 BC.
Mommsen 1899 provides a detailed reconstruction of this episode. See also Hill
2010:229-230. Appius Claudius Pulcher was the elder brother of Clodius, who was
murdered by Milo in 52 (as Chapter 19 will describe). He had served in Asia under
Lucullus (who had married his sister Claudia) during the Third Mithridatic War
ca. 72-71.

[39] Cicero concluded his letter to Atticus by saying that if Brutus did not approve,
"there is no reason why I should be friendly with him," noting that Brutus's uncle
Cato certainly would approve, being a long-time opponent of moneylenders and of
Caesar's and Crassus's bailout of the publican tax collectors on their Asia contracts.

other property as security. ... The creditor in this instance becomes the equivalent of a tax farmer on a limitless contract ... seiz[ing] their capital ... and enjoying its yield forever.[40]

Brutus's arrangement was by no means novel. A decade earlier Pompey had enriched himself during his conquest of Syria between 65 and 63 when he was empowered to designate which king would take the throne in Cappadocia. He followed what had become normal Roman practice in asking who would pay him more. The winner turned out to be Ariobarzanes II (the son of Mithridates' foe Ariobarzanes I), who ruled from 63 to 51.

> Cicero found a later heir, Ariobarzanes III [51-42], still repaying the debt over a decade later: the 33 talents (792,000 sesterces) handed over *per month* did not even cover the interest Pompey was charging. With ceremonial magnanimity, he confirmed the suppliant Tigranes to the throne of Armenia for a fee of 6,000 talents (144 million sesterces), and the eventual sum apparently outstripped even this. ... These payments were not paid to the Roman treasury, but into the private purses of the imperators in question.[41]

Tan characterizes the strategy of Pompey and Brutus to be one of "creating 'debt farms' out of military campaigns," using local Roman administration and armed forces to enforce collection of the money owed by Rome's provinces, forcing provincials to borrow money after their temples and reserves had been sacked. "Diplomacy proved itself a cash cow straddling the lines of legality."[42] That is why Romans were hated throughout their provinces.

---

[40] Tan 2017:77-78. As for Cicero, Beard 2015:328 notes that he "left Cilicia in 50 BCE with more than 2 million sesterces in local currency." We do not know how he got it, perhaps from selling captives as slaves after a minor military victory. On his way back to Italy, he deposited it with a company of *publicani* in Ephesus. But as civil war broke out, he lent it in 48 to Pompey, and there is no indication that he ever got it back.

[41] Tan 2017:9, citing Cicero, *Letters to Atticus* 6.1.3 and 6.3.5, Appian, *Mithridatic Wars* 104, and Plutarch, *Pompey* 33.4.

[42] Tan 2017:76 and 79. He points out (p. 77, fn35): "There is little epigraphic evidence for predatory creditors, but then it is unsurprising that inscriptions were not erected to those who were preying upon local finances." The problem was ongoing. Jones 1964:124, citing Cassius Dio, *Roman History* 62.2 and Tacitus, *Annals* 13.42, reports: "Seneca is said to have lent 10,000,000 *denarii* at exorbitant rates of interest to the Britons."

But plunder and booty were not enough. The property Romans most wanted was human slaves. Rome stole the freedom of provincials as well as their monetary reserves. The Gauls saw themselves as defending their realm against Rome in order to escape slavery. Caesar's *Gallic Wars* expresses the resentment felt by the Gauls in 52 BC through the leader Critognatus (in Caesar's wording):

> The Cimbri, after laying Gaul waste and inflicting great calamities, at length departed from our country and sought other lands; they left us our rights, laws, lands, and liberty. But what other motive or wish have the Romans than, induced by envy, to settle in the lands and states of those whom they have learned by fame to be noble and powerful in war, and impose on them perpetual slavery? For they never have carried on wars on any other terms.[43]

Roman exploitation of the provinces did not help Rome avoid its own debt crisis, however. Verboven dates this crisis from the summer of 54, "when huge sums [were] borrowed to buy the electorate for the consulship of 53." Interest rates doubled from 4 to 8 percent. Elections were suspended when Clodius was murdered in January 52. The Senate called in Pompey and his soldiers to prevent widespread revolt. By the summer of 51, "Atticus was unsuccessful in finding a loan for Cicero to repay a debt of 800,000 HS [sesterces] he owed to Caesar," having difficulty collecting from his own debtors. "Late in 51 or early in 50, the Senate decreed a maximum interest rate of 12%," that is, 1% a month, simple interest.[44] The tribunes passed a law confirming the senatorial interest decree.

But this act was insufficient to revive credit, and land prices declined as lending dried up in response to the instability. In the next decade Caesar would introduce moderate debt and land reforms seeking to address the credit crisis, but these benefited mainly well-to-do land buyers on credit. His reforms will be discussed in the next chapter.

A coda regarding Rome's provinces in Greece and Asia

Caesar returned to Rome in 49 and defeated the Senate army commanded by Pompey, who fled to Egypt. When Caesar visited Egypt

---

[43] Caesar, *Gallic Wars* 7.77. The war leader, Vercingetorix, led 80,000 troops at Alesia. Critognatus's words were spoken in a debate over whether to surrender or fight. Brunt cites Caesar's boast that his wars provided 1,000,000 slaves. This figure was not disputed, although it obviously means simply a great number.

[44] Verboven 2003:2, citing Cassius Dio, *Roman History* 61.37.1.

the next year, Pompey's severed head was brought to him as a trophy. Pompey was buried with the inscription: "How pitiful a tomb for one so rich in temples," an allusion to the wealth he had looted from the territories he had conquered.[45]

Joining up with Caesar in 48, Mark Antony ravaged Greek cities and temples, depleting their monetary reserves and decimating Greek culture.[46] Rome's destructive exploitation was thus social as well as financial. In Asia Minor in 47, however, Caesar "cut taxes by a third; moreover, by simply delegating to local cities the task of collecting and transporting tax payments, he avoided the costs of establishing a [Roman] replacement bureaucracy."[47]

Later, some additional help came from Augustus, who as Octavian cancelled the Asian province's tribute debts and restored revenue to the Temple of Artemis at Ephesus, as well as "objects that Antony had removed: the famous Ajax to Rhoeteium, Myron's Apollo to Ephesus, his Athena and his Heracles to Hera of Samos, though he kept the Zeus for Rome; he allowed, it is said, Cos a remission of 100 talents of its tribute in return for the Venus Anadyomene. ... He was no less ready to help meet the emergencies of fire and earthquake, and encouraged senators also to assist. On one occasion he paid the annual tribute of Asia out of the patrimonial funds."[48] Yet notwithstanding Caesars' tax cut for Asia and Augustus's later help, immense booty and tribute continued to flow into Rome from the provinces, helping empower Rome's oligarchy to destroy what was left of the Republic.

A long circle was being closed. Rome's army re-organization under Marius, based on hiring troops loyal to their generals (and the inducement of booty and land distribution), had led to Sulla's coup rolling back plebeian gains and concentrating oligarchic power in the Senate. Crassus (who was mainly after money) set the stage for Pompey (serving the conservative Senate, but feared), and finally Caesar's return in 49, hoping to arrange a moderate compromise. But domestic politics had broken down.

---

[45] Appian, *Civil War* 86.

[46] Broughton 1938:585 and 684.

[47] Tan 2015:218. See Broughton 1937:538, Appian, *Civil War* 5.4, and Cassius Dio, *Roman History* 42.6.

[48] Broughton 1938:587, 679 and 711.

19
Caesar's Moderate Debt and Land Legislation, 49-44 BC

Caesar arrived in Gaul in 58, and within three years extended Roman sway as far north as Britain. In Rome, Pompey and Crassus were elected to their third joint consulship for the year 54, defeating L. Domitius Ahenobarbus (married to Cato's sister) who campaigned to deprive Caesar of his command. The re-elected consuls increased Caesar's legions from four to ten (adding an eleventh in 53), renewed his command for five more years as already noted, and provided funds for his troops, along with enough money to pay appropriate bribes to senators and other supporters.[1]

Caesar is reported to have said: "Soldiers and money: If you lack one, you will soon lack the other."[2] As Chapter 18 describes, he is said to have killed 400,000 men, sold uncounted numbers of captives into slavery, and taken so much gold that when he returned to Rome in 49, its price fell by somewhere between one-sixth and one-quarter.[3] He was elected consul for the year 48, and re-elected for 46, 45 (as sole consul) and 44 (with Mark Antony).

Clodius removes Cicero and Cato from Rome

Soon after Caesar left Rome in 58, Cicero was punished for his extra-judicial killing of Catiline's followers. Cicero's nemesis was Publius Clodius Pulcher, the younger brother of Appius Claudius Pulcher. Cicero had attacked him in 62 after Clodius was caught in Caesar's home infiltrating an all-female ritual of the Bona Dea and accused of trying to seduce Caesar's wife Pompeia (leading Caesar to divorce her).

---

[1] Plutarch, *Julius Caesar* 21 describes the alliance as being forged in 56 when Crassus and Pompey met with Caesar at Lucca (on Italy's northern border with Gaul). Pompey remained in Rome, delegating to Caesar command of his troops in Spain. See also Plutarch, *Crassus* 14-15 and *Pompey* 51.

[2] Cassius Dio, *Roman History* 42.49.5.

[3] Appian, *Civil War* 2.8 and Suetonius, *Julius Caesar* 54.2, discussed in Frank 1933:325 and Verboven 2009:109. No gold was turned over to the Roman treasury.

Clodius bribed his way to an acquittal, but retained a deep hatred of Cicero. With his patrician reputation darkened, he changed his clan name Claudius to the plebeian-sounding Clodius. Caesar had presided over the adoption ceremony in his role of *pontifex maximus*, with Pompey officiating as augur, and both leaders had backed Clodius's election as tribune for 58.[4]

After gaining popularity by introducing a free grain dole for Rome's urban population, Clodius passed laws to prevent anyone like Bibulus using augury to postpone popular assembly business, and to exile any Roman guilty of putting citizens to death without trial.[5] The obvious target was Cicero, who quickly left Rome. A follow-up law required him to stay at least 400 miles away.

Clodius also re-established the legality of political street clubs, stirring up his own mob (no doubt made up largely of sympathizers of Catiline's debtor revolt) to destroy Cicero's house on the Palatine Hill. Clodius replaced it with a shrine to the goddess Libertas, personification of the principle of freedom under the law that Cicero had violated. Clodius then got Cato out of the way by appointing him to a lucrative governorship in Cyprus in 58, where Cato (accompanied by Brutus, as Chapter 18 has described) spent his time making money for himself as well as for the Roman treasury before returning to the Senate in 56.

Crassus was made governor of Syria for five years when his term as consul ended in 55. He used the appointment to loot a few rich temples in 54, but then led his 40,000-man army to a disastrous defeat in which he was killed by the Parthians. His co-consul Pompey was given command of Rome's two Spanish provinces for a similar term. But the year 54 also saw Pompey's wife Julia die prematurely. He married the daughter of Q. Metellus Scipio, ending the First Triumvirate by aligning himself with Senate conservatives against Caesar, whose popularity was rising as a result of his military conquests and presumed sympathy with Catiline and the plight of Roman debtors.

T. Annius Milo, a supporter of Cicero, had been elected plebeian tribune in 57 and allowed Cicero to return to Rome. Milo married Sulla's daughter Fausta in 54, and in 53 ran for consul for the year 52 against Pompey's candidates, while Clodius ran for the praetorship. Both men had street gangs that had been fighting for five years, and their conflict caused the elections in 53 to be postponed for seven

---

[4] Watts 2018:207-208. His change of family made him the "son" of a new father younger than himself.

[5] Watts 2018:209 and Mommsen 1958:321 and 328.

months. Matters came to a head in January 52, when Milo and his gang happened to meet Clodius and his followers on the Appian Way. Milo ordered his gladiators to kill Clodius.

News of the attack led to a riot, and a mob set a Senate building on fire – and then paraded by Pompey's house to support him against Milo's allies. The Senate condemned Milo, Cicero's attempt to defend him being outvoted. Rising civic unrest, still largely over the debt issue, led the Senate to appoint Pompey sole consul for 52.

Caesar hoped to run for the consulship in 49 as his command in Gaul was nearing its end in December 50. He brought his troops to Ravenna, south of Venice near Cisalpine Gaul's border with Italy. His *Commentary on the Civil War* (*Bellum Civile*), Appian's *Civil War*, Cassius Dio's *Roman History* and Suetonius's biography of *Julius Caesar* all contrast his attempt to negotiate a peaceful return to Roman politics with the Optimate preparations to mount a civil war to block his candidacy.

The ensuing fight pushed Rome's debt and landlordship arrangements into a crisis, which ended with Pompey, Cato and their supporters fleeing Italy and soon losing their lives.

Caesar's return to Rome is met by a financial crisis

Having kept Caesar away from Rome for nine years, the Senate certainly did not want him to return with an army. Arriving near the border with Italy, Caesar was brought news by G. Scribonius Curio, plebeian tribune for 50, describing the Senate's preparations for armed resistance, to be led by Pompey. Caesar gave Curio a letter to take to the Senate, proposing to disband his army if Pompey would do the same. However, he warned, "if Pompey should retain his command he would not lay down his own, but would come quickly and avenge his country's wrongs and his own injuries." Appian reports that "this was satisfactory to Pompey, but the consuls refused."[6] The Senate directed Caesar to relinquish command of his legions to his adversary Ahenobarbus, who took the field with 4000 men.

Mark Antony succeeded Curio as plebeian tribune at the beginning of January 49. Summoning a meeting of the Senate on January 3, 49, he read out Caesar's letter, which the senators viewed as a declaration of war. Four days later, after extensive debate, the consul Claudius Marcel-

---

[6] Appian, *Civil War* 32. See also Caesar's own account in *Civil War* 1.1-9 and Cassius Dio, *Roman History* 41.36-38. Watts 2018:221-228 provides a summary of these events.

lus rejected Caesar's attempt to run for consul that year. His co-consul
C. Lentulus Crus, who had been chief prosecutor of Clodius in the Bona
Dea scandal, supported Metellus Scipio's urging to declare a state of
emergency. Caesar was named a public enemy and thus subject to the
senatus consultum ultimum, the law that had justified the killing of Gaius
Gracchus and Catiline's followers.[7] Lentulus ordered Curio and Mark
Antony out of the Senate, and they fled for their lives, seeing a detach-
ment of Pompey's army standing around the Senate-house. They made
their way to Caesar the next night, disguised as slaves in a hired car-
riage.[8]

The next day, consul Marcellus (without authorization from the
Senate) offered Pompey the command of all Roman troops in Italy,
together with money and power to raise levies for troops and more
funding throughout Italy. That meant that if Caesar disbanded his own
troops, he would expose himself to attack from his enemies.[9] On January
10 or 11 he led a legion of 5,000 men and 300 horses from Ravenna
across the Rubicon, the stream that formed Italy's boundary with Cisalpine Gaul.

Proceeding toward Rome, Caesar wrote that crowds turned out to
welcome him. His troops promised "to defend their general, and the
tribunes of the commons, from all injuries" and even agreed "to forego
their pay, which Caesar had promised to double on the outbreak of the
civil war."[10]

The Senate turned much of Italy against itself by "imposing levies
throughout Italy, demanding arms, and exacting money from the
municipal towns and violently taking it from the temples. All distinctions between things human and divine were confounded."[11] As Appian
described: "With the fury of party rage the senators levied additional
contributions on the allied cities, which they collected with the greatest
possible haste," demanding that cities turn over their monetary reserves
and precious metals to the Senate so that Pompey could "assemble
130,000 Italian soldiers, chiefly veterans who had had experience in war,
and to recruit as many able-bodied men as possible from the neighbor-

---

[7] Caesar, *Civil War* 1.2 and 1.5.

[8] Appian, *Civil War* 33. See also Caesar, *Civil War* 1.2.

[9] Appian, *Civil War* 32.

[10] Caesar, *Civil War* 1.7. Mommsen 1958:381-395 notes that Caesar supported
needy soldiers and paid the subaltern officers and troopers out of his own funds.

[11] Caesar, *Civil War* 1.6.

ing provinces." They voted Pompey all the money in the public treasury to pay for the war, "and their own private fortunes in addition if they should be needed to pay the soldiers."[12]

But when Caesar seized advantageous positions, the Senate "panicked and repented that it had not accepted Caesar's proposals, which it at last considered fair."[13] Caesar made a last-ditch attempt to restore peace by repeating his earlier offer: "Let Pompey go to his own province; let them both disband their armies; let all persons in Italy lay down their arms; let all fears be removed from the city; let free elections, and the whole republic be resigned to the direction of the Senate and Roman people." But when the Optimate hard-liners made it clear that they wanted Caesar alone to disarm, he sent Mark Antony to raise troops, staying with two legions at Ariminum, modern Rimini, just over the Rubicon border on the Adriatic coast.[14]

Italian cities backed Caesar, not his rivals. Curio recaptured the town of Iguvium (modern Gubbio in Umbria) "with the cheerful concurrence of all the inhabitants. Upon receiving an account of this, and relying on the affections of the municipal towns, Caesar drafted all the cohorts of the thirteenth legion from the garrison and set out for Auximum." The city's leaders told Rome's Senate legate, Attius Varus, that they refused to fight against Caesar. The legate's troops deserted him, and either joined Caesar's army or went home.[15]

Back in Rome, the consul Lentulus emptied the treasury and fled. So did the other consul, Marcellus, and most of the magistrates. As Caesar marched southward along Italy's east coast, local officials "cheerfully received him, and aided his army with every necessity," he wrote.[16] His 12th legion joined his march toward Corfinium, where he caught up with Ahenobarbus, who had been sent as his replacement in command of Gaul but whose soldiers had begun to mutiny. "The inhabitants of Corfinium captured him at the gates as he was trying to escape," and sent deputies to Caesar "to say that they were ready to throw open their

---

[12] Appian, *Civil War* 34.

[13] Appian, *Civil War* 36.

[14] Caesar, *Civil War* 1.9-11. Caesar complained about the Senate's inequitable proposal that Pompey "should merely promise to go to his province, without naming the day on which he would set out" or even promising to meet with Caesar, making "the expectation of peace appear very hopeless."

[15] Caesar, *Civil War* 1.12-13.

[16] Caesar, *Civil War* 1.14-15 and 1.18.

gates, to do whatever he should order, and deliver up Domitius [Aheno-barbus] alive into his hands."[17]

Rather than confronting Caesar, Pompey marched to Brundisium in February 49 to sail across the Adriatic to the Illyrian peninsula, ordering all the troops that the Senate had raised throughout Italy to join him. But the town's citizens were irritated by his demands, and favored Caesar. "As soon as they were aware of Pompey's depar-ture, while his men were running up and down, and busied about their voyage, they made signs from the tops of the houses: Caesar, being apprised of the design by them, ordered scaling-ladders to be got ready, and his men to take arms."[18] His soldiers reached the port and captured two of Pompey's ships full of soldiers, but Pompey managed to sail away in March. "Cicero facetiously complained that no one had ever done more to make urban property prices collapse than Pompey when he had abandoned Rome."[19]

Lacking ships to pursue Pompey, Caesar marched to Spain in April 49, and commanded the magistrates of the free towns to procure him ships and have them convoyed to Brundisium. He delegated Valerius to take one legion to Sardinia, whose governor, Marcus Cotta Curio, deserted the island. Caesar sent three legions to Sicily, where Cato had been placed in charge of the Republican army. Fleeing Sicily, Cato bewailed that Pompey "had undertaken an unnecessary war" after having assured the Senate that he could easily defeat Caesar.[20]

Having dispersed his opponents, Caesar returned to Rome in December 49. Optimate families feared that he would seize their property as Sulla had done to his own opponents, while many poorer Romans hoped that he would cancel their debts by decree. With typical hyperbole Cicero wrote in May 49: "I foresee a bloodbath ... an onslaught on private property, the return of exiles and cancellation of debts."[21]

A credit crisis already had been mounting since 54, as Chapter 18 has described, and lending dried up even more in fear of what Caesar might do. Land prices plunged as wealthy families called in their loans and hoarded their silver and gold in preparation to leave Italy. The credit

---

[17] Appian, *Civil War* 38 and Caesar, *Civil War* 1.20 and 1.24. See also Plutarch, *Caesar* 32 and Cassius Dio, *Roman History* 41.

[18] Caesar, *Civil War* 1.24 and 1.28.

[19] Cicero, *Letters to Atticus* 7.17.1 (February 49), cited in Collins and Walsh 2015:154.

[20] Caesar, *Civil War* 1.29-30.

[21] Yavetz 1983:65, citing Cicero, *Letters to Atticus* 10.8.2.

market collapsed.[22] "Friends and foes saw in Caesar a second Catiline,"
summarizes Mommsen. "Was there any wonder that even grave and politically impartial men expected amnesty for all exiled criminals, cancelling
of creditor's claims, comprehensive mandates of confiscation, proscription, murder – nay, even a plundering of Rome by the Gallic soldiery?"[23]

But Caesar did not emulate Sulla. He allowed all the exiles except
Clodius's murderer Milo to return, and restored civic rights to the
children of those who had suffered in the time of Sulla – mainly opponents of the Optimates.[24] By proclaiming this amnesty he hoped to
demonstrate his moderation, and to co-opt his opponents by appointing them as magistrates. Most notable among these appointments were
two of Pompey's followers, Cassius and Brutus, who ended up stabbing
Caesar in 44.

Caesar's debt laws help aristocrats who bought land with mortgage credit

As with Solon in Athens half a millennium earlier, hopes for general
debt cancellation were disappointed. By the time Caesar left Rome later
in 49, "the moneylenders, bankers and wholesale merchants were among
Caesar's most loyal followers."[25] He held their support, just as he had
done when he bailed out the *equites* and investors in their companies
from their Asian contracts during his consulship a decade earlier, in 59.

Once Caesar had cleared his path to run for the consulship for the
year 48, he dealt with the civil war's economic disruption. Food prices
had risen and there was near famine in Rome. As noted, interest rates
had soared and land prices fell sharply, and would continue to do so
throughout the next four years of his rule. Lending had dried up, with
the cutback in credit actually dating from the fight over the consulship
for 53.[26] Creditors were especially unwilling to lend money after the
Senate limited the legal rate of interest to 12 percent in 51 to counter

---

[22] Watts 2018:228. See Caesar, *Civil War* 3.20, Appian, *Civil War* 2.48 and Cassius
Dio, *Roman History* 41.37.3.

[23] Mommsen 1958:407. Pompey and the Optimates trivialized the reason for
Caesar's program, "believing or pretending to believe that Caesar had been driven
to civil war by the impossibility of paying his debts." Cicero, *Letters to his friends* 8.7
likewise attributed Curio's support to Caesar paying off Curio's debts – Cicero as
usual belittling of any economic or social logic opposing Optimate policy.

[24] Caesar, *Civil War* 1.32-33 and Plutarch, *Julius Caesar* 37. Cassius Dio, *Roman
History* 41.36 provides more details.

[25] Yavetz 1983:54. See Suetonius, *Julius Caesar* 42.

[26] Verboven 2003:1-5. See also Chapter 18 at fn44.

the "dearness" of credit (*caritas nummorum*). Andreau points out that this "proves that the maximum of 88 BC (whatever it was [being $8^{1}/_3$ percent according to Frank]) was no longer being applied."[27]

There was no shortage of money, but it was hoarded. In addition to paying his soldiers, Caesar coined massive amounts of gold.[28] But the wealthy were reluctant to lend, fearing that Caesar might confiscate land pledged as collateral, preventing borrowers from being able to pay their creditors, as had occurred in the crisis under Sulla four decades earlier.

There has been some confusion among modern writers imagining that the collapse of land prices reflected a general deflation of coinage and hence of general price levels. Many economic writers conflate payment in "hard" money (coinage) to buy food and other products with credit to buy land. But what is deflated in credit crises is credit to purchase land or other assets, not actual coinage. These are two distinct spheres of monetary and credit circulation.[29]

No copies of Caesar's debt laws responding to this credit crisis have been preserved. Documentation of his financial reforms during his rule from 49 to his death in 44 is limited to scattered passages in his own narrative and those of later writers, namely Cassius Dio, Suetonius and Plutarch, and there is Tacitus's description of Emperor Tiberius's financial reform in AD 33, which is said to have emulated Caesar's reforms. These summaries focus more on the aims of Caesar's acts than on

---

[27] Andreau 1999:92. See Frank 1933:269-271.

[28] Verboven 2003:7-11, citing Orosius, *Histories against the Pagans* 6.15.5. In 49, Caesar found 4,135 pounds of gold, and 900,000 pounds of silver in the treasury, "enough to coin 75,600,000 *denarii*."

[29] Today's Quantity Theory of Money fails to distinguish between bank credit created to buy assets (and hence affecting primarily property prices) and money spent on goods and services, affecting product prices and wages. Collins and Walsh 2015 follow today's monetarist theory in assuming that falling land prices resulting from Rome's collapse of credit for investment in land must have been accompanied by price deflation for Roman goods and services across the board. But there is no reason to believe that Roman lending for real estate purchases (or its cutback) spilled over into the economy at large to affect prices of food or other products, or of labor. A parallel today is the post-2009 and 2020 surge in Federal Reserve money creation (Quantitative Easing and direct asset purchases) to support real estate, stock and bond prices that soared to record highs, while consumer prices and wages remained fairly stable through 2020.

their details, obliging modern historians to try to reconstruct what happened.[30] Cassius Dio spelled out the problem that Caesar faced:

> Creditors who had lent money, it seems, being now in need of large sums because of the civil strife and the wars, were collecting their loans most relentlessly, and many of the debtors for the same reasons were unable to pay back anything, even if they wished to do so, since they did not find it easy to sell anything or to borrow more.[31]

As Caesar himself described the situation, seeing that "credit was beginning to fail in Italy, and the debts could not be paid, he determined that arbitrators should be appointed: and that they should make an estimate of the possessions and properties [of the debtors], how much they were worth before the war, and that they should be handed over in payment to the creditors."[32] That settlement would save the reputations and credit of the debtors by rolling back mortgage debts in proportion to the collapse of land prices. Debtors were able to pay their creditors with land evaluated at the price that it was worth before the civil war, that is, when the loans initially were taken out. This debt writedown brought debts and creditor claims in line with land prices.

Creditors lost about one-fourth of their nominal money claims for payment, but their purchasing power over land remained stable, so they recovered an equivalent land valuation for the sums that they had lent. This principle was similar to the 75 percent rollback under the Valerian Law of 86 in the Sullan debt crisis (see Chapter 15). But in Caesar's case there had been no debt-financed real estate bubble that collapsed, merely a steady decline in land prices as Rome's political crisis deteriorated after 53. There was no shortage of money, but it was not being lent out or invested in land, given the risk of civil war.

Caesar's *Lex Julia de bonis cedenalis* that gave effect to his debt reform may have been proclaimed as late as 45-44, or else was a renewal of a

---

[30] Yavetz 1983:64 notes: "There is no conclusive proof for a series of *Leges Juliae*, indeed not even for a single *Lex Julia*." Elliott 2015:272 writes: "The details of these laws are only known through their revival in AD 33 – their original purpose and stipulations are likely to remain forever veiled."

[31] Cassius Dio, *Roman History* 41.37.

[32] Caesar, *Civil War* 3.1. As Cassius Dio, *Roman History* 41.37 paraphrases this: "He ordered that securities should have a fixed valuation according to their worth, and he provided that arbiters for this purpose should be allotted to persons involved in such a dispute."

ruling from as early as 49. In any case, Frederiksen's classic 1966 article has helped untangle the workings of his bankruptcy law (debt reform), which benefited mainly the well-to-do, by introducing

> a new procedure in settlement of debt, *cessio bonorum*. By this a debtor might admit insolvency before a praetor or other magistrate, and with the magistrate's permission might then "cede" his land and goods in settlement of his debt, retaining enough to keep him alive. He did not thereby suffer *infamia* and entirely avoided personal execution; no second action could be brought for the same debts unless the debtor had acquired substantial money in the meantime; and in other ways he was offered protection.[33]

Plutarch and Appian barely allude to this legislation, despite their common emphasis on debt problems.[34] Suetonius added a dimension that has confused historians. In addition to Caesar's technical adjustment allowing indebted landlords to "satisfy their creditors according to a valuation of their possessions at the price which they had paid for them before the Civil War," he claims that Caesar permitted them to "deduct from the principal any interest that had been paid in cash or assigned in writing – an arrangement which wiped out about a fourth part of their indebtedness."[35] Tacitus (*Annals* 6.16) likewise wrote that the reform by Tiberius in AD 33 cancelled all interest charges, claiming that this was based on a ruling by Caesar that had come to be ignored, stipulating that no claims for back interest were legally collectible and should be deducted from the principal that was owed. Yet Caesar's own civil war narrative did not mention cancelling interest payments.[36]

---

[33] Frederiksen 1966:135. Verboven 2009:107-108 follows this reading. "If the praetor agreed, the creditor was obliged to accept the transfer at the estimated pre-war value." This *cessio bonorum* is akin to what Caesar had arranged in Spain in 61 (Plutarch, *Julius Caesar* 12, noted in Chapter 18).

[34] Herz 2015:246 notes that "the juristic treatment of *cessio bonorum* suggests that the doctrine might have been curtailed, at least in Italy," although it seems to have persisted in Egypt. "By the third century when Ulpian and Modestinus discuss the practice, both picture it as a temporary stay of enforcement that does not release the debtor from liability attaching to after-acquired property," although they "disagree on the propriety of a basic living allowance being exempt from creditors." But their contemporary jurists Cassius and Sabinus view the discharge as permanent.

[35] Suetonius, *Julius Caesar* 42.

[36] On this episode generally see Plutarch, *Julius Caesar* 37, Appian, *Civil War* 2.198, Cassius Dio, *Roman History* 41.37, and the discussion in Lewis and Reinhold 1951

Discussing the *Lex Julia*, Mommsen praised Caesar for being the first
to give "an insolvent the right – on which our modern bankruptcy regulations are based – of formally ceding his estate to his creditors," and
surviving free to make a new start.[37] But modern bankruptcy laws do
not let debtors write down their debts in proportion to the fall in land
prices, as Caesar's law had done. They seek payment of the full value
of the original money principal that creditors claim, to be paid by liqui-
dating the debtor's assets at prevailing market prices, which in a crash
will be distress prices. The severe U.S. price deflation of the 1880s and
'90s led to bankruptcy for many farmers "crucified on a cross of gold."
Likewise, the Great Depression of the 1930s led to a large transfer of
land and real estate to creditors, as did the 2008 financial crash.

Trying to follow a middle road, the *Lex Julia* applied to debtors who
could not pay their obligations because of merely temporary pressures
stemming from the fall of land prices during Rome's civil warfare.
Debtors would not become *infamis* or subject to bondage if prices for
their property failed to cover their original mortgage balance. But smallholders without sufficient property to cede to their creditors, and who
could not have paid even under *normal* circumstances, are likely to have
fled their localities to avoid the consequences of their indebtedness.

Coelius and Dolabella try to lead new revolts to cancel debts of the less affluent in 48-47

After being appointed dictator by the praetor Lepidus in 48, Caesar
spent only a whirlwind eleven days in Rome before resigning his dictatorship to start his new consulship and departing to confront his
enemies militarily. In January 48 he led his army to Brundisium to cross
the Adriatic and fight Pompey, defeating him in what is now southern

---

II:288. Frank 1933:312 attributed to 49 what more likely was proclaimed in 45-44.
He follows Suetonius in writing that Caesar attempted to restore credit by "permitting debtors to go into bankruptcy on the basis of pre-war evaluations of their
property," and "by permitting the interest already paid on debts to be deducted
from the principal." Verboven 2003:3 believes that Caesar made the decree soon
after he returned in 49. Brunt 1971b:144 states that, "in my view Caesar himself
on his return renewed it in 47 with an upper limit of 500 *denarii*; he also relieved
debtors by letting them deduct interest paid from the capital owed, apparently up
to 25%." This writedown appears to have applied to all debtors, not only those who
borrowed to buy land.

[37] Mommsen 1866 IV:556.

Albania in August. Cicero and Brutus surrendered after the battle, and Pompey took refuge in Egypt.

Caesar pursued Pompey there, and was greeted in September by Cleopatra's brother, who presented him with Pompey's severed head and seal-ring, apparently expecting that this would gain Roman support for Ptolemy XIII's claim to the Egyptian throne. Caesar was so appalled that he had Pompey's assassins put to death.

Cato and Metellus Scipio fought on for a few years in North Africa, and finally were defeated in 46 at Thapsus, each committing suicide shortly after the battle. Caesar spent much time in Egypt, making only sporadic appearances in Rome until October 45 when, having been co-consul in 46 and sole consul for 45, he returned to be elected consul for his fifth term in 44, with Mark Antony his co-consul.

But earlier, as soon as he left Rome in 48, other politicians sought to advance themselves by trying to mobilize a new following to demand remission of rents and other debts. M. Coelius Rufus (82-48) and P. Cornelius Dolabella (85/80-43) sought power by picking up Catiline's call for outright debt cancellation.

Coelius, the son of an *equite* banker in Puteoli, had been briefly associated with Catiline and was a tribune of the plebs in 52, and *curule aedile* in 50. He backed Caesar so strongly against Pompey in the civil war that Caesar in 48 gave him the office of *praetor peregrinus*, judging suits involving foreigners and non-citizens. Cassius Dio states that Coelius wanted the top-ranking position of *praetor urbanus*, the praetor in charge of disputes among Roman citizens, with authority ranking just behind that of the two consuls. When Caesar assigned this position to Gaius Trebonius, Coelius made his own play for power. Undertaking the cause of poorer debtors,

> he gave notice to whomever owed anything that he would assist them against their creditors, and to all who dwelt in other people's houses that he would release them from payment of the rent. Having by this course gained a considerable following, he set upon Trebonius with their aid and would have slain him, had the other not managed to change his dress and escape in the crowd. After this failure Coelius privately issued a law in which he granted everybody the use of houses free of rent and annulled all debts.[38]

---

[38] Cassius Dio, *Roman History* 42.22 and Odgers 1930. Coelius apparently proposed debt relief after September 48.

When nobody stepped up to lodge an appeal to have his debts cancelled, Coelius "promulgated a law that all debts should be discharged
in six equal payments, of six months each, without interest."[39] Finding
himself opposed by Caesar's co-consul Servilius and other magistrates, and raising

> less than he expected to raise the passions of the people, he dropped it,
> and promulgated two others; one, by which he remitted the annual rents
> of the houses to the tenants, the other, an act of insolvency: upon which
> the mob made an assault on Gaius Trebonius, and having wounded
> several persons, drove him from his tribunal.
>
> The consul Servilius informed the senate of his proceedings, who
> passed a decree that Coelius should be removed from the management
> of the republic.[40]

Cassius Dio adds that Servilius removed the tablets recording Coelius's laws and "would not permit Coelius to do anything in his capacity
as praetor, but assigned the duties pertaining to his office to another
praetor, debarred him from the Senate, dragged him from the rostra
while he was delivering some tirade or other, and broke his chair in
pieces."

Seeing little path for success in Rome, Coelius decided to join Milo,
who had returned to Italy despite Caesar's ban and was recruiting disaffected men and ravaging Capua and other cities in Campania. Coelius
asked Servilius "for leave of absence, even saying that he wished to
proceed to Caesar," but the consul sent a tribune with him to make sure
that he did not encourage any rebellious act.[41]

> When they reached Campania, and found that Milo had been
> defeated near Capua and taken refuge on Mount Tifata, Coelius gave up
> his plan of going farther, the tribune was alarmed and wished to bring
> him back home. Servilius ... declared war upon Milo in the Senate and
> gave orders that Coelius should remain in the suburbs, so that he might
> not stir up any trouble. Nevertheless, he did not keep him under strict
> surveillance, because the man was a praetor. Thus Coelius made his

---

[39] Caesar, *Civil War* 3.20. Mommsen 1958:489 wrote that: "After his proposed law
which granted debtors an interest-free respite of six years failed to pass," Coelius
"proposed a second law cancelling all claims arising out of loans and current house
rents."

[40] Caesar, *Civil War* 3.20-21.

[41] Cassius Dio, *Roman History* 42.23-24.

escape and hastened to Milo, and he would certainly have created some disturbance had he found him alive.

But Milo had been killed in Apulia. Coelius went to Brutium, hoping to form a league in that district, but was killed by the soldiers that Caesar had left to protect Italy.[42]

The defeat of Coelius and Milo left the problem of debt and landlessness unresolved. In January 47, Dolabella, from a prominent patrician family, revived Coelius's campaign to abolish debts and back rents. He had married Cicero's daughter Tullia (becoming her third husband), and although having backed Pompey at first, he had joined Caesar by 48. He emulated Clodius's strategy of being adopted by a plebeian so that he could be elected tribune. On the day that the popular assembly was to discuss his debt-relief law, a crowd of artisans, small shopkeepers, freedmen and also soldiers joined to barricade the Forum to prevent the assembly being dispersed. The oligarchic wing of the Populares, headed by the tribunes Trebellius and Asinius Pollio, defeated the proposal, and the Senate authorized Mark Antony – Rome's senior official as Caesar's Master of the Horse – to use his soldiers to "disperse Dolabella's bands, [resulting in] a loss of 800 killed. It was years since Rome had seen such a slaughter."[43]

By attacking Dolabella, Antony made himself unpopular with Romans hoping for debt and rent relief. Caesar was still away, and no curule magistrates to administer Rome in his absence were elected in 47 until after his return in September from a war in Anatolia over Pontus, in which he defeated Pharnaces, the son of Mithridates.[44]

Caesar's triumphs and legislative reforms

Back in Rome, Caesar found himself faced with mutinous troops complaining of their long length of service, demanding more money and even killing two of their officers. Caesar defused the situation by giving each man a thousand drachmas and allotting them land in Italy. He also eased popular discontent by pardoning Dolabella and, on being chosen

---

[42] Cassius Dio, *Roman History* 42.25 and Caesar, *Civil War* 3.22.

[43] Caesar, *Civil War* 3.20-22, Plutarch, *Antony* 9, Appian, *Civil War* 2.48, Cassius Dio, *Roman History* 41.37, and Ferrero 1909 II:273, 291-293 and 260-261.

[44] Cassius Dio, *Roman History* 42.31.

consul for the third time, for the year 46, selected Lepidus as his colleague instead of Antony.[45]

Caesar soon left Rome once again, this time for Africa to defeat
Metellus Scipio and Cato at Thapsus in February 46. Returning for his
third dictatorship – granted for an unprecedented ten years – he was
awarded four triumphs, bunched together in a weeks-long spectacle
starting in April 46,

> one for his Gallic wars …; one for the Pontic war against Pharnaces; one
> for the war in Africa against the African allies of L. Scipio, in which the
> historian Juba (the son of King Juba), then an infant, was led a captive.
> Between the Gallic and the Pontic triumphs he introduced a kind of
> Egyptian triumph, in which he led some captives taken in the naval
> engagement on the Nile.[46]

Appian describes the booty that was displayed, out which Caesar
minted the largest supply of gold coins in Roman history, increasing
their proportion of Rome's overall money supply to one quarter.

> It is said that money to the amount of 60,500 silver talents was borne
> in the procession and 2,822 crowns of gold weighing 20,414 pounds,
> from which wealth Caesar made apportionments immediately after the
> triumph, paying the army all that he had promised and more. Each
> soldier received 5000 Attic drachmas [*denarii*], each centurion double
> that amount, and each military tribune and prefect of cavalry fourfold
> that sum. To each plebeian citizen also was given an Attic mina [one
> hundred *denarii*].[47]

---

[45] Plutarch, *Antony* 9-10 and *Caesar* 51, and Cassius Dio, *Roman History* 42.30.
Antony married Clodius's widow Fulvia. Dolabella proved to be quite a survivor,
often changing sides from one party to another. Caesar brought him along as one
of his generals in his campaigns in North Africa and Spain, and even proposed to
transfer his consulship to Dolabella in 44. Antony protested, but later welcomed
him as one of his own supporters when Dolabella received the consulship after
Caesar's assassination. Antony gave him command of Syria, where Dolabella died
in a battle against Cassius in Laodicea.

[46] Appian, *Civil War* 101. Celebrating the end of four wars – in Gaul (over Vercingetorix), Egypt, Pontus (over Pharnaces) and Numidia (over king Juba, Cato and
Scipio) – the triumphal spectacle brought booty from all. In March 47, Caesar had
celebrated a similar triumph in Alexandria with Cleopatra.

[47] Appian, *Civil War* 102. The celebration is said to have run 40 days, adding to
Caesar's popularity. Alongside the triumphs, he provided splendid public banquets
with abundant meat dishes. Verboven 2003:10-11 states that the gold was enough to
coin 816,560 *aurei* worth 20,414,000 *denarii*. Gold had not previously been minted

The vast tribute on display showed that Caesar had rescued Rome's finances, which his opponents had depleted in their war against him. And to remind Romans of how he had defeated his domestic Optimate opponents, his parade included actors depicting Cato killing himself and Metellus Scipio committing suicide and throwing himself into the sea.

Suetonius describes how Caesar distributed his booty and revived Coelius's proposal in 48 to abolish rents for a year in the face of Rome's housing scarcity:

> To every foot soldier in his veteran legions, besides the two thousand sesterces paid him in the beginning of the civil war, he gave twenty thousand more, in the shape of prize-money. He likewise allotted them lands, but not in contiguity, that the former owners might not be entirely dispossessed. To the people of Rome, besides ten *modii* of corn, and as many pounds of oil, he gave three hundred sesterces a man, which he had formerly promised them, and a hundred more to each for the delay in fulfilling his engagement. He likewise remitted a year's rent due to the treasury, for such houses in Rome as did not pay above two thousand sesterces a year; and through the rest of Italy, for all such as did not exceed in yearly rent five hundred sesterces.[48]

Caesar left for Spain to fight the followers of Pompey and other Optimates in November 46, defeating them in March 45. It was during the ensuing year back in Rome that Caesar returned to his agenda for restructuring Rome's economy and society. Like Marius and Pompey, Caesar sought land for his veterans. Seeing little public land left unallocated in Italy but not wanting to confiscate privately-held land, Caesar settled (according to Suetonius) 80,000 soldiers and other citizens in colonies. His 13th legion was settled in Italy, but Carthage and Corinth were the main recipients of soldiers, as well as Spain and Gaul, where Caesar's 10th legion became the basis for a new colony at Narbo (modern Narbonne).

Cassius Dio reports that Caesar first selected "those who had chosen to be farmers and would, hopefully, remain settled on their land." The

---

regularly, although it was used for large payments in place of silver coins. Caesar's triumphal spectacles culminated in "a combat of elephants, twenty against twenty, and a naval engagement of 4000 oarsmen, where 1000 fighting men contended on each side." Scheidel 2007:330 calculates the booty payout to 50,000 soldiers at 5,000 dinars per man to have totaled 250 million dinars.

[48] Suetonius, *Julius Caesar* 38-39, Appian, *Civil War* 102, and Caesar, *Civil War* 3.21. Cassius Dio, *Roman History* 42.51 dates Caesar's mortgage-debt writedown to reflect the purchasing power of money in terms of land from this time.

settlers were barred from selling their land for twenty years to prevent them converting their land into money and streaming to Rome (as had happened before the Catilinarian uprising).[49] To keep the rest of the population in Italy, he ruled that no free Roman between 20 and 40 years old be absent from Italy for more than three years at a time.[50]

Caesar's reported rulings on bankruptcy and interest may have been proclaimed in the five months from October 45 to his assassination in March 44 – his longest stay in Rome during 49-44. Suetonius describes him as reiterating his *Lex Julia* (discussed above) enabling mortgages to be paid by transferring land at the pre-civil war land prices, and added the ability of debtors to deduct the interest they had paid from what they owed their creditors, "by virtue of which provision about a fourth part of the debt was lost."[51] These were the laws that some historians (as also noted above) believed were part of his rulings in 49.

With land prices falling as property was thrown onto the market to raise the funds to pay creditors calling in their loans, Caesar directed that two-thirds of all capital assets be held in the form of Italian real estate. That created a demand for land, at least by the wealthy.[52] And to increase the demand for (free) labor, Caesar decreed that "on the ranches not more than two-thirds of the laborers could be slaves." At least one third of the herdsmen were to be men of free birth.

To raise public revenue, Caesar imposed tariffs on foreign imports, while laying plans for building projects, headed by a vast temple to Mars, public theaters, a city lake and draining the mosquito-ridden Pontine marshes southeast of Rome (a project completed by Augustus).[53]

---

[49] Cassius Dio, *Roman History* 42.55, discussed in Yavetz 1983:143. Appian, *Civil War* 3.2.5 wrote that this regulation was repealed by Brutus and Cassius after Caesar was killed.

[50] Suetonius, *Julius Caesar* 42, in Brunt 1971b:234-65 and 559-561.

[51] Suetonius, *Julius Caesar* 42.

[52] Frank 1933:312. See Suetonius, *Julius Caesar* 42 and 44.3, and Tacitus, *Annals* 6.16-17. Verboven 2003:3 believes that it was soon after Caesar returned in 49 that he "decreed that debtors would be allowed to repay their debts with a transfer of land assessed at pre-war prices and he forbade anyone to hold more than 60,000 sesterces in cash." That left really only one thing to buy: land. The idea was to convert coinage into land to re-inflate its price. But the details and timing of Caesar's actions remain obscure.

[53] Suetonius, *Julius Caesar* 42-44. Frank 1933:339-340 summarizes Caesar's spending program, beginning with bread and circuses, doles, banquets, public dinners, combats of gladiators and stage-plays, keeping his own and his state

Caesar's behavior became increasingly regal after the Senate confirmed him as dictator for life early in 44. "Sitting on the rostra in his gilded chair" at the Lupercalia festival of Pan on February 15, "adorned with the royal apparel and resplendent in his crown overlaid with gold, Antony with his fellow-priests saluted him as king and binding a diadem upon his head, said: 'The people offer this to you through me.'" In a pose of modesty as if resisting popular will, Caesar sent the crown to the Temple of Jupiter.[54]

Despite being a virtual king, Caesar did not use his dictatorship to do what most Romans had wanted for five centuries: debt relief and security from forfeiture of their self-support land and eviction for debt arrears. Although these acts were widely expected of Caesar, they never were his program. Nonetheless, on the midmonth Ides of March, he was killed in the Senate by those whom he had tried the most to appease, Rome's leading Optimates, including Brutus, while Trebonius distracted Mark Antony in conversation outside.[55]

The aftermath

The threat of armies fighting over the debt conflict had shrunk from Catiline's revolt to that of Coelius, and debt protests played no role in the struggle among the rivals seeking to take the place of Caesar. His reforms had fallen short of alleviating the debt burden, but no new populist leaders arose seeking to consolidate their power by overthrowing the elites like Greece's 7th-century reformer-tyrants had done, much less (repeating Mommsen's words) "to make war on property itself, and either to intimidate their creditors by threats or to get rid of them by conspiracy and civil war." As Mommsen concluded:

---

accounts together like an oriental monarch. Suetonius also wrote that Caesar "conferred citizenship on all who practised medicine at Rome, and on all teachers of the liberal arts, to make them more desirous of living in the city and to induce others to resort to it." Caesar reduced the dole (from 320,000 to 150,000 Roman citizens), while increasing the demand for (free) labor by decreeing that no more than two-thirds of laborers on ranches could be slaves, as noted above.

[54] Cassius Dio, *Roman History* 44.11. See also Suetonius, *Julius Caesar* 79, and for background, Lintott 2009.

[55] As a fitting epilogue, Trebonius then left for the post Caesar had promised him, proconsul of Asia, there raising money and troops for Brutus and Cassius to help fight Caesar's supporters. Dolabella also went as proconsul to Asia, where he looted so outrageously and killed the governor who tried to block him that he was declared a public enemy and killed by Cassius, his successor as proconsul.

> The relations of debtor to creditor returned almost to the same point at which they had stood in the worst time of the social crisis of the fifth century; the nominal landowners held their lands virtually by sufferance of their creditors; the debtors were in servile subjection to their creditors, so that the humbler of them appeared like freedmen in the creditor's train and those of higher rank spoke and voted even in the Senate at the nod of their creditor-lord.[56]

The aftermath of Caesar's assassination in 44 saw his adopted heir Octavian defeat the armies of Brutus, Cassius and Mark Antony, and in 27 the Senate gave him the titles augustus and princeps. Octavian was careful to avoid depicting his role as "king." Rome's oligarchy had been using "kingship" as a term of invective for half a millennium, because "kingship" meant the power to overrule the oligarchy, above all by acting to preserve social order by cancelling debts and redistributing land. Octavian therefore presented himself as merely the princeps, "first citizen." Mindful of how Rome's magnates accused Caesar of seeking the crown, his adopted son Octavian had no intention of laying himself open to criticism on the basis of that long-established label. He was just another citizen, Augustus, restoring peace to the Roman Republic, not the long class war that had marked the Republic.

Nonetheless, the Empire he put in place left the Senate as little more than a ceremonial membership club for the elite. But this did not clear the path for popular reform. Policy infighting over debt and land laws had ended.

Historians celebrate the next few centuries as the peak of Rome's glory, but it was only a coda to the crisis in which the Republic had ended. Yet the Republic is still typically celebrated as a prototype of democracy, and its Augustinian era's sequel as a Golden Age, as if Rome's oligarchic, military and extractive character and decline from the 3rd to 5th centuries AD was not imprinted in its DNA from the very beginning. But as the Italian historian Guglielmo Ferrero (1871-1942) wrote over a century ago about how the debt crisis played out after Caesar's death, Rome's

> debts were steadily accumulating, and it was impossible for Italy to shake them off. Not even the spoils of a second Gaul or Asia would have sufficed. Yet the age of expansion seemed definitely closed; before long there would be no more unexpected importations of gold and silver captured in war; debtors could place little hope in legislative assistance,

---

[56] Mommsen 1866 IV:615. See Cassius Dio, *Roman History* 41.38.

and would soon be forced to meet their claims by their own efforts. When this point was reached the liquidation of this immense mass of debt would automatically follow. [57]

Today's modern writers downplay the role of debt and its relationship with land tenure, focusing instead mainly on the lives and achievements of the wealthy at the top, as if their amassing of wealth reflected a victory of economic and technological efficiency. To be sure, Ferrero noted,

> There were many upper class families who might still manage to keep afloat by playing off their creditors against their debtors and reducing their scale of living. Not so the middle class. The houses they had built and the slaves they had bought and trained with so much care during the last twenty years would pass into the hands of a small group of capitalist creditors, and with them would disappear the industrious and intelligent bourgeoisie which had been slowly formed during the last half century.

The recent generation of historians of classical antiquity have followed the lead of modern economists to sidestep the debt dynamics that polarize economies. This is in contrast to what Mommsen, Ferrero, Toynbee and their generation emphasized, and what Rome's own historians stressed as they described Rome's debt crises and the intransigence of its creditors. As Ferrero summarized:

> the solution of the problem of debt ... could only be achieved by one of those revolutionary strokes which recur periodically in the history of nations. There was no other way out. ... the abolition of debt ... like a surgical operation ... is the more dangerous and painful the longer it has been delayed.

Rome never did solve its debt problem, leaving the Empire to suffer the momentum of economic polarization inherited from the Republic. Today's West likewise has not succeeded in coping with debt in a way that saves its economies from polarizing. That similarity and the reason for it – the West's inheritance of Rome's pro-creditor legal philosophy – is the main relevance of Roman history for today's world.

---

[57] Ferrero 1909 II:266. See also II:291-293 and 260-261. The longer the abolition of debts was postponed, he wrote, the worse matters became. Ferrero's summary shows how much more concern was paid to debt problems a century ago than is the case with most modern monetary and fiscal studies of Rome. He was often nominated for the Nobel Prize in Literature.

20
The Empire's Fiscal Squeeze and Money Shortage, 1ˢᵗ to 3ʳᵈ Centuries AD

Comparing the virtues and defects of democracy, oligarchy and monarchy, Herodotus (3.82) had Darius describe what leads oligarchies to become monarchies: "In an oligarchy, the fact that a number of men are competing for distinction in the public service leads to violent personal feuds; each of them wants to get to the top and see his own proposals carried, so they quarrel. Personal quarrels lead to open dissension and then to bloodshed, and the only way out is a return to monarchy."

That is what happened during the in-fighting from Caesar's murder in 44 to the Senate's conferring upon Octavian the titles augustus and princeps in 27 BC. After Caesar no more aristocratic rivals attempted to take the populace into their camp by promoting democracy in the way that Aristotle described aristocratic families as having done in Athens. Rome's oligarchic voting system blocked the citizenry from having much effective political force, and the fate of the Gracchi, Marius, Catiline and Caesar had shown Senate power to be strong enough to be immune to democratic reforms to alleviate the debt and land problems.

Military bloodshed had settled matters ever since Marius had created an army-for-hire. Fighting among rival generals was not over political or ideological differences, but was for power and wealth, and was waged by troops loyal to their paymasters. That is how Octavian conquered his rivals to create Rome's new principate. The battle that culminated in the principate was not fought over how to restructure the Roman state in the abstract, but simply reflected the dynamics of internecine opportunism.

Rome's imperial regime was different from the earlier Near Eastern monarchies. Their rulers had proclaimed Clean Slates cancelling back taxes and debts owed by smallholders, returning self-support land and liberating bondservants. But just as the Roman oligarchy's long-standing opposition to kingship (*regnum*) had aimed at preventing any political authority reversing the concentration of land and creditor power, so did Rome's emperors. "'Whoever does not want the existing state of affairs to be changed, is a good citizen and a good man,' says Augustus."[1] But

---
[1] Macrobius, *Saturnalia* 2.4.18.

by not changing the polarizing status quo by cancelling debts, emperors supported the concentration of land in Rome's great estates. During Rome's imperial "golden age" of the first two centuries of emperorship, smallholders fell into debt and became *coloni* (sharecroppers), itinerant laborers or mercenaries, or ran away. They were victims of the emperor's bureaucracy just as they had been victims of oligarchic power during the Republic. Rome remained an oligarchy, increasingly based more on land ownership employing *coloni* labor than creditor power as opportunities for financial gain-seeking dried up.

Stripping the economy to pay soldiers

Roman politics had been controlled by army commanders since Sulla's coup in 82. This continued after Caesar's death, with his former co-consuls Lepidus and Antony, along with his adopted son Octavian, appointed to manage the Roman state as the Second Triumvirate, each with his own army. Antony seized 175 million *denarii* that Caesar had left in the treasury, outbidding Octavian for soldiers at 500 *denarii* each.

Octavian marched on Rome from Campania with Caesar's veterans late in 44 BC, and again in summer 43 with eight legions and auxiliaries. Brutus and Cassius left for the East to plunder its cities. Calling themselves *Liberatores*, they "had to confiscate and proscribe brutally in order to keep their promises to their soldiers."[2] But at the Battle of Philippi in Macedonia in October 42, Cassius lost to Antony, and Brutus lost to Octavian's army. Both losers committed suicide.

Antony remained in the East, hoping to bring Brutus's and Cassius's territories under control. Crossing the Aegean to Pergamum, he reminded its leaders that (as Appian relates): "When the publicans, who farmed these [tax] collections by the authority of the Senate, wronged you by demanding more than was due, Caesar remitted to you one-third of what you had paid to them and put an end to their outrages. He turned over to you the collection of the taxes from the cultivators of the soil." Antony then chastised them for letting themselves be looted by giving "vast sums of money to the murderers of your benefactor and against us, who were seeking to avenge him,"[3] explaining that it was now his turn to make demands:

> We need money and land and cities as rewards for our soldiers. There
> are twenty-eight legions of infantry which, with the auxiliaries, amount

---

[2] Frank 1933:312 and 339-342, and Ste. Croix 1981:361-362

[3] Appian, *Civil War* 5.4.

to upwards of 170,000 men, besides cavalry and various other arms of
the service. The vast sum that we need for such a vast number of men
you can easily imagine. Octavian has gone to Italy to provide them with
the land and the cities – to expropriate Italy, if we must speak plainly.
That we may not be under the necessity of expelling you from your
lands, cities, houses, temples, and tombs, we have assessed you for contribution – not of all that you have (for you could not pay that), but a
part ... what you contributed to our enemies in two years (and you gave
them the taxes of ten years in that time) will be quite sufficient for us;
but it must be paid in one year, because we are pressed by necessity.

The Greeks ... declared that they had been subjected to force and
violence by Brutus and Cassius, and that they were deserving of pity,
not of punishment; that they would willingly give to their benefactors,
but that they had been stripped by their enemies, to whom they had
delivered not only their money, but, in default of money, their plate and
their ornaments, and who had coined these things into money in their
presence. Finally, they prevailed by their entreaties that the amount
should be reduced to nine years' taxes, payable in two years. It was
ordered that the kings, princes, and free cities should make additional
contributions according to their means, respectively.

Antony "gave relief to the cities that had suffered most severely," and
"in Syria he delivered the cities from tyrants one after another." But
after Cleopatra joined him he dedicated his efforts to supporting her
ambitions for Egypt.[4] Although he married Octavian's sister Octavia in
40, Antony relocated to Egypt with Cleopatra, hoping to use its wealth
to back his own territorial ambitions in Rome's Eastern provinces. If he
had managed to create his own Egypt-centered realm, that might have
divided Rome into two empires. But his effort failed when Octavian
defeated him at the Battle of Actium in 31.

Having emerged victorious over Antony, Octavian returned to Rome
and sold off what remained of the property he had confiscated from
his rivals.[5] He assigned Africa to Lepidus, who nonetheless mounted
some opposition in Sicily but went into exile after his troops defected to
Octavian, who now faced the problem of how to meet the demands of

---

[4] Appian, *Civil War* 5.7-9.

[5] Ferrero 1909 III. Chapter XI emphasizes that "the proscriptions arranged in
43-42 by Antony, Lepidus and Octavian were not dictated by political revenge, but
by the desire to get rid of the richest men in Italy and confiscate their capital and
their credit."

his soldiers for the land and rewards they had been promised, and who were threatening to revolt if not paid more.

> Octavian said that he would not engage them in any more civil wars, which had fortunately come to an end, but in war against the Illyrians and other barbarous tribes, ... from which war the soldiers would acquire great riches. They said that they would not go to war again until they had received the prizes and honors of the previous wars. He said that he would not even now postpone the honors, but that he had distributed many prizes, and now gave additional crowns to the legions, and purple-bordered garments and the dignity of chief councilors to the centurions and tribunes in their native towns.
>
> While he was distributing other awards of this kind, the tribune Ofillius exclaimed that crowns and purple garments were playthings for boys, that the rewards for soldiers were lands and money. The multitude cried out "Well said"; whereupon Octavian descended from the platform in anger. The soldiers gathered round the tribune, praising him and railing at those who did not join with them, and the tribune said that he alone would suffice to defend so just a cause. After saying this he disappeared the following day, and it was never known what became of him.
>
> Octavian praised those who remained with him ... saying ... that they would be discharged rich, and that he would give them 500 drachmas per man now. Having thus spoken, he exacted tribute from Sicily to the amount of 1600 talents, appointed propraetors for Africa and Sicily, and assigned a division of the army to each of these provinces.[6]

Many soldiers seemed near mutiny and began attacking Octavian's supporters, but both parties recognized their mutual dependence on each other – a relationship on which the Empire would be based for the next five centuries:

> The chiefs depended on the soldiers for the continuance of their government, while, for the possession of what they had received, the soldiers depended on the permanence of the government of those who had given it. Believing that they could not keep a firm hold unless the givers had a strong government, they fought for them, from necessity, with good-will.
>
> Octavian made many other gifts to the indigent soldiers, borrowing from the temples for that purpose, for which reason the affections of the army were turned toward him, and the greater thanks were bestowed upon him both as the giver of the land, the cities, the money and the houses – and as the object of denunciation on the part of the despoiled ...

---

[6] Appian, *Civil War* 5.126-129.

Local populations suffered as Roman soldiers proved as predatory land grabbers as their commanders. Appian describes communities "crying out against Octavian, saying that the colonization was worse than the proscription, since the latter was directed against foes, while the former was against unoffending persons."[7]

Back in Rome, Octavian distributed cash to pacify his troops and consolidate their support. This payment constituted the last great wave of the military bonuses that Walter Scheidel calculates as representing a sharp increase in wage income from Sulla in 81 to 29 BC, near the end of the Republic. That long-extended rise reflected the army's main reliance on citizens who had lost their own plots of land and volunteered for the army as a source of income and booty. In the wake of Marius's recruitment of a mercenary army, Sulla's warlordism had inspired "an arms race of cash incentives. Campaign bonuses for common soldiers rose from 800 denars in 69 BC (7 times annual pay) to 1,500 in 61 BC (13 times) to 5,000 in 46 BC (22 times the newly doubled stipend of 225 denars/year), with multiples assigned to cavalrymen and officers. Base bonuses of 5,000 denars were again promised in 43 and 42 BC, and actually paid out on the latter occasion."[8] Scheidel calculates that "as much as one-third of the entire Roman citizenry of this period" benefited from these payments:

Table 1 Major military bonuses, 69 to 29 BC

Year	Amount (denars)	Recipients	Total (million denars)
69 BC	800	15,000	12
63 BC	950	15-20,000?	14-19
61 BC	1,500	40,000	60
49 BC	500	50,000	25
46 BC	5,000	50,000	250
43 BC	500	25,000	12.5
	500	25,000	12.5
	500	25,000	10
	2,500	40,000	100

---

[7] Appian, *Civil War* 5.12-16.

[8] Scheidel 2007:330-332. Especially striking are the peak distributions in 61 (Pompey's victory over Mithridates and the pirates, and the resulting reparations and booty), 46 (Caesar's victory in North Africa over Metellus Scipio), 43 and 42 (payments to troops by the generals buying military support in the turmoil after Caesar's assassination), and finally by Augustus to restore peace (and pacify Rome's restless troops) after defeating his rivals.

42 BC	1,000	20-30,000	20-30
	5,000	80,000	400
36 BC	500	<150,000>	<75>
30 BC	250	(50,000+)	(12.5+)
29 BC	1,000	120,000	120
Total		c. 400,000?	c. 1,100

But civil warfare and foreign conquest, along with major military bonuses, basically came to an end as the new "stable monarchical regime obviated the needed for competitive military spending. ... Domestic peace, overseas colonization, and gradual demilitarization deprived the imperial heartland of further profits."

Augustus's empire and tax remission

Octavian "proclaimed peace and good-will, remitted the unpaid taxes, and released the farmers of the revenue and the holders of public leases from what they owed."[9] That wiped out the fiscal arrears that had accumulated prior to Rome's civil war.

Amnesties of unpaid taxes and other debts by new rulers have occurred throughout history. Roman emperors after Octavian typically "began their reigns with gestures of generosity or at some early point tried to establish themselves in the public mind as open-handed, by lowering the rate of some given levy, as Tiberius halved the one per cent auction tax and Gaius abolished it in Italy. ... Claudius, too, though at the end of his reign, granted five years' relief to bankrupt Byzantium, and Nero declared all of Greece free of tribute."[10]

But these tax remissions did not apply to debts owed to private creditors. The epoch of populist debt revolts and agitation for pro-debtor reforms was over. Partly this was because less lending was occurring. Debtors had already lost their land, and the supply of credit shrank as the rising imperial tax burden left little revenue either to lend or repay loans.

---

[9] Appian, *Civil War* 5.130. See the discussion in Frank 1940:13, 23 and 28-29, pointing out that in addition to using the treasures that poured in from Egypt after 28 and from other provinces to support Roman make-work employment programs, Augustus "annulled all the State claims – that is to say, not merely the arrears of taxation, but the private claims of knights proscribed in 43, which had been confiscated by the State."

[10] MacMullen 1987:737, citing Tacitus, *Annals* 12.62-63. The challenge, he adds, was to remain popular while taxing enough to maintain the empire as new conquests ended and the flow of booty dried up.

Octavian was given the titles augustus and princeps at the beginning of the year 27 BC, four years after consolidating power in the wake of his victory over Antony. He ruled for 41 years, and the empire that he bequeathed to Tiberius and subsequent successors through Marcus Aurelius (who died in AD 180) has long been celebrated for consolidating its control over a vast area extending from the North African coast up through Spain and Gaul to Britain, and across to the Black Sea downward to Syria and Asia Minor, encompassing a population of 50 to 60 million (a fifth to a sixth of the world's total at that time) and lasting for four centuries.[11]

But this period also saw the Roman core hollowed out, in much the same way as had occurred during the Republic. As Rostovtzeff put matters, nobody asked "whether it was worthwhile to save the Roman Empire in order to make it a vast prison for scores of millions of men."[12] Looking at the economic structures at work, Ernst Badian asked: "If the Roman empire had broken up before 31 BC, what historian would have shed a tear for it?"[13] It might have broken up in the way that Alexander's empire fractured among competing generals, ultimately to be absorbed by other empires.

The aftermath of the Republic saw the distribution of land, money, credit and wealth continue to polarize during the five centuries from Augustus to the deposition of the last nominal emperor, Romulus Augustus, in 476. Rome's ultimate dissolution was the outcome of the debt burden and growing proto-feudal latifundia estates, but most attention has focused on – and indeed, celebrated – how the Empire extended its reach even as it dissolved, integrating Europe into a single Christian culture.

Tiberius's mortgage relief, AD 33

The fiscal surpluses hoarded by Tiberius (who ruled from AD 14 to 37) drained money from the rest of the economy, filling his treasury with 2.7 billion sesterces as he cut back public spending. Suetonius (ca. 49-122) wrote that he "seldom gave discharges to the veteran soldiers. ... Nor did he ever relieve the provinces by any act of generosity, excepting Asia,

---

[11] Hopkins 1978:1.

[12] Rostovtzeff 1926:478.

[13] Badian 1972:92.

where some cities had been destroyed by an earthquake."[14] Fiscal austerity had slowed the issue of new Roman coinage since 10 BC under Augustus, while spending on luxuries by the wealthy was sending gold and silver eastward.[15]

By AD 33 the shortage of credit was aggravated by what seems to have been a revival of the anti-usury laws attributed to Caesar discussed in Chapter 19. The only references to these supposedly earlier laws are what Tacitus and Suetonius reported in their descriptions of what Tiberius did. Tacitus wrote that Caesar revived two earlier Roman laws that had long been ignored: one capping the annual rate of interest (which Tacitus believed was 10 percent, not 12 percent), and the other requiring property owners to hold two-thirds of their total estate in Italy.

What occurred under Tiberius was a shortage of credit similar to that which occurred after Caesar had returned to Rome. Once again, creditors called in their loans, causing land prices to crash as indebted landholders had to sell land to pay. To bail out landholders who had bought property on credit, "Tiberius put together a state-backed rescue package of loans via the Roman banking system to stabilize the price of land, restore credit and ensure that the fortunes of heavily leveraged elites remained mostly intact."[16] Blaming the usurers, Tacitus described the mortgage relief program announced by Tiberius:

> A powerful host of accusers fell with sudden fury on the class which systematically increased its wealth by usury in defiance of a law passed by Caesar the Dictator ... a law long obsolete because the public good is sacrificed to private interest. ... The senators, not one of whom was free from similar guilt, threw themselves on the emperor's indulgence. He yielded,

---

[14] Suetonius, *Tiberius* 48-49, adding that Tiberius obtained money by confiscating the estates of prominent individuals "in Gaul, Spain, Syria and Greece upon such despicably trifling and shameless pretenses, that against some of them no other charge was preferred but that they held large sums of ready money as part of their property. Old immunities, the rights of mining and of levying tolls, were taken from several cities and private persons. And Vonones, king of the Parthians, who had been driven out of his dominions by his own subjects, and fled to Antioch with a vast treasure, claiming the protection of the Roman people, his allies, was treacherously robbed of all his money, and afterwards murdered." Suetonius granted that "when some large houses being burnt down upon Mount Coelius, he indemnified the owners," but these probably were members of Rome's own aristocratic elite.

[15] Frank 1940:32.

[16] Elliott 2015:268 and 272, adding that the original purpose of Caesar's debt laws "are likely to remain forever veiled."

and a year and six months were granted, within which everyone was to settle his private accounts conformably to the requirements of the law.

Hence followed a scarcity of money ... being locked up in the imperial treasury or the public exchequer. To meet this, the Senate had directed that every creditor should have two-thirds of his capital secured on estates in Italy. Creditors however were suing for payment in full ... the usurers had hoarded up all their money for buying land. ... many were utterly ruined. The destruction of private wealth precipitated the fall of rank and reputation, till at last the emperor interposed his aid by distributing throughout the banks a hundred million sesterces, and allowing freedom to borrow without interest for three years, provided the borrower gave security to the State in land to double the amount.[17]

Tiberius's treasury lent cash-poor aristocrats and other indebted land-lords 100 million sesterces (about 3 percent of its holdings) to pay their creditors within three years, in a market where the wealthy were told to invest two-thirds of their assets in Italian land, thus bidding up its price and letting indebted landlords sell out and avoid bankruptcy.[18]

Aiding indebted landowners in this way did not help the landless poor or other rural and urban debtors. The effect of promoting these buyouts was to accelerate the spread of latifundia owned by the richest families. Colin Elliott emphasizes that neither Tiberius "nor the land-holders who benefitted from the rescue package much cared about its financial or economic impact" in terms of an expansionist Keynesian-style fiscal policy based on "an abstraction ('the economy')."[19] The main concern of Tiberius – and of subsequent Roman emperors bailing out indebted elites – was to protect their wealth and status, not that of the citizenry at large. "When a great family lost its money and was threatened with exclu-sion," Seneca wrote, Tiberius "ordered them all to explain to the Senate why they were in debt, and under this condition he granted them specific sums," sometimes paying the family's debts out of his own funds.[20]

Rome's subsequent emperors cancelled tax debts mainly to relieve local officials and elites, who had become the main debtors to the treasury. "The resistance of the rich to the tax-collector had become so

---

[17] Tacitus, *Annals* 6.16-17. Suetonius, *Tiberius* 48 gives a similar narrative, citing this as one of the few generous acts of Tiberius.

[18] Suetonius, *Tiberius* 48, in Lewis and Reinhold 1951:209-210.

[19] Elliott 2015 274-278, citing Crawford 1970 for earlier making this point.

[20] Veyne 1990:358, citing Seneca, *De Beneficiis* 2.7-8. Such actions and tax abate-ments were a royal *liberalitas*. Seneca's view of Tiberius was more sympathetic than that of Suetonius.

"endemic in the later empire," notes *The Cambridge Ancient History*, that "In Gaul Julian [emperor 331-363] refused to declare a tax amnesty for late payment because, he said, 'As is well known, it is the poor who are forced to pay in full without any relaxation at the beginning of an indiction.'"[21]

Rome's tax squeeze aggravates land concentration

Augustus stripped the Senate of effective power and reduced its members to a state of dependency on himself. By starting what became a state bureaucracy to collect tribute and taxes directly, he ended the privilege of Senate leaders to enrich themselves by collecting this revenue. The Senate's designated governors and *publicani* were replaced by civic officials who became equally rapacious, often "more to be feared than the barbarians" from the 4th century onward.[22] The imperial leadership taxed most of the economy's surplus and spent it mainly on paying troops and mercenaries (and also on the grain dole).

This administrative shift had begun already with Caesar, who "helped the cities of Asia by abolishing the farming of the basic tax ... the cities no doubt paid less, and paid it to Caesar's agents without the help of *publicani*."[23] The tax-collecting companies finally disappeared by the 3rd century AD, as did the major banking families. "Financial phenomena linked with the aristocracy disappear from view," Andreau finds. "The number of bankers known from inscriptions decreases sharply. Not one is attested after the first century AD outside Rome and the major ports (Ostia, Portus, and Aquileia)."[24]

The largest debts took the form of tax arrears, which mounted up beyond the ability of many localities to pay as emperors raised taxes to cope with the declining inflow of military booty and tribute. But there are few records to measure indebtedness from the 3rd century onward, largely because debts and arrears mounted up without lending taking place.

The source of credit and the character of debtors shifted after the 2nd

---

[21] Whittaker and Garnsey 1998:198-199. The authors add that "the law codes prove that the system was further manipulated by the *principales* within the decurion class to bring bankruptcy to their lesser colleagues." Julian tried to clean up and reduce the centralized Roman administrative bureaucracy that enforced this system.

[22] MacMullen 1987:752.

[23] Badian 1968:116-117.

[24] Andreau 1999:136-137. He notes (p. 194): "In the Athenian classical period, [the slave banker] Pasion possessed one of the largest fortunes in the city. That was not the case with the Italian bankers of the period of Augustus."

century. "Banking in the traditional sense declined," notes Arietta Papaconstantinou, but small-scale credit by landlords and rural moneylenders continued. The paucity of documentation has led this rural credit
to be largely ignored, and is one reason why historians of this period
have focused on the tax burden, which certainly was the major cause of
indebtedness and forfeiture of land. Most studies of professional bankers
and money have had little to say about "practices of individuals related
to credit ... Contrary to the image given by literary texts, which are
essentially urban and mention primarily the large financial operations of
big merchants, landowners or high officials, papyri unsurprisingly show
that rural society and the entire agricultural system were also largely
dependent on credit."[25] The most significant outcome "was the transfer
of land ... as the result of unpaid debts ... from the rural smallholder to
the large urban landowner."[26]

Debt and land-transfer records were on paper, and the records of tax
arrears to the *aerarium* (the central repository of public state money) and
fiscus (the emperor's own personal treasury, established by Augustus)
often were burned in times of distress. After Augustus's reign "the data
on which to base an estimate of the yield of taxes direct and indirect, of
inheritances, and of rents from crown lands, recede beyond our reach,"
summaries MacMullen.[27] But the overall picture is clear. The Empire
was impoverished by taxes, which the wealthiest landowners shifted
onto smallholders and local families, who had little land to pledge as collateral for money loans. The Late Roman Empire's colonate saw smallholders fall prey to large landowners as clients, ultimately to be reduced
to serfdom. Most debts were not the result of money loans, but took the
form of short-term balances owed by sharecroppers and smallholders for
unpaid taxes and cultivation costs incurred during the crop year. Often
the landlord billed the tenant-debtor for the tax levy, which he himself
may not have actually paid. Pliny the Younger (AD 61-113) described
how arrears mounted up from these levies despite large reductions of
rent. That led to deepening clientage that left tenants with little incentive even to try to extricate themselves from hopeless debt.

---

[25] Papaconstantinou 2016:614 and 618, noting that debt acknowledgements rarely
"mention the reason for which loans were made, or use vague expressions such as 'in
my time of need,' or 'when the need arose.'"

[26] Papaconstantinou 2016:637.

[27] MacMullen 1976:102; see also 1974:49 emphasizing the lack of economic records
in the 1ˢᵗ and 2ⁿᵈ centuries AD, a point raised already by Rostovtzeff 1926:145.

> Several tenants no longer have any concern to reduce a debt which they despair of being able to pay off; they even seize and consume whatever is produced, acting like people who think they no longer have to be thrifty since it is not their own property. The growing evils, therefore, have to be faced and relieved. There is one method of remedying them – to lease not for a rent in money but on shares, and then to place some of my men to superintend the work and guard the produce.[28]

Economic dependency was aggravated as over-cropping led to soil erosion, especially on small holdings in Italy's rural economy.[29] Finley cites the concern of Pliny the Elder (AD 23-79, uncle of Pliny the Younger) about "how far a ten-iugerum [six-acre] holder could resist breaching the traditional alternating fallow system, regardless of the deleterious consequence to the fertility of his land."[30]

Many latifundists divided their estates into parcels and leased them "to the growing class of free tenant farmers (*coloni*), often ex-slaves. ... Gradually formalized by imperial legislation, this institution, called the colonate, contained the seeds of manorial serfdom and was one of the most significant heritages of the Roman world to feudal times."[31]

Pliny the Younger described this dynamic in a letter mentioning an estate he intended to buy: "The previous owner quite often sold off the tenants' pledges for their debts; and while he reduced the debt of the tenants (*coloni*) for a time, he depleted their resources for the future, on account of the loss of which they began to run up their debts again." Unable to work their way out of debts to their landlord, tenants could not acquire viable farms of their own. Smallholders who still owned their land faced the usual "pressures pushing them toward dependence on richer, more powerful neighbors: the need for loans, for protection and for temporary jobs to supplement their income" in the face of imperial demands for taxes and creditor demands for their labor service.[32]

Families "unable to meet the demands for tribute abandoned their homes and fields, or were thrown into jail, or sold their children into

---

[28] Pliny the Younger, *Letters*, Book 9, #37 (abridged), in Lewis and Reinhold 1951 II:166. On arrears see also #36 to Calvisius Rufus, and #61 to Priscus, available at https://www.gutenberg.org/files/2811/2811-h/2811-h.htm#link2H_4_0010.

[29] Frank 1940:363-366.

[30] Finley 1973:105, citing Pliny the Elder, *Natural History* 18.

[31] Lewis and Reinhold 1951 II:166.

[32] Garnsey and Saller 1987:112, citing Pliny the Younger, *Letters* 3.19.6. However, notes Andreau 1999:53, we have no recorded details of rural or urban usury on this small scale.

slavery."[33] The alternative to such loss of liberty was to leave their land
and migrate to Rome, to be fed by the grain dole supplied by Egypt and
further west in North Africa. "In the long run," writes Papaconstantinou
of this period's land tenure,

> the rural credit economy, and especially the integration within it of
> goods, property, labour and services, could not but result in the slow
> dispossession of the economically weak, as they would very naturally use
> every unit of exchange they could possibly employ in order to obtain the
> necessary cash to remain within the system. Borrowing for labour was
> the last resort. Technically, of course, the line between paid labour and
> labour owed as repayment for a loan is very fine indeed.[34]

The emperors thus reduced their subjects to the same state of dependency that had occurred in Republican Rome, and the imperial periphery was much as Caesar had described:

> Throughout all Gaul there are two orders of those men who are of any
> rank and dignity: but the *plebs* is held almost in the condition of slaves,
> and dares to undertake nothing of itself, and is admitted to no deliber-
> ation. Most of them, when they are pressed either by debt, or the large
> amount of their tributes, or the oppression of the more powerful, give
> themselves up in vassalage to the nobles, who possess over them
> the same rights without exception as masters over their slaves.[35]

The fiscal amnesties of Hadrian and Marcus Aurelius

Hadrian (117-138) and Marcus Aurelius (161-180) were sufficiently
pragmatic to proclaim tax remissions: Hadrian near the start of his
reign in 118, and Marcus near the end of his rule in 178. Hadrian's act
after becoming emperor in 117 followed what had become the usual
practice of emperors giving a donative to their soldiers to hold their
loyalty. Hadrian had to cope with rumors that Trajan (his cousin)
had not named him as his heir, and also had to put down a plot on his

---

[33] MacMullen 1976:101. Elsewhere (1974:9) he notes the reports of much bullying
of the weak: beatings, maulings, and even murder, as well as robbery, theft and
general intimidation.

[34] Papaconstantinou 2016:639, focusing on conditions in Egypt. He elaborates (p.
618): "The most common loans in rural Egypt were short-term loans for the acquisition of seed at sowing time, or for other forms of agricultural investment. Those were
generally repayable at harvest, in money, produce, labour, or various combinations
of the three. Money was also very commonly borrowed for the payment of taxes."

[35] Caesar, *Gallic Wars* 6.13.

life aiming to prevent his accession. To gain the support of his other subjects, Tacitus reports, "Hadrian cancelled a countless sum of money owed to the fisc by private debtors in Rome and Italy, and also vast sums of arrears in the provinces, and he burned the records of indebtedness in the Forum of the deified Trajan in order to strengthen the general sense of security."[36]

An inscription reports that Hadrian was "the first of all *principes* and the only one who, by remitting 900 million sestertii owed to the fiscus, provided security not merely for his present citizens but also for their descendants by this generosity."[37] This event was commemorated in a *sestertius* coin depicting a lictor setting a torch to publicly burn the treasury's debt records.[38]

The major beneficiaries of this debt amnesty were local tax officials and public contractors who had failed to meet the fiscal guarantees they had promised for regions where it was their responsibility to collect

---

[36] Tacitus, *Annals* 12.63.5-7. Cassius Dio, *Roman History* 71.32.2 gives a similar report, forming the basis for *Historia Augusta, Life of Hadrian* 6-8. Said to have been compiled early in the 4th century, it repeats that "Hadrian then made a donation of six gold *aurei* to all Roman citizens on top of the three *aurei* that had already been given while the emperor was away. Further measures included a reform of a law assigning the property of condemned people to the public treasury (*aerarium publicum*) in lieu of the emperor's treasury (*fiscus privatus*) (HA Hadr. 18.7)."

[37] *Inscriptiones Latinae Selectae* (ed. Hermann Dessau, Berlin: 1892), ILS 309.

[38] On another coin, the reverse shows Hadrian on a platform, seated in his chair of state, while an official distributes money with the legend *liberalitas Aug* (imperial generosity) *in exergue.*

revenue. A marble relief found in the Roman Forum in 1872 depicts
Hadrian "seated on the Rostra giving the edict to burn the debt records
of the arrears of taxes owing by the provincials, or canceling the debts
due to the *fiscus* from individuals in Rome and Italy."[39]

Sixty years later, in 178, Marcus Aurelius repeated Hadrian's remission of tax arrears, extending back to the year 133. Cassius Dio reports
that Marcus

> remitted all debts owed by anyone to the emperor's private treasury or
> to the public treasury for a period of forty-five years, not including the
> fifteen years of Hadrian; and he ordered all the documents relating to
> these debts to be burned in the Forum. He also gave gifts of money to
> many cities, including Smyrna, which had suffered terrible destruction
> by an earthquake; and he assigned the task of rebuilding that city to a
> senator of praetorian rank.[40]

Such acts of liberality were necessary in the face of Rome's fiscal
demands. Constantine's Triumphal Arch in Rome, erected in 315,
shows him distributing money, probably from his triumphal procession.
But these tax amnesties were *ad hoc* proclamations. There is no record
of advocacy for a general debt cancellation, although occasional local
revolts broke out against local autocratic rule. No philosopher, scholar,
lawyer or politician suggested any rationale for debt writedowns or
reforms broadening land tenure to reduce economic polarization.

Reflecting the economy's polarization, most moneylending was to the
well-to-do, as few others had property left to borrow against. "Loans are
not made to people in need," Plutarch observed by the 2nd century AD,
"but to those who wish to acquire some superfluity for themselves." The
landholding elite were the major beneficiaries of imperial amnesties
for tax arrears, and that remained the case for the next few centuries.
A wealthy estate owner who was powerful enough to delay payment
might wait for Rome to remit back taxes, as it might do to avoid civil
unrest, for example. "Arrears piled up on the local account books till a
general amnesty started another round of his triumphant intransigence,"
describes MacMullen. "Summoned to court, he ignored the summons or
bought acquittal for himself or his dependents 'who call in the patron-

---

[39] Illustrated in Rostovtzeff 1926:314. For more illustrations and related discussion
see https://followinghadrian.com/2018/07/24/the-early-reforms-and-economic-poli-
cies-of-hadrian-hadrian1900/, depicting "a line of Praetorian Guards carrying up bundles
of records and throwing them on the heap to which a lictor is putting the torch."

[40] Cassius Dio, *Roman History* 72.32.

age of the mighty,' *potentiorum patrocinium*. Inside municipal administration, he saw to it that those weaker, that is, poorer than himself had
to shoulder the heavier burdens, despite a stream of laws and protests
from the emperors."[41] When the wealthy were powerful enough not to be
forced to pay, the tax squeeze was levied on artisans, service providers
and local officials.

From Diocletian (284-305) onward, smallholders were tied more
tightly to the land as *coloni*, locking in the concentration of land tenure
as a means of squeezing out a surplus to support imperial spending on
the army and the dole. With the less affluent population reduced to clientage, only the wealthy qualified for loans. To borrow, after all, a man
needed property to pledge – and if he had some, Plutarch advised, then
"he ought not to be borrowing." He blamed debtors for trying to live
in luxury beyond one's means, warning that "We enslave ourselves by
mortgages and notes."[42]

But the real economic slavery was suffered by the poor. Smallholders did not borrow money to spend on themselves. Their debts took
the form mainly of arrears for taxes and charges during the crop year.
Instead of giving them aid, emperors supported the landlords by forgiving them their own arrears, but did not annul what small debtors owed.
The effect thus was the opposite of that sought by the Republic's revolts
demanding debt cancellation, and of the amnesties that Near Eastern
rulers had proclaimed for millennia, cancelling debts owed by smallholders, mainly *to* the wealthy. Protection of debtors and their family
landholdings is what had made the earlier Near East more resilient than
Rome, whose emperors supported the oligarchy.

The Empire's deepening tensions and oppression

Even the Empire's 2nd-century "golden age" prosperity with its five
"good" emperors, Walbank has pointed out, had "serious popular discontent and sharpened contrasts. We read of class conflicts at Smyrna,
Rhodes and Sardis, of riots and arson in Prusa" in Asia Minor where

---

[41] MacMullen 1976:210-211, after pointing out (p. 209) that the small landholder
"was less and less often to be met with. In Egypt, taxation was to blame. He surrendered his property to somebody better able to make it pay, enrolling himself
as a tenant." In sum: "The ability of the large landholder to rise above the times
he owed in part to his self-sufficiency. ... Moreover, he served as government to
himself, judging, preaching to, imprisoning, or exploiting his dependents as if he
constituted the Dominate in miniature."

[42] Plutarch, *Moralia* 827D (Loeb Classical Library, 1936 X:317 and 320).

Goths already were invading. These "good emperors" merely "limited
the task of the State to that of 'night watchman' for the business-man."[43]
Economic dependency became a road to serfdom after Marcus Aurelius's son Commodus was assassinated in 192. Five emperors emerged
from the army in just one year. A Phoenician general, Severus (193-211),
seized power by executing senators who opposed him. Acting on the
same principle that Augustus and his fellow Triumvirate members had
followed, Severus is said to have advised his sons: "Enrich the soldiers,
scorn all others."

Severus established a dynasty that put the nobility "out of the way.
... The emperor now ruled by means of his army; presently the armies
would rule through their appointees on the throne, and since there were
several armies – each eager for the donative that always followed the
enthronement of a favorite – a season of civil wars was inevitable."[44]
Contrary to what Herodotus wrote about kingship providing stability,
Rome's imperial monarchy was headed by generals vying for control,
leading troops loyal to themselves as employers.

Reversing the situation that had existed in antiquity when absentee
landlords lived in their townhouses off rents from the rural agricultural
economy, the Late Roman landowning families largely stood aside,
wanting simply to be left in peace on their own estates to collect rents
from their estates and the urban land they owned, while avoiding taking
responsibility for city political life as *curiales*. Local populations thus
were drained both by the imperial tax authorities and by the aristocracy
of country estate owners consolidating their power over dependent labor
and renters.[45]

"No Augustan golden age followed," Rostovtzeff concluded a century
ago. Industry did not flourish, because prices were set "ruinously low for
the artisans," and in any case "customers were few, the market became
more and more restricted, and the state more and more oppressive.
Apart from the production of some standardized articles for the masses
and some luxuries for the few rich, industry lived on the orders of the
state." [46]

---

[43] Walbank 1969:101, 61-62 and 64, and 23.

[44] Frank 1940:90.

[45] Walbank 1969:123.

[46] Rostovtzeff 1926:469 and 471.

Monetary and debt strains in the Late Roman Empire

During the Republic and the first two centuries under the emperors, the traditional source of silver and gold for Roman coinage was tribute, loot and taxes extracted from the territories that Rome conquered. But war booty and tribute diminished after the Empire reached its limit by the time of Trajan's death in 117. There was less and less bullion to pay the troops and for the grain dole – the *Cura Annonae* to feed about 200,000 Roman poor. Rome's response was to increase the domestic tax burden and to adulterate the coinage.

By the 3rd century, money was flowing out of the Empire to hire mercenaries and pay foreign tribes not to invade, and to buy luxuries from the East. The wealthiest families lived off their landed estates, especially in North Africa and southern Italy, regions providing grain to Rome. Shipping the grain from North Africa for the Roman dole was the only commerce that the government conducted directly. Most trade was conducted by Near Easterners, and consisted largely of luxury imports paid for by the reserves of silver and gold that the wealthy had accumulated during the centuries of conquest. "By the lowest reckoning," wrote Pliny, "India, China and the Arabian Peninsula take from our empire 100 million sesterces every year – that is the sum which our luxuries and our women cost us."[47]

Rome's trade deficit and fiscal gap forced it to debase its silver coinage, starting in Nero's reign (54-68) when the silver *denarius* was reduced by about 20 percent. By the 190s about half the silver content of Roman coinage had disappeared, and by the 260s the *denarius* contained barely detectable amounts of silver. This depreciation of the coinage led prices to jump tenfold in the 270s. Diocletian issued a Price Edict in 301 collecting many taxes and rents in kind and setting maximum prices for basic commodities that the government needed to buy, but this squeezed producers whose input costs were soaring. That disrupted market production further, leading to "a succession of abrupt cuts in the weight of base-metal coins, right through into the 320s."[48]

---

[47] Pliny the Elder, *Natural History* 12.41 (English translation. Parker 2002:73). In Book 6 he estimates that about half the eastward flow of Roman silver and gold coins was to India.

[48] Elliott 2020:79-82 and MacMullen 1976:108-115. Elliott attributes the monetary collapse to "the plague in the 250s, the abduction and murder of the emperor Valerian in 260, the fragmentation of the empire into separatist states, numerous foreign incursions and invasions and domestic brigandage," capped by mutinies by the army seeking higher pay from whatever generals promised them the most.

Diocletian's price controls were a purely fiscal measure, not a policy of forward planning to increase productive enterprise. The currency depreciation and resulting price inflation caused moneylending to largely dry up as claims for payment quickly lost their purchasing power. Large estates able to accumulate rent, profit and other revenue did not become financial centers, but hoarded gold and silver as commodities and stores of (rising) exchange value, or bought more land. Egyptian records show that "loans of money are made for shorter terms in the third century and still more markedly so in the fourth, when house leases grow shorter, too, and land leases begin to stipulate payment in advance."[49]

In the closing years of the Late Roman Empire just before Constantine's imperial reign, Diocletian (284-305) prohibited the nobility from serving in the imperial army. His objective was to break Rome's historical domination of the army by the wealthy landowning oligarchy. The ban boosted the power of the generals and led to the increased hiring of mercenaries.

At the imperial level, generals paid Germanic and other mercenaries to fight against other generals. The "barbarians" ended up more as recipients of Roman money than as tributaries. But the hiring of mercenaries stopped when there were no more conquerable lands from which the Empire could extract tribute as a paying proposition. Rome moved its administrative core north, to Milan and to Trier near the Rhine to administer the Western Empire from Gaul to Britain, while Constantinople became the basis for the Byzantine Empire. All these regions experienced a dissolution into manors that survived by becoming self-sufficient. As economic polarization widened between the wealthy few and their subjects, families ran away, or welcomed the Vandals and other "barbarians" moving south to Rome and North Africa in the 5th century.

---

[49] MacMullen 1976:118. He adds that "it seems likely that the small creditor class and urban professional (a teacher, for instance), but neither the peasant nor the magnate, suffered as the result of inflation."

Part III

Epilogue

If their enemy have wealth, they have greed; if he be poor, they are ambitious. ... To plunder, butcher, steal – these things they misname empire.
> – Tacitus, *Agricola* 30, citing the words of Calgacus of Scotland, ca. AD 83.

The Persians regard lying as the second among wrongdoings, and being in debt as the first.[1]
> – Herodotus, *The Histories* I.138.

In a country well governed, poverty is something to be ashamed of. In a country badly governed, wealth is something to be ashamed of.
> – Confucius.

By the 5th century Rome's Empire had become a shell. Its administrative capitals had shifted northward, beyond Milan to Trier and Constantinople. In the wake of rival Roman generals hiring Germanic tribes as mercenaries to carve out their own lands, the Vandals took the opportunity to conquer Rome and North Africa.

"Barbarians" always had been at the gates. What changed the balance of power was the degree to which Rome had been weakened from within by creditors monopolizing the land and reducing debtors to a state of abject dependency. The closing books of the New Testament described the early centuries of the Roman Empire as an End Time, but Christianity's denunciations of the hubristic arrogance of wealth ended after Constantine made it Rome's state religion in 321. The maldistribution of land, money and other wealth was accepted as the natural social order.

Even as recent scholarship has reinforced understanding of how Roman oligarchic wealth broke "free" of public oversight and ended up

---

[1] In other words, moneylending forces debtors to lie to avoid payment, while creditors habitually lie and cheat.

destroying liberty, today's neoliberal philosophy idealizes a free market as one that provides liberty mainly to the wealthy to act as they wish in their own self-interest as their transactions dominate "the market." Public regulation to restrain their self-seeking is deemed to "distort" this market by adding to "transaction costs." Such regulation is denounced as "socialism," much as Roman oligarchs denounced populist-reformers as "seeking kingship."

Projecting this modern economic ideology back to Rome, the neoliberal ideal of minimizing transactions costs meant abolishing all restraints on oligarchic land grabbing and the expropriation of the property of debtors. There was a real cost, of course, in the form of serfdom and imperial collapse. To neoliberals, these costly results are "externalities," irrelevant to their market models, which pretend that economic welfare will be maximized by individuals acting in their own self-interest. But in antiquity, Stoic and then Christian ethics were influential enough that not even the Roman oligarchy went as far as modern free marketers in idealizing selfishness as a positive force of economic efficiency. As Christianity became the Roman State religion accepted by its economic elites, its moral focus shifted away from economic selfishness to personal egotism and the healing redemption of making bequests of one's economic gains to the Church. As Augustine put matters: "Get rid of pride and wealth will do no harm."[2]

---

[2] Augustine, Sermon 37.4, Kessler, *Reichtumskritik*, p. 399, cited in Brown 2005:24.

21
Rome's End Time Leads the Church to Ban Usury, 4th Century AD

A century ago Michael Rostovtzeff blamed Rome's decline on allegedly anti-oligarchic levelling policies destroying what he and others called "the middle class," a fuzzy category including subsistence landholders, craftsmen and public officials trying simply to survive. But the Empire's polarizing economy had no real equivalent to a modern-style middle class.[1] Rostovtzeff treated the oligarchy as a victim being squeezed by imperial tax collectors. But Plato wrote that "an oligarchy becomes 'two cities,' Rich and Poor, as great wealth is opposed to extreme poverty for the masses, and almost everyone outside the ruling class is a pauper."[2] Rome's oligarchy thus was a perpetrator, not a victim, especially as many wealthy estates were politically strong enough to avoid taxes while squeezing free self-supporting families, turning them into clients, bondservants and ultimately serfs.

The emperors actually focused their tax levies on civic and temple reserves, because these were the easiest to grab. What was deranged was public and social infrastructure, and Rostovtzeff himself quoted the 3rd-century historian Herodian's description of how Maximinus (235-238),

> after reducing most of the distinguished houses to penury, found that the spoils were few and paltry and by no means sufficient for his purposes, he attacked public property. All the money belonging to the

---

[1] Rostovtzeff 1926:487 and 472. MacMullen 1974:89 criticizes Herbert Hill's 1952 book on the *equites*, *The Roman Middle Class in the Republican Period* (Oxford), on the ground that what Hill called Rome's middle class was less than 0.1 percent of the population. "Senators had to have property worth 250,000 times the day's wage of a laborer; *equites* qualified for their rank by less than half of that estate." MacMullen added: "The absurdity of the title points to the difficulty experienced by our modern selves in coming to grips with a world utterly different from our own. We should guard against a blind insistence that there *must* be a middle class and that it must be sought where we are used to finding it today."

[2] Ste. Croix 1981:286-287, citing Aristotle, *Politics* 3.3 at 1276b 3-4, and Plato, *Republic* 8 at 551d and 552b-d.

cities that was collected for the victualling of the populace or for distribution among them, or was devoted to theaters or to religious festivals,
he diverted to his own use; and the votive offerings set up in the temples,
the statues of the gods, the tributes to heroes, all the adornments of the
public buildings, everything that served to beautify the cities, even the
metal out of which money could be coined, all were melted down.[3]

This looting was hardly a new phenomenon. Cleopatra had financed
her struggle against Rome in 20 BC by confiscating Egypt's hierarchic
lands and wealth that the temples had accumulated.[4] Roman emperors
raised funds by selling off public land that had not already been taken.
Most sales were to the wealthy.

The Empire's monetary depreciation and resulting price inflation
reduced the value of tax revenue based on fixed monetary levies, and
also the value of rental income for leases held by cities and temples. This
shrank funding for civic philanthropy, and by the end of the 3rd century
the temples had exhausted their resources on emergency charity.[5] In
Asia Minor, new construction was limited to walls to protect against
robbers.[6]

Rostovtzeff wrote a classic melodramatic description of how the fiscal
burden was shifted onto local officials held responsible for meeting the
emperor's tax quotas. After the reforms of Diocletian (co-emperor from
286 to 305), "the only possible advance was to the position of a *curialis*,
which in fact was a move downwards."

> The *curiales* (those who were eligible for the municipal council and the
> magistracies) formed a group of richer citizens (with a minimal census
> of 25 iugera of land) responsible to the state ... both for the welfare,
> peace, and order of the city and for the fulfilment by the population of
> all its obligations towards the state. Like the tillers of the soil, each of the
> *curiales* personally formed a single unit for purposes of taxation, and the
> whole of the *curiales* formed one large unit, representing the amount of

---

[3] Herodian, *History of the Roman Empire from the Death of Marcus Aurelius* 7.3:3-6,
translated by Rostovtzeff 1926:399-400. See Broughton 1938:911.

[4] Johnson 1936:146 and 639.

[5] Jones 1974:139 notes: "The main losers by the inflation were charitable trust
funds, such as the *alimenta* and many civic endowments invested in mortgages
and fixed rent charges. The other important loser was the imperial government ...
The state was thus forced back onto an economy in kind, paying its soldiers and
civil servants mainly in food and clothing, and making levies in kind to supply its
needs."

[6] Broughton 1938:912.

tax and of compulsory work demanded from the population of the city. ... Their responsibility was not only material but personal. Thus they had strictly to observe the rule of *origo*, to remain in their city and not seek to escape to another place of residence, and in dying they had to substitute for themselves another taxable and responsible unit in the person of their children.[7]

Max Weber called this an "authoritarian liturgical state," treating its subjects "as purely fiscal units,"[8] owing labor services via the corvée and being victimized by local power relationships. To gain income was to make oneself a target of the fiscal authorities or other predators. As Rostovtzeff described the situation:

> If a peasant succeeded in improving his land and adding to it, he knew that his fate was to be promoted to the position of a *curialis*, which meant slavery, oppression, and in the last resort ruin. Better to produce enough to support his family and not make useless efforts to better his position. ... The tenant of a large landowner was content to perform his duties and to enjoy the protection, and the oppression, of his master. The fate of his neighbor, the free peasant, was not attractive enough to induce him to strive to become one. ... Thus the reigning mood was resignation, and resignation never leads to prosperity.[9]

MacMullen, by contrast, describes wealthy families and local officials as "a sort of Mafia type ... exuberantly formidable, brutal, and threatening," in cahoots

> to "shake down" the defenseless without excuse or in the name of tax collection. A farmer after a bad year of illness or crop destruction by animals, or after the bursting of his irrigation ditches in a spring flood, borrows at usurious rates, and he and his family are soon obliged to sell out and become tenants or sharecroppers. A bailiff is now their master since, more often than not, the new owner himself lives in the city. A villager who 'makes it' aspires to a life of urban idleness, and emigrates; the city man with money to invest buys into one of the villages nearby, comes to own it entire, or owns pieces of property in a number of villages.[10]

---

[7] Rostovtzeff 1926:468 and 472.

[8] Weber 1909.

[9] Rostovtzeff 1926:470.

[10] MacMullen 1974:12 and 15. Such experience is well documented from Byzantium (Hudson 2018).

Even for moderate landholders, Frank summarizes, "real estate had come to be considered a dangerous possession, ready funds were being hidden or hoarded, money was scarce, and interest rates rose."[11] Commerce shrank except for the grain trade and luxuries, yet the senatorial class "built large and beautiful fortified villas in the country and dwelt there, surrounded by their family, their slaves, a real retinue of armed clients, and thousands of rural serfs and dependants."[12] These large plantations became self-sufficient and basically self-governing, with their owners leasing out the land of entire villages to renters who worked on their estates.

The colonate ossifies into feudalism

Keeping slaves in sexually segregated barracks made sense as long as landowners viewed "the cost of maintaining women and rearing children [as] a dead ballast on working capital."[13] But as the seizure of war captives declined, reducing their supply and thus raising their price, slavery (and its sexual segregation) gave way to sharecropping arrangements in which serflike workers, *coloni*, owed service on the land of their patrons.

The Theodosian Code, published in 438, is a compilation by Theodosius II and his co-emperor Valentinian III of Roman laws enacted since 312. Its first reference to serfs being bound to the soil is a ruling from 322. The Code of Justinian in 534 spelled out the legal, fiscal and debt obligations imposed on *coloni*, who were tied to their designated estates to prevent flight from the land. They could not be sold like slaves, but their labor obligations remained attached to the land if it were sold. The effect was to make *coloni* "remain for life as renters, that is, to accept *adscription* to the soil and become serfs. It was not long before the sons of serfs had to assume the same status, and serfdom because almost universal."[14]

Coloni were "not sturdy independent peasants of the old Italian type, but tenant-farmers, successors of the obsolescent slave class ... too poor to pay rent for their land or to buy their own implements and seed; these they obtained from the landlord and, as 'share-croppers,' repaid him in

---

[11] Frank 1940:18.

[12] Rostovtzeff 1926:475.

[13] Weber 1909.

[14] Frank 1940:217 and 302-303. See also Chapter 20 at fn31. Justinian was the Eastern Roman emperor from 527 to 565.

kind, and, in some provinces such as Africa, by services on his private land."[15] This tenant-farming system was known as the colonate.

A *colonus* was responsible for taxes levied on the land. That often obliged him to incur debt and become an *adscripticius*, obliged "to perform tasks on the estate (*ruralia obsequia*), till the land, or perform the work of a *colonus* ... under the *potestas* of the estate owner; he was prohibited from litigating against his estate owner."[16] However, the East Roman Empire blocked creditors from using debt to pry away the land of *coloni*, including *adscripticii* who were allowed to own their own land. To stabilize tax payments, "in 535 Justinian forbade money-lenders to take the land from their farmer debtors."[17] But landlords devised a legal loophole to sell a *colonus* by creating a tiny "land plot" that could be sold with the serf attached to it.

By the late 3rd century the combination of sharecropping obligations, debt service and taxes that fell mainly on the poor had led to a flight from the land.[18] Many fugitives found work as mercenaries or joined military brigades revolting against large landlords. The Empire's first major "peasant revolt" of this sort occurred in Gaul and Spain in the late 2nd century, gathering force under Maternus, a former Roman soldier who led a group of deserters from Commodus's army around 187. As his contemporary Herodian described:

> At first they attacked and plundered villages and farms, but when Maternus had amassed a sizable sum of money, he gathered an even larger band of cutthroats by offering the prospect of generous booty and a fair share of the loot. As a result, his men no longer appeared to be brigands but rather enemy troops.
>
> They now attacked the largest cities and released all the prisoners, no matter what the reasons for their imprisonment. By promising these men their freedom, he persuaded them to join his band in gratitude for favors received. The bandits roamed over all Gaul and Spain, attacking

---

[15] Walbank 1969:54 and 57.

[16] Sirks 2008:131-134 spells out the Justinian Code's details.

[17] Sirks 2008:130, noting that Justinian forbade this and ordered the return to debtors of lands on which creditors had foreclosed in the provinces of Thrace, Illyricum and Mysia Secunda.

[18] This reached such proportions that the Justinian Code stipulated that "any harborer of fugitives who uses them as if they were his own *coloni* ... must pay the taxes due by them: the rationale evidently was that whoever profits from them also must carry the burden" (Sirks 2008:132).

the largest cities; a few of these they burned, but the rest they abandoned after sacking them.[19]

Maternus and his troops marched on Rome around 190 in an attempt to seize the emperorship from Commodus, but his troops had little interest in fighting for his personal glory and beheaded him. Other rebel leaders emerged in various regions. E. A. Thompson has collected the scant Roman descriptions of such revolts, emphasizing that their leaders were more than brigands. They took over large areas and expropriated the landowners. Around 205-207, for instance, an Italian leader, Bulla, mobilized some 600 freedman and runaway slaves and plundered Italy. Apparently supported by local populations, he warned landlords "that if they would put a stop to brigandage, they must feed their slaves," who after all composed a large part of his own force.[20] Runaways from Gaul and Hispania joined such leaders as an alternative to serfdom. They must have had local support as they seized estates, and are reported to have enslaved some owners on their own land.[21]

The worst looters, of course, were the soldiers who grabbed the emperorship, plunging the next few centuries into almost constant military and fiscal crisis. Elaborating on the looting of Maximinus (235-238) noted above, Herodian described how the emperor confiscated the wealth of the rich to pay his soldiers, realizing that not doing so would run the risk of him being assassinated by his own troops.

> After Maximinus had impoverished most of the distinguished men and confiscated their estates, which he considered small and insignificant and not sufficient for his purposes, he turned to the public treasuries; all the funds which had been collected for the citizens' welfare or for gifts, all the funds being held in reserve for shows or festivals, he transferred to his own personal fortune. The offerings which belonged to the temples, the statues of the gods, the tokens of honor of the heroes, the decorations on public buildings, the adornments of the city, in short, any material suitable for making coins, he handed over to the mints.

---

[19] Herodian, *History* 1.10.1-2.

[20] Thompson 1952:14-15, citing Cassius Dio, *Roman History* 76.10, the sole source on Bulla.

[21] Thompson 1952:12, summarizing the little that was acknowledged in print about these revolts. Official reports rarely cite the logic of their opponents and of popular support. Drinkwater 1992 criticizes the idea of a "great revolt" with a common class-interest doctrine, and indeed Thompson notes the absence of a class-based reform program among the rebels and their leaders.

... Although no fighting was going on and no enemy was under arms anywhere, Rome appeared to be a city under siege. ... The soldiers too were disgusted with his activities, for their relatives and fellow citizens complained that Maximinus was acting solely for the benefit of the military.[22]

This imperial looting led to protests in the most prosperous provinces, and a revolt was organized to unseat him. Maximinus ended up being killed by his own soldiers while marching on Rome in 238. The ensuing tumultuous year saw six emperors seek power, a fight that has been cited as starting "the crisis of the 3ʳᵈ century."

The speed at which the Roman Empire's "Golden Age" turned into raw grabitization shows how hollow its polarized economy had become. With *coloni* tied to the land and hence not available for conscription, the Empire's generals from Gaul to the Danube hired Gauls, Germans and other mercenaries to fight against armies fielded by rival generals, also hiring them to carve out their own mini-kingdoms. The deaths caused by this infighting are said to have far exceeded those caused by barbarian invasions led by chieftains operating on their own.[23] The generals who were able to grab the Empire found that it was dissolving into parts. The barbarian leaders ultimately proved better able to organize the world they were taking over, winning support – or at least non-resistance – from local populations.

One of the few reported peasant revolts occurred in Gaul and Spain in 283, by rebels taking the name of Bacaudae. Their revolt extended into the 5ᵗʰ century. We first hear of them when the new Emperor Diocletian appointed Maximian as co-ruler in the West in 286 to put down their uprising. There were no slave revolts such as had occurred in Sicily in the late 2ⁿᵈ century BC, but slaves are reported to have joined debtors rebelling or defecting to invaders. When a Gothic army defeated that of Rome at Adrianople (now Edirne, at modern Türkiye's border with Bulgaria) in 378, local guides brought the victors "to the villas of great landowners, who were then plundered by a coalition of Gothic soldiers and local residents. When in 408 the Romano-Gothic military leader Alaric for the first time besieged the city of Rome [besieging it again in

---

[22] Herodian, *History* 7.3.5. Maximinus was called the Barracks Emperor, being the first to have come neither from the senatorial nor equestrian class. The dividing line between emperors and barbarians was becoming blurred.

[23] Kulikowski 2020.

409 and eventually sacking it in 410], his forces were swollen by many debtors who had left the imperial capital to join his army."[24]

Matters came to a head in the 5th century throughout the Empire, not merely at the hands of Alaric's Visigoths. Armoricans (a Celtic tribe in what is now modern Brittany) mounted a great revolt from 407 to 417. The Gallic Bacaudic leader Tibatto led a rebellion manned largely by slaves in 435-437 and again in 442, while Donatists and circumcellions were revolting in North Africa. The main source of information about the Bacaudae is Salvian (400-490; discussed in the next chapter), a Christian from Gaul educated at the Empire's northern capitol in Trier who described the milieu in which revolts were occurring in the 440s:

> Among all this the poor are laid waste, widows groan, orphans are trampled down, to such an extent that many of them, including those who are not of obscure birth and have had a liberal education, flee to the enemy, so that they should not die through the affliction of public persecution. They seek Roman humanity among the barbarians because they cannot bear barbaric inhumanity among the Romans.[25]

A recent dissertation notes that "the Bacaudae are known to have fostered good relations with barbarians; in Spain the Bacaudae in northern Tarraconensis fought against Rome alongside the Suevi, whilst in 448 Eudoxius, another Bacaudic leader, sought refuge from Attila."[26] Elaborating further on reasons for rebellion and flight to the barbarians, Salvian (5.34–35) describes the wealthy as preventing the poor from benefitting from remissions of unpaid tax and "depicts the independent peasantry as saddled with unbearable taxes which forced them to cede their property and freedom to wealthy patrons (who might, of course, be responsible for collecting those taxes), in order to escape the tax collector." Far and wide, he wrote,

> they migrate either to the Goths or the Bacaudae, or to other barbarians everywhere in power; yet they do not regret having migrated. They

---

[24] Weisweiler 2022.

[25] Salvian, *De gubernatione Dei* (*On the Government of God*) 5.21, quoted in Lambert 2013:265. Salvian was from Roman Gaul, attributing Rome's decline to punishment by God for its bad behavior. He described "small landowners who are unwilling to abandon their land and possessions [as having] no protection against the depredations of the tax-collectors except to put themselves under the 'protection' of a powerful landowner, thus losing both their property and their free status" (5.38–45, quoted in Lambert 2013:263).

[26] Burrows 2017:177.

prefer to live as freemen under an outward form of captivity than as captives under an appearance of liberty. Therefore, the name of Roman citizens, at one time not only greatly valued but dearly bought, is now repudiated and fled from, and it is almost considered not only base but deserving of abhorrence.[27]

A long cycle was being closed. Early Rome, apparently offering liberty and economic opportunity, had gained settlers and runaways, enabling it to grow and ultimately field an army that conquered the ancient world. But Rome now was driving its own population to run away. Their freedom had been lost, first through debt and loss of their land, and then by oppressive taxes, extracted as much by local officials as by what remained of the imperial Roman state. The social order that Rome's oligarchy had put in place was disintegrating as its polarizing debt, land tenure, tax structure and military infighting led to the revolts, invasions and migrations to the "barbarians" that ended the Empire.

The End Time of oppressive gain-seeking backed by Roman force

With its oppressive taxes to pay for the military subjugation of its subjects reduced to clientage and peonage, Rome's Empire was coming to be seen as the enforcer of hell on earth, with the oppressive greed and luxury of its landowning elite destroying any hope for social cohesion. Even many well-to-do were driven to Christianity, finding it express-ing an ethic similar to what had been Stoicism's ideal of moderation and mutual aid (at least among fellow aristocrats) as opposed to the wealth-grabbing, usury and military violence that Christians perceived as an End Time. For many of the poor and less wealthy, the slaves and *coloni*, the only alternative to rebelling or running away seemed to be withdrawal in one form or another – monastic isolation or even martyr-dom, which was becoming widespread as dying did not seem so awful under the then-existing oppression.

Much as kingship had been denounced under the Republic, Roman authorities persecuted Christianity not so much as a religion as a poten-tially revolutionary moral program opposed to Roman landlordship and

---

[27] Salvian, *De gubernatione Dei* 5:8, quoted in Burrows 2017:202 and 178. Burrows adds that Augustine's student Orosius (*History Against the Pagans* 7.41.7) "famously stated that many Romans preferred a poverty stricken *libertas* among the bar-barians to *tributaria solicitude* within Roman society." See Jones 1974:774-778 and Whittaker and Garnsey 1998:199-201 for similar statements by Ambrose (340-397, Bishop of Milan) and his contemporary Basil, Bishop of Caesarea in Asia Minor.

creditor power. The horror that Roman elites felt in the face of Christian
ideals was akin to how Latin American landowners felt about the Liberation Theology of the 1960s, or indeed how socialism is perceived today
as an existential threat to the neoliberal economics of financialization
and privatization.

Emperor Dacias (249-251) intensified the persecution of Christians
who refused to accept the primacy of Roman gods. Many became
martyrs by resisting. The persecution intensified under Valerian (253-
260), who issued a decree in 257 directing the Christian clergy to
perform sacrifices to the Roman gods or face banishment. The next
year he seized the property and ordered the execution of Christians who
refused allegiance to the Roman deities.

An important early Christian leader was Cyprian (210-258), a lawyer
from a wealthy Numidian Berber family who converted in 245 and
became Bishop of Carthage in 249. As the next chapter will describe,
the Numidian region of North Africa was flourishing by providing the
grain to feed Rome, while also being the most feudalized part of the
Empire. That combination made it a rising center of Christianity. When
Cyprian was brought before the Roman proconsul and told to sacrifice
to the Roman gods, he refused even when threatened with death. He
was decapitated by the sword as a warning to those who resisted Roman
authority.

In the face of life's economic and moral injustice, such persecution
hardened the tradition of martyrdom in Christians who saw their
Church as an island of purity and mutual aid in a society sinking into
the End Time. Matthew 5.10 had preached: "Blessed are those who
suffer persecution on account of justice." And Ephesians 6:11-23, written
by the Apostle Paul or a follower ca. AD 62, blamed Rome as responsible for the End Days: "Put on the whole armor of God, so that you
may be able to stand against the wiles of the devil. For our struggle is
... against the rulers, against the authorities, against the cosmic powers
of this present darkness, against spiritual forces of wickedness in the
heavenly places."

This ethic was expressed most poetically in the New Testament's
closing verses of Revelation, written toward the end of the emperorship of
Domitian (81-96). Verse 17 describes Rome as the Whore of Babylon, "the
great prostitute, who sits on many waters. With her the kings of the earth
committed adultery," becoming servants not only of Rome but of its drive
to amass land and riches in ways that impoverished their victims.

An angel explains the imagery of "the woman and of the beast she
rides." The woman "is the great city that rules over the kings of the

earth," and the beast has seven heads, corresponding to the seven hills of Rome and its seven kings. But the beast's day will soon end, and will bring its rider, the Roman-oriented elite "to ruin and leave her naked." Verse 18 forecasts that when the kings who "shared her luxury see the smoke of her burning, they will weep and mourn over her ... The merchants of the earth will weep and mourn over her because no one buys their cargoes any more – cargoes of gold, silver, precious stones and pearls, fine linen, purple silk and scarlet cloth" and other luxuries, along with the "bodies and souls of men."

"They will say, 'The fruit you longed for is gone from you. All your riches and splendor have vanished, never to be recovered.' The merchants who sold these things and gained their wealth from her ... will weep and mourn" for the loss of their Great City. A mighty angel will appear and overthrow it, chiding it with the words: "Your merchants were the world's great men. By your magic spell all the nations were led astray."

Gibbon's *Decline and Fall of the Roman Empire* put much of the blame for its decay on Christianity for its passivity and hopelessness. But Christianity's rejection of the self-indulgent Roman world was an understandable reaction against Rome's armed defense of its laws making debt and monopolization of land irreversible, and the oligarchic ethic claiming that this was the natural path to a successful economy. Christianity emerged from that world as a response to an oligarchic autocracy from which the only escape seemed to be withdrawal. It was not Christianity that provided a pall of passivity and fatalism over an otherwise dynamic Empire. Rather, it was the Empire's blind alley of wealth addiction and selfishness that caused this mood and led many Roman elites and finally Emperor Constantine to embrace Christianity, which they hoped might bring a redeeming ethic.

The Council of Nicaea prohibits usury by the Christian clergy in 325

Christians were not in a position to change the rules of landlordship and clientage, but at least they could renounce usury, starting with their own clergy, and their monasteries could provide interest-free loans to laypeople.[28] The Council of Elvira (in Spain, near Granada), dated between 300 and 309, forbade its clergy from practicing usury. Canon 20 (of 81) stipulated: "If any clergy are found engaged in usury, let them be censured and dismissed. If a layman is caught practicing usury, he may

---

[28] Papaconstantinou 2016:617 provides examples from Egypt.

be pardoned if he promises to stop the practice. If he continues this evil practice, let him be expelled from the church."[29] The rule applied only to the 19 Spanish bishops in attendance, but a few years later, in 314, the Council of Arles (in Roman Gaul) also forbade usury.

Rome ended the ban on Christianity in 311, and a decade later, in 321, Constantine converted and made Christianity the state religion. The Empire that Christians had spent centuries demonizing suddenly was transformed into their protector, to the point where Roman officials even were asked to adjudicate disputes among rival groups to decide which theology should be deemed to be Christian orthodoxy.

The Council of Nicaea was convened in 325 under Constantine's sponsorship to help end schisms within the Church. It is best known for opposing Arian theology with the Nicene Creed asserting that Christ was created by God out of his own body ("of the substance of the Father") and thus was eternal, not coming into existence only at the moment of his birth in Bethlehem. Defining Christ as always existing, as part of God, removed Jesus from the worldly Jewish conflicts of his own time. The Council did, however, maintain the policy of Elvira and Arles forbidding the clergy to practice usury. Canon 17 ruled that officials found guilty were to be removed:

> Forasmuch as many enrolled among the Clergy, following covetousness and lust of gain, have forgotten the divine Scripture, which says, "He hath not given his money upon usury," ... the holy and great Synod thinks it just that if after this decree anyone be found to receive usury, whether he accomplish it by secret transaction or otherwise ... or by using any other contrivance whatever for filthy lucre's sake, he shall be deposed from the clergy and his name stricken from the list.[30]

Subsequent councils also deplored usury, but clerics who practiced it were let off with a warning, not deposed. In 345 the First Council of Carthage (whose main aim was to condemn the Donatists, as Chapter 22 will discuss) declared that taking interest was reprehensible for all Christians, not only for members of the clergy. Canon 5 ("On Avarice") stated:

> The cupidity of avarice (which, let no one doubt, is the mother of all evil things), is to be henceforth prohibited, lest anyone should usurp

---

[29] http://legalhistorysources.com/Canon%20Law/ElviraCanons.htm.

[30] https://www.christian-history.org/council-of-nicea-canons.html#17. For a summary of the Church Councils dealing with usury see *The Excursus on Usury*, relying heavily on the Belgian Canonist Zeger Bernhard Van Espen (1646-1728), available at https://orthodoxchurchfathers.com/fathers/npnf214/npnf2121.htm.

another's limits, or for gain should pass beyond the limits fixed by the fathers, nor shall it be at all lawful for any of the clergy to receive usury of any kind. ... And what is reprehensible in laymen is worthy of still more severe censure in the clergy.[31]

However, no penalties were imposed for violating this canon. The Cappadocian bishop Basil "the Great" (330-379) is illustrative of this softening of punishment. On the one hand he described how, "Taking advantage of the latter's poverty, the usurer has managed to persuade the borrower to undertake to pay an interest whose term amount is not revealed, and which is so great as actually to be impossible to pay, so that in effect the borrower is contracting a voluntary servitude for life."[32] But Basil also wrote that: "A taker of usury, if he consent to spend his unjust gain on the poor, and to be rid for the future of the plague of covetousness, may be received into the ministry."[33]

This tolerance continued within the Church. At Constantinople in 692 the Council of Trullan (Canon 10) ruled that: "A bishop, presbyter or deacon who receives usury ... let him desist or be deposed,"[34] but an epitome of this canon permits the sinner not to be deposed if he stops practicing usury. The Church hierarchy ended up simply urging creditors, landlords and other wealthy Christians to donate charitably to the poor, via the clergy. The Romanized Church urged charity from the rich, not redistribution of their land and property claims that Roman law had legitimized.

The theological impact of making Christianity Rome's imperial religion

It was inevitable that upon Christianity becoming the state religion, Church and state would accommodate themselves to each other. Rome's 5ᵗʰ-century emperors backed Augustine and other Church leaders who accepted the existing feudal distribution of land and wealth, along with Rome's legal principles locking in hereditary landlordship power and the corresponding dependency of the *coloni*. As a state religion, Christianity was co-opted to no longer oppose the *rentier* wealth of the Empire's

---

[31] https://www.newadvent.org/fathers/3816.htm.

[32] St. Basil, *Commentary on Psalm 14*, cited in Avila 1983:56.

[33] St. Basil, *Epistles* 188, Canon 14, at https://www.newadvent.org/fathers/3202188.htm.

[34] https://www.documentacatholicaomnia.eu/03d/0691-0691,_Synodum_Constantinopolitanum,_Canones_%5bSchaff%5d,_EN.pdf.

ruling elite. Church leaders denounced rebels opposing the wealthy as heretics and schismatics.

Augustine of Hippo, Cyril of Alexandria and other bishops did not advocate social reform to redistribute land and monetary wealth as Roman Catholicism took shape, mainly in North Africa. Catholic leaders denounced and persecuted as schismatics Jewish Christians, North African Donatists, Egyptian Nestorians, Northern European followers of Pelagius, and Arians. The existing status quo of property rights and serfdom was defended. The economic message of earlier Christians, and Jesus Christ himself, had become heretical.

By ruling that Jesus always had existed as God, the Nicene Creed downplayed his Jewish context and Jesus's own hope to revive the Mosaic tradition of the Jubilee Year. There was no awareness of the parallel between Jesus's first sermon announcing that he had come to restore the Jubilee Year and the Lord's anticipated return restoring equity on earth.[35] That Near Eastern-Jewish background was absent from the Christianity that developed from Rome to North Africa, Gaul and Western Europe. As the next chapter will describe, Augustine's theology changed the meaning of the Lord's Prayer to focus on forgiveness of original sin and sexual self-indulgence, not on the worldly debt amnesty that Jesus had advocated.

The political tendency of states throughout history has been to subordinate religion and culture to serve the vested interests. It was not Christianity that corrupted the Roman Empire; rather, it was becoming the state religion of the Empire and its landowning elites that diverted Christianity away from the pro-debtor message of Jesus and his followers. A world free of avarice and money-greed would have to await the Lord's return to restore a Golden Age at the end of history, as such a world was unattainable in the face of Roman oppression and indeed in the Empire's aftermath in coming centuries.

By the end of the 4th century usury had declined as commercial activity shrank throughout the Roman Empire, and the Church had forbidden the practice, at least by its clerics (who were forgiven if they apologized and promised to stop engaging in moneylending). What also shrank was new warfare, and with it the capture of slaves from defeated territories. As life on the land stabilized on merely a subsistence level, slaves on Rome's latifundia estates were reorganized to become serfs with their own cottages and families in an attempt to stop the depopulation.

---

[35] I describe Jesus's first sermon and the altered meaning of the Lord's Prayer and its background in *"... and Forgive Them Their Debts"* (2018).

22

Romanized Christianity Supports the Oligarchy, 4th and 5th Centuries AD

The Empire's collapse was not simultaneous in all regions nor universal. North Africa, the Hispanic provinces, Gaul, and the Byzantine East enjoyed rising agricultural productivity and land prices, while Italy's population and economy was declining.[1] By the time the Visigoths' leader Alaric sacked Rome in 410, many of the wealthiest families had moved to North Africa in what now comprises Libya (Numidia), Tunisia and Algeria. As large as all Italy, the region's vast estates had been supplying Rome with most of the grain for its *Cura Annonae* dole since the 2nd century.

The native Berber population (the name deriving from Greek *barbaros*, "babbler")[2] had worked as sharecroppers already under the Phoenicians. From 396 BC onward, Numidian farmers and herders around Carthage are reported to have revolted against Phoenician demands for tribute and taxes. Rome's destruction of Carthage in 146 BC was followed by a Roman elite overlayering the mixed Berber-Punic population and carving the land into latifundia estates over the next few centuries. The estates' high economic productivity went hand in hand with a proto-feudal concentration of wealth and land tenure. "The massive landholdings of the emperor and of the nobility of Rome," notes Peter Brown, kept the region "underdeveloped by Roman standards. Their villages were denied any form of corporate existence and were frequently named after the estates on which the villagers worked, held to the land by various forms of bonded labor."[3]

As declining Roman warfare reduced the capture of slaves, raising their price after the 2nd century AD, large landowners adopted patron-client arrangements to obtain labor, using debt leverage to lock labor into a state of peonage. Smallholders who ran into debt were obliged to

---

[1] Bowersock 1988:173 and 176.

[2] Hence the term Berber or Barbary Coast since the 16th century. In Arabic the region is called the Maghreb, "The West [of Egypt]."

[3] Brown 2012:327, 330 and 366.

become *coloni* tenant farmers or seasonal migrant workers. Resentment and open fighting against Roman landlords and creditors found its counterpart in opposition to the Christian bishops who made an accommodation with Rome. The resulting schism within the Church capped the long protest that had spanned Roman history from the Secession of the Plebs in 494 to Catiline's revolt in 64-62 BC and the "peasant uprisings" in Gaul and Hispania in the 3rd to 4th centuries AD.

Christianity in North Africa

North Africa had a strong Christian tradition, and more bishoprics than Rome. Tertullian (155-220), born into a wealthy pagan family in or near Carthage, is usually regarded as the first Christian to write in Latin, and coined the term *trinity*. He was the teacher of Cyprian (210-258), from a similar Berber/Punic background, who was executed for resisting Roman authority, as Chapter 21 has described. Lactantius (ca. 250–325) was the region's third major early Church Father.

This North African flowering of Christianity occurred during the Empire's persecution of the religion, which peaked in 303-304 under Diocletian, who continued the policy of ordering Christians to turn over their holy books upon pain of punishment and even death. Many Numidians refused to do so and were imprisoned or became martyrs. Their followers accused Christians who complied with the Roman authorities of being *traditores*, "traitors" to the faith – and in practice, supporters of Roman property and oppression.

In 311, Galerius (East Roman emperor 305-311) ended the persecution of Christians in the last year of his rule. That same year saw one of the *traditores*, Caecilian, appointed Bishop of Carthage. The "rigorist" Numidian bishops denounced him for having turned over copies of his scriptures to the Roman authorities. He was excommunicated, and Donatus of Casae Negrae was appointed bishop in his place.

Ecclesiastical infighting intensified after 313, when the Edict of Milan by Constantine (306-337) and his co-emperor Licinius (308-324) reiterated the Church's legal status and ordered confiscated church property to be returned. The question was, which group would be in control of these assets. The followers of Donatus, being the most popular in North Africa, asked Roman officials for support against their rivals, but Constantine declined to get involved, and left it to the Council of Arles in 314 to decide who was legitimately Christian and therefore entitled to the returned property.

The council's bishops, mainly from Gaul and Italy, sided with Rome and reappointed the *traditore* Caecilian as Bishop of Carthage, excommunicated Donatus and declared his followers to be heretics.[4] From this time forward Roman emperors and officials ruled against them. Constantine issued a ruling against the Donatists in Milan in 316, and the next year ordered the Church to unify under pro-Roman leadership. This reflected the Empire's main concern: to promote the Church's acceptance of the wealth and dominance of the landed Roman aristocracy.

This concern became urgent as anti-creditor revolts were spreading throughout rural Numidia, spearheaded by the Donatists' circumcellion followers, mainly itinerant Berber and Punic poor opposing creditors and owners of the region's great estates.[5] One of their harshest critics, Bishop Optatus of Milevis, described their character ca. 340:

> The records of debts had lost their force, no creditor at that time had the freedom to enforce payment, all were terrified ... [The circumcellions] besieged the creditors with dangers, so that those who should have had suitors on account of their loans were forced into groveling prayers through fear of death. Each one hastened to write off even his greatest debts.[6]

---

[4] Eusebius, *Church History* 10.5.21024. For a list of rulings relating to this episode emanating from the Council of Arles and discussion of subsequent infighting see Lenski 2016:171 and *passim*. Barkman 2014:41 notes that "The names 'Melitians' [in Egypt] and 'Donatists' are pejorative titles given to these groups by their opponents and were not used by the groups when talking about themselves. Rather, both the 'Melitians' and the 'Donatists' saw themselves either as simply 'Christians' or as 'the Church of the martyrs.' The act of naming the members of a faction after their leader was a common rhetorical tool and represented a step closer to identifying them as 'heretics.'"

[5] The major study emphasizing the role played by this rural revolt remains Frend 1952. This view of Donatism as class conflict was put forth already by Karl Kautsky 1925:449. Latourette 2007:139 emphasizes that the theological conflict was along ethnic and economic class lines, setting the "non-Latin and the Catholics [against] the Latin elements in the population."

[6] Optatus, *Against the Donatists*, quoted in Hoover 2008:220, fn49, citing Edwards 1997:69. Lenski 2017:136 notes that the uprising in 340 mobilized mainly impoverished tenants reduced to debt bondage, citing Shaw 2011:781-782: "it is most probable that the documents, the tabulae, that were being destroyed were records of debts owed by peasant workers to landlords." Boicu 2019:94 characterizes the circumcellions as "the avant-garde of the Donatist Church," adding that "without the support of these 'gangs of savages' Donatism would have been crushed rapidly by imperial forces."

A. H. M. Jones has described the Donatists and their allied "storm troopers," the circumcellions, as being "at bottom a social movement," and to many "a revolutionary uprising of the poor against the rich," combining religious and social protest. Its most radical supporters, the circumcellions

> gave their protection to tenant farmers against their landlords, to debtors against their creditors, and to slaves against their masters. 'No one was allowed to be safe on his estates. The bonds of debtors lost their force, no creditor was free to exact his money at that time.' ... Their houses were burnt down, they themselves were forced to work at the mill like slaves, or torn from their carriages and compelled to run behind while their slaves drove. ... The circumcellions were recruited from the poor peasantry, and were no doubt not averse from paying off old scores against oppressive landlords and extortionate moneylenders when they had a good excuse for doing so in the name of religion.[7]

Donatists set up their own churches, attracting a majority in many towns. Constantine tried to restore peace by stopping taking sides in 321, the year in which he converted to Christianity and made it the state religion. His grant of toleration enabled North African cities to have two churches, Donatist and the more pro-Roman. But the schism was revived and intensified in 347, when Constantine's son Constans (337-350) sent two officials to Carthage "to distribute funds for the churches of Africa and for almsgiving." The Donatists accused them of favoring the pro-Roman congregations. As *The Cambridge Ancient History* describes: "The bishop of Bagai summoned up bands of circumcellions and confronted the officials, who replied by sending in soldiers – the bishop was among the victims. Other Donatist martyrs soon followed. ... to the Donatists the age of persecution and martyrdom had returned, and Constans was the reincarnation of his pagan predecessors."[8] In August the Roman proconsul of Africa issued a decree "ordering the unity of all the churches under

---

[7] Jones 1959:294 (repeated in Jones 1974:324), citing Martroye 1904-1905. He adds a caveat: "There is no evidence that the Donatist church ever proclaimed any revolutionary programme of community of goods or freeing of slaves or remission of debt," but points out (p. 282) that within the African provinces Donatism "was both widespread and persistent ... and at some periods dominating the whole country, and surviving despite many persecutions for close on three centuries to our certain knowledge, and probably longer." Its leaders included the well-to-do, not only the lower strata of the population. For a similar view see Ward-Perkins 1998 in *The Cambridge Ancient History*, Vol. 13, p. 384.

[8] Hunt 1998:25, drawing largely on the narrative of Optatus.

the Catholic bishop of Carthage." The Roman commission removed
Donatus as bishop and exiled him to Gaul, where he died ca. 355.

This show of imperial force "to compel the dissidents into union with
the mainstream church ... galvanized the Donatist cause for generations
to come."[9] The term "Catholic" designated the pro-Roman party that
triumphed. It meant "universal," in the sense of being exclusionary of
any doctrine not authorized by the orthodox bishops.[10] The Donatists
did not see themselves as seceding from the Church, however, but as
representing what had long been its mainstream supporting the economically oppressed and denouncing blatant wealth and hubris.

The Donatist controversy splits the North African Church

The struggle between North African Donatists and the new Catholic
orthodoxy is documented almost solely on the theological plane. The
Donatists insisted that Church officials should be "spotless." This meant
specifically that "lapsed" clergy who had surrendered copies of their
scriptures to the Romans or had committed crimes needed to be re-bap-
tized in order to be re-admitted to the Christian body, implicitly under
Donatist authority.

Most historians have treated this schism as an esoteric part of the 4th
and 5th centuries' theological debate, but underlying it was the conflict
between Roman landlords and indebted Berber-Punic tenants. The
interface with the church concerned the willingness to die as martyrs
to defend the idea of Christian purity in the Romanized world around
them. "Martyrdom is fundamental to the whole picture," Lenski has
noted. "The entire controversy was born of conflicts over who had
suffered sufficiently for the faith ... by refusing to collaborate with a persecuting Roman state." At issue was "sacred victimhood."[11]

Jones has framed the debate in terms of the political and economic
interests at work: "What the sectaries actually said in public, so far as our

---

[9] Lenski 2016:170, adding (p. 175): "It was in this period that Donatism spread
outward from Africa to establish footholds in Rome and in Spain," citing Frend
1952:169-171. Boicu 2019:94 notes that "opponents of the imperial judgment were
threatened with harsh retaliation, while rigorous bishops were to be sent into exile
(the case of Donatus Magnus), or even put to death through public execution (the
case of Marculus and 9 other bishops)."

[10] Marone 2007-2008 notes that: "[I]t was the struggle with the Donatists which
first drew out the full theological significance of the epithet Catholic and passed it
on to the schoolmen as an abiding possession."

[11] Lenski 2016:187.

record goes, was ... 'The Donatist Church is the true Catholic Church, and we will never communicate with *traditores*,' but what they thought, we are asked to believe, was: 'We are Africans and hate the Rome Government; we will have nothing to do with the Romans and will maintain our African Church and if possible set up our African state.'"[12]

On a yet deeper level, Tilley describes the Donatists as viewing themselves as the Chosen Ones, part of the *collecta* of Israel, liberated from oppression by a pagan government and church. They denounced the economic world to which Augustine, Bishop of Hippo, was accommodating by siding with Rome during what they saw as the End Time marked by economic unfairness and oppression.[13] The Church was seen as rejecting the position that it had held at its origins four centuries earlier.

Augustine's political base in the Roman landlord class

Along with Cyril of Alexandria (patriarch from 412 until 444), Augustine (354-430) gave Christianity its subsequent Western form as a state religion, mediated increasingly by wealthy elite families administering both Church and state. When he became Bishop of Hippo in 395, Donatists substantially outnumbered the orthodox church in Numidia. Hippo, west of Carthage, was North Africa's second largest port. The Augustinians did not challenge the polarization of wealth, but "appealed to the Haves to play patron," notes MacMullen.[14] They "were not in the business of questioning anyone's title to land," summarizes Garnsey, "unless, that is, they were heretics" such as the Donatists.[15]

Augustinian and Donatist theology shared the same scripture, liturgies, martyrs, calendars and holidays, and both opposed the Arians and Manichaeans. But the only writing that has survived relating to the Donatist opposition is Augustine's caricature, capped by his description of the circumcellions response to economic oppression:

---

[12] Jones 1966c:3.

[13] Tilley 1997:177-179. Frend 1952 notes that: "For the Donatists, apocalyptic conviction took the form of violence towards landowners and the rich in general, as representatives of the present (Satan-dominated) age." Hoover 2018:332-333 provides a review of the historiography of Donatism blending social and religious concerns.

[14] MacMullen 1974:124.

[15] Garnsey 2007:94. He adds (p. 88): "The Church accepted the existing social hierarchies, the patriarchal family, the subordination of women, and slavery. This was the case even before the community of Christians came to include people of social and economic prominence."

> What master was not forced to fear his slave if his slave sought refuge
> under the protection of the Donatists? . . . Who was able to demand a reck-
> oning from a slave who consumed his provisions or from a debtor who
> asked the Donatists for help and defense? ... The homes of the innocent
> who had offended them were either razed to the ground or destroyed by
> fires. ... What official breathed easily in their presence? What banker was
> able to demand what they were unwilling to pay?[16]

Augustine's fight against the Donatists reversed Christianity's role
as a movement protecting the poor against the wealthy. The Church
embraced the status quo, and instead of the debt relief that had been
central to Jesus, it only recommended charitable contributions out of
what the aristocracy extracted from the economy.

Failing to evangelize the Donatists by his public preaching, Augustine resorted to violence. Brown characterizes him as perhaps "the first
theorist of the Inquisition"[17] inasmuch as his appeal to state authority
to oversee Church doctrine provided the moral rationale for Emperor
Theodosius (379-395) and Ambrose (Bishop of Milan, 374-397) to use
state power, including violence, to support Church leaders who, in turn,
reconciled Christianity with Roman property and clientage practices. As
Walter Nigg has summarized, Augustine's application of the principle
"*Cogite intrar* – compel them to enter," created a precedent by which "All
those instrumental in the ferocious suppression of the heretics [and the
Jews] in the Middle Ages could call upon [his] authority ... – could and
did. The violence and cruelty unleashed by this one man was beyond
measure."[18]

Augustine claimed that persecuting heretics and pagans would consolidate a spirit of unity, by suppressing ideas different from those
of the bishops who won Roman approval at the ecumenical councils
that shaped Christian doctrine. The suppression started in 405 with
the Edict of Unity issued by Emperor Honorius (393-423) banning
Donatism as sectarian. In 410 a council of bishops blocked a proposal
for a new Edict of Toleration, and Donatists were ordered to turn over
their buildings to Augustine's church. That led the next year to the
Council of Carthage, and although the 289 Donatist bishops outnumbered the 267 orthodox Catholic bishops, the Roman tribune in charge,
Flavius Marcellinus, banned the Donatists from holding Church proper-

---

[16] Augustine, Letter 185.4.15 (Teske III:188), quoted in Hoover 2008:219, fn48.

[17] Brown 2000:236.

[18] Nigg 1962:116-117.

ty.[19] In 412 an imperial edict declared Donatism a crime, and Donatists were stripped of civil rights in 414.

Augustine's focus on original sin, not on how property maldistribution causes poverty

Augustine's concept of Christian morality was limited to personal sinfulness and selfishness, not the creditor power and landlord monopoly that earlier Roman historians described as destroying the Republic. Personal sins could be forgiven, but not debt. Redemption could take the form of giving away one's wealth, especially to the Church, but there was no thought of forgiving monetary debts. Augustine's theology changed the entire meaning of the Lord's Prayer, as Peter Brown has spelled out in detail:

> As Éric Rebillard has demonstrated so persuasively, Augustine believed that the life of a Christian was a life of continual penance. The pious Christian was a human hedgehog. He or she was covered from head to foot with the tiny, sharp spines of daily, barely conscious *peccata minutissima*—tiny little sins. It was to expunge these that the Christian should pray every day Forgive us our trespasses as we forgive those who trespass against us (Matthew 6:12).
>
> ... This aspect of the piety of Augustine has been exhaustively studied, now almost half a century ago, by Anne-Marie La Bonnardière. In a masterly article, she pointed out how this crucial passage in the Lord's Prayer was seized upon by Augustine, in the opening years of the Pelagian controversy, as the touchstone of orthodoxy. Recited by the baptized before receiving the Eucharist, the phrase Forgive us our trespasses left no room for the Pelagian claim that some baptized Christians, at least, could live without sin. To Augustine, the prayer was a daily reminder of a daily state of sinfulness, which cried out for daily forgiveness.[20]

Neither Augustine nor other Church Fathers proposed land redistribution to those who had lost it. They probably did not understand that Jesus's first sermon (Luke 4) called for a Jubilee Year bringing debt forgiveness and land redistribution in accordance with Leviticus

---

[19] Smither 2006, and Burns and Jensen 2014:85-87. O'Donnell 2005:80-81 and 224 seeks to de-mythologize Augustine, describing his "putch" at this council meeting as his greatest personal triumph by "destroying the morale and the organization of the native African Christian Church, the so-called Donatists. ... He set a style for ambitious churchmen aligned with state authority that had hitherto been seen mainly in the Greek east."

[20] Brown 2005:20-21, citing Augustine, *Enarratio in Psalm* 103 sermon 3.18 (of December 403).

25. Instead, the focus of Mosaic law on debt relief and land redemption
that was at the center of Jesus's preaching played no role as the Church
reached an accommodation with the vested interests to receive charity
from them, but not challenge their economic control.

Refraining from criticizing the property rights that shaped the distribution of landholding and led to clientage and poverty, Catholic
Christianity implicitly backed the power of creditors and landowners
over debtors and tenants. "By saying with Christ, 'Render to Caesar the
things that are Caesar's, and to God the things that are God's,'" commented Fustel de Coulanges, Christianity chose not to challenge "the
laws of property, nor the order of succession, nor obligations, nor legal
proceedings. It placed itself ... outside all things purely terrestrial,"[21]
leaving Roman-based law intact.

Augustine "never directly concerns himself with the legal reform
of property rights and laws," notes one modern historian of property.
"Instead he explores what ownership ought to mean and how it should
be ethically regarded by all."[22] What was attacked as destroying social
equity was not concentrated land tenure and harsh debt laws but
personal greed and selfish ambition as a universal human trait and
indeed, sin.

A utopian strain had earlier revived the Stoic ideal of a golden age.
Seneca (4 BC-AD 65), tutor to Nero and also a creditor at usurious rates,
pontificated:

> There was once a fortune-favored period when the bounties of nature lay
> open to all, for men's indiscriminate use, before avarice and luxury had
> broken the bonds that held mortals together, and they, abandoning their
> communal existence, had separated and turned to plunder.[23]

Already in the 6th-century BC, Theognis of Megara had expressed a
reaction against social injustice similar to what Stoic philosophers and
Christians would voice:

> Everything here has gone to the ravens and perdition.
> And not one of the immortal and blessed gods is responsible to us
> for this ... but the violence [*bie*] of men and their baneful private inter-

---

[21] Fustel de Coulanges 1980:385 and 387.

[22] Avila 1983:109.

[23] Seneca, Letter to Lucilius #90.36. See also 90.3 and *passim*. In the New Testament, Acts 4:31-35 shows how Christianity aimed at reviving this ethic.

ests [*kerdos*] and their outrage [*hubris*] have plummeted them from much
nobility [*polla agatha*] into debasement [*kakotes*].[24]

The Stoic version of history had roots in Greek philosophy describing money-wealth as addictive, as Chapter 7 has discussed, making its
possessors hubristic and selfish with money-greed at society's expense.
The story of the Roman Republic culminating in the Empire and its fall
reads like a dramatization of this moral philosophy.[25] Lactantius framed
the dynamic of history in terms of a similar conflict between selfishness
and the ethic of mutual aid:

> The source of all these evils was cupidity, bursting forth from the
> contempt of true virtue. The greedy did not share with others, they even
> seized public property as their own, drawing in all things for their own
> private gain. Products which individuals were making for the use of
> all were taken into the homes of the few. In order to enslave the many,
> the greedy began to appropriate and accumulate the necessities of life
> and keep them tightly closed up, so that they might keep these bounties
> for themselves. They did this not for humanity's sake (which was not
> in them at all), but to rake up all things as products of their greed and
> avarice. In the name of justice they made unfair and unjust laws to
> sanction their thefts and avarice against the power of the multitude. In
> this way they availed as much by authority as by strength of arms or
> overt evil.[26]

A revulsion against luxury and hubris – abusive wealth-seeking by
the elites, arrogance that took the form of injuring others – created a
moral reaction in early Christians to eschew wealth altogether, in favor
of mutual aid.[27] That always has been the core of religious ethics, and
was in line with Rome's Stoic ethic, which was egalitarian among the
aristocratic elites themselves (for instance, in their interest-free *eranos*
loans "among gentlemen"). The ethic of ostensibly floating above the

---

[24] Theognis 833-836, in Figueira and Nagy 1985:53.

[25] Garnsey 2007:44.

[26] Lactantius, *Divine Institutes* 5.6.7-9 (1964:72).

[27] The reaction against inequality and drudgery was by no means limited to
Roman Christendom. Richard Payne 2022 describes how peasant revolts against
Persia's 6th-century Sasanian rulers sought to create ("restore") an egalitarian
Zoroastrian order as a protest against the extreme polarization that widened the
gap between luxury and poverty. The morality of economic balance rejected silk
garments, silver wine vessels and other status symbols of the elites. Interest was
condemned, as it had been under Christianity and would be under Islam.

exploitative commercial and financial world and not dirtying one's hands by making money directly through usury and commerce explains why many wealthy families became Christians and supplied most of the Church's bishops.

Lactantius added that war leaders were celebrated and even deified for destroying cities and enslaving their inhabitants, yet "if anyone strangles one man, he is held as an evildoer and criminal, and it is not considered fitting that he be admitted to even the earthly dwelling place of the gods." A century later in *The City of God* (Book 4) Augustine added the story of a pirate who had been seized and was said to have justified himself to Alexander the Great: "For what I do with a petty ship, I am called a robber, whilst thou who dost it with a great fleet are styled emperor." He summarized:

> Justice being taken away, then, what are kingdoms but great robberies? For what are robberies themselves, but little kingdoms? The band itself is made up of men; it is ruled by the authority of a prince, it is knit together by the pact of the confederacy; the booty is divided by the law agreed on.

To many Christians it seemed that the only alternative to self-aggrandizing egotism and greed was to withdraw from the selfish world. There were violent protests from Gaul and Spain to North Africa, but no proposals for economic and political restructuring to make land and credit part of a more equitable social order. There was no movement like that of the early Greek reformer-tyrants to save smallholders from clientage and debt bondage by overthrowing local autocrats, breaking up their land monopoly and banning debt slavery and the colonate.

Brown describes those who spoke of themselves as *pauperes* as being mainly the non-rich or *plebs media*, the precarious well-to-do plebeians living on the edge. The word *paupertas* did not mean "poverty" so much as the loss of one's status based on property ownership. "Perhaps you have been made utterly poor and destitute," wrote Augustine. "You had some little family property that had supported you, which was taken away from you by the tricky dealing of a rival. You groan, you grumble against the times you live in. ... Yesterday, this person was groaning that he had lost his property. Today, backed by a greater patron, he is grabbing the property of others."[28]

But Augustine did not seek to reform the economic forces that led people to lose their property and status. Instead of promoting laws to

---

[28] Augustine, Sermon 13.8, cited in Brown 2012:346.

protect smallholders and the poor, his Church urged the wealthy to act generously and charitably – with the charity to be mediated by the clergy, not by donors or the state acting independently of the Church.[29] Giving to the poor was to take the form of giving to the monks and priests who organized the Church in the name of the poor. The clergy in effect became the paradigmatic "poor." The misery suffered by the secular poor was depicted as punishment for humanity's original sin, not the sinfulness of wealth.

Neither Augustine nor any other contemporary orthodox Christian leader spoke in the spirit of the Biblical prophets who called for "repentance" by the Jews for having diverged from the Lord's laws forbidding selfish behavior and commanding the Jubilee Year. Their defeat by Assyria and Babylonia was blamed on them having sinned against the Law of God for having permitted the oligarchy to monopolize the land and reduce the population to bondage.[30] Jesus's preaching followed this focus on social injustice and criticized the selfishness of the Judaic wealthy that led to debt dependency. He devoted his first sermon to announcing that he had come to proclaim the Jubilee Year. But no members of the Romanized Church echoed Isaiah 5:12 by denouncing the Empire's latifundists for "add[ing] house to house and join[ing] field to field till no space is left and you live alone in the land." Augustine instead focused on personal sin, with an idiosyncratic focus on sexual indulgence that has remained characteristic of his church.

In Egypt, largely under Cyril of Alexandria, worship of the virgin Mary (an element often seen as transposing Egyptian Isis worship) replaced the classical justice goddess Nemesis punishing hubris (mainly of the rich and powerful). This Christian Mariolatry, emphasizing the compassionate Mother of Jesus/God, helped exclude Jewish Christians as part of Cyril's anti-Semitism. It also excluded the idea of a justice goddess protecting the weak and poor, a figure going back to Nanshe

---

[29] Finley 1973:88 emphasizes that neither the Stoics nor Augustine and other Christian bishops called for abolition of slavery. "The stress is on the master's moral obligation to behave, for his own sake, with self-restraint and moderation, at least as much as on the humanity of the slave." Today's billionaires who receive most growth in income and wealth defend themselves by endowing charitable foundations. This is not a sign that the economy is working well, but that it is *not* doing so, and therefore is obliged to rely on charity from the rich instead of internal prosperity, which is blocked precisely by the behavior of the wealthy in seeking to further enrich themselves.

[30] See Borg 1987:122 and 163-164, and Crossan 1994.

of Lagash in Bronze Age Sumer, who was followed by counterpart justice goddesses for thousands of years down to Greece and Rome. The dimension of social justice as a religious commandment to protect the poor and their self-support land from the rich was replaced by Christian compassion taking the form of charity by the rich – to the Church, at their own personal discretion.

Salvian and Pelagius criticize landlord exploitation of smallholders and the poor

The Gallic Christian Salvian described the poverty confronting most of the population ca. 440, the year in which Leo I became pope:

> Faced by the weight of taxes, poor farmers found that they did not have the means to emigrate to the barbarians. Instead, they did what little they could do: they handed themselves over to the rich as clients in return for protection. The rich took over title to their lands under the pretext of saving the farmers from the land tax. The patron registered the farmer's land on the tax rolls under his (the patron's) own name. Within a few years, the poor farmers found themselves without land, although they were still hounded for personal taxes. Such patronage by the great, so Salvian claimed, turned free men into slaves as surely as the magic of Circe had turned humans into pigs.[31]

Much as Biblical prophets had blamed Judea's defeats by Assyria and Babylon on the failure of its kings to save society from creditors dispossessing the poor, Salvian blamed Rome for allowing landlords to drive their tenants and debtors to flee to join the Teutonic tribes fighting its generals. But the Roman elite, whose politically correct moral philosophy claimed to abhor selfishness and greed, were unwilling to lighten their *rentier* claims. "Are we surprised that the barbarians capture us," Salvian asked, "when we make captives of our own brothers?"[32]

A kindred attitude was voiced by Augustine's major adversary Pelagius (354-418), from Britain (probably Wales; his name meant "sea" in Welsh). He moved to Rome around 380, holding views more in tune with the culture of Gaul and other northern reaches of Rome's Empire. Decrying the Age of Avarice, his *De devitiis* ("On Riches," written between 408 and

---

[31] Salvian, *De gubernatione Dei* 5.9.45, paraphrased in Brown 2012:433-450.

[32] Brown 2012:433-434, 442, 446 and 450, citing Salvian *De gubernatione Dei* 5.9.46. He notes (p. 136) that Salvian was striking a common theme. Ambrose (340-397) had "represented a new departure" by blaming Rome's decline on the greed of great landowners, much as Pliny accused the latifundia of ruining Italy.

414) anticipated the French anarchist Proudhon's claim that "Property is Theft." There was no guiltless wealth, because its essence was to exploit and impoverish society: "Take away the rich and you will find no poor," he claimed. "Every inheritance had its own, dark history. ... The lush 'flowers of wealth' pushed their roots deep into 'a bed of crime.'" In sum, "the possession of riches ... can hardly have been acquired without some injustice," anticipating Balzac's observation that behind every great fortune lay some long-forgotten crime. His contemporary Jerome (ca. 347-420, translator of the Bible into Latin), wrote along similar lines: "a rich man is either a wicked man or the heir of a wicked man."[33]

Christians who followed Pelagius's critique of wealth "seem to have come from the lower layer of the nobility, which," notes Brown, "was a fertile breeding ground of mavericks." This was in the tradition of Solon and other early Greek reformers, as well as many Judaic prophets and Donatists, and indeed similar to the Russian *intelligentsia* in the early 20th century and to the well-to-do that formed the socialist cadre in modern times.

This class of lower-level nobility supplied most of the clergy.[34] Like Pelagius, they viewed the cause of most human suffering to be worldly wealth, above all that of landlords and creditors. But they believed that even the wealthy possessed the free will to live a life free of sin. If egotism were bad in itself, God would not have imbued man with ambition and a desire for acclaim. The key choice was whether to use wealth in ways that served society by being generous or that injured others by acting selfishly.

In contrast to Pelagius and most of the clergy, Augustine blamed his epoch's social crisis and the End Time not on the oligarchy's land grabbing and usury, but on mankind's collective original sin inborn from the fall of Adam. His followers did not question the existing distribution of land and monetary wealth. No personal effort or political reform could erase this sinful legacy. It was on this ground that Augustine condemned Pelagius for claiming that Christians could save themselves by subsidizing good works or doing such works themselves.[35]

---

[33] Pelagius, *De devitiis* 7.3 and 7.6, and Jerome, Letter 120.1.7, in Brown 2012:312-314.

[34] Brown 2012:24, 343-344 and 317. He points out (p. 319) that Jerome linked the absolute poverty of Christ to the poverty of the monks. But Christianity's early adherents were drawn largely from the professional groups that traditionally formed *collegia* for social meetings, mutual aid and burials. In later times, bishops tended to come from the ranks of town councilors and other prosperous classes.

[35] Pelagius is said to have defended his view that wealth was evil, not man, by citing Deuteronomy 24:16: "Each is to die for his own sin," not that of his fathers.

It was long normal for Roman politicians to seek votes by making lavish donations to finance games, the major entertainment and social occasion for most cities, often going into debt to do so (as did Caesar and as discussed in Chapters 17 and 18). Public philanthropy was a related instance of *noblesse oblige*. But Augustine claimed that only his Church could be entrusted to use wealth in a truly Christian way. Individuals acting on their own to show their good spirit by social spending was seen as a sinful manifestation of pride.

Going to the opposite extreme, many ascetics withdrew into monasteries as an alternative to worldly life. The Church's passivity regarding economic reform – except for condemning usury by the clergy and denouncing it for society in general – was what led Roman officials to back Augustine against Donatus and Pelagius.

Stripping Debt Cancellation from the Lord's Prayer

Pelagius's "notion that a human being might use his or her free will to live without sin flouted the daily recitation of the Lord's Prayer: *Forgive us our sins*," observes Brown, reiterating the point (noted above) that: "Recited by the baptized before receiving the Eucharist, the phrase *Dimitte nobis debita nostra* – Forgive us our sins [*debita*] – left no room for the Pelagian claim that baptized Christians could live without sin. To Augustine, the prayer was a daily reminder of a state of sinfulness, which cried out for daily forgiveness."[36]

This Augustinian sin was alien to what early Near Eastern rulers forgave when they proclaimed amnesties for debts owed to the palace, temples and private creditors, and also alien to what archaic communities forgave when they gave amnesties pardoning offenders who owed *wergild*-type compensation debts. Inflicting personal injury was the archaic concept of "sin." Archaic *wergild*-type laws called for personal monetary redemption by paying compensation to the injured parties.[37]

Brown 2012:370-376 describes how Augustine pressured Pope Zosimus to excommunicate Pelagius and his followers after Innocent I died in 417. Demanding that a larger Council of Carthage with over 200 bishops be convened in 418, Augustine "masterminded a putch, denying free will" in getting the emperor to condemn Pelagius and his follower Caelestius. In 421 the First Council of Ephesus declared Pelagius a heretic, and his writings on freedom of the will were destroyed.

[36] Brown 2012:361-362.

[37] I review the semantics in Hudson 2018, Chapter 4. The aim of enforcing such obligation-debts was to prevent families from causing social disorder by taking revenge on each other by resorting to feud justice.

The word for offense/sin came to be a metonymy for such repara-
tion debts. The German word *Schuld* expresses this conflation of sin/
injury and its restitution debt, which is found in most Indo-European
languages, and also in Babylonian and Hebrew.[38] But for Augustine,
debita did not mean monetary debt as it had originally meant. Rather,
it referred to the need to atone for the sin of Adam's self-indulgence.[39]
That stripped from the Lord's Prayer its call to "forgive them their
debts" that reflected Jesus's focus on the debt amnesty at the core of the
Jubilee Year (Leviticus 25). It was replaced with the idea of payment
to expiate a sin/offense, with the Church receiving the payment, inter-
jecting itself into the dynamic of personal salvation, while leaving the
world's monetary debts intact, not subject to forgiveness either by the
Church or by any civic authority. The poor as well as the rich were
deemed sinful, simply for being born.

Romanized Christianity thus made a sharp break from the preach-
ings of Jesus advocating debt cancellation in the tradition of the Jubilee
Year debt amnesty. Except for Roman tax amnesties, debt forgiveness
was no longer politically feasible in an era when most debts were owed
to private creditors. Despite Christian denunciation of these creditors
and usury, personal debtors were not saved from losing their economic
liberty to their creditors.

Jesus's worldly fight for debt cancellation also was sidestepped by
Cyril, patriarch of Alexandria (412-444), who led the other schism split-
ting the 5th-century Church over the threefold nature of Jesus, the Lord
and the Holy Spirit. In the schism, Cyril insisted on Trinitarianism and
that the Nestorians be denounced as heretics. As discussed in Chapter
21, the First Council of Nicaea in 325 had deemed it a heresy to say that
Jesus was begotten at a moment in time and hence did not always exist.
Spiritualizing Jesus as eternal God incarnate shifted the focus away
from his call for debt forgiveness, especially his fight against the Pharisees who advocated the *prosbul* clause obliging debtors to waive their
rights to have their debts forgiven in the Jubilee Year of Leviticus 25.

---

[38] In German, *e.g.*, "*Schuld kann vergeben werden, aber Schulden bleiben bestehen.*"

[39] Brown 2012:179. He notes (p. 376) that Emperor Julian "the Apostate" (361-363)
accused Augustine of denouncing sex as "a demonic urge, planted irrevocably in the
human body." Even among married couples, it was tainted. Stoicism had nothing
like Augustine's abhorrence of sexual sinfulness. Indeed, Brown points out (2012:518),
celibacy was not inevitable in Christianity. Many early bishops were married.

To cap matters, Cyril's emphasis on Mariolatry helped exclude Judaism from Christian theology.[40]

These transformations of Christianity effectively negated its early ideal of protecting the poor from being reduced to dependency by creditors and land appropriators addicted to wealth and dominance. That protection had been a central focus of all archaic religion. Its ideal and its associated values, and even literal phraseology of protecting widows and orphans, the weak and poor, were transmitted to classical antiquity by the major temples, Stoic philosophy and Christianity. But these values became increasingly hollow as less and less attention was paid to the social dynamics that followed from increasing oligarchic selfishness. Eventually Augustine would give his already noted sermon, *Tolle superbiam diviiae non nocebunt*: "Get rid of pride and wealth will do no harm."[41] But wealth was accumulated precisely as an embodiment of one's pride, increasingly by making the weak and poor more dependent, indebted and enserfed.

Fiscal consequences of the Church as economic administrator

Leo I (440-461), made pope a decade after Augustine died, was called "the Great" for centralizing papal authority and supporting Augustine and Cyril against the Donatists, Pelagius and followers of Nestorius of Constantinople.[42] He claimed that only baptism and relinquishing wealth to the Church could save the Christian world from liability for the inborn sins that made everyone sinful. Leo "always treated wealth as a providential fact of life. It had to be accepted on a 'No questions asked' basis. How wealth had been obtained was no longer an issue for him. What mattered was how it would be used," by and for the Church, whose landed estates became islands in a sea of poverty, in which "[t]he rich were expected to be generous and good natured; the poor were to be suppliant and grateful."[43]

---

[40] The way that Christianity took the "African branch" of Augustine and Cyril was emphasized in the 19th century by John W. Draper's *History of the Intellectual Development of Europe* (1863), and later by Robert Briffault's *Rational Evolution* (1930). I discuss this in Hudson 2010.

[41] Augustine, Sermon 37.4, Kessler, *Reichtumskritik*, p. 399, cited in Brown 2005:24.

[42] Nestorius was driven out of the Church by the often violent Cyril at the Council of Ephesus in 431, but retained a major influence on the Persian Sassanids.

[43] Brown 2012:465 and 56.

Deathbed confessions and donations of property became increasingly popular.[44] At the point where one's life was nearing its end, priests reminded the mortally sick or dying to think of the eternal afterlife. Donors were urged to seek approval from the Lord by giving to the Church, rather than giving in the classical way of making philanthropic gifts to their city (which would be commemorated by an inscription citing the donor's name if the gift was large enough). Giving became "a religious transaction," to be reciprocated with an appropriate place in heaven.

Such testamentary bequests left family heirs disinherited. That led to a flourishing legal practice in contesting deathbed wills, and also undercut civic fiscal balance.[45] Land given to the Church was tax-exempt, obliging communities to maintain their fiscal revenue by raising taxes on secular property. That made the Church an increasing tax burden on communities, as well as a fiscal overhead.

By supplying princes of the Church, wealthy families protected their economic interests, ruling by virtue of their landed wealth and pro-creditor debt laws, just as they had done throughout Roman history. The Church's insistence that bishops and clergy not own property or fortunes of their own encouraged wealthy families to assign Church careers to their younger members, not the firstborn heirs.[46]

Like modern corporate business executives and the old Soviet managerial class, bishops managed the wealth of their organization, not their own property.[47] This separation of the ownership of Church property from its management ostensibly achieved what Socrates had advocated for "philosopher kings," having no money and property of their own so that they would not fall subject to wealth addiction.[48] But the aristocratic

---

[44] Brown 2012:xxv. By Martin Luther's time (1483-1546), obtaining salvation by giving to the Church bureaucracy had degenerated into the notorious business of selling indulgences.

[45] Brown 2012:495 cites the complaint of the Frankish King Chilperic of Neustria (ruled 561-584): "Behold, our fisc has remained poor and our riches are passed over to the churches."

[46] Brown describes how wealthy families used the Church to absorb male and female heirs into monastic life, abstaining from procreation and thus leaving hereditary fortunes intact for the remaining relatives.

[47] That is the distinction that Adolph Berle and Gardner Means would draw in their 1932 book *The Modern Corporation and Private Property* to describe how U.S. corporate management was becoming separated from shareholder ownership rights.

[48] Garnsey 2007:40 notes that Averroes, the 12th-century Islamic philosopher from Andalusia, "proceeds as does Plato to issue the warning that Guards must be like sheepdogs rather than wolves: they must use their superior power and strength to

Church leaders retained the class perspective and worldview of their siblings. The separation of ownership from the management of Church property and income did not save economies from poverty, or even from greed. Being in charge of how to spend Church income enabled clerical elites to become a bureaucracy managing Church land, workshops and money. While this was not their own personal property, they lived off its revenue, benefitted from its increase and often were themselves accused of avarice, reflecting the Church's rising wealth and its temptations.[49]

The Romanized Church thus became a sector alongside and symbiotic with the state, sanctifying (and materially benefitting from) the status quo of land ownership and hereditary wealth. Protesters seeking reforms to create a fair and equitable society were deemed heretical.

The Vandals replace the Romans with little resistance

In 429 a reported force of 80,000 Vandals (a Germanic tribe driven into the Roman Empire after the Huns invaded their territory early in the 4th century) entered North Africa. The Berber and Punic population seem to have offered little resistance, having no love for their landlord-run state.[50] The Vandal siege of Hippo during the spring and summer of 430 prevented the crops from being harvested, causing a famine in which Augustine was one of the victims.

The Vandals made Hippo their first capital, and their kingdom expanded for the next two decades. They were Christians but their theology was Arian, claiming that Jesus did not exist before he was born, in contrast to Nicene Christianity. This argument about the nature of Christ provided an excuse for the Vandals to take over Augustinian churches and place their clergy in control, looting the monasteries of their coinage and precious metals.

The Vandals established a North African kingdom that included Sicily, Sardinia, Corsica and Malta by 439, and they looted Rome in 455 with much more destruction and looting than had occurred in Alaric's 410 attack. In 476, Genseric (ruled 428-477) negotiated peace with Con-

---

protect rather than exploit them to do harm." He adds (p. 17): "The ban on private property comes first, well before the regulations on women and the family."

[49] Brown 2012:487 and 490. He adds (p. 493): "All over the West, the clergy lost out to their bishop," acting merely as councilors, often disgruntled. He adds (p. xxv) that Jerome saw the problem, noting that the Church "has grown great in power and riches and has shrunk in spiritual energy."

[50] Cameron 2000:553-559. See also Merrills and Miles 2010:181. The figure of 80,000 men is from Procopius, *Wars* 3.5.18-19.

stantinople, and in 483 Huneric (477-484) closed all the Nicene churches and turned them over to Arian clergy.

The Vandals and Berbers became a combined military force and made North Africa a center of public construction, learning, literature and science. Throughout the Empire, in fact, the "barbarians" brought "cloisonne jewelry, felt-making, the ski, the use of soap and butter, the construction of tubs and barrels, the cultivation of rye, oats, spelt and hops, and the discovery of the heavy plough, the stirrup and the horse-shoe." Water wheels and windmills developed as new sources of power, and the valved bellows revolutionized smelting.[51]

These improvements did little to help the *coloni*, however. *Adscripticii* were still tied to the landowner's estate and unable to leave without per-mission, with no rights to sue their patron. By the late 6th and 7th centu-ries houses throughout the former Roman Empire stopped leaving much archaeological evidence. Dirt floors became the norm, except for the homes of bishops and kings with the old mosaic or marble floors, and the technique of building in mortared stone and brick was lost.

Many basic skills disappeared, even wheel-pottery for a few centuries. "The economy that sustained and supplied a massive middle and lower market for low-value functional goods had disappeared, leaving sophis-ticated production and exchange only for a tiny number of high-status objects."[52] Although the Eastern Empire issued new copper denomina-tions, coinage almost disappeared in the West, where silver and gold became "collectables" to store value. The final stage of Rome's debt-rid-den economy thus operated on barter. Without a market, good-quality low-value items disappeared. And as Scheidel has summarized, without a system of financing public administration, "Monumental structures fell into disrepair; previously thriving cities emptied out; Rome itself turned into a shadow of its former grand self, with shepherds tending their flocks among the ruins. Trade and coin use thinned out, and the art of writing retreated. Population numbers plummeted."

How is one to measure the period's gross domestic product (GDP) under these circumstances? There are suggestions that the valuation of luxury items was so great that, even as the underlying economy for most of the population was ground down, "the economy" (as viewed and measured by modern historians) seems not to have been all that bad. "The new Germanic rulers operated with lower overheads and proved

---

[51] Walbank 1969:122-123.

[52] Ward-Perkins 2005:109-113 and 117-118.

less adept at collecting rents and taxes. Forensic archaeology reveals that people grew to be taller, likely thanks to reduced inequality, a better diet and lower disease loads. Yet these changes didn't last."[53]

The aftermath

The East Roman Emperor Justinian (527-565) conquered the Vandal kingdom in 534 and incorporated it into his own Byzantine Empire. Strong Byzantine emperors in the 9th and 10th centuries were able to prevent a creditor oligarchy from emerging to block their power to protect indebted smallholders. Western Christendom's commerce and credit were only revived by the vast monetary inflow of Byzantine silver and gold looted by the Crusaders when they sacked Constantinople in 1204.

Just as temples from the Bronze Age through classical antiquity had been in charge of minting, refining and attesting to the purity of monetary silver, two new Church orders, the Knights Templar and Hospitallers, emerged from the Crusades to re-establish credit practices. The Templars became Europe's largest bankers, sanctioned by the Church and by the fact that their debtors were the upper nobility embarking on the Crusades, and kings needing to wage papal wars and pay Peter's Pence and other papal tribute.

It was at this time that the medieval Churchmen defended commercial "interest" as legitimate when charged on productive credit extended to borrowers who used their loans to make a profit for themselves, in contrast to usury that impoverished debtors. No such distinction between productive and unproductive credit existed in antiquity (although such a distinction was implicit in the fact that Near Eastern rulers only annulled personal "grain" debts, not commercial "silver" debts). Antiquity's vocabulary had no words to distinguish between predatory usury and legal commercial interest charges, or between productive and unproductive credit.

Italian banking families close to the papacy emerged in the 13th century to play an increasing role in financing royal wars throughout Europe. In due course the need to refinance these debt arrangements became a lever to pry away royal land, mines and other property. Royal domains and the public commons succumbed to the same fate as private-sector borrowers, losing land, natural resources and basic infrastructure to creditors.

---

[53] Scheidel 2021, "The Road from Rome."

The 18th and 19th centuries saw classical political economy refine the logic for reversing the ability of wealthy medieval and Renaissance creditor families to shift taxes off themselves onto agriculture and industry, just as Roman elites had done. Instead of giving fiscal favoritism to the *rentier* elite, the French Physiocrats, Adam Smith, David Ricardo, John Stuart Mill and subsequent 19th-century political economists developed the logic for taxing away the land's rent or simply nationalizing land, natural resources and basic infrastructure outright so as to create a market free from *rentier* income.

In contrast to classical antiquity's view that it was natural to privatize the land's rental yield and let its ownership become concentrated by turning smallholders into indebted tenants and ultimately into serfs, the 19th century's classical economists depicted the landlord class as socially unnecessary. They deemed land rent – and by logical extension, monopoly rent and financial extraction (interest and other fees and penalties) – to be unearned and not necessary for production, contrasting this unearned *rentier* income with normal business profits. No such conceptual distinction between earned and unearned income, rents and mercantile profits existed in antiquity.

In the 19th and early 20th centuries tax reform to free economies from their *rentier* overhead required political reform to replace the authority of the upper house of parliament dominated by the hereditary landlord class (such as the House of Lords in England) with that of a more broadly elected popular house (such as the House of Commons). That democratic drive shaped the perspective of Theodor Mommsen, who blamed Rome's oligarchic Senate for having blocked the reforms that were needed to save the Republic. Many subsequent classicists whose works have been cited in the preceding chapters likewise blamed the oligarchy for its oppression of Rome's own population and that of its provinces.

Reform did not come either from within the Empire or from Christianity as it became the Roman State religion. The wealthy held onto their property with dependent labor attached to it. Neither Romanized Christianity nor most subsequent economic reformers went so far as to advocate a general widespread debt cancellation or land redistribution as earlier antiquity had hoped for. There is almost no reference to the policy of royal debt amnesties that had kept Near Eastern kingdoms resilient for millennia, nor to Jesus's call for a Jubilee Year. There is still a widespread idealism about an egalitarian Golden Age, but it lacks any recognition of the archaic royal aim of restoring financial balance by wiping away the accrual of arrears and other debts.

In the Bronze-Age Near East interest charges were accepted as a

normal phenomenon as long as they remained subject to the safety
valve of Clean Slates alleviating personal and agrarian debts when their
buildup threatened to force smallholders into widespread bondage and
concentrate land ownership.[54] Interest-bearing debt did not disappear.
Debt was allowed to begin accumulating once again, but the tradition of
Clean Slates kept it from destabilizing archaic economies.

Greece and Rome made a great break that set the West on a different trajectory of credit and land tenure. The results were so destructive
that they ended up leading to an abhorrence of usury so extreme that
all interest-bearing debt was denounced, even that for financing commercial enterprise. Yet the Roman legal system, giving creditor claims
priority over the property rights of debtors, remains the basis of modern
Western thinking about property and market efficiency.

That worldview has led Western economies to experience a modern
debt crisis resulting from the exponential buildup of personal, corporate, government and international debt since 1945, and especially since
1980. Today's financial polarization and the widening gap between the
wealthy *rentier* One Percent and the 99 Percent is akin to the economic
polarization that occurred after antiquity's oligarchies broke free of
control and oversight by overthrowing and preventing any reappearance
of kingship.

Aristotle was right in stating that democracies tend to evolve into
oligarchies. Democracies have not been as successful as strong states
(denounced in today's West as autocracies) in resisting oligarchy and
minimizing economic polarization. When Roman oligarchs accused
advocates of debt cancellation and land redistribution of "seeking
kingship," they meant what today's financial neoliberals pejoratively call
"autocracy," meaning any central power able to regulate or tax creditors
and absentee landlords to protect the economy at large from destructive
polarization.

The political rhetoric used today by Western neoliberal "free market"
economies that call themselves democracies (but which in reality are
electoral oligarchies) against the state-centered "autocratic" or "authoritarian" economies of China, Russia and their allies closely resembles
that of Greek and Roman oligarchies when they used "tyranny" and
"kingship" as pejoratives in opposing popular reformers.

---

[54] The Sumerian term ca. 2500 BC for such a Clean Slate proclamation was
amargi, "return to the mother [condition]," an implicit norm with no outstanding
personal debt balances (but leaving commercial debts in place).

The nominal political "democracies" of the modern West have failed to check the power of creditors and other *rentiers*. They have become oligarchies. In each, a *rentier* class has concentrated political and law-making power in its own hands, seeking its own short-term gains instead of steering the economy toward overall prosperity. That problem confronting today's Western economies is the same as that faced by those of the ancient Greeks and Romans, and indeed has its very roots in the world they created. That is what makes classical antiquity so relevant for understanding the financial and economic, political, rhetorical and philosophical dynamics that have led to the modern world's crisis.

23
Roman History and Modern Ideology

Blaming the fall of the Roman Empire on barbarians at the gates, or even on the internecine fighting among generals for the emperorship, is like tracing a sick man's death from the moment he died – his falling body temperature and the convulsions of rigor mortis. We need to begin earlier to determine just when the deterioration began and how it weakened Rome's body and spirit. "Not the Antonine Age, which [Gibbon] had originally seen as Rome's peak," nor "the Augustan Age or the Ciceronian Age or the time of the Punic Wars or, for that matter, the reign of Constantine can serve as the point from which Rome began an irreversible fall," reflects Glen Bowersock.[1] Rather, Rome's infirmity can be traced back to the birth of the Republic. Overthrowing kingship in 509 BC left no authority able to prevent the landed oligarchy from enriching itself by reducing most of the population to clientage and dependency over the next five centuries.

Rome's problem actually had its genesis in the West's break from Near Eastern practice when it adopted interest-bearing debt without any authority empowered to cancel it when needed to restore economic resilience and prevent creditor oligarchies from emerging. Many early societies reversed the polarization of land ownership and wealth by cancelling debts and redistributing land, as Bronze Age Near Eastern rulers and the Greek "tyrants" did, and as Roman reformers advocated. But today's economic ideology echoes Rome's legal philosophy in upholding the principle of absolute creditor rights: all debts must be paid, without regard for the social consequences. This approach is more sympathetic with the views of Rome's oligarchy than with those of its leading historians who framed Roman history as a Greek tragedy, attributing its decline and fall to the oligarchy's selfishness and violence that held most of the population in debt and kindred forms of dependency.

Instead of the moral disapproval expressed by ancient writers, today's free-enterprise individualism shares Ayn Rand's idealization of selfishness in viewing society as driven forward by acquisitive enterprise seeking to make as much money as possible. Monopolization of land,

---

[1] Bowersock 1988:166.

credit and the public domain is depicted as part of the West's success story, while its *rentier* underside is downplayed.

Walter Scheidel dismisses the tradition of Livy, Dionysius of Halicarnassus, Plutarch and others as having provided "little in the way of credible overarching assessments of socio-economic development beyond the obvious facts of unprecedented levels of capital accumulation among the elite, the expansion of chattel slavery, and urban growth (all of which attracted considerable moral opprobrium)." Brushing away their focus on debt and land grabbing, he characterizes their narratives as reflecting "aristocratic feuds ... pieced together from now-lost sources by Greek-speaking provincials several centuries after the fall of the republic, who, remote from the original context, struggled to re-fashion their distant partisan sources into speciously coherent narratives ... shaped by the conventional topoi of greed, hybris, and class struggle."[2] It is as if the literary history of Rome's struggles over debt and land, the secessions of the plebs, political assassinations and over-reaching by the rich and powerful is all fiction.

Why did antiquity's own philosophers, poets and historians condemn wealth addiction? Why did so many members of the elite embrace Stoic philosophy and subsequent Christianity if they did not agree with the criticisms of self-centered egotism and hubris described by the historians whose writings Scheidel disparages?

I attended a public lecture by Prof. Scheidel at Columbia University in 2017 where, in the question period, he insisted that debt was not a significant factor in Rome's decline. The audience let out a gasp, recognizing how radically at odds his claim was with the histories they had read. In *The Great Leveler*, published that same year, he wrote that since the Stone Age, equality has been achieved only by external causes: the four "great levelers" of mass warfare, violent revolution, lethal pandemics and state collapse. There is no acknowledgement of the ability to reverse the concentration of wealth by writing off debts and returning land to smallholders, or by progressive tax policy.

To the extent that wealthy elites block peaceful economic reform, they indeed leave no alternative but violent revolution. But the long-normal practice of Near Eastern realms reversing economic polarization by royal debt remission and land redistribution, the prototypes for the

---

[2] Scheidel 2007:340. He further explains (p. 322): "Ancient literary sources for this period, composed by aristocrats or their clients, tend to focus on the undesirable consequences of imperial success – 'luxury,' social mobility and civil discord, ultimately resulting in warlordism and autocracy."

Biblical Jubilee Year, plays no role in Scheidel's analysis. It is as if such reforms were fictions, not the reality for millennia in the Near East and then a central focus of real-life political struggles in classical antiquity.

Recent studies of credit and debt in antiquity have broadened understanding of early banking, money and coinage, but compared to late 19th- and early 20th-century classical historians, this research focuses less on the political revolts that occurred over debt and land tenure. Research has concentrated on estimating broad economic measures: wage levels relative to price indexes, population density, free/slave employment ratios, and size corresponding to modern Gross National Product. Ancient historians did not think in terms of these kinds of statistical measures.

Complaining that "there are no ancient statistics, and quantifiable evidence is uneven in quality and coverage and generally scarce," Scheidel outlines a model "derived from ancient numerical data, material evidence, and consideration of the logical corollaries of adequately documented features such as conscription, urbanization, emigration, and redistribution."[3] With no sources available to quantify economy-wide debt relations, he cites the greater economic efficiency of "large 'rational' slave estates" as the main force driving smallholders off their land. In his reading, smallholders left the land because they could obtain higher income in Rome with its dole. "Recent scholarship has finally begun to privilege 'pull' factors over the traditional 'push' scenario of an erosion of family farms through conscription." There is no mention here of debt foreclosure or eviction. Scheidel describes incomes declining when the Empire ended the wars that had provided a bonanza of booty for soldiers on the one hand, but also a huge influx of slaves to farm the land of the economic elite, enabling large estates to displace smaller subsistence farms. That left veterans either to be resettled in new colonies or move to Rome.[4]

Bowersock's view that "the world of Late Antiquity can be seen not as a world in decline from some previously lofty standard, but as a world

---

[3] Scheidel 2007:322.

[4] Scheidel 2007:336 and 322, fn1, citing Hopkins 1978:1-15 regarding the effects of military conquest: "foreign wars, fought by peasant conscripts, undermined the viability of the family farm and fueled urbanization whilst providing the elite with capital and captives that were used to establish large, 'rational' slave estates producing cash crops for urban and overseas markets, a process that ultimately fanned political conflict over access to land that compromised the stability of the political system of the Republic."

in transition"[5] is shared by many recent writers. In their view, Rome did not really fall. In fact, the Empire's dissolution has been celebrated as ending slavery and oppressive imperial taxes, opening the way for liberty from the state. New nation-states emerged, whose rising commercial rivalry put in place economies based on domestic growth with public investment and social spending.

Rome did of course decline and fall, giving way to new polities, but there remains a continuity from Rome's oligarchic state to the modern world, which has inherited Rome's pro-creditor legal philosophy. Today's legal principles and economic ideology follow Rome in upholding the sanctity of debt claims and making the loss of land to creditors irreversible. These principles have permitted and led to the defining economic feature of Western economies: running up an exponentially increasing debt burden owed to a *rentier* oligarchy.

Pro-creditor policy was the main reason why Rome lost its resilience as compared to the earlier Near Eastern societies with their redistributive policies. But that policy has remained the West's distinguishing ideological feature. A related continuity from Rome is in the fiscal sphere. Oligarchies always have minimized social spending on public services, along with the taxes levied to finance them. Rome's Optimates kept social spending at the discretion of the rich, limited mainly to their show of civic philanthropy or staging games to gain popularity for elections. The effect of such fiscal restraint and lack of government support to meet basic needs historically has obliged citizens to rely on patrons or moneylenders for credit. That remains the case today. So does the oligarchic drive to free wealth from strong government and regulatory oversight, with today's "free market" ideology viewing public regulation as playing only an autocratic role, much as that of Rome vilified the policy of cancelling debts and redistributing land as being that of tyrants seeking kingship.

The predatory oligarchic ideal of a free market

Cicero's attack on advocates of debt cancellation and land redistribution sounds like modern libertarian rhetoric: "The men who administer public affairs must first of all see that everyone holds on to what is his, and that private men are never deprived of their goods by public acts." He writes that L. Marcius Philippus, who tried to distribute public land to Rome's plebeians in 104 BC, "deserved to lose his civil rights, pointing as [his proposal] did to an equalization of goods. What greater

---

[5] Bowersock 1988:167.

plague could there be than that? For political communities and citizenships were constituted especially so that men could hold on to what was theirs."[6] And also, indeed, what they appropriated from the public domain and smallholders.

This attitude is the essence of today's free-market ideology that has come to imbue modern classical scholarship. An overview chapter in *The Cambridge Economic History of the Greco-Roman World* (2007) points out that the basic assumption underlying "the 'methodological individualism' that distinguishes Neoclassical Economics is that individuals and their stable preferences are the irreducible starting points of analysis, while the rational efforts of individuals to maximize their personal preferences (what is referred to as Rational Choice theory) provide the basis of all economic analysis."[7]

It is in this spirit that the New Institutional Economics speaks of "minimizing transaction costs" for securing property rights. It takes as its "point of departure interaction among individuals, defined as 'transaction,'" notes Andre Bresson. The main aim is to lower the cost of enforcing creditor and property rights, headed by "the cost of contracts and the settlement of legal conflicts (attorney's fees, court costs)."[8] Claiming that efficiency and prosperity are maximized by providing security of credit and property contracts, the school's founder, Douglass North, views the economy from the vantage point (and indeed as being limited to) individuals borrowing, pledging, buying and selling property – voluntarily and hence implicitly with a mutual gain. He focuses on "changes in contractual behavior, resource allocation and income distribution" in terms of transaction costs, which he approvingly sees as falling as contracts increasingly protect enforcement of financial and property rights.[9] He does not address the power relationships at work. It is as if the "efficiency" of lowering transaction costs for creditors to increase their fortunes is synonymous with efficiency for the economy to prosper over time.

---

[6] Cicero, *De Officiis* 2.21.73, cited in Roselaar 2010:18. See also *De Officiis* 2.12.43 and 2.23.80, and Garnsey 2007:114-115.

[7] Frier and Kehoe 2007:115, pointing out the kinship of the New Institutional Economics with the Chicago School's "free market" Law-and-Economics individualism grounded in the Coase Theorem since the 1960s. The authors acknowledge (p. 127) that Roman law rewarded "particular groups within society at the expense of others, but without fostering growth." But they do not explain what the problems were.

[8] Bresson 2016:19-20.

[9] North 1977:710.

In practice, endorsing unconditional legal support for property rights often means supporting the "right" of debtors to pledge and lose their property (and in early Rome, their liberty) to foreclosing creditors. The Roman oligarchy certainly sought to minimize restraints on transactions that protected debtors against bondage and expropriation, such as laws limiting the appropriation of public land to 500 iugera, and annual interest charges to just $1/12^{th}$. When the honest judges Scaevola and Rutilius tried to enforce the law and prevent illegal seizure of civic property in Asia Minor, the publican *equites* maneuvered to get them removed (as Chapter 14 has described). Was such "freedom" from public "interference" a desirable example of minimizing transaction costs?

Minimizing transaction costs means enabling creditors to foreclose readily on property and income pledged by debtors as collateral. Contracts and laws minimizing such expenses reflect power relationships, typically benefiting the wealthiest classes, such as by removing the right of debtors to request easier terms when distressing circumstances arise. Legalizing the transfer of income, land or other property from the weaker to the stronger locks in these power arrangements, leaving weaker parties with no recourse or appeal to mutual aid.

People living on mere subsistence do not have a choice. For them, "the market" and its contracts are a take-it-or-leave-it deal with bankers or with suppliers of basic needs. Modern narratives assume that debtors and creditors are interacting voluntarily to obtain mutual gains. In a sense, any market transaction is implicitly "formed by mutual consent," even though the relationship is unequal and even where the weaker party has little choice but to enter the transaction. Thus, as Seth Bernard has recognized, even *nexum* debt bondage was "a contractual relationship," notwithstanding that the alternative often was starvation and a loss of life. The *nexum* "institution was at some basic level conceived of as useful to both creditor and debtor, however uneven the risks involved." According to Bernard, falling into debt slavery and losing one's land was "an exchange," and "should be seen not as something Roman smallholders tried to avoid, but as a widespread strategy for exchanging labor, land, or capital within existing social hierarchies."[10]

But this ignores the reality that under circumstances such as those leading to *nexum* debt bondage the contractual outcomes were much like the robber's offer: "Your money or your life." Debtors had little voice in writing the laws that set the terms of their market "choice." The power and dependency relationships dictated by Rome's *rentier* oligarchy had

---

[10] Bernard 2016:323.

the effect of polarizing land and wealth ownership instead of promoting domestic prosperity by protecting the resilience of debtors.

The New Institutional Economics sidesteps this issue by assuming that widening inequality reflects efficient markets; otherwise (so the argument goes), it would not have emerged dominant and "fittest." By that circular reasoning *any* distribution of property, credit and debt must have succeeded because it is the most efficient. But Rome's pro-creditor rules were enacted because of oligarchic power relations, and often imposed by force and violence. They were not promulgated because they were the most efficient for the economy at large.

The oligarchic pro-creditor drive was the dynamic that Rome's early historians blamed for the Republic's decline and fall. The West today is driven by the same basic dynamic and has adopted similar policies to those of Rome to disable any checks to the power of its oligarchies. Contractual market rules sanctify the right of creditors to foreclose on the collateral that debtors are obliged to pledge, and to lose irreversibly when they cannot pay. In antiquity this collateral included the debtors' personal liberty as well as their self-support land, which they lost when harvests were bad or other misfortunes led them to fall into arrears. Debt contracts and land-appropriation rights turned labor, land and money into market "commodities" bought and alienated freely and irreversibly. The resulting debt bondage and monopolization of the land imposed enormous social costs.

The broad social context of market structures

No ancient philosopher or even politician asserted that usury or land grabbing was economically efficient and in the public interest. There was no theory of overall macroeconomic relations, market demand, "economic growth" or debt deflation in Rome's tribute-seeking economy. Instead, classical antiquity's "political correctness" followed Solon, Socrates, Aristotle and the Delphic oracle in warning that the acquisition of wealth, especially by moneylending, was addictive and socially injurious.

In contrast, analyzing society as if it were simply a scale model of personal drives for self-enrichment ignores these concerns and excludes the logic of public regulation for the benefit of society as a whole. The drive to free creditors and monopolists from regulatory oversight has seen individualistic economics become the modern mainstream: "*The Cambridge Economic History of the Greco-Roman World* was based more on Douglass North than Moses Finley," notes Peter Temin – that is, more on microeconomic price theory than the dominance of social relations in shaping the behavior of individuals and class conflict.[11]

Assuming that debt is a result of borrowing to invest the proceeds productively, free-market economists do not distinguish between fair and unfair markets, productive and unproductive credit. They assume that loans are payable, with interest, out of the gains that debtors make from their productive investment. But in today's economies most bank credit is extended to buy real estate already in place, or financial securities already issued, with the proceeds raised from their issue long since spent. In classical antiquity the only productive loans that financed business ventures were commercial "bottomry" loans. Investment in publican tax-collecting companies and loans enabling absentee landlords to buy real estate did not help the economy grow, but resulted in financial and property crashes.

The "modernist" assumption of mutual benefit for debtors as well as creditors downplays the problem of forfeiting land and other collateral as a result of bad harvests, personal misfortune, warfare or an economic crash. Indeed, the tendency of creditor claims to grow faster than the ability to pay leads to the *insecurity* of land tenure and other property of debtors. That debt dynamic is what incited Roman attempts at social reform – the failure of which paved the road to literal serfdom. It is hard to see that as "survival of the fittest."

The main reason why economies polarize is their failure to restrain creditor power and land grabbing. It therefore is unsurprising that the most basic economic conflict throughout history has been that of creditors and landed oligarchies against the rest of society. The defining economic character of any era is how it deals with the dynamics of debt and loss of the debtors' means of livelihood. A resilient economy requires restoring balance by public intervention from "above" the market to prevent creditors from impoverishing debtors. But the *rentier* classes fight to gain control of the political and law-making sphere and prevent democratic, royal or socialist governments from providing economic resilience by checking their self-seeking. This fight is decisive in shaping the context within which market transactions and resource allocation operate.

---

[11] Temin 2013:viii.

Oligarchic vs. democratic concepts of liberty

The inscription on America's Liberty Bell, "Proclaim liberty throughout the land," is a translation of Hebrew *deror*, from Leviticus 25 calling for proclamation of the Jubilee Year at the center of Mosaic law. The word is cognate to Akkadian *andurarum*, referring to the royal Clean Slate proclamations common in the Near East from the third to the first millennia BC. But Moses Finley notes that it is "impossible to translate the word 'freedom,' *eleutheria* in Greek, *libertas* in Latin, or 'free man,' into any ancient Near Eastern language, including Hebrew, or into any Far Eastern language either, for that matter."[12] The Near Eastern counterpart, including the Hebrew *deror* translated on America's Liberty Bell, meant the liberty of debtors from bondage and liability to creditors (along with return of self-support land) as part of an economy-wide restoration of economic balance.

To Rome's creditors and landowners, however, liberty meant the right to deprive debtors and clients of their own freedom – all under the law. As Ste. Croix has noted: "The *libertas* of the Roman aristocrat meant the rule of a class and the perpetuation of privilege." He cites Tacitus's comment that: "Nobody ever sought power for himself and the enslavement of others without invoking *libertas* and such fair names."[13]

At issue is freedom and liberty for whom. Abraham Lincoln explained this as the great issue prompting the American Constitution's 13th Amendment freeing the slaves:

> We all declare for liberty; but in using the same *word* we do not all mean the same *thing*. With some the word liberty may mean for each man to do as he pleases with himself, and the product of his labor; while with others the same word may mean for some men to do as they please with other men, and the product of other men's labor. Here are two, not only different, but incompatable things, called by the same name – liberty.[14]

---

[12] Finley 1975:28, cited in Larsen 2015:101.

[13] Ste. Croix 1989:368, citing Tacitus, *History* 4.74. He adds (p. 366), citing Tacitus, *Annals* 1.75: "Under the Principate the word *libertas*, in the mouth of a member of the Roman governing class like Tacitus, meant essentially *libertas senatus*, the freedom of the Senate. ... If the common herd acted of their own volition against the interests of their rulers, that would be not *libertas* but *licentia*, mere licence: a charge of illegality would almost certainly be brought against it."

[14] Abraham Lincoln addressing a crowd in Baltimore on April 18, 1864, in *Collected Works of Abraham Lincoln*, Vol. 7 (New Brunswick, N.J.: 1953):302-303.

The neoliberal self-interest ideal views "liberty" for the wealthy as the right to deprive debtors and others of their own liberty and property. Arnold Toynbee described how Rome's patrician idea of liberty was limited to the oligarchy's freedom *from* civic bodies or kings powerful enough to check its power to indebt and impoverish the citizenry. "The patrician aristocracy's monopoly of office after the eclipse of the monarchy had been used by the patricians as a weapon for maintaining their hold on the lion's share of the country's economic assets; and the plebeian majority of the Roman citizen-body had striven to gain access to public office as a means to securing a more equitable distribution of property and a restraint on the oppression of debtors by creditors."[15] The latter attempt failed, and European and Western civilization is still living with the aftermath.

Lacking the prospect of royal amnesties annulling personal debts as in Sumer, Babylonia and their neighboring realms, Greeks and Romans falling into debt lost their land tenure and fell into bondage without hope of any authority liberating them. *Eleutheria* and *libertas* came to signify freedom from bondage, but not liberation from liability to creditors. That is why, as Finley noted, the great political cry throughout antiquity was not for "*libertas*" but for debt cancellation and land redistribution.

That kind of liberty was achieved only rarely, as when Greece's archaic "tyrants" overthrew their local aristocracies. Subsequent oligarchies used the word "tyrant" as a term of invective, much as Roman elites accused reformers of "seeking kingship." Yet liberating Greek populations from debt bondage was a precondition for democracy, and kingship was the golden age of Roman growth, which was followed by the tumultuous 5th century of class conflict after the oligarchy overthrew Rome's last king, Tarquinius Superbus in 509, within a year of Cleisthenes's reported rewriting of Athens' constitution.

Oligarchic opposition to democracy and kingship

One hardly can discuss democracy without putting it in the context of oligarchy and aristocracy. Aristotle described democracy as arising as a challenge to the leading families' monopolization of wealth and political power. But it was transitory, tending to evolve into oligarchy, which

---

[15] Toynbee 1965 I:316. Rome's richest and most powerful administered the courts in their own favor and simply ignored the laws, broke contracts and dodged taxes. Contracts were only for the weak.

sought to make itself into a hereditary aristocracy. In due course, some families sought to gain power by taking the *demos* into their camp, sponsoring a new transition to democracy. That is what Cleisthenes the Alcmeonid did in Athens in 508 BC.

No such democratic restructuring occurred in the Roman Republic. Politicians advocating debt reforms were killed for trying to make Rome more democratic, most notably the Gracchi, Catiline and Julius Caesar. Rome's oligarchy created an election system in which voting rights were proportional to landholding and wealth, and limited public administration to the patrician elite, excluding non-patricians from serving as magistrates or on juries – with the perennial fallback of assassinating reformers that threatened their "rights."

Any form of government – democracy, oligarchy or kingship – is an arena in which private wealth, most notably that of creditors and landholders, vies for control against strong rulers, monarchs or civic authority whose interest lies in protecting the general population from wealthy patrons appropriating their labor and land. A key defining factor for any society is how it treats debt dynamics, along with land tenure and tax policy. Will creditor and property interests be subordinated to the common weal, or will governments support their *rentier* claims at society's expense? At stake is whether to deter or permit (indeed, encourage) economic polarization. The central focus of historiography therefore should be to place policy choices regarding debt, land tenure and taxation in the context of this eternal conflict between strong government and private wealth.

The prime task of any democracy, oligarchy or monarchy is to preserve itself. For democracies and monarchies (or today's socialist economies) this requires preventing oligarchic accumulation of creditor power and wealth. There are many ways to do this, but when Herodotus (3.80-82) juxtaposed monarchy to democracy and oligarchy, he did not remark on how Near Eastern monarchies had maintained stability for millennia by keeping debt dynamics in check and by land redistribution – the same policies that classical antiquity's advocates of democracy were demanding.[16]

---

[16] Modern monarchies are not like those of the Bronze Age Near East. Since Rome, kings and emperors have been the head of their *rentier* aristocracy, ruling autocratically in the interest of their nobility (or foreign sponsors), not promoting prosperity for their population at large. The closest equivalent in the modern world to Bronze Age rulership would be socialist economies, now that democracies and

"Monarchy" thus does not necessarily mean autocracy that oppresses most of the population. It can preserve its control by blocking the emergence of creditors and large landowners strong enough to break free and monopolize society's wealth and control of land and labor. That check on the power of wealthy families is the most important criterion in evaluating the politics of monarchy or other state-controlled civil government.[17]

The debt relief and reversal of land transfers by Bronze Age rulers, and also by Byzantine emperors in the 9th and 10th centuries, disprove Scheidel's claim that the only ways to reverse inequality are external crisis, violent revolution or state collapse. When coupled with his statement that debt was not a significant problem contributing to Rome's economic polarization (he blamed the Empire), the political message is to disparage the ability of internal reform to counter economic polarization and to accept it as a natural result of how free markets work.

That message of surrender to polarization is part of the ideology by which oligarchies seek to preserve themselves, claiming that their taking over economic planning from government ("regulatory capture") is the most productive form of social organization, not a harbinger of the End Time.

The historiographic blind spot of pro-creditor ideology

One might expect that today's debt problems would create greater interest in Roman history, especially since the West's pro-creditor legal philosophy has been inherited from Rome. But precisely because the causes of Rome's economic struggles are so kindred to those of today, modern economic ideology shies from confronting how similar the West's debt dynamics are to those of Rome, producing a similar polarization of wealth and consequent economic austerity. Imbued with modern neoliberal ideology reflecting its pro-creditor biases, classical scholars cannot endorse the narratives of Livy, Plutarch and their contemporaries without levying a similar critique against modern Western economies.

---

oligarchies have adopted pro-creditor laws whose effect is to indebt and polarize their income and wealth.

[17] There may be hybrid forms. India has been called an "electoral autocracy" in which citizens can vote for just which politician with autocratic power shall occupy the nation's highest administrative office. China's policy of "Common Prosperity," popularized by Xi Jinping since 2020, aims at reversing the country's economic polarization by high wealth taxes and social redistribution policies.

Given the similarities between the economies of Rome and today's West, Margaret Thatcher's TINA – There Is No Alternative to the neoliberal "free market" ideal – implies that the economic polarization of Rome under its oligarchy was a result of efficient markets. Scheidel's conclusion is that more egalitarian economies can only be created by external checks or violent revolution, not by domestic policy reform. He implies that the five centuries of Rome's revolts seeking reform of debt and land tenure could not have succeeded peacefully, and doubts that the attempted revolts occurred in the way that Rome's own historians described. In any case, if one believes that policies to resist free market forces are inefficient, and that today's pro-*rentier* ideology really promotes overall wealth by debt leverage, the inference is that the moral drawn by ancient historians criticizing money addiction is too "socialist" to be taken seriously and there was no reasonable path that Rome could have taken to avoid economic polarization.[18]

Recent reassessments of Roman history make the point that the Empire's collapse was part of an evolution leading via European nation-states to the modern Western world. This Western world is indeed the product of antiquity's oligarchic collapse. It has inherited Rome's legal philosophy giving creditor claims priority over the livelihood and property of debtors, enabling creditors to absorb most of the economy's wealth. Contract law is still administered by the wealthiest classes, who view the sanctity of their creditor claims to be an intrinsic element of the natural order.

Today's version of this individualistic pro-creditor ideology denies social-democratic, royal or socialist regimes legitimate power to regulate and check the *rentier* classes.[19] It portrays their concentration of wealth as a victory of the fittest, not as the road to serfdom. That Hayekian

---

[18] Like Chicago-style neoliberal doctrine, the New Institutional Economics speaks of minimizing transaction costs without acknowledging that economic rent is a cost, being unearned income obtained corrosively or, as Aristotle put it, in a "sterile" way.

[19] At the end of his popular article "The Road from Rome," Scheidel writes that the Empire and its aftermath at least freed the world from the "ancient scourge" of "divine kingship." I have no idea whether he knows that the commandment of the gods for Hammurabi and similar Near Eastern kings to follow was the command to cancel debts, liberate bondservants and restore land to debtors who had lost it – the economic solution that Rome's oligarchy fought to prevent during its entire Republic.

label is applied only to democratic regulatory power to check *rentiers*, not to *rentier* oligarchies.

Neoliberal historians depict the progress of Western civilization as a long fight to remove government's regulatory role, leaving economies "free" for the power of *rentier* wealth to shape markets and politics. Today's mainstream ideology defines liberty and free markets to mean freedom *from* public regulatory authority, and hence, freedom *for* economic rent (income not socially necessary for production) to be charged without government constraint. This freedom for *rentiers* is juxtaposed to autocracy, which to Frederick Hayek simply meant strong government forward planning, as he accused any public regulation and government planning of leading society down the road to serfdom.

This anti-state historiography downplays how the Near Eastern takeoff managed to avoid the loss of liberty to which Western oligarchies have succumbed. The Bronze Age takeoff has been characterized as Oriental Despotism, rejected as "autocracy," while classical antiquity's oligarchies are euphemized as democratic.

Is Western civilization pursuing a failed economic model?

Something is amputated in assuming that Western civilization started in Greece and Rome around 750 BC. The implication is that these new economies were created *de novo*, not recognizing how land tenure, money, interest-bearing debt, prices, weights and measures (initially to denominate taxes and other debts) and much commercial and contract practice were innovated in the Bronze Age Near East,[20] and how radical it was for Greek and Roman oligarchic aristocracies to adopt these practices without the palatial control that had maintained resilience in earlier economies.

Excluding awareness of Western civilization's Near Eastern background, particularly its palatial regulation of debt relations, blocks knowledge of how truly radical antiquity's oligarchies were in "freeing" themselves from civic checks. The result is a misunderstanding, indeed a complete lack of understanding, of how Western civilization has come to be structured in a way that is causing a modern debt crisis whose political and economic dynamics are strikingly akin to those of Rome.

---

[20] I discuss this development elsewhere, in *"... and forgive them their debts"* (2018) and my forthcoming *Temples of Enterprise*. For the Western free-market bias in historiography see David Gress, *From Plato to NATO* (1998).

Most popular treatments label the political structures that emerged in the ancient Mediterranean "democracies" simply because there were no more kings. (Sparta had two, but they were subject to check by an aristocratic *gerousia* council.) Democracy usually is defined as a political system in which the majority of citizens are able to elect leaders to legislate policies that the majority wants. That rarely has happened. Throughout classical antiquity there was a constant popular call for what Near Eastern rulers had regularly proclaimed. Palatial economies were not democratic, but their rulers recognized the need to cancel agrarian debts and restore widespread land tenue for the taxpaying population. But despite almost constant fighting for reform, the *demos* in Greece and Italy failed to achieve similar liberty from debt bondage and expropriation.

One can easily draw a parallel with today's world. Today's voters want debt relief, higher wages, and for governments to meet their basic needs in a less polarized and predatory economy. But in the United States they are unable to get a political party even to sponsor public health care, to say nothing of progressive taxation of the financial, real estate and monopoly sectors.

Western democracy has not prevented oligarchies from arising and enacting policies that indebt and impoverish much of the population. Nominally democratic voting systems for electing public officials have not been accompanied by *economic* democracy to minimize the rise of personal debt and dependency on a creditor and landlord class gaining control of public regulation and lawmaking. Instead, the word "democracy" has become a euphemism for electoral oligarchy "free" from state regulation.

Strong states have been able to avoid the polarization of wealth and land ownership that nominal political democracies have failed to prevent. And when they do so, such states are deemed autocratic and antithetical to democracy. Communist China is deemed to be an autocracy, but under party rule its money and debt creation has aimed at promoting widespread economic growth. What the West really deems autocratic is China's success in preventing *rentier* interests from taking over the economy and government. In the language of today's American diplomacy, "democracy" has come to mean "free markets" and an economy open to U.S. multinational companies and creditors. In practice that often means client oligarchies or military autocracies that block democratic reformers from restraining predatory rent-seeking.

Where does that leave the historic role of classical Greek and Roman antiquity? The answer is best expressed by reference to Aristotle's description of democracy as the stage immediately preceding oligarchy. Classical antiquity bequeathed to subsequent Western civilization the legal and political structure of economically polarizing creditor oligarchies, not democracy in the sense of social structures and policies that promote widespread prosperity. Antiquity's great transition to the modern world lay in replacing kingship not with democracies but with oligarchies having a pro-creditor legal philosophy. That philosophy permitted creditors to draw wealth into their own hands, without regard for restoring economic balance and long-term viability as occurred in the Near East through Clean Slates. The modern West is dominated by similar creditor oligarchies: to the extent that today's "free market democracies" have economic planning, it is increasingly done by the financial sector seeking to concentrate in its own hands as much income, land and money as possible at the expense of the indebted population at large.

These are the oligarchic dynamics that Rome's own historians blamed for the Republic's decline and fall. Rome's collapse was the forerunner of the debt crises, economic polarization and austerity caused by subsequent Western oligarchies. The West's pro-creditor laws and ideology inherited from Rome make repeated debt crises transferring property and control of government to financial oligarchies inevitable. That is why a knowledge of the economic history of the Bronze Age Near East and classical antiquity is so important – to demonstrate that there is indeed an alternative to *rentier* oligarchies, and that it succeeded over prolonged periods of time. Classical antiquity's most fundamental role in the evolution of Western civilization was to block the tradition of rulers ("the state") overriding *rentier* power to prevent or reverse the polarization of wealth and income. This flaw has remained the political hallmark of societies calling themselves democracies ever since.

BIBLIOGRAPHY

ANCIENT TEXTS

In citing modern historians I often retain their own translations for ancient texts. The following list provides accessible online references or other standard translations.

* available online at Perseus Digital Library: http://www.perseus.tufts.edu/hopper/collection?collection=Perseus:collection:Greco-Roman.
** available online at LacusCurtius: Into the Roman World: https://penelope.uchicago.edu/Thayer/E/Roman/home.html.
*** available at Internet Archive: https://archive.org/.

Aeschylus, *Agamemnon*, translated by Herbert Weir Smyth, Loeb Classical Library (1926).*
    " *Eumenides*, translated by Herbert Weir Smyth, Loeb Classical Library (1926).*

Appian, *Roman History*, translated by Horace White, Loeb Classical Library (1913), of which *Civil War* is available at LacusCurtius and *The Mithridatic Wars* at https://www.livius.org/sources/content/appian/appian-the-mithridatic-wars/.

Aristophanes, *Clouds*, translated by George Theodoridis (2007), available at https://www.poetryintranslation.com/PITBR/Greek/Clouds.php#highlightclouds.
    " *Ecclesiazusae*, translated by George Theodoridis (2004), available at https://www.poetryintranslation.com/PITBR/Greek/WomenInParliament.php#highlightaristophanes.
    " *Ploutos (Wealth)*, translated by George Theodoridis (2008), available at https://www.poetryintranslation.com/PITBR/Greek/Wealth.php#highlightaristophanes.

Aristotle, *Politics,* translated by H. Rackham, Loeb Classical Library (1932, repr. with corrs. 1944).*
    " *Rhetoric*, translated by John Henry Freese, Loeb Classical Library (1926).*

Pseudo-Aristotle, *Constitution of the Athenians*, translated by J. M. Moore in *Aristotle and Xenophon on Democracy and Oligarchy* (London, 1975).***
    " *Oeconomica*, translated by G. Cyril Armstrong, Loeb Classical Library (1935).*

Athenaeus, *The Deipnosophists, Or Banquet of The Learned of Athenaeus*, translated by Charles Burton Gulick, Loeb Classical Library, 7 vols. (1927-1941), available at http://www.attalus.org/info/athenaeus.html.

Caesar, Julius, *Civil Wars (Bellum Civile)*, translated by A. G. Peskett, Loeb Classical Library (1914).**
    " *The Gallic War (De Bello Gallico)*, translated by H. J. Edwards, Loeb Classical Library (1917).**

Cassius Dio, *Roman History*, Loeb Classical Library, 9 vols. (1914-1927).**

Cicero, M. Tullius, *De Legibus*, translated by C. W. Keyes, Loeb Classical Library (1928).***
    " *De Officiis*, translated by Walter Miller, Loeb Classical Library (1913).**
    " *De Re Publica*, translated by C. W. Keyes, Loeb Classical Library (1928), available at http://www.attalus.org/info/republic.html.
    " *De Senectute*, translated by William Armistead Falconer, Loeb Classical Library (1923).*
    " *Letters to his friends* and *Letters to Atticus*, in *The Letters of Cicero; The Whole Extant Correspondence in Chronological Order*, translated by Evelyn S. Shuckburgh, 4 vols., George Bell & Sons (London, 1908-1909).**
    " *Orations: Against Verres, Cataline Orations, Pro Flaccus, Pro Fonteio, pro lege Manilia*, in *The Orations of Marcus Tullius* Cicero (Vols. I & II), translated by C. D. Yonge, Henry G. Bohn (London, 1856).*
    " *Philippics*, in *The Orations of Marcus Tullius Cicero* (Vol. IV), translated by C. D. Yonge, George Bell & Sons (London, 1903).*

Demosthenes, *Against Timocrates*, in *Demosthenes*, translated by A. T. Murray, Loeb Classical Library (1935).*

Dessau, Hermann, ed., *Inscriptiones Latinae Selectae* (Berlin, 1892), ILS 309.***

Diodorus Siculus, *Bibliotheca historica (Library of History)*, translated by C. H. Oldfather, C. L. Sherman, C. Bradford Welles, R. M. Geer and F. R.

Walton, Loeb Classical Library, 12 vols. (1933-1967).**

Diogenes Laertius, *Lives of the Eminent Philosophers*, translated by R. D. Hicks, Loeb Classical Library, 2 vols. (1925).*

Dionysius of Halicarnassus, *Roman Antiquities*, translated by Earnest Cary, Loeb Classical Library, 7 vols. (1937-1950).**

Eusebius, *Ecclesiastical History*, translated by Kirsopp Lake and J. E. L. Oulton, Loeb Classical Library, 2 vols. (1926, 1932).***

Gellius, *Attic Nights*, translated by John C. Rolfe, Loeb Classical Library (1927).*

Herodian, *History of the Roman Empire from the Death of Marcus Aurelius to the Accession of Gordian III,* translated by Edward C. Echols, University of California Press (Berkeley and Los Angeles, 1961), available at https://www.livius.org/sources/content/herodian-s-roman-history/herodian.

Herodotus, *The Histories*, translated by A. D. Godley, Loeb Classical Library, 4 vols. (1920-1925).**

Historia Augusta, Life of Hadrian, translated by David Magie, Loeb Classical Library (1921).**

Lactantius, *The Divine Institutes, Books I-VII*, translated by Sister Mary Francis McDonald, The Fathers of the Church series, Catholic University of America Press (Washington, 1964).

Livy, *History of Rome*, translated by Rev. Canon Roberts, E. P. Dutton & Co. (New York, 1912).*
    " translated by B. O. Foster, Frank Gardner Moore, Evan T. Sage, and Alfred Cary Schlesinger, Loeb Classical Library, 14 vols. (1919-1959).***

Macrobius, *Saturnalia, Volume I: Books 1-2*, translated by Robert A. Kaster, Loeb Classical Library (2011).

Pausanias, *Description of Greece*, translated by W. H. S. Jones and H.A. Ormerod, Loeb Classical Library, 4 vols. (1918-1935).*

Plato, *Apology*, translated by Harold North Fowler, Loeb Classical Library (1914).*
>   " *Laws*, translated by R. G. Bury, Loeb Classical Library, 2 vols. (1926).*
>   " *Phaedrus*, translated by Harold North Fowler, Loeb Classical Library (1914).*
>   " *Republic*, translated by Francis MacDonald Cornford, Oxford University Press (Oxford, 1941).***
>   " *Timaeus*, translated by R. G. Bury, Loeb Classical Library (1929).*

Pliny the Elder, *Natural History*, translated by John Bostock and H. T. Riley, Bohn's Classical Library, Henry G. Bohn (London, 1855).*

Pliny the Younger, *Letters*, translated by William Melmoth (1746), available at https://www.gutenberg.org/files/2811/2811-h/2811-h.htm#link2H_4_0010.

Plutarch, *Moralia*, translated by Frank Cole Babbitt, P. A. Clement, H. B. Hoffleit, Edwin L. Minar, Jr., F. H. Sandbach, W. C. Helmbold and Harold North Fowler, Loeb Classical Library, Vols. III, VIII, IX, X (1931-1969).***
>   " *Parallel Lives of the Greeks and Romans*, translated by Bernadotte Perrin, Loeb Classical Library (1923).**

Polybius, *The Histories*, translated by W. R. Paton, Loeb Classical Library, 6 vols. (1922-1927).**

Procopius, *Wars*, translated by H. B. Dewing, Loeb Classical Library, 5 vols. (1914-1928).**

Sallust, *The War with Catiline*, in *Sallust*, translated by J. C. Rolfe, Loeb Classical Library (1921, rev. 1931).**
>   " *Histories,* in *Sallust*, translated by J. C. Rolfe, Loeb Classical Library (1921, rev.1931).**

Salvian, *De gubernatione Dei*, in *The Writings of Salvian, The Presbyter*, translated by Jeremiah F. O'Sullivan, The Fathers of the Church series, The Catholic University of America Press (Washington, 1947).

Seneca the Younger, *Ad Lucilium Epistulae Morales* (*Moral Letters to Lucilius*), translated by Richard M. Gummer, Loeb Classical Library, 3 vols. (1917-1925).***

Suetonius, *Lives of the Twelve Caesars*, translated by J. C. Rolfe, Loeb Classical Library, 2 vols. (1913, 1914).**

Tacitus, *Agricola, Germania, Dialogue* on *Oratory*, translated by M. Hutton and W. Peterson, revised by R. M. Ogilvie, E. H. Warmington and Michael Winterbottom, Loeb Classical Library (1914, rev. 1970).
    " *Annals*, translated by Clifford H. Moore and John Jackson, Loeb Classical Library, Vols III, IV, V (1931-1937).**

Tacticus, Aeneas, *On the Defense of Fortified Positions*, translated by W. A. Oldfather - The Illinois Greek Club, Loeb Classical Library (1923).**

Thucydides, *The Peloponnesian War*, translated by Richard Crawly, Everyman's Library: J. M. Dent & Sons; E. P. Dutton & Co (London and New York, 1910).*

Xenophon, *Constitution of the Athenians*, translated by J. M. Moore in *Aristotle and Xenophon on Democracy and Oligarchy* (London, 1975).***
    " *Hellenica*, translated by Carleton L. Brownson, Loeb Classical Library, 2 vols. (1918, 1921).*
    " *The Politeia of the Spartans*, translated by J. M. Moore in *Aristotle and Xenophon on Democracy and Oligarchy* (London, 1975).***
    " *Memorabilia*, translated by E. C. Marchant, Loeb Classical Library (1923).*
    " *Oeconomicus*, translated by E. C. Marchant, Loeb Classical Library (1923).*
    " *Ways and Means: A pamphlet on Revenues*, translated by H. G. Dakyns in *The Works of Xenophon*, Macmillan and Co. (1897), available at http://lucianofsamosata.info/demonax.info/doku.php?id=text:on_revenues.

BIBLIOGRAPHY

MODERN WORKS

Africa, T. W. (1961), "Aristonicus, Blossius and the City of the Sun," *International Review of Social History* 6:110-124.

Anderson, Greg (2005), "Before *Turranoi* Were Tyrants: Rethinking a Chapter of Early Greek History," *Classical Antiquity* 24:173-222.

Andreades, Andreas Michael (1933), *A History of Greek Public Finance* (Cambridge, MA).

Andreau, Jean (1968), "Banque grecque et romaine dans le theatre de Plaute et de Terence," *Melanges d'archaeologie et d'histoire* 80:461-526.
    " (1984), "Histoire des metiers bancaires et evolution econo-mique," *Opus* 3:99-114.
    " (1987), *La Vie financiere dans le monde romain. Les metiers de manieurs d'argent* (Rome).
    " (1999), *Banking and Business in the Roman World* (Cambridge).
    " (2006),"Existait-il une Dette publique dans l'Antiquité romaine?", in J. Andreau, G. Béaur and J.-Y. Grenier (dir.), *La Dette publique dans l'Histoire*, Journées du Centre de Recherches Historiques (26-28 Novembre 2001), Paris, Comité pour l'Histoire économique et financière de la France (C.H.E.F.F.):101-114.
    " (2012), "Personal endebtment and debt forgivness [sic] in the Roman empire," December 17, 2012, Committee for the Abolition of Illegitimate Debt (CATDM), available at https://www.cadtm.org/Personal-endebtment-and-debt.

Andrewes, A. (1956), *The Greek Tyrants* (London).
    " (1977), "Kleisthenes' reform bill," *The Classical Quarterly* 27:241-248.

Asheri, D. (1963), "Laws of inheritance, distribution of land and political constitutions in ancient Greece," *Historia* 12:1-21.

Astour, Michael (1972), "The Merchant Class of Ugarit," in D. O.

Edzard, ed., Gesellschaftsklassen *im Alten Zweistromland und in den angrenzenden Gebieten*, (Munich) (=ABAW 75):11-26.

Austin, Michael Merwin (1981), *The Hellenistic World from Alexander to the Roman Conquest: A Selection of Ancient Sources in Translation* (Cambridge).

Austin, M. M. and P. Vidal-Naquet (1977), *Economic and Social History of Ancient Greece: An Introduction* (London).

Avila, Charles (1983), *Ownership: Early Christian Teaching* (Maryknoll, NY).

Badian, Ernst (1968), *Roman Imperialism in the Late Republic* (Ithaca).
    " (1969), "Quaestiones Variae," *Historia* 18:447-491.
    " (1983), *Publicans and Sinners: Private Enterprise in the Service of the Roman Republic* (Ithaca).

Bagnall, Roger and Peter Derow (2008), *The Hellenistic Period: Historical Sources in Translation* (Malden, MA and Oxford), available at https://epdf.tips/the-hellenistic-period-historical-sources-in-translation-blackwell-sourcebooks-i.html.

Barkman, Heather (2014), "The Church of the Martyrs in Egypt and North Africa: A Comparison of the Melitian and Donatist Schisms," *Journal of the Canadian Society for Coptic Studie*s 6:41-58.

Barlow, Charles T. (1978), "Bankers, moneylenders and interest rates in the Roman Republic," PhD. thesis (Chapel Hill, NC).
    " (1980), "The Roman Government and the Roman Economy, 92-80 B.C.," *American Journal of Philology* 101:202-219.

Beard, Mary (2015), *SPQR: A History of Ancient Rome* (New York and London).

Benveniste, Emile (1973), *Indo-European Language and Society* (Coral Gables, FL).

Bernard, Seth (2016), "Debt, Land, and Labor in the Early Republican Economy," *Phoenix* 70:317-338.

Berriman, A. E. (1953), *Historical Metrology* (London and New York).

Billeter, G. (1898), *Geschichte des Zinsfusses im griechisch-romischen Altertum bis auf Justinian* (Leipzig, repr. Wiesbaden, 1970).

Bintliff, J. (2006), "Solon's reforms: an archaeological perspective," in Blok and Lardinois (2006).

Blok, Josine and A. Lardinois, eds. (2006), *Solon of Athens. New Historical and Philological Approaches* (Leiden and Boston).

Blok, Josine and Julia Krul (2017), "Debt and its Aftermath: The Near Eastern Background to Solon's Seisachtheia," *Hesperia* 86:607-643.

Boeckh, August (1857 [1842]), *The Public Economy of Athens* (Boston and London).

Boersma, Johannes (2000), "Peisistratos' Building Activity Reconsidered," in Heleen Sancisi-Weerdenburg, ed., *Peisistratos and the Tyranny: A Reappraisal of the Evidence* (Amsterdam):49-56.

Bogaert, Raymond (1968), *Banques et Banquiers dans les Cités Grecques* (Leiden).
  " (1988), "Les Operations en nature des banques en Egypte greco-romaine," *Ancient Society* 19:213-224.

Boicu, Dragos (2019), "The Consolidation of Donatism in the First Half of the Fourth Century," *Subbto* 64:83-100.

Borg, Marcus J. (1987), *Jesus: A New Vision* (New York).

Bossier, Gaston (1897), *Cicero and his Friends: A Study of Roman Society in the Time of Caesar* (London).

Bourriot, Felix (1976), *Recherches sur la nature du genos* (Paris).

Bowersock, Glen W. (1988), "The Dissolution of the Roman Empire," in Norman Yoffee and George L. Cowgill, eds., *The Collapse of Ancient States and Civilizations* (Tucson):165-176.

Brandbourg, Gilles (2015), "The later Roman Empire," in Monson and Scheidel (2015): 258-281.

Bravo, Benedetto (1974), "Commerce et noblesse en Grece archaique," *Dialogues d'histoire ancienne* 10:99-160.
" (1977), "Le monde de l'emporion," *Dialogues d'histoire ancienne* 3.
" (1985), "Les Travaux et les jours et la cite," *Annali della scuola normale superiore di Pisa* 15:705-65.

Bresson, Alain (2016), *The Making of the Greek Economy: Institutions, Markets, and Growth in the City-States* (Princeton).

Bringmann, K. (1985), *Die Agrarreform des Tiberius Gracchus* (Stuttgart).

Brock, Roger and Stephen Hodkinson, eds. (2000), *Alternatives to Athens: Varieties of Political Organisation and Community in Ancient Greece* (Oxford).

Broughton, T. R. S. (1938), "Roman Asia Minor. The First Mithridatic War, 89-84 BC," and "Roman Asia Minor," in Tenney Frank, *Economic Survey of Ancient Rome*, IV: *Roman Africa, Syria, Greece and Asia* (Baltimore).
" (1952), *The Magistrates of the Roman Republic: 99 B.C.-31 B.C.* (New York).

Brown, Peter (2000), *Augustine of Hippo: a Biography* (Berkeley).
" (2005), "Augustine and a Crisis of Wealth in Late Antiquity," *Augustinian Studies* 36:1:5-30.
" (2012), *Through the Eye of a Needle: Wealth, the Fall of Rome, and the Making of Christianity in the West, 350-550 AD* (Princeton).

Brunt, Peter A. (1971a), *Social Conflicts in the Roman Republic* (London and New York).
" (1971b), *Italian Manpower: 225 BC-AD 14* (Oxford).

Burns, J. Patout Jr. and Robert M. Jensen (2014), *Christianity in Roman Africa* (Grand Rapids, MI).

Burrows, Michael Harvey (2017), "Lower-Class Violence in the Late Antique World," PhD. dissertation, Leeds University, https://core.ac.uk/download/pdf/83935118.pdf.

Butera, C. J. (2010), "'The Land of the Fine Triremes:' Naval Identity and *Polis* Imaginary in 5th Century Athens," PhD. dissertation, Duke University, https://dukespace.lib.duke.edu/dspace/handle/10161/3132.

Cameron, Averil (2000), "The Vandal conquest and Vandal rule (A.D. 429-534)," in Averil Cameron, Bryan Ward-Perkins and Michael Whitby, eds., *The Cambridge Ancient History, XIV: Late Antiquity: Empire and Successors, A.D. 425-600* (Cambridge).

Cameron, H. D. (1964), "The debt to the earth in the *Seven Against Thebes*," *Transactions and Proceedings of the American Philological Association* 95:1-8.

Cartledge, Paul A. (1979), *Sparta and Lakonia. A Regional History 1300-362 B.C.* (London).
   " (2002), "The Political Economy of Greek Slavery," in P. Cartledge, E. Cohen, and L. Foxhall, eds., *Money, Labour and Land. Approaches to the Economies of Ancient Greece* (London):156-166.

Cavaignac, Eugene (1908), *Études sur l'Histoire Financière d'Athènes au Ve Siècle: Le Trésor d'Athènes* (Paris).
   " (1923), *Population et capital dans le monde antique* (Strasbourg).

Cavanagh, William (2018), "An Archaeology of Ancient Sparta, with Reference to Laconia and Messenia," in Powell (2018):61-92.

Cecchet, Lucia (2017), "Debt Cancellation in the Classical and Hellenistic *Poleis*: Between Demagogy and Crisis Management," in *The European Legacy* 28:127-148, available at https://doi.org/10,1080/10848770,20 17m1402516.

Christien, Jacqueline (2002), "Iron Money in Sparta: Myth and History," in Powell and Hodkinson (2002):171-190.

Cline, Eric H. (2014), *1177 B.C.: The Year Civilization Collapsed* (Princeton).

Cohen, Edward E. (1992), *Athenian Economy and Society: A Banking Perspective* (Princeton).

Collins, Andrew and John Walsh (2015), "Debt Deflationary Crisis in the Late Roman Republic," *Ancient Society* 45:125-170.

Cornell, Tim J. (1995), *The Beginnings of Rome: Italy and Rome from the Bronze Age to the Punic Wars (c.1000-264 BC)* (London and New York).
   " (2005), "The Value of the Literary Tradition Concerning

Archaic Rome," in Raaflaub (2005):47-74.

Costouros, G. J. (1979), "Early Greek accounting on estates," Working Paper No. 21 in E. N. Coffman, ed., *Working Paper Series Vol. II*, 1-6, Academy of Accounting Historians (Richmond, VA).

Crawford, Michael H. (1968), "The edict of M. Marius Gratidianus," Proceedings of the Cambridge Philosophical Society, n.s. 14: 1968:1-4.
   " (1970), "Money and exchange in the Roman world," *Journal of Roman Studies* 60:40-48.
   " (1974), *Roman Republican Coinage* (Cambridge).
   " (1985), *Coinage and Money Under the Roman Republic: Italy and the Mediterranean Economy* (Methuen).

Crossan, John Dominic (1994), *The Essential Jesus: Original Sayings and Earliest Images* (San Francisco).

Cunningham, William (1911), *An Essay on Western Civilization in its Economic Aspects*, 2 vols. (Cambridge).

Curtius, E. (1870), "On the religious character of Greek coins," *Numismatic Chronicle* 10:91-111 (translated by B. V. Head; original title "Uber den religiosen Character der griechischen Münzen").

D'Arms, John (1981), *Commerce and Social Standing in Ancient Rome* (Cambridge, MA).

David, E. (1981), *Sparta between Empire and Revolution, 404-243 BC* (New York).
   " (1984), *Aristophanes and Athenian Society of the Early Fourth Century BC* (*Mnemosyne* suppl., Leiden).

Davies, J. K. (1981), *Wealth and the Power of Wealth in Classical Athens* (New York).
   " (2009), "Ancient Economies," in Andrew Erskine, ed., *A Companion to Ancient History* (Oxford):436-446.

Deloume, Antonin (1890), *Manieurs d'Argent* à Rome *jusqu'à l'Empire: les grandes compagnies par actions des publicains, les financiers maîtres dans l'État, les millions de Cicéron, les actionnaires, le marché, le jeu sous la République: étude historique* (Paris).

Demandt, Alexander (1984), *Der Fall Roms. Die Auflösung des römischen Reiches im Urteil der Nachwelt* (Munich). The list is available at http://courses.washington.edu/rome250/gallery/ROME%20250/210%20Reasons.htm.

Dickens, G. (1912), "The Growth of Spartan Policy," *Journal of Hellenic Studies* 32.

Dinsmoor, William Bell (1934), "The Repair of the Athena Parthenos: A Story of Five Dowels," *American Journal of Archaeology* 38:93-106, available at http://penelope.uchicago.edu/Thayer/E/Journals/AJA/38/1/Athena_Parthenos*.html.

Donlan, Walter (1985), "The Social Groups of Dark Age Greece," *Classical Philology* 80:293-308

Dossey, Leslie (2010), *Peasant and Empire in Christian North Africa* (Berkeley).

Drews, Robert (1983), *Basileus: The Evidence for Kingship in Geometric Greece* (New Haven and London).

Drinkwater, J. F. (1992), "The Bacaudae of fifth-century Gaul," in J. Drinkwater and H. Elton, eds., *Fifth-Century Gaul: a crisis of identity?* (Cambridge):208-17.

Dudley, D. R. (1941), "Blossius of Cumae," *Journal of Roman Studies* 31:94-99.

Duplouy, Alan and Roger W. Brock, eds. (2018), *Defining Citizenship in Archaic Greece* (Oxford).

Eckstein, A. M. (1987), "Nabis and Flamininus on the Argive Revolutions of 198 and 197 B.C," *Greek, Roman and Byzantine Studies* 28.2:213-233.

Eddy, Samuel (1977), "The gold in the Athena Parthenos," *American Journal of Archaeology* 81:107-111.

Eder, Walter (2005), "The Political Significance of the Codification of Law in Archaic Societies: An Unconventional Hypothesis," in Raaflaub

(2005):239-267.

Edwards, M. W. (1997), *Optatus: Against the Donatists. Translated Texts for Historians Vol. 27* (Liverpool).

Elliott, Colin P. (2015), "The Crisis of A.D. 33: past and present," *Journal of Ancient History* 3(2):267-281.
    " (2020), "The Role of Money in the Economies of Ancient Greece and Rome," in S. Battilossi, Y. Cassis and K. Yago, eds., Springer *Handbook of the History of Money and Currency* (Singapore).

Eyre, Christopher (2005), "Village Economy in Pharaonic Egypt," in A. K. Bowman and E. Rogan, eds., *Agriculture in Egypt from Pharaonic to Modern Times*, Proceedings of the British Academy 96 (Oxford):33-60.

Ferguson, John (1975), *Utopias of the Classical World* (Ithaca).

Ferrero, Guglielmo (1909 [1902]), *Greatness and Decline of Rome*, 5 vols. (New York). Notes are from Vol. 2: Julius Caesar, unless otherwise noted.

Figueira, Thomas J. (1981), *Aegina: Society and Politics* (New York).
    " (1985), "The Theognidea and Megarian Society," in Thomas J. Figueira and Gregory Nagy, eds., *Theognis of Megara: Poetry and the Polis* (Baltimore).
    " (1988), *The Power of Money: Coinage and politics in the Athenian empire* (Philadelphia).
    " (2002), "Iron money and the ideology of consumption in Laconia," in Powell and Hodkinson (2002):137-190.
    " (2018), "Helotage and the Spartan Economy," in Powell (2018):565-595.

Fine, J. V. A. (1951), *Horoi: Studies in Mortgage, Real Security, and Land Tenure in Ancient Athens* (Athens).

Finley, Moses I. (1951), *Studies in Land and Credit in Ancient Athens: 500-200 BC. The Horos Inscriptions* (New Brunswick, NJ).
    " (1963a), *The Ancient Greeks* (London).
    " (1963b), "Land, Debt, and the Man of Property in Classical Athens," *Political Science Quarterly* 58.
    " (1968), "*A History of Sicily. Vol. I: Ancient Sicily to the Arab Conquest* (New York).

" (1973), *The Ancient Economy* (Berkeley and Los Angeles).

" (1977), *Aspects of Antiquity*, 2nd ed. (London).

" (1981), *Economy and Society in Ancient Greece* (London; New York: 1983).

Fisher, Nick R. E. (1992), *Hybris: A study in the values of honour and shame in Ancient Greece* (Warminster).

Flower, Michael (2002), "The Invention of tradition in Classical and Hellenistic Sparta," in Powell and Hodkinson (2002):192-207.

Forrest, W. G. (1966), *The Emergence of Greek Democracy: 800-400 BC* (New York).

" (1968), *A History of Sparta: 950-192 BC* (London).

" (2000), "The Pre-polis Polis," in Brock and Hodkinson (2000):119-136.

Forsdyke, Sara (2006), "Land, labor and economy in Solonian Athens," in Blok and Lardinois (2006).

Forsythe, Gary (2005), *A Critical History of Rome: From Prehistory to the First Punic War* (Berkeley and Los Angeles).

" (2018), *Primary Sources for Ancient History, Vol. II: The Roman World* (Pittsburgh).

Fournir, Eric (2019), "Persecuting Heretics in Late Antique North Africa: Tolerant Vandals and Intolerant Bishops," in Yaniv Fox and others, eds., *Inclusion and Exclusion in Mediterranean Christianities, 400-800* (Turnhout, Belgium).

Fowler, W. Warde (1927), *Social Life at Rome in the Age of Cicero* (New York).

Frank, Tenney (1933), *An Economic Survey of Ancient Rome, Vol. I: Rome and Italy of the Republic* (Baltimore).

" (1940), *An Economic Survey of Ancient Rome, Vol. V: Rome and Italy of the Empire* (Baltimore).

Frederiksen, M. W. (1966), "Caesar, Cicero and Debt," *Journal of Roman Studies* 56:128-141.

French, Alfred (1956), "The Economic Background to Solon's Reforms," *The Classical Quarterly* 6:11-25.
  " (1957), "Solon and the Megarian Question," *The Journal of Hellenic Studies* 77:238-246.
  " (1963), "Land Tenure and the Solon Problem," *Historia* 12:242-247.
  " (1964), *The Growth of the Athenian Economy* (London).

Frend, William Hugh Clifford (2000 [1952]), *The Donatist Church. A Movement of Protest in Roman North Africa* (Oxford).

Frier, Bruce W. and Dennis P. Kehoe (2007), "Law and Economic Institutions," in Walter Scheidel, Ian Morris and Richard Saller, eds., *The Cambridge Economic History of the Greco-Roman World* (Cambridge).

Fuchs, Andreas (1993), *Die Inschriften Sargons II aus Khorsabad* (Göttingen).

Fuks, Alexander (1966), "Social Revolution in Greece in the Hellenistic Age," *Parola del Passato* 21:437-448.
  " (1984), *Social Conflict in Ancient Greece* (Leiden).

Fustel de Coulanges, Numa Denis (1980 [1864]), *The Ancient City: A Study on the Religion, Laws, and Institutions of Greece and Rome* (Baltimore).

Gabba, Emilio (1991), *Dionysius and The History of Archaic Rome* (Berkeley).

Gabrielsen, Vincent (1994), *Financing the Athenian Fleet: Public Taxation and Social Relations* (Baltimore).
  " (2008), "The Public Banks of Hellenistic Cities," in Verboven, Vandorpe and Chankowski (2008):115-130.

Gallant, T. W. (1982), "Agricultural systems, land tenure and the reforms of Solon," *Annual of the British School at Athens* 77:111-124.

García-Bellido, M. P., L. Callegarin and A. Jiménez, eds. (2011), "Barter, Money and Coinage in the Ancient Mediterranean (10th-1st c. BC)," Anejos de Archivo Español de Arqueología 58, Madrid: Consejo Superior de Investigaciones Científicas.

Gardner, Percy (1913), "Coinage of the Athenian Empire," *Journal of Hellenic Studies* 33.

"   (1918), *A History of Ancient Coinage: 700-300 BC* (Oxford).

Garnsey, Peter (2007), *Thinking about Property: From Antiquity to the Age of Revolution* (Cambridge).

Garnsey, Peter, and Richard Saller (1987), *The Roman Empire: Economy, Society and Culture* (Berkeley and Los Angeles).

Gelb, Ignace J. (1967), "Approaches to the Study of Ancient Society," *Journal of the American Oriental Society* 87:1-8.

Gibbon, Edward (1776), *History of the Decline and Fall of the Roman Empire*, available at https://www.gutenberg.org/files/25717/25717-h/25717-h.htm.

Glotz, Gustav (1930), *The Greek City and Its Institutions* (London).

Goelet, Ogden (2002), "Fiscal Renewal in Ancient Egypt: Its Language, Symbols and Metaphors," in Hudson and Van De Mieroop (2002).

Gomme, A. (1956), *A Historical Commentary on Thucydides* (Oxford).

Gray, Vivienne J. (1996), "Herodotus and Images of Tyranny: The Tyrants of Corinth," *American Journal of Philology* 117:361-389.

Grote, George (1859), *History of Greece* (New York).

Haldon, John (2015), "Late Rome, Byzantium, and early medieval western Europe," in Monson and Scheidel (2015):345-389.

Hansen, Mogens Herman (2005), *The Imaginary Polis: Symposium, January 7-10, 2004* (Copenhagen).

Harmatta, J., ed. (1984), *Proceedings of the VIIth Congress of the International Federation of Classical Studies*, 2 vols. (Budapest).

Harris, E. M. (1997), "A New Solution to the *Seisachtheia*," in Mitchell and Rhodes (1997):55-60.
"   (2002), "Did Solon Abolish Debt-Bondage?" *The Classical Quarterly* 52.2:415-430.

Harris, W. V., ed. (2008), *The Monetary Systems of the Greeks and Romans* (Oxford).

Harvey, David (2003), *The New Imperialism* (Oxford).

Hatzfeld, Jean (1966), *History of Ancient Greece* (New York).

Head, Barclay V. (1887), *Historia Numorum: A Manual of Greek Numismatics* (Oxford).

Heather, Peter (2005), *The Fall of the Roman Empire: A New History of Rome and the Barbarians* (Oxford).

Heichelheim, Fritz (1964), *An Ancient Economic History, from the Palaeolithic Age to the Migrations of the Germanic, Slavic, and Arabic Nations*, 3 vols. (Leyden).

Heltzer, Michael (1984), "Private Property in Ugarit," in Alfonso Archi, ed., *Circulation of Goods in Non-Palatial Context in the Ancient Near East* (Rome).

Herz, Zachry (2015), "The Effect of Bankruptcy Law on Roman Credit Markets," *Business & Bankruptcy Journal* 2:207-240.

Hill, George (2010), *A History of Cyprus*, 4 vols. (Cambridge).

Hill, Herbert (1952), *The Roman Middle Class in the Republican Period* (Oxford).

Hinard, François (1985), *Les Proscriptions de la Rome républicaine* (Rome).

Hinsch, Moritz (2016), "Private Debts in Classical Greece," delivered at the international conference on "Debt: The First 3500 Years" in Tübingen, Germany, June 11, 2016.

Hocart, A. M. (1952), *The Life-Giving Myth* (London).

Hodkinson, Stephen (2000), *Property and Wealth in Classical Sparta* (London).
　　" (2005), "The Imaginary Spartan Politeia," in Hansen (2005):22-81.
　　" (2018), "Sparta: An exceptional Domination of State over

Society?" in Powell (2018):29-57.

Hodkinson, Stephen and Ian Macgregor Morris, eds. (2012), *Sparta in Modern Thought: Politics, History and Culture* (Swansea).

Holladay, J. (1977), "The followers of Peisistratus," *Greece and Rome* 24:40-56.

Hollander, David B. (2007), *Money in the Late Roman Republic* (Leiden).

Hooper, Finley (1979), *Roman Realities* (Detroit).

Hoover, Jesse A. (2008), "The contours of Donatism: theological and ideological diversity in fourth century North Africa," available at https://www.academia.edu/1829408/The_contours_of_Donatism_theological_and_ideological_diversity_in_fourth_century_North_Africa?email_work_card=view-paper.
    " (2018), *The Donatist Church in an Apocalyptic Age* (Oxford), available as his doctoral dissertation, Baylor University, https://baylor-ir.tdl.org/bitstream/handle/2104/9160/Jesse_Hoover_phd.pdf?sequence=1&isAllowed=y.

Hopkins, Keith (1978), *Conquerors and Slaves* (Cambridge).

Howgego, Christopher (1992), "The Supply and Use of Money in the Roman World 200 B.C. to A.D. 300," *Journal of Roman Studies* 82:1-31.

Hudson, Michael (1992), "Did the Phoenicians Introduce the Idea of Interest to Greece and Italy – And if So, When?" in Kopcke and Tokumaru 1992:128-143.
    " (1999), "From Sacred Enclave to Temple to City," in Michael Hudson and Baruch Levine, eds., *Urbanization and Land Ownership in the Ancient Near East* (Cambridge, MA):117-191.
    " (2000a), "How Interest Rates Were Set, 2500 BC-1000 AD: *Máš, tokos* and *fœnus* as metaphors for interest accruals," *Journal of the Economic and Social History of the Orient* 43 (2000):132-161.
    " (2000b), "Music as an Analogy for Economic Order in Classical Antiquity," in Jürgen Backhaus, ed., *Karl Bücher. Theory, History, Anthropology, Non-Market Economies* (Marburg):113-135.
    " (2010), "Entrepreneurs: From the Near Eastern Takeoff to the Roman Collapse," in David S. Landes, Joel Mokyr and William

J. Baumol, eds. *The Invention of Enterprise: Entrepreneurship from Ancient Mesopotamia to Modern Times* (Princeton).

" (2011), "Simon Patten on Public Infrastructure and Economic Rent Capture," *American Journal of Economics and Sociology* 70:873-903.

" (2018), "*...and forgive them their debts: Credit and Redemption From Bronze Age Debt Remissions to the Jubilee Year* (Dresden).

" (2019), "Origins of Money and Interest: Palatial Credit, not Barter," Springer *Handbook of the History of Money and Currency* (Singapore). Also available at michael-hudson.com.

" (2020), "Debt, Land and Money, From Polanyi to the New Economic Archaeology," in Radhika Desai and Kari Polanyi Levitt, eds., *Karl Polanyi and Twenty First Century Capitalism* (Manchester).

" (2021), "Land Tenure: From Fiscal Origins to Financialization," in Daivi Rodima-Taylor and Parker Shipton, eds., *Land and the Mortgage: The History, Culture, and Property of Belonging* (Oxford and New York).

Hudson, Michael and Marc Van De Mieroop, eds. (2002), *Debt and Economic Renewal in the Ancient Near East* (Baltimore).

Humm, Michel (2005), *Appius Claudius Caecus. La république accomplice* (Rome).

Humphreys, S. C. (1978), *Anthropology and the Greeks* (London).

Hunt, David (1998), "The successors of Constantine," in Averil Cameron and Peter Garnsey, eds., *The Cambridge Ancient History, XIII: The Late Empire, A.D. 337-425* (Cambridge):1-43.

Husselman, E. M. (1961), "Pawnbrokers, accounts from Roman Egypt," *Transactions and Proceedings of the American Philological Association* 92:251-266.

Hutchinson, Lester (1967), *The Conspiracy of Catiline* (New York).

Ioannatou, M. (2006), *Affaires d'argent dans la correspondance de Cicéron, L'Aristocratie sénatoriale face à ses dettes* (Paris).

Irwin, Elizabeth (2005), *Solon and Early Greek Poetry: The Politics of Exhortation* (Cambridge).

Jacoby, F. (1909), *Fragmente der griechischen Historiker* (Boston and Leiden).
" (1949), *Atthis: The Local Chronicles of Ancient Athens* (Oxford).

James, C. L. R. (1994), *C. L. R. James and Revolutionary Marxism: Selected Writings 1939-1949* (Chicago).

Jebb, R. C. (1880), "Delos," *Journal of Hellenic Studies* 1.

Johnson, Allan Chester (1936), *Roman Egypt, to the Reign of Diocletian* (Baltimore).

Jones, A. H. M. (1959), "Were Ancient Heresies National or Social Movements in Disguise?" *Journal of Theological Studies*, n.s. 10.2 (October 1959):280-298.
" (1959), "Overtaxation and the Decline of the Roman Empire," *Antiquity* 33:39-43.
" (1964), *The Later Roman Empire, 284-602: A Social, Economic and Administrative Survey* (Oxford).
" (1966a), *The Decline of the Ancient World* (London).
" (1966b), *The Greek City from Alexander to Justinian* (Oxford).
" (1966c), *Were Ancient Heresies Disguised Social Movements?* (Philadelphia).
" (1967), *Sparta* (Oxford).
" (1974), *The Roman Economy: Studies in Ancient Economic and Administrative History* (Oxford).

Jones, David (2006), *The Bankers of Puteoli: Finance, Trade and Industry in the Roman World* (London).

Jursa, Michael and Juan Carlos Moreno Garcia (2015), "The ancient Near East and Egypt," in Monson and Scheidel (2015):115-166.

Kallet-Marx, Robert M. (1995), "Quintus Fabius Maximus and the Dyme Affair (Syll. 684)," *The Classical Quarterly* 45:129-153.

Kautsky, Karl (1925), *Foundations of Christianity: A Study of Christian Origins* (New York).

Kay, Philip (2014), *Rome's Economic Revolution* (Oxford).

Keaveney, Arthur (2005 [1982]), *Sulla: The Last Republican*, 2nd ed. (London and New York).

Kelly, J. M. (1970), "A hypothesis on the origin of <u>mutuum</u>," *The Irish Jurist* 5:156-163.

Knorringa, H. (1961 [1926]), *Emporos. Data on Trade and Traders in Greek Literature from Homer to Aristotle* (Amsterdam).

Knox, Alfred D. (1929), *Herodes, Cercidas and the Greek Choliambic Poets* (London and New York).

Kolb, F. (1977), "Die Bau-, Religions-Und Kulturpolitik Der Peisistratiden," *Jahrbuch des Deutschen Archäologischen Institute* 92:99-138.

Kopcke, Gunter and Isabelle Tokumaru (1992), *Greece Between East and West: 10th-8th Centuries BC* (Berlin).

Kraay, C. (1968), *Essays in Greek Coinage Presented to Stanley Robinson* (Oxford).

Krentz, Peter (1982), *The Thirty at Athens* (Ithaca).

Kristensen, Karen. R. (2004), "Gortynian Debt Bondage. Some New Considerations on IC IV 41 IV-VII, 47 and 72 I.56-II.2, X. 25-32," *Zeitschrift für Papyrologie und Epigraphik* 149:73-79.

Kulikowski, Michael (2020), *The Tragedy of Empire: From Constantine to the Destruction of Roman Italy* (Cambridge, MA).

Kurke, Leslie (1999), *Coins, Bodies, Games and Gold* (Princeton).

Laberbe, J. (1971), "L'appartion de la notion de tyrannie dans la Grèce archaique," *Antiquité classique* 40:471-504.

Lambert, David (2013), "Salvian and the Bacaudae," in Steffen Diefenbach and Gernot Michael Müller, eds., *Gallien in Spätantike und Frühmittelalter. Kulturgeschichte einer Region* (Berlin):255-276.

Larsen, J. A. O. (1938), "Roman Greece," in Tenney Frank, *An Economic Survey of Ancient Rome, Vol. IV* (Baltimore).

Larsen, Mogens Trolle (2015), *Ancient Kanesh: A Merchant Colony in Bronze Age Anatolia* (Cambridge).

Latourette, Kenneth Scott (2007), *A History of Christianity* (Peabody, MA).

Laum, Bernard (1952), "Geschichte der öffentlichen Finanzwirtschaft im Altertum und Frühmittelalter," in Wilhelm Gerloff and Fritz Neumark, eds., *Handbuch der Finanzwirtschaft* (Tübingen):231-235.

Lenski, Noel (2016), "Imperial Legislation and the Donatist Controversy: From Constantine to Honorius," in Richard Miles, ed., *The Donatist Schism* (Liverpool):166-219.
    " (2017), "Peasant and Slave in Late Antique North Africa, c. 100-600 CE," in Rita Lizzi Testa, ed., *Late Antiquity in Contemporary Debate* (Newcastle upon Tyne):113-155.

Lewis, N. (1941), "Solon's Agrarian Legislation," *American Journal of Philology* 62.2:144-156.

Lewis, Naphtali and Meyer Reinhold (1951, 1990), *Roman Civilization: Selected Readings* (New York).

Lewis, Sian (2012), *Periander of Corinth*, in R. S. Bagnall, K. Brodersen, C. B. Champion, A. Erskine and S. R. Huebner, *The Encyclopedia of Ancient History* (Wiley).

Lintott, A. (2009), "The Assassination," in M. Griffin, ed., *Companion to Julius Caesar* (Chichester):72-82.

Lo Cascio, E. (1979), "Carbone, Druso e Gratidiano: la gestione della res nummaria a Roma tra la Lex Papiria e la Lex Cornelia," *Athenaeum* 57:215-238.

Lowry, S. Todd (1987), *The Archaeology of Economic Ideas* (Durham).
    " (1979), Recent Literature on Ancient Greek Economic Thought," *Journal of Economic Literature* 17:65-86.

Lyttkens, C. H. (1994), "A Predatory Democracy? An Essay on Taxation in Classical Athens," *Explorations in Economic History* 31:62-90.

Mackil, Emily (2015), "The Greek *polis* and *koinon*," in Monson and Schiedel (2015):469-491.

MacMullen, Ramsey (1974), *Roman Social Relations, 50 B.C. to A.D. 284* (New Haven).
" (1976), *Roman Government's Response to Crisis: AD 235-337* (New Haven).
" (1987), "Tax-Pressure in the Roman Empire," *Latomas* 46:737-754.
" (2000), *Romanization in the Time of Augustus* (New Haven).

Magie, David (1950), *Roman Rule in Asia Minor, to the end of the Third Century after Christ* (Princeton).

March, Duane A. (1989), "Cicero and the 'Gang of Five,'" *The Classical World* 82:225-234.

Marone, Paula (2007-2008), "The Use of the Term 'Catholic' in the Donatist Controversy," *Pomoerivm* 6:81-91.

Martroye, F. (1904-1905), "Un tentative de révolution sociale en Afrique," *Revue des questions historiques* 76 (1904):353-416, and 77 (1905):1-53.

Mattern, Susan P. (1999), *Rome and the Enemy: Imperial Strategy in the Principate* (Berkeley).

Mayor, Adrienne (2010), *The Poison King: The Life and Legend of Mithradates, Rome's Greatest Enemy* (Princeton).

Meikle, S. (1989), "Et in Arcadia Chicago," *Polis* 8:25-34 (review of Lowry 1986).

Merrills, Andrew and Richard Miles (2010), *The Vandals* (Chichester and Malden, MA).

Meritt, Benjamin D. (1937), *Documents on Athenian Tribute* (Cambridge, MA).
" (1961), *The Athenian Year* (Berkeley and Los Angeles).

Michalopoulos, Miltiadis (2016), *In the Name of Lykourgos: The Rise and fall of the Spartan Revolutionary Movement, 243-146 BC* (Barnsley).

Middleton, J. Henry (1888), "The Temple of Apollo at Delphi," *Journal of Hellenic Studies* 9-10:282-322.

Migeotte, Leopold (1984), *L'emprunt public dans les cités grecques* (Quebéc and Paris).

Millett, Paul (1991), *Lending and Borrowing in Ancient Athens* (Cambridge).

Mitchell, L. and P. J. Rhodes (1997), *The Development of the Polis in Archaic Greece* (London).
  " (1971), "Solon's Coinage," *Arethusa* 4:25-47.

Momigliano, Arnaldo (1963), "An Interim Report on the Origin of Rome," *Journal of Roman Studies* 53.
  " (2005), "The Rise of the plebs in the Archaic Age of Rome," in Raaflaub (2005):168-184.

Mommsen, Theodor (1866 [1854-1856]), *History of Rome* (reprinted Free Press, Glencoe, 1958). Available on-line at Project Gutenberg.
  " (1899), "Der Zinswucher des M. Brutus," *Hermes* 34:145-150.
  " (1911), *The History of Rome*, translated by E. A. Freeman, 4 vols. (London and Toronto).
  " (1958), *The History of Rome, An account of events and persons from the Conquest of Carthage to the End of the Republic*, translated by Dero A. Saunders and John H. Collins (Cleveland).

Monson, Andrew and Walter Scheidel, eds. (2015), *Fiscal Regimes and the Political Economy of Premodern States* (Cambridge).

Moore, J. M. (1975), *Aristotle and Xenophon on Democracy and Oligarchy: Translations with Introductions and Commentary* (London).

Morris, Ian (2002), "Hard Surfaces," in P. Cartledge, E. Cohen and L. Foxhall, eds., *Money, Labour and Land. Approaches to the Economies of Ancient Greece* (London):8-43.

Morris, Sarah (2003), "Imaginary Kings: Alternatives to Monarchy in Early Greece," in Kathryn A. Morgan, ed., *Popular Tyranny: Sovereignty and Its Discontents in Ancient Greece* (Austin):1-24.

Mossé, Claude (1969), *La Tyrannie dans la Grèce antique* (Paris).
" (1973), *Athens in Decline 404-86 BC* (London).

Mullett, M. E. (1988), "Byzantium: a friendly society?" *Past and Present* 118:3-24.

Murray, Oswyn (1990), "The Solonian law of *hubris*," in Paul Cartledge, Paul Millett and Stephen Todd, eds., *Nomos: Essays in Athenian Law and Politics* (Cambridge):139-145.

Nafissi, Massimo (2018), "Lykourgos the Spartan 'Lawgiver': Ancient Beliefs and Modern Scholarship," in Powell (2018):93-123.

Nagy, Gregory (1985), "Theognis and Megara: A Poet's Vision of his City," in Thomas J. Figueira and Gregory Nagy, eds., *Theognis of Megara: Poetry & the Polis* (Baltimore):22-81.

Nicolet, Claude (1966), *L'ordre equestre ~ l'epoque republicaine* (Paris).

Nichols, Mary P. (1987), *Socrates and the Political Community: An Ancient Debate* (Albany).

Nigg, Walter (1962), *The Heretics* (New York).

North, Douglass C. (1977), "Markets and Other Allocation Systems in History: The Challenge of Karl Polanyi," *Journal of European Economic History*:703-716.

Ober, Josiah (1989), *Mass and Elite in Democratic Athens: Rhetoric, Ideology, and the Power of the People* (Princeton).
      " (2006), "Solon and the *Horoi*: Facts on the Ground in Archaic Athens," in Blok and Lardinois (2006):441-456.
      " (2007), "'I Besieged That Man': Democracy's Revolutionary Start," in Raaflaub, Ober and Wallace (2007):83-104.
      " (2015), "Classical Athens," in Monson and Scheidel (2015):492-522.

Odgers, Merle M. (1930), "Marcus Caelius Rufus," *Classical Weekly* 23 (April 7):161-166.

O'Donnell, James (2005), *Augustine: A New Biography* (New York).
      " (2009), *The Ruin of the Roman Empire: a new history* (New York).

Offer, Avner and Gabriel Söderberg (2016), *The Nobel Factor: The Prize in Economics, Social Democracy and the Market Turn* (Princeton).

Ogden, Daniel (1997), *The Crooked Kings of Ancient Greece* (London).

Ogilvie, R. M. (1965), *A Commentary on Livy. Books 1-5* (Oxford).

Oliva, Pavel (1971), *Sparta and her Social Problems* (Amsterdam and Prague).
    " (1981), *The Birth of Greek Civilization* (London).

Ollier, François (1933-1943), *Le mirage spartiate*, 2 vols. (Lyon and Paris).

Olmstead, A. T. (1948), *History of the Persian Empire* (Chicago).

Oppenheim, A. Leo (1949), "The Golden Garments of the Gods," *Journal of Near Eastern Studies* 8:172-193.

Osborne, R. G. (1988), "Social and economic implications of leasing land and property in classical and Hellenistic Greece," *Chiron* 18:279-323.

Papaconstantinou, Arietta (2016), "Credit, Debt and Dependence in Early Islamic Egypt," in Jean-Luc Fournet and Arietta Papaconstantinou, eds., *Mélanges Jean Gascou: textes et études papyrologiques* (Paris):613-642.

Parker, Grant (2002), "Ex Oriente Luxuria: Indian Commodities and Roman Experience," *Journal of the Economic and Social History of the Orient* 45(1):40-95.

Payne, Richard (2022), "Zoroastrian Materialism: Religion, Empire, and their Critics in Graeber's Late Axial Age," in Weisweiler (2022).

Pleket, H. W. (1971), "Review of Bogaert 1968," *Mnemosyne* 24:433-437.

Pomeroy, Sarah B. (1994), *Xenophon, Oeconomicus. A Social and Historical Commentary* (Oxford).

Powell, Anton (2018), ed., *A Companion to Sparta* (Hoboken, NJ).
    " (2018a), "Sparta: Reconstructing History from Secrecy, Lies and Myth," in Powell (2018):3-28.

Powell, Anton and Stephen Hodkinson, eds. (2002), *Sparta Beyond the Mirage* (London).

Pritchett, W. Kendrick (1974), *The Greek State at War, Part II* (Berkeley and Los Angeles).
    " (1977), "Loans of Athena in 407 BC," *Ancient Society* 8:33-47.
    " (1979), *The Greek State at War, Part III: Religion* (Berkeley and Los Angeles).

Quirke, Stephen and Carol Andrews (1988), *The Rosetta Stone: Facsimile Drawing with an Introduction and Translation* (New York and London).

Raaflaub, Kurt A. (2003), "Stick and Glue: The Function of Tyranny in Fifth-Century Athenian Democracy," in K. Morgan, ed., *Popular Tyranny: Sovereignty and Its Discontents in Ancient Greece*:59-94.
    " (2005), "The Conflict of the Orders in Archaic Rome: A Comprehensive and Comparative Approach," in Raaflaub (2005):1-46.
    " ed., (2005), *Social Struggles in Archaic Rome* (Oxford).
    " (2007), "The Breakthrough of *Dēmokratia* in Mid-Fifth-Century Athens," in Raaflaub, Ober and Wallace:105-154.

Raaflaub, Kurt A., Josiah Ober and Robert W. Wallace, eds. (2007), *Origins of Democracy in Ancient Greece* (Berkeley).

Rawson, Elizabeth (1975), *The Spartan Tradition in European Thought* (Oxford).

Renger, Johannes (1972), "Flucht als soziales Problem in der altbabylonischen Gesellschaft," *Gesellschaftsklassen*:167-82.

Ridgeway, David (1993), *The First Western Greeks* (Cambridge).

Rhodes, P. J. (1972), *The Athenian Boule* (Oxford).
    " (1982), "Problems in Athenian *eisphora* and liturgies," *American Journal of Ancient History* 7:1-19.
    " (2000), "Oligarchs in Athens," in Brock and Hodkinson (2000):119-136.

Rose, Peter W. (2012), *Class in Archaic Greece* (Cambridge).

Roselaar, Saskia T. (2010), *Public Land in the Roman Republic: A Social and Economic History of* Ager Publicus *in Italy, 396-89 BC* (Oxford).

Rosenstein, Nathan (2004), *Rome at War: Firms, Families, and Death in the Middle Republic* (Chapel Hill and London).

Rostovtzeff, Michael (1926), *The Social and Economic History of the Roman Empire* (Oxford).
    " (1941), *The Social and Economic History of the Hellenistic World*, 3 vols. (Oxford).

Rothbard, Murray (1995), *Economic Thought before Adam Smith* (Hants, England).

Roussel, Denis (1976), *Tribu et cité: Etudes sur les groupes sociaux clans les cités grecques aux epoques archaique et classi*que (Paris).

Royer, J. P. (1967), "Le Probleme des dettes a la fin de la republique romaine, " *Revue historique de droit francais et etranger* 45:193-240, 407-450.

Ruzé, Francoise (2018), "The Empire of the Spartans (404-371)," in Powell (2018):320-353.

Ryan, S. X. (1994), "The Quaestorships of Q. Curius and C. Cornelius Cethegus," *Classical Philology* 89:256-261.

Sagstetter, Kelcy (2013), *Solon of Athens: The Man, the Myth, the Tyrant?* PhD. dissertation, University of Pennsylvania, available at http://repository.upenn.edu/cgi/viewcontent.cgi?article=2081&context=edissertations.

Salmon, J. B. (1984), *Wealthy Corinth: A History of the City to 338 B.C.* (Oxford).
    " (1997), "Lopping Off the Heads? Tyrants, Politics and the *Polis*," in Mitchell and Rhodes (1997):32-38.

Sampson, Gareth C. (2013), *The Collapse of Rome: Marius, Sulla and the First Civil War (91-70 BC)* (Barnsley).

Sancisi-Weerdenburg, Heleen (2000), ed., *Peisistratos and the Tyranny: A Reappraisal of the Evidence* (Amsterdam).

Savunen, Lisa (1993), "Debt Legislation in the Fourth Century B.C.," in U. Paananen, et al., eds., *Senatus Populusque Romanus: Studies in Roman Republican Legislation* (Helsinki):143-159.

Schatzman, I. (1975), *Senatorial Wealth and Roman Politics* (Brussels).

Schavione, Aldo (2000), *Ancient Rome and the Modern West* (Cambridge, MA).

Scheidel, Walter (2007), "A Model of Real Income Growth in Roman Italy," *Historia: Zeitschrift für Alte Geschichte* 56:322-346.
    " (2017), *The Great Leveler: Violence and the History of Inequality from the Stone Age to the Twenty-First Century* (Princeton).
    " (2019), *Escape from Rome: The Failure of Empire and the Road to Prosperity* (Princeton), summarized in "The Road from Rome" (2021).
    " (2021), "The Road from Rome," available at https://aeon.co/essays/how-the-fall-of-the-roman-empire-paved-the-road-to-modernity.

Schepens, Guido, Felix Jacoby and Jan Radicke, eds. (1999), *Die Fragmente Der Griechischen Historiker Continued*, Part IV Fascicle 7 (Leiden).

Schur, W. (1926), "Zur Vorgeschichte des Ptolemaerreiches," *Klio* 20.

Schütrumpf, E. (1987), "The rhetra of Epitadeus: a Platonist's fiction," *Greek, Roman and Byzantine Studies* 28:441-457.

Scullard, H. H. (1951), *Roman Politics, 220-150 BC* (Oxford).
    " (1980), *A History of the Roman World from 753 to 146 BC* (London).

Sealey, Raphael (1976), *A History of the Greek City States ca. 700-338 BC* (Berkeley).

Shapiro, H. A. (1989), *Art and Cult under the Tyrants in Athens* (Mainz am Rhein).

Shaw, Brent (2011), *African Christians and Sectarian Hatred in the Age of Augustine* (Cambridge).

Sherk, Robert K., ed., (1984), *Rome and the Greek East to the death of Augustus* (Cambridge).

Sherwin-White, A. N. (1977), "Roman Involvement in Anatolia, 167-88 B.C.," *Journal of Roman Studies* 67:62-75.

Shimron, Benjamin (1972), *Late Sparta: The Spartan Revolution 243-146 BC* (Buffalo).

Shipley, Graham (2000), *The Greek World After Alexander, 323-30 BC* (London and New York).

Shipton, Kirsty (2008), "Bankers as Moneys Lenders: The Banks of Classical Athens," in Verboven, Vandorpe and Chankowski (2008):93-114.

Singor, H. W. (1988), review of "Basileus. The Evidence for Kingship in Geometric Greece by R. Drews," *Mnemosyne*, Fourth Series, Vol. 41, Fasc. 1/2:218-222

Sirks, A. J. B. (2008), "The Colonate in Justinian's Reign," *Journal of Roman Studies* 98:120-143.

Slobodian, Quinn (2008), *Globalists: The End of Empire and the Birth of Nationalism* (Cambridge).

Smither, Edward L. (2006), "Persuasion or Coercion: Augustine on the State's Role in Dealing with Other Religions and Heresies," *Faculty Publications and Presentations*, Paper 14, available at http://digitalcommons.liberty.edu/lts_fac_pubs/14.

Snodgrass, Anthony (1980), *Archaic Greece: The Age of Experiment* (London).

Ste. Croix, G. E. M. (1989 [1981]), *The Class Struggle in the Ancient Greek World* (Ithaca).
    " (2004), in David Harvey and Robert Parker, eds., *Athenian Democratic Origins and Other Essays* (Oxford).

Steel, Catherine (2013), *The End of the Roman Republic, 146 to 44 BC: Conquest and Crisis* (Edinburgh).

Steinkeller, Piotr (2002), "Money-Lending Practices in Ur III Babylonia," in Hudson and Van De Mieroop (2002).

Steinkeller, Piotr and Michael Hudson, eds. (2015), *Labor in the Ancient*

World (Dresden).

Stone, I. F. (1988), *The Trial of Socrates* (Boston and Toronto).

Tan, James (2015), "The Roman Republic," in Monson and Scheidel (2015):208-228.
    " (2017), *Power and Public Finance at Rome, 264-49 BC* (Oxford).

Tarn, William W. (1923, revised ed. 1961), "The Social Question in the Third Century," in J. B. Bury, E. A. Barber, Edwyn Bevan and W. W. Tarn, *The Hellenistic Age: Aspects of Hellenistic Civilization* (Cambridge), available at https://archive.org/stream/hellenisticageas00buryuoft/hellenisticageas00buryuoft_djvu.txt.

Taylor, Lily Ross (1968), *Party Politics in the Age of Caesar* (Berkeley and Los Angeles).

Temin, Peter (2013), *The Roman Market Economy* (Princeton).

Tengström, Enim (1964), *Donatists and Catholics, Social, Economic and Political Aspects of a North African Church Division* (Gothenberg).

Thompson, E. A. (1952), "Peasant Revolts in Late Roman Gaul and Spain," *Past and Present* 2:11-23.

Thompson, W. E. (1978), "The Athenian investor," *Rivista di Studi Classici* 36:402-423.
    " (1979a), "A view of Athenian banking," *Museum Helveticum* 36:224-241.
    " (1979b), "An aspect of Athenian public finance," *Acta Clasica* 22:149-153.
    " (1982), "The Athenian entrepreneur," *L'Antiquite classique* 51 :53-85.

Thomsen, Rudi (1957-1961), *Early Roman Coinage and its Evidence*, 3 vols. (Copenhagen).
    " (1964), *Eisphora: A Study of Direct Taxation in Ancient Athens* (Copenhagen).
    " (1977), "War Taxes in Classical Athens," Colloques Nationaux du C.N.R.S. #936 (Paris):135-147.
    " (1980), *King Servius Tullius: a historical synthesis* (Copenhagen).

Tigerstedt, Eugène Napoleon (1965-1974), *The Legend of Sparta in Classical Antiquity*, 2 vols. (Stockholm).

Tilley, Maureen A. (1997), *The Bible in Christian North Africa: The Donatist World* (Minneapolis).

Toynbee, Arnold (1913), "The Growth of Sparta," *Journal of Hellenic Studies* 33:254-275.
" (1939), *A Study of History* (Oxford).
" (1965), *Hannibal's Legacy* (Oxford).
" (1969), *Some Problems in Greek History* (London).

Ure, Percy (1922), *The Origin of Tyranny* (Cambridge).

van Wees, Hans (1999), "The Mafia of Early Greece. Violent Exploitation in the Seventh and Sixth Centuries," in K. Hopwood, ed., *Organized Crime in Antiquity* (London):1-51.
" (2000), "Megara's Mafiosi: Timocracy and Violence in Theognis," in Brock and Hodkinson (2000):52-67.
" (2004), *Greek Warfare. Myths and Realities* (London).
" (2006), "Mass and Elite in Solon's Athens: The Property Classes Revisited," in Blok and Lardinois (2006):351-389.
" (2013), *Ships and Silver, Taxes and Tribute: A Fiscal History of Archaic Athens* (London and New York).
" (2018a), "Luxury, Austerity and Equality in Sparta," in Powell (2018):202-235.
" (2018b), "The Common Messes," in Powell (2018):236-268.

Veenhof, Klaas (1982), "The Old Assyrian Merchants and Their Relations with the Native Population of Anatolia," in Hans-Jorg Nissen and Johannes Renger, eds., *Mesopotamien und Seine Nachbarn* (Berlin).

Ventris, Michael and J. Chadwick (1956), *Documents in Mycenaean Greek* (Cambridge).

Verboven, Koenraad (2002), *The Economy of Friends. Economic aspects of* amicitia *and patronage in the Late Republic* (Brussels).
" (2003), "54-44 BCE: Financial or Monetary Crisis," in Elio lo Cascio, ed., *Credito e Moneta nel Mondo Romano* (Bari):49-68.
" (2009), "Currency, Bullion and Accounts: Monetary Modes in

the Roman World," *Revue Belge de Numismatique et de Sigillographie* 155:91-124.

Verboven, Koenraad, Katelijn Vandorpe and Véronique Chankowski, eds. (2008), *Pistoi Dia Tèn Technèn: Bankers, Loans and Archives in the Ancient World. Studies in Honour of Raymond Boghaerty* (Leuven).

Versnel, H. S. (1970), *Triumphus: An Inquiry into the Origin, Development and Meaning of the Roman Triumph* (Leiden).

Vervaet, Frederik Juliaan (2004), "The lex Valeria and Sulla's empowerment as dictator (82-79 BCE)," *Cahiers du Centre Gustave Glotz* 15:37-84.

Veyne, Paul (1990), *Bread and Circuses* (London).

Villard, Pierre (2007), "L'(AN)DURāRU À L'ÉPOQUE NÉO-ASSYRIENNE," Revue d'assyriologie et d'archéologie orientale 101:107-124.

von Reden, Sitta (2010), *Money in Classical Antiquity* (Cambridge).
   " (2012), "Money and Finance," in Walter Scheidel, ed., *The Cambridge Companion to the Roman Economy* (Cambridge):266-286.

von Ungern-Sternberg, Jürgen (2005a), "The Formation of the 'Annalistic Tradition': The Example of the Decemvirate," in Raaflaub (2005):75-97.
   " (2005b), "The End of the Conflict of the Orders," in Raaflaub (2005):312-332.

Wade-Gery, H. T. (1930), "A note on Kleon's finance," *The Classical Review* 44:163-165.

Walbank, F. W. (1969), *The Awful Revolution: The Decline of the Roman Empire in the West* (Liverpool).
   " (1982), *The Hellenistic World* (Cambridge, MA).

Wallace, R. W. (2007), "Revolutions and a New Order in Solonian Athens and Archaic Greece," in Raaflaub, Ober and Wallace (2007):49-82.

Walsh, Patrick Gerard (1974), "Livy," *in Greece and Rome: New Surveys in the Classics*, No.8.

Ward, C. Osborne (1907 [1887]), *The Ancient Lowly: A History of the Ancient*

Working People from the Earliest Known Period to the Adoption of Christianity by Constantine (Chicago), available at https://catalog.hathitrust.org/Record/007704751.

Ward, Lorne H. (1988), "Origins of the Class Structure in Pre-Etruscan Rome, c. 750-c.550 BC," *Science and Society* 52:413-440.

Ward-Perkins, Bryan (1998), "The Cities," in Averil Cameron and Peter Garnsey, eds., *The Cambridge Ancient History, XIII: The Late Empire, A.D. 337-425* (Cambridge):371-410.
" (2005), *The Fall of Rome and the End of Civilization* (Oxford).

Warren, J. B. L. (1863), *Essay on Greek Federal Coinage* (London).

Watts, Edward J. (2018), *Mortal Republic: How Rome Fell Into Tyranny* (New York).

Weber, Max (1976, 2013 [1909]), *The Agrarian Sociology of Ancient Civilizations*, available at https://archive.org/stream/max_weber_the_agrarian_sociology_of_ancient_civilizations/%28Verso%20World%20History%20Series%29%20Max%20Weber-The%20Agrarian%20Sociology%20Of%20Ancient%20Civilizations-Verso%20%282013%29_djvu.txt.

Weisweiler, John (2022), "Monetization, Marketization and State Formation: The Later Roman Empire as an Axial Age Economy," in J. Weisweiler, ed., *Debt in the Ancient Mediterranean and Near East: Credit, Money and Social Obligation c. 700 BCE-700 CE* (New York).

Wenzer, Ken C. (2003), *Land as an Economic Factor and its Biblical Origins* (Lincoln, NE).

West, Martin L. (1992 [1972]), *Iambi et elegi Graeci ante Alexandrum cantati. 2: Callinus, Mimnermus. Semonides. Solon. Tyrtaeus. Minora adespota* (Oxford).
" (1993), *Greek Lyric Poetry. The poems and fragments of the Greek iambic, elegiac, and melic poets (excluding Pindar and Bacchylides) down to 450 B.C.* (Oxford).
" (1997), *The East Face of Helicon: West Asiatic Elements in Greek Poetry and Myth* (Oxford).

Whittaker, C. R. and Peter Garnsey (1998), "Rural life in the later Roman empire," in Averil Cameron and Peter Garnsey, eds., *The*

Cambridge Ancient History, XIII: The Late empire, A.D. 337-425 (Cambridge):277-311.

Wickham, Chris (2009), *The Inheritance of Rome: A History of Europe from 400 to 1000* (London).

Will, Edouard (1967), *Histoire politique du monde hellénistique (323-30 avant J.C.)* (Paris).

Willetts, R. F. (1955), *Aristocratic Society in Ancient Crete* (London).

Wunsch, Cornelia (2002), "Debt, Interest, Pledge and Forfeiture in the Neo-Babylonian and Early Achaemenid Period: The Evidence from Private Archives," in Hudson and Van De Mieroop (2002):221-255.

Yavetz, Z. (1963), "The failure of Catiline's conspiracy," *Historia* 12:495-499.
   " (1983), *Julius Caesar and his Public Image* (Ithaca).

Subject Index

Name Index – People(s)

Name Index - Places

Ingram Content Group UK Ltd.
Milton Keynes UK
UKHW050801070623
423024UK00010B/26

9 783949 546129